"Every once in a while, you come across a book that matt_ continues to be updated with the latest information possible. This is what you have in your hands with *Correctional Counseling and Rehabilitation* by Salisbury and Van Voorhis. Helping people get the tools and skills they need to successfully reenter society is about investing in them as people, the communities they return to, and our community more generally. This book does that and does it masterfully. With COVID-19 ravaging the correctional system, this book is all the more important for students, policymakers, and practitioners."

Alex R. Piquero, *Ph.D., University of Miami, Department of Sociology &*
Criminology, Arts & Sciences Distinguished Scholar

"This book, *Correctional Counseling and Rehabilitation*, is a masterpiece. It consists of theoretical frameworks, treatment modalities, and most recent cutting-edge evidence-based practices for treating justice-involved people in institutional settings and in the community.

Salisbury and Van Voorhis go the extra mile and provide a critical analysis to include the importance of race and culture. They highlight the significance of providing multicultural counseling for racially and ethnically diverse correctional populations, as opposed to an ethno-centrism perspective.

This text is so well designed and orchestrated, that any ordinary person can read it and truly understand the meaning of corrections and treatments for individuals in justice systems."

Leroy Curtis Johnson, *M.S.W., Assistant Professor (clinical),*
University of Utah, College of Social Work

Correctional Counseling and Rehabilitation

This text presents the foundations of correctional treatment and intervention, including overviews of the major therapeutic modalities that are effective when intervening with justice-involved individuals to reduce ongoing system involvement and improve well-being. The text also focuses on diagnosis of mental illness, correctional assessment and classification, case planning strategies, and the necessary counseling and human service skills for working alongside system-involved people.

Specific chapters focus on working with women, individuals struggling with substance abuse, and clients with severely antisocial behavior such as psychopathy. Written to help students prepare for a career in correctional counseling or forensic social work, the book also assists working professionals (e.g., institutional and community corrections staff) to determine which strategies might be most effective with their clients. Revised using person-centered language, the tenth edition includes a new chapter focused on the necessary relational skills that probation and parole officers must have to be agents of behavior change. The content is divided into four parts: (1) A Professional Framework for Correctional Counseling; (2) Client Assessment, Diagnosis, Classification, and Case Planning; (3) Contemporary Approaches for Correctional Counseling and Treatment, and (4) Effective Correctional Interventions for Special Populations.

This book is appropriate for upper-level undergraduates and graduate students in Criminal Justice and Criminology, Psychology, and Social Work programs, as well as correctional practitioners looking for professional development to enhance behavior change among clients.

Emily J. Salisbury, Ph.D., is an Associate Professor and the Director of the Utah Criminal Justice Center at the University of Utah College of Social Work. She is trained as an applied criminologist and focuses her research on the science of correctional treatment interventions, particularly among system-involved women. The Utah Criminal Justice Center is an interdisciplinary research center that provides organizations with research, training, and technical assistance grounded in scientific evidence to prevent and reduce crime and victimization among all communities, with an understanding that approaches must be tailored to the contextual needs of organizations and the diverse populations they serve.

Dr. Salisbury's research focuses on correctional policy, risk/needs assessment, and treatment intervention strategies, with a particular focus on system-involved women, gender-responsive practices, and trauma-responsive care. As a result of her scholarship on behalf of women, she was awarded the Marguerite Q. Warren and Ted B. Palmer Differential Intervention Award from the American Society of Criminology Division on Corrections and Sentencing.

Patricia Van Voorhis, Ph.D., is Professor Emerita of Criminal Justice at the University of Cincinnati. Dr. Van Voorhis has published extensively, including two books and many articles in the leading criminology and criminal justice journals. She has provided expertise to federal, state, and local agencies on topics pertaining to correctional effectiveness, program implementation, evaluation techniques, women offenders, risk assessment, and correctional classification. She has directed numerous federal- and state-funded research projects on inmate classification, gender-responsive assessment, program implementation, and cognitive behavioral interventions, and continues to pursue a rigorous consulting and research agenda in retirement. Dr. Van Voorhis is the recipient of many awards, including the prestigious American Society of Criminology August Vollmer Award, which recognizes a criminologist whose research scholarship has contributed to justice or to the treatment or prevention of criminal or delinquent behavior.

Correctional Counseling and Rehabilitation

TENTH EDITION

Emily J. Salisbury
Patricia Van Voorhis

Routledge
Taylor & Francis Group

NEW YORK AND LONDON

Cover image: Getty Images

Tenth edition published 2022
by Routledge
605 Third Avenue, New York, NY 10158

and by Routledge
4 Park Square, Milton Park, Abingdon, Oxon, OX14 4RN

Routledge is an imprint of the Taylor & Francis Group, an informa business

© 2022 Taylor & Francis

First edition published by Anderson Publishing Company 1987
Ninth edition published by Routledge 2016

Library of Congress Cataloging-in-Publication Data
Names: Van Voorhis, Patricia, author. | Salisbury, Emily J., author.
Title: Correctional counseling and rehabilitation / Emily J. Salisbury & Patricia Van Voorhis.
Description: Tenth edition. | New York, NY : Routledge, 2022. |
Patricia Van Voorhis appears as the first named author on earlier editions. |
Includes bibliographical references and index.
Identifiers: LCCN 2021050206 (print) | LCCN 2021050207 (ebook) |
ISBN 9780367404345 (hardback) | ISBN 9780367406455 (paperback) |
ISBN 9780367808266 (ebook)
Subjects: LCSH: Correctional psychology. |
Prisoners–Counseling of. | Psychotherapy.
Classification: LCC HV9276 .V35 2022 (print) |
LCC HV9276 (ebook) | DDC 365/.661–dc23/eng/20220127
LC record available at https://lccn.loc.gov/2021050206
LC ebook record available at https://lccn.loc.gov/2021050207

ISBN: 978-0-367-40434-5 (hbk)
ISBN: 978-0-367-40645-5 (pbk)
ISBN: 978-0-367-80826-6 (ebk)

DOI: 10.4324/9780367808266

Typeset in Berling and Futura
by Newgen Publishing UK

Access the companion website: www.routledge.com/cw/salisbury

To the individuals who lost their chance of personal growth and change, who died and will die from COVID-19 and COVID-19 related complications while living and working in correctional institutions across the globe.

Contents

Preface

At the time of writing, the COVID-19 crisis is ravaging the globe, with the Delta variant sickening those who are not vaccinated and threatening to mutate yet again. I am particularly concerned about the children and adults who are detained in correctional settings and for the many dedicated and professional staff who supervise and work alongside them.

Thousands of people's judicial sentences were converted to possible death sentences during 2020 and into 2021 due to their detention. While some state governments and the Federal Bureau of Prisons successfully and carefully released some incarcerated people early, at the outset of the pandemic, our carceral systems are so bloated in the United States that none of it made much difference in the aggregate, though it most certainly did for each individual and their families. Increased population density inside correctional settings and elevated prevalence of cardiac and respiratory conditions increased the exposure risk for incarcerated people and staff.

Estimates of infection in the United States indicate that the COVID-19 case rate for incarcerated populations is 5.5 times higher than for people in the general population (Saloner, Parish, Ward, DiLaura, & Dolovich, 2020). Nearly 3,000 incarcerated people and staff have died thus far, and this is likely a significant undercount since most prison and jail systems are only counting deaths while in custody and deaths directly related to COVID-19, rather than those that occur after release or that are COVID-related deaths (Turcotte, Sherman, Griesbach, & Hinga Klein, 2021). To me, it serves as a heavy reminder that our hegemonic, pseudo-solution to crime through mass incarceration continues to have life and death consequences, never more real than now, with far too many individuals caught up in correctional systems that cannot easily respond to major public health emergencies.

While this is not a correctional health textbook per se, I want to emphasize that as long as justice-involved people and the practitioners who work with them behind walls and in the community are at greater risk of contracting the coronavirus, the work of positive behavior change and public safety will be threatened. Most clients are only going to do the hard, painful work to reflect on the harms they have committed if they feel safe and relatively healthy. The pandemic continues to threaten this challenging, deeply personal work by forcing many people to stick to their survival strategies that have gotten them this far in life.

As a result, I feel an obligation now, more than ever, to promote the effective strategies that can help people gain their rightful place as mother or father; wife or husband; daughter or son to their families—their rightful place to a life that most justice-involved people have only ever dreamed of living. As correctional scholars who have worked alongside countless agencies and the clients they serve, Pat and I know full well that there will be many system-involved people who beat the odds and fight their ways to personal and psychological growth with the guidance of well-educated practitioners. Our sincere hope is that this text continues to serve in that role.

The tenth edition of this text is dedicated to the individuals who lost that additional chance of personal growth and change, who died and will die from COVID-19 and COVID-19 related complications while living and working behind bars.

Several substantial revisions have been made for the tenth edition. First, we made a concerted effort to use person-first, or person-centered, language throughout the book (Bedell et al., 2019). We felt it important to model more humanistic language, especially since we come from a counseling and therapeutic perspective. After listening to many formerly incarcerated people about this issue, I am convinced that using terms like "offender," "criminal," and "inmate" inflict undue emotional duress on people who are making strides toward change and also contribute to cultures of harm—and so they have been consciously avoided. Unfortunately, they cannot always be eliminated because much of our classic disciplinary terminology includes these labels in the titles of assessments and major areas of inquiry, an illustration of just how pervasive these terms are. The shift to person-centered language is not to diminish the harms that many system-involved people have engaged in, but to recognize that these stigmatizing labels can disrupt the therapeutic alliance and assimilate correctional professionals into cultures that forget they are delivering *human services*. We do not wish to perpetuate these cultures.

Additionally, the Table of Contents has been reorganized slightly to reflect what we feel is a more straightforward presentation of content. Part I remains an introduction to the professional skills necessary for correctional counseling. A new chapter has been added to this section, titled "Community Corrections Officers as Change Agents" (Chapter 3), to highlight the important behavioral change role that probation and parole officers are increasingly expected to accomplish, beyond their law enforcement role, in an era of evidence-based corrections. Chapter 4 (Correctional Treatment: Accomplishments and Realities) has been moved up to introduce readers to the evidence of correctional rehabilitation as foundational knowledge for the remaining chapters.

Part II has been modified and now reflects "Client Assessment, Diagnosis, Classification, and Case Planning" whereas Part III introduces readers to the contemporary modalities used with clients in the system. Part IV focuses on the specific needs of clients who require distinct treatment approaches.

Additionally, a glossary has been appended to each chapter, as well as various Online Learning Enhancements that instructors and students may use to dig deeper into chapter content. A companion website with video content, PowerPoint slide decks, a test bank, flashcards, and other instructional aids is also available online at www.routledge.com/cw/salisbury.

E. J. Salisbury

REFERENCES

Bedell, P. S., So, M., Morse, D. S., Kinner, S. A., Ferguson, W. J., & Spaulding, A. C. (2019). Corrections for academic medicine: The importance of using person-first language for individuals who have experienced incarceration. *Academic Medicine, 94,* 172–175.

Saloner, B., Parish, K., Ward, J. A., DiLaura, G., & Dolovich, S. (2020). COVID-19 cases and deaths in federal and state prisons. *JAMA, 324,* 602–603.

Turcotte, M., Sherman, R., Griesbach, R., & Hinga Klein, A. (2021, July 21). The real toll from prison Covid cases may be higher than reported. *The New York Times.* Retrieved from www.nytimes.com/2021/07/07/us/inmates-incarcerated-covid-deaths.html?searchResultPosition=4

Acknowledgments

We would like to thank our new contributing authors to the textbook. Many thanks to Lori Brusman Lovins, Bobbie Ticknor, Linsey Belisle, Whitney Howey, and Ben Marrufo for contributing their expertise to several chapters in the tenth edition. Their contributions were kindly facilitated by Brenda Vose who is a colleague and friend to the authors and the text. We would also like to recognize Ashley Shank who engaged in the diligent work of improving the text with person-centered language and created the chapter glossaries. Next, Jaclyn Parker Keen deserves special acknowledgment for significantly improving the ancillary materials that make the content and ideas more accessible to instructors and students. Of course, our team at Routledge has also been integral to the book's publication—we thank Kate Taylor and her team for their attention to detail and communication during the production phase. Lastly, we wish to give much appreciation to Ellen Boyne, our editor at Routledge, for giving us the time and flexibility to finish the tenth edition under extreme and uncertain conditions during the COVID-19 pandemic.

PART I

A Professional Framework for Correctional Counseling

The purpose of Part I of this text is to encourage the reader to develop a personal sense of what correctional counseling is about. Prior to presenting specific strategies and theories of counseling in later chapters, we wish to devote some time to what the career is like. Such an awareness includes a general understanding of essential counseling skills and responsibilities. It is also important to examine more specifically the professional context of correctional counseling; that is, how it relates both formally and informally to the rest of the correctional process. Part I also discusses a number of challenges unique to correctional counselors in comparison with counselors working with people who are not involved in the justice system. Part I concludes with how community corrections staff, though not called "counselors," are increasingly expected to possess basic counseling skills to improve the likelihood of their client's success and behavioral change.

In Chapter 1 (The Process of Correctional Counseling and Treatment), several key professional and human dimensions of the counseling relationship are presented. The chapter discusses the importance of timing, motivation, effective risking, and the characteristics of a therapeutic relationship. Readers are introduced to the essentials of effective communication and the importance of developing sensitivity to gender and ethnic differences. The authors show how varied the counseling function is across different correctional settings (community versus institutional), as well as across different contexts such as probation, parole, education, recreation, institutional counseling, psychotherapy, and spiritual counseling.

Chapter 2 (Understanding the Special Challenges Faced by the Correctional Counselor) helps readers to better understand the world of corrections through the eyes of the correctional counselor. Particular attention is paid to such job stressors as prison overcrowding, excessive paperwork, involuntary clients, large caseloads, conning behaviors of incarcerated people, and staff burnout. Readers are introduced to valuable strategies for coping with challenging environments and system-impacted people who are resistant to treatment. A discussion of ethics and standards of practice for counselors is crucial to anyone in the role of therapist or counselor.

Finally, Chapter 3 (Community Corrections Officers as Change Agents) reminds readers that community corrections officers are human service agents, and as such, the chapter

DOI: 10.4324/9780367808266-1

focuses on the critical relational and motivational interviewing skills these staff must possess for client behavioral change, even though they are not counselors or clinicians. The dual role orientation is an important concept in this reading, noting the effectiveness of shifting probation and parole officers' function from purely enforcement agents to change agents as well. Justice-involved people on community supervision have far better outcomes when their supervising officer displays firm, fair, *and caring* supervision strategies with appropriate professional boundaries while teaching clients skills.

Part I encourages the reader to become personally involved in the correctional counseling process, to understand that there is an inevitable blending of personal beliefs, professional feelings, and practice. To the extent that the goal of this part is realized, the remainder of the book will become more interesting and meaningful. Correctional counseling is more than learning about counseling techniques. It is also vitally involved with learning through experience: clarifying and developing one's own feelings and beliefs concerning helping others, particularly those impacted by the justice system.

CHAPTER 1

The Process of Correctional Counseling and Treatment

Michael Braswell, Jennifer L. Mongold, and Emily J. Salisbury

KEY TERMS

case management	Motivational Interviewing
change talk	professional humility
community-based counselors	psychotherapy
effective risking	storytelling
institutional counselors	therapeutic intention and outcome
meta-analysis	timing

What does it mean to be a correctional counselor? A related question could be "What does it mean to be a well-integrated, helpful human being?" In its broadest context, correctional counseling is about helping persons who are troubled in one way or another and in most cases "in trouble." School teachers and guidance counselors, concerned neighbors, family members, and other grounded and compassionate persons may proactively intervene in the troubled lives of youth and adults. Such actions in some instances may help in ways that keep troubled individuals out of the justice system altogether. In a more professional and specific context, correctional counselors have studied both the science and art of human behavior and been trained to utilize therapeutic intervention strategies. At the outset, it seems important to note that a well-educated and well-trained counselor who is also a compassionate and helpful human being will end up being a better, more effective counselor. Conversely, no matter how highly educated one might be or what level of technical competence one might possess, without the human component—genuine care and commitment to the helping process—therapeutic outcomes for both the client and the counselor will fall short.

Correctional counseling and treatment services span numerous correctional and pretrial settings, including correctional institutions, community-based residential settings, probation and parole, human service programs that contract with correctional agencies, and, most recently, specialized mental health, veterans, and drug courts. In addition, more recent restorative justice programs include more informal community settings that include victims, justice-involved people, their neighbors, and criminal justice professionals (Van Ness & Strong, 2015; Wozniak, Braswell, Vogel, & Blevins, 2008).

DOI: 10.4324/9780367808266-2

Correctional counseling requires a combination of skill, knowledge, and experience—all of which shape the counselor's professional attitude and style. Each system-impacted person presents the counselor with a unique counseling situation and challenge that, in many instances, offers little promise of an adequate resolution. For example, imagine yourself the counselor in the following case (Braswell, Miller, & Cabana, 2006):

> John has been in prison for two years. He is a likable guy who works in the prison library. Usually quiet, John has a remarkable talent for repairing damaged books. He has saved the prison library hundreds of dollars by his efforts.
>
> As his counselor, you try to see him at least once a month to find out how he is getting along. He always indicates that he is doing all right and that he is optimistic regarding his parole hearing, which is only nine months away. John has some reason to feel good about his chances for making parole—this is his first time being involved in the justice system. As a result of getting into a drunken brawl at a bar and seriously injuring another man, he was sentenced to six years in the state penitentiary. Although John had experienced severe drinking problems for a number of years, fighting had never been a part of the problem. Since being in prison, he has completed intensive substance use therapy, joined Alcoholics Anonymous, and has even successfully completed several college-level courses in library science. Needless to say, counseling John is a pleasant experience for the most part because of his own motivation.
>
> However, in the last several weeks John's behavior and attitude have changed. His wife, who has been visiting him faithfully every Sunday, has not shown up for the last two visitation days. The cell block rumor is that she is seeing another man and is planning to file for divorce. To make matters worse, the man she is involved with is an alcoholic himself. John has quit coming to work and keeps to himself in the cell block. He has also been losing weight and looks haggard and distraught.

As his counselor you want to help, but John, who has always been quiet, has now become even more withdrawn. You are not sure how to approach him. You have considered talking to his wife or his parents. If John's depression continues to worsen, his behavior may become unpredictable. He might become aggressive and get into a fight with someone in the cell block or he might turn his anger inward and attempt suicide. You have to approach him, but how? You have to do something in an attempt to help him, but what?

As a correctional counselor, you are aware that the odds are substantially against a marriage surviving the extended imprisonment of one of the spouses. Yet John is your client, and he is distraught. Will his unhappiness explode in a cell block confrontation, endangering the safety of prison staff or other incarcerated people? Or will it, perhaps, result in an internal explosion in the form of emotional illness or self-inflicted injury? Although your therapeutic options and resources are limited, you will have to do the best you can. Will your counseling efforts be successful in resolving John's crisis? If they are not, will you and John be able to live with the consequences? The chapters in this text will attempt to:

1. Introduce you to some of the professional and human dimensions of the correctional counseling process.

2. Help you to better understand characteristics of justice-involved clients and correctional counselors.

3. Explore the role of diagnosis and classification in the treatment of people involved in the justice system.
4. Examine a variety of correctional counseling approaches.
5. Explain how correctional counseling has changed in theory and practice.
6. Consider selected special issues and problems in counseling the system-impacted population.

GOALS OF CORRECTIONAL COUNSELING AND TREATMENT

This book focuses on "correctional" counseling and treatment. While it seems that current politics favor the term "correctional," the idea of "correctional" counseling may not be compatible with what most counselors consider the legitimate interest and purposes of helping people impacted by the justice system. For instance, is the primary goal of counselors who work in prison one of correcting individuals for successful readjustment to the outside world, or is their primary role concerned with adjusting them to the institutional world of the prison? Or should correctional counselors be concerned with both possibilities, including the client becoming more responsible and peaceful whether he or she eventually gets out of prison or spends the rest of his or her life incarcerated? Similarly, does the basic goal of probation and parole officers revolve around therapeutically correcting people under their supervision, or are they more concerned with the enforcement of the conditions of probation and parole? More fundamentally, one might ask whether there is any substantial evidence that counselors could "correct" system-involved people if they wanted to. In fact, correctional counselors often relate frustration over their inability to conduct interventions geared to helping people reform and change the course of their lives. For example, prison case managers and counselors tell of devoting most of their time to facilitating incarcerated people's adjustment to the institution rather than to their more long-term adjustment to a normal/prosocial life on the outside (see Chapter 2). Similarly, probation and parole officers maintain that their time is overburdened by enforcement of the conditions of probation and parole, leaving little time for assisting clients with reintegration and community adjustment. Given the conflicts counseling staff face, institutional and outside-world adjustments are not necessarily mutually exclusive.

The goals of correctional counseling and treatment are challenged by the convergence of several realities:

1. Political and scholarly debate concerning the effectiveness of therapy and treatment interventions (e.g., Andrews & Bonta, 2010; Cullen & Gendreau, 2000; Lipsey, 1992, 2009; Martinson, 1974; Van Voorhis, Cullen, & Applegate, 1995).
2. A litigiously based drive for hypervigilant, if not excessive, agency accountability (Hepburn, 1989).
3. Declining fiscal and personnel resources resulting from prison overcrowding and severe cuts to local, state, and federal correctional treatment budgets.
4. A failure by the general public and lawmakers to understand that correctional health care is the very definition of public health care. This failure became even more apparent during the COVID-19 pandemic.

What seems to be a more appropriate focus is to view correctional counselors as helping professionals who attempt to apply their skills and expertise in correctional and related settings. In doing so, they try to focus on the strategies that are likely to reduce future offending. The primary goal of these counselors appears to be one of intervening therapeutically with various clients, the majority of whom happen to be involved in the justice system. To name a few, these interventions may address prison adjustment, reentry, risk of future offending, trauma, family concerns, substance use, education and employment, and mental health concerns. In addition, counseling interventions are not just about guiding people toward prosocial behavior but also about creating opportunities for them to experience personal and social transformation (Ward & Maruna, 2007; Wozniak et al., 2008).

THE COUNSELING PROCESS

Correctional counseling and psychotherapy are comprised of a process that involves four essential qualities:

1. a sense of timing and good communication
2. effective risking
3. therapeutic intention and outcome
4. professional humility

In order for one to develop a sense of **timing**, the counselor needs, first, to pay—careful—attention to whatever the client is communicating. Communication is the lifeblood of relationships. It is the way we get to know each other. Communication includes what we say and do not say; what we hear and do not hear. It includes the way we look, dress, and feel. In this regard, Virginia Satir's work continues to have meaning for us today. In defining communication, Satir (1972) states, "Communication covers the whole range of ways people pass information back and forth; it includes the information they give and receive, and the ways that the information is needed. Communication covers how people make meaning of the information" (p. 20).

There are six basic elements of communication that everyone contributes to the communication process (exceptions to this would include persons with such disabilities as visual or hearing impairment):

1. The body is an element of communication that moves and has form and shape. How a person moves, as well as his or her physical appearance, can provide the correctional counselor with significant information. An unclean physical appearance, for example, might be indicative of depression—or an indication the client does not feel safe and is trying to deter others from approaching. The body language of crossed arms may be indirectly signaling to keep our distance.

2. Values are another element of communication. They are usually reflected in a person's behavioral habits and verbal communication, especially concerning what people "ought and ought not to do."

3. Another important element of communication are the expectations a person brings to an experience. These expectations are, for the most part, based upon past experiences and

are inclined to influence the way a person perceives his or her own and others' communication. Sometimes negative expectations (e.g., all justice-involved people are bad and untrustworthy) can contribute to a person experiencing poor communication and human relations skills and eventually might encourage a destructive self-fulfilling prophecy.

4. The sense organs (i.e., eyes, ears, nose, mouth, and skin) enable a person to see, hear, smell, taste, and be touched.

5. Words and a person's voice combine to provide that individual with the ability to talk, which is essential to all verbal communication.

6. Finally, the brain stores the knowledge a person has acquired from past experiences. All of these elements work together in each person's communication process (Satir, 1972).

Good communication does not occur automatically. Communication can be constructive or destructive. To be an effective and helpful communicator, one must be skilled at listening, interpreting, and expressing oneself. As much as possible, when interacting with others, the counselor needs to listen in a nonjudgmental manner. Because the client is typically involved in the justice system, it is easy to come to view such a relationship in terms of "us versus them." The client, however, has already been judged and found guilty. As counselors, we need to be clear and open-minded in an effort to establish a basis for trust with the person we are working with if we are to have any hope of establishing a basis for meaningful communication.

Many counselors, particularly those who work with system-involved people, may find it difficult to pay adequate attention to their clients' communication. Perhaps this difficulty is, to a large extent, the result of the counselor's professional and personal attitude, an attitude that is a reflection of the counselor's dual responsibility (i.e., security and treatment) and, as mentioned previously, the retributive feelings of society in general. Indeed, we live in a social system that is often punishment-oriented. In addition, the counselor who works in a correctional setting is typically concerned first with security/custody needs of the agency and community, and second with the treatment and rehabilitation needs of the client.

A part of the basis for meaningful communication also includes being sensitive to, and able to interact with, an ethnically and culturally diverse population. In the United States, as counselors, we often are inclined to filter everyone and everything through our dominant culture—white, male, middle-class, heterosexual values. However, we are a pluralistic society that includes a diversity of people with myriad experiences. Different groups of individuals have their own values and ways of communicating. Yonas and Garland (1994) suggest four ways to sensitize helping professionals particularly to ethnic variations:

1. Sensitize practitioners to ethnic variations in approaches to problem-solving.

2. Provide greater understanding of the general perspectives, common problems, and specific needs of the people from specific ethnic backgrounds.

3. Clarify the likely sources and probable nature of conflicts between service providers and clients from specific ethnic groups.

4. Suggest ways in which the organizational structure and operating procedures of the criminal justice system complement or come into conflict with the values, orientations, and lifestyles of people from specific ethnic backgrounds.

Gender responsivity has become another concern for correctional counselors. This concern emerges from increasing accusations that prevailing correctional treatment focuses primarily on male clients and ignores female clients (Chesney-Lind, 2000). Or at best, the current intervention and assessment models were developed for males and applied to females with insufficient thought to relevance or effectiveness (Morash, Bynum, & Koons, 1998; Van Voorhis, 2012). Females impacted by the justice system have different problems to deal with than justice-involved males. Six out of 10 women in state prisons have sexual or physical abuse in their past. Another issue for girls and women impacted by the system is the role of motherhood. In 1999, there were an estimated 615,500 mothers under correctional supervision with approximately 1.3 million children under age 18 (Greenfeld & Snell, 1999). These different aspects of the woman's life can create special problems that need to be addressed differently in the therapeutic environment and treatment. Bloom, Owen, and Covington (2003) put forward several guiding principles for gender-responsive policies and programs, and more are discussed in Chapter 13. Those most relevant to correctional treatment and counseling are as follows:

1. Acknowledge that gender makes a difference.
2. Create environments based on safety, respect, and dignity.
3. Develop interventions that are relational in their approach, focusing on healthy connections to children, family, significant others, and the community.
4. Address substance use, trauma, and mental health issues in an integrated and culturally relevant manner.

While effective communication skills and a sensitivity to racial, ethnic, sexual orientation, and gender differences and identities are essential to developing a sense of timing, depth of meaning and insight often comes from stories. Counseling embodies a variety of therapeutic skills and knowledge, but those elements often come alive through stories. In a sense, counseling is also **storytelling** and story listening. Stories allow us to experience ourselves and others in a more personal and dynamic context. Like their ancient counterparts, modern counselors listen, ask questions, and, in a manner of speaking, tell stories (Kurtz & Ketcham, 2002). In citing an archetypal story, Kurtz and Ketcham (2002) write, "the shortest distance between a human being and Truth is a story" (p. 142). The transcendent potential of stories concerning therapeutic possibilities and personal insight and transformation has been examined and explored by other therapists and social change agents (Berg & Quinney, 2005; Dass & Gorman, 1985; Kopp, 1977; Lozoff, 1999).

For the counselor to develop a sense of timing, he or she must be able to respect "where clients are" in terms of their value systems, life experiences, and needs, yet not necessarily respect "what the clients have done" in terms of their behavior. Respecting and understanding where the client is helps the counselor to have a more accurate perception of the general condition of the system-impacted person and aids in the implementation of a meaningful treatment strategy. Listening to the client's feelings, stories, and concerns is essentially a clinical art that enables the counselor to build a base relationship with his or her client that can increase the potential for positive change to occur. Developing the ability to fully listen to a client requires both patience and perseverance. Giving advice to a client before adequately understanding what he or she is trying to communicate is like a physician attempting to provide medical treatment before an adequate assessment has been rendered concerning the nature of the patient's illness. In fact, giving advice to clients is not always a productive goal in the counseling experience. Far better strategies include leading clients to consider making their own decisions for their continued success. Perhaps, in the final analysis, counselors would do well to remember the old adage: "It is not so much 'what' you say as it is 'when' and 'how' you say it."

In recent years, many of these recommendations have come together in a counseling process referred to as **Motivational Interviewing**. Motivational Interviewing was developed for use with substance-using clients, but has been more widely adopted in the field of corrections. Motivational Interviewing is defined as a "client-centered, directive method for enhancing intrinsic motivation to change by exploring and resolving ambivalence" (Miller & Rollnick, 2002, p. 25). Rather than teaching a new skill, or exploring a client's past, Motivational Interviewing is intended to focus on the client's concerns and hopes in the "here and now." As the term implies, the intent of Motivational Interviewing is to enhance the client's intrinsic motivation to change. This is done through a process of eliciting and selectively reinforcing times when clients demonstrate "**change talk**" or their own self-motivational statements. The counseling process seeks to wake up or bring forth motivation inside a client who, on some level, already wants to change, or remains ambivalent about doing so.

Many readers would be quick to recognize that we really do not hear much change talk from those involved in the justice system; we are more likely to hear resistance. However, empathic interviewers who listen reflectively to understand the clients' feelings and perspectives accurately, without judging or blaming, often help clients to better open up to their own experiences and share them with a counselor. If the client-counselor relationship is accepting and empathic, these client disclosures often reveal an ambivalence about change rather than the standard denial of problems.

Motivational Interviewing techniques discourage counselors from arguing for change, assuming the expert role, criticizing, shaming or blaming, interrogating the client, or rushing the process (Stinson & Clark, 2017). Instead counselors are encouraged to develop discrepancies voiced by the client. It is important to stress that the discrepancies must be client-centered, a discrepancy between the client's present behavior and his or her goals and beliefs. For example, when Jane voices that her substance use is keeping her from regaining custody of her children. In this discrepancy, Jane, not the counselor, is presenting the reason for changing. Motivational Interviewing recognizes that people are more persuaded to change by what they hear themselves say than by what they hear others telling them to do. The counselor may have initially called attention to the discrepancy, but all along it was Jane's discrepancy, not one created by the counselor's value system, the rules of probation, or the demand of family members.

What if clients defend against or deny any discrepancy between their behavior and their goals? Motivational Interviewing teaches counselors to "roll with resistance." Arguing will only strengthen defenses and denials. The counselor keeps the discussion going, continues to explore problems, but does not turn that resistance into an argument or an opportunity for a power struggle. The counselor's patience with resistance (timing) increases the chances that clients will, in time, become more open to discrepancies and the need to change. As the language shifts to change talk, it becomes possible for the counselor to reinforce the client for that talk and to shift counseling to a process of building self-efficacy and maintaining motivation. Readers will have the chance to learn more about Motivational Interviewing in Chapter 3.

Effective risking is a skill or an ability that the counselor attempts to impart to his or her client. The offense that brings the client to the counselor could be viewed as the primary "symptom" of other, deeper conflicts. An important goal of the counseling relationship is to help the justice-involved client develop more acceptable ways of relating to his or her environment.

Risking in a general sense is not new to many people impacted by the system. Every time they have tried to commit crimes they have risked arrest and possible imprisonment. Risking in a therapeutic sense—a serious effort to substantially change one's attitude and behavior—is a commitment no one, whether they are justice-involved or not, would take lightly. Such a risk, if unsuccessful, could prove to be devastating to a person's emotional stability and, perhaps, physical survival. For instance, in cases of intimate partner violence, it is a significant risk for a woman to attempt to leave her abusive relationship because this is the time when women are at a heightened risk of being lethally harmed. A great deal of safety planning needs to occur before taking such a risk. In other words, problems that have taken a lifetime to evolve rarely can be changed quickly or with a single decision. Incarcerated people face the additional problem of feeling as though they cannot appear to conform too closely to establishment values. They must keep up the proper image in the cell block or face, in some cases, potentially violent consequences. The key to taking risks is to learn to take risks effectively. Some system-involved people often act impulsively without thinking through their actions in terms of what the consequences may be. The counselor should attempt to help the client assess the costs of his or her actions. In other words: If I choose to take a risk, what will it cost me? The costs may be measured in time (e.g., a possible prison sentence), money, more positive or negative relationships, or even life or death. In a more general sense, we could ask ourselves if "the price we are paying for the life choices we have made is worth it." Figure 1.1 illustrates an instructional tool for helping clients determine the costs and benefits of engaging in a particular behavior. For every behavior, there are both positive and negative short- and long-term consequences. Assisting clients to understand these is part of the behavior change process.

When evaluating the potential costs of a particular risk, the correctional counselor can help the client make a more relevant and effective choice by examining three fundamental existential questions: "Who am I?" "Where am I going?" "Why?" These questions provide a counseling focus that is both "here and now" and responsibility based. "Who am I?" can provide a catalyst for helping the client to put into better perspective the successes and failures of his or her past, as well as the as-yet unrealized hopes and fears of the future in the context of the present—the "here and now." "Where am I going?" suggests two questions: "Where do I currently see myself?" and "Where do I see myself in the future?" These questions apply in particular to people who are justice-involved to help them with risk-taking regarding vocational and career decisions. "Why" enables the counselor to help his or her client experience a greater sense of responsibility and accountability for the choices he or she makes and the risks he or she takes. In fully exploring the "why" of a person's choice, the counselor can help the individual clarify his or her priorities and make a more informed decision in terms of personal meaning and responsibility to others.

Of course, in the end one has to act. Kurtz and Ketcham (2002), in discussing what is perhaps the most successful long-term treatment for alcohol abusers, wrote, "An axiom of A.A. [Alcoholics Anonymous] is 'Bring the body, the mind follows'" (p. 91). For many incarcerated people, the prison they are sentenced to is not as foreboding as the psychological prison their experiences and choices have placed them in. It is true for both system-involved and law-abiding persons that are bound by fear and anger from past interpersonal/psychological wounds, prison becomes more a state of mind than a building of concrete and steel. It takes a lot of courage and encouragement to persist in trying a different approach and response.

BEHAVIOR: _____

CONSEQUENCES

	+	−
SHORT-TERM		
LONG-TERM		

FIGURE 1.1 Cost-benefit analysis instructional tool.

Understanding **therapeutic intention and outcome** is essential to effective therapeutic relationships and has a lot to do with whether a justice-involved person changes for the better. Rather than base one's perception of effectiveness completely on short-term outcomes, the counselor also focuses on the attempt to put his or her good intentions into action through modeling, empathy, and genuineness. Notice, for example, how often people try to do the right thing because they want the respect of parents and friends more than they want just a good grade in college or a job promotion. Good relationships often motivate people to action. In the context of therapeutic relationships, clients also transfer both positive and negative feelings to the counselor as a part of the dynamics of the relationship process. How the counselor responds to these feelings will have a substantial impact on any potential attitude change on the part of the client.

The therapeutic relationship is also important during times when the system-impacted client's life just does not seem fair. The support of the therapeutic relationship sustains the client during times when, despite their best efforts, life is discouraging. As van Wormer (1999) observes, "Sometimes one encounter or one supportive relationship—whether it be a teacher, social worker, or priest—can offer a turning point in a life of crime" (p. 51). Bo Lozoff (1999) writes, "A staff person who's calm and strong and happy is worth his or her weight in gold. People who are living examples of truthfulness, good humor, patience, and courage are going to change more lives—even if they're employed as janitors—than counselors who can't get their own lives in order" (p. 52). In commenting on the work of Mother Teresa, Tim Ward (in O'Reilly, O'Reilly, & O'Reilly, 2002) offers sound advice to the counselor when he writes, "Do the task at hand without delusions that you can cure all suffering" (p. 190).

Professional humility plays an important role in the success of therapy as well as the effectiveness of the therapist or counselor. In truth, the words *humility*, *humor*, and *humanity* all come from the same root word and are key aspects to accepting responsibility for what we human beings have done to each other and our willingness to change. Rohr (in Kurtz & Ketcham, 2002) challenges us to let go of three needs: the need to be in control, the need to be effective, and the need to be right. It is easy to get carried away with one's accomplishments. Success with one type of treatment for a particular client does not necessarily translate into success with that treatment for other clients. Counselors have the ability to reach many people, but not every person will respond to a counselor's efforts, no matter how well intentioned or prepared the counselor is. These are important caveats to consider for the beginning counselor as well as for the seasoned veteran therapist. Professional humility is a way to stay grounded with successes as well as failures.

It is important that the correctional counselor be committed to his or her therapeutic effort and intention. Indeed, to persevere—to continue trying—may be more important to long-term correctional rehabilitation and stability than more immediate treatment outcomes. Life does not necessarily offer rewards or guarantees for people who try to do the right thing. For example, the justice-involved client who appears to have become rehabilitated may return to prison in short order after committing other crimes. Conversely, a person who seemed unresponsive to treatment may complete his or her sentence and lead a reasonably productive, crime-free life for any number of reasons. In cases in which the counselor has done all she or he can do to help the client and the intervention does not succeed, there should be no regrets. If professional humility reminds us of anything, it is that, in the final analysis, we do not control outcomes. All we can do is all we can do.

TYPES OF CORRECTIONAL COUNSELING

Within correctional settings, counselors are generally divided into two categories: (1) community-based and (2) institutional.

Community-based counselors include probation and parole service professionals (even though they are not certified clinicians), halfway house counselors, case managers for drug courts or mental health courts, and probation or parole officers with specialized caseloads (e.g., for mental health clients, justice-involved women, or persons convicted of sex offenses). Counselors working in pretrial or supervised release settings could also be included in this group. Other, yet very important, professional resources include mental health centers, public schools, employment agencies, volunteers, day reporting programs, private helping centers (e.g., alcohol and other drug counseling), and pastoral counselors and other faith-based agencies and organizations.

Probation is perhaps most utilized as an alternative to sentencing adjudicated juveniles and convicted adults to correctional institutions. Essentially, probation consists of mandating a person to a community-based treatment or other correctional program rather than incarceration. Probation officers are responsible for managing and supervising people who have been placed on community-based orders (e.g., community service, home detention, etc.) by the courts.

Parole officers supervise and monitor people who have been released on parole from prison or jail. Unlike probation officers, who usually work with people before incarceration, parole officers work with people after they have been incarcerated for a period of time. The work of some parole officers actually begins prior to release as they prepare people for their return home.

The treatment and counseling functions of probation and parole have increased in recent years. For example, these officers are often required to conduct intake risk/needs assessments (see Chapter 6) or screen for mental health, trauma, or substance use problems. In addition, many probation and parole officers now facilitate cognitive behavioral treatment groups on topics such as anger management, healthy relationships, cognitive skills, or life skills (see Chapters 9 and 10). Finally, both probation and parole officers are responsible for monitoring and assessing the compliance of people on probation and parole with court-ordered conditions of release. If people fail to comply with conditions of release, both probation and parole officers may initiate revocation proceedings (i.e., a process that responds to violations of the conditions of probation or parole) against such people.

It is important to note that the roles of both probation and parole officers are, to some extent, conflictual in nature. These professionals are faced with reconciling the competing roles of public safety and the rehabilitation and reintegration of people involved in the system (Purkiss, Kifer, Hemmens, & Burton, 2003). In other words, probation and parole officers are charged with ensuring public safety, while at the same time being asked to help their clients. One problem with this dual role centers on the issue of counselor/client confidentiality. If the client is aware that his or her probation/parole officer must investigate and enforce the conditions of probation/parole, building a truly confidential relationship is likely to be significantly reduced. The confidentiality dilemma of "treatment versus security" is a conflict that all correctional counselors share to some extent. More discussion on the dual role of parole and probation officers is discussed in Chapter 3.

Institutional counselors and treatment professionals often include: intake assessment staff, institutional parole officers, psychologists, psychiatrists, social workers, counselors, case managers, chaplains, educators, vocational instructors, and recreation specialists. These professionals will work with the incarcerated person to varying degrees, depending on his or her individual needs. However, the majority of incarcerated people are usually assigned to a counselor (sometimes referred to as a prison case manager or an institutional parole officer) with whom they should have considerable interaction during their incarceration. Like their community counterparts, institutional counselors are responsible for supervising and monitoring justice-involved people.

However, these individuals also perform a number of other important duties, which include:

1. Monitoring and assessing incarcerated people's adjustment problems.

2. Assessing risk and needs, or administering institutional custody assessments.

3. Developing and recommending interventions considered most beneficial for the rehabilitation of incarcerated people.

4. Advising and counseling incarcerated people regarding their problems and monitoring and evaluating their progress.

5. Communicating with incarcerated people's families and contacts in the community to maintain established bonds outside the institution.

6. Planning for community reentry upon the incarcerated person's release from prison.

In addition, counselors prepare reports for parole boards and make recommendations concerning an incarcerated person's release. More importantly, they play a crucial role in the person's transition from the institutional setting to community life. For example, counselors provide discharge planning so that, upon release, people on parole can be referred to community-based programs that fit their individual needs. Ideally, institutional and community-based counselors coordinate their efforts to make a client's transition from the correctional institution to the community easier.

Another institutional counselor who often plays an important role in the client's life is the prison chaplain. Chaplains perform a number of duties, including conducting religious and funeral services, counseling troubled clients, conveying news of family tragedies to clients, and helping to link people on parole to community religious or faith-based resources. However, the chaplain's primary focus is often to help incarcerated people survive the stresses of prison life.

In correctional institutions, there are four basic categories of treatment programming:

1. education
2. recreation
3. counseling/casework
4. psychotherapy

The educational specialist working in a prison or the correctional educator in general is confronted with a highly challenging population of potential students. Both juveniles (Hodges, Guiliotti, & Porpotage, 1994) and adults (Kirsch, Jungeblut, Jenkins & Kolstad, 1993) involved in the justice system evidence lower literacy levels than their counterparts in the general population. The failure of many of these people within the mainstream educational system is primarily the result of unidentified or unaddressed learning disabilities (Corley, 1996; Parkinson, Dulfano, & Nink, 2003). Research has also demonstrated a link between inadequate education of incarcerated people and prior employment (Whitehead, Jones, & Braswell, 2008). In one study, a substantial percentage of incarcerated people were either unemployed or working part-time prior to their arrest. In addition, 70% of them reported incomes less than $15,000 per year (Harlow, 2003).

Unfortunately, traditional educational approaches do not work with most system-involved people, and matching people with the appropriate instructional or educational programs often presents a considerable challenge for correctional educators. However, being able to meet these educational challenges translate into a significant payoff for society. Research consistently demonstrates that incarcerated people who participate in educational programs have lower recidivism rates (Davis, Bozick, Steele, Saunders, & Miles, 2013) and better community adjustment (McCollum, 1994).

Even so, many national organizations, such as the American Correctional Association (ACA) and the Correctional Education Association (CEA), have noted a number of deficiencies in the educational opportunities available in prison, and they continue to push for changes within correctional education. The United Nations Economic and Social Council (UNESC), for example, endorses correctional education standards, which include:

1. All incarcerated people should have access to education.
2. People in prison should have access to literacy programs, basic education; vocational training; creative, religious and cultural activities; recreational education and activities; social education; higher education; and library facilities.

3. Prison administrators and managers should facilitate and support education as much as possible.

4. Disincentives to incarcerated people who participate in approved formal educational programs should be avoided.

5. Wherever possible, people who are incarcerated should be allowed to participate in education outside prison.

6. Where education has to take place within the prison, the outside community should be involved as fully as possible.

7. Vocational education should aim at the greater development of the individual and be sensitive to trends in the labor market.

8. Creative and cultural activities should be given a significant role because they have a special potential for enabling incarcerated people to develop and express themselves.

9. Educational opportunities should aim at developing the whole person, bearing in mind the incarcerated person's social, economic, and cultural background (National Institute of Correctional Education, 2004).

The latter portion of these standards recognizes the importance of allowing an incarcerated person to reach his or her full potential and develop as a "whole" person by providing as many educational opportunities as possible. However, providing educational opportunities is not enough. Because many people who are incarcerated may believe that society views them as failures, not worthy of further investment, their success may hinge on the relationships they build with correctional educators or other treatment professionals. As with client-counselor relationships, the interpersonal skills the educator brings to his or her relationship with a justice-involved person will often determine success or failure (van Wormer, 1999). The attitude of educators, especially in correctional settings, may represent a "make or break" point regarding a person's willingness to commit to learning. If a teacher is judgmental, he or she simply reinforces the "guilty as charged" motif reflected in the typical perceptions and experiences incarcerated people tend to have with the system. If a teacher encourages and inspires, the odds increase that at least a number of incarcerated students will respond in kind. Feelings and intuition, critical thinking skills and knowledge, and imagination, creativity, and wonder are all important elements in encouraging people in prison to experience learning and themselves in a new way (Braswell & Whitehead, 2002; Moriarty, 2008).

One of the authors had an older incarcerated person under his supervision who refused to attend basic education classes even though the person in question was functionally illiterate. After several weeks of pondering the challenge, the counselor found a way to motivate the client to begin learning to read and write. Realizing the client was more or less a sports fanatic who loved to quote batting averages, won-lost records, and other sports statistics he gleaned from television sports news, the counselor offered to appoint him assistant sports editor for the prison newsletter, contingent upon his successful completion of the basic education program. What the client had vigorously resisted in the past, he began to enthusiastically embrace. The result was that he completed basic education and continued in the educational process.

Recreational programs offer distinct advantages over other treatment programs. For instance, one does not have to be able to read and write to participate in and learn from recreational programs. Even physically disabled people involved in the system can engage in a variety of recreational activities (e.g., arts and crafts, music, table games). A major problem

FIGURE 1.2 Incarcerated people at a state penitentiary work with General Education Diploma (GED) test materials.
Source: AP Photo/Greg Wahl-Stephens.

regarding correctional recreation has been one of perception. Too often, the correctional recreation specialist has been no more than an athletic "coach," coordinating a few recreational activities such as softball, basketball, and weightlifting, which are meaningful to only a small percentage of the incarcerated population.

The "treatment versus security" dilemma is nowhere more evident than in the area of correctional recreation. If a correctional institution does not utilize a varied and comprehensive recreation program, people are left with a substantial amount of idle time and very few appropriate outlets for venting any frustrations or tensions they might be experiencing. Such a situation can, of course, result in an increase in physical and emotional conflicts among incarcerated people, ranging from sexual assaults to personal depression. Indeed, if a correctional institution operates a varied and comprehensive recreational program, new problems as well as benefits will probably occur. More recreational programs and activities result in a more complex scheduling process. Meals, work assignments, education programs, and other aspects of institutional life need to operate smoothly in conjunction with recreational activities. Another concern is for the security of recreational events. Inadequate and ineffective supervision could result in a security and treatment nightmare.

A number of innovations have occurred in recreation and related programming that have implications for corrections. Outward Bound and therapeutic wilderness programs have been used with system-impacted juveniles eligible for incarceration (Wilson & Lipsey, 2000). The programs provide a rugged outdoor experience, usually of one or two weeks in duration, in which youths engage in:

1. physical conditioning (e.g., running and hiking)
2. technical training (e.g., lifesaving, solo survival)
3. safety training
4. team training (e.g., rescue and firefighting)

An important aspect of the program is teaching the youths that they are capable of doing more than they think they can do and that they can learn to trust and help others. Results are mixed as to whether these programs can successfully reduce recidivism long-term with adolescents (Clem, Prost, & Thyer, 2015), but programs appear to be more effective when they incorporate therapeutic components such as individual counseling and family therapy (Wilson & Lipsey, 2000).

Counseling and case management functions and process (the subject of the remainder of this book) provide a cohesiveness that enables institutional and other programmatic activities to run as smoothly as possible. Traditionally, counselors work with both individual clients and conduct group counseling sessions relating to different kinds of problems (e.g., drug use, sexual offending, problem-solving, anger management, and suicide prevention). Formally and, more importantly, informally, counselors function as "crisis intervenors." From the newly arrived client who is anxious and depressed, to the incarcerated person who has just been turned down for parole, the counselor must intervene in a diverse and varied array of interpersonal situations. Counselors try to help clients adjust to and function in the institution with a minimal amount of interpersonal frustration and deterioration. Effective treatment or rehabilitation does occur, but in the context of many challenges. For example, treatment is often secondary to general crisis intervention and maintenance functions. In addition, some justice-involved people genuinely want to change; others do not. Some people come to a point in their lives where they want to chart a more positive and meaningful course; others are comfortable with their antisocial behavior and engage in counseling as a means of improving their situation in prison and their chances of getting out as soon as possible.

The use of correctional counseling as opposed to **psychotherapy** has been an issue of continuing debate. Arguments have been raised regarding the differentiation of the two along lines of theory behind the technique (e.g., psychoanalysis as psychotherapy); degree of emotional disturbance and psychopathology (i.e., more serious disturbances require psychotherapy); clinical work setting (e.g., medical or educational); and level of professional education and training (e.g., the M.D. psychiatrist is a psychotherapist; the Ph.D. or Psy.D. psychologist is a psychotherapist; and the M.A. counseling psychologist is a counselor). Generally speaking, psychotherapists have doctorate degrees (M.D., Ph.D., Psy.D.). In a fundamental sense, however, it is often difficult to determine where counseling stops and psychotherapy begins, especially in correctional settings where most treatment practitioners are counselors with M.A. (master of arts) degrees or social workers with M.S.W. (master's in social work) degrees. This is not to suggest that there is little difference between the M.D. psychiatrist who can prescribe medication and who has completed a psychiatric residency and an M.A.-level counselor. There are obvious and significant differences between the two. It is rather an attempt to point out that, in reality, most institutional and agency clinical treatment professionals who provide counseling or psychotherapy services that are available to justice-involved people are trained at a master's level of expertise.

EFFECTIVENESS OF CORRECTIONAL COUNSELING AND TREATMENT

Historically, there has been considerable debate among practitioners and researchers regarding the effectiveness of counseling and treating people involved in the justice system. However, whether counseling is effective may depend to a large extent on what meaning one gives the word "effective." For some people, effective counseling and treatment is whatever keeps the prison routine running smoothly, with little regard for preparing the system-impacted person to return and readjust to the outside community. For others, effective treatment programs are equated with whatever programs are cheapest to implement and maintain in terms of financial costs. Finally, for many policymakers, members of the general public, and correctional practitioners, reductions in recidivism represent the benchmark measure of effectiveness.

Regardless of one's perspective, the role, function, and degree of success attributed to correctional treatment programs have represented areas of heightened controversy, with support ranging from heavy emphasis on rehabilitation and community reintegration (Andrews & Bonta, 2010; Cullen & Gendreau, 2000; Cullen, Wright, & Applegate, 1996; MacKenzie, 2006; Lipsey, 2009; Palmer, 1992; Smith, Gendreau, & Schwartz, 2009) and restorative justice (Van Ness & Strong, 2015) to very little reliance, if any, on correctional counseling and treatment programs (Dilulio, 1991; Farabee, 2005; Whitehead & Lab, 1989).

A number of approaches have been used to try to measure the effectiveness of justice-involved treatment. The most respected approaches include long-term, post-treatment, follow-up measures; experimental designs (using control groups); and personality or attitudinal change as measured by psychological tests. In examining these approaches, it is apparent that the most accepted evaluation techniques are driven by quantitative methodology (Van Voorhis, 2006). One of the most respected evaluation methodologies utilizes the statistical technique of meta-analysis. **Meta-analysis** affords an opportunity to summarize results across many studies, thereby combining many research samples into one large sample and creating a summary statistic (effect size) that gauges the effectiveness of all or specific types of program modalities. Meta-analyses correct for many of the methodological problems of individual studies, including low base rates and small sample sizes (Lipsey & Wilson, 2001). As will be seen in later chapters of this book, particularly Chapter 4, a series of meta-analyses offers strong recommendations regarding the effectiveness of behavioral, social learning, and cognitive behavioral interventions for people impacted by the system (e.g., Andrews et al., 1990; Lipsey, 1992, 2009; MacKenzie, 2006; Sherman et al., 1997).

Undoubtedly, both practitioners and researchers will continue to debate the merits of program evaluation techniques. It is also likely that they will continue to question the effectiveness of correctional counseling and treatment programs. However, there seems to be a general consensus among many practitioners and researchers regarding the elements that comprise an effective counseling or treatment program. These elements include:

1. Focusing intensive interventions on high-risk rather than low-risk clients who are often harmed by meeting other system-involved people and interruptions to the prosocial influences in their lives (see Chapter 6).

2. Utilization of behavioral and cognitive behavioral interventions (see Part III Chapters 8–11).

3. A high degree of treatment integrity and program quality, where staff adhere to program designs and professional standards (see Chapter 7).

4. A method for matching characteristics of the client, therapist, and program—referred to as the principle of responsivity (see Chapter 6).

5. A cooperative treatment community where health care, education, vocational, recreational, mental health, and substance use professionals work together in a comprehensive, integrated approach in intervening with justice-involved people and promoting prosocial, productive behavior.

6. Administrative and institutional support in providing adequate resources and opportunities to develop and implement meaningful treatment and related programs.

7. A variety of practical life skills and treatment experiences that reinforce personal accountability and relevance both within the institution and in the community.

8. Program evaluation to (a) identify and understand which programs work and which do not, (b) monitor the strengths and weaknesses of effective programs, and (c) identify opportunities for improvement.

9. Relapse prevention strategies to assist the client in the community upon completion of the formal phase of a treatment program in a correctional facility (see Chapter 12).

10. Well-trained treatment staff who have attained appropriate educational credentials.

CONCLUSION

Correctional counselors are involved in both community-based and institution-based programs for justice-involved people. The nature of their job involves both security and treatment functions. The fact that these functions are often in conflict with each other can be frustrating to counselors. Even so, the primary goal of most correctional counselors continues to be one of intervening therapeutically to address prison adjustment, reentry, risk of future offending, substance use, trauma, family concerns, mental health, and employment.

The scope and purpose of correctional counseling covers a dynamic range of professional expertise and responsibility that continues to evolve and challenge the creative energies of the counselor who chooses to work in a correctional environment. Even so, successful counselors possess good communication skills and timing and an ability to motivate system-impacted people to change. These skills must utilize empathy, an ability to reflectively listen to clients' concerns, and a skilled ability to help clients discover how their behaviors are interfering with their hopes and goals. Successful counseling also involves assisting clients to "risk" the process and prospects of change in a realistic and planful manner. Therapeutic intention is essential and involves the counselor's use of commitment, good modeling, empathy, and genuineness. Finally, professional humility is required of counselors, as they understand and accept that some clients will change and some will not, and most will go through a series of goal attainments and setbacks.

While there historically has been debate about the effectiveness of treatment programs with system-involved people, the evidence over the last 50 years is clear: We can no longer talk about improving public safety without including treatment and rehabilitation policies and practices as a scientifically supported part of the equation. This book will make clear to readers that there is a science to how correctional counseling and rehabilitation is achieved—successful programs must adhere to empirically supported principles of effective client intervention, demonstrate a good deal of professionalism, high quality, and fidelity to their underlying program designs.

Discussion Questions

1. What challenges do correctional counselors face that other counselors outside of the field of corrections may not have to deal with?

2. What are the essential abilities that a correctional counselor or therapist needs to possess?

3. What is Motivational Interviewing and why might it be helpful with people involved in the justice system?

4. What is meant by gender-responsivity, and how might it be demonstrated?

5. What are the six basic elements of communication, and how do they relate to the "abilities" in question 2?

6. What are four ways in which correctional counselors become more sensitive to the ethnic and cultural diversity of justice-involved people?

7. Discuss the crucial role that education specialists play as part of the correctional counseling and treatment team.

ONLINE LEARNING ENHANCEMENTS

The Alliance for Higher Education in Prison is an organization that promotes the educational needs of incarcerated people. For readers located in the United States, consider looking into the higher education programs in your home state. www.higheredinprison.org/national-directory/stats-view

GLOSSARY OF KEY TERMS

case management   the coordination of services by correctional counselors to provide quality mental health care that is customized accordingly to a client's setbacks or persistent challenges and to aid them in their recovery and/or reentry

change talk   statements by the client that indicate commitment to, consideration of, or motivation for change

community-based counselors   treatment professionals who work with justice-involved clients in the community; these may include probation and parole service professionals, halfway house counselors, case managers for drug courts or mental health courts, and probation or parole officers with specialized caseloads

effective risking   a skill or an ability that the counselor attempts to impart to his or her client about taking appropriate, careful behavioral risks during the change process

institutional counselors   treatment professionals who supervise and monitor incarcerated clients; these may include intake assessment staff, institutional parole officers, psychologists, psychiatrists, social workers, counselors, case managers, chaplains, educators, vocational instructors, and recreation specialists

meta-analysis a statistical analysis that combines the results of multiple scientific studies

Motivational Interviewing a client-centered counseling approach in which the counselor enhances the client's intrinsic motivation to change by helping them explore and resolve ambivalence

professional humility an essential quality of correctional counseling in which the counselor understands and accepts that some clients will change while others will not; a way for counselors to stay grounded with client successes as well as failures

psychotherapy a basic category of treatment programming in which mental health problems are treated by talking with a psychiatrist, psychologist, or other mental health provider; most psychotherapists possess doctorate degrees (M.D., Ph.D., Psy.D.) as opposed to master's degrees

storytelling a therapeutic technique in which counselors listen to and tell stories to better experience themselves and clients in a more personal and dynamic context

therapeutic intention and outcome an essential quality of correctional counseling in which the counselor, rather than basing assumptions of effectiveness on short-term outcomes, attempts to put his or her good intentions into action through modeling, empathy, and genuineness

timing an essential quality of correctional counseling in which the counselor pays careful attention to what the client is communicating; respects "where clients are" in terms of value systems, life experiences, and needs; and demonstrates patience with client resistance

CHAPTER 2

Understanding the Special Challenges Faced by the Correctional Counselor

William N. Elliott, Jeffrey L. Schrink, and Emily J. Salisbury

KEY TERMS

burnout	multicultural counseling
cognitive behavioral interventions	power and control
collateral information	redirection
contextual demands	reframing
crisis intervention	reversal of responsibility
dual/multiple relationships	special needs clients
ethnocentrism	stereotype
"here and now" style	thinking errors
interpersonal boundaries	treatment versus security dichotomy

The following vignettes were extracted from a 23-year-old criminology graduate's first 90 days on the job as a correctional counselor in a state-operated juvenile correctional facility.

1. The counselor took a group of juveniles involved in the justice system to a nearby county juvenile detention center to conduct peer counseling with the youth at the county facility. At one point during the discussion, the counselor walked up behind one of the county detainees, a rather frail-looking 10-year-old boy, and placed his hand on the youth's shoulder. The boy screamed in terror and ran into the corner of the group room and assumed the fetal position.

2. After only six weeks on the job, the counselor approached the assistant superintendent of the institution and passionately requested that a youth be considered for an early release from custody. The following week, the assistant superintendent informed the counselor that the youth, while watching a movie with other system-impacted youth at a local theater, had stolen a pack of cigarettes from a woman's purse. This theft jeopardized the opportunity for other youth involved in the system to visit the theater.

DOI: 10.4324/9780367808266-3

3. The counselor, following his orientation training, was directed by the superintendent to surreptitiously record an interview with two juveniles. The superintendent believed that the juveniles had engaged in sexual contact with an incarcerated adult who was regarded as a "trustee."

4. Two months after the counselor assumed his position, a colleague transferred to another division of the Department of Correction. The counselor was thus left with two caseloads totaling 100 youth and all of the attendant responsibilities: admission summaries, progress reports, telephone calls, supportive counseling, crisis intervention, classification team meetings, etc.

The new counselor featured in these vignettes was the first author who, with a recently awarded graduate degree in hand and assistance from the second author, had secured a counseling position with a state correctional facility for male youth. Each situation not only served as a painful, albeit necessary, learning experience, but also as a vivid illustration of the special challenges that face the correctional counselor. In the first illustration, the counselor discovered that basic counseling principles and techniques were woefully inadequate in the treatment of people involved in the justice system (in this case a youth who had been the victim of sexual abuse by his father). Prior childhood trauma is highly prevalent among incarcerated children and adults.

In the second vignette, the counselor learned too late that he had fallen prey to ingratiation (Elliott & Verdeyen, 2002), a subtle form of resistance to treatment. The youth had told the counselor that he wished that the counselor had been his father. This endeared the counselor to the youth so much that the youth was not held as accountable for program achievement as other juveniles. In the third instance, the counselor was confronted by the first of many ethical dilemmas (client confidentiality) inherent in correctional counseling. In the final scenario, the counselor was besieged by a huge caseload with excessive paperwork, two of the many **contextual demands** confronting the correctional counselor.

PRELIMINARY CONSIDERATIONS

Before examining the four special challenges cited previously, it is important to define correctional counseling for the purposes of this chapter. Correctional counseling is understood by the authors as an intensive, purposeful, interactive process between a counselor, who is professionally prepared to deal with the special problems posed by a correctional environment, and a client, who has been found guilty of committing a crime or active delinquency and placed in a correctional facility. Although academic and experiential qualifications for correctional counselors may vary across jurisdictional boundaries, most corrections departments require at least an undergraduate degree in criminology/criminal justice or a social or behavioral science. Additionally, higher job classifications have been developed to attract individuals with relevant clinical experience or graduate degrees in counseling and related fields. The caliber of individuals who work as correctional counselors runs the gamut from highly dedicated professionals who take their work seriously to those who just put in the hours to get their paychecks.

Additionally, many of the principles outlined in this chapter and throughout the text are not just for counselors working with justice-involved populations. They also apply more broadly to anyone who works alongside such individuals, such as custody staff, community corrections officers (i.e., probation and parole officers), volunteers, and programming facilitators.

PRINCIPLES AND TECHNIQUES

Beginning correctional counselors are often admonished to forget everything they have learned about traditional counseling techniques. Traditional counseling strategies are dismissed as either irrelevant or susceptible to manipulation by clients involved with the justice system. The authors disagree with the notion that standard counseling methods are inherently useless or ineffective. Rather, conventional counseling principles and techniques must be applied in a unique manner to system-involved populations. For example, it is universally agreed that a warm, collaborative relationship between the counselor and client is required if counseling interventions are to be successful. This is no less true in correctional counseling. However, the correctional counselor must build a relationship through which he or she can guide the client toward more responsible decisions and prosocial behavior.

The importance of establishing a meaningful relationship with the client cannot be overstated. In fact, it is so important that the next chapter in this text is entirely dedicated to it (Chapter 3). Myers and Jackson (2002) assert that, without personal involvement on the part of the counselor, there will be no significant connection with the client and, therefore, counseling will not hold the client's attention. In discussing the appropriateness of this relationship, however, it is important to introduce the notion of **interpersonal boundaries**. A boundary is the invisible line that separates individuals according to their needs, feelings, emotional health, privacy concerns, and other human issues. Counselors examine interpersonal boundaries according to their appropriateness. For example, it would be inappropriate for a stranger to ask us about the intimate details of our lives. However, such discussions are typically not inappropriate with a spouse. Similarly, it is appropriate for parents to exercise authority over their children, but not appropriate for them to exercise such authority over other adults. Counselors also cautiously maintain appropriate boundaries with clients. It is appropriate to develop a therapeutic relationship with clients but inappropriate to develop a sexually intimate relationship with a client, or even one that could be called a friendship.

Unfortunately, many correctional counselors are reluctant to build personal involvement with clients because they fear becoming overly emotionally involved with them. Indeed, managing interpersonal boundaries with justice-involved clients is important for several reasons, not the least of which is preventing manipulation and exploitation (Elliott & Verdeyen, 2002). However, a trusting and open working relationship is not synonymous with emotional overinvolvement and poor boundary management. To the contrary, a collaborative relationship between the counselor and client is seen as a necessary precursor to successful counseling (Harris, 1995). The counseling relationship, or therapeutic alliance, has been systematically shown to be related to positive outcomes in treatment (Drapeau, Korner, & Brunet, 2004).

In traditional counseling, a lot of time is spent both inquiring about and listening to clients' complaints about the actions of other people, the world they live in, and so forth; the list is endless. The authors contend that it is less productive to probe at length for problems. Correctional counselors who sacrifice valuable time and energy exploring the client's past for antecedents of current problems may be ignoring a more likely cause of behavior. That is, it is typically a "here and now" style of thinking that supports and maintains antisocial behavior (Walters, 1990). Moreover, complaining is often an effort to avoid talking about the issues that really need to be discussed, whether the client realizes this or not. The authors suggest that such historical investigations are not only fruitless but at times counterproductive. While there are appropriate times in counseling for understanding how past experiences affect current maladaptive behavior (e.g., in trauma therapy), a sense of accountability for current and future decisions is paramount for justice-involved clients to embrace. While we cannot change clients' past experiences, counselors can guide clients toward healthy cognitive behavioral techniques to view, cope, and heal from their past.

The authors strongly endorse group counseling as the preferred modality for providing treatment to clients involved with the justice system. Groups provide the client with a wealth of new information gathered from interactions with other individuals who can relate to the client's current situation and issues. In addition, groups create an external feedback mechanism (participants challenging and supporting each other) with the prospect of internalization somewhere down the line (Walters, 2001). Moreover, group members will typically refuse to accept excuses from, and are not bashful about offering hard-hitting feedback to, their peers (Myers & Jackson, 2002). Correctional counselors who lack requisite training and experience are encouraged to conduct psychoeducational groups that are highly structured and largely didactic in nature (Elliott & Walters, 1991, 1997). Typically, such groups are time-limited and offer a specific curriculum, including a workbook for participants (Caputo, 2004).

Whenever possible, counselors are advised to seek collateral information regarding the clients they are treating. Indeed, counselors should find out as much as they can about a client's behavior in his or her housing unit, classroom, work area, or elsewhere. Such investigations can be enlightening because many clients often present themselves in a more favorable light in the presence of authorities. Some might call it deceitful, or manipulative behavior, on the part of the client, but good counselors understand that these behaviors typically emerge because clients have had to navigate survival on the streets and the web of social support institutions (e.g., foster care, welfare, etc.). Clients may also be in denial about just how dire their situation truly is. Therefore, it is crucial that the counselor rely on something other than the client's self-report. Reading the client's central file, observing his or her behavior in different contexts, and talking with other staff who know the client are ways in which the counselor can form a reliable and comprehensive impression of the client (Elliott & Verdeyen, 2002). Housing unit officers are especially valuable sources of information because they spend more time with the client than any other staff.

Whether counseling clients in groups or individually, the correctional counselor must adopt and adhere to some kind of conceptual framework for his or her treatment efforts. Unfortunately, there is no "magic bullet" for effectively treating clients. However, focal cognitive behavioral interventions directed at specific antisocial thinking styles have the best efficacy at reducing antisocial behavioral risk and recidivism (McMackin, Tansi, & LaFratta, 2004; see Chapters 8–11).

Yochelson and Samenow (1976) originally described 52 specific thinking errors uncovered in their intensive case studies of incarcerated people housed at St. Elizabeth's Hospital in Washington, D.C. Walters (1990) modified and consolidated these thinking errors into a set of eight interactive "criminal" thinking patterns, which serve as the centerpiece of his comprehensive theory of antisocial behavior. Yochelson and Samenow's model has widespread popularity among counselors in several state institutions, whereas Walters's (1990)

TABLE 2.1 Eight primary criminal thinking patterns	
Walters (1990)	*Elliott and Verdeyen (2002)*
Mollification	The Blaming Game
Cutoff	I Feel Nothing
Entitlement	I Should Get What I Want
Power Orientation	I'm in Charge
Sentimentality	Look at Me Being Good
Superoptimism	I Can Get by with Anything
Cognitive Indolence	That's Too Much Work
Discontinuity	I Talk One Way and Act Another

theory figures prominently in the Federal Bureau of Prisons Psychology Treatment Programs. Regardless of the model selected for use, it is clear that challenging the cognitive distortions or "thinking errors" employed by clients to justify their offending is an integral part of treatment (Houston, 1998).

Elliott and Verdeyen (2002) have adapted the Walters (1990) model in a manner that renders it "user-friendly" to correctional counselors who seek to challenge antisocial thinking exhibited by clients in groups. In Table 2.1, Walters's eight primary criminal thinking patterns are listed in the left-hand column while the corresponding cognitive distortions described by Elliott and Verdeyen appear in the right-hand column. As noted above, the authors of this chapter encourage the correctional counselor to focus his or her efforts on incipient anti-social thinking regardless of the treatment context. However, the counselor is warned that doing so will require a maximum degree of patience and commitment. After all, in some cases, the protective shield of justifications, rationalizations, and excuses used by clients has been developed over the course of a lifetime of violating the laws of society (Walters, 2001).

RESISTANCE TO TREATMENT

Some counseling texts suggest that the counseling relationship can only occur with the mutual consent of both the client and counselor. This is perhaps the ideal relationship, but it is not often found in many contexts, especially corrections. Many system-impacted clients are, after all, confined in institutions against their will; participation in correctional counseling is, by definition, arguably involuntary. However, even if some clients do voluntarily involve themselves in counseling programs, the counselor may still be confronted by fierce resistance. Antisocial behavior is highly reinforcing (Walters, 2001) and ego syntonic, that is, consistent with the client's view of right or wrong (Harris, 1995). Therefore, the client may see no reason to change or is ambivalent to change, and presents little motivation to do so during treatment. Moreover, the very nature of the prison environment promotes an "us versus them" atmosphere in which people who are incarcerated may view counselors as "cops" and counseling sessions as "snitch sessions" (Morgan, 2003).

Resistance to treatment can assume many forms. Harris (1995) identifies some of the more common ones: withholding information, missing appointments, discrediting or dismissing the counseling process, failing to do homework assignments, and declining to cooperate with the counselor in overt or covert ways. The level of engagement that the client expresses during therapy will affect the progress of the treatment (Levenson & Macgowan, 2004). Of course, many clients are outwardly compliant, which can also be a form of resistance (Stanchfield, 2001). It may not be obvious for quite some time that such clients are merely going through the motions and saying the right words while failing to internalize any of the information presented during counseling sessions. Elliott and Verdeyen (2002) describe 12 specific types of resistance that correctional counselors can expect to confront. These "dirty dozen" **power and control** tactics employed by clients in counseling are presented in Table 2.2. Many correctional counselors understandably become impatient with and

TABLE 2.2 The dirty dozen: power and control tactics exhibited by incarcerated people in counseling

Tactic	Example
Testing	Client completes the first few and last few pages of a workbook just to see if the counselor actually reads the workbook.
Diversion	Client asks the counselor for help with an in-class assignment while another client sets the clock ahead by 15 minutes.
Extortion	Client threatens to file a complaint against the counselor unless she (counselor) immediately enrolls the client in a psychoeducational group.
Sphere of Influence	Client obtains documentation from an influential citizen to support the claim that he requires residential substance use treatment solely to receive a one-year sentence reduction.
Disreputation	Client circulates a petition calling for the reassignment of a counselor labeled as "racist."
Rumor Clinic	Client spreads a rumor that the counselor is an alcoholic and is thus unfit to conduct substance use groups.
Solidarity	Several clients refuse to attend group counseling sessions because of the expulsion of a group member.
Negotiation	Client offers to clean the counselor's office in exchange for retaking a drug education examination that he (client) had failed.
Revenge	Client damages the TV/VCR in a group room after she is expelled from a group because of poor attendance and disruptive behavior.
Ingratiation	Client tells counselor that she (counselor) is responsible for motivating the client to turn his life around.
Splitting	Client tells female counselor that a male colleague said that women had no business working with incarcerated males.
Boundary Intrusion	Client compliments counselor on her perfume and asks if her husband or boyfriend likes it.

Source: Elliott, W., & Verdeyen, V. (2002). *Game Over! Strategies for Managing Inmate Deception.* Lanham, MD: American Correctional Association.

frustrated by these encounters with resistance. They either dismiss the client as unmotivated for counseling or respond irritably and try to coerce the client into adopting a receptive attitude and cooperative behavior (Harris, 1995). The latter approach inevitably sets the stage for a power struggle between the counselor and client that signals the death knell for successful counseling. Such power struggles and the confrontation they entail are counterproductive for several reasons. First, research has consistently shown that confrontation arouses defenses, activates resistance, and deteriorates into a means of attack and an attempt to tear someone down (Elliott, 2002). Second, clients will always emerge victorious from power struggles because the mere act of engaging the counselor in such a conflict reinforces a client's inflated sense of self-importance (Elliott & Verdeyen, 2002). Finally, power struggles often reveal the counselor's vulnerabilities or "hot buttons" and, therefore, must be actively avoided to prevent the undermining of the counselor's credibility.

It is thus imperative that correctional counselors become adept at managing resistance and using indirect methods for engaging clients in the counseling process. Elliott (2002) has identified three such strategies that simultaneously challenge incipient antisocial thinking and prevent futile and protracted struggles for control. Elliott refers to these strategies as the "3Rs" of managing client resistance to counseling: redirection, reframing, and reversal of responsibility. The "3Rs" are illustrated in Table 2.3.

Whether or not the counselor chooses to adopt the "3Rs," he or she is encouraged to remember that one of the most important elements in managing resistance is to avoid extended debates with clients. Counselors should point out the self-defeating nature of clients' behavior and clarify the short- and long-term consequences of continuing to engage in such behavior. However, the counselor cannot force the client to make the decision to adopt a prosocial lifestyle. All he or she can really do is supply the client with information

TABLE 2.3 The "3Rs" of managing client resistance to counseling

Strategy	Techniques
Redirection: Return focus of attention to task/issue at hand.	1. Ignore resistance. 2. Employ underfocusing (Stanchfield, 2001). 3. Focus on client's contribution to problem/conflict. 4. Focus on current/relevant issues. 5. Solicit other group members' reactions to client's resistance.
Reframing: Encourage client to adopt a different perspective about the source of his/her resistance.	1. Address semantics. 2. Place a positive spin on the resistance. 3. Place a negative spin on the resistance. 4. Relabel resistance in terms of its underlying antisocial thinking pattern(s).
Reversal of Responsibility: Reflect client's resistance back to him/her in a manner that assigns personal responsibility and demands accountability.	1. Paraphrase resistance with attention to its underlying (antisocial) meaning. 2. Ask challenging, open-ended questions. 3. Encourage client to make a value judgment regarding his/her resistance. 4. Deliver responses as tentative observations.

Source: Elliott, W. (2002). Managing offender resistance to counseling. *Federal Probation, 66*, 172–178.

and feedback. The choice to continue a pattern of antisocial behavior or create a prosocial way of life is the exclusive province of the client (Walters, 2001).

ETHICAL PROFESSIONAL BEHAVIOR AND DILEMMAS

The American Counseling Association's *2014 ACA Code of Ethics* provides cursory knowledge on the ethical standards of care counselors must follow, as well as the core professional values and principles when working in a counseling role. Box 2.1, 2.2, and 2.3 outline the core professional values, principles of professional and ethical behavior, and sections of the *Code of the Ethics*. Other human service professional organizations have their own standards of practice and care, such as the National Association of Social Workers' (2021) *Code of Ethics*, the National Commission on Correctional Health Care's (2015) *Standards for Mental Health Services in Correctional Facilities, 2015*, and the American Correctional Association's (2021) *Performance-Based Expected Practices for Adult Correctional Institutions*, fifth edition.

Box 2.1 American Counseling Association: Core Professional Values

1. enhancing human development throughout the life span
2. honoring diversity and embracing a multicultural approach in support of the worth, dignity, potential, and uniqueness of people within their social and cultural contexts
3. promoting social justice
4. safeguarding the integrity of the counselor–client relationship
5. practicing in a competent and ethical manner

Box 2.2 American Counseling Association: Principles of Professional Ethical Behavior

1. autonomy, or fostering the right to control the direction of one's life
2. nonmaleficence, or avoiding actions that cause harm
3. beneficence, or working for the good of the individual and society by promoting mental health and well-being
4. justice, or treating individuals equitably and fostering fairness and equality
5. fidelity, or honoring commitments and keeping promises, including fulfilling one's responsibilities of trust in professional relationships
6. veracity, or dealing truthfully with individuals with whom counselors come into professional contact

---

Box 2.3 American Counseling Association: Sections of the
Code of Ethics

Section A: The Counseling Relationship
Section B: Confidentiality and Privacy
Section C: Professional Responsibility
Section D: Relationships with Other Professionals
Section E: Evaluation, Assessment, and Interpretation
Section F: Supervision, Training, and Teaching
Section G: Research and Publication
Section H: Distance Counseling, Technology, and Social Media
Section I: Resolving Ethical Issues

Competent and well-intentioned correctional counselors sometimes struggle both with each other and with themselves over what appear to be conflicting ethical demands that arise when abstract ethical standards collide with the practical realities of counseling within the correctional environment. Some argue that such dilemmas naturally arise because of a basic and unavoidable conflict between two opposing philosophies: **treatment** and **security**. Because the primary mission of correctional institutions is custody and security, counselors are often required to assume roles and responsibilities in addition to and perhaps inconsistent with that of counselor or helper. The so-called treatment/custody dichotomy is but one of several ethical dilemmas to be examined in this section.

The Treatment versus Security Dichotomy

The premise that treatment and security interests are mutually in conflict is debatable and seems to be based on a narrow definition of "security." The purpose of maintaining effective security and control within a correctional facility is more than preventing escape. Another primary goal is to protect incarcerated people from each other and themselves, thus promoting the safety and general welfare of all concerned (Manchak, Skeem, & Rook, 2014). This is hardly inconsistent with a treatment philosophy. Indeed, the authors of this chapter would argue that treatment can only occur within an environment characterized by safety, security, and structure. More guidance on this dichotomy, which could also be characterized as care versus control, is provided in Chapter 3.

Definition of the Client

The nature of correctional counseling, given the many and varied tasks counselors are asked to perform, suggests that there are several potential "client" definitions—is it the individual we are working with, or the organization we work for? The crux of the ethical issue is typically couched in terms of the counselor's perceived divided, or dual, loyalties between the competing interests of the client and those of the institution (Magaletta, Patry, Dietz, & Ax, 2007). The objectives and interests of each party can overlap. In reality, both the individual and the institution are clients of the counselor in varying ways, and these loyalties can affect the therapeutic alliance depending upon how they are navigated (Merkt et al., 2021).

Dual or Multiple Relationships

One of the most common ethical dilemmas voiced by correctional treatment professionals concerns the problem of **dual** or **multiple relationships**. Specifically, when required to relieve a correctional officer in a housing unit or participate in a search for contraband in an institution, many counselors push the ethical "panic button." Dignam (2003, p. 50), however, argues that a counselor may indeed feel uncomfortable when performing tasks that are unrelated to treatment, "but performing a task that is merely different from a clinician's typical regimen is not tantamount to behaving unethically, at least not in the context of dual or multiple relationships." Unless it can be convincingly demonstrated that clients' welfare would be somehow jeopardized or that they could be exploited in the process, the performance of security-related tasks does not pose significant ethical problems.

BOUNDARIES OF COMPETENCE AND MAINTAINING EXPERTISE

Given the complex and diverse nature of populations impacted by the justice system, it is ethically imperative that correctional counselors be sufficiently knowledgeable and competent to treat clients. Counselors can begin or continue to meet this ethical obligation by supplementing their training and experience in areas pertinent to working with justice-involved clients. Independent study options include reading on topics such as using person-first or person-centered language (Bedell et al., 2019) with justice-involved clients, the principles of Motivational Interviewing (Stinson & Clark, 2017; see also Chapter 3), culturally responsive cognitive behavioral therapy (Hays & Iwamasa, 2006), trauma-responsive practices (Benedict, 2014), and understanding the distinct needs and promoting the safety of LGBTQI+ populations (Jenness, Sexton, & Sumner, 2019; Kahle & Rosenbaum, 2021). It is equally important for counselors to realize that they cannot be all things to all people. The full range of client needs and problems can be found in prisons, and counselors need to be careful that they function within the boundaries of their expertise (Dignam, 2003).

Confidentiality

It is axiomatic that confidentiality is essential to the counseling relationship, as it provides the client with the comfort of knowing that what is said during sessions will not be repeated outside the counseling context. However, when counseling takes place within a jail or prison, confidentiality often conflicts with institutional security. For example, if a client discloses his or her intent to escape during a counseling session, the counselor must decide whether to breach confidentiality. Obviously, in such a situation, the counselor will be under intense pressure to divulge the information to a third party, most likely administrative or custodial personnel. Agency policy may even dictate that the counselor be required to disclose information that might constitute a threat to institutional safety or security. Moreover, there is a statutory requirement known as the "duty to warn," which requires that confidentiality be superseded by the need to protect an identifiable third party from harm (Walsh, 2003). At the same time, ethical standards governing the counseling profession maintain that counselors report to proper authorities when clients indicate an intention to harm themselves or others. This standard applies regardless of whether the client is involved in the justice system.

Given the reality that there are relatively severe limits on a system-involved client's privacy and confidentiality, it can be argued that the more important ethical issue for counselors is to ensure that all recipients of services are fully aware of such limits. Obviously, informing clients of limits and restrictions on privacy and confidentiality should occur prior to engaging in the counseling process (Dignam, 2003). At a minimum, counselors need to clarify for themselves and with the client what communications will be kept strictly confidential and what protections they do and do not have in the counseling relationship (Harris, 1995).

CONTEXTUAL DEMANDS

There are a host of issues and demands arising from the correctional environment itself. These confront the counselor on a routine basis and make his or her job that much more difficult and stressful. The counselor's ability to effectively negotiate these demands will, to a large degree, determine his or her susceptibility to the **burnout** that so often afflicts helping professionals. Several of the most prominent of these contextual demands are examined in this section.

Working in a Bureaucracy

A prison is the epitome of a bureaucracy. It is an organization dominated by rules and paperwork, often ignoring individuals in favor of procedures and precedents (Pollock, 1998). Moreover, correctional organizations, both institutional and community-based, adhere to a paramilitary style of management with a vertical chain of command (Elliott & Verdeyen, 2002). Obviously, some people feel more comfortable working within, and adapt more readily to, such a structure than others. Correctional treatment professionals may especially have a difficult time coping with the regimentation and rigidity so endemic to correctional operations. Counselors who attempt to "buck the system" run into the proverbial brick wall and end up frustrated, disillusioned, and of little or no value to offenders. Counselors who, on the other hand, devote their time and energy to carving out a niche for themselves within the bureaucracy will become valuable members of the correctional "team."

Handling Excessive Paperwork

The written or electronic record is the single most important item in the criminal justice system. No matter how insignificant or important the event, nearly everything that is done for, by, or to a client either originates or culminates in some type of correctional report or record. The exact nature and function of the reports and records and the kind of person responsible for developing and maintaining them vary somewhat depending on the stage of the criminal justice system involved. At the correctional level, it is the counselor who is most responsible for collecting information and writing reports. Several different types of records and reports must be periodically developed for each client. Because there are so many clients on a typical caseload, the resulting paperwork can often be enormous. Time spent on paperwork reduces the opportunities for the counselor to interact with the client. Unfortunately, some ineffective counselors have learned to hide behind this paperwork. On the other hand, correctional-based computer management software has reduced the time to write reports and data entry. Nevertheless, keeping accurate and updated records is a substantial part of the role.

Managing Large Caseloads

Counselors are often expected to maintain a caseload that may exceed 100 clients. The sheer size of the caseload is further exacerbated by the fact that there is usually a fairly rapid turnover of the clients on the caseload. If the average stay of a person in an institution is two years and a counselor has a caseload of 125 clients, the counselor may never really get to know any of the clients before they are discharged.

Not only is the caseload large, but it is also diverse. The counselor must accept any and all clients assigned, and few opportunities exist for developing a specialized caseload. Often the clients have little in common beyond the fact that they have been convicted of a crime and sentenced to some type of correctional facility or program. It is not unusual for a counselor in an institution housing adults convicted of felonies to have clients on his or her caseload who have been convicted of murder, robbery, rape, child molestation, drunk driving, public intoxication, and any number of other offenses.

Under such pressure, it may be tempting for the correctional counselor to focus on the clients with whom he or she enjoys interacting rather than with those clients who need help the most. Clients should be seen because they need to be seen, not because they want to structure their free time around the counselor. Similarly, they should not be seen just because the counselor likes to interact with them and is able to rationalize that he or she cannot help everyone on his or her caseload anyway. Figure 2.1 illustrates this problem further.

FIGURE 2.1 Dr. Kay Jackson stands in front of the New Jersey Adult Diagnostic and Treatment Center in Avenel, the state's prison for people convicted of sex offenses. Dr. Jackson told the media that her resignation was a protest over dangerously high caseloads, insufficient administrative support for the therapists, ongoing "chaos" resulting from major changes in the prison's therapy programs, and "discomfort in the work environment."
Source: AP Photo/*Star-Ledger*, William Perlman.

Responding to Racial and Ethnic Disproportionality

Black adults are imprisoned at a rate five times that of white adults, and almost twice the rate of Hispanic adults (Carson, 2020) and there is no indication that this racial and ethnic disproportionality is going to abate anytime in the near future. This can complicate the efforts of correctional counselors supervising clients of a different race or ethnicity because they, like most people, have a tendency to resort to ethnocentrism when dealing with others who are different from themselves. Ethnocentrism involves judging other people on the basis of one's own beliefs rather than those of others. Closely related to ethnocentrism is the all-too-common human tendency to stereotype others; that is, to judge people on assumed group characteristics rather than to see them and react to them as individuals. Obviously, ethnocentrism and stereotyping are prescriptions for failure in a correctional setting.

The correctional counselor can avoid many of the problems relating to ethnocentrism and stereotyping if he or she assumes a more racially and ethnically sensitive approach. Such an approach is often referred to as "culturally responsive" or multicultural counseling (Hays & Iwamasa, 2006). Specifically, correctional counselors need to try to broaden and deepen their knowledge and understanding of diverse groups so that they can appreciate where these individuals "are coming from" and then begin to see them as individuals rather than as some larger group. This is true not only for racial/ethnic identities but also for gender-identities and sexual-orientation. The American Correctional Association has also chosen to address ethnocentrism by changing existing sections of the ethics code to reflect a better understanding of the special problems associated with multicultural counseling (ACA, 2021).

Working with Special Needs Clients

Novice correctional counselors are often surprised to find that their caseloads consist of clients with severe mental illnesses, developmental disabilities, and substance use problems. Increasingly, such "special needs clients" are found in prison populations and present unique treatment needs and challenges to counselors. Counselors working with female clients will be confronted by additional demands in that such clients often present a variety of family and social problems, including their relationships with their children and histories of physical or sexual abuse. However, there are also many strengths among these clients. Far more detail is provided on working with women clients in Chapter 13.

One of the fastest-growing subpopulations since the 1960s has been justice-involved people with mental illness. Although there is wide variation in measurement, it has been estimated that as much as 31% of incarcerated people in U.S. state prisons have a form of mental illness (Prins, 2014). This does not include the high rates of mental illness that are also found among people detained in U.S. jails (Steadman, Osher, Clark Robbins, Case, & Samuels, 2009). Correctional institutions have often been cited as inappropriate environments for treating people with mental illness (Council of State Governments, 2002), and they frequently do not get the intensive treatment they require in these settings. Thus, diversionary efforts continue to be made, particularly through using the Sequential Intercept Model (Abreu, Parker, Noether, Steadman, & Case, 2017; Munetz & Griffin, 2006) promoted by the Substance Abuse and Mental Health Services Administration (SAMHSA; Comartin, Nelson, Smith, & Kubiak, 2021).

Of the 1.4 million people confined in state and federal prisons in 2018, 14% of people housed in state prisons and 46% of people housed in federal prisons were incarcerated for drug-related offenses (Carson, 2020). Of course, many links have been drawn between substance use, crime, and violent behavior (DeMatteo, Filone, & Davis, 2015; Raskin White, Loeber, Stouthamer-Loeber, & Farrington, 1999; Raskin White, 2016). Individuals addicted to substances report significantly greater antisocial activity and have more extensive criminal justice records than those not addicted to drugs or alcohol, while those with greater histories of antisocial activity are more likely to report prior substance use (Peters & Matthews, 2003). In recognition of the scope of substance use problems among people in jail and prison, correctional counselors should regard substance use treatment as an essential element of counseling services offered to the incarcerated population. Chapter 12 provides additional guidance for serving individuals with serious substance use.

One of the most widely accepted findings in the criminological research is that men are arrested at a higher rate than women (Holtfreter, Reisig, & Morash, 2004). Females involved in the system are much more likely to seek counseling services, and actively seek counseling to address issues of prior sexual/physical abuse and separation from their children (Hislop, 2001). Accordingly, the correctional counselor who works with women will be expected to provide a gender-responsive counseling services to a significant portion of the population. Chapter 13 focuses particular attention on the treatment of justice-involved women.

Providing Crisis Intervention and Reentry Services

Counseling incarcerated clients with deeply ingrained antisocial tendencies is a daunting task, and true cognitive and behavioral change may not be possible in many cases (Harris, 1995). Therefore, working with such clients, especially in institutions, often boils down to **crisis intervention**, that is, helping clients manage incipient crises.

Correctional institutions are unquestionably stressful environments and system-impacted people must deal with a host of issues resulting from incarceration and having a criminal record. These include, but are certainly not limited to, separation from family members, imposition of structure in one's life, loss of previous coping strategies (e.g., alcohol and drug use), and fear of the prison environment itself (e.g., physical or sexual violence) (Morgan, 2003). Some people thrive under the environmental structure and the "inmate code" (i.e., unwritten rules of conduct) (Elliott & Verdeyen, 2002). Many simply adapt and blend into the environment, while many others experience significant adjustment difficulties and internal distress. Accordingly, crisis intervention and brief supportive counseling services are necessary to assist this latter group in adjusting to their newfound lives in correctional institutions.

Adjustment difficulties, of course, are not limited to newly incarcerated people; rather, chronic anxiety and stress are inevitable byproducts of incarceration (Morgan, 2003). People with both short- and long-term sentences will encounter various stressors and life issues they must handle. For example, it is not uncommon for family members or significant others to discontinue communication with incarcerated people, thus depriving the latter of a valuable source of social support (Pettus-Davis et al., 2017). Even people nearing their release experience apprehension and anxiety, a process referred to as "getting short." Issues such as becoming reacquainted with family members, finding a job, and avoiding antisocial behavior become primary areas of concern (Pettus-Davis, 2021). The Institute for Justice Research and Development at Florida State University has produced many studies and publications on the important drivers of success for reentry, called the 5-Key Model for Reentry (Pettus, Veeh, Renn, & Kennedy, 2021).

FIGURE 2.2 The 5-Key Model for Reentry.
Source: Image reproduced with permission from the Institute for Justice Research and Development, Florida State University.

The correctional counselor working among institutional settings will, at some point in his or her career, be called upon to provide crisis support services to clients who engage in self-harm and suicide attempts. Self-harm occurs with relative frequency among prisoners, but is especially prevalent among those with serious mental illness and female incarcerated populations (Hawton, Linsell, Adeniji, Sariaslan, & Fazel, 2014). A U.S. Bureau of Justice Statistics report from 2020 revealed that over 1,000 people died in jails in 2016, with over half of them being largely preventable, and with suicide being the leading cause of death (Carson & Cowhig, 2020a). Jail suicides occur far more frequently than suicides in state prisons in the U.S. and in the general population (Carson & Cowhig, 2020b).

It is thus necessary for counselors to be thoroughly familiar with the demographic, historical, situational, and psychological risk factors for self-harm and suicide. The Vera Institute of Justice reports that men detained in jail are 50% more likely to commit suicide than women detained in jail, and incarcerated people who are white are six times more likely to commit suicide compared to incarcerated people who are Black and three times more likely than those who are Latinx (Pope & Delany-Brumsey, 2016).

In prisons throughout the world, the strongest clinical risk factors for suicide are: suicidal ideation, history of attempting suicide, and current psychiatric diagnosis. Institutional risk factors are: occupation of a single cell and having no social visits. Criminological risk factors include: remand status, serving a life sentence, and being convicted of a violent offense, especially homicide (Zhong et al., 2021).

Surviving the Brutality of the Prison Environment

It is obvious that prisons are brutal environments. Correctional workers witness overt displays of violence, receive verbal abuse and threats, and observe or, if necessary, participate in the application of physical force to manage a disruptive incarcerated person. Such exposure to violence and aggression may be a bitter pill for many counselors to swallow; after all, many enter the correctional field to "help" clients and "find the good" in them. However, virtually everyone who has made correctional work his or her career has experienced a "normalization" process (Welo, 2001) that can diminish the shock, disgust, fear, and anger experienced after witnessing violence and other antisocial behavior. Still others find that they simply cannot ethically navigate the dual loyalties and human suffering that occurs among institutional correctional environments (Buser, 2020).

Unfortunately, correctional counselors are additionally subjected secondarily to the violence and the destructiveness perpetrated by clients. Counselors are expected to familiarize themselves with the presentence investigation reports and other documents concerning the clients assigned to their caseload increasing their exposure to secondary and vicarious trauma. Such reports are replete with the "horror stories of [the clients'] crimes, the victim impact statements, [and] the anguish of their family members" (Welo, 2001, p. 166). Repeated exposure to accounts of the pain and misery caused by clients can lead to cynicism, disillusionment, and ultimately, burnout (Elliott & Verdeyen, 2002). Thankfully, the promotion of self-care for staff in corrections is alive and well, and readers who are interested in this profession should seek out agencies that understand the importance of mitigating secondary trauma through a health and wellness organizational culture.

FINAL CONSIDERATIONS

This chapter has been devoted to an exploration of the numerous and diverse challenges faced by the correctional counselor. It is hoped that the reader now has a keen appreciation for the complexities inherent in developing counseling strategies that are effective with a population that outwardly often behaves in resistant and hostile ways, but underneath need staff to walk alongside them on their journey to behavioral change. It will be important to resolve the various ethical dilemmas endemic to counseling in a correctional institution, and negotiate the unique contextual demands of counseling in a institutional environments and other correctional settings (e.g., probation and parole field offices). However, this discussion would be incomplete without attending to the issue of burnout prevention.

In a concerted effort to assist the correctional staff in not succumbing to burnout and its deleterious physical and emotional consequences, Elliott and Verdeyen (2002) have offered 10 strategies for burnout prevention and career satisfaction. These strategies, dubbed "The Ten Commandments for Prison Staff," are listed in Box 2.4. Finally, the authors of this chapter recommend that the correctional counselor do his or her best to maintain and exercise a healthy sense of humor. Even so-called gallows humor can be an effective way of distancing oneself from shocking, disgusting, or dangerous situations, and preventing unwarranted emotional and behavioral responses to such situations (Kauffman, 1988).

Box 2.4 Ten Commandments for Prison Staff

1. Go home safe and sound at the end of the day.
2. Establish realistic expectations (for self, clients, and other staff).
3. Set firm and consistent limits.
4. Avoid power struggles.
5. Manage interpersonal boundaries.
6. Don't take things personally.
7. Strive for an attitude of healthy skepticism.
8. Don't fight the bureaucracy.
9. Ask for help (from supervisors and colleagues).
10. Don't take your work home with you.

Source: Elliot, W., & Verdeyen, V. (2002). *Game Over! Strategies for Managing Inmate Deception*. Lanham, MD: American Correctional Association

---

Discussion Questions

1. Discuss the importance of identifying and challenging antisocial thinking when counseling clients who are involved in the justice system.
2. Why do you think group counseling is the preferred modality in the treatment of system-impacted clients?
3. What are some of the ethical dilemmas facing the correctional counselor? How can they be successfully resolved?
4. Discuss some of the contextual demands encountered by the correctional counselor that make the job more stressful.
5. Separate into five groups and assign one of the 5-Keys to each group from the 5-Key Model of Reentry seen in Figure 2.2. Each group should consider the specific obstacles that formerly incarcerated people face for their assigned Key and brainstorm possible solutions.

ONLINE LEARNING ENHANCEMENTS

In this YouTube video from "Transforming Criminal Justice for the 21st Century," hosted by the Institute for Justice Research and Development, Lamont Carey promotes the idea, "Keep Your Hustle, but Change Your Product." Mr. Carey uses spoken word to highlight the importance of strengths and transferable skills of formerly incarcerated people. www.youtube.com/watch?v=NdaNTnpfUII

GLOSSARY OF KEY TERMS

burnout job stress that may occur after prolonged exposure to the emotional hazards of being in a helping profession; typically characterized by emotional exhaustion, lack of motivation, depersonalization, and feelings of ineffectiveness

cognitive behavioral interventions psychosocial interventions utilized by counselors to target unhealthy or antisocial thinking patterns in an effort to help clients change their thinking and/or behavior

collateral information information pertaining to a client's behavior in his or her housing unit, classroom, work area, or elsewhere; correctional counselors are encouraged to collect such information to verify information provided by the client

contextual demands a host of difficult issues and demands arising from the correctional environment that the counselor must navigate on a routine basis

crisis intervention methods for helping clients manage incipient crises; crisis intervention is particularly important for institutionalized clients due to a host of stressful issues resulting from incarceration

dual/multiple relationships an ethical dilemma commonly faced by correctional treatment professionals in which counselors perform tasks unrelated to the treatment of clients

ethnocentrism the practice of judging other people on the basis of one's own beliefs rather than those of others

"here and now" style a style of thinking common in clients that involves living in the present and typically supports and maintains antisocial behavior

interpersonal boundaries limits or guidelines that people create to identify safe, reasonable, and permissible ways for other people to behave toward them

multicultural counseling a counseling method in which the counselor assumes a racially and ethnically sensitive approach to treating clients

power and control tactics commonly employed by resistant clients who attempt to take control of the counseling session and/or counselor-client relationship

redirection one of the "3Rs" of managing client resistance to counseling in which the counselor attempts to return the focus of attention to the task/issue at hand

reframing one of the "3Rs" of managing client resistance to counseling in which the counselor encourages the client to adopt a different perspective regarding the source of his/her resistance

reversal of responsibility one of the "3Rs" of managing client resistance to counseling in which the counselor reflects the client's resistance back to him/her in a manner that assigns personal responsibility and demands accountability

special needs clients clients that present unique treatment needs and challenges to counselors, such as those with severe mental illnesses, developmental disabilities, and substance use problems

stereotype the act of judging people on assumed group characteristics rather than seeing and reacting to them as individuals

thinking errors erroneous thinking patterns employed by clients to justify their offending behavior

treatment versus security dichotomy the assumption that the treatment needs of clients are naturally at odds with maintaining security and control within correctional institutions

CHAPTER 3

Community Corrections Officers as Change Agents

Linsey A. Belisle and Emily J. Salisbury

Individuals on probation and parole make up the largest correctional population in the United States; in 2018, there were 6.7 million adults under U.S. correctional control, including 4.5 million adults under community supervision (Jones, 2018). With over two-thirds of the correctional population under community supervision, it is crucial to shift the professional responsibilities of probation and parole staff to reflect (1) community supervision as human service work and (2) officers' roles as change agents. Although we would never expect correctional officers (either institutional or community officers) to serve in a clinical role like social workers, many of the human service principles from social work and behavior change are integral characteristics for staff to motivate clients to change antisocial behavior. Therefore, although this text is primarily about the correctional counseling role, we now know that teaching community corrections staff the skills of both law enforcement *and* change agents improves clients' outcomes on officers' caseloads in the community.

DOI: 10.4324/9780367808266-4

COMMUNITY SUPERVISION AS HUMAN SERVICE WORK

If you search for a human services job or career, alongside more commonly known human services roles such as social worker or substance use counselor, it is likely that community supervision officers (i.e., parole or probation officer) will also be included in the list. This may come as a shock for some, as supervision agencies have taken a more surveillance and law enforcement approach to supervision over the past few decades. Mass probation led to overwhelming caseloads and strained resources (Phelps, 2017). Alongside these increases in caseloads and limited resources, the overarching "get tough on crime" sociopolitical context pushed many community corrections agencies to abandon the rehabilitative foundation of community supervision in favor of a surveillance and law enforcement approach (Cullen, Jonson, & Mears, 2017). Lovins, Cullen, Latessa, and Jonson (2018) compare this approach to surveillance as the supervision officer being the referee—he or she is only there to blow the whistle when a violation or offense occurs. But there is overwhelming evidence to suggest that just being a referee (i.e., surveilling and enforcing alone) has little to no impact on reducing recidivism and changing behavior, ultimately placing public safety at risk (see Chadwick, Dewolf, & Serin, 2015; Cullen, Pratt, Turanovic, & Butler, 2018; Drake & Aos, 2012).

The surveillance only approach not only fails to reduce recidivism but also fails to adhere to the goals of human service work. Human service work provides a wide range of services to the community. It is rooted in the pursuit of helping individuals become more self-reliant and self-sufficient through assistance in learning new skills, providing resources or referrals to treatment/services (Moffat, 2011). To do so, human service professionals follow a series of steps: (1) evaluate needs, (2) develop a treatment/case management plan, (3) activate the plan, and (4) provide support along the way (Moffat, 2011). Instead of seeing community supervision officers as referees, in which their only role is to supervise and enforce compliance, it is crucial that community supervision agencies evolve to better reflect human service work, integrating their dual roles of law enforcement and change agents (Lovins et al., 2018). To do so, means implementing evidence-based corrections centered on rehabilitative efforts and practices that are rooted in core correctional practices.

CORE CORRECTIONAL PRACTICES

One of the advancements in the correctional treatment literature is the development and empirical support surrounding core correctional practices. Andrews and Kiessling (1980) identified five core components of effective correctional intervention: (1) appropriate use of authority, (2) appropriate modeling and reinforcement, (3) skill-building and problem-solving, (4) effective use of community resources, and (5) relationship factors (see Table 3.1). These components are rooted in social learning theory (see Chapter 10) and are conducive to establishing therapeutic interactions and relationships, ultimately creating a space supporting positive behavioral change in correctional settings (Dowden & Andrews, 2004). These practices are critical for all staff who work directly with justice-involved clients, including correctional counselors, social workers, and institutional and community corrections officers.

Appropriate use of authority is the concept of officers and staff being "firm but fair" when working with individuals under supervision (Andrews & Kiessling, 1980; Dowden & Andrews, 2004). Officers should use their authority to establish themselves as an

TABLE 3.1 Core correctional practices

Core Correctional Practices	Description
Appropriate use of authority	→ All staff, including officers, should be "firm but fair." → Use authority to provide clear structure and guidelines, avoid controlling and shaming clients.
Appropriate modeling and reinforcement	→ All staff, including officers, model prosocial behavior. → Staff should engage in role-playing and opportunities to model, practice, and reinforce prosocial skills/attitudes.
Skill-building and problem-solving	→ Use structured, cognitive behavioral learning techniques to improve client's skills.
Effective use of community resources	→ Connect clients with resources in the community to address clients' needs.
Relationship factors	→ Relationship between the staff/officer and client. → Focus on establishing a professional and productive relationship through mutual respect.

Table adapted from Andrews and Kiessling (1980) and Dowden and Andrews (2004).

authoritative figure, but it is crucial that they not become authoritarian and understand the distinction (see Box 3.1 below; Skeem, Eno Louden, Polaschek, & Camp, 2007). Examples of appropriate use of authority would be clear communication of expectations and guidelines, rewarding compliance (because if we want a behavior to continue, we reinforce/reward it; see Chapter 8), being respectful, and avoiding shaming or attempting to control clients (Dowden & Andrews, 2004).

The second core component, appropriate modeling and reinforcement, has two parts. The first part, appropriate modeling, requires that: (1) supervision officers and staff actively model prosocial attitudes/behaviors and (2) intervention staff (social workers, counselors, case managers) participate in role-playing exercises to allow clients to practice prosocial skills. The second part of this focuses on reinforcement. Staff must utilize positive/negative reinforcement and positive/negative sanctions when working with clients; officers need to reward achievements and appropriately disapprove of actions or behaviors that do not support the positive progression toward clients' goals (Dowden & Andrews, 2004).

The third core component, skill-building and problem-solving, utilizes structured learning and evidence-based techniques to support skills development and problem-solving abilities (Andrews & Kiessling, 1980; Dowden & Andrews, 2004). Much more is discussed in Part III of this book about the theoretical principles and modalities underlying how and why we teach clients new skills. Although there are various ways correctional professionals can improve clients' skills and problem-solving abilities, they should be done so in a structured, cognitive behavioral, and experiential way. For example, the use of cost-benefit analyses can help clients see the pros and cons of a decision or behavior, and through this process, they can learn to make better, more informed decisions.

The fourth component, effective use of community resources (also referred to as advocacy and brokerage), is a critical component of core correctional practices (Andrews & Kiessling, 1980; Dowden & Andrews, 2004). Case management and correctional staff are often responsible for connecting their clients with appropriate treatment and services within the community (or in correctional institutions) to help address both criminogenic (i.e., crime producing) and non-criminogenic client needs.

The last component, relationship factors, relates to the quality of the relationship between the staff member and the client (Andrews & Kiessling, 1980; Dowden & Andrews, 2004). This relationship should remain professional, maintain healthy boundaries, and be genuine, respectful, open, warm, and understanding. This is arguably the most crucial factor, as Dowden and Andrews (2004) claim that correctional interventions are most effective when mutual respect between the officer/staff member and the client exists. One study indicated that parolees randomly assigned to parole officers who received training on building collaborative relationships were more likely to have fewer subsequent drug use days and technical violations over time compared to the control group (Blasko, Friedmann, Giuranna, Rhodes, & Taxman, 2015). Given the emphasis on the relationship, this component is revisited below in the dual role orientation section.

While core correctional practices have been broadly applied to various interventions and environments (e.g., community supervision of juveniles and adults, correctional institutions), these components have significant implications for adherence to the risk-needs-responsivity model (see Chapters 4, 6, and 7; Bourgon, Chadwick, & Rugg, 2020), and can directly contribute to the reduction of recidivism and the adoption of prosocial behaviors (Chadwick et al., 2015; Dowden & Andrews, 2004; Latessa, Smith, Schweitzer, & Labrecque, 2013; Lowenkamp, Holsinger, Robinson, & Alexander, 2014; Robinson, Van Benschoten, Alexander, & Lowenkamp, 2011; Robinson et al., 2012). In their meta-analysis, Dowden and Andrews (2004) found adherence to core correctional practices in human service programs was related to better outcomes, including reductions in recidivism. Similarly, a more recent meta-analysis found lower recidivism rates for clients of community supervision officers who were trained in core correctional practices compared to officers who had not been trained (Chadwick et al., 2015). Just over one-third (36%) of clients who were supervised by a trained officer reoffended, whereas about 50% of individuals on the non-trained officers' caseloads reoffended (Chadwick et al., 2015). This highlights the importance of training supervision officers and direct-service staff in core correctional practices, as these components increase their ability to act as change agents and thereby increase the likelihood of their clients' success under supervision.

MODELS OF SUPERVISION TO INCREASE USE OF CORE CORRECTIONAL PRACTICES

Various models of supervision, based on structured curricula, have been developed specifically for community corrections staff. These models provide a standardized model for translating best practices, including core correctional practices, with clients on community supervision caseloads. For example, Bonta and colleagues (2010) developed a training program called the Strategic Training Initiative in Community Supervision (STICS). STICS is a three-day curriculum that teaches community supervision officers how to interact and supervise their clients more effectively. Rooted in core correctional practices, STICS teaches officers how to build rapport with clients, target antisocial attitudes, model prosocial behavior, appropriately use reinforcement, and utilize cognitive behavioral techniques and interventions (Bonta et al., 2010; Bourgon et al., 2020). Similarly, the Staff Training Aimed at Reducing Re-arrest (STARR) curriculum was developed by the U.S. Probation and Pretrial Services in 2009. This program was designed specifically for federal community supervision officers and focuses on teaching officers techniques and skills rooted in core correctional practices (see Clodfelter, Halcomb, Alexander, Marcum, & Richards, 2016; Lowenkamp et al., 2014; Robinson et al., 2012).

Effective Practices in Community Supervision (EPICS) is another model similar to STICS and STARR that teaches community supervision officers how to integrate evidence-based practices, such as core correctional practices, into their interactions with clients as well as their overall approach to supervision (Latessa et al., 2013; Smith, Schweitzer, Labrecque, & Latessa, 2012). Officers are taught how to implement EPICS with every officer–client interaction. The structured approach includes four components: check-in, review, intervention, and homework (University of Cincinnati Corrections Institute [UCCI], n.d.). The check-in allows officers to determine any immediate needs/crises, as well as gauge client compliance with conditions of supervision, doing so in an effort to build the "firm and fair" rapport. The review component focuses on skills covered in the previous session and explores how the client utilized those skills. If the client did not utilize the skills, officers then work with them to address barriers to the successful application of the skills. The intervention step allows for the identification of ongoing needs and "at-the-desk" skills for teaching clients to address these needs. The last component, homework, provides an opportunity for the client to role-play and practice the skills, see the skills modeled by the officer, and then give specific homework related to the skill to complete prior to the next meeting (UCCI, n.d.).

FIGURE 3.1 Stuart Walker and Leticia Longoria-Navarro from the Multnomah County Department of Community Justice practice learning the EPICS model before implementing it with clients.
Source: Photo Credit: Leah Nash; Reproduced with permission from Governing.com from "The Changing Relationship Between Ex-Criminals and Their Parole Officers." (www.governing.com/archive/gov-probation-parole-states-community-supervision.html)

These models (STICS, STARR, and EPICS) have demonstrated their ability to improve supervision officers' use of core correctional practices to varying degrees—ultimately enhancing their abilities to interact with clients and promoting positive, prosocial changes among their clients (see Bourgon et al., 2020; Bonta et al., 2011; Labrecque & Smith, 2017; Latessa et al., 2013; Lowenkamp et al., 2014; Robinson et al., 2011; Robinson et al., 2012; Smith et al., 2012). For example, officers who received 40 hours of the STARR training were more likely to utilize effective intervention strategies with their clients and saw a 25% reduction in relative risk of failure rates with their clients compared to the officers who did not receive the training (Robinson et al., 2012). When examining the impact of EPICS, Latessa, Smith, Schweitzer, and Labrecque (2013) found that clients of officers who did not receive EPICS training were almost two times more likely to be arrested and one-and-a-half times more likely to be reincarcerated compared to clients with officers who routinely implemented the skills taught in EPICS. These studies clearly show that when officers are aware of and trained on the core correctional practices, they become more effective change agents; they engage in evidence-based interventions with clients to maintain accountability while promoting positive behavioral changes.

DUAL ROLE ORIENTATION

As described in the previous sections, community supervision officers are required to wear two hats: They hold clients accountable while also being tasked to engage in structured interventions with clients to build skills. For far too long, community supervision officers were only asked to be law enforcers; but merely enforcing the law does not adhere to best practices in corrections and creates obstacles for building a professional relationship that promotes positive change. On the other hand, just focusing on providing interventions without holding clients accountable also fails to produce the best outcomes. For example, Paparozzi and Gendreau (2005) categorized parole officers into three groups based on how they approached supervising clients: (1) social work approach, (2) law enforcement approach, or (3) a combination of the two. Parole officers who were categorized as either taking a social work approach or a law enforcement approach had worse client outcomes than officers who were categorized as having both a social work and law enforcement approach. Clients of officers whose approach to supervision was a combination of the two were up to three times less likely to be revoked than clients on the other officers' caseloads (Paparozzi & Gendreau, 2005; see also Skeem & Manchak, 2008). These findings highlight the importance of embracing community supervision officers' **dual role orientation**, blending control with care (Skeem et al., 2007; Skeem & Manchak, 2008).

Skeem and colleagues (2007) discuss this concept of blending control with care by focusing on the relationship established between the officer and the client, as the quality of this relationship has implications for behavioral change and compliance. Skeem and colleagues (2007) found the ideal dual role orientation relationship to be firm (the officer is **authoritative** but not **authoritarian**; see Box 3.1), fair (client feels like they are treated fairly), and caring (client feels like their supervision officer cares about their success and well-being). When supervision officers take this approach, their clients are more likely to trust their supervision officers. This trust is strongly related to increased compliance of conditions and decreased likelihood of recidivism (Kennealy, Skeem, Manchack, & Louden, 2012; Skeem et al., 2007).

Box 3.1 Authoritarian vs. Authoritative Traits

Authoritarian Traits	Authoritative Traits
→ Has a command presence.	→ Has a command presence.
→ Demands too much all the time.	→ Uses authority with respect, fairness, and care.
→ Rigid adherence to rules/conditions.	→ Flexible to problems that arise.
→ Inflexible to any problems that emerge.	→ Recognizes that violations are natural, teachable moments.
→ Disparaging use of power and control.	→ Uses power and control responsibly and ethically.
→ Infrequently, if ever, uses professional discretion.	→ Knows how to use their professional discretion depending on the situation.
→ Takes disrespect from clients personally.	→ Takes disrespect from clients in a "matter of fact" way.

Another way to think about this relationship is to consider supervision officers as coaches. The traditional law enforcer approach makes officers out to be referees. For instance, they are not invested in the outcomes, they remain neutral, and are only there to blow the whistle when someone steps out of line (e.g., committing a violation of supervision or a new crime; Lovins et al., 2018). When we think about these qualities in a supervision officer, they become an officer who is not invested in clients changing and only there to enforce compliance. This approach does not blend care with control or adhere to the core correctional practices discussed earlier.

Lovins and colleagues (2018) suggest that a supervision officer's job can be better described as being a coach. As shown in Box 3.2, coaches care about players on their teams and they are invested in the outcome (i.e., they want to win the game). They get to know each person on their team, know their strengths and weaknesses, and know how to motivate them. Coaches utilize players' strengths while they also continually work to improve their skills through practice. Critically, coaches also hold players accountable, using both positive and negative reinforcement as well as punishment and sanctions—in other words, they are permitted to discipline their players when they step out of line. It is not as if coaches try to become best friends with their players—they can "bench" them anytime necessary and take them out of the game (i.e., put out a warrant for arrest). The best coaches tend to be firm, fair, and caring. Supervision officers who approach their jobs as coaches will naturally interact with their clients in a way that is much more aligned with blending care and control as well as the core correctional practices (Lovins et al., 2018).

For community supervision to be as effective as possible, it is crucial that agencies and supervision officers retire the referee whistle, pick up the coaching playbook, and approach their interactions and client relationships as a coach (Lovins et al., 2018). When agencies and supervision officers do so, the role of a coach (i.e., change agent) allows for a relationship to develop that blends both care and control to have the most effective client outcomes. The dual role orientation is crucial in helping the community supervision system become more

Box 3.2 Differences Between the Referee and Coaching Roles

Referee Role	Coaching Role
→ Rule-enforcer with a firm and fair attitude.	→ Rule-enforcer with a firm, fair, and caring attitude.
→ Objective, neutral party who is not invested in the outcome of any player or game.	→ Subjective, non-neutral party invested in players' success/winning.
→ Closely watches for and calls the "fouls."	→ Closely watches for errors or missteps and can "bench" (discipline) any player.
→ Does not develop a relationship with players.	→ Develops a motivating relationship with players using a dual role orientation and mutual respect.
→ Not concerned with individual strengths or deficits among players.	→ Identifies strengths and deficits among players and teaches new skills based on individual needs.
→ Does not provide reinforcement or rewards to players.	→ Reinforces and rewards players for improved performance and skill.

evidence-based. Whetzel and Lowenkamp (2011) reminded us of this by stating, "To become an evidence-based system, perhaps the first lesson we [community supervision officers] must learn is that our effectiveness as change agents depends, to some degree, upon us, on who we are and how we treat offenders" (p. 15). Evidence-based supervision means blending control with care and treating clients in a firm, fair, and caring manner (Skeem et al., 2007).

MOTIVATIONAL INTERVIEWING

Many of the ideas discussed in this chapter are also in line with Motivational Interviewing's goals and purpose. There are many people who feel that justice-involved clients cannot change unless they are fully motivated to do so. That may be somewhat true, but the reality is that there are steps we can take as staff to help motivate clients toward change. In other words, it is not as if community corrections staff are not part of the process of motivating clients. In fact, much of what probation and parole staff do on a daily basis with clients motivates them either toward or away from behavioral change. Think about it. When someone with authority over you, tells you that "you should stay away from people who aren't good for you" or "you need to quit using drugs," how does that make you feel? Does it make you feel motivated to change or perhaps motivated not to change? Does it make you feel like that person understands your situation or is merely judging your situation?

Motivational Interviewing is a way of being and communicating with people to facilitate intrinsic motivation to change their behavior. It is a way of communicating with clients about change (Miller & Rollnick, 2013) with an understanding that long-term change does not occur by forced compliance or by telling people what they "should" do. Its central goal is to increase clients' intrinsic motivation to change, rather than promoting change due to extrinsic motivators that are external to the person (e.g., not to get arrested again, to get off probation). Motivational Interviewing begins with an understanding that most people are simply *ambivalent* to change, not necessarily *resistant* to change, although, with many clients, it may initially sound and feel like resistance. Ambivalence is typical in the change process, and it means that most times, people are unsure if they want to change; most clients know right from wrong, and know the arguments both for and against changing their behavior. Our goal is to guide them toward making arguments for change in their own words, for their own reasons. This is only accomplished through mutually respectful relationships—the kind we build with clients through core correctional practices and the dual role orientation.

In their text, *Motivational Interviewing with Offenders* (2017), Stinson and Clark indicate that the spirit of Motivational Interviewing has four central elements that highlight the importance of mutually respectful relationships among interactions between staff members and clients: (1) Partnership, (2) Acceptance, (3) Compassion, and (4) Evocation. Although these elements may sound as if they are related to conducting clinical therapy, they are actually reflective of doing any kind of human service work effectively—whether it is in the world of dentistry (Gillam & Yusuf, 2019), teaching (Snape & Atkinson, 2016), or correctional treatment (Stinson & Clark, 2017).

Partnership

Again, many of these elements may sound foreign to corrections staff who are most familiar with using their law enforcement role in supervision. For instance, the first element, Partnership, conveys an understanding that staff and clients are working together in a

FIGURE 3.2 Officer Andrew Skidmore from Multnomah County Department of Community Justice in Portland, Oregon meets with a 24-year-old client who has been under supervision for more than two years.
Photo Credit: Leah Nash; Reproduced with permission from Governing.com from "The Changing Relationship Between Ex-Criminals and Their Parole Officers." (www.governing.com/archive/gov-probation-parole-states-community-supervision.html)

collaborative way toward positive change. This is quite different to simply telling the justice-involved individual to meet the conditions of supervision, "or else." The work is really being done together—this requires staff to understand that they will always have authority and power over their clients by virtue of their position, but to attempt to step out of an authoritarian and "expert" role and relationally position themselves alongside the client. Motivational Interviewing is something that staff engages in *with* clients rather than *on* clients (Stinson & Clark, 2017).

Acceptance

The second element involves Acceptance of the person for whomever he/she/they are today, but not necessarily acceptance of criminal actions. This is a challenge with clients who have engaged in very serious antisocial criminal behavior. Judgment for the crimes committed is a reality with which correctional staff must often wrestle. It is important to remember that clients have already been sentenced by a judge and that it is better to judge behavior rather than the person. Miller and Rollnick (2013) indicate four ways to foster acceptance. First, we must recognize the **absolute worth** of all clients on our caseload, regardless of what they may have done in their past. To do this work, we have to seriously interrogate ourselves about whether we truly believe this. In the words of Bryan Stevenson, the well-respected capital defense attorney and author, "Are people really more than the worst thing they have ever done?" Acceptance will not work well if staff cannot get past feelings of judgment and condemnation.

Second, Acceptance also requires **accurate empathy**, which indicates a genuine curiosity about learning who the client is and their inner world. This requires a suspension of our own values and attitudes and to focus on the client's perceptions as they personally view it. Empathy is the ability to let go of our own worldview to truly attempt to see and feel the client's worldview and accept it for what it is. Communicating this to justice-involved individuals takes careful attention because it can easily come off as sympathy or pity, which will only strain the relationship. Stinson and Clark (2017) sum it up as, "You listen to people the way they want to be listened to" (p. 21).

Autonomy-support is the third way to convey Acceptance. One of the best ways to think of autonomy-support is to consider that people are the experts in their own lives: No one else has lived the life that you have, and so you are in the best position to make the choice you need. Allowing clients to have the power of choice to do what they think is best will elicit more change than strictly telling them what to do. An inherent problem with this is that correctional and criminal justice systems are not known for giving people choice and autonomy. Yet, at the end of the day, even if systems try to control and surveil people in the strictest sense, individuals can still find ways to be defiant. Forcing compliance has never been effective at facilitating long-term behavior change. A good example of this is the probation officer telling a new client to "Just be honest with me. If you're honest with me, then this whole thing will go a whole lot smoother for both of us." Seems appropriate on its face. However, a better message to a new client might be, "Just keep showing up—keep coming to these appointments as best you can and let me know if you can't ahead of time. I'd like for you to be honest with me too, but I understand that honesty first requires trust, and we aren't there yet."

The fourth component of Acceptance is **affirmation**, which asks staff to communicate their support of clients when appropriate and to recognize that many have been through incredibly difficult challenges before they came to be under correctional supervision (Stinson & Clark,

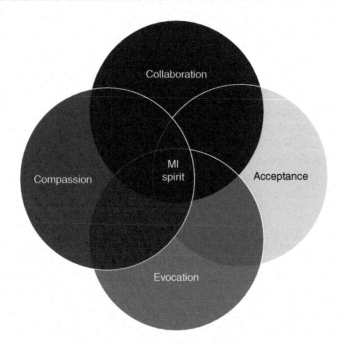

FIGURE 3.3 The Spirit of Motivational Interviewing.
Source: Reproduced with permission from SAGE Publishing

2017). Most justice-involved people have been victims themselves at one point in time (if not at multiple points in their lives; Lauritsen, Sampson, & Laub, 1991) and have overcome significant adversity. This, of course, does not mean that they should not be held accountable for their crimes, but that in many cases, these adversities created the conditions under which committing criminal acts were easier choices for them to make. In other words, people who come from privileged backgrounds generally have more positive opportunities and positive role models early in their lives compared to individuals with less privilege. With many clients, the fact that they are even alive can be viewed as a strength and affirming their resilience.

Compassion

Not many people feel compassion for individuals who have committed criminal offenses, and it may seem counterintuitive, or even a relational boundary violation, to show compassion for people on our caseloads. However, compassion is a key ingredient to fostering healthy rapport, relational safety, and trust among clients and staff. Compassion has many meanings, but perhaps the best for our purposes is the spiritual quote from the Nobel Peace Laureate Archbishop Desmond Tutu:

> *My humanity is bound up in yours for we can only be human together. We are different precisely in order to realize our need of one another.*

What is conveyed here is love and forgiveness. For our purposes, it really means we should do our best to embrace the notion that all people are worthy of love and forgiveness, not that we have to love and forgive our clients. The former would certainly be a boundary violation, and the latter would likely be viewed as judgmental and odd by clients. Different from empathy, compassion connotes patience with, and a connection to, human frailties (Stinson & Clark, 2017). Perceiving clients as unworthy of forgiveness and undeserving of opportunities for a better life makes it hard to believe that people can change. Staff who show compassion toward clients must have a strong sense of self and understand that it will oftentimes not be well received by clients, at least at first. This is because many justice-involved people have never had anyone in their lives genuinely care about them, let alone show compassion. It may feel especially suspicious to clients who have been continually harmed and abandoned by people who should have cared for them, such as parents or intimate partners.

Evocation

Finally, Evocation indicates a belief that individuals already have within them everything they need to move toward positive change. While undoubtedly many clients will need to learn new prosocial skills to sustain change, all the "ingredients" are already there to accomplish their goals. This is truly where a strengths-based approach to correctional work comes in. Strengths-based approaches recognize that all people have strengths and abilities within them to change, regardless of what they have done or been through in their past. It moves past a deficit model of change, which focuses only on the problems that need to be changed (e.g., substance use, antisocial friends, etc.) and instead begins from a position of the strengths that all of us have. Stinson and Clark (2017) remind us that our goal with Evocation is to help clients activate those strengths, values, and abilities to move forward.

CONCLUSION

The twenty-first century was met with a wave of criminal justice reform, with a primary focus on rehabilitation through the implementation of evidence-based correctional practices. When considering community corrections reform, agencies must retire the supervision-only mindset and shift the professional responsibilities of probation and parole staff to reflect (1) community supervision as human service work and (2) officers' roles as change agents.

When officers adopt a human service focus and take on the role of change agents—including the use of core correctional practices (Andrews & Kiessling, 1980; Dowden & Andrews, 2004), Motivational Interviewing (Stinson & Clark, 2017), and establish a dual role orientation (i.e., establish a firm, fair, and caring relationship with clients; Skeem et al., 2007)—their clients are more likely to complete their supervision and abstain from future criminal justice-involvement. This, in turn, creates safer communities and reduces the number of individuals in the justice system.

In other words, it is no longer acceptable for custody and supervision staff to consider themselves as solely law enforcers, whereas the mental health and social work staff are the change agents. Long-term behavior change does not occur through control mechanisms and coercive tactics—they emerge from structured, skill-based interventions delivered by staff who walk alongside the client to both hold accountability and hope for change.

Perhaps one of the best ways that captures this dual role orientation is the newest tagline for the American Probation and Parole Association (APPA): *A Force for Positive Change.*

The spirit of this statement demonstrates the importance of the dual role. It also sends the message to all who work in community corrections that they are integral to reducing crime and recidivism. With over 6 million adults under community supervision (Jones, 2018), its impact on public safety cannot be understated.

Discussion Questions

1. Choose one of the 5 Core Correctional Practices and discuss why it is important for behavioral change among clients.
2. What does being "firm, fair, and caring" mean to you?
3. Describe what is meant by the "dual role orientation."
4. When a person is authoritative, how is that different than being authoritarian?
5. Review Box 3.2 and come up with more distinctions between being a referee versus a coach. First, think in terms of sports and/or learning an instrument, and then relate these traits back to dual role orientation of community corrections officers.
6. Engage in 5 minutes of focused free writing, note down everything that comes to mind with the prompt, "What is Motivational Interviewing?" Do not write using sentences—instead, write ideas and thoughts without worrying about grammar or spelling.

ONLINE LEARNING ENHANCEMENTS

Bryan Stevenson's TED talk *We Need to Talk About an Injustice* provides an opportunity to discuss the motivational interviewing concepts of acceptance and absolute worth. https://www.ted.com/talks/bryan_stevenson_we_need_to_talk_about_an_injustice?language=en

GLOSSARY OF KEY TERMS

absolute worth one of the four aspects of Acceptance in Motivational Interviewing; a belief in the inherent value and potential of every human being

acceptance a central element in Motivational Interviewing that promotes mutually respectful relationships between staff and client; staff acceptance for who the client is today, without judgment and is fostered through the concepts of absolute worth, accurate empathy, autonomy-support, and affirmation

accurate empathy one of the four aspects of Acceptance in Motivational Interviewing; an active interest in, and effort to understand, the client's internal perspective; to see the world through the client's eyes and the conviction it is worthwhile to do so

affirmation one of the four aspects of Acceptance in Motivational Interviewing; statements and actions that recognize client strengths and acknowledge behaviors that lead in the direction of positive change

ambivalence a normal cognitive obstacle in the behavior change process that takes the form of a conflict between two courses of action (taking steps toward changing behavior vs. not taking steps toward changing behavior), each of which has costs and benefits

authoritarian a characteristic of human service providers that does not promote healthy and positive professional relationships with clients because authority is used in overbearing and inappropriate ways

authoritative a characteristic of human service providers that promotes healthy and positive professional relationships with clients through firm, fair, and caring interactions

autonomy-support one of the four aspects of Acceptance in Motivational Interviewing; accepting the client's inherent capacity to make informed personal decisions (i.e., autonomy) and actively supporting it

community corrections a broad term used to encompass agencies that are supervising justice-involved individuals in the community, this includes both probation and parole agencies

community supervision officer a term that refers to officers supervising justice-involved clients in the community, this includes both probation or parole officers

Compassion a central element in Motivational Interviewing that promotes mutually respectful relationships between staff and client, conveying patience with, and a connection to, human frailties

core correctional practices the five components of effective correctional intervention: (1) appropriate use of authority, (2) appropriate modeling and reinforcement, (3) skill-building and problem-solving, (4) effective use of community resources, and (5) relationship factors

evidence-based corrections intentionally using the scientific evidence from correctional psychology to implement policies, practices, and procedures that are most likely to reduce recidivism

Evocation a central element in Motivational Interviewing that promotes mutually respectful relationships between staff and client; the staff member's belief that individuals already have within them everything they need to move toward positive change

dual role orientation the practice of blending care and control when working with clients; holding them accountable while also engaging in effective interventions to promote behavioral change

"get tough on crime" a philosophy/approach starting in the 1980s that was based on the assumption that being more punitive would prevent crime, which led to the implementation of punishment oriented policies and practices

human service work a broad term that includes professions that focus on helping clients (could be individuals, groups, or communities) improve their lives

Partnership a central element in Motivational Interviewing that promotes mutually respectful relationships between staff and client through collaborative interactions

models of supervision the various curricula developed to create structured interactions between corrections staff and clients in order to promote the core correctional practices (STICS, STARR, and EPICS)

Motivational Interviewing a person-centered, goal directed method of communication for eliciting and strengthening intrinsic motivation for change

strengths-based approaches interventions that start with an understanding that all people have strengths and abilities within them to change, regardless of what they have done, or been through, in their past

CHAPTER 4

Correctional Treatment: Accomplishments and Realities

Paula Smith, Paul Gendreau, and Claire Goggin

KEY TERMS

actuarial assessment
"appropriate" interventions
clinical subjective/intuitive assessment
Correctional Program Assessment
   Inventory 2000 (CPAI–2000)
dosage

need principle
principles of effective intervention
"punishing smarter" strategies
responsivity principle
risk principle
therapeutic integrity

The purpose of this chapter is to summarize the treatment outcome evaluation literature with respect to our knowledge about the success of various types of treatment strategies in reducing recidivism. In addition, we provide some data on the quality of correctional treatment programs routinely found in the corrections field.

ACCOMPLISHMENTS

One of the impressive accomplishments in the area of correctional rehabilitation is that so much useful knowledge has been generated in a relatively short period (see Gendreau, 1996a). In the 1960s, corrections professionals had little idea of "what worked." There were few treatment outcome evaluation studies at that time and little indication of effectiveness by any type of intervention (Martinson, 1974). In his review of the literature, for example, Martinson (1974) analyzed the results from 231 studies of correctional treatment programs. He concluded "that with few and isolated exceptions, the rehabilitative efforts that have been reported so far have had no appreciable effect on recidivism" (p. 48). Although his "nothing works" credo had a tremendous impact on popular and professional thinking, it should be noted that Martinson's (1974) review had a number of shortcomings. Only 138 of 231 studies reported recidivism as an outcome. Of these, only 73 were based on recognizable treatment categories. Indeed, probation, imprisonment, and parole were among the treatments being tested, which begs the question of how these interventions can be defined

DOI: 10.4324/9780367808266-5

as "treatment." Furthermore, the number of outcomes per treatment type was limited, with considerable modality differences among them (i.e., counseling, psychotherapy, skills development, group methods, milieu therapy; Cullen & Gendreau, 2000). This essentially means that given the low number of studies in each of the categories that we would now consider "treatment," the Martinson study actually would not have been considered so definitive on the possible drawbacks of treatment. Moreover, the study did not include the kind of treatment intervention that we know now to be most effective—cognitive behavioral programming. Thankfully, we are now working with a "what works" credo to help build knowledge instead of the "nothing works" concept that only seeks to destroy it (Cullen & Gendreau, 2001).

Presently, a huge evaluation literature exists that can only be summarized adequately by quantitative research synthesis techniques (also known as meta-analysis). There are at least three dozen of these quantitative reviews available, and they encompass approximately 1,000 studies (McGuire, 2002). Assessments of these quantitative reviews have been undertaken for the purposes of generating a set of guidelines, or **principles of effective intervention** with system-impacted clients (e.g., Andrews, 1995; Andrews & Bonta, 2010; Bonta & Andrews, 2017; Gendreau, 1996b; Gendreau & Andrews, 1990). A brief summary of the results of the meta-analyses and the principles of effective intervention are outlined below.

Results of the Meta-analyses

How successful are we at rehabilitating justice-involved clients? First, summarizing across all evaluation studies, regardless of their nature, it has been reported that about 64% of the programs studied reduce recidivism, with the average reduction being 10% (cf. Lipsey, 1992). This outcome, in itself, is noteworthy. If only cynics in criminal justice were not so parochial (Gendreau & Ross, 1979), they would be astonished to learn that results of this magnitude are often deemed quite acceptable in a wide variety of other service delivery areas (Lipsey & Wilson, 1993; Rosenthal & DiMatteo, 2001). But it is not sufficient to simply summarize across all studies; the next step is to determine what characteristics, if any, reliably distinguish studies that reduce recidivism from those that do not. If we can do this—find some order in this universe—then we can make enormous strides in engineering better treatment services for clients in the future. Fortunately, we can. Studies that share certain programmatic features, or what are called "appropriate" interventions (Andrews et al., 1990), reduce recidivism by approximately 25–30% (Bonta & Andrews, 2017; Andrews, Dowden, & Gendreau, 1999), whereas studies designated as "inappropriate" produce slight increases in recidivism. Appropriate treatment programs also produce substantial reductions in other measures of antisocial behavior (e.g., prison misconduct) that are correlated with recidivism (French & Gendreau, 2006). Finally, appropriate treatment programs set in the community generally produce two to three times greater reductions in recidivism than prison-based programs (Andrews et al., 1990).

The Principles of Effective Intervention

What are these appropriate treatments? Much of the detail of these treatments are provided throughout this text, but it is important to first provide the reader with an overview of these principles before diving deeper into each. Given the intended audience of this text, for a detailed presentation of these issues it is recommended that the reader consult Bonta and Andrews (2017), Cullen and Gendreau (2000), Gendreau (1996b), and Andrews (1995). The reader is also encouraged to inspect exemplary individual studies (e.g., Alexander, Pugh, & Parsons, 1998; Bourgon & Armstrong, 2005; Gibbs, Potter, & Goldstein, 1995; Goldstein, 1999; Gordon, Graves, & Arbuthnot, 1995; Henggeler, Schoenwald, Borduin, Rowland, & Cunningham, 1998). Listings of these and others can be found, for the most part, in Andrews et al. (1990, pp. 403–404), Andrews et al. (1999), and Gendreau (1996b, pp. 114–120). The principles of effective intervention underlying appropriate treatments are as follows:

1. The treatment is based on behavioral strategies (e.g., radical behavioral, social learning, or cognitive behavioral) (Andrews et al., 1990; French & Gendreau, 2006; Gendreau, 1996b; Gendreau, Little, & Goggin, 1996). As such, program facilitators should engage in the following therapeutic practices: prosocial modeling, effective reinforcement and disapproval, problem-solving techniques, structured learning procedures for skill-building, effective use of authority, cognitive self-change, relationship practices, and Motivational Interviewing (Stinson & Clark, 2017). It is important to note that meta-analyses of the correctional treatment literature have *consistently* favored cognitive behavioral interventions over other treatment modalities (see Lipsey & Cullen, 2007; Smith et al., 2009). Cognitive behavioral interventions are discussed at length in Part III of this textbook. In a review of the results of a meta-analysis, Smith et al. (2009) noted that approximately 73% (or 16/22) of the mean effect size estimates were greater than $r = 0.15$. Using the Binomial Effect Size Display (BESD) statistic, an $r = 0.15$ means that the success rate of the treatment represents a 15% reduction in recidivism over the control condition (Rosenthal & Rubin, 1979; see also Gendreau & Smith, 2007; Smith, et al., 2009). In contrast, "other" treatment modalities (i.e., non-behavioral) were associated with much smaller reductions in recidivism with approximately 88% (or 7/8) less than $r = 0.15$.

2. The program has a manual that describes the theory and data justifying the program, as well as a curriculum that details the discrete steps to be followed in presenting the material (for an example of a comprehensive program manual, see Gibbs et al., 1995).

3. The treatment is located, preferably, in the client's natural environment (or represents an *"in vivo"* intervention).

4. The treatment is multimodal. In other words, the program offers a variety of interventions and is equipped to minister to a range of client needs, particularly criminogenic needs (needs associated with recidivism).

5. The intensity of treatment should be approximately 100 hours of direct service over a three- to four-month period (see also Andrews & Bonta, 2010; Bourgon & Armstrong, 2005).

6. The treatment emphasizes positive reinforcement contingencies for prosocial behavior and is individualized as much as possible. Clients should spend at least 40% of their program time acquiring prosocial skills. Furthermore, the ratio of reinforcers to punishers should be at least 4:1 (see Gendreau, French, & Gionet, 2004).

7. The behaviors targeted are those that are predictive of future antisocial behavior and are dynamic in nature (e.g., antisocial attitudes and antisocial peers; see Bonta, 2002; Gendreau et al., 2004; Gendreau, Goggin, French, & Smith, 2006; Simourd, 2004). This is the **need principle** (see Chapter 6). In identifying such problems, it is crucial for programs to use valid actuarial assessments (Gendreau, Goggin, & Smith, 2002).

Furthermore, and this point cannot be stressed enough, it is the medium- to higher-risk clients who will benefit the most from treatment. This is the **risk principle** (see Chapter 6).

8. The treatment should be designed to match key client characteristics and learning styles with relevant therapist characteristics and program features to facilitate the learning of prosocial values. This is the **responsivity principle** (see Chapter 6).

9. Once the formal phase of treatment has ended, continuity through aftercare on an as-needed basis is required. Especially with chronic problems such as sex offenses and substance abuse, relapse prevention program models are useful (Dowden, Antonowicz, & Andrews, 2003).

10. Several system factors must be in place for effective service delivery (see Andrews & Bonta, 2010; Gendreau, Goggin, & Smith, 2001). These center on the quality of program implementation, the training and credentials of program directors and staff, the degree to which the organization engages in interagency communication and advocacy brokerage, the involvement of program directors in the design and day-to-day operations of the program, the degree to which the organization engages in meaningful attempts at knowledge dissemination to line staff, the participation of staff in program decision-making, the care taken to monitor changes in clients' behavior for effective case management, and the quality of the therapeutic practices of the staff. Lowenkamp, Latessa, and Smith (2006) conducted 38 evaluations of community-based residential programs. The results indicated that the "program implementation" domain was strongly associated with treatment effectiveness ($r = 0.54$).

Finally, the principles above apply to both juvenile and adult samples and, on the basis of more limited evidence, to females and minority groups. The components of the responsivity principle, however, may differ considerably across different samples of correctional clients (see Smith et al., 2009, and Chapter 6 for a review).

WHAT DOES NOT WORK

In comparison with appropriate treatment programs, the programmatic features underlying inappropriate strategies are as follows:

1. Inappropriate programs are based on psychodynamic, non-directive, and medical-model treatments. As well, programs that are based on threats, inculcating fear, and/or **"punishing smarter" strategies**, such as boot camps, drug testing, electronic monitoring, restitution, and shock incarceration, have been unmitigated failures (Andrews et al., 1990; Gendreau 1996b; Gendreau, Goggin, & Fulton, 2000; Gendreau et al., 1993; Smith, Goggin, & Gendreau, 2002).

2. Sociological perspectives that singularly target the importance of respect for a client's culture, diversion from the correctional system, or providing access to legitimate opportunities for the disadvantaged are associated with slight increases in recidivism (cf., Bonta & Andrews, 2017; Gendreau et al., 2004). While respecting a client's culture is important for any therapeutic alliance to occur, it is not enough to change behavior. Further, diversion programs can be successful, but only if they divert clients who are low-risk for recidivism,

or divert medium- and high-risk clients to intensive treatment interventions based on the principles of effective intervention listed above.

3. Programs that intensively treat low-risk clients or target behaviors that are weak predictors of antisocial behavior (e.g., self-esteem with male clients) rarely demonstrate effectiveness (Andrews, Bonta, & Hoge, 1990; Gendreau et al., 1996).

THE REALITIES OF CORRECTIONAL TREATMENT

While it is one thing to document the fact that certain types of exemplary treatment programs (published in the research literature) can have a meaningful effect on reducing recidivism, another reality exists: It is highly likely that these exemplary studies are far from representative of the programming typically found in government and private agencies in the field (Gendreau & Goggin, 1991; Lab & Whitehead, 1990). In an attempt to address this crucial issue, the **Correctional Program Assessment Inventory 2000 (CPAI-2000)** was developed to measure **therapeutic integrity**, or program quality (Gendreau & Andrews, 2001). The instrument now consists of 131 items derived from the "what works" literature reviewed previously. The CPAI-2000 assesses programs on eight dimensions: organizational culture, program implementation/maintenance, management/staff characteristics, client risk-need practices, program characteristics, several aspects of core correctional practices, interagency communication, and evaluation. The CPAI-2000 documents the strengths and weaknesses of a program in each of the dimensions and provides an overall percentage score of program quality.

The CPAI (and its subsequent revised versions) has been applied to more than 550 correctional treatment programs (Gendreau et al., 2001; Lowenkamp, 2004; Lowenkamp et al., 2006). Two studies, one involving a meta-analysis (Nesovic, 2003), and the other based on an analysis of numerous treatment programs in Ohio (Lowenkamp, 2004), determined that scores on the CPAI were highly predictive of recidivism (r < 0.25 to 0.50).

Results of the CPAI Research

In 1990, the CPAI was administered to 170 adult correctional substance use programs (Gendreau & Goggin, 1991). Program respondents were instructed to provide the authors with a complete dossier of all facets of their functioning, as well as answer a detailed questionnaire. The 101 programs that responded produced a mean CPAI score of 25%. Programs that were community-based (versus those in prisons) and "contracted out" (versus those run by institutions) had higher scores on the CPAI, but even in these two cases, mean CPAI scores were less than 40%. Two programs received a very satisfactory score, eight were judged to be satisfactory, and 12 almost received a passing grade (40–49%).

The fact that only 10% of programs received a satisfactory grade seemed somewhat low, given that the survey was conducted within a correctional organization that was considered a leader in correctional rehabilitation. Subsequently, another survey (Hoge, Leschied, & Andrews, 1993) was undertaken of agencies providing services for juvenile clients within a Canadian province that has had a very progressive history in correctional service delivery. Adequate data for the purposes of scoring the CPAI were available for 135 programs. The overall mean CPAI score for all programs was 35%. Furthermore, the mean percentage scores on the CPAI subcomponents were all less than 50%, with the evaluation component recording by far the lowest scores (20%). CPAI scores did not differ whether scoring was based on a file review or an actual site visit by the evaluators. The researchers also found that programs with a specialized focus (e.g., substance abuse, sex offending) produced slightly higher CPAI scores (39% versus 32%). Programs in probation settings had lower CPAI scores than institution-based programs. As with the Gendreau and Goggin (1991) study, few programs (10%) scored as satisfactory or better. Of some encouragement is that a new provincial innovation in service delivery—intensive community-based interventionist agencies that targeted the youth and family—was generally (7 out of 9) of satisfactory or very satisfactory quality. A modified version of the CPAI, called the Correctional Program Checklist (CPC), has been administered to a number of individual programs by the team at the University of Cincinnati Corrections Institute led by Edward Latessa.

The pessimistic conclusion reached in the earlier surveys remains the same. What should be done about this sorry state of affairs? One school of thought is to declare a pox on the treatment enterprise and essentially "throw in the towel" (Lab & Whitehead, 1990). On the other hand, a productive strategy for dealing with the issue is to begin the arduous task of identifying the most frequently occurring programming deficits for programs "in the field" with the objective of rectifying the problems (Gendreau & Goggin, 1991).

We now turn to a brief summary of the major program deficiencies we and our colleagues have catalogued in our evaluations.

The shortcomings listed in what follows have occurred at least 50% of the time; regrettably, in some cases the incidence is 70% or more. The reader will quickly recognize the fact that some of the chapters in this text (see Chapters 6 through 10) and the literature reviewed previously in this chapter speak directly to several of the concerns described. The major deficiencies, with commentary where appropriate, are as follows:

1. *Implementation*
   a. Program directors and staff are not adequately familiar with the literature. Moreover, they do not conduct a thorough review of the literature on the proposed treatment and its effectiveness prior to implementing the program. As a result, they may find themselves "following a hunch," repeating the mistakes of others, or chasing the latest panacea (see Van Voorhis et al., 1995).
   b. The professional credibility (i.e., training, experience with successful programs) of program designers is often suspect.
   c. Granted, the corrections literature is still relatively sparse in the program implementation area, though it is improving (e.g., Duwe & Clark, 2015; Gendreau, 1996b; Salisbury, Sundt, & Boppre, 2019; Taxman & Belenko, 2012); however, there is extensive literature on technology transfer that demonstrates how to establish programs effectively in other social science/service and management fields (Backer, Davis, & Soucy, 1995) that invariably is ignored by program designers in corrections.
2. *Client Preservice Assessment*
   a. Somewhat surprisingly, given all that has been written about **actuarial risk assessment** (Bonta, 1996, 2002), the traditional **clinical subjective/intuitive assessment** persists. Indeed, there is virtually no recognition of the classic literature concerning the inadequacy of this approach to assessment (e.g., Little & Schneidman, 1959; Meehl, 1954).

b. Among the programs that employ actuarial systems (or tests) to assess clients, it is not unusual to find a preoccupation with static risk factors (e.g., previous offending history, type of offense), while the assessment of dynamic risk factors (e.g., attitudes, values, and behaviors) is overlooked. It is impossible to monitor treatment effectiveness unless the latter are assessed because they represent the targets for behavioral change (Gendreau et al., 1996).

c. There is still confusion as to which dynamic factors should be appraised. Programs still place major importance on the assessment of self-esteem, anxiety, and depression, which are among the weakest predictors of recidivism for male offending populations (though they have shown strength as predictors for female offending populations—see Chapter 13), while directing negligible attention to robust predictors, such as antisocial attitudes (Gendreau et al., 1996).

3. *Program Characteristics*

a. Programs either did not use any appropriate treatments (i.e., those known to be effective) or they diluted the overall effectiveness of the program by employing inappropriate strategies along with effective ones. In one specific instance (Gendreau & Goggin, 1991) it was found, similar to the findings of Hester and Miller's (2003) comprehensive analysis of the alcoholism treatment literature, that the most frequently used interventions were empirically established failures.

b. The **dosage** level (i.e., intensity) of treatment is often insufficient (e.g., several hours per week). Clients simply do not spend enough time in treatment.

c. The responsivity principle is almost totally neglected. This lack of attention to individual differences is striking; it reflects a long-standing bias in theory development in criminology (see Andrews & Wormith, 1989) and evolving management practices in corrections that are macro-level and input-output-oriented with little concern directed toward the needs of the individual client (Gendreau et al., 1996). In these common instances, clients are treated as if they are all alike (see Chapter 6).

d. Very few programs incorporate a meaningful system of reinforcers (see Chapter 8).

e. Relapse prevention strategies are underutilized (see Chapter 12).

f. A sound index of therapeutic integrity in a program is a treatment manual that outlines, in ample detail, the theory underlying the treatment, the daily treatment task schedule (i.e., lesson plan, homework exercises, teaching aid materials), and the process evaluation assessment tools. The manual should be of sufficient quality that an "external" therapist should be able to come into the program and conduct a class session with relative ease. Such manuals are, in our experience, quite rare. Furthermore, few programs monitor, in any quantifiable way, the quality of the instruction per se. We are aware of only three measures developed in this regard (i.e., Gendreau & Andrews, 2001; Mitchell & Egan, 1995; UCCI, 2005, 2015).

g. Many programs have experienced problems finding any relevant/useful community services to which clients may be referred for ongoing service.

4. *Staff Characteristics*

The foregoing should be read more as an indictment of the lack of quality control exhibited by employers and the paucity of relevant training programs in academic settings. For the most part, we have found treatment staff to be dedicated and eager to upgrade their skills when the opportunity presents itself.

FIGURE 4.1 Two residents of the Virginia Center for Behavioral Rehabilitation stand on a rooftop and threaten to hang themselves unless they can talk to a state official about their treatment at the psychiatric facility, November 2011, in Burkeville, Virginia.
Source: AP Photo/Steve Helber.

a. It is not unusual to find staff hired for a treatment program on characteristics other than clinical experience and training relevant to the task at hand. Program staff commonly have less than a university degree; postgraduate training is rare. In addition, we have not discovered one hiring protocol in the United States or Canada that employed an actuarial assessment of the characteristics (e.g., clarity, honesty, empathy, fairness; see Gendreau & Andrews, 2001) that have been found to be associated with effective counseling skills (see Chapters 1 through 3).

b. Time and again, when questioning staff, we have encountered large gaps in knowledge regarding:

(i) the criminological theories of antisocial behavior and the psychological theories of personality and their relevance to treatment (see chapters from Part III in this text); and

(ii) basic concepts of classical and operant conditioning (see Chapter 8), without which it is impossible to undertake any sort of effective counseling.

These are strong comments to be sure, but with respect to this last point, how could it be otherwise when some programs have difficulty identifying a varied menu of reinforcers and punishers, let alone demonstrating awareness of the principles of how to reinforce and punish behavior? Seldom have we seen the classic texts on the modification of behavior referenced by programmers (Masters, Burish, Hollon, & Rimm, 1987; Matson & DiLorenzo, 1984; Spiegler & Guevremont, 2002). Therefore, in our opinion, much of what goes on under the guise of cognitive therapy really consists of nondirective "chats" with no guarantee that prosocial behavior is reinforced and antisocial behavior is not reinforced or punished. Recommended reading on how counselors should function as competent role models can be found in Chapters 3 and 8 of this text and in Bonta and Andrews (2017).

5. *Evaluation*

a. Systematic and thorough evaluation practices are, for all intents and purposes, nonexistent. Process evaluation, or how the client is progressing in treatment, is sporadic at best; follow-up outcome evaluation is even more so.

b. Consumer/client satisfaction surveys are infrequent.

CONCLUSION

There is only one avenue to pursue to alleviate the shortcomings outlined in this chapter, and it is better education and training. This topic has been discussed in detail elsewhere (Gendreau, 1996a). Unfortunately, there are few opportunities for training in correctional client assessment and treatment. There are, at best, only a handful of academic psychology/criminal justice/forensic social work programs in the United States that have an in-depth curriculum in the correctional treatment area. Nevertheless, it does not need to be a Herculean task to bring about needed changes (e.g., Ax & Morgan, 2002; Gendreau, 1996a; Henggeler, Schoenwald, & Pickrel, 1995). A few key academic programs and a greater awareness of how to effect knowledge dissemination (Gendreau, 1995, 1996b) will, in our view, lead to a new generation of treatment programs that will be better able to benefit the clients and protect the public.

Discussion Questions

1. Realistically speaking, how effective can we expect correctional treatment programs to be? Is this more or less effective than for other interventions in human services?

2. What client problems and behaviors should programs target for purposes of intervention? What problems should not be targeted?

3. What would be the characteristics of a "high-quality" correctional treatment program?
4. Why should program directors and staff be familiar with the treatment effectiveness literature prior to designing a program?
5. What types of knowledge should correctional treatment staff possess to perform their jobs effectively?

ONLINE LEARNING ENHANCEMENTS

Washington State Institute for Public Policy (WSIPP) Benefit-Cost Clearinghouse
WSIPP is a nonpartisan public research group located in Olympia, Washington state. They are a team of multidisciplinary researchers who conduct applied policy research for the state legislature in a creative and collaborative environment. Their Benefit-Cost Clearinghouse includes a consistently updated array of studies and meta-analyses investigating the effectiveness of interventions focused on juvenile and adult correctional populations, substance use, child welfare, public health, and education. Studies are not limited to Washington state, and the site provides a reliable source for determining evidence-based correctional programs. www.wsipp.wa.gov/BenefitCost

GLOSSARY OF KEY TERMS

actuarial assessment an assessment instrument that statistically predicts the likelihood of recidivism by employing psychometric methods to assess clients

"appropriate" interventions correctional treatment interventions that have been shown to reduce recidivism by approximately 25–30%

clinical subjective/intuitive assessment an unstructured risk assessment that relies on clinical judgment to determine the likelihood of recidivism rather than actuarial methods

Correctional Program Assessment Inventory 2000 (CPAI–2000) an instrument that is used to measure therapeutic integrity by assessing programs on eight dimensions: organizational culture, program implementation/maintenance, management/staff characteristics, client risk-need practices, program characteristics, several aspects of core correctional practices, interagency communication, and evaluation

dosage the intensity level, or number of hours of prescribed correctional treatment

need principle a correctional counseling principle that maintains that needs related to future offending should receive high priority as clients are matched to programs

principles of effective intervention a set of guidelines underlying the appropriate treatment of correctional clients

"punishing smarter" strategies correctional programs such as boot camps, drug testing, electronic monitoring, restitution, and shock incarceration; such programs have proven to be ineffective in the treatment of correctional clients

responsivity principle maximize the client's ability to learn from a rehabilitative intervention by providing cognitive behavioral treatment and tailoring the intervention to the learning style, motivation, abilities, and strengths of the individual

risk principle a correctional counseling principle that maintains that clients should be provided with treatment and supervision levels that align with their level of risk; intensive treatment efforts should be directed toward high- and medium-risk clients, while low-risk clients should not be assigned to institutional placements or intensive treatment interventions that expose them to criminogenic influences

therapeutic integrity the quality of correctional treatment programs

PART II

Client Assessment, Diagnosis, Classification, and Case Planning

This book endeavors to present a wide array of individual and group correctional treatment strategies. Yet none of the strategies or techniques presented in this book will work with all justice-involved people all of the time. Juveniles and adults represent a highly heterogeneous group of individuals who differ from one another according to their treatment needs, the danger they pose to others, their ability to cope with certain correctional environments, their amenability to specific counseling styles, their willingness to participate in correctional treatment programs, and their likelihood of recidivating. Failure to identify and to plan for these differences can be both dangerous and expensive for correctional agencies.

It is dangerous, for example, to fail to identify potentially violent correctional clients prior to their committing harmful acts against others. At the other end of the behavioral continuum, it is expensive, ineffective, and unjust to assign low-risk clients to correctional environments that are too restrictive.

The next two chapters will discuss how correctional systems can accommodate the treatment and security needs of correctional clients by: (1) clinical identification of clients who are mentally ill; and (2) systematic testing or screening of all correctional clients for risk potential and treatment needs.

Chapter 5 presents an important overview of the major categories of mental illness and intellectual disability. In recent years correctional agencies have had to deal with a growing proportion of intellectually disabled and mentally ill people. This growth is, in part, the result of the "war on drugs," which in many states required mandatory sentencing of people convicted of drug offenses. Reductions in funding for community mental health services have also created a situation in which prisons are now the largest providers of mental health services in the country. Such clients can pose a serious threat to others if they are dangerous, or, conversely, may themselves be highly vulnerable to being victimized by other incarcerated people. At the same time, prisons can greatly aggravate mental health conditions if the mentally ill are not appropriately cared for. A mental health-related diagnosis should be a major factor in determining correctional placement. Carbonell, Anestis, and Salisbury point

DOI: 10.4324/9780367808266-6

out in Chapter 5 that although mental illness assessments and diagnoses must be formulated by licensed psychologists or psychiatrists, it is, nevertheless, extremely important for correctional staff to be trained to recognize symptoms. Otherwise, referrals to appropriate services do not occur in time to prevent tragedies or other problems. Their chapter also gives valuable advice about how staff should report concerns.

A second strategy of identifying important differences between clients is discussed in Chapter 6. In contrast to the methods discussed in Chapter 5, Chapter 6 discusses classification strategies that are administered to all members of a correctional setting, usually upon admission. Risk assessment instruments, for example, are administered shortly after conviction and classify people according to high, medium, and low potential for absconding, violating conditions, and committing new offenses. Chapter 6 also devotes considerable attention to screening clients for needs that should be addressed in correctional treatment programs. Correctional practitioners are advised to give priority to those needs that are related to future offending. New developments in correctional assessments are also discussed, such as gender-responsive risk assessments and assessments specific to special populations such as people convicted of sex offenses.

As noted before, failure to utilize appropriate classification strategies can result in higher costs to correctional agencies. Not all people on probation, for example, need to be monitored on a weekly basis. Only high-risk clients need intensive supervision. Others need not receive undue amounts of scarce resources. Similarly, incarcerated people with high anxiety may respond differently to therapy than do people who are aggressive and committed to antisocial behavior. Van Voorhis observes that it makes good sense to assign clients to the treatment options that best fit their needs and psychological characteristics. The alternative, treating people as if they are all alike, often creates a situation in which the program is not as successful as it could be. Simply put, the successes of clients who are assigned correctly may be canceled out by failures of the clients who are incorrectly assigned, but who nevertheless might have succeeded in another type of program.

Chapter 7 shifts the focus away from assessment and diagnosis to the role of individual counselors as they work with individual correctional clients. How does a counselor apply the assessments and theories presented throughout this book to a solid case management plan for each client? How does the counselor collaborate with each client in determining the goals of correctional supervision and treatment? How can the counselor use his or her knowledge to motivate clients to change and to design a course of action that will impart new skills, attitudes, and directions? With this chapter we return to where we began the book, with discussions of how important correctional counselors can be to correctional clients.

CHAPTER 5

Assessment and Diagnosis of Correctional Clients

Joyce L. Carbonell, Joye C. Anestis, and Emily J. Salisbury

KEY TERMS

antisocial personality disorder
avoidant personality disorder
bipolar disorder
borderline personality disorder
competency to stand trial
dependent personality disorder
DSM-5
dynamic assessments
dysthymic disorder
guilty but mentally ill
histrionic personality disorder
intellectual disability
major depressive disorder
manic disorder
Millon Clinical Multiaxial Inventory-IV
 (MCMI-IV)
Minnesota Multiphasic Personality
 Inventory-3 (MMPI-3)

mood disorders
narcissistic personality disorder
not guilty by reason of insanity
 (NGRI)
obsessive-compulsive
 personality disorder
paranoid personality disorder
personality disorder
projective tests
psychotic disorders
schizoid personality disorder
schizophrenia
schizotypal personality disorder
static assessments
substance use disorder
Thematic Apperception Test (TAT)
Wechsler Adult Intelligence Scales IV
 (WAIS-IV)

DOI: 10.4324/9780367808266-7

INTRODUCTION

Mental health assessments attempt to answer questions about how and why people think, feel, and behave in different ways. Such assessments try to describe how an individual copes with stress, perceives a stimulus or event, how he or she may feel emotionally at a given time, what kinds of concerns or interests he or she may have, his or her ability to pay attention or concentrate on a given task, his or her ability to remember different events that have occurred recently or in the past, how he or she relates to other people, and his or her ability to solve problems or think about different issues. While these are the general purposes of assessments, they are very similar to the diagnosis and assessment issues that arise when dealing with justice-involved people. A person may be assessed before trial, after trial, while incarcerated, or when on probation or parole. The questions range from traditional issues concerning intellect and emotional functioning that are relevant to someone's functioning while incarcerated, to psycho-legal issues such as insanity and competency.

Assessments, no matter what the purpose, are snapshots of an individual at a given time. While assessments can provide information about an individual's underlying personality or intelligence, which is less subject to change over time, they can also reflect how the individual is thinking, feeling, and functioning at the time that he or she takes the test or is interviewed.

Think about a snapshot that shows a smiling young man dressed in prison garb. By looking at the picture we can say that the man appeared happy at the time the picture was taken, although we do not know why he was happy. In a similar way, an assessment can tell you that individuals may feel distressed, depressed, anxious, fearful, or angry at the time that they were assessed, but it might not apply to how they felt the week prior to or after the assessment. Such assessments are considered to be **dynamic assessments**. That is, they can change over time.

Other assessments, however, are more stable. For example, if the photograph shows that the man has a beard, it would probably be safe to say that he had a beard before the picture was taken. Depending on the length of his beard, we may feel comfortable making a statement regarding how long he had had the beard. Similarly, if he has green eyes, we would assume that his eyes were green before and after the picture was taken. In the same manner, some assessments provide information regarding an individual's underlying style of relating to the world, including such things as how this person relates to society as a whole, his or her tendency to use alcohol or other drugs, his or her style of solving problems, and other issues concerning this person's basic personality style. These assessments are called **static assessments** because they do not change much, if at all, over time.

If the one snapshot of the young man can tell us something about that moment in time, then it is easy to see how actually knowing the man might provide even more information. For example, if you knew him you could tell the photographer that the reason behind his happiness was that he had just been granted early release. Thus, the daily information that you observe, combined with the evaluation performed by the mental health professional, can give a more complete picture than either would alone.

In summary, assessments by mental health professionals attempt to answer questions about how and why people think, feel, and behave in different ways. They do this by providing information about how the individual being tested was feeling, thinking, and functioning at the time the assessment was administered and by integrating this information with the daily observations provided by the correctional counselor or other staff.

Many problems that occur in correctional settings may actually increase the need for mental health services (American Bar Association, 1989, 2011; National Commission on Correctional Health Care, 2015). It is important for correctional counselors, case managers, and other staff to be able to recognize certain signs and symptoms and to use this information to make appropriate referrals. Although not all types of mental illness can be discussed in this chapter, we will cover the major categories and use three case examples to illustrate. As we move through the chapter we will refer to these incarcerated people as we explain how assessment works. The three people are:

James, a 19-year-old white man who burglarized a bakery with several other slightly older men, is serving his sentence in a state institution. Other than some minor driving violations, this is his first encounter with the criminal justice system. James appears to others to be very quiet and mostly a loner. He does not ask many questions and answers others with brief replies. He has frequent minor rule infractions and has trouble adjusting when the prison routine changes. He is often the subject of practical jokes and at times lashes out at others.

Marianna, a 30-year-old Hispanic woman, is in jail. She and her husband have been accused of importing cocaine into the country. The jail staff note that she has not been eating and seems depressed. Her attorney has raised questions regarding her competency to stand trial.

Horace is a 45-year-old Black man who is in his fourth year of imprisonment, having been convicted of second-degree murder. He is viewed as "strange" by others incarcerated with him and staff, and he believes that he has special powers. Although he is not generally a management problem, he does become testy whenever the prison routine is altered for any reason.

THE ROLE OF THE CORRECTIONAL STAFF

Correctional staff can play an important role in the assessment of people who are incarcerated or on community supervision by serving as sources of information for the mental health professional. As noted earlier, the mental health professional may see the client for only a brief period, compared to the correctional staff or probation officers, who may see them numerous times over the course of many months. They will know important things about the client that will aid in a mental health assessment, and they may be the first to suspect that they need assessment and possibly treatment. Thus, it is the observation and intervention of correctional personnel that frequently lead to assessment and treatment for the client. In deciding to refer someone for a mental health assessment, it is important to start with what you already know, and what you know is what you have observed.

Correctional staff members are in a unique position to observe the behavior of incarcerated people because they have the opportunity to interact with and see them in a variety of situations and contexts. This opportunity to observe allows the correctional staff to gather important information about the client's behavior that can assist mental health professionals in making a mental health assessment. Correctional officials play a crucial role, and their ability to observe and communicate accurately is of great importance. They must know what is important information to communicate to the mental health professional and how to communicate that information.

A common problem with observation is that observers tend to make assumptions about what they see and report their assumptions rather than the behavior of the person observed (Eysenck & Eysenck, 1983). Another way of thinking about this is to realize that many people report their interpretation of events, rather than describe the event itself. In addition, people tend to merge information from an event they witnessed with information they learned later, thus making their final report less reliable (Greenspan & Loftus, 2020). When asked to report on what they observed, the information that is reported is a combination of the observed information and the subsequent information.

James, who was described earlier, does not make eye contact. One staff member describes him as sullen, and another staff member reports that he is shy and withdrawn. Both have seen the same behavior, but they are reporting their interpretation of the behavior, not the behavior itself. At the same time, the person who describes James as sullen because he does not make eye contact may overhear someone else indicate that James does not pay attention to instructions, and the officer may add this to his or her description even though it is not a behavior the officer has observed. It is the description of observed behavior that is the most important to communicate to the mental health professional.

A description of Horace would be more useful if it described the things that he did and said rather than simply stating that he is strange, as this does not convey any specific information. In fact, labels sometimes tell us more about the person using them than they do about the person being labeled. Although you might believe that Marianna is depressed, it is important to note what she is doing or not doing that has led you to that belief.

In general, it is better to provide too much information rather than leave out pieces that might be important. So when in doubt, pass on the information. Be as specific as possible about what you have observed. Ask yourself the following questions about the behavior that you wish to describe:

1. How often does the behavior occur? Is it a daily event or does it only occur several times a week?
2. Does it occur only in certain contexts, like at work or in the housing unit?
3. Does it involve only certain people, such as other incarcerated people or staff?
4. When does it occur? Does it happen only after phone calls or visits? Does it happen at other times too?

Reporting your specific observations is the most helpful approach. In the case of James, reporting that James does not make eye contact, instead of reporting that James does not pay attention when addressed, is a more accurate report of what you have actually seen. With Marianna it would be helpful to describe her crying in terms of how often and when, and report her statements regarding her wish to die. For Horace, rather than noting that he is strange, you could describe his statements about aliens and obtain copies of the writings he has been doing regarding his alien friends.

Because there is such a wide variety of behavior possible, it will help to know something about the major diagnostic categories that are used by mental health professionals. The next section will describe a few of the major categories that are listed in the *Diagnostic and Statistical Manual of Mental Disorders*, Fifth Edition, generally known as the DSM-5 (American Psychiatric Association, 2013).

THE DSM-5

The DSM-5 is the "bible" of mental health diagnostics. Although the correctional counselor or case manager is not expected to diagnose, it helps to know basic information about the major mental health categories. The DSM-5 begins with a cautionary statement, noting that the criteria are offered as guidelines and that, "Use of DSM-5 to assess for the presence of a mental disorder by nonclinical, nonmedical, or otherwise insufficiently trained individuals is not advised" (American Psychiatric Association, 2013, p. 25). Although armchair diagnoses are common, they are frequently incorrect. Mislabeling may cause numerous problems in the correctional setting for both the client and the staff.

In addition, it is important to remember that although the DSM-5 allows mental health personnel to use labels to put people into categories, there is a great deal of overlap between categories, and many people have multiple diagnoses. Because there are numerous criteria for each diagnosis and a person does not have to meet all of the criteria to be diagnosed as having a certain problem, people with the same diagnoses may look quite different from one another. For example, if a person must have three of nine symptoms to be diagnosed with the disorder, two different people could each have three of the symptoms, but have completely different symptoms. In spite of these problems, diagnostic categories provide important information and assist in developing treatment plans.

There are 21 major diagnostic classes in the DSM-5, but only a few will be covered here. In addition, there is a category for "other conditions that may be a focus of clinical attention." Although the previous edition of the DSM (DSM-IV-TR; American Psychiatric Association, 2000) was widely known for using a multiaxial system in which people were diagnosed along several different dimensions, or axes, the DSM-5 moved to a nonaxial documentation of diagnosis. Previously, Axis I described the most well-known clinical disorders (e.g., depressive and anxiety disorders, schizophrenia disorders), Axis II described personality and intellectual disorders, while Axis III disorders described medical or neurological conditions that may influence a psychiatric problem (e.g., a medical diagnosis of cancer may induce a depressive disorder).

The DSM-5, the most updated version, excludes these axial designations, and thus Axis III has been combined with Axes I and II. Although there is not enough space to discuss all of the categories of mental disorders, those described here will be those that are of most importance in correctional settings because they are the most common, or because they are the most disruptive to the management and security of a correctional setting. Keep in mind that many people will have more than one diagnosis, and that, in spite of diagnostic criteria, there can still be disagreement about what diagnosis best fits a person.

Mood Disorders

Mood disorders are the common cold of mental health, but can range in intensity from mild to severe. While it is common for people to experience feelings of depression at times and elation at other times, in a mood disorder these feelings are more intense and disrupt daily functioning for a longer period. These disorders include the depressive disorders, such as major depression and dysthymia, manic disorders, and the bipolar disorders.

A person with major depressive disorder experiences a depressed mood nearly every day; episodes of crying; lack of interest or pleasure in almost all activities nearly every day; a lack of appetite or significant weight loss (or gain) without an attempt to diet; an inability to sleep or a constant desire for sleep; agitation or feelings of fatigue and lethargy; feelings of worthlessness or guilt; problems with thinking, concentration, attention, and memory; and recurrent thoughts of death or suicidal ideation. Some individuals who experience a severe episode of major depression may also experience some symptoms of psychosis.

A **dysthymic disorder** is also a depressive disorder but tends to be more chronic in duration. A person with dysthymia will appear to be chronically depressed and irritable, but not at the level of severity required for a diagnosis of depression. People who are dysthymic may complain of trouble sleeping, loss of appetite, problems with concentration and decision-making, and low self-esteem.

While a depressive disorder is characterized by an experience of intense depression, a **manic disorder** is characterized by an experience of intense elation or sometimes an irritable mood. During a manic episode the individual experiences a period of elevated or irritable mood that lasts at least one week. The individual may experience feelings of grandiosity, a decreased need for sleep, pressured speech, a feeling that his or her thoughts are racing, difficulties with attention, physical or mental agitation, and an overinvolvement in activities that are experienced as pleasurable without regard to any risk involved. A **bipolar disorder** is one characterized by the occurrence of manic episodes and depressive episodes in alternation. It is easy to see, from this description, how an individual with a manic disorder or in a manic phase could become involved with the criminal justice system or have difficulties coping with incarceration.

Depression is a common mental health problem in correctional settings. Feelings of depression are frequently associated with losses, and incarceration generally involves a series of losses for those who are incarcerated. While some will experience brief episodes of depression that will dissipate without intervention, anyone who appears to have depressed or elevated moods that are more prolonged than is typical should be referred for mental health assessment. Marianna, who was discussed earlier, is an example of someone who should be referred for evaluation.

In Marianna's case, the correctional counselor noticed that she had not been eating and appeared to be sad. This prompted further observation, which included checking on her sleeping habits and talking with her. The correctional staff on night shift reported that Marianna was awake most of the night crying. When the correctional counselor asked her how she was doing, she became very tearful and stated that she felt hopeless about her current situation. Although Marianna denied feeling suicidal, she stated that she wished she were dead. A referral was made to the mental health staff for further evaluation. The referral included what Marianna had said and what the counselor had observed, as well as what the correctional staff had observed.

Psychotic Disorders

Unlike mood disorders, some of which may occur in response to environmental variables, **psychotic disorders** are almost always preexisting, although they may be exacerbated by the conditions of incarceration. Additionally, people on medication to control the symptoms of a psychotic disorder may not reveal this at the time of their arrest, and thus may come to a correctional setting without having had their medication for some time. An additional difference between psychotic and mood disorders is that mood disorders can be seen as extending along a continuum from a normal mood change to a pathological mood change, but psychoses are qualitatively, not quantitatively, different from normal behavior and feelings. Thus, while you may be able to describe a person as mildly depressed or severely depressed, you would not describe a person as "just a little psychotic."

Psychotic disorders are those in which the person has an impaired sense of reality. Schizophrenia, for example, is a psychotic disorder and one with which most people are familiar. Because many of the other psychotic disorders have symptoms in common with schizophrenia, schizophrenia will be used as the example for psychotic disorders. When they hear the term "schizophrenia," most people think of hallucinations (seeing, hearing, smelling, or feeling things that are not there) or delusions (having erroneous beliefs that involve a misinterpretation of an event or experience). These are called "positive" symptoms of schizophrenia and include other symptoms, such as disorganization in speech and behavior. The "negative" symptoms of schizophrenia include having flat affect, impairments in the ability to produce speech and thoughts, and what is called avolition, or problems in initiating activities. A person who is schizophrenic may have loose associations and thus may relate words or concepts that to others do not seem to be connected. They may engage in ritual-like behaviors, and their emotional responses may be incongruous to the situation. Although people with schizophrenia may be able to get along with others, it is difficult for them to establish relationships with others. Counselors and other incarcerated people may not feel rapport or empathy with them. But in spite of the unusual nature of some of their behavior and symptoms, their behavior can vary greatly. While at times they may be incapable of carrying on a rational conversation, later they may be quite capable of writing a reasonable and well-written request for medical service (Kaplan & Sadock, 2000).

Horace is a good example of a person with schizophrenia who is in a correctional setting. Others see him as strange, and while he is not openly disliked, there is no one who is close to Horace. He is easily upset by small changes in routine because he has many small rituals each day that may go unnoticed by other people, but have great significance to Horace. Many of his requests and demands are incomprehensible to the staff because they involve his delusional beliefs about aliens and his own special powers. He is socially withdrawn and is frequently seen talking to himself or looking off into space, both of which may be the result of hallucinations. Most of Horace's problems occur when his schedule is disrupted or he interprets an action or incident in a delusional fashion, causing him to behave erratically in the eyes of others. Yet Horace is able to follow a schedule reasonably well, and at times has relatively normal conversations with his case manager. His case manager is aware of the problems he creates and took the opportunity to refer Horace during a relatively calm time when he was amenable to the referral.

It is important to be aware that a person who is psychotic acts on information that is not shared by others. As a result, he or she is seen as unpredictable. It is not useful to challenge their beliefs or their perceptual distortions. People who are delusional or psychotic are frequently frightened and suspicious of others. Perhaps the best approach is to neither confirm nor deny, but to listen and recognize what impact those beliefs or distortions may have on the client's behavior. If you make the mistake of pretending to believe the delusions or hallucinations, you then may be challenged as to why you are not acting on them. If you try to argue about such matters, you will only lose the cooperation of the client. As with Horace, it is easier to make the referral when the client is less overtly disturbed and more likely to cooperate. As the correctional counselor or case manager, you can provide the mental health staff with the description of the behaviors that have led to your concern. Because such behaviors are intermittent in nature, your ability to describe and report the actual behaviors is essential.

Intellectual Disability

Although intellectual development disorder (previously referred to as mental retardation in DSM-IV-TR) was traditionally thought of as having an intelligence quotient (IQ) score below a certain level, diagnostic criteria today involve not only the IQ score but also include deficits in adaptive functioning and require that the disability was apparent in the developmental years (American Psychiatric Association, 2013). For a person to be considered intellectually disabled, his or her IQ score must be about 70 or below and be accompanied by deficits in adaptive behavior. A person with an IQ of 73 could be considered disabled if adaptive functioning is also poor, but a person with an IQ of 70 might not be described as disabled if his or her adaptive functioning is good. Because adaptive functioning refers to how effectively individuals cope with common life demands and how well they meet the standards of personal independence expected of someone in their age group, sociocultural background, and community setting (American Psychiatric Association, 2013), a person with intellectual deficits will have difficulty coping with the demands of a correctional setting, be it jail, prison, or probation. This is complicated by the fact that most mentally challenged defendants or incarcerated people do not wish to be labeled as "stupid" and may develop ways of trying to hide their intellectual and adaptive deficits. A mentally disabled person may learn to survive in prison by being aggressive because he or she cannot cope in other ways, having failed to master social and cognitive skills (Conley, Luckasson, & Bouthilet, 1992).

The largest group of incarcerated people with intellectual disabilities is likely to be in the mild severity range. At the high end of this range, people can generally learn basic literacy and vocational skills, while at the low end they may have more difficulty with learning basic academic and job skills. Even at the high end of this range, people with intellectual disabilities will need support and guidance, particularly when their environment is stressful. Although some studies indicate that only about 2% of incarcerated people are intellectually disabled, others indicate that the prevalence in the prison population is approximately 10% (Smith, Algozzine, Schmid, & Hennly, 1990). Even if the number of mentally challenged people in a given institution is small, this population requires more staff attention than others and is more likely to be victimized (Denkowski & Denkowski, 1985; Linhorst, McCutchen, & Bennett, 2003).

Given the problems that intellectual disability can cause for both the client and the staff, it is essential for correctional staff to identify people who may be intellectually disabled or marginally competent and are not receiving appropriate services. Identification is difficult because there is no specific personality or physical feature that always occurs with individuals with intellectual deficits. Some people are placid, and others are aggressive and impulsive because they have poor communication skills and are unable to make their needs known (American Psychiatric Association, 2013).

Although there are no personality characteristics that always identify a person with intellectual developmental disorder, there are behavioral clues. Such people may indicate that they understand a question or a command, but will be unable to repeat it back in their own words; they may have poor reading skills and use only simple words when communicating (Bowker, 1994). They may have trouble following complex directions or understanding abstract concepts, and they are more likely to be impressionable and thus be more easily victimized and manipulated. They may demonstrate delayed adjustment to the routine of the institution and to any changes in the institutional routine.

James, whose case was described earlier, is an example of someone whose intellectual functioning should be evaluated. He has trouble following directions and does not verbalize well or frequently. He is the object of practical jokes, to which he responds with anger. As with many incarcerated people who are mildly disabled, James is unlikely to reveal to his case counselor that he has a history of special education or that he has trouble reading. His poor writing skills make it difficult for him to make written requests, thus increasing his sense of frustration. Referring James for assessment would determine whether he is functioning at a low level and might assist in referring him to appropriate educational services that would enhance his ability to cope.

Personality Disorders

Personality can be thought of as an individual's ongoing style of relating to the world. This involves how an individual perceives events, relates to self and others, and copes with stress. The DSM-5 defines a **personality disorder** as "an enduring pattern of inner experience and behavior that deviates markedly from the expectations of the individual's culture. This enduring pattern is inflexible and pervasive across a broad range of personal and social situations" (American Psychiatric Association, 2013, pp. 645–646). Personality disorders begin in adolescence or early adulthood and lead to an impairment in functioning.

There are 10 specific personality disorders, each with its own set of diagnostic criteria. These disorders are grouped into clusters based on common descriptive similarities. Cluster A, the "odd-eccentric" cluster, contains the personality disorders of **paranoid personality disorder, schizoid personality disorder,** and **schizotypal personality disorder.** These disorders are characterized by a pervasive mistrust of others, a preference for isolation over social relationships, an inability to experience or display a wide range of emotions, a pervasive tendency to distort perceptions and information, odd and/or magical thinking, an unusual appearance, and behaviors that are eccentric or bizarre.

Cluster B, which covers the "dramatic-emotional" dimension, contains the diagnoses of **antisocial personality disorder, borderline personality disorder, histrionic personality disorder,** and **narcissistic personality disorder.** In general, these disorders are marked by a disregard for the normal expectations of society or social relationships; a lack of empathy for others, or an inability to take on the perspective of another; impulsivity; irritability, or mood swings; irresponsible behaviors; deceitfulness; interpersonal relationships that are very intense, unstable, and frequently violent; substance use; difficulties with controlling emotions or modulating emotional displays; a tendency to engage in self-destructive behaviors; a desire to be the center of attention at all times; and a sense of low self-worth that gets communicated as either grandiosity or as self-degradation.

The last cluster, C, which covers the "anxious-fearful" dimension, includes the personality disorders of **avoidant personality disorder, dependent personality disorder,** and **obsessive-compulsive personality disorder.** These disorders have common features that include social inhibition, feelings of inadequacy, fear of rejection or ridicule, an excessive need to be taken care of, difficulty with making autonomous decisions or independent actions, fear of abandonment or being alone, a preoccupation with details or organization, a tendency to be inflexible in values, and a desire for perfectionism that interferes with an ability to perform.

Incarcerated people with personality disorders present many problems in institutional settings. People with personality disorders may be incarcerated due to their difficulties with societal expectations and with making good decisions, and the same behaviors that led to their incarceration are likely to be repeated in the institutional setting. In general, their ability to cope with stressful events is very poor and their judgment tends to worsen as their stress levels increase. People with personality disorders may be manipulative and impulsive, and may actually harm themselves or make a suicidal gesture when angry or unable to cope with stress. Frequently, these people come to the attention of correctional staff when they break the rules or harm themselves out of anger or an attempt to manipulate for some privilege. When these types of behaviors are present with a persistent pattern, or any time someone is in danger of harming himself/herself or others, a referral to a mental health professional is warranted. It is useful to keep in mind that people with personality disorders are perceived as very difficult and frustrating to manage and supervise. While it is common to find this group of people frustrating, this frustration should not stand in the way of referral to a mental health professional for assessment.

Substance Use Disorders

Substance use is a broad category that can include use of alcohol, prescription drugs, or street drugs. According to the DSM-5, the hallmark feature of a **substance use disorder** (SUD) is "a cluster of cognitive, behavioral and physiological symptoms indicating that the individual continues using the substance despite significant substance-related problems" (American Psychiatric Association, 2013, p. 483). Diagnosis of a SUD is based on a pattern of pathological behavior related to use of the substance. Pathological behavioral criteria are categorized into four groupings including: (1) impaired control; (2) social impairment; (3) risky use; and (4) pharmacological criteria.

Moreover, substance use can vary in intensity and severity. The DSM-5 categorizes severity based on the number of symptom criteria a person has and can range between mild, moderate, or severe. Although the DSM-5 divides substance-related disorders by the type of substance being used, many people use more than one substance and may also have another disorder in addition to their substance use. One substance may be used to counteract the effect of others. Regardless of whether the person is diagnosed with a substance use disorder, the long-term use of some substances can cause serious medical problems and organic brain damage, leading to more problems with day-to-day functioning. Thus, a person with a history of using substances, but who has ceased using drugs, may still be affected by previous use.

Seventy-four percent of people in state prisons who had mental health problems used drugs or were dependent on alcohol (Bureau of Justice Statistics, 2006). The Bureau of Justice Statistics (2006) indicates that drug users have a greater involvement in crime than non-drug users, and that they are unlikely to have received treatment. Heavy alcohol use is also common among arrestees. Thus, a correctional counselor or case manager will face a large number of clients with histories of drug use and with a low likelihood of having received treatment for that drug use. Because of the profound impact of substance use on behavior, it is important for correctional counselors and other staff to be aware of the various signs of use of different drugs and the types of behaviors that are associated with each. Although treatment of substance use disorders is difficult, structured programs are of help to some individuals, and referrals for evaluation should be made for those who appear to be current users or those who have histories of drug addiction and appear to be adversely affected by the long-term effects of their disorder.

TRAUMA

In the last 15 years, criminal and juvenile justice reform advocates, as well as academic researchers, have begun to make progress in forcing correctional leaders to understand the critical role that prior and current trauma play in affecting clients' behavior in institutional settings as well as in the community. Indeed, among a national sample of incarcerated men, one out of six reported physical and sexual abuse in childhood. Over half (56%) indicated physical trauma during childhood (Wolff & Shi, 2012).

Mental and behavioral problems in adulthood are significantly increased by trauma exposure during childhood and adolescence. A recent meta-analysis that included 56 samples with a total of 21,099 prisoners worldwide found that male prisoners have a 5-fold higher point prevalence rate of post-traumatic stress disorder (PTSD) compared to the general population (Baranyi, Cassidy, Fazel, Priebe, & Mundt, 2018). This resulted in an estimate of more than 300,000 prisoners in the United States with PTSD.

Research with justice-involved girls and women also indicates far higher prevalence of traumatic experiences compared to the general population. As outlined in Belisle (2021, p. 38),

> Compared to boys, girls experience trauma/abuse/victimization at higher rates, experience it at an earlier age and over more extended periods of time (Belknap, 2007; Belknap & Holsinger, 2006; Dierkhising et al., 2013; Saar et al., 2015). Girls in the juvenile justice system are four times more likely to experience sexual assault or rape, twice as likely to experience sexual abuse or forced displacement (Dierkhising et al., 2013), and more likely to witness abuse (including emotional, physical, or sexual abuse) than system-impacted boys (Belknap & Holsinger, 2006).

Prior studies also demonstrate high rates of trauma exposure among women and girls in jails, prisons, and juvenile facilities as well as those on probation (Belknap & Holsinger, 2006; Browne, Miller, & Maguin, 1999; DeHart, Lynch, Belknap, Dass-Brailsford, & Green, 2013). Jails are typically operated by local governments (e.g., counties) and hold persons awaiting trial or serving shorter sentences, whereas prisons are operated by state or federal governments and hold those convicted of crimes. Focusing on women in jails, Green, Miranda, Daroowalla, and Siddique (2005) interviewed 100 women inmates and found that an overwhelming majority (98%) reported trauma exposure, most commonly partner violence (71%) or childhood trauma (62%).

Mental health symptoms related to traumatic stress or PTSD create significant cognitive behavioral disadvantages and impairments among prisoners, adding to the already major challenge in returning to society (Sadeh & McNiel, 2015). There is significant concern for difficulties with emotional regulation, dissociation, and interpersonal instability among chronically or repeatedly traumatized individuals (Van der Kolk, Roth, Pelcovitz, Sunday, & Spinazzola, 2005). Further, the combination of PTSD and SUDs has been associated with recidivism (Ardino, 2012), and there is a high correlation between PTSD and SUDs, as well as between childhood trauma and SUDs (Khoury, Tang, Bradley, Cubells, & Ressler, 2010). This suggests an increased risk for rearrest for traumatized former prisoners.

Because trauma is so prevalent among justice-involved individuals, it is imperative that correctional staff understand how the brain operates under chronic stress and cumulative trauma to drive dysfunctional and antisocial behavior among clients—dysfunctional behavior that perhaps was one's attempt at coping with prior harmful events and experiences, such as substance use or self-harming behavior to numb out emotional pain. Although only clinical staff with appropriate certification should assess how trauma may be affecting clients' daily functioning, we are beginning to see a larger effort among policymakers and correctional systems to build awareness of trauma-responsive correctional environments. For instance, in 2021 the U.S. Bureau of Justice Assistance hosted a series of webinars for correctional staff focused on creating trauma-responsive correctional settings. Details on these webinars can be found in the Online Learning Enhancements at the conclusion of this chapter.

SUICIDE

Suicide is not a diagnostic category, but it is an important issue for correctional counselors because of the increased incidence of suicide in correctional settings. Suicide can be associated with almost any category of mental disturbance, including substance use. Some categories of mental disorder may increase the probability of suicide, but one cannot rule out the possibility of suicide based on the presence or absence of a particular disorder.

Suicide is of particular concern in jails. Synopses of studies of jail suicides indicate that it is the leading cause of death in jails and that the suicide rate in jails is considerably higher than in the general population (Carr, Hinkle, & Ingram, 1991; Noonan & Ginder, 2014; Winkler, 1992). The rate of suicide in prisons also seems to be higher than that in the general population, but not as disproportionately high as it is in jails, and it may vary depending on whether the prison is state or federal (Kennedy, 1984). Kennedy (1984) suggests that suicide may be a reaction to the depression and anxiety that accompany incarceration and suggests that the anxiety surrounding impending release may also be a risk factor, particularly with people in prison (see Figure 5.1). However, it is important to note that suicide rates have been decreasing, perhaps as a result of improved assessment and identification of behavioral indicators and referral to mental health services. For example, Noonan and Ginder (2014) reported that suicide rates in local jails declined 17% between 2000 and 2012.

While there is no single indicator that will always alert the mental health professional to suicide, most people who commit suicide have spoken about it to someone. Statements regarding feeling hopeless and helpless should be a cause for concern and referral for evaluation. In addition, some clients will give away possessions before a suicide and will attempt to put their affairs in order. The initial period of incarceration appears to be the time of the highest risk, particularly for those who are newly involved in the justice system and for intoxicated people. In prisons, loss of a relationship, such as a divorce or a break-up, is also associated with suicide (Arboleda-Florez & Holley, 1989; Way, Miraglia, & Sawyer, 2005).

All suicidal statements and attempts should be taken seriously. Although some argue that suicide attempts and statements are manipulative actions, they can have serious consequences

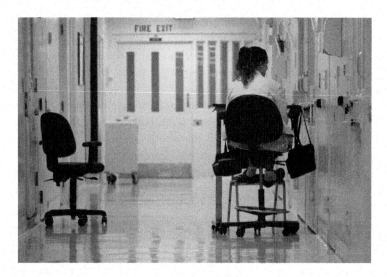

FIGURE 5.1 A medical worker keeps a vigil outside an isolation cell containing a person who authorities fear might attempt suicide, at California State Prison, Sacramento, in Folsom, California. Source: AP Photo/Rich Pedroncelli, File.

because people can die accidentally or deliberately kill themselves. Perhaps it is useful to remember that someone who is willing to risk injury and death to get attention is in need of intervention. Although depressed people are at risk for suicide, so are many people who do not show signs of depression. Given the potential seriousness of a suicide attempt or a completed suicide, it is essential to refer for assessment those who have expressed suicidal ideation either through verbalizations or behavior.

TECHNIQUES OF ASSESSMENT AND DIAGNOSIS

Once the client is referred to a mental health professional, a variety of techniques may be used to evaluate the problem. The nature of the problem, the characteristics of the client (e.g., reading and attention span), and the training of the mental health professional dictate what type of assessment will be done. A psychiatrist is likely to conduct an interview and take a history. A clinical psychologist is also likely to conduct an interview and take a history. Psychologists are also likely to use a variety of assessment instruments, depending on the nature of the presenting problem. Two of the major categories of testing instruments used are those that evaluate intelligence and those that evaluate personality characteristics. The interpretation of most assessment instruments depends on information collected during the interview, so interviews will be discussed first.

Interviews

The interview is the basic method for collecting background information about a person. How the interview is conducted depends on the orientation of the interviewer (e.g., behavioral, psychoanalytic) and the purpose of the interview. Interviews, although they vary greatly, generally elicit biographical information, information about current life experiences, symptom information, and social history, thus helping the examiner place the test results in the context of the client's life. Although very useful, interviews are generally not standardized and thus different interviewers might elicit different information from the same interviewee.

To help alleviate this problem, several structured interviews have been developed and are used to aid in diagnosis. These interviews are often structured around the diagnostic system and lead to a diagnosis. For example, the series of Structured Clinical Interviews for DSM-5 (SCID-5) give detailed instructions to the interviewer about what questions to ask for diagnosis and indicate what additional questions to ask, depending on the answers to the previous questions. The SCID-5-RV (Research Version) (First, Williams, Karg, & Spitzer, 2015a) is the most comprehensive version in the series of SCID-5 interviews containing more disorders than other versions, as well as subtypes and severity criteria. The SCID-5-CV (Clinical Version) (First, Williams, Karg, & Spitzer, 2015b) assesses only the most common disorders observed in clinical settings. The SCID-5-PD (Personality Disorders) (First, Williams, Benjamin, & Spitzer, 2015) should be used to assess each of the personality disorders.

Intelligence Testing

Intelligence is a concept that has long been debated, and opinions range from those holding that it is a measure of genetic potential to those holding that it is simply a measure of acculturation. David Wechsler, who developed one of the most widely used intelligence tests, believed that intelligence is global in nature and relevant to personality (Groth-Marnat, 2003). Evaluations to determine an IQ score take many different forms and range from group-administered tests that may not require any writing or reading, to individually administered tests. It is important to remember that the tests alone do not classify a person as intellectually disabled because there must also be a deficit in adaptive functioning. Although there are measures of adaptive functioning available, they are generally of little use in correctional settings because the behaviors assessed are not relevant to life in an institution.

The "group" tests such as the *Revised Beta Examination*, Second Edition (Kellogg & Morton, 1978) and the Shipley-2 (Shipley, Gruber, Martin, & Klein, 2009) are useful for screening, but do not tell us many specifics about a client. An individual test gives the examiner more opportunity to observe the client and it may help the examiner to understand why they have performed in a certain way. Does the client work slowly or experience difficulty in comprehending the instructions? Was the client ill on the day the test was taken and not functioning well? Or were they just unwilling to cooperate? However, in spite of these issues, group tests serve an important function and provide a good estimate of intelligence scores for most clients.

Individual tests of intelligence are more costly to administer, but provide more information about an individual. The **Wechsler Adult Intelligence Scales IV (WAIS-IV)** (Wechsler, 2008) is the standard assessment instrument for adults. It is a multidimensional test and assesses many different abilities. It takes an hour or more to administer, but provides the examiner with a detailed picture of a person's intellectual strengths and weaknesses. A person's score on the WAIS-IV compares the individual to the average person and gives us a picture of how that individual compares to others in the same age group. Information about a client's skills and weaknesses can help correctional staff in finding the appropriate vocational, counseling, and job placements for them.

Intelligence tests do not measure the person's academic achievement and, in many institutions, academic testing is given by the education service when people enter the prison. The intelligence score is a useful piece of information to use in conjunction with the academic testing because it helps correctional staff make a prediction of what the person's academic achievement could be with the appropriate educational assistance.

Personality Tests

Personality tests are usually divided into two major categories—projective and objective tests. **Projective tests**, such as the Rorschach (Exner, 2002), are not as commonly used as objective personality tests, like the **Minnesota Multiphasic Personality Inventory-3** (MMPI-3; Ben-Porath & Tellegen, 2020), because they are time-consuming to administer, score, and interpret. Projective tests must be administered individually and scored individually, making them less attractive in settings where large numbers of people need to be evaluated or screened. Because there are valid and reliable group-administered instruments for personality, projective tests are not common in institutional settings where large numbers of people may need to be evaluated. There are many other projective tests, such as the **Thematic Apperception Test (TAT)**, projective drawings (Groth-Marnat, 2003), and a variety of incomplete sentence blanks. All of them are considered projective because they present the subject with an ambiguous stimulus upon which he or she must "project" an idea or an image.

The MMPI-3 is the most commonly used objective personality test instrument and is widely administered among mental health, medical, forensic, and public safety settings. The MMPI-3 has several hundred questions that requires that a client be able to read at the fifth-grade level or comprehend the material when presented on audiotape. The MMPI-3 and its predecessors, the MMPI and MMPI-2, have been widely used in correctional settings. An early typology was developed for use with incarcerated people based on the original MMPI (Megargee & Bohn, 1979). It was updated for the MMPI-2 (Megargee, Carbonell, Bohn, & Sliger, 2001) and has been helpful in understanding correctional populations. It provides an efficient means of classifying clients into groups that provide information about their institutional and personal adjustment.

Finally, the **Millon Clinical Multiaxial Inventory-IV** (MCMI-IV; Millon, Grossman, & Millon, 2015) is designed to be used exclusively with populations that exhibit psychological symptoms or are actively involved in therapy. Thus, it is not useful as a screening instrument.

LEGAL ISSUES AND MENTAL HEALTH ASSESSMENT

The purpose of a mental health assessment is to provide a picture of a person's mental state and his or her current level of functioning. While these assessments are useful, they do not always relate directly to what could be called psycho-legal issues—issues where psychology and the law overlap. Decisions about legal issues such as competency to stand trial, insanity, and diminished responsibility almost always involve the input of mental health professionals, but simply diagnosing a client does not necessarily provide an adequate answer for questions concerning these issues. In fact, a diagnosis may provide little useful information. There is an "imperfect fit" between legal issues and diagnostic issues. As noted in the DSM-5:

> In most situations, the clinical diagnosis of a DSM-5 mental disorder such as intellectual disability (intellectual development disorder), schizophrenia, major neurocognitive disorder, gambling disorder, or pedophilic disorder does not imply that an individual with such a condition meets legal criteria for the presence of a mental disorder or a specified legal standard (e.g., for competence, criminal responsibility, or disability). For the latter, additional information is usually required beyond that contained in the DSM-5 diagnosis, which might include information about the individual's functional impairments and how these impairments affect the particular abilities in question. It is precisely because impairments, abilities, and disabilities vary widely within each diagnostic category that assignment of a particular diagnosis does not imply a specific level of impairment or disability.
>
> (American Psychiatric Association, 2013, p. 25)

In spite of this imperfect fit, mental health and the law are inextricably intertwined. The insanity defense, although frequently the subject of television movies, is rare. It is used in less than 1% of cases and successful only 15–25% of the time (Walker, 2001; Zapf, Golding, & Roesch, 2006). To be found **not guilty by reason of insanity (NGRI)** one must meet specific criteria, and those criteria vary from state to state. However, the general notion behind NGRI is that the defendant lacks the appropriate mental state to be convicted because he or she has not chosen to do wrong; they have done so as a result of mental illness. Guidelines for NGRI generally specify that the person must be unable to appreciate the wrongfulness of the act or could not conform his or her conduct to the requirements of the law. Thus, a diagnosis alone does not answer this question. The mental health professional can, however, offer information about a person's functioning and how that person might react in various situations that, combined with the diagnostic information, can assist the court in reaching an appropriate decision.

Because the notion of NGRI is disturbing to many people, other psycho-legal remedies have been offered. In spite of the rarity and lack of success of the NGRI defense, highly publicized cases may make the general public believe that many "guilty" people (people who have committed acts but without the appropriate mental state) go free. A solution to this concern is the **guilty but mentally ill** verdict, in which a person can be found guilty in spite of his or her mental state, but also receive treatment in a prison or forensic hospital. It is a compromise position that allows the defendant to be found guilty, while, in theory, it maximizes the probability that this person will receive treatment. This issue may be of more concern to correctional staff because people with a guilty but mentally ill verdict will, in many cases, be sent to a prison setting, where their mental illness may be a barrier to adjustment.

The other major issue in the psycho-legal arena is **competency to stand trial**. The issue in competency is basically whether the defendant can understand the charges and the proceedings well enough to assist in his or her own defense. A person who cannot assist in his or her own defense cannot be tried because of the possibility of not receiving a fair trial. Because a person cannot be tried in his or her absence, a person who is "mentally absent" from the proceedings cannot be tried either. There are many diagnoses that are relevant to this issue, including intellectual development and psychotic disorders, but, once again, they only provide information about the diagnosis and functioning level. The final decision on these psycho-legal issues is always in the hands of the judge or the jury.

While NGRI refers to the mental state of the defendant at the time of the crime, competency refers to mental state at the time of the trial. In addition, NGRI has the finality of an acquittal, whereas competency can be reassessed. It is possible, in other words, for a defendant to be assessed as incompetent at one point and competent at another point, as with the case of a person with schizophrenia who becomes stabilized after receiving appropriate medications.

Overall, it is important to remember that insanity and competency are legal terms, and not mental health concepts. Persons who are diagnosed with a mental disorder more often than not are considered sane and competent.

CONCLUSION

In summary, correctional personnel play an essential role in the timely and appropriate referral of clients to mental health resources. The correctional counselor, the probation officer, and other correctional staff provide information about the client's day-to-day functioning and behavior, thus providing an important and necessary context in light of which the mental health professional can interpret the results of their assessment. By becoming familiar with the various diagnoses and their manifestations, correctional staff will be able to assist clients in obtaining the appropriate services and provide valuable input to the mental health professional.

In addition to making referrals, the correctional counselor and others can use their understanding of the assessment process and the results to assist the client in developing a better level of adjustment while incarcerated or on probation. Correctional counselors and staff are in a unique position to assist in the evaluation process and to use the results of that assessment. In summary, mental health evaluations are used to make decisions about placement, need for treatment, need for medication, and legal status, but they would be incomplete without the input of the correctional counselors and other staff who provide the context for the evaluation.

Discussion Questions

1. Why is it important for correctional staff to have some knowledge of mental illness?
2. What is the difference between a static assessment and a dynamic assessment?
3. What types of problem behaviors warrant the referral of a correctional client to a psychologist/psychiatrist or mental health unit?
4. What types of mistakes should we seek to avoid in observing and reporting a correctional client's behavior to mental health officials?
5. What procedures are typically followed in diagnosing mental illness?
6. What behavioral symptoms indicate that an individual may be contemplating suicide?
7. Why is a diagnosis of mental illness not enough to secure a verdict of NGRI?
8. How is incompetence different from NGRI?

ONLINE LEARNING ENHANCEMENTS

Mental Health in the Correctional System: Making Choices for Safety and Well-Being
This flexible, online workshop series includes 20 modules covering 25 hours of free training. Its focus is specifically for correctional staff to learn the basics of managing the correctional environment with individuals who have serious mental illness and trauma-related backgrounds. Topics include deinstitutionalization and its relationship to criminal justice, creating environments based on safety and respect, clients' legal rights, common medications and malingering, self-injury and crisis prevention, trauma-informed correctional practices, and managing workplace stress. The series was developed by an academic expert on correctional mental health, Dana DeHart, Ph.D. at the University of South Carolina College of Social Work. http://cmhtraining.sc.edu

Understanding Intellectual and Developmental Disabilities in People Involved with the Criminal Justice System
Hosted by the Council of State Governments Justice Center, this webinar discusses differences and similarities between various kinds of behavioral diagnoses and intellectual/developmental disabilities (I/DD), how to identify someone with I/DD, and tips to work more effectively with people with I/DD in correctional settings. https://csgjusticecenter.org/events/understanding-intellectual-and-developmental-disabilities-in-people-involved-with-the-criminal-justice-system/

U.S. Bureau of Justice Assistance Webinar Series on Becoming Trauma Informed with Dr. Stephanie Covington
Hosted by the U.S. Bureau of Justice Assistance, this three-part webinar series delivered by a trauma and psychology expert covers the Adverse Childhood Experiences research, how to move from being trauma-informed to trauma-responsive, and practical skills for working with clients with significant prior victimization.

Part 1: Becoming Trauma Informed: Understanding the ACE Study
https://cossapresources.org/Media/Webinar/07a75be7–9501–438e-80d7–2edcbc3d3ce0

Part 2: Becoming Trauma-Informed and Moving to Trauma Responsive
https://cossapresources.org/Media/Webinar/afbecb49–4e13–4d8f-8513–3c610d7f6e3e

Part 3: Trauma Specific Services—Programs that Work
https://cossapresources.org/Media/Webinar/afbecb49–4e13–4d8f-8513–3c610d7f6e3e

Organizations to Follow and Become More Involved With

- International Association for Correctional and Forensic Psychology
- The Arc's National Center on Criminal Justice and Disability

GLOSSARY OF KEY TERMS

antisocial personality disorder   a cluster B ("dramatic-emotional") personality disorder characterized by a long-term pattern of disregard for, or violation of, the rights of others; a low moral conscience is often apparent, as well as a history of crime, legal problems, or impulsive and aggressive behavior

avoidant personality disorder a cluster C ("anxious-fearful") personality disorder characterized by anxiety in personal relationships and social situations; feelings of inadequacy and severe sensitivity to rejection or criticism are often apparent

bipolar disorder a mood disorder characterized by the occurrence of manic episodes and depressive episodes in alternation

borderline personality disorder a cluster B ("dramatic-emotional") personality disorder characterized by a long-term pattern of unstable relationships, a distorted sense of self, and strong emotional reactions

competency to stand trial a legal principle that ensures the protection of a criminal defendant's right to a fair trial; a defendant is deemed competent to stand trial when they can understand the charges and the proceedings well enough to assist in their own defense

dependent personality disorder a cluster C ("anxious-fearful") personality disorder characterized by a pervasive psychological dependence on other people to meet emotional and physical needs

DSM-5 (*Diagnostic and Statistical Manual of Mental Disorders*, Fifth Edition) – a manual for assessment and diagnosis of mental disorders; frequently utilized by correctional counselors in understanding basic information about the major mental health categories

dynamic assessments mental health assessments that have the capability of changing over time

dysthymic disorder a depressive disorder that tends to be more chronic in duration; those with this disorder will appear to be chronically depressed and irritable, and may complain of trouble sleeping, loss of appetite, problems with concentration and decision-making, and low self-esteem

guilty but mentally ill a compromise verdict in which a person can be found guilty in spite of their mental state, but also receive treatment in a prison or forensic hospital

histrionic personality disorder a cluster B ("dramatic-emotional") personality disorder characterized by constant attention-seeking, seductive behavior, and exaggerated behaviors and emotions

intellectual disability a disability characterized by significantly impaired intellectual or adaptive functioning; for a person to be considered intellectually disabled, their IQ score must be about 70 or below and be accompanied by deficits in adaptive behavior

major depressive disorder a mood disorder characterized by a persistently depressed mood that is often accompanied by loss of interest in enjoyable activities, low self-esteem, changes in sleeping and eating habits, problems with concentration, and feelings of worthlessness or guilt

manic disorder a mood disorder characterized by an experience of intense elation or sometimes an irritable mood

Millon Clinical Multiaxial Inventory-IV (MCMI-IV) a brief self-report inventory designed to be used exclusively with populations that exhibit psychological symptoms or are actively involved in therapy

Minnesota Multiphasic Personality Inventory-3 (MMPI-3) a commonly used objective personality test that assesses personality traits and psychopathology; it is widely used and has enjoyed success in correctional settings

mood disorders disorders that persistently and severely impact a person's emotional state beyond common feelings of depression at times and elation at other times; these disorders include the depressive disorders, such as major depression and dysthymia, manic disorders, and the bipolar disorders

narcissistic personality disorder a cluster B ("dramatic-emotional") personality disorder characterized by a long-term pattern of exaggerated feelings of self-importance, excessive need for admiration, and lack of empathy for others

not guilty by reason of insanity (NGRI) a plea by a criminal defendant who admits the criminal act, but claims that he or she was mentally disturbed at the time of the crime and lacked the mental capacity to have intended to commit a crime

obsessive-compulsive personality disorder a cluster C ("anxious-fearful") personality disorder characterized by excessive attention to detail or organization, perfectionism, and a need for control over one's environment

paranoid personality disorder a cluster A ("odd-eccentric") personality disorder characterized by paranoid delusions and a pervasive mistrust of others

personality disorder an enduring pattern of inner experience and behavior that deviates markedly from the expectations of the individual's culture; this enduring pattern is inflexible and pervasive across a broad range of personal and social situations

projective tests a category of personality tests that present the subject with an ambiguous stimulus upon which he or she must "project" an idea or an image

psychotic disorders disorders in which a person has an impaired sense of reality

schizoid personality disorder a cluster A ("odd-eccentric") personality disorder characterized by a lack of interest in social relationships, a preference for isolation, secretiveness, emotional coldness, detachment, and apathy

schizophrenia a psychotic disorder characterized by "positive" symptoms such as hallucinations, delusions, and disorganization in speech and behavior; as well as "negative" symptoms such as having flat affect, impairments in the ability to produce speech and thoughts, and problems in initiating activities

schizotypal personality disorder a cluster A ("odd-eccentric") personality disorder characterized by severe social anxiety, paranoid ideation, unconventional beliefs, a lack of emotion or inappropriate emotional responses, and peculiar speech or modes of dress

static assessments mental health assessments that do not change much, if at all, over time

substance use disorder a cluster of cognitive, behavioral, and physiological symptoms indicating that the individual continues using the substance despite significant substance-related problems

Thematic Apperception Test (TAT) a projective personality test that uses a series of provocative yet ambiguous pictures about which the subject is asked to tell a story

Wechsler Adult Intelligence Scales IV (WAIS-IV) a multidimensional, standard assessment of intellectual ability for adults; a person's score on the WAIS-IV compares the individual to the average person and depicts how that individual compares to others in the same age group

CHAPTER 6

An Overview of Correctional Classification Systems

Patricia Van Voorhis, Emily J. Salisbury, and Ben Marrufo

KEY TERMS

Adult Internal Management System (AIMS)
correctional classification
criminogenic needs
differential treatment
dynamic risk factors
gender-responsive
general responsivity
Jesness Inventory
Level of Service/Case Management Inventory (LS/CMI)
Megargee MMPI-based Typology
myth of efficiency
needs-assessment systems
needs principle
Ohio Risk Assessment System (ORAS)

psychological classification systems
reliability
responsivity assessment
responsivity characteristics
risk assessments
risk factors
risk principle
risk/needs assessment
seamless classification systems
specific responsivity
static risk factors
treatment amenability
typology
validity
Women's Risk/Needs Assessment (WRNA)

The previous chapter discussed the need to identify or diagnose correctional clients with mental illness to appropriately provide for their supervision and needs. In cases in which mental illness or intellectual disability is suspected, clients are referred to psychologists or psychiatrists or to a mental health unit for an in-depth assessment. In this chapter we again discuss assessments, but here we focus on assessment and classification procedures that are administered to *all* clients within a given correctional unit.

To understand the need for such assessments, we must first appreciate that correctional clients are a highly heterogeneous group, with diverse treatment needs and security considerations. The task of classifying people according to risk, treatment needs, and other special considerations (e.g., mental and physical health) begins as soon as the client starts his or her sentence.

DOI: 10.4324/9780367808266-8

In recent years, **correctional classification** has been greatly aided by systematic assessment and testing procedures. Prior to the advent of agency-wide classification, correctional classification was primarily a clinical process in which counselors and case managers based decisions on their professional judgment of a client's dangerousness, treatment needs, treatment amenability, or likelihood of escaping or absconding. While their assessments sometimes may have been correct, critics faulted this process as time-consuming, inequitable, subjective, and discretionary (Bonta, 1996; MacKenzie, 1989). We also have learned that professional opinion alone is not as accurate as professional opinion supported by properly constructed and validated tests (Grove & Meehl, 1996). The importance of assessment and prediction techniques becomes evident when we understand that even under the best clinical settings, predictions of the risk of future offenses are wrong at least two out of three times (Steadman et al., 2000).

Structured tests and procedures for classifying justice-involved adults and juveniles offer an alternative to the more subjective use of professional judgment. A variety of correctional classification systems are available for security, custody, and treatment purposes. The administrative procedures and formats for each system are equally varied, ranging from behavioral checklists that staff complete after a brief period of observation to semi-structured interviews and paper-and-pencil tests. The common points among all of the classification systems are:

1. They are usually administered to all clients in a correctional institution or program, usually at the point of intake and at regular intervals thereafter.
2. They form the basis of a **typology** of clients in the program, in which each "type" on the typology categorizes clients according to similar needs or risk levels.
3. Some level of staff training is required to administer the system.
4. The classification process is governed by agency policies that set forth uniform and efficient procedures, applying the same criteria to all clients in an expeditious way.

Thus, clients are classified into subgroups, or types, and each subgroup is relatively similar, whereas the institution or program population as a whole is largely distinct. With the population now classified into similar subgroups, correctional practitioners have a much-needed tool to assist them in predicting future behaviors, identifying needs, and planning treatment.

PURPOSES AND PRINCIPLES OF EFFECTIVE CLASSIFICATION

In this chapter, we will discuss classification systems and what makes them effective. Early classification systems were highly subjective in nature, relying on the professional "gut feelings" of correctional and clinical staff and not on any empirical data (Bonta & Andrews, 2017). Bonta (1996) referred to these as first generation assessments. Second generation risk assessments were those that dealt with static risk factors (e.g., criminal history, age, substance use history, etc.). A **static risk factor** is one that cannot be changed over time with intervention. Second generation assessments were able to differentiate clients as low risk to recidivate versus high risk to recidivate, but did not focus on **dynamic risk factors** (Bonta & Andrews, 2017), which are amenable to change through intervention and incorporated into third generation assessments (e.g., antisocial attitudes, current substance use, unhealthy intimate relationships, etc.).

Andrews, Bonta, and Hoge (1990) developed principles that would assist classification of clients based on their risk to recidivate. The risk-need-responsivity principles would help develop third generation assessments, which are based on empirical data and focused on both the client's risk to recidivate as well as intervention needs. Fourth generation assessments are more comprehensive (Bonta & Andrews, 2017) with a case planning component, which will be discussed further in Chapter 7.

The systems described in this chapter were designed for a variety of organizational needs, and the purposes met by each classification system differ somewhat from system to system. Unfortunately, it is not unusual to find agencies using systems for the wrong purpose. For example, institutional systems typically do not predict new offenses in the community. "What do you want the classification system to do?" is a question that needs to be answered prior to selecting or constructing a classification system (Hardyman, Austin, & Peyton, 2004).

Careful attention to some guidelines for classification and treatment will help to sort out some of this confusion and allow us to use correctional classification systems effectively (Bonta & Andrews, 2017). In summarizing a number of classification studies, Andrews et al. (1990) put forward the following principles of classification—risk, needs, and responsivity—which we will refer to frequently throughout this chapter. In fact, these core concepts will emerge throughout the text, as they are the core principles of effectively intervening with justice-involved people.

THE RISK PRINCIPLE

At first glance, the risk principle speaks to a fundamental purpose of corrections: to protect society and to keep correctional populations safe. This, of course, is achieved by separating the dangerous from the vulnerable elements of a correctional population or assigning people to minimum-, medium-, or maximum-security institutions or community supervision levels on the basis of their predicted likelihood of recidivism, escape, or other misconduct (Clear, 1988; Levenson, 1988). Because few people cause more concern for the criminal justice system than the incarcerated person who escapes, the parolee who commits a new offense, or the arrestee who fails to show for trial, we have a clear need to identify high-risk clients. Public safety is widely perceived to be the most important purpose of correctional classification (Feeley & Simon, 1992; Van Voorhis & Presser, 2001).

In more recent years, however, the risk principle has come to have important implications for correctional rehabilitation as well. Research shows us that intensive correctional treatment programs are more successful with high- and medium-risk clients than with low-risk ones. That is, in intensive treatment programs, higher-risk clients are more likely to show greater reductions in recidivism (as a group) than less serious, low-risk clients (Andrews et al., 1990; Bonta, Wallace-Capretta, & Rooney, 2000; Lipsey, 2009; Brusman Lovins, Lowenkamp, Latessa, & Smith, 2007; Lowenkamp & Latessa, 2002).

Your response to this observation might be, "Well, of course, high-risk clients have more 'room' for improvement!" But this is only part of the picture. The risk principle also notes that low-risk clients tend to do more poorly in intensive correctional treatment than if they had not been assigned to such a group. Why is this the case? First, low-risk clients have many prosocial attributes. Premature introductions to intensive correctional programming only serve to introduce them to antisocial role models who model antisocial attitudes and behaviors. Especially in the case of institutional programs, such treatment also interferes with many of the very characteristics that make these individuals low-risk—family, education, employment, and prosocial associates.

Thus, the treatment implications of the risk principle are:

1. Identify high-, medium-, and low-risk clients.
2. Direct intensive treatment efforts (not just intensive security) to high- and medium-risk clients.
3. Wherever possible, avoid assigning low-risk clients to institutional placements or intensive treatment interventions that expose them to criminogenic influences.

THE NEEDS PRINCIPLE

In corrections, we have an ethical responsibility to attend to the basic needs of system-impacted people. And in most correctional agencies, we view addressing a broad array of needs as a routine task of case management and counseling. Effective counselors or case managers will seek to determine what services a client should receive, relative to housing, substance abuse services, job development, education, medical assistance, and mental health. Often they use objective needs assessments to identify such needs on a case-by-case basis.

Bonta and Andrews (2017) remind us, however, that this process often omits a second question: Which needs are associated with a client's likelihood of engaging in criminal behavior? Are we recognizing and treating the needs that are *most likely* to get him or her into trouble again? The needs principle maintains that needs related to future offending should receive high priority as we match clients to programs. Such needs are also risk factors and have come to be called **criminogenic needs.**

Of all the needs we could consider to be criminogenic needs, which ones are most important? For over the past 20 years, scholars and policymakers have asserted that the three most important dynamic risk factors (also called criminogenic needs) are antisocial values/beliefs/attitudes, antisocial associates/friends, and antisocial personality characteristics (e.g., weak self-control, impulsivity, negative emotionality, irritability, interpersonally antagonistic, risk-seeking, callous disregard for others, etc.; Andrews, Bonta, & Hoge, 1990; Dowden & Andrews, 2000; Gendreau et al., 1996). Such priorities were determined by early risk assessment studies that found antisocial attitudes, associates, and personality traits to have the highest correlations with recidivism.

Box 6.1 The Central Eight Risk Factors (Bonta & Andrews, 2017)

1. criminal history
2. antisocial attitudes and thinking patterns
3. antisocial personality traits (e.g., weak self-control, impulsive, irritable, interpersonally antagonistic, risk-seeking, callous disregard for others, etc.)
4. antisocial peers/friends

5. family/marital problems

6. education/employment problems

7. substance abuse

8. poor use of leisure/recreational time

Unfortunately, the early studies were focused primarily on the needs of justice-involved men (Bloom, Owen, & Covington, 2003; Hardyman & Van Voorhis, 2004; Morash, Bynum, & Koons, 1998; Reisig, Holtfreter, & Morash, 2006). More recent research with system-involved women encourages strong attention to poverty, current mental health symptoms, trauma, unhealthy intimate relationships, parental stress, and substance abuse (see Chapter 15; Van Voorhis et al., 2010; Wright, Salisbury, & Van Voorhis, 2007).

Apart from the question of which needs are most important, the needs principle guides case managers and counselors to give high priority to risk factors for future antisocial involvement. Moreover, if we focus our programming efforts on reducing these needs, we stand a good chance of reducing recidivism. Programs that treat criminogenic needs are far more effective than those that either do not treat them or choose to focus on individual problems (e.g., cooking skills) that are not related to future offending (Andrews et al., 1990; Lowenkamp & Latessa, 2002; Smith et al., 2009).

THE RESPONSIVITY PRINCIPLE

It is not enough for a case manager or counselor to identify the client's level of risk and criminogenic needs. There are other factors that can assist or impede us in providing treatment to clients. These additional factors make up the responsivity principle. The responsivity principle can be broken down into two areas, **general responsivity** and **specific responsivity.**

General responsivity refers to delivering treatment programs and interventions to the style and capabilities of the client (Bonta & Andrews, 2017). For most clients, this means adopting a modality that uses cognitive behavioral interventions and cognitive social learning strategies. Decades of research in correctional rehabilitation indicates that the default modality for the treatment of offending behavior should be those using cognitive behavioral and social learning interventions (see the chapters from Part II of this text—Chapters 8–10), unless there is evidence to suggest that a client will not do well with such interventions, which leads us to specific responsivity.

The second component of the responsivity principle is specific responsivity. Specific responsivity deals with the client's psychosocial attributes. These attributes are not necessarily risk factors, but they do have an impact on a client's **treatment amenability** or their success in treatment (Hubbard, 2007). Some of these factors include intelligence, anxiety, mental health, learning abilities, cognitive maturity (Hubbard, 2007; Van Voorhis, 2006), motivation to change, age, and cultural identification (James, 2015). But they can also include things like access to transportation, housing, food, clothing, childcare, and so on. We must address these specific factors if we want to ensure a program is successful. Failure to address the client's specific characteristics could lead them to becoming barriers to effective treatment (Gendreau, 1996b; Van Voorhis, 2006). Another tenet of specific responsivity is that treatment should be provided to the clients based on their personality and their interpersonal style (Wormith and Zidenberg, 2018).

We must also ensure that we match counselors or facilitators to clients. For example, let's say we have a counselor who works best with clients who are substance dependent. This counselor is empathetic to the substance dependent clients and is able to build rapport fairly easily with this population. This same counselor, however, does not do well with violent offenders. The counselor does not seem effective with this population. Would you want to place a client who has violent offenses in a group with this specific counselor? Of course not. You want to match the counselor's style with the client's learning style as best as possible. This is a main premise of the responsivity principle, though it is not always achievable due to staffing capacity.

Taxman (2014) adds an additional principle of responsivity: systemic responsivity. Systemic responsivity is ensuring that the agency, institution, or jurisdiction has the appropriate programming in place to address the client's risk and need profiles (Taxman, 2014). Jurisdictions need to ensure that there are appropriate services in place for all clients' needs, not just a one size fits all program. Identifying all responsivity factors of an individual will ultimately give case managers a better, more holistic, picture of the client's treatment needs.

Most responsivity characteristics are not risk factors. But they are as important to counselors and case managers as risk factors are, because if responsivity characteristics are not addressed, we never get an opportunity to address the risk factors. Consider the following example:

> After completing an intake interview and a risk assessment, Cassandra's probation officer learned that she has been abusing alcohol and other drugs for several years. In addition, she does not have a high school education. A reasonable conclusion would be to require attendance in a substance abuse program and the receipt of a GED [General Educational Development test] while Cassandra is on probation. However, Cassandra, a single parent, does not have access to adequate transportation and childcare. She cannot afford a car, and her children are far too young to leave home alone. Neither childcare nor transportation is a risk factor for future antisocial behavior. However, without addressing these two issues, Cassandra will not be able to attend substance abuse therapy or GED classes. She will not, in other words, have access to services that will help her change in ways that make her less likely to reoffend.

The importance of the responsivity principle is not new to corrections, however, it is seldom incorporated into correctional treatment or evaluations of correctional programs. It is probably the least followed principle of effective intervention among correctional and forensic agencies, and the least evaluated among researchers, particularly with regard to specific responsivity and program fidelity. This lack of adherence plays out in important ways when it comes to the gender and race of clients. Historically a client's gender and race have been subsumed as specific responsivity factors (Bonta & Andrews, 2017), which has meant that these attributes are seldom considered in the design of offending interventions for women, people of color, and women of color.

In an effort to highlight the importance of cultural inclusiveness, some correctional scholars are beginning to argue that gender and race should be at the forefront of our understanding of risk, need, and responsivity (RNR), and that placing gender and race within the realm of specific responsivity does not give enough weight to the importance of these characteristics in the criminal legal system (Boppre, 2019; Salisbury, Boppre, & Kelly, 2016). While there is little evidence to suggest that the RNR model does not apply across gender and race, there is evidence that the entire model should be tailored to women and people of color.

For instance, the notion of risk for recidivism means something very different for women compared to men because women are far less likely to engage in criminal offending, which is related to the risk principle. With regard to the risk and need principles, women have additional criminogenic needs that predict their ongoing recidivism, but that are not predictive of men's offending (e.g., symptoms of depression and anxiety; Van Voorhis, Wright, Salisbury, & Bauman, 2010). Depression and anxiety in a traditional RNR model would be labeled as specific responsivity factors, but for women, these is growing evidence that these are risk/criminogenic factors and important in the trajectory of women's offending patterns (Salisbury & Van Voorhis, 2009). There are additional psychosocial areas that seem to operate this way for women (e.g., prior and current trauma, unhealthy intimate relationships). More detailed information on this topic can be found in Chapter 13. Note that very little research has been done as of yet with gender-nonconforming and transgender offending populations in terms of specific responsivity, though there is certainly significant reason to do so given their disproportionately high rates of victimization and incarceration (Jenness, Sexton, & Sumner, 2019).

It is also important to consider the lack of high-quality, widely disseminated program curricula specifically designed for people of color in the system. The vast majority of programs and interventions have been designed with white men in mind, and applied to other individuals of color and women. While many of these popular programs have been shown to be effective with non-normative offending groups and across the globe, there is reason to believe that if we started with these populations in mind, curricula would be more effective at reducing future recidivism. This is the case with justice-involved women—there is meta-analytic evidence that interventions tailored to women's relational learning styles (that are also cognitive behavioral in nature) are most effective with women clients compared to those that are not tailored to women (Gobeil, Blanchette, & Stewart, 2016).

For those interested in a cognitive behavioral program specifically designed for African American clients, the Habilitation Empowerment and Accountability Therapy (HEAT) curriculum is gaining recognition for improved treatment completion and retention rates (Marlowe et al., 2018). HEAT was created by Darryl Turpin and Guy Wheeler, drug court professionals from Kentucky and Florida respectively, who consistently observed African-American men doing poorly in traditional drug court interventions designed for white offending populations. The program is a nine-month, trauma-informed, strengths-based curriculum for young African-American men comprised of three components: family, self, and community. Although the curriculum is highly focused on addressing substance abuse, it also incorporates numerous culturally specific dynamics in African-American communities, and reviews African-American history throughout the lessons, noting the traditional cultural strengths of the Black community. A women's version of the program is also available, called Habilitation Empowerment Recovery (HER).

Another considerable problem when we fail to consider the notion of responsivity includes a potential for routinely "masking" a treatment effect (Van Voorhis, 1987). We repeatedly hear of programs that "failed," when in fact they probably succeeded with certain types of clients and failed with others—for the group as a whole, then, the successes were canceled by the failures.

For example, in what's become a classic evaluation of a popular cognitive behavioral program, Van Voorhis and her associates employed the Jesness Inventory (Jesness, 1996) to classify adult male parolees into the following four personality styles:

Asocial: Parolees with internalized antisocial values, beliefs, and attitudes. Crime is a lifestyle.

Neurotic: Highly anxious parolees, whose antisocial behavior represents the acting-out of an internal crisis. Crime for these people often has more of a personal and private meaning and is not necessarily for personal gain. Dysfunctional, self-defeating coping responses play a role in getting these individuals into trouble.

Dependent: Immature and easily manipulated parolees. They get into trouble through their own naiveté and in the course of being too easily led by other justice-involved people.

Situational Offenders: These parolees have prosocial values and less extensive criminal careers. They get into antisocial behavior on a situational basis, when they are unable to cope with certain life events, or through substance abuse.

When these parolees were assigned to Ross and Fabiano's (1985) cognitive skills program (Reasoning and Rehabilitation), some types were clearly more successful than others (see Figure 6.1; Van Voorhis, Spiropoulos, Ritchie, Seabrook, & Spruance, 2013).

Figure 6.1 also shows that the cognitive skills program was most appropriate for dependent and situational clients. Neurotic program participants, on the other hand, fared worse than members of the comparison group who did not participate in the program. Notice also

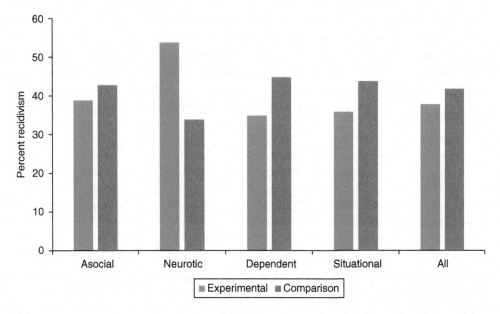

FIGURE 6.1 Percent returning to prison following cognitive skills programming by specific personality types.
Source: Van Voorhis et al. (2013)

that the program did not appear to be very successful with the group as a whole. However, a more accurate picture is that it worked with some participants but not with others. We do not know why high-anxiety clients performed so poorly. According to their pre-program assessments, they needed the program, but they just could not succeed in it. Perhaps there was too much confrontation.

In the future, this program could refer neurotic clients to a program more suitable to their needs. Such a practice would involve practitioners in doing exactly what the classification system was designed to do—matching clients to programs from which they can benefit. Alternatively, the cognitive program could be altered to better accommodate or work with high-anxiety individuals. Again, perhaps some facilitators were a bit too confrontational.

OTHER PURPOSES

Correctional administrators also use classification to help allocate such resources as staff, treatment options, and bed space. Classification also streamlines decision-making, so we can assign individuals to institutions, living units, case managers, and treatment options in an efficient manner. For instance, when clients are sent to prison, they are first classified by their sex/gender. Historically, prison systems have used a person's sexual anatomy to determine where they will be housed—in either a men's or women's facility. However, this practice is slowly being revisited by prison systems due to transgender and intersex community advocacy, scholarship with incarcerated people who are transgender (Jenness, Sexton, & Sumner, 2019), and civil lawsuits.

In fact, after a major lawsuit, as of July 1, 2021, the state of New Jersey will permit male/female housing placement to be determined by gender identification rather than strictly by genitalia (Porter, 2021). This issue is quite a complex one, and jail and prisons systems are still navigating best practices. There are many things to consider, including how to handle whether a man convicted of serial rape suddenly indicates he identifies as a woman, but in actuality wants access to female victims, as was once the case in the state of Nevada. The potential victimization of incarcerated women when transferring men who identify as women into their facilities is also cause for concern. Recently, an incarcerated woman sued the Illinois Department of Corrections for failing to protect her from sexual assault by a transgender inmate who was transferred to her unit (Masterson, 2020). Similar incidents have been observed in the United Kingdom with the case of Karen White. Despite the complexities, the fact remains that transgender women housed in male facilities are among the most brutalized and victimized (Jenness et al., 2019). Some states such as Oregon have been legally mandated to house transgender prisoners convicted of sexual crimes with other transgender people or with those who are non-cisgender (i.e., gender nonconforming; Wilson, 2019).

As we review different types of commonly used classification systems, we will revisit the core principles of risk-need-responsivity frequently. Readers will notice, however, that sometimes a classification model can meet more than one of the three principles. For example, a criminogenic need is also a predictor of future offending, so it is a risk factor as well as a need. And a responsivity factor can also be a need (e.g., transportation), but one that is not related to future offending.

TYPES OF COMMONLY USED CLASSIFICATION SYSTEMS

The choice of a classification system depends on the purpose for which it is being chosen. An overview of the array of correctional classification systems available and the purposes served by each is shown in Table 6.1. We discuss each type of system below.

Risk Assessment Systems

The earliest and most commonly used instruments for classifying correctional clients were **risk assessments** designed to predict new offenses or prison misconducts. As early as the 1970s, the U.S. Parole Commission was employing the Salient Factor Score (SFS) to classify people on parole into high, medium, and low levels of risk of reoffending (Hoffman, 1983). Institutions were using custody classification systems models based on the National Institute of Corrections Model Prisons Project (National Institute of Corrections [NIC], 1979) to classify incarcerated people to maximum, medium, and minimum custody.

Even though the NIC classification system was developed over 40 years ago, many prison systems still continue to use it to determine custody classification, despite the fact that risk/needs assessment systems improve prediction of antisocial behavior. As summarized in Table 6.2, the system is administered to all incarcerated individuals upon admission and then

TABLE 6.1 An overview of correctional classification approaches		
Type of System	*Purpose: Institutional Corrections*	*Purpose: Community Corrections*
Risk Assessments	Used for custody classification to predict institutional misconduct for assignment to maximum-, medium-, and minimum-custody institutions. Paroling authorities may also use it to determine release onto parole.	Predict new offenses for assignment to high-, medium-, and low-risk caseloads.
Needs Assessments	Used for case planning and case management; identifies client needs for programming referrals.	Used for case planning and case management; identifies client needs for programming referrals.
Risk/Needs Assessments	A limited number of prison systems in the United States use it for custody classification. Primarily used for treatment and reentry planning. Paroling authorities may also use to determine release onto parole.	Predict new offenses with needs that are also risk factors. Determines assignment to high-, medium-, and low-risk caseloads.
Responsivity Assessments	Assessments of IQ, maturity, personality, and other attributes likely to interfere with a client's ability to participate in certain programs.	Assessments of IQ, maturity, personality, and other attributes likely to interfere with a client's ability to participate in certain programs.

TABLE 6.2 Factors considered in institutional custody classification systems

Intake Classification System	Reclassification
Past institutional violence	Past institutional violence
Severity of current offense	Severity of current offense
Severity of prior convictions	Severity of prior convictions
Escape history	Escape history
Prior felonies	Prior felonies
Stability (age, education, employment)	Stability (age, education, employment)
Time to release	Prison misconduct
	Program/work performance
	Time to release

readministered approximately one to two years thereafter. Classification specialists score each item, add the scores, and consult guidelines to determine what institutional custody level matches the score. It is noteworthy that most of the factors listed in Table 6.2 are static risk factors—they do not change over time. Reclassification assessments attempt to correct for this. Items such as prison misconduct, time to serve, and accomplishments in institutional treatment programs can reduce or increase one's custody assignment. Similarly, some systems change scores or weights on the static items for purposes of reclassification. With the item not counting for as many points on the reclassification instrument as it does on the intake classification system, custody assignments can drop.

A host of validation studies found these custody classification systems to be predictive of institutional misconduct. In other words, they were **valid**, particularly for incarcerated men (Hardyman, Austin, & Tulloch, 2002). In recent years, however, scholars have discouraged the use of these systems for incarcerated women in female prisons (Bloom et al., 2003; Hardyman & Van Voorhis, 2004; Morash, Bynum, & Koons, 1998; Van Voorhis & Presser, 2001). Most states have not validated these assessments for women (Van Voorhis & Presser, 2001), and when they do, they often learn that the system must be redesigned to be valid. Current custody classification systems also tend to overclassify women by assigning them to custody levels that are too harsh for the rather minor level of misconducts that women typically commit (Van Voorhis, Salisbury, Wright, & Bauman, 2008). Officials should choose, instead, a risk/needs assessment because women's needs tend to be more predictive of serious prison misconduct than static offense-related factors (Van Voorhis et al., 2010; Wright et al., 2007; Wright, Van Voorhis, Salisbury, & Bauman, 2012).

Most institutional custody classification systems also offer no recommendations for programming and correctional treatment. Similarly, they do not predict recidivism in the community. Therefore, it would not be entirely correct to assume that people classified as minimum custody are the best candidates for work release, early release, or furloughs. Community risk assessment instruments are needed for this purpose, or a risk/needs assessment.

Needs Assessment Systems

Classifying clients into separate institutional custody levels or community supervision levels on the basis of risk alone would not provide enough information to guide decisions pertinent to treatment, adjustment to prison, and community reentry. Needs-assessment systems attempt to offer such treatment-relevant information. Figure 6.2 shows an example of an institutional needs assessment form. This form is used to record staff assessments of clients' problems as well as the magnitude of those problems.

Needs assessments provide: (a) systematic and objective identification of client needs; (b) information needed to link people to services that promote behavioral change and prevent physical, psychological, or social deterioration; (c) a tool for individualized case planning; and (d) information needed to allocate agency and programming resources (Clements, McKee, & Jones, 1984). At the same time, needs assessments are absolutely essential to prisoner reentry programs (Austin & McGinnis, 2004; Hardyman & Van Voorhis, 2004; Parent & Barnett, 2003).

Needs most likely to be identified by these instruments include those related to health, intellectual ability, mental health, education, employment, and alcohol and drug abuse. Like risk assessment models, needs assessments are designed to be administered at intake and at regular intervals throughout the correctional terms. It is important to note that these assessments were never designed to be the final assessment of a serious problem such as mental or physical health; instead, they are intended to triage clients, identifying those who need more intensive assessments.

The most common forms of needs assessment ask a correctional case manager or counselor to rate each need according to the extent to which, if any, the problem interferes with daily functioning (see Figure 6.2). In response to the alcohol abuse item, for example, a case manager might be prompted to indicate whether there is: (a) no alcohol abuse; (b) occasional abuse, some disruption of functioning; or (c) frequent abuse, serious disruption, needs treatment. Understandably, some have faulted such items as requiring too much subjectivity and being likely to lead to problems with the reliability of the instrument.

More acceptable approaches would more closely follow guidelines established by the American Correctional Association, which emphasize the importance of providing objective criteria for each level of need and informing determinations with additional information provided by assessments, presentence investigations, medical reports, psychological evaluations, and other documents (Clements et al., 1984; Hardyman & Van Voorhis, 2004; Hardyman et al., 2004). Alternatively, many agencies use established screens, especially for mental health, substance abuse, and education. Substance abuse, for example, may be assessed by instruments such as: (a) Substance Abuse Subtle Screening Inventory (SASSI-3; Miller & Lazowski, 1999); (b) Adult Substance Use Survey (ASUS; Wanberg, 1993; Wanberg & Milkman, 1998); (c) the Addiction Severity Index (ASI; McLellan, Kushner, Metzger, & Peters, 1992); (d) Drug Abuse Screening Test (DAST; Center for Addiction and Mental Health, 1999); or (e) Michigan Alcoholism Screening Test (Selzer, 1971). Mental health screenings often utilize the Minnesota Multiphasic Personality Inventory 2 (MMPI-2; Butcher, Dahlstrom, Graham, Tellegen, & Kaemmer, 1989), the Symptom Checklist 90 (SCL90; Derogatis, 1994), or the Millon Clinical Multiaxial Inventory-IV (MCMI-IV; Millon et al., 2015), to name just a few.

What we do with the needs assessment is as important as the assessment itself. Unfortunately, many assessments sit in files or on computers and are not used to their fullest

```
                    INITIAL INMATE CLASSIFICATION
                      ASSESSMENT OF NEEDS

NAME _____        NUMBER _____
        Last              First      MI

CLASSIFICATION CHAIRMAN _____        DATE ____ / ____ / ____


TEST SCORES:                                                    I.Q.

                                                               Reading

                                                                Math

NEEDS ASSESSMENT: Select the answer that best describes the inmate.

HEALTH:
1 Sound physical health,    2 Handicap or illness that   3 Serious handicap or chronic
  seldom ill                  interferes with functioning   illness, needs frequent medical   code
                              on a recurring basis          care

INTELLECTUAL ABILITY:
1 Normal intellectual ability, 2 Mild retardation, some   3 Moderate retardation, indepen-
  able to function               need for assistance          dent functioning severely limited  code
  independently

BEHAVIORAL/EMOTIONAL PROBLEMS:
1 Exhibits appropriate      2 Symptoms limit adequate    3 Symptoms prohibit adequate
  emotional responses         functioning, requires         functioning, requires significant   code
                              counseling, may require       intervention, may require
                              medication                    medication or separate housing

ALCOHOL ABUSE:
1 No alcohol problem        2 Occasional abuse, some     3 Frequent abuse, serious
                              disruption of functioning     disruption, needs treatment      code

OTHER DRUG ABUSE:
1 No drug problem           2 Occasional abuse, some     3 Frequent abuse, serious
                              disruption of functioning     disruption, needs treatment      code

EDUCATIONAL STATUS:
1 Has high school diploma   2 Some deficits, but potential 3 Major deficits in math
  or GED                      for high school diploma        and/or reading, needs           code
                              or GED                         remedial programs

VOCATIONAL STATUS:
1 Has sufficient skills to  2 Minimal skill level, needs 3 Virtually unemployable, needs
  obtain and hold satisfactory enhancement                  training                          code
  employment
```

FIGURE 6.2 Assessment of client needs.

potential (Miller & Maloney, 2013; Viglione, Rudes, & Taxman, 2015). That is, the client never gets to the service or program the assessment says he or she needs. Observe, for example, the results of an evaluation of a community correctional work-release program (see Figure 6.3). The first column shows the proportion of people in the program who were assessed as having

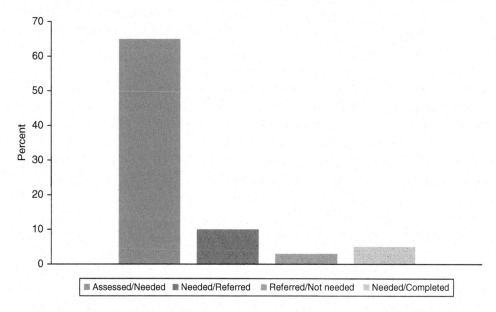

FIGURE 6.3 Matching of clients to antisocial thinking/cognitive skills programming.
Source: Van Voorhis & Spiropoulos, 2003.

antisocial beliefs, values, and attitudes. The second column shows the proportion of people with antisocial attitudes who were placed in a program for antisocial thinking and cognitive skills prior to their release. The third column shows the proportion of people who were in such a program, but had not been assessed as needing the program. The final column shows the proportion of people who needed the program and actually completed it. Figure 6.3 shows quite clearly that this agency did not (or could not) use the needs assessment to match clients to the cognitive skills program. Unfortunately, this is a common problem. In many agencies, assessments are administered and then ignored.

This is incredibly important in terms of determining effectiveness of programs. In a classic statewide study of halfway houses, for example, Lowenkamp and Latessa (2002) reported that halfway houses that matched clients to programs on the basis of sound needs assessments achieved much greater reductions in recidivism than those that did not.

Risk/Needs Assessments

In a growing number of community correctional agencies, risk and needs assessments are being combined into a single instrument. In contrast to the first and second generation assessments, these newer instruments contain dynamic items; scores can change over time. Such classification models constitute the third and fourth generation of systems. Examples of such systems include the Level of Service Inventory-Revised (LSI-R; Andrews & Bonta, 1995) and its more recent version, the **Level of Service/Case Management Inventory (LS/CMI**; Andrews, Bonta & Wormith, 2004), as well as the Correctional Offender Management Profiling for Alternative Sanctions (COMPAS; Brennan, Dieterich, & Oliver, 2006). The list of dynamic risk/needs assessment also includes several recent assessments that are available in the public domain and do not have to be purchased from assessment companies, including the **Ohio Risk Assessment System (ORAS**; Latessa, Smith, Lempke, Makarious, & Lowenkamp, 2010), and the **Women's Risk Needs Assessment** (Van Voorhis et al., 2010). In contrast to the needs assessments discussed in the previous section, **risk/needs assessments** include only those needs that are also **risk factors**. This is to help ensure that staff give focused attention to reducing criminogenic needs, thereby increasing the likelihood that they will also reduce recidivism.

Even so, scholars and practitioners alike have raised questions about the applicability of assessments such as the LS/CMI and the COMPAS to women offenders (Blanchette & Brown, 2006; Van Voorhis et al., 2010; Van Voorhis, 2012). Although the aforementioned assessments are known to be valid or predictive of women's recidivism, sources observe that they are not as relevant to the needs of women offenders as they should be. Specifically, the tools do not assess current symptoms of depression, parental stress, self-efficacy, abuse, and dysfunctional relationships. In response, the National Institute of Corrections developed the Women's Risk/Needs Assessment (WRNA) suite of instruments. The new **gender-responsive** assessments have been validated on samples of justice-involved women and have been found to make statistically significant improvements to the earlier tools designed for men, such as the LSI-R (Van Voorhis et al., 2010; Wright et al., 2007). Box 6.2 shows the risk/ needs factors assessed by the WRNA. To date, the WRNA has been adopted in more than 50 jurisdictions. A shortened version of the WRNA, the Inventory of Needs (ION, but now referred to as the Gender Informed Needs Assessment; GINA) was recently developed and validated for use in pretrial settings (Gehring & Van Voorhis, 2014).

Box 6.2 Women's Risk/Needs Assessment

RISK FACTORS

- Criminal History
- Antisocial Thinking
- Antisocial Associates
- Employment/Financial
- Education
- Housing Safety
- Anger
- Mental Health History
- Current Depression (symptoms)
- Current Psychosis (symptoms)
- History of Substance Abuse
- Current Substance Abuse
- Family Conflict
- Relationship Dysfunction
- Victimization as an Adult

- Child Abuse
- Sexual Abuse
- Parental Stress

STRENGTHS

- Self-efficacy
- Parental Involvement
- Educational Assets

Source: Van Voorhis, P., Wright, E., Salisbury, E., & Bauman, A. (2010). Women's risk factors and their contributions to existing risk/needs assessment: The current status of gender responsive assessment. *Criminal Justice and Behavior, 37* (3), 261–288.

As you can see from Box 6.2, a few strengths of clients are also identified to build client motivation and mobilize them for case planning purposes. Symbolically, measuring clients' strengths is an indication that we recognize that people are more than their deficits—more than their risks and needs. Very few risk/need assessments also identify strengths. Well-established tools that do, however, include the Service Planning Instrument (SPIn; Orbis Partners, 2003), the Service Planning Instrument for Women (SPIn-W; Orbis Partners, 2005), and the Youth Assessment and Screening Instrument (YASI; Orbis Partners, 2000). Importantly, strengths are not simply the opposite of risk factors—for instance, a low score on an antisocial attitudes scale does not mean that the client has strong prosocial attitudes. When measured appropriately, strengths actually are protective factors insulating clients from recidivism, and they are becoming increasingly important to measure in determining an accurate prediction of risk for reoffending (Brown, Robinson, Wanamaker, & Wagstaff, 2020).

ASSESSING RESPONSIVITY

As noted earlier, being responsive to treatment means that clients are able to participate in a given correctional program or setting. That is, it fits their learning styles, intellectual and emotional capabilities, cultural needs, and they have no insurmountable barriers to succeeding in the program. Individual situations and characteristics that are barriers to correctional adjustment and success in correctional interventions are referred to as responsivity characteristics. When we do not address these, some clients will be set up to fail.

Some responsivity factors do not have to be assessed. For example, we will not need to find a test to determine whether a single mother needs childcare or transportation to attend a substance abuse program. Other situations will require responsivity assessments. For example, programs that require clients to prepare written homework assignments and recognize the connection between their thoughts and their behavior will need to assess intelligence, as low-functioning individuals have difficulty succeeding in such situations. Intelligence screens such as the Culture Fair Test (Cattell & Cattell, 1973), the Shipley Institute for Living Scale-2 (Shipley et al., 2009), or the Beta III (Kellogg & Morton, 2009) are frequently used for this purpose. Educational programs often use the Wide Range Achievement Test (WRAT-4; Wilkinson & Robertson, 2006) to determine an individual's reading level. Increasingly, we are noticing that correctional programs that engage in confrontational interventions with clients may not succeed with highly anxious people (e.g., see Listwan, Sperber, Spruance, & Van Voorhis, 2004). A personality assessment, such as any of those discussed below, will help identify such clients.

The earliest form of assessments for responsivity involved assessments of personality characteristics. During the 1970s and 1980s, a number of correctional psychologists worked to develop psychological assessments to facilitate the notion of **differential treatment** (Jesness & Wedge, 1983; Megargee & Bohn, 1979; Quay, 1984; Quay & Parsons, 1972; Warren, 1971, 1983). Grounded, as all classification research is, in the notion that justice-involved people are not all alike (Palmer, 1978, 2002), the assessments developed by these scholars classified people according to personality or conceptual/cognitive maturity (Jesness & Wedge, 1983; Warren, 1983). These and later studies found that different "types" made varying adjustments to prison (Bohn, 1979; Megargee & Bohn, 1979; Megargee et al., 2001; Quay, 1984; Van Voorhis, 1994) and had distinct responses to specific types of correctional interventions (Palmer, 1974, 2002; Van Voorhis et al., 2002; Warren, 1983).

This section offers three examples of **psychological classification systems** that are used in correctional settings. To furnish a broad overview of different types of systems, this section introduces: the **Jesness Inventory** (formerly Interpersonal Maturity Level or I-level; Jesness, 2003; Warren & the Staff of the Community Treatment Project, 1966); Quay's Adult Internal Management System (AIMS; Quay, 1984); and the Megargee MMPI-based Typology (Megargee & Bohn, 1979; Megargee et al., 2001).

The three systems differ in terms of the types of psychological characteristics and criteria that form the basis of the respective typologies. Some are developmental typologies, and others are personality-based. One, Megargee's MMPI-based Typology, includes categories that include incarcerated people who are psychologically disturbed. Some of the systems tap a combination of factors (e.g., maturity, personality, pathology). The systems also differ in their methodology of administration. The AIMS requires staff observation while the Jesness Inventory and the MMPI-2 are taken directly by the client.

The **Jesness Inventory-Revised** (Jesness, 2003) began with the theoretical work of Sullivan, Grant, and Grant (1957) and originally used a model called the Interpersonal Maturity Level (I-level). The instrument is now an actuarial measure of I-level, which is a part of the Jesness Inventory (Jesness, 2003). The instrument contains 160 true/false items, and was originally developed for adolescents, but may now be used with adults as well (Jesness, 2003).

The classification scheme consists of four levels that characterize individuals on a cognitive developmental/maturity sequence pertaining to self and interpersonal perspectives. In addition to the four levels, the classification system also has personality subtypes within the levels. Therefore, the psychological characteristics tapped by the classification system are: (a) cognitive development or interpersonal maturity and (b) personality. We will present each in turn.

The developmental component of I-level shares assumptions common to several other ego and cognitive developmental (stage) theories as set forth by Loevinger (1966), Piaget (1948), Kohlberg (1976), and others. These theories maintain that cognitive development:

1. Involves changes in qualitative thought processes that describe how one thinks (not what one thinks).

2. Occurs through a developmental sequence of stages that are the same for all persons.

3. Occurs in the direction of increasing complexity (i.e., one's thinking becomes more complex with development).

4. Represents an underlying logic at each developmental stage that appears to be consistent across situations.

5. Occurs through stages that are hierarchical integrations that enable individuals to comprehend all stages below and one stage above their diagnosed stage of reasoning.

Because development can cease at any point along the continuum, a cross-section of the population, theoretically, would show a distribution of persons at all stages.

The levels of interpersonal development range from the least mature stage of the newborn infant (I_1) to a theoretically ideal stage of interpersonal maturity that is rarely attained (I_7). A description of the socio-perceptual frame of reference that characterizes each level shows how individual perceptions of and reactions to others change with the development of the personality. Warren (1983) refers to the frame of reference embodied in each level as a "relatively consistent set of expectations and attitudes, a kind of interpreting and working philosophy of life." This way of making sense of one's environment, then, is relatively consistent across situations until the individual matures into the next level, where a new cognitive frame of reference is integrated with previous experiences and perspectives.

Four levels apply to youth and adult populations. Phil Harris's (1988) abbreviated description of levels 2(I_2), 3(I_3), 4(I_4), and 5(I_5) follows.

I_2 is a stage typical of very young children. Major concerns center on differentiating persons from objects. Other persons are viewed solely as sources of gratification (e.g., as "givers" and "takers," evidencing no understanding of others nor an ability to predict or influence the behavior of others).

I_3 youths have learned that they have power; their behaviors affect the responses they receive from others. Much of their activity centers on learning how power is structured. They tend to apply stereotypical rules and simple formulas when interacting with others.

I_4 youths operate from a set of internalized values. They are aware of feelings and motives in themselves and in others and their relevance to communication and relationships with others. They tend to be rigid in their application of rules and to be concerned with their own uniqueness.

I_5 individuals are considerably less rigid in their application of rules than are persons at I_4; they tend to see gray areas in situations and are tolerant of viewpoints different from their own. The most distinguishing characteristic of this stage is empathy—the capacity to experience the world from the perspective of another person.

An overview of these characteristics presents a compelling case for differential responses to the correctional clients under our supervision. A counselor would not, for example, expect an I_3 youth client to readily understand what it was like to be "in the shoes of" the dorm mate who was hurt last night. Similarly, an I_4 youth may be defensive about any failure on his part to measure up to his expectations of himself. These expectations may be either prosocial or antisocial, but by knowing his I-level diagnosis, we would predict the youth to be holding on to these values in a consistent manner.

Although the levels outlined above have some applicability to cognitive behavioral interventions (see Chapter 9) and can be useful guides to counselors or social workers, the I-level personality subtypes (or Jesness Inventory Subtypes) are in more frequent use. These might also be termed the personality-based adaptations found to be evidenced at each of these levels. Harris's (1988) descriptions are as follows:

I_2: *Asocial Passive:* Responds to unmet demands by withdrawing, whining, or complaining.
   Asocial Aggressive: Responds to unmet needs with open aggression.
I_3: *Immature Conformist:* Conforms to whomever has the power at the moment and sees self as less powerful than others.
   Cultural Conformist: Conforms exclusively to a specific group of peers.
   Manipulator: Counteractive to any source of power, adult, or peer. Extremely distrustful of others.
I_4: *Neurotic Acting-Out:* Internally conflicted due to negative self-image. Responds to internal conflict by putting up a facade of super-adequacy and maintaining a high level of activity. Attempts to keep others at a distance through distracting behavior or verbal attack, even though he or she may be very sociable.
   Neurotic Anxious: Also internally conflicted due to a negative self-image. Responds to internal conflict with guilt, anxiety, or depression. Tends to be introspective and frequently attempts to engage others in gaining self-understanding.
   Cultural Identifier: As part of his or her socialization process, certain antisocial values were internalized that permit a range of antisocial acts.
   Situational-Emotional Reaction: Responds to a current crisis, situation, or an emotional change that is recent in origin. This individual, however, has a prosocial value system.
I_5: The subtypes of this group are identical to those found at I_4.

The treatment applications of the Jesness Inventory involve classifying people and then assigning them to case managers and counselors who have been specially trained to work with that "type" of individual. Semel (2016) provides a thorough review of the instrument, its psychometric properties, and how it is complementary to the risk-need-responsivity model. The Jesness Inventory types are also helpful in determining an appropriate treatment strategy and living environment (Palmer, 1974, 2002; Warren, 1971, 1983).

Additional research with adults found that the personality types listed above could be greatly simplified by collapsing the Jesness Inventory types into four: (a) asocial; (b) neurotic; (c) dependent; and (d) situational. Clients classified into these types have been observed to: (a) make dramatically different adjustments to prison (Van Voorhis, 1994); (b) have different long-term recidivism rates (Listwan, Van Voorhis, & Ritchey, 2007); (c) make sense of their convictions for child molestation in different ways (Sperber, 2004); and (d) respond to a cognitive behavioral program differently (see Figure 6.1; Van Voorhis et al., 2013). The responsivity principle would suggest that counselors could use the assessment information as a tool for better treatment and supervision planning.

The **Adult Internal Management System** (AIMS; Quay, 1984) differs from all of the other systems because the classification does not directly involve input from the client. Instead, staff complete two behavior observational checklists. The first, the Life Histories Checklist, consists of 27 items designed to be answered after a review of the individual's background reports and perhaps a brief interview. The second instrument, the Correctional Adjustment Checklist (CAC), is completed by a staff member and is based on staff observation of the client over a brief period in the correctional setting. It contains 41 items.

Scores on the two checklists are combined, and the client is classified into one of five personality types:

1. aggressive-psychopathic
2. inadequate-dependent
3. neurotic-anxious
4. manipulative
5. situational

Names have since been changed to the less descriptive Alpha I, Alpha II, Sigma I, Sigma II, and Kappa, and correspond to their respective rates of institutional misconduct. A similar system exists for use with juveniles (Quay & Parsons, 1972). The AIMS manual identifies a number of treatment issues for each type, but the most common application of the system has been for separation of incarcerated people into housing units, especially separating predatory people from vulnerable ones. For this purpose, the system is more aptly termed a management rather than a treatment tool. Three studies have examined the effectiveness of the system for purpose of client management. All reported reduced disciplinary infractions (Bohn, 1979; Levenson, 1988; Quay, 1984). Although these studies are quite dated, the AIMS is still widely used among institutional correctional settings.

The **Megargee MMPI-based Typology** (Megargee & Bohn, 1979; Megargee et al., 2001) was developed for use with juveniles and adults. As the title implies, the classifications are obtained from results of the Minnesota Multiphasic Personality Inventory (MMPI). The classification system was developed by Edwin I. Megargee and his associates at Florida State University as a means of classifying large correctional populations. It involves separating MMPI profiles into 10 categories on the bases of profile configurations, slopes, shapes, and elevations. The scoring rules for doing this are available in a book titled *Classifying Criminal Offenders with the* MMPI-2: *The Megargee System* (Megargee et al., 2001).

The MMPI-based system offers a means of efficiently identifying individuals who exhibit certain forms of psychological disturbance. The Megargee System serves as both a classification function for all incarcerated individuals and as a tool in further assessing those who appear to be suffering from more serious forms of mental illness.

To understand how these systems address responsivity, imagine two adults on your caseload. One has been classified as neurotic, the other as asocial (with antisocial beliefs, values, and attitudes). We will notice fairly quickly that the man classified as neurotic cannot tolerate criticism well, is highly defensive, and seems to have more difficulty trusting us than the man classified as committed to crime. He is quick to misunderstand our discussions and intentions. We may even notice that any type of criticism of the neurotic client results in an increase rather than a decrease in his acting-out behavior. The asocial client, on the other hand, needs to know that we are "not buying" his antisocial thinking. He needs to hear from us when we notice his antisocial attitudes getting him into trouble. Simply put, what works for one backfires with the other. A similar phenomenon may occur as we make treatment referrals. A certain type of treatment program may work for the neurotic client but may be exploited by the more manipulative one.

FUTURE DIRECTIONS IN CORRECTIONAL CLASSIFICATION

Correctional classification and assessment is an area that continues to evolve. Three new directions are particularly noteworthy. In addition to the development of the gender-responsive Women's Risk/Needs Assessment (discussed previously) we should also discuss the development of risk models for specific types of individuals, for example, persons convicted of sex offenses, psychopaths, and substance users. A second new direction is the development of seamless classification systems in which the same assessment is used across probation, institutional, and parole assignments—sometimes even at pretrial.

Studies of specific types of clients, such as violent individuals, those with psychopathy, people convicted of sex offenses, and with specific criminogenic needs, have produced numerous additional assessments to support the case management and supervision of these individuals. These include, for example: (a) the Hare Psychopathy Checklist-Revised (Hare, 2003); (b) the Sex Offender Needs Assessment Rating (SONAR; Hanson & Harris, 2000); (c) the Static-99 (Hanson & Thornton, 1999); (d) the Spousal Assault Risk Assessment Guide (SARA; Kropp, Hart, Webster, & Derek Eaves, 1997); and (e) the Criminal Sentiments Scale (Simourd, 1997). Assessments for substance use were listed earlier in this chapter. People convicted of sex offenses, especially, often appear to be low risk on conventional risk/needs assessments, but high risk on the SONAR or the Static-99. This is because they have a different set of risk factors that is not tapped by conventional risk/needs assessments (see Chapter 14).

Another new direction suggests that seamless classification systems could one day replace the use of separate systems for community and institutional agencies. For example, an instrument such as the LS/CMI, ORAS, WRNA, or the COMPAS could be administered at a pre-sentence point and readministered at regular intervals thereafter. It would follow the client into a correctional facility and back out to parole. As circumstances change, such as when programs are completed or abstinence is achieved, the dynamic risk/needs scores would be readministered. The value of such a model is particularly relevant to reentry and transition programs designed to address the needs of record numbers of people in prison who are now returning to their communities (Petersilia, 2003). Suggestions such as those formulated in the NIC Transition Model (Parent & Barnett, 2003) include using such assessments to: (a) begin planning for release as soon as people are admitted to prison, and (b) assure continuity of care throughout the correctional term and beyond.

Box 6.3 Validity and Reliability: What Do We Mean?

Throughout this chapter we frequently use the terms **validity** and **reliability.** Because these concepts are essential to the task of treating correctional clients equitably, we want to assure that readers have a reasonable understanding of these terms.

WHEN IS A CLASSIFICATION SYSTEM VALID?

A classification system is valid when it measures what it promises to measure. Correctional risk assessments, for example, promise to predict recidivism or prison misconduct—depending on the system. Clients are placed in high-, medium-, or low-risk levels according to their prediction score. If the prediction score or levels are accurate, those who are classified as high risk should incur more new offenses than those who are classified as low risk. This is called predictive validity. To determine if this is the case, a researcher will take data from a sample of clients and follow them for at least 12 to 24 months, keeping track of any new offenses during that period. When the data have been analyzed, we should see something like Figure 6.4.

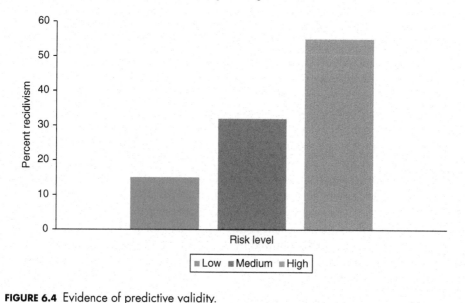

FIGURE 6.4 Evidence of predictive validity.

In other words, over time high-risk clients really were at greater risk of committing new offenses than low-risk ones. If we saw something different, such as columns showing that each group had the same rate of recidivism or something other than the "ascending stairs," we would conclude that the system was invalid. Importantly, it is crucial to also test predictive validity with subgroups of people, such as women and minorities, to ensure the systems are working as equitably for them as the majority correctional populations.

Validity also requires that the system correlates or reaches a similar classification as another measure of the same construct—in this case, risk. This second form of validity is called *construct validity*. We would have construct validity, for example, if, in a sample of individuals classified according to both the ORAS and the LS/CMI, most clients achieved the same classification on both assessments. If the ORAS gave a different risk classification than the LS/CMI for many clients, we would conclude that the instrument did not have construct validity.

Why do we frequently discuss validity as an ethical consideration? In corrections, the lives of individuals can be profoundly affected by their correctional classification. Individuals facing trial, for example, can either be released on their own recognizance or jailed, depending on the results of a risk assessment instrument. Risk assessments sometimes also determine early prison release or whether a person on probation will be placed on electronic monitoring. Similarly, prison classification systems determine whether someone will be placed in a minimum-custody facility or in a medium- or maximum-custody facility with less freedom of movement and fewer privileges.

When Is a Classification System Reliable?

A classification system is reliable when two tests of the same individual produce the same classification. This could be when one individual takes a test twice or when one or two individuals administer an assessment on two separate occasions. We want similar results. We are especially concerned with questions that ask for too much judgment on the part of an interviewer. This chapter, for example, refers to a question that asks interviewers to determine whether a client's substance use is causing minor levels of disruption or major levels of disruption. Would two interviewers score that item the same? To check on the reliability of an assessment, draw a random sample of 50 clients who agree to be assessed twice by two independent counselors or case managers. Take the assessments and count the number of cases in which the assessment results were the same for each assessment. There will be 50 pairs of assessments here; at a very minimum, 80% of them should show the same classification regardless of the person administering the assessment.

A final new direction challenges the practice of assigning clients to programs one need at a time. For example, if a high-risk client is first referred to a cognitive behavioral program, then to a mental health program, followed by a substance abuse program, with no concern for whether these needs were co-occurring or needed to be addressed in some therapeutically relevant sequence, we would truly be taking an overly simplistic view of the case. Recently, a number of researchers have subjected risk/needs measures to various types of factor and cluster analyses, and found that they co-occur in meaningful ways (e.g., Brennan, Breitenbach, & Dieterich, 2008; Brennan, Breitenbach, Dieterich, Salisbury, & Van Voorhis, 2012; Taxman & Coudy, 2015). The implication here is that risk factors should be treated in the context of other risk factors. Stephanie Covington's work (e.g., Covington 2008a, 2008b) with women involved in the justice system is a fitting example. Covington maintains that, for many women, substance abuse occurs with mental health, trauma, and relationship issues. These all must be addressed, and sometimes the treatments must occur simultaneously. To target one issue—the substance use, for example—with one program—relapse prevention, for example—would miss treating a very big portion of the causal dynamics of the woman's substance abuse.

CONCLUSION

The classification systems discussed in this chapter are not an exhaustive list. Rather, they give an overview of the systems in place in corrections. As you can see, correctional classification is a major area in criminal justice research that is assisting in creating new and empirical assessments. Classification assessments have become a valuable tool for corrections and case managers as they assist in identifying a client's risk, need, and responsivity factors. Assessing these factors allows correctional staff to identify treatment programs that match the individual client's needs, which allows for better treatment outcomes. Failure to address these factors could lead the client to not be successful in treatment.

This is not to suggest, however, that correctional classification efforts have always been successful, or that systems can be implemented easily. In fact, future consumers of these systems should be alerted to the reality of some very serious mistakes that have been made with systems that appeared, at least on paper, to be easily implemented. A myth of efficiency appears to have marred many attempts to classify correctional populations. The myth of efficiency works on the desire to find a classification system that can be completed so easily that the agency does not need to concern itself with overburdening an already overworked staff. The myth might hold, for example, that the probation officer who has a caseload of 100 people need not complain about being required to complete a risk assessment instrument because it only takes three minutes to fill out the form. Indeed, the risk assessment instrument shown in Figure 6.2 appears to be clear and easy to complete. Why would an agency have problems with it when the questions are so straightforward? Yet this level of simplicity can also be a system's shortcoming, because the form can be filled out so quickly, the staff need not give it any thought. Unfortunately, even these simple systems have incurred problems with inaccuracy (Austin, 1986; Buchanan, Whitlow, & Austin, 1986).

Most important, there has been ongoing controversy surrounding the problematic use of assessment and classification instruments among system-involved people of color, particularly African American men. Although this is a highly complex issue, one of the main problems stems from heavily weighted criminal history items in the instruments that disproportionately increase risk levels of Black men, not because they have engaged in more crime, but rather due to historically racist policing and prosecutorial practices within poor, urban communities and limited opportunities for upward social mobility (Eckhouse, Lum, Conti-Cook, & Ciccolini, 2019). This is a multifaceted and continuously unfolding problem, particularly in the United States.

Potential users of these systems should also be warned of the problems in borrowing a risk assessment instrument from one jurisdiction and implementing it in another with no consideration for how well it fits a new population (Clear, 1988; Jones, 1996). Researchers have warned that the cut-off points separating risk levels could change substantially across settings and geographic areas. Thus, for a prediction instrument to be as accurate as possible, it must be validated to each new location (Wright, Clear, & Dickson, 1984). As was learned in a series of studies on women, the system may be completely invalid and inaccurately assigning people to unnecessarily austere correctional settings (Hardyman & Van Voorhis, 2004). For a description on how to investigate risk assessments for agency adoption, the National Institute of Justice recently published a report on the topic, specifically focused on ensuring principles of fairness, efficiency, and effectiveness for correctional clients (Bucklen, Duwe, & Taxman, 2021).

In conclusion, classification appears to make good sense from both a management and a treatment perspective. But as with any program strategy, treatment integrity is an issue. All of the systems listed above have carefully established guidelines regarding their use, and problems have resulted from not adhering to those guidelines. Yet there have also been numerous instances of successful implementation, which have served to improve the functioning of correctional programs.

Box 6.4 A Case Study

In this and the previous chapter, we presented a number of tools for achieving a good understanding of correctional clients. Correctional classification tools help us to identify risk, needs, and responsivity characteristics that must be considered in treatment plans. They offer counselors valuable insights into a client's challenges and strengths.

Prior to referring clients to appropriate interventions, correctional case managers and counselors must first decide upon treatment goals and a course of planned intervention. This involves reviewing a client's social and offending history as well as any classification scores, mental health reports, or educational assessments. These form the basis of a treatment plan, the foundation upon which key client needs are set forward and goals of supervision and counseling are determined. Treatment plans typically contain the following components:

I. background and social history

II. offending history and dynamics of incidents

III. description of the current offense

IV. risk scores and results of needs and responsivity assessments

V. treatment goals

VI. treatment approaches for addressing client needs

Consider Jason's situation:

Assume that you are asked to develop a treatment plan for Jason, one that will hopefully point him in a more positive and meaningful direction. In addition to accounting for Jason's social and offending history, the treatment plan will furnish any relevant mental health and classification information and detail the criminogenic needs that you plan to have addressed during Jason's prison term. In this case, you have not observed any behaviors that would prompt you to refer Jason to the prison's mental health unit for an interview and assessments. He did, however, complete several assessments offered through the correctional system's classification unit. These included a Level of Service Inventory (LSI-R; Andrews & Bonta, 1995), an IQ assessment, and a Jesness Inventory (Jesness, 1996). Results of these assessments are as follows:

Classification and Assessment: Jason's score on the LSI-R indicated that he was at a medium-high risk of reoffending. This risk classification makes Jason appropriate for the institution he is in and also suggests that Jason is a candidate for many of the types of intensive treatment programs targeted to criminogenic needs. In addition, the LSI-R serves as a case management tool because it prioritizes the criminogenic needs that should be targeted while Jason is incarcerated. Jason's main criminogenic needs are: (a) antisocial associates; (b) antisocial attitudes; (c) limited work skills; (d) educational limitations; and (e) problematic family relationships.

The Jesness Inventory classified Jason as a CFC (Cultural Conformist). CFCs are described as people who: (a) see little reason to question their way of life or change their behavior; and (b) rarely admit to having serious personal problems. When they *do* admit to personal problems, they blame them on others (e.g., police, schools, and lawyers). CFCs are oriented to their peers for social approval and satisfaction of needs. They often possess antisocial values that are highly supportive of their offending behavior.

Jason's IQ score on the Culture Fair Test (Cattell & Cattell, 1973) was 118, clearly above average. Jason is an avid reader, especially of sports and adventure stories.

To staff in the classification unit, Jason did not appear to be a candidate for any substance abuse interventions. On further observation, however, this may need to be re-evaluated. You have just learned, for example, that Jason received a disciplinary citation for stealing fruit to make an alcoholic beverage. Your concern leads you to a plan to further discuss Jason's alcohol and other drug use, perhaps even to administer a substance abuse screening instrument. It is not uncommon for clients to misrepresent their substance abuse in intake interviews, and for treatment practitioners to learn of the problem later.

At present, you decide to focus on the following criminogenic needs:

- antisocial attitudes, supportive of antisocial and offending behavior
- limited cognitive skills, e.g., poor problem-solving and decision-making skills
- limited educational attainments or job skills
- aggressive attitudes and behavior
- orientation to antisocial rather than to prosocial peers or family members

While these may not represent all of the criminogenic needs identified by the LSI-R, they are your priorities at the present time. These may change over time, as Jason improves or as different criminogenic needs (such as substance abuse) become apparent.

You also note that Jason has the following strengths:

- above-average intelligence
- good physical health
- affirmation from his sister
- enjoyment of reading and remorse over his failure to complete high school

Thus, you write the following treatment goals:

1. To reduce criminogenic thought patterns.
2. To build problem-solving and decision-making skills.
3. To build skills for managing anger.
4. To encourage Jason's relationship with prosocial individuals (e.g., his sister, key correctional staff, and incarcerated people who model anti-criminogenic behaviors).
5. To complete the GED and some college-level courses.

Discussion Questions

1. What are the common points of the classification systems?
2. What purposes are served by correctional classification?
3. What is the difference between a static classification system and a dynamic classification system? Why is the difference important?
4. What do the authors mean when referring to the "myth of efficiency"?
5. Distinguish among the risk principle, the needs principle, and the responsivity principle. How is each important to correctional treatment efforts?
6. How might an accurate needs or responsivity assessment make a correctional treatment program more effective?
7. What is meant by the statement that a classification system should be valid and reliable?
8. Why is it unethical to use a classification system that is not known to be valid?

ONLINE LEARNING ENHANCEMENTS

Who Should Get Parole? FiveThirtyEight, a website more generally focused on political polling and sports predictions, created a risk assessment simulator for the average person to determine the rate of false negatives and false positives they would be willing to entertain among parolees. The Parole Simulator is an interactive way to explain the challenges behind risk assessment and the myth of perfect prediction.

How the Parole Simulator Works: https://fivethirtyeight.com/features/how-our-parole-simulator-works/

Parole Simulator: https://fivethirtyeight.com/features/prison-reform-risk-assessment/#who-should-get-parole

GLOSSARY OF KEY TERMS

Adult Internal Management System (AIMS)   a correctional classification system that does not directly involve input from the client, but instead involves staff completion of two behavior observational checklists

correctional classification   the ongoing process of collecting and evaluating information about correctional clients to determine risk, needs, and responsivity characteristics that must be considered in treatment plans

criminogenic needs   characteristics, traits, or issues that directly relate to one's likelihood of reoffending

differential treatment   the notion of treating correctional clients according to their individual needs, personalities, and levels of cognitive maturity

dynamic risk factors   risk factors related to one's likelihood of recidivism that can be changed over time

gender-responsive   a concept of ensuring that risk/needs assessments are tailored to the gender-specific needs of correctional clients

general responsivity   refers to the fact that cognitive social learning interventions delivered in a firm, fair, and caring manner are the most effective way to teach people prosocial behaviors

Jesness Inventory   a psychological classification system that classifies individuals according to their personality type; upon classification, individuals are then assigned to case managers and counselors who have been specially trained to work with that "type" of individual

Level of Service/Case Management Inventory (LS/CMI)   a risk/need assessment tool that identifies the criminogenic needs of correctional clients that should be targeted in treatment

Megargee MMPI-based Typology   a classification system developed for use with juveniles and adults; classifications are obtained from results of the Minnesota Multiphasic Personality Inventory (MMPI)

myth of efficiency   the false notion that quick, easy to complete risk assessments should be prioritized over more complex assessments that tend to be more reliable

needs-assessment systems   classification systems that help guide decisions pertinent to correctional clients' treatment needs, adjustment to prison, and community reentry

needs principle   a correctional counseling principle that maintains that needs related to future offending should receive high priority as clients are matched to programs

Ohio Risk Assessment System (ORAS)   a risk/needs assessment that is available in the public domain and does not have to be purchased from assessment companies

psychological classification systems   classification systems that identify psychological characteristics and formulate the basis of developmental or personality-based typologies; used in correctional settings to identify appropriate responses to correctional clients

reliability   a concept referring to a classification system's ability to produce the same classification when two tests of the same individual are administered

responsivity assessment   assessments of IQ, maturity, personality, and other attributes likely to interfere with a client's ability to participate in certain programs

responsivity characteristics   individual situations and characteristics that are barriers to correctional adjustment and success in correctional interventions

risk assessments instruments used to predict risk of recidivism or institutional misconduct among correctional clients; clients are placed in high-, medium-, or low-risk levels according to their prediction score

risk factors factors related to an individual's risk of future offending or antisocial behavior

risk principle a correctional counseling principle that maintains that clients should be provided with treatment and supervision levels that align with their level of risk; intensive treatment efforts should be directed toward high- and medium-risk clients, while low-risk clients should not be assigned to institutional placements or intensive treatment interventions that expose them to criminogenic influences

risk/needs assessment an assessment that includes only those needs that are also risk factors; risk/needs assessments help correctional counselors focus attention on reducing criminogenic needs, thereby increasing the likelihood that they will also reduce recidivism

seamless classification systems classification systems in which the same assessment is used across probation, institutional, and parole assignments

specific responsivity refers to adjusting the cognitive social interventions to account for the strengths, personality, motivation, learning style, and gender/race characteristics of the individual

static risk factors risk factors related to one's likelihood of recidivism that cannot be changed over time

treatment amenability a client's likelihood of achieving success in a correctional program

typology a classification according to type; correctional clients are categorized according to similar needs or risk levels

validity a concept referring to a classification system's ability to measure what it promises to measure

Women's Risk/Needs Assessment (WRNA) a gender responsive assessment that is tailored to the risk/needs factors of system-impacted women

CHAPTER 7

Case Planning and Case Management

Patricia Van Voorhis

KEY TERMS

activities	Principles of Effective Intervention
assessment-based	responsivity principle
case plan	risk effect
congruence	risk principle
continuity of care	screen
empathy	seamless service delivery
goal	strengths-based approach
graduated sanctions	tasks
interpersonal boundaries	therapeutic relationship
needs principle	warmth and openness

What do the lessons of this book mean when it comes to our day-to-day interactions with correctional clients? Most of what has been presented comes together into a **case plan** that sets forward the goals, expectations, and directions of the correctional term. Most of these directions will direct the client, for example, as when a case management plan indicates that a client will attend a substance use class. Case management plans also list the case manager's[1] responsibilities (e.g., make the referral to the substance use class, work to get the client into a community college program, or secure a more detailed mental health assessment). When conducted properly, case plans provide a clear structure and focus to clients and treatment personnel. Clients will know what is expected of them and with proper encouragement from case managers they will embrace their goals. A good case plan also represents collaborative decision-making that involves the case manager and the client. The results of those decisions are then well documented.

Case planning is the next step following the administration of a dynamic risk/needs assessment. In developing the plan, the counselor or case manager examines assessment results for high-scoring need categories and then develops an action plan for addressing the needs. There is a structure to formulating the plan, one that is fairly standard across the helping professions. In Figure 7.1, for example, we see the usual spaces for identifying

DOI: 10.4324/9780367808266-9

CASE PLAN

Case Plan Origin Date:		Client Name: ID#:			
Case Manager(s):		Risk Level			
Risk Factor:					
Goal(s):					
Responsivity Factor(s) (Barriers):					
Strengths:					
Tasks:	Activities:		Start Date:	Goal Date:	Success Date:

Case Manager Signature: Client Signature:

_____   _____

FIGURE 7.1 Case plan.

the client (e.g., name, ID). One sheet is completed for each goal addressed. The risk level is noted (high, medium, or low). Then the case manager or counselor works with the client to determine goals, tasks (steps the client will take), and activities (steps the staff will take in assisting the client with the task) toward reaching those goals, all in the spirit of first identifying responsivity factors (see Figure 7.2 for more detail). In planning these tasks, case managers must also determine whether there are roadblocks to the desired tasks. For example, a referral to a substance use intervention is not likely to be successful if transportation or childcare issues are going to make it difficult to attend. These are responsivity issues or barriers that must be addressed to accomplish the tasks. The case plan is updated on a regular basis as goals are achieved or roadblocks are encountered.

The process set forward in Figure 7.2 is a basic visualization of the case management process. Many guidelines must be added. Various chapters in this book have had a lot to say about how these case plans should be conducted. These are reviewed in what follows along with some additional considerations.

GUIDELINES FOR CASE PLANNING

There are a number of evidence-based professional guidelines to follow as we plan a course of guidance and treatment for correctional clients. First and foremost, many of the Principles of Effective Intervention (see Chapter 4; Gendreau & Goggin, 1996; Andrews & Bonta, 2010) should be considered in developing case plans. Moreover, research shows us that clients

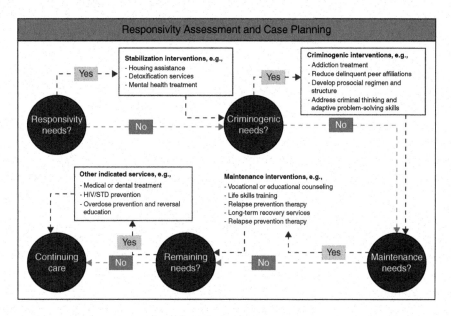

FIGURE 7.2 Responsivity assessment and case planning.
Source: SAMHSA's GAINS Center for Behavioral Health and Justice Transformation.
Reproduced with permission from Policy Research Associates, Inc., operator of SAMHSA's
GAINS Center. Marlowe, D. (2018, July 17). Responsivity assessment and case planning.
SAMHSA's GAINS Center Newsletter. Policy Research Associates. www.prainc.com/risk-need-
responsitivity/.

who are managed according to these principles have better outcomes than those whose
case manager simply followed a hunch in the course of setting the conditions of supervision. Case plans should also be assessment-based. That is, the case manager should use an
assessment rather than a judgment call to determine whether a client should be referred to
a specific intervention.

State-of-the-art case plans are also updated on a regular basis. If a client's task is accomplished, it is noted on a revised case plan, and another, perhaps more difficult, step is identified as a new task. It may take many tasks to achieve a goal. In this way, clients are tracked
over time, through a process of updating the case plan according to the accomplishments or
difficulties encountered by the client. In many cases, the case plan is transferred to another
case manager in another agency. For example, when incarcerated people are released, the
case management plan should follow the client to wherever he or she is receiving post-
release supervision.

With correctional clients, case planning involves more than a course of treatment.
Counseling and treatment must also take place in the context of appropriate supervision and
structure. Correctional clients must meet supervision requirements that are consistent with
their risk level. They must be monitored accordingly to determine whether the conditions
of supervision are being adhered to, and they must be subjected to sanctions when those
conditions are violated.

Finally, a good **therapeutic relationship** is the foundation of state-of-the-art case planning,
as was emphasized in Chapter 3. Case planning is far more than simply filling out the form

shown in Figure 7.1. Motivational Interviewing, effective collaboration with the client, building self-efficacy, and effective re-enforcement all play a role in helping clients plan and execute a course of change.

Use of Assessments

Case plans should be **assessment-based**. They should never be based upon a case manager's judgment of whether a problem exists. We may sometimes think that we can judge a client's risk level on the basis of our lengthy experience in working with justice-involved people, but this is not the case. Research tells us that clinical judgments of who is high risk or low risk, who is depressed, substance-dependent, and so on, are not reliable unless they are accompanied by an assessment. This has been known since the 1950s, when researchers discovered that psychiatrists diagnosing mental illness tended to disagree with each other (Grove & Meehl, 1996). A similar finding was observed among correctional practitioners who attempted to determine risk or needs subjectively (Bonta, Law, & Hanson, 1998). It is also important to note that programs that assess risk and needs are more effective than those that rely upon professional judgment calls.

In terms of day-to-day practice, then, the case plan (Figure 7.1) should not list a risk level or a need, unless a dynamic risk/needs assessment such as the LSI-R (Andrews & Bonta, 1995), the LS/CMI (Andrews et al., 2004), WRNA (Van Voorhis et al., 2010), COMPAS (Brennan et al., 2006), or ORAS (Center for Criminal Justice Research, 2009) determines that it actually is a need. However, in doing so, we need to recognize that the need domains of these assessments only **screen** for certain needs. When clients score high on substance use, education, or mental health, there is a need for further assessments. The dynamic risk/needs assessments are short, relative to the time needed for a full mental health, education, or substance use battery of tests designed to gather the specific nature of these problems. The dynamic risk/needs assessments show us that a problem exists in a specific domain, but they cannot show us the nature of the problem. Other domains, such as housing, antisocial friends, and employment, of course, do not require further assessments. The dynamic risk/needs assessment gives us most of the information we need in the case of those needs.

Principles of Effective Intervention

The **Principles of Effective Intervention** offer a very rich set of guidelines for developing case plans. Most relevant in this regard are the risk, need, and responsivity principles. Recall (Chapters 4 and 6) that the **risk principle** stated that intensive interventions should be reserved for high-risk, perhaps medium- and high-risk, correctional clients. Figure 7.3 offers supporting evidence. In an evaluation of a day-reporting center (DRC) program among probationers (Van Voorhis & Groot, 2010), it can be seen that the most substantial reductions in post-program recidivism were for clients classified as medium- or high-risk. It is extremely important to note what happened to the low-risk group, however. After 24 months, the low-risk group who received the DRC program showed *higher* post-program recidivism than low-risk clients who did not receive the program. This is the **risk effect** in action. Intensive correctional interventions are intended for high-risk clients. Such programs reduce the recidivism of high-risk clients, but they tend to increase the recidivism of low-risk ones. The stability of the

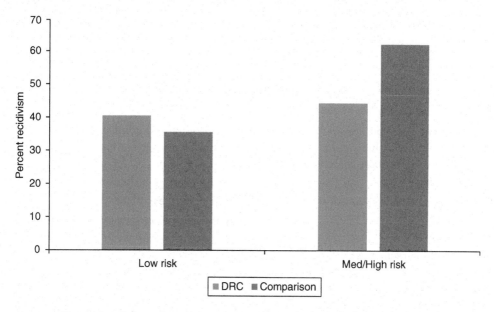

FIGURE 7.3 Illustration of the Risk Principle among day-reporting centers.
Source: Van Voorhis and Groot (2010)

risk effect was seen in a large meta-analysis conducted by Mark Lipsey (2009). The program quality that had the strongest effect on program effectiveness in Lipsey's study was the risk principle. Programs that reserved intensive services and interventions for high-risk individuals had much better outcomes than those that did not consider risk in their case planning.

This has clear implications for case planning. We should triage medium- to high-risk clients into the more intensive case management process that we discuss in this chapter. Many agencies are doing this by administering a set of screening questions to all new admissions. In contrast to the full risk/needs assessments, such as the LSI-R, the LS/CMI, WRNA, COMPAS, or ORAS, screeners seldom contain more than 15 questions. These questions are administered to all clients at intake. The screener identifies low-risk individuals, who then do not receive the full assessment. Only those who score medium risk and high risk on the screener receive the full, dynamic risk/needs assessment. That assessment then will identify the needs that contribute to the high scores. Therefore, the case planning process discussed in this chapter pertains primarily to medium- to high-risk clients. With few exceptions, elaborate case plans do not need to be prepared for low-risk clients.

Why do low-risk people do poorly in our state-of-the-art correctional programs? They do poorly because they do not have the criminogenic needs that medium- and high-risk clients have. If they did, they would not score as low-risk. They are low-risk for a reason because they have fewer criminogenic needs to target and have many prosocial attributes—these might include stable employment, family support, and prosocial friends. If they did not have these, they would not have scored as low-risk. Requiring low-risk individuals to attend a cognitive restructuring program to change attitudes that they do not have only serves to introduce the antisocial thinking styles to them. In addition, when low-risk people attend programs with other correctional clients, they have the potential to form new friendships with antisocial individuals who might model inappropriate attitudes and behaviors.

Then what should be done for low-risk clients? In so far as is possible, given the constraints of the criminal sentence, low-risk individuals should be kept as close to the prosocial influences in their lives as possible.

1. Do not assign policies and conditions that interfere with employment.
2. Do not assign policies or conditions that interfere with family stability.
3. These likely will be individuals with few criminogenic needs, but they might score high on one or two risk/need factors. Depending upon the need, plan for job development, vocational education, educational or substance use services in non-correctional community settings.
4. Those returning from prison should return to prosocial families and neighborhoods as soon as possible. Halfway houses are needed by high-risk returning incarcerated clients, not by low-risk ones.
5. Supervision requirements should be minimal, for example, call-in or kiosk reporting. Keep low-risk clients out of the probation waiting room and group treatment settings.

The risk principle tells us who we are going to primarily work with: medium- and high-risk clients. Once that group has been identified for more intensive case management, we then choose the needs that will be the focus of the case plan. Recall from Chapter 6 that we are going to give priority to needs that are related to future offending. These are also called risk factors or criminogenic needs. Generally, we will not be planning for needs that are not related to future offending, such as cake decorating, attractiveness, or wilderness skills. The needs we will be interested in are those that appear on the assessment. These were discussed in Chapter 6, but are repeated in Box 7.1. We will be following the needs principle. Goals will be developed that are based upon high-scoring risk/need scales.

Box 7.1 Women's Risk/Needs Assessment (WRNA)

RISK FACTORS

- Offending History
- Antisocial Thinking
- Antisocial Associates
- Employment/Financial
- Education
- Housing Safety
- Anger
- Mental Health History
- Current Depression (symptoms)
- Current Psychosis (symptoms)
- History of Substance Use

- Current Substance Use
- Family Conflict
- Relationship Dysfunction
- Victimization as an Adult
- Child Abuse
- Sexual Abuse
- Parental Stress

STRENGTHS

- Self-efficacy
- Parental Involvement
- Educational Assets

Source: Van Voorhis, P., Wright, E., Salisbury, E., & Bauman, A. (2010). Women's risk factors and their contributions to existing risk/needs assessment: The current status of gender responsive assessment. *Criminal Justice and Behavior, 37* (3), 261–288.

If we have properly focused on medium- to high-risk correctional clients, we will notice that each one has multiple needs. Requiring clients to address all of these needs at once will be overwhelming and unrealistic. This also sets them up to fail the conditions of supervision. The need to prioritize the client issues we will work on in the immediate future will require a good deal of counselor expertise. The following might be helpful considerations:

1. Do any of these needs threaten client safety or survival, for example, domestic violence, acute mental health problems, or substance dependence? It goes without saying that these should receive high priority.
2. What does the client believe to be important? Involving the client in this decision has a number of advantages. Most importantly, encouraging clients to take responsibility for the decisions affecting their lives motivates the change process and builds self-efficacy. It also models decision-making, problem-solving, and the importance of taking responsibility for change.
3. Has the court established any requirements?
4. Is the client scoring higher on some domains than others?
5. Some domains are stronger predictors of recidivism than others, for example, antisocial peers, antisocial attitudes, anger, employment/financial (especially with respect to women).
6. What is the proper order of interventions? Mental health issues should be stabilized before or while treatment for substance dependence is undertaken; vocational training may need to precede employment requirements.
7. What services are available at the time the case management plan is developed? If an agency has a GED program, but vocational training is not available until clients are

released to the community, the GED program should take priority. What if there are no program resources? It may be the task of program personnel to build them. Many dedicated program directors have built viable partnerships with outside social services, for example, community colleges, mental health agencies, employment services. Moreover, we have noted many evidence-based curricula throughout the previous chapters.

It is not enough to identify a problematic risk factor for intervention to be followed by goal setting, and then tasks and activities to meet the goal. If clients are unable to engage in those tasks, they will not be able to participate in executing the case plan. Recall that the **responsivity principle** guides case managers and counselors to take into consideration potential barriers to participating. These may involve learning styles, intelligence, motivation, and the demands of everyday life, such as transportation, financial wherewithal, and childcare needs. Ethnicity brings important cultural issues to the treatment group, and many of these can be viewed as strengths. For example, some ethnic groups have a strong sense of community that can be tapped when a member is in need. Women tend to do better in groups that take their relationships into consideration (see Chapter 13; Bloom et al., 2003; Van Dieten, 2008). The case plan should make note of and address problems that can interfere with a client's responsivity to treatment.

The Evolving Case Plan

This would be a good time to say that Figure 7.2 is oversimplified, as case planning for medium- to high-risk clients must be updated on a regular basis. Ideally, clients will begin to change while serving a period of supervision or residential stay. They accomplish some of the initial activities and must move on to next steps. They may complete a class or successfully address a need, for instance getting a job. Similarly, a very difficult problem (e.g., substance dependence or a mental health issue) may stabilize so they can address other goals more successfully. Even though the problem is stabilized, we will need to continue to monitor against relapse. They may be released from our supervision to another agency, such as parole. In such cases, the plan must be updated so that the client can move on to other goals. Opportunities may not be available until the conclusion of supervision.

Unfortunately, not all clients are this successful. Some will commit violations and be sent to prison. Some will be sanctioned to a brief period of time in jail, but will return to our caseload. Others will fail to attend the service we referred them to or will be fired from the job we worked to help them secure. Still others will need to have ongoing involvement with other social service agencies. Substance-dependent and/or some mentally ill clients will have chronic needs. These clients may be receiving services for the remainder of their lives. We may need to get them started on that path.

Thus, in many instances, a client will be seen by the same case manager from the time he or she is admitted to a correctional term until discharge. There are, however, a number of scenarios where the client, particularly very serious or very troubled clients, will be transferred to others. Here the notion of **continuity of care** is crucial. As the term implies, continuity of care involves continuity of service over time, sometimes even after a client's correctional term expires.

When do we need to be concerned about continuity of care? First, whenever we have a client with a chronic problem, such as mental health, intellectual disability, substance dependence, or antisocial sexual urges, we will need to involve other community services in a plan of care. For example, we may need to partner with a community mental health agency for mental health services. We will continue to work with the client as well. However, when the period of correctional supervision ends, the client may continue to need the ongoing assistance of community mental health services. The client may come back to us at a later date, when charged with another offense.

Continuity of care is a very clear issue for reentry programs. Initiatives to fund reentry programs began nearly a decade ago to deal with large numbers of incarcerated people released to their home communities from correctional facilities. The National Institute of Corrections operationalized one such model with its Transition from Prison to Communities Initiative (Parent & Barnett, 2003). The reentry programs assert that reentry planning must begin as soon as a client is admitted to prison, with a dynamic risk/needs assessment that identifies needs and leads to a case plan. Clients and treatment staff should work on goals designed to reduce risk/needs, but likely will not have enough time to achieve all goals. Shortly prior to release, then, a final case plan is prepared and "handed" off to a parole agency. A new case manager then will be able to begin where the prison treatment staff left off, finishing goals that could not be finished in prison and starting new tasks that are better met in community settings.

Continuity of care may also involve more general situations where a needed program is not available at one point in time, but may become available at another time or another facility upon transfer. When governments do a good job of tending to continuity of care, we refer to them as providing a **seamless service delivery** approach. That is, there is no interruption of service when clients leave an agency or status and move to another. One of the best ways to facilitate the seamless approach is to use the same dynamic risk/needs assessment and case planning format regardless of where the client is in the system—specialty courts, probation, parole, or prison. Many states are doing this. The advantage is that all agencies speak the same language.

Another essential tool for addressing continuity of care is a network of outside community providers. If we think of all the risk/need factors listed in Box 7.1, it is difficult to imagine a correctional agency administering to all of them. How, for example, can a probation office serve as a community college? It cannot. It must develop constructive and collaborative working relationships with outside service providers. Indeed, most correctional agencies will need support from outside job development services (U.S. Department of Labor), employers, community mental health, health clinics, community colleges, transitional housing authorities, child welfare agencies, public schools, libraries, neighborhood centers, public transportation, childcare agencies, recreation centers, and welfare/public assistance agencies. More often than not, these partnerships are the work of energetic program directors and staff at the local level. That network is also essential to clients who require wraparound services discussed in approaches for justice-involved women (see Chapter 13) and families receiving Multisystemic Therapy® or family functional therapy (see Chapter 11).

An innovative example of a seamless case management partner system using software and technology comes from the Singapore Prison Service. The illustration in Figure 7.4 demonstrates the ideas behind having a continuum of care and case management for supervisees in the community. One of the obstacles to wraparound services for clients is organizations' abilities to share client data and information among relevant stakeholders, and various information systems that are not compatible. In part, because Singapore is a small island nation with only one jurisdiction, it is far easier to implement such an innovation compared to the United States. However, significant efforts are being made at a national level in the United States to assist criminal justice and behavioral health agencies in local jurisdictions adopt a similar model. See the Online Learning Enhancements for an example from the U.S. Council of State Governments Justice Center.

Supervising and Sanctioning Correctional Clients

Up to this point, we have discussed case planning and case management primarily from a therapeutic and helping standpoint. There is, however, an obvious distinction between correctional clients and clients served by other social service agencies. Correctional clients have broken the law, they likely have hurt others physically or financially, and many will do it again. Thus, correctional case managers and counselors have an obligation to protect communities by supervising clients at a level commensurate to their risk to society. The dynamic risk/needs assessment will provide a risk score. It is essentially the sum of all individual risk/need factors demonstrated by the client. Additionally, the correctional agency will likely have supervision and/or residential guidelines for each level of risk. In community correctional agencies, the structure of supervision and the level of monitoring increase as risk increases. In residential settings, freedom of movement, privileges, and architectural environments become tighter as risk increases.

This structure is relevant to treatment success as well as to safety and security. The structure provides an appropriate level of containment that helps to keep the client from being distracted from treatment goals. Well-designed treatment programs lose a good deal of effectiveness when an appropriate structure is not present.

Related to this is the issue of how we should respond to clients who violate conditions of supervision. This is an important matter for counselors in community corrections. The practice of revoking community-based correctional clients to prison on the basis of technical violations rather than serious offenses is a problematic one. Indeed, a substantial proportion of prison populations consist of individuals revoked from probation or parole (see Wodahl, Ogle, & Heck, 2011). The use of **graduated sanctions** is becoming an accepted response to this problem. Graduated sanctions are:

> structured, incremental responses to non-compliant probationers (or other types of offenders) while they are under supervision. They are designed to give the probation officer the ability to respond quickly to non-compliant acts through a series of actions such as one day in jail, more drug testing, more reporting, or a curfew. The sanctioning process uses modest steps to restrict the offender's liberty to deter future non-compliant acts and to ensure the integrity of the court order.
>
> (Taxman, Soule, & Gelb, 1999)

Graduated sanctions are used extensively in juvenile corrections, and have expanded to specialty courts (drug courts, especially), residential settings, probation, and parole. At their best, graduated sanctions should follow the principles of operant conditioning (see Chapter 8). As such, correctional officials should have a menu of sanctions that increase in severity to fit the magnitude of the violation. As with punishments occurring in the operant conditioning paradigm, the sanctions should occur with certainty, consistency, and proportionality to the violation, and within very close time proximity to the offense (Taxman et al., 1999). Graduated sanctions have contributed to the effectiveness of drug courts (Finigan,

1998; Harrell & Cavanagh, 1998) and work especially well when designed to accompany evidence-based treatment programs.

Merry Morash's book, *Women on Probation and Parole* (2010), illustrates this very poignantly as she describes the difference between the supervision styles of officers in a "gender-responsive county" versus a "traditional county." In the gender-responsive county, officers would sanction women for violations, relapse ("dirty" urine tests), and failure to attend substance use interventions. For example, a woman found to be in relapse could be picked up and required to serve a period of time in jail, away from drugs and drug-using opportunities. Upon release, she would be expected to return to substance use treatment. The treatment requirements may have been modified to reflect the nature of the violation. For example, the woman may return to residential substance use services rather than the non-residential program she violated. Sometimes the cycle from treatment to sanction would repeat itself several times, but in many instances it eventually leads to more stability, improved commitment to therapy, and success. Thus, the sanctions and the containment offered by the sanctions were an important part of the case plan for high-risk, substance-dependent women. The highly skilled group of probation officers also carefully planned the sequence of interventions. For example, goals relative to the stabilization of mental health and substance use were sought before job training and employment.

In addition, the gender-responsive county provided interventions for healthy relationships, trauma, parenting, and other gender-responsive needs. However, substance dependence is a chronic problem from which it is extraordinarily difficult to recover. Recovery often occurs in fits and starts, and this should be acknowledged by a sanctioning process that does not give up on clients at the first sign of difficulty (Marlowe, 2009). Many of the women interviewed indicated that they needed to have their relapses interrupted by the jail time, as they were beginning to slide downhill. Moreover, they noted that the expectations were very clear. They felt that the officers were present, attentive to their needs, and cared about their success. Many relied upon the officers to help them resolve very difficult problems of daily life. In the course of modeling effective decision-making and problem-solving, officers helped clients become more adept at negotiating these problems on their own. The officers were also very encouraging; reinforcing accomplishments was seen as essential. If this approach sounds familiar, it should! The importance of being "firm, fair, and caring" during the behavioral change process was emphasized in Chapter 3.

In the traditional county, relapse often involved a revocation to prison. Monitoring was not very structured or consistent, so clients could be on a downhill slide for quite some time before their condition was detected. Clients reported that they were pretty much on their own without much of a relationship with their officer. Expectations were far from clear to the clients, and when they were finally apprehended, the sanction involved a revocation to prison and sometimes an end to the substance use therapy. They became, in other words, one of the many who account for growing prison populations. People whose probation or parole was revoked comprise a very large proportion of prison intakes (Travis & Lawrence, 2002).

The lessons of the gender-responsive county and the traditional county teach us that the case plan must carefully address needs in the context of risk. Justice-involved clients must know that they are going to be sanctioned fairly for violations. The level of monitoring must increase with risk, and should be noted on the case plan. Clients should be informed of sanctions and have a clear understanding of the expectations.

Finally, it is not all about punishment, or even mostly about punishment. Encouragement and reinforcement should be ever-present as clients start to make even modest improvements. Even at the point of starting a program or showing up to a probation appointment, it is possible to define them as individuals who are working on growth and change. Chapter 4 referred to program/agency quality assessments such as the Correctional Program Assessment Inventory (CPAI) (Gendreau & Andrews, 2001). The CPAI and similar assessments actually score programs on whether staff reinforce clients. The guidelines maintain that reinforcements should outnumber punishers by a factor of four to one.

The Case Management Relationship and Process

Having discussed some of the more technical aspects of case planning, it is important to stress the process of case management because much of this work occurs in meetings that involve a therapeutic relationship with clients. What should these interactions look like? How should counselors and case managers relate to clients as members of this planned change process? High-risk clients pose special challenges here, but they are the individuals who should be receiving the most services. Even so, their assessments will indicate that they have many risk/need factors. Some of these, such as substance use, will be chronic and especially challenging to deal with. High-risk clients also pose a risk to community safety, so they will need to be more intensively monitored.

At the outset, this relationship and process needs to be **collaborative**. There are a number of benefits to involving the clients. First, the case manager should model effective planning and decision-making around life and day-to-day issues. Correctional clients often have very poor skills in decision-making and goal-setting (see Chapter 9). The counselor should be aware that helping a client set goals is not just an exercise in paperwork, but rather a lesson in how this will need to be done for the remainder of the client's life.

Collaboration also strengthens the client's commitment to the goals. Clients who have a role in setting the priorities of their case plan have more investment than they would have in a top-down, authoritative model where they have no voice. Collaboration also affords clients an opportunity to explain constraints and to identify areas of support. We will learn, for example, whether they need transportation or whether a family member can provide childcare. Because the client is present for the formulation of the case plan, expectations will be clearer and our ability to hold the client accountable for violations will be easier.

High-risk clients have many needs that we cannot address all at once. Setting too many goals is a prescription for failure, as clients incur violations when they are not able to do the undoable. Moreover, it is very discouraging to hear a long list of problems and defects during post-assessment meetings. Hearing that one has one defect after another is no way to boost self-efficacy or confidence in one's ability to change. Therefore, a large part of the process involves **setting priorities**. We will have to give attention to problems that pose the greatest risk for future offending. Court requirements may need to be explained and addressed. Practical considerations abound, for example, what programs are available and what are the impediments to success (responsivity issues). We probably can only work on a few risk factors at a time.

Benefits are also to be gained from a **strengths-based approach** that involves both working from existing strengths (e.g., education, employment, parental involvement, family support) as well as building new ones (self-efficacy, decision-making skills). In keeping with emerging research on positive psychology (Seligman, 2002; Sorbello, Eccleston, Ward, & Jones, 2002; van Wormer, 2001), which is finding many advocates among writers of gender-responsive approaches (Blanchette & Brown, 2006; Bloom et al., 2003; Morash, 2010; Van Dieten, 2008), we have to be building client resilience and empowering clients to make changes. A steady diet of discussing one's deficits can be so discouraging that we are more likely to create fear, dependency, avoidance, and anxiety rather than any desire to change.

What about the nature of the therapeutic relationship itself? In his classic book, *The Helping Interview* (originally published in 1969), which has been in print for decades, Alfred Benjamin discusses the importance of trustworthiness, genuine empathy, congruence, respect, honesty, warmth and openness, and boundaries. These are many of the traits discussed in the first three chapters of this book. Some of these concepts are self-evident; some are not. Individuals with **congruence**, for example, present to the world a person who they actually are. They are not putting on airs or pretending to be someone they are not or imitating the feelings of another individual. For the most part, congruent people are more trustworthy than people who are trying to be someone they are not.

Empathy was discussed in Chapters 1 and 3 as an ability to take the perspective of another person, even when we have not experienced some of the discouragements of his or her life. It is not sympathy, which involves identifying with the client by indicating that you have the same thoughts or feelings. Instead, it involves skillful, reflective listening that clarifies and amplifies the person's own experiences without injecting the counselor's feelings. Empathy conveys some level of acceptance, but identifying with or always agreeing with the client will be counterproductive.

Recall that Donald Andrews (1980) explained the value of **warmth and openness** when he compared the effectiveness of warm, approachable probation officers to distant and authoritarian officers. The warm and approachable officers were more likely to impact the behavior of their clients than the distant, unapproachable officers. In fact, the distant officers had little to no influence on the future behaviors of their clients (see the discussion of role models in Chapter 10). This does not mean "making nice" all the time. Counselors and case managers have to maintain good **boundaries** with clients (see Chapter 2). For example, Andrews's warm and open case managers were also firm but fair. They were not overly revealing of their personal lives. A boundary was defined in Chapter 2 as "the invisible line that separates individuals according to their needs, feelings, emotional health, privacy concerns, and other human issues." Counselors must maintain a professional boundary; their relationship with the client is only appropriate to the job responsibilities at hand: supervision and providing resources to the change process. Intimacy, giving the client so much attention that the counselor cannot manage his or her own life or job, or too much caretaking, all step over the line.

On a related note, the *Collaborative Case Work for Women* curriculum (Van Dieten, 2008) underscores the relational needs of system-involved women. Working on the notion that women tend to give high priority to their relationships with others (Bloom et al., 2003; Gilligan, 1982), counseling and case management should recognize the primacy of women's relationships with children, significant others, friends, and families of origin. This concern extends to the counselor as well. The need for the counselor to model a healthy, caring professional relationship with good boundaries is paramount.

As noted in Chapter 3, Motivational Interviewing (Miller & Rollnick, 2002) is another approach that should be incorporated into the case management process. Motivational

Interviewing has been discussed at several points throughout this book. It is being adopted by many correctional agencies as they seek to teach counselors and case managers how to best develop clients' intrinsic motivation to change. We do this by asking open-ended questions, expressing empathy, uncovering clients' ambivalence about whether to change, and identifying discrepancies in the clients' actions and lives. Counselors are taught that arguing with clients only builds resistance. It is far better to roll with resistance, affirm the client as a person, reflect or paraphrase his or her feelings, highlight ambivalence, and reinforce "change talk" and client self-efficacy when it is heard. The attempt is to uncover the client's readiness and motivation to change. This will not happen when we argue, assume the expert role, label, or criticize, shame, or blame.

With the advent of managed care in the medical and mental health profession came the insurance mandate for psychologists to prepare treatment plans on a frequent basis to secure insurance reimbursements for client care. To assist with the paperwork, a series of treatment planners was published by John Wiley and Sons. Three of them might prove useful to correctional counselors and case managers, *The Probation and Parole Treatment Planner* (Bogue, Nandi, & Jongsma, 2003), *The Addiction Treatment Planner* (Perkinson & Jongsma, 2006), and *The Juvenile Justice and Residential Care Treatment Planner* (McInnis, Dennis, Myers, O'Connell Sullivan, & Jongsma, 2002). The planners list goals that correspond with many of the risk/need factors discussed throughout this book. Commensurate with each goal are recommended interventions. The treatment planners will be seen by many as too scripted. If used as the only tool for case planning, they likely would undermine rather than help the therapeutic relationship with clients. If used as a supplemental tool, however, they contain many "at the desk" interventions that may prove useful to some client situations. For example, for a person on probation who has a conviction for domestic violence and a very high anger score on a dynamic/risk needs assessment, the treatment planner recommends a long-term goal of "improving awareness and understanding of anger: How is it triggered and its consequences." A task for this goal was for the client to "attend an anger management class." An activity that the probation officer could use in a probation meeting was to "process principles the client has learned in didactic sessions held in the class; apply these principles to his/her daily life through role playing or modeling" (Bogue, Nandi, & Jongsma, 2003, p. 19). There are many more goals, tasks, and activities in the planner that deal with anger. The treatment planners also may assist case managers' efforts to individually reinforce work conducted in treatment programs.

In the next section of this chapter, we apply many of the suggestions discussed to this point to a case study. This is one of the case studies used in the staff trainings for the Women's Risk/Needs Assessment (WRNA) (Van Voorhis et al., 2010), so the example and the tools are from that approach.

A CASE STUDY

The following is a case study for Melanie Jones. Melanie has just been admitted to a reentry prison unit after serving a portion of her sentence. Scores on the WRNA indicate that she is high risk. Therefore, she will receive intensive supervision and a good deal of case planning. For a workshop on case planning using the following "Melanie" vignette, see the Online Learning Enhancements at the conclusion of this chapter.

Name: Melanie Jones	Age: 25	Race: Caucasian
Charge: Possession of Methamphetamines		
Sentence: Prison 24 months; community supervision 24 months		

Melanie was on misdemeanor probation for a previous possession conviction (marijuana) when she was caught in possession of methamphetamines. She has been convicted twice of possession of other drugs in the past, and each time was sentenced to probation and drug treatment. She has never successfully completed drug treatment. Her first arrest occurred when she was 19.

Melanie acquired a GED as a requirement of her probation and was working part-time at a fast food restaurant prior to her arrest. She had been employed there for three months, but reports that she was getting bored with doing the same activities every day. Prior to this job, Melanie had worked at various part-time positions as a cashier. She rarely stayed at the same job for more than three or four months, and she never wanted to be employed full-time. Melanie says that she gets bored with work and eventually quits or gets fired. She has been fired twice in the past year; both employers found out that she came to work drunk or high. Melanie says that she would not have to get drunk or high before work if it were not so boring.

Melanie does not want a full-time job because working 40 hours a week would cut into the time she spends with her boyfriend, Justin. She and Justin have been dating since she was a sophomore in high school. They have a 2-year-old son together and live together. Justin repairs cars at the local garage part-time. In the meantime, he makes and sells meth. Melanie sometimes helps him cook the drugs, but mostly helps run them. Melanie's parents do not like Justin. They report that Melanie was a great kid. She was on the honor roll and headed to college before she got mixed up with Justin. Despite their disapproval of Justin, they "put up" with him because of Melanie's son, Jake. Her parents take care of Jake now that Melanie is incarcerated. They report that he spent a lot of time with them prior to her incarceration too.

Melanie's parents have threatened to try to take full custody of Jake if Melanie does not go to treatment and stop using drugs. Melanie does not want to lose Jake, but she does not believe that she is addicted to alcohol or other drugs. She has been to treatment twice before, and she did not like it. In each case she left treatment after a couple of weeks. She does not feel that treatment applies to her because she does not use *that* much, and her drug use would not be a problem if it were not illegal. Besides, she does not know who she would hang out with if she did not drink or use drugs. All of her friends live around the neighborhood and use drugs. Two of her friends sometimes help Justin make meth, and their other friends use drugs and are small-time dealers. Melanie does not use meth because "it's hard on your body." However, she and her friends do smoke marijuana, use cocaine, and take pills. But Melanie thinks of these as just minor drugs—she notes that "it's not like she's using crack or heroin."

Melanie is very afraid that if she did not do drugs or if she quit hanging out with her friends, Justin would quit dating her. She reports that she is very happy with Justin, and they get along great. Sometimes when he is stressed out or drinking, Justin has gotten angry with Melanie.

She reports that she deserves it when he hits her because she talks back and is not grateful for everything he provides to her and Jake. Melanie wants to get pregnant again because she believes that this will improve her relationship with Justin.

Since Melanie has been incarcerated, her parents have cared for Jake. They report that they have not seen Justin since he dropped Jake off after Melanie was taken into custody. They encourage Melanie to take treatment seriously and offered to let her live with them when she gets out of prison. They bring Jake to visit her every weekend. Justin has spoken with Melanie on the phone three times since she has been in prison. He has been to visit her once. During that visit he blamed her for being stupid enough to get caught and threatened to kill her if she gave him up to the police. She has not had contact with Justin now in over six months.

Melanie has been incarcerated now for 18 months. She just completed the Women's Risk Needs Assessment as the initial part of her reentry planning. She has six months left to prepare for release and will then serve 24 months under community supervision. She has not been participating in any programming since her incarceration began.

In addition to a risk/needs score, the WRNA produces a case management score sheet, which helps case managers to identify the most serious needs. If a score exceeds the cut-off, threshold score, it is checked as a risk/need factor that is appropriate for intervention. These cut points were set over the course of the WRNA validation studies, which identified a point on the risk-needs scales where scores reached a tipping point and started to correspond to offense-related outcomes over a two-year period. For Melanie, the case management score sheet found that the scores surpassed these cut points on the following domains: antisocial attitudes, employment/financial, housing safety, antisocial friends, anger/hostility, history of mental illness, depression, adult victimization, substance use, relationship dysfunction, and parental stress. Melanie also scored high on the following strengths: parental involvement, family support, and self-efficacy.

Supervision Strategy

As noted in the case study, Melanie has just come in for reentry planning after serving 18 months of a 24-month sentence. In this unit, prison case managers work to develop a case plan for programs and services that will start during the final six months of Melanie's sentence. The case manager occasionally works with a parole officer from Melanie's home community. Given Melanie's high risk, she was placed in one of the higher custody units in prison, but the only service she received was stabilization of her depression. While that was a commendable accomplishment, case managers will note that there are 10 additional needs to work with. There is a good deal of time available for programs in prison, but not enough to address 10 needs. It is unfortunate that Melanie did not work on any other programs during the past 18 months.

Nevertheless, Melanie will be released as a high-risk woman with some very serious needs. Given the high substance use score, Melanie will participate in an intensive residential substance use program while she serves the remainder of her sentence. She does not believe she needs this, so her case manager has a good deal of work to do to remind Melanie that the program was court-mandated and that it would be in Melanie's best interests to attend it. In her discussions with Melanie, the case manager will utilize the techniques of Motivational Interviewing.

Upon release, Melanie will be transferred to a halfway house, where an intensive substance use intervention will continue. She is not likely to be released to independent living until she has completed six months at the halfway house. The prison program, the halfway house, and the parole office have a highly structured plan of graduated sanctions that will be imposed in the event that Melanie violates conditions of her supervision.

Case Planning of Risk/Need Factors

Much of the case planning process at this point will involve the needs principle. As per the case management guidelines discussed in the previous section of this chapter, case managers have involved Melanie in the case planning process. The case managers have been careful to avoid portraying Melanie as a person with many problems and defects, but Melanie is aware that there is a lot to work on and she wants to know about the other problems. The case manager is careful to outline the opportunities that are still available in the prison and those that could become available while Melanie is in the halfway house and later on parole. The case manager works hard to help Melanie understand the need to take "one thing at a time." She also reminds Melanie of her strengths: her involvement with her son and the support from her family of origin. The case manager is also careful to praise Melanie for her concern and interest in working on some additional problems. Melanie has fairly high self-efficacy (a strength) and the case manager wants to maintain Melanie's confidence.

Here is where the case plan (Figure 7.1) comes in. Note that there is one case plan for each need and goal that Melanie will work on. At the top of the plan, there are lines where

CASE PLAN

Case Plan Origin Date: *September 10, 2014*		Client Name: ID#: *Melanie Jones*				
Case Manager(s): *Gail Montoya*		Risk Level *High*				
Risk Factor: *Substance abuse*						
Goal(s): *Eliminating Drug and Alcohol Use*						
Responsivity Factor(s) (Barriers): *Motivation*						
Strengths: *Self-efficacy in many areas of her life*						
Tasks:	Activities:			Start Date:	Goal Date:	Success Date:
1. Attend Residential Drug Therapy	1. Arrange referral and admission			9/15/14	9/17/14	
	2. Motivational interviewing for denial and ongoing support of treatment activities			9/10/14	11/1/14	
2. Submit to random drug tests	1. Oversee random drug tests			9/10/14	3/1/15	

Case Manager Signature: _____   Client Signature: _____

FIGURE 7.4 Case plan.

the case manager will need to indicate the risk factor, the goal, the responsivity factor, and the relevant strength. To define some of the other terms, the **goal** speaks to the long-term and states the desired behavioral change for the need being addressed. **Tasks** identify the short-term, immediate steps to reaching the broader goal. These should be stated in objective and behavioral terms. They have to be measurable. They also should have a time frame to them. Since tasks are relevant to the client's behavior, it goes without saying that they should be achievable and realistic. **Activities** refer to the case manager's actions relative to the task. There should be at least one activity for each task, and there could be several. Activities could pertain to supervision, program referrals, or in-person meetings. Note that each activity and task should have a start date, a planned completion date (goal date) and a success date, and the actual date of completion.

Returning to Melanie, it is already known that she will have to attend the inpatient substance use program, and Melanie understands that this was court-mandated. As such, Figure 7.4 shows the initial case plan for the broader goal of eliminating the use of illicit substances. The case manager has already noted that Melanie has a good deal of self-efficacy, but is in a good deal of denial about her substance use. Therefore, we see motivation marked as a responsivity issue and self-efficacy noted as a strength. There are two tasks noted and three activities. One task is to attend the substance use treatment program at the prison. That is Melanie's responsibility. The case manager, however, has the responsibility of referring Melanie to the class, assuring her eligibility, and securing a space for her. The case manager is also going to utilize Motivational Interviewing for the next several months to support the work of the treatment. In addition, arranging and monitoring urine tests will be the responsibility of the case manager. Start dates and goal dates are also noted.

The broad goal probably will not be attained by the time Melanie is released to a halfway house, so the case plan with be transferred to a community case manager at that point. This could be Melanie's future parole officer, a case manager at the halfway house, or both. But we can foresee additional tasks, such as attending a relapse prevention program and a support group while at the halfway house. Melanie may also be required to attend aftercare once she is released on parole. All of this is to say that the case plan will evolve over time if the case managers do an effective job of tracking the case and attending to continuity of care.

What about Melanie's concerns for other needs? She states that she wants to do a better job of parenting her son. The case manager is aware of the fact that there is a very good parenting skills class at the halfway house, and Melanie expresses some interest in it. The plan is to defer that goal until Melanie is released to the halfway house. In the meantime, however, the case manager is going to incorporate discussions about the effects of Melanie's drug use on the well-being of her son. This is not going to be an argument, but will be integrated into the Motivational Interviewing process that she and Melanie will work on during their meetings. Melanie is fortunate that Jake visits every weekend; she is able to maintain her relationship with him through this ongoing contact.

It might, however, be a very good time to work on issues of healthy relationships. Melanie states that she wants to be safe when she returns home, and she wishes that Justin would be a better partner to her. The reentry unit has a group that works on healthy relationships, and Melanie has time and the desire to attend it. Therefore, the case manager prepares another case plan for a goal pertaining to healthy relationships. This is one of the goals that was initiated by Melanie.

The case manager also sees a good deal of antisocial thinking in Melanie's excuses for not working, her denial of the seriousness of her substance use, and her desire to return to friends who also use drugs. The case manager knows that there is a component of the substance use program that deals with antisocial thinking. She also knows that staff do a good job of correcting antisocial thinking. She develops another case plan for antisocial thinking and knows that she will replicate some of the antisocial thinking interventions at her desk as well. Importantly, the case manager also knows that Melanie will need a lot of praise and reinforcement for every step that she takes.

One of the common mistakes at this point would be to refer Melanie to *any* needs-based program that is available and has space. Of course, we already know that Melanie will be matched to programs on the basis of assessed need, so that is one indication that she will not receive a "one-size fits all" approach to her issues. But the reentry case manager was very astute in recognizing that substance users are not a homogeneous group of clients. Services must be targeted to level of risk, severity of need, and where clients might be located in the change process. Note, for example, that it will be some time before Melanie receives a relapse prevention program.

Another tool for assisting programmatic efforts to match clients to programs is a Decision Matrix (see Table 7.1). These must be prepared at a local level because they categorize programs available in the agency and from outside partners. The matrix arrays these options by need, the severity of the need, and the risk level of the client. Preparation of the matrix also requires that agency staff secure a thorough understanding of the programs and services with which they work. The matrix and their knowledge of these programs greatly contributes to assuring that clients are properly matched to services.

TABLE 7.1 Sample decision matrix

	Substance Use			Employment			Education			Parental Stress			Peer			Etc.
	L	M	H	L	M	H	L	M	H	L	M	H	L	M	H	
Service																
ALMA	*			*			*	*		*	*					
Next Step				*	*	*	*	*	*					*		
Project Hope		*	*	*						*	*			*		
Sun Valley		*			*											
Turning Key										*	*		*	*		
Supervision																
Curfew		*	*		*		*	*						*	*	
UA	*	*	*											*	*	
EMU		*	*	*	*		*	*						*	*	
Collateral Contact	*	*	*	*	*		*	*		*	*		*	*		

CONCLUSION

Unfortunately, our collaborations with various correctional agencies show us that the skills of good case management are not as evident as we would wish. Too often we see clients who never get beyond the assessment stage to a case plan. Additionally, it is not uncommon for case managers to develop one plan that is never updated and does not evolve over time. The case, in other words, is not tracked over time. Problems also occur when low-risk clients are not triaged out of intensive case planning. A review of case plans may also show us that low-risk clients are being referred to programs attended by many high-risk clients, who then model criminogenic habits and attitudes to the low-risk clients. Finally, case managers who stay mired in an authoritarian approach to clients will not be heard by high-risk/high-need clients.

In closing, much of what has been discussed throughout this book comes together in an applied sense in client case planning. It is a fortunate correctional client who has a case manager who is well versed in behavioral therapy, social learning, and cognitive behavioral approaches, as well as the state-of-the-art practices for addressing women clients, substance use and dependence, sex offending, and antisocial personalities. Case managers who effectively track and plan for medium- and high-risk clients, introduce them to life-changing interventions, and form effective therapeutic relationships change many lives (Lipsey, 2009).

Discussion Questions

1. What is meant by assessment-based case planning? Why should case plans be assessment-based?
2. Differentiate between goals, tasks, and activities.
3. What does it mean to provide strength-based counseling? Why is it important?
4. What is the risk effect? If the risk effect is occurring, will a program evaluation show that the program as a whole reduced recidivism over time?
5. Which of the Principles of Effective Intervention receives the most attention as we develop case management plans? Why is this the case?
6. What is the value of using the same risk/needs assessments throughout a jurisdiction— using the same assessments for prisons, community-based facilities, probation, and parole?
7. Which of the examples of risk/need factors are most likely to need careful planning to assure continuity of care?
8. Why is it important to encourage clients to collaborate with case managers in the development of a case plan?
9. Discuss the importance of case plans being created collaboratively with the client rather than simply telling the client the steps he/she should take toward the goal.

ONLINE LEARNING ENHANCEMENTS

Utah Criminal Justice Center Workshop Series: Case Planning to Target Criminogenic Needs
This online workshop series hosted by the Utah Criminal Justice Center features one of the co-authors of this textbook (Emily J. Salisbury) and includes three video workshops

(30 minutes each) discussing and modeling the process of case planning for targeting criminogenic needs. Vignettes are embedded in the videos reflecting two mock-client stories from which to create case plans. Issues of responsivity, strength, tasks, and activities are modeled to create case plans.

Webinar 1: "Introduction to Case Planning"
www.youtube.com/watch?v=_p49td0Z8rU&t=849s

Webinar 2: "Applying Case Planning: Part I"
www.youtube.com/watch?v=6XCf4StswpQ&t=9s

Webinar 3: "Applying Case Planning: Part II"
www.youtube.com/watch?v=ajfJqxSgoAU&t=245s

The Council of State Governments Justice Center: Collaborative Comprehensive Case Plan
This website provides excellent information on building collaborative and comprehensive case plans across systems, with useful elements to consider along the way, including interagency information sharing, staff training, and others. https://csgjusticecenter.org/publications/collaborative-comprehensive-case-plans/

GLOSSARY OF KEY TERMS

activities the case manager's actions relative to tasks assigned to clients; activities could pertain to supervision, program referrals, or in-person meetings

assessment-based when case managers use assessments rather than judgment calls to determine whether a client should be referred to a specific intervention

case plan a collaborative plan between the correctional client and case manager that sets forward the goals, expectations, and directions of the correctional term; case plans will direct the client and list the case manager's responsibilities, providing a clear structure and focus to clients and treatment personnel

congruence a state in which an individual presents to the world a person who they actually are

continuity of care the continuity of service or treatment for correctional clients over time, sometimes even after a client's correctional term expires

empathy an ability to take the perspective of another person, even when one has not experienced some of the discouragements of his or her life

goal the long-term desired results and behavioral change for the need being addressed in a client's case plan

graduated sanctions structured, incremental responses to noncompliant correctional clients while they are under supervision

interpersonal boundaries limits or guidelines that people create to identify safe, reasonable, and permissible ways for other people to behave toward them

needs principle a correctional counseling principle that maintains that needs related to future offending should receive high priority as clients are matched to programs

Principles of Effective Intervention a set of evidence-based guidelines underlying the appropriate treatment of correctional clients; includes the core principles of risk, need, and responsivity among others

responsivity principle a correctional counseling principle that maintains that programs should accommodate client characteristics and situations that are likely to become barriers to success in a given correctional program

risk effect a phenomenon in which recidivism increases in low-risk clients who receive intensive correctional interventions intended for high-risk clients

risk principle a correctional counseling principle that maintains that clients should be provided with treatment and supervision levels that align with their level of risk; intensive treatment efforts should be directed toward high- and medium-risk clients, while low-risk clients should not be assigned to institutional placements or intensive treatment interventions that expose them to criminogenic influences

screen to evaluate a correctional client in order to assess their individual criminogenic needs

seamless service delivery a process in which correctional agencies tend to continuity of care with no interruption of service when clients leave an agency or status and move to another

strengths-based approach a strategy in which therapists and case managers focus on clients' positive attributes and existing strengths as well as building new ones

tasks short-term, immediate steps assigned to correctional clients to help them reach their broader goals

therapeutic relationship the close and consistent working relationship between correctional clients and therapists; a good and effective therapeutic relationship entails trustworthiness, genuine empathy, congruence, respect, honesty, warmth and openness, and boundaries

warmth and openness an ideal quality in which therapists are approachable and genuine with their clients

NOTE

1 The terms counselor and case manager are used interchangeably throughout this chapter.

PART III

Contemporary Approaches for Correctional Counseling and Treatment

The four counseling and treatment approaches presented in this section form a core set of modalities that are known to reduce recidivism if they are delivered correctly. They largely reflect the principle of general responsivity.

Chapter 8 presents the behavioral approaches of classical and operant conditioning. While classical conditioning is not widely used in corrections, except occasionally for special populations (e.g., sex offenders), operant conditioning, in the form of token economies, is pervasive, especially in correctional settings for youth. And, of course, later key components of social learning and cognitive behavioral approaches grew out of the earliest behavioral models—classical and operant conditioning. The key concepts (techniques of effective reinforcement and appropriate punishment and disapproval) are so effective that many agencies are now training all correctional staff to use them.

The cognitive therapies focus on "thinking processes" (Chapter 9). These strategies target dysfunctional perceptions, attitudes, and beliefs that, in turn, support and encourage dysfunctional behavior. In correctional settings, cognitive restructuring programs seek to change "thinking errors" that support antisocial behavior. Another approach works on cognitive skills, maintaining that justice-involved juveniles and adults often demonstrate deficient thinking skills that can be improved in treatment settings.

Social learning models (observational learning approaches) are discussed in Chapter 10. It focuses on the fact that in addition to cognitions, rewards, and punishers, people also frequently learn simply by watching others. The chapter maintains that observational learning is the most common form of human learning. Learning from this perspective, however, is most likely when careful attention is given to providing: (a) role models with good relationship skills; (b) opportunities to practice newly learned skills and behaviors; (c) specific performance feedback; and (d) client reinforcement for learning the new behaviors. Social learning theory provides the theoretical foundation for popular skills development programs and anger management programs.

DOI: 10.4324/9780367808266-10

Finally, family therapy models look to the family system as a vehicle for reforming people. Chapter 11 focuses on family treatment programs, which may be the most appropriate response to clients who come from dysfunctional family systems. Chapter 11 introduces the notion of systems theory and discusses how it works in both the development of family problems and in the therapies that work to address these problems. Systems therapy, as exemplified by the Structural, Communication, Strategic, and Conjoint Family Therapy approaches, operates from a noticeably different paradigm than the more linear approaches discussed in previous chapters. A frequently used family therapy model for correctional clients is Multisystemic Therapy® (MST). MST borrows from the earlier models of family therapy, but also provides wraparound services to clients and their families. Chapter 11 also devotes considerable attention to parenting skills classes, such as those offered by the Oregon Social Learning Center, where parents are taught the key strategies of radical behavioral and social learning approaches.

CHAPTER 8

Behavioral Interventions

Bobbie Ticknor

KEY TERMS

aversion therapy	law of effect principle
behavioral approaches	negative reinforcement
behaviorism	operant conditioning
classical conditioning	positive reinforcement
conditioned response	punishment
conditioned stimulus	relapse prevention
contingency contract	stimulus control
covert sensitization	token economy
exposure therapy	unconditioned response
extinction	unconditioned stimulus

Addressing problematic behavior is a main concern in correctional counseling. Covert behaviors are private actions not observed by others. This includes emotions, physiological responses, and cognitions. Overt behaviors are the actions that other people directly observe. Other terms used to describe these concepts include internal and external behavior. Cognitive theory (discussed in Chapter 9) is concerned with the internal cognitions that produce external behavior while behavior theory primarily focuses on the observable actions of the individual.

Behavior therapies are also markedly different from traditional psychoanalytical approaches. Behavior interventions, also referred to as behavior therapy or behavior modification, tend to focus in the moment when a behavior is exhibited whereas psychoanalytical models aim to treat the pathology of the problematic behavior. The behavior therapist focuses on identifying the conditions that impact the client's actions rather than the causes of the behavior. The client-therapist relationship is a collaboration where clients become active participants in their treatment. The therapist will offer several treatment options to clients who will then decide what will most meet their needs based on their own experiences and preference. The therapist also assists clients in learning various techniques for change. Behavior therapy is not a single technique, but a series of different approaches to target specific behaviors. There are many approaches the therapist can use for the discontinuation of problematic behaviors. Common techniques in correctional rehabilitation include modeling

DOI: 10.4324/9780367808266-11

and role-play, using targeted reinforcement and punishment, desensitization exercises, and learning how to problem solve.

Behavior models were developed using many of the concepts explored in early learning theories. According to these perspectives, all behavior is learned, including antisocial behavior. The roots of modern behavior therapy were derived from experimental work conducted in the early twentieth century by scientists such as Ivan Pavlov, John B. Watson, Mary Cover Jones, and Edward Thorndike. These early pioneers studied animals in laboratory experiments in efforts to further understand learning and what techniques could be used to change behavior. It was theorized human and animals learned in similar ways. Behavioral approaches emphasize the scientific study of observing the interaction between behavior and environmental stimuli. These theories focus on how humans are conditioned to respond to different events and assume all human behavior (including criminal behavior) is learned and can be unlearned. While some approaches to psychology focus on cognitions, behavioral approaches generally disregard this information and focus on observing and measuring behavior with the goal to ultimately predict and control actions. Contemporary behavior therapy was derived primarily from the work on classical and operant conditioning.

CLASSICAL CONDITIONING

Classical, also known as Pavlovian or respondent, conditioning was discovered by Ivan Petrovich Pavlov. After his graduate studies, Pavlov was invited to direct the Department of Physiology at the Institute of Experimental Medicine in 1890. He conducted the bulk of his research on the physiology of digestion and went on to win the 1904 Nobel Prize in Physiology or Medicine for his work in this area (Clark, 2004). One of his best-known experiments, and the discovery that ultimately led to the formation of classical conditioning, focused on digestion in dogs.

During the late nineteenth century, Pavlov was researching salivation in dogs while they were being fed as part of his work on conditioned reflexes. He originally predicted the dogs would salivate in response to receiving food because it is a reflexive process and is not consciously controlled. Pavlov discovered the dogs would begin salivating in the absence of the stimuli of being presented food and concluded their response was not a purely physiological process as he predicted. He theorized the dogs were demonstrating a learned response that was produced by seeing the lab assistants who would typically bring the food. He refocused his research in efforts to learn more about how these responses were learned. This ultimately led to the formation of classical conditioning.

At its core, classical conditioning involves automatic or reflexive responses to a stimulus. A neutral stimulus (NS) does not trigger a response. An unconditioned stimulus (UCS) does elicit a response that is consistent and natural. This is referred to as an unconditioned response (UR). You may have experienced this when you have smelled one of your favorite foods and became hungry. A NS can be presented with an UCS to become what is referred to as a conditioned stimulus (CS). A conditioned response (CR) is produced when the participant reacts the same to the CS and UCS. For example, Pavlov's dogs originally only salivated (UCR) when they were given the food (UCS) until he began to ring a bell (CS) just before feeding them. The dogs began to associate the ringing bell with food and would salivate

(CR) when they heard it even if they were not being presented with food. Pavlov (1927) was able to invoke a reflexive response to a stimulus that was previously neutral. This is known as acquisition and is a learned behavior. Classical conditioning serves as the foundation for various types of treatment modalities. Some of these, such as aversion and exposure therapy, are still used in correctional counseling today.

Aversion Therapy

A common form of therapy derived from the basic principles of classic conditioning is aversion therapy. The goal of this therapy is to reduce maladaptive behavior by associating it with an undesired stimulus. An aversive stimulus, or something that is considered unpleasant, is introduced when the problem behavior is presented and is terminated when the behavior stops. As a result, the client begins to associate the problematic behavior with the disagreeable stimulus until the behavior itself becomes aversive. This type of therapy has been predominantly used in correctional counseling for substance abuse treatment or for those who commit sexual offenses.

Aversion therapy can be used as a technique for reconditioning deviant sexual arousal. This represents a stable dynamic risk factor often associated with sexual recidivism (see Chapter 14; Hanson & Harris, 2000; Hanson & Morton-Bourgon, 2004; Mann, Hanson, & Thornton, 2010). Specific techniques used during treatment with this population include olfactory aversion, masturbatory reconditioning, and verbal satiation (Gray, 1995; Laws, 2001; Marshall, Marshall, Serran, & Fernandez, 2006). Although some of these strategies have been criticized and new approaches, such as cognitive behavioral therapy and the Good Lives Model, have been proposed for this population as more effective solutions, these techniques are still used today (Sandhu & Rose, 2012).

Aversion therapy has also been explored for substance abuse treatment. Taste aversion is a common method used for clients with alcohol use disorder and is associated with a significant reduction in heavy post-treatment drinking (Frawley, Howard, & Elkins, 2017; Howard, 2001). Chemical and covert sensitization has been associated with reductions in cravings for cocaine (Bordnick, Elkins, Orr, Walters, & Thyer, 2004). While aversion therapy can be an effective tool for some patients and substances, the research is mixed on its consistent efficacy for all patients and other substances such as opioids and nicotine (Pacini, Maremmani, & Maremmani, 2020).

Exposure Therapy

Exposure therapy, also developed on the principles of classical conditioning, is used to treat anxiety. This includes generalized anxiety disorder (GAD), phobias, post-traumatic stress disorder (PTSD), panic disorder, and agoraphobia. During therapy, the client confronts underlying intense or maladaptive responses to a specific event. Responses are typically characterized by uneasiness and physiological reactions when the client thinks about the event. Exposure therapy can also be used to treat negative emotions such as anger. Clients use imaginal therapy to expose themselves to the anxiety-inducing stimulus. They may also use interoceptive exposure where the primary focus of therapy is on the bodily symptoms experienced during anxiety. Patients are exposed to the source of their anxiety until they have been desensitized. Exposure can be brief, lasting a few seconds or minutes, or prolonged, from 15 minutes up to an hour. The goal of exposure therapy is to recondition the response so the individual can engage in the activities they have been avoiding.

Anxiety disorders are extremely common in the general population, but they are also diagnosed at high rates for both justice-involved adults and juveniles. Roughly 14% to 20% of incarcerated people in the U.S. federal system and 22% to 30% of people in U.S. state prisons have symptoms of an anxiety disorder (National Commission on Correctional Health Care, 2002). Approximately, 90% of those who are in long-term solitary confinement also suffer from anxiety (Haney, 2003). Nearly a third of adult incarcerated women meet the DSM-5 criteria for an anxiety disorder (Morgan, Fisher, Duan, Mandracchia & Murray, 2010; Pimlott, Beeble, & Bybee, 2009). Other research suggests one-third of female and one in five male juveniles in custody also suffer from the disorder (Abram, Teplin, McClelland, & Dulcan, 2003; Teplin et al., 2006). Research has found those who suffer from high anxiety have trouble adjusting to the prison environment and do not respond well to programming. Without treatment, these individuals have behavior problems while incarcerated and higher recidivism rates once released back into the community (Listwan-Johnson, Gentry Sperber, Murphy Spruance, & Van Voorhis, 2004).

Aversion and exposure therapy are two common treatment modalities developed from the core principles of classical conditioning. They focus on how the interaction between the person and the environment can be manipulated to bring about behavior change. Classical conditioning paved the way for approaches such as behaviorism. This work was conducted by psychologist John B. Watson several decades later, offering the next step in the evolution of contemporary behavior therapy.

Behaviorism

Inspired by the work of Ivan Pavlov, John B. Watson was an American experimental psychologist who studied biology, physiology, and the behavior of animals. He joined the private research university Johns Hopkins University in Maryland in 1908 where he merged this research to include the behaviors of children. Classical behaviorism was popularized in 1913 after a series of lectures given by Watson at Columbia University that were later published in *Psychological Review*, a scientific journal that publishes articles on theory (Kreshel, 1990).

Behaviorism is a learning theory that assumes all behavior is acquired through conditioning. As with classical conditioning, this process occurs through interaction with the environment. Additionally, behaviorists believe behavior should be studied in a systematic and observable manner. Watson also argued the entire field of psychology needed to rethink its approach to introspective studies on behavior that were not directly observable. In his landmark paper, *Psychology from the Standpoint of a Behaviorist*, Watson (1913) argued psychology should "never use the terms consciousness, mental states, mind, content, introspectively verifiable, imagery and the like" (p. 116). He went on to argue any behavior can be modified with proper conditioning techniques regardless of individual traits or cognitions.

Behaviorism remained relevant for several decades and greatly impacted the field of psychology. Interestingly, Watson eventually left his academic job and joined corporate America. He was asked to resign from Johns Hopkins in 1920 after having an affair with a research associate. He later joined J. Walter Thompson, a large advertising agency in the United

States, and was vice president of the company by 1924. Here, he used his background to apply psychological theories to advertising practices (Kreshel, 1990). Watson continued his work in psychology, human behavior, and advertising until he retired in 1947. His original propositions have been largely credited with establishing psychology as a scientific discipline and the foundation of modern behavior therapy. It was not until work on operant conditioning by Edward L. Thorndike, at the turn of the twentieth century, and B.F. Skinner, in the 1930s, that the science was reshaped once again.

OPERANT CONDITIONING

Operant conditioning, also referred to as instrumental conditioning, is a theory that uses rewards and punishment to manage behavior. The theory was coined by American psychologist Burrhus Frederic Skinner, commonly known as B.F. Skinner, in 1937. While Skinner is known as the father of operant conditioning, his work was based on Thorndike's (1898) law of effect. This principle suggested behaviors that result in a satisfying outcome are more likely to become established patterns whereas those that produce negative or discomforting effects will become less likely to occur. This seemingly simple concept led to the development of both operant conditioning and the aforementioned school of behaviorism.

Like Thorndike, Skinner also studied learning in animals. He used the *Skinner Box*, also known as an operant conditioning chamber, to experiment on rats and various other animals. The purpose of the box was to analyze animal behavior by observing when a task was performed, pairing the task with a reward, and measuring how long it would take for the animal to learn the desired behavior. Each box contained a lever the rat could operate to obtain food or water. The goal was to teach the rat to press the lever to get the reward. The rats inadvertently pushed the lever at the beginning but ultimately learned doing so would result in getting the food or water. Once the behavior was learned, the rats would then repeat the desired behavior, pressing the lever independently. From this research, Skinner recognized the influence of effects, or consequences. He argued behavior is learned through the manipulation of the environment and the impact of positive or negative consequences resulting from one's actions. As such, operant conditioning focuses on the use of reinforcements and punishments as tools for learning and behavior change. It is primarily focused on how the consequences of behavior affect learning, rather than how prior conditions affect learning, as in classical conditioning.

Reinforcement

Nevertheless, even Pavlov recognized the importance of reinforcement for sustained learning in classical conditioning studies. The term reinforcement was first used in 1903 by Pavlov to describe the need to use reinforcers when US and CS are presented together. Without periodic reinforcement, the CS will decay and the CR will undergo extinction. The concept of reinforcement was expanded upon in operant conditioning. At its core, a reinforcer is something that can be used to increase a targeted behavior. If the behavior does not increase, it is not, by definition, reinforced. Reinforcers might include things like verbal praise, tangible items, valued activities, and many others. There is no limitation to what a reinforcer can be as long as it is desirable and obtainable.

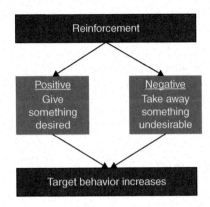

FIGURE 8.1 Types of reinforcement.

Reinforcers can be characterized as either positive or negative. **Positive reinforcement** occurs when the subject is given something perceived as valuable or pleasurable when they perform the desired action. **Negative reinforcement** removes an aversive stimulus, or something that is uncomfortable or unpleasant. There are several recommended principles for effectively using reinforcement:

1. Reinforcers should be contingent on the client's performing the target behavior.
2. The reinforcement should be administered immediately after performing the target behavior.
3. Reinforcers should be administered consistently.
4. The client should be made aware that the reinforcer is a consequence of the target behavior.
5. Continuous reinforcement should be used initially, followed by intermittent reinforcement.
6. Natural reinforcers should be used in therapy.
7. Reinforcers should be kept potent (Spiegler & Guevremont, 2010, p. 137).

As shown by these guiding principles, how reinforcement is used is extremely important. This is of particular relevance for criminal justice agencies. The desired target behavior must be clearly communicated to clients, and reinforcers should be presented immediately following the demonstration of that behavior. The reinforcers used must be individualized for each client, be something they consider valuable, and be consistently and fairly given across all treatment staff. However, they should be given more intermittently as behavior becomes learned—otherwise clients can become desensitized to the reinforcers (they lose their potency, or value). The agency itself must have a culture willing to support programs designed using the principles outlined in operant learning theory. Many programs adopt a contingency management (CM) model to address the needs of clients and put these principles into practice.

CM is a type of behavioral therapy where reinforcements are given when positive behavior is demonstrated. CM has its roots on Norfolk Island in the South Pacific in the mid-1800s (Gendreau & Listwan, 2018). This type of program has been commonly used in correctional rehabilitation to manage behavior in juvenile facilities and for substance abusers. There are some basic practices required to increase the success of CM programs (Alessi, 2013). First, an objectively verifiable target behavior must be identified. Second, the target behavior must

Institutional reinforcers

- ☐ Verbal praise/Feedback
- ☐ Indirect praise
- ☐ Food/Snacks
- ☐ Additional free time
- ☐ Lunch with staff member
- ☐ Field trip
- ☐ Extra visit/Telephone call

- ☐ Extended recreation time
- ☐ Items from commissary
- ☐ Badges, ribbons, certificates
- ☐ Prized job assignments
- ☐ Weekend passes
- ☐ Extra shower time
- ☐ Television/Radio privileges

Community reinforcers

- ☐ Verbal praise/Feedback
- ☐ Indirect praise
- ☐ Bus tokens
- ☐ Gift certificates
- ☐ Extended curfew
- ☐ Less frequent meetings with staff

- ☐ Badges, ribbons, certificates
- ☐ Gym pass
- ☐ Stationery for resume
- ☐ Letter of recommendation
- ☐ Partial payment of rent or utilities
- ☐ Tuition reimbursement

FIGURE 8.2 Examples of reinforcers in corrections.

be observed frequently to ensure proper reinforcement is provided. Third, the reinforcer must be given immediately following the targeted behavior. Finally, reinforcers are withheld if the target behavior is not performed. An example applying these principles is the positive behavior interventions and supports (PBIS) framework.

The PBIS Framework

The PBIS is a tiered-system used in several criminal justice agencies, mostly juvenile justice facilities, across the United States. Each agency designs their program based on specific behavioral expectations with their clients. The treatment staff use reinforcement and real-time behavioral data to make purposeful decisions for additional treatment options and changes to the program (Jolivette & Nelson, 2010). There are three tiers in the program. Tier I, referred to as the Universal Tier, is the starting point for all youth who enter the residential facility. The behavioral expectations are explained to the client along with the daily programming expectations and the specific reinforcers that will be used. The Targeted Tier (Tier II) focuses only on those youth who are at-risk for problematic behaviors. Staff use a variety of techniques, such as verbal de-escalation, additional reinforcement, and additional programming, to correct the maladaptive behaviors. The final tier, Intensive Tier III, is for a small set of youth who display severe problem behaviors. The goal for treatment staff is to assist these youth with reducing harm to self and others. Facilities who have implemented the PBIS framework have reported increased engagement and motivation, treatment staff-client relationship satisfaction, staff self-efficacy, and a decrease in misconduct and problematic behaviors at the facility (Alonzo-Vaughn, Bradley, & Cassavaugh, 2015; Fernandez, McClain, Brown Williams, & Ellison, 2015; Kimball, Jolivette, & Sprague, 2017; Jolivette, Swoszowski, McDaniel, & Duchaine, 2016).

In February of 2013, the Georgia Department of Juvenile Justice (DJJ) launched their PBIS program. The DJJ piloted the program at eight long-term secure youth development campuses (YDCs) and 19 short-term regional youth development centers (RYDCs). These agencies served approximately 1,400 youth daily. They used several data-based tools inherent in the PBIS framework. The *Dashboard* provided various graphs to capture all the details when behavioral incidents were occurring. Using this data, the team actively made changes to the program including supervision patterns, retraining staff when needed, reiterating behavior expectations with the youth, and increasing the use of reinforcements when clients were engaging in the targeted behaviors. The *Radar Report* helped staff to identify, intervene, and monitor youth who were high-risk for engaging in negative behavior or were not responding to the plan expectations outlined in Tier I. Those involved in the project reported more efficient and effective daily, weekly, and monthly meetings; a decrease in problematic behavior across the facilities; and increased staff job satisfaction (Fernandez et al., 2015).

The Arizona Department of Juvenile Corrections also employed a Behavioral Intervention Team using the PBIS framework. Alonzo-Vaughn and colleagues (2015) focused on Tier II youth to evaluate the impact of the framework on reducing violence at a juvenile residential facility. The program focused on education, staff support, mindfulness, honesty, and overall behavior modification. Reinforcements, referred to as Mane Catch Tickets, were given to clients who demonstrated targeted behaviors. They found many youths responded positively to the reinforcements provided during the program. There were significant reductions in violence throughout the facility and increased effectiveness of the treatment program.

Programs that use the principles outlined in operant conditioning and contingency management are built on collaboration, communication, and involvement. They tend to be proactive and preventative. This involves having well-trained staff who can apply the requirements of the program, including the appropriate and consistent distribution of reinforcers. The agency itself must have a commitment to the strategy and provide ongoing training for treatment staff as needed. This can be challenging for many agencies. There may be political or motivational factors that can hinder the development of these programs. Additionally, it cannot be assumed all treatment staff are qualified based simply on the formal education they may have received (Gendreau & Listwan, 2018). These programs require careful planning, proper piloting trials, and good stakeholder relationships. CM programs can be effective at rehabilitation but are not without their difficulties to implement (Gendreau, Listwan, Kuhns, & Exum, 2014). Program quality and treatment fidelity matter (Lowenkamp et al., 2006). A breakdown in any of these areas can decrease the overall effectiveness of the program and fail to produce a meaningful change in problematic behaviors.

Punishment

The second tool used by treatment staff can involve the use of punishments, or punishers. Punishment can be defined as "any consequence of a specific behavior that reduces the likelihood that the behavior will be repeated, or repeated at the same rate, in the future" (Marlowe & Kirby, 1999, p. 4). The target behavior, in this sense, becomes the problematic behavior. To be effective, punishment should be applied consistently, immediately, and at the proper intensity (Hineline & Rosales Ruiz, 2013). Additionally, the effective use of punishment also requires treatment staff to be aware of and monitor unwanted side effects such as negative emotional reactions, avoidance behaviors, or retaliatory behavior (Spiegler & Guevremont, 2010).

Punishment can also be positive or negative. Positive punishment is the presentation of something that is undesirable when the client performs an action that is not aligned with the

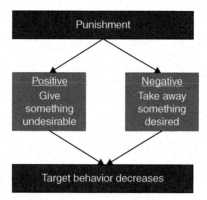

FIGURE 8.3 Types of punishment.

target behavior. In other words, an aversive stimulus is presented to discourage the problem behavior. This might include verbal scolding or implementing new rules or restrictions on the individual. Negative punishment removes a favorable stimulus. Here, the negative punishment reduces the problem behavior by removing something that is pleasant to the client. In corrections, this might include removing visits to the commissary or extra privileges previously earned. It is important to note that removing services or treatment should not be used as a punisher. Furthermore, threatening or adding additional treatment programming as a punishment is also not an effective use of this tool and can negatively impact behavior change and motivation.

As with reinforcers, there are guiding principles to the effective use of punishment.

1. The punisher should occur immediately after the target behavior is performed.
2. The punisher should be administered every time the target behavior occurs.
3. The client should be aware of the contingency between the target behavior and the punisher.
4. Reinforcement should not closely follow the delivery of the punisher.
5. The punisher should be proceeded by a warning cue (Spiegler & Guevremont, 2010, p. 167).

As shown above, using punishment in correctional settings must also be done with intention. Again, the client should be clearly made aware of the behaviors that would result in punishment. The administration of the punishment should be consistent and immediate. Treatment staff must also be trained on how to deliver effective punishment focusing on the goal to change behavior and not for the purposes to cause mental or physical pain (Gendreau & Smith, 2012). One notable recent attempt at using punishers in treatment is the Honest Opportunity Probation with Enforcement (HOPE) Program out of Hawai'i.

The HOPE Model

The HOPE model, also known as a "swift, certain, and fair" (SCF) program, was developed in 2004 in the state of Hawai'i. Treatment staff use graduated sanctions, or punishers, to deter probationers from violating supervision conditions. This involved close monitoring, frequent drug testing, and the use of punishers for violations to program rules. Generally speaking, other treatment and services were not predominately used or only available to those who were identified most at-risk and in need. The original findings of the effectiveness of the HOPE model boasted significant reductions in drug use, arrests, and revocations (Hawken & Kleiman, 2009). This led to the program being widely praised as an evidence-based practice to reduce probation violations, substance use, new arrests, and revocations to prison. A later six-year follow-up study reported less dramatic effects than the original study found, however (Hawken et al., 2016).

Additional programs were established to test the HOPE model in other regions of the United States. Lattimore and colleagues (2016) studied over 1,500 probationers across four sites in Saline County, Arkansas; Essex County Massachusetts; Clackamas County, Oregon; and Tarrant County, Texas, in 2012. These researchers found participants in the HOPE model did not have significant reductions in arrests. The HOPE participants did have fewer arrests for property offenses (15% vs. 20%) and drug charges (12% vs. 15%), but these were not significant findings. Humphries and Kilmer (2020) noted some issues in the design of the multisite study. First, they argued only one site actually implemented HOPE as designed from the original study. They also noted that Lattimore and colleagues did not talk about other important outcomes that were found at several sites. Specifically, there were fewer positive drug tests for the HOPE participants, but this was not highlighted in their 2016 report.

Programs such as HOPE generally talk in terms of behavior change but are often modeled on deterrence theory. This has historically been the guiding principle for the use of punishment in corrections and largely ignores the wealth of literature on classical and operant conditioning. There is a clear line of research to suggest punishers are an effective tool in dealing with problematic behavior (see Hineline & Rosales-Ruiz, 2013). That said, the use of punishers should be carefully considered and employed in conjunction with reinforcers. Reinforcers should far outnumber punishers by a factor of four to one (Gendreau et al., 2014). Previous research has clearly demonstrated correctional programs should combine both reinforcement for prosocial behaviors and strategies to decrease antisocial behaviors, as well as teaching new skills and behaviors (addressed in greater detail in Chapters 9 and 10). These interventions are considerably more effective than programs that rely on punishment alone (Gendreau, 1996a; Marlowe & Kirby, 1999; Wodahl et al., 2011). There are a number of additional techniques that are often combined with the use of reinforcers and punishers with varying effects on changing behavior.

ADDITIONAL TECHNIQUES

In addition to the techniques mentioned in the programs above, there are other tools used in contemporary behavioral models that can impact the use of reinforcement and punishment. Contingency contracts define target behaviors, possible reinforcers, and set expectations. Token economies use tokens and backup reinforcers to reinforce behavior. Point systems use a similar model. Level systems manage behavior by clients progressing through different levels that traditionally open additional privileges. Skill training focuses on social and life skills needed to function better in society. Each technique employs a variety of reinforcers and punishers that can be offered in both the community and institutional setting.

Contingency Contracts

Contingency contracts, or behavior contracting, outline specific behavioral expectations for the client and the process for administrating reinforcements. The goal of the contract is to be a motivating tool for behavior change. The contingency contract is used to clearly communicate the targeted behaviors, defines what reinforcers will be given when the behaviors are performed, and outlines the punishers if the client engages in problematic behavior. It represents a mutual agreement between the client and treatment staff where the client is heavily involved in the planning process. The agreement should consider both the individual experiences and preferences of the client. Such a contract is different from a case plan as discussed in Chapter 7, but certainly could be one of the Tasks and Activities within a case plan.

There are several specific components to the contract. First, the task must be clearly defined noting who will be responsible for the task, typically the client. A time frame should be attached to the task to ensure it progresses in a timely manner. The specific behaviors attached to the task should be defined in collaboration with the client and the treatment staff. Next, the specific reinforcer should be identified along with the person responsible for administrating the reward. A time frame should also be given for the distribution of the reinforcer and exactly the terms in which it will be given. Both the client and treatment staff can add comments or decide on revisions within the contract. Finally, both the client and the therapist should sign and date the contract to show their commitment and agreement. Figure 8.4 shows an example of a typical contingency contract. It may be as simple as this form with handwritten notes or the contract may be a part of a larger computerized case management system.

A contingency contract specifies the *contingent* relationships between completion of the behavior and the reward to be given. Contingency contracts have been used in a variety of fields to help manage behavior including criminal justice. Contracting has been successfully implemented in a variety of programs including drug and mental health courts, juvenile justice, and community sanctions (Bralley & Prevost, 2001; Petersilia, 2007; Predergast, Podus, Finney, Greenwell, & Roll, 2006; Taxman, Shepardson, & Byrne, 2004; Wilson, Mitchell, & MacKenzie, 2007). Contingency contracts are used in corrections and often in conjunction with other strategies such as token economies (TE) and level systems. Box 8.1 and 8.2 at the conclusion of the chapter also illustrate the use of a contingency contract using a case study.

Token Economies

The first comprehensive token economy system was developed by Ayllon and Azrin (1968) in the early 1960s at the Anna State Psychiatric Hospital in Illinois. A token economy is a system of CM with the purpose of managing and changing behavior based on the principles of operant conditioning. As with other operant learning strategies, the goal of the token economy system is to motivate the clients to change their behavior and refrain from problematic behaviors. Clients earn tokens, or small reinforcers such as a chip or voucher, for adaptive behavior. They later can exchange their tokens for larger reinforcers, also referred to as backup reinforcers. The tokens themselves become conditioned reinforcers because they are later traded in for desired backup reinforcers. The client learns to exhibit the adaptive behavior to obtain tokens and avoid maladaptive behaviors that could result in the loss of tokens.

```
                              CONTRACT
    — — — — — — — — — — — — — — — — — — — — — — — — — —

            TASK                              REWARD

    WHO: _____            WHO: _____

    TASK: _____           TASK: _____

    WHEN: _____           WHEN: _____

    HOW WELL: _____       HOW MUCH: _____

    _____                 _____

    _____                 _____

    — — — — — — — — — — — — — — — — — — — — — — — — — —

    SIGNATURE: _____   DATE: _____

    SIGNATURE: _____   DATE: _____


    COMMENTS ON AGREED UPON TASK: _____

    _____

    _____

    _____

    AGREED UPON REVISIONS TO TASK: _____

    _____

    _____

    _____
```

FIGURE 8.4 Example contingency contract.

Token economies are often used more in group settings than individual. There are four basic practices central to a token economy system (Spiegler & Guevremont, 2010). First, an individualized list of target behaviors should be established indicating the number of tokens the client can earn or lose for each behavior. Second, a broader list of reinforcers should be developed that can be used for all clients. Third, a currency system should be established that can be tangible or symbolic. Lastly, the rules and procedures for the token economy should be clearly explained to each client. It may also be helpful to have a display detailing the process.

A token economy only works as well as the motivation that accompanies it. A reinforcer must be something desired by the individual. Common reinforcers can come in several categories. Tangible items are physical objects and might include food, money or gift cards, sanitation kits, etc. Social reinforcers include praise, acceptance, additional phone time with social supports, etc. Certain activities might also be good reinforcers. For example, participating in a sports game or additional library visits might be an attractive incentive for some clients. A printed menu displaying each reinforcer and the cost is helpful. See Figure 8.2 for a broader list of possible community and institutional reinforcers.

Level Systems

A level system is a behavioral approach that categorizes participants in levels based on their behavior. The client advances through the levels by performing more targeted behaviors and fewer problem behaviors. They receive access to more privileges as their level increases. Their level will be decreased if the client engages in behaviors deemed unacceptable by the program. Reinforcement is also different within each level. There are generally more restrictions to desired items in lower levels. Level systems are often paired with a point system, a type of token economy where clients are provided points instead of tokens when they perform targeted behaviors. These systems are broadly used in juvenile justice.

Point and level systems also use reinforcement and punishment. As with other programs discussed, reinforcers are used to teach new behaviors, replace undesirable and problematic behavior, and build positive relationships with the youth and treatment staff. Common punishers include the use of time-outs and response cost. A time-out involves removal of the youth from the physical space where the maladaptive behavior occurred. This not only isolates them from others but also works as a cooldown period. The response cost involves removing reinforcers to decrease the negative behavior.

Some concerns have been raised with both token economies and point and level systems. There is research to suggest these programs might increase conflicts between staff and the youth, bring about inconsistencies in the distribution and immediacy of reinforcers and punishers by staff, and not provide long-term benefits (Mohr, Martin, Olson, Pumariega, & Branca, 2009). Additionally, these programs can be perceived or become punitive because they tend to focus primarily on bad behavior (Spiegler & Guevremont, 2010). As with other programs discussed in this chapter, those programs that are most successful provide individualized treatment, ongoing communication with clients, additional training and booster sessions for treatment staff, and ongoing evaluation (Mohr et al., 2009).

Additionally, level systems often do not work as effectively with girls in detention compared to boys, in part due to their relational interpersonal nature (for more, see Chapter 13). If they create strong friendship bonds at their current level and earn their way behaviorally to get promoted to the next level, they have been known to sabotage their success to stay with their group of friends, even if it means not obtaining more privileges. This is a case of not understanding that the friendship bond is more reinforcing for the girls compared with additional privileges.

Skill Training

Skill training is another common type of behavior intervention provided during correctional counseling. These programs focus on specific skills that can be contributing to the client's problem behaviors. Correctional programming often includes sessions for life or social skills. Life skill training can focus on a variety of skills such as critical thinking, decision-making, coping, or problem-solving. Social skills focus on the client's interactions with others. This might include skills such as effective communication and active listening. Other skills taught might include basic life needs such as managing a budget, using a computer, or filing out a job application. Key components of skill training include modeling, prompting, shaping, role-play, feedback, and practice.

During this treatment approach, trained therapists teach a variety of skills to help clients deal with problematic behaviors. Each skill is broken down into steps so it can be replicated. Modeling is a way to teach the skill through observation. Participants observe the skill being taught then imitate it in a scenario that pertains to their own experiences. This is known as role-playing (see Chapter 10 on social learning theory for more information on modeling and role-play). Participants role-play the scenario then receive feedback or directions for corrective action. Another key component of skill training is the use of practice, also referred to as behavior rehearsal. This starts with the role-playing exercise. Participants are also given homework where they seek additional opportunities to practice their newly acquired skills. Reinforcement is used throughout the role-play, feedback, and practice stages to further assist the client in learning the skill and demonstrating the target behaviors.

TECHNOLOGICAL INNOVATIONS IN BEHAVIOR THERAPY

The techniques mentioned in this chapter represent activities used during individual or group sessions between a client and the treatment staff. There are various technological advances that have been developed to augment these traditional modalities. Computer and mobile apps have gained popularity over the last decade due to their wide distribution and affordability. Another emerging technology in correctional rehabilitation is the use of virtual reality (VR). These innovations are not meant to replace existing treatment models. They are simply tools to enhance current evidence-based practices in correctional counseling.

Computer and Mobile Apps

Computer and mobile apps influence nearly every part of our lives. This is also the case for many under the control of the criminal justice system. Many states are using the technology to provide mental health services, substance abuse treatment, and educational opportunities. Smartphone devices are assisting with supervision by offering location tracking, remote reporting, and event management. There are apps that provide reinforcement in the form of text messages or emails for meeting goals and demonstrating desired behaviors (Spohr, Taxman, & Walters, 2015). Finally, computer and mobile apps are being used to connect clients with the resources they need once released (Bush, Armstrong, & Hoyt, 2019).

Patterson and colleagues (2017) noted several specific web- and mobile-based apps that have been useful for treatment. The Computerized Assessment of Substance Abuse (CASA) was created by the Correctional Service of Canada and helps practitioners identify individual treatment needs and available resources. The Addiction-Comprehensive Health Enhancement Support System (A-CHESS) was developed by the University of Wisconsin–Madison's Center for Health Enhancement Systems Studies to monitor health issues related to substance abuse. The Therapeutic Education System (TES) is based on the community reinforcement approach that focuses on increasing reinforcement for non-drug-using behaviors. The Fluency-Based Computer-Delivered Program for Behavioral Intervention and

Assessment for opioid users is a computer-based treatment model used to promote self-efficacy through skill-building, self-monitoring, and progress-tracking activities.

Virtual Reality

Another relatively new technology being used for correctional rehabilitation is virtual reality (VR). VR refers to any computer-generated environment that uses two- or three-dimensional (2D or 3D) visualization and transmission devices to provide user input within a virtual world (Ticknor & Tillinghast, 2011). This environment can be accessed using a mobile phone, laptop, tablet, or head-mounted display (HMD). Participants maneuver the virtual world using a touch screen, keyboard, or hand controller(s).

The most common use of VR in treatment has been through virtual reality exposure therapy (VRET) (Maples-Keller, Bunnell, Kim, & Rothbaum, 2017; Rothbaum, Rizzo, & Difede, 2010). VRET is being used to improve on traditional exposure therapy by providing an immersive virtual environment where the client can experience the events or objects that cause their disorder but do so in a safe and controlled environment (Botella et al., 2007; Botella, Fernandez-Alvarez, Guillen, Garcia-Palacios, & Banos, 2017). Opris and colleagues (2012) performed a meta-analysis comparing VRET to classical evidence-based interventions. They found the VRET participants performed better than controls and were equally effective at treating anxiety as the traditional treatment modalities. Riva, Wiederhold, and Mantovani (2018) reviewed 25 recent studies on VRET and concluded VR was an effective tool to enhance traditional ET and the technology "compares favorably to existing treatment in anxiety disorders, with long-term effects that generalize to the real world" (p. 9).

Another area where VR has been extensively studied is with substance use. A common form of treatment for substance abuse involves cue-based exposure therapy (CET) (Cho et al., 2008). CET exposes the patient to the triggering substance (e.g., the sight of alcohol) and teaches them coping skills to deal with urges. Clinicians are incorporating VR with cue-exposure therapy (VR-CET) to treat individuals diagnosed with alcohol and/ or drug dependence by exposing patients to relevant contextual environments (Bordnick et al., 2009).

Finally, VR is beginning to be used in behavior therapy for some of the concepts previously outlined in this chapter. A pilot study, nicknamed Virtual Environment for the Treatment of Offenders (VETO), was conducted by the present author (see Ticknor, 2017). This pilot represented a feasibility study to evaluate whether VR could be used to enhance traditional cognitive-behavior therapy for justice-involved juveniles. Study findings suggested the juveniles were motivated by use of the technology, the functionality allowed more realistic modeling and role-play, the facilitator was able to give broader feedback as the simulation was recorded and could be replayed, and several reinforcers could be used directly in the virtual environment to enhance learning. This offered study participants a safe and controlled, yet realistic, environment to learn and practice new skills. While using this technology is relatively new, several other researchers are now exploring the effectiveness of using VR for behavior modification (see the work of VanGelder, Riva, and Wiederhold).

These interventions offer behavior therapists several advantages. First, having additional options means treatment can be available to a larger population. This includes those who live in rural areas or do not have access to quality care (Ticknor, 2019). Additionally, many of these solutions can also be achieved with limited resources (Chaple et al., 2014). This might assist agencies in dealing with the resources needed to achieve proper treatment dosage with their clients. That said, there are several additional considerations for using the technology for treatment. There may be some ethical implications for patient or client privacy (Patterson et al., 2017). Additionally, there may be additional costs associated with hardware, software, and training for the technology (Ticknor, 2019). Finally, some technology might induce physiological stress for the client (Ticknor, 2018).

CONCLUSION

Behavior therapy is not a single technique. These interventions are based on generations of research on classical and operant conditioning and provide several tools that treatment staff can use to change behavior. This type of treatment can be effective in behavior modification with some important guiding principles. Any agency designing a program must have a culture supportive of this model. This means setting clear guidelines on behavior expectations, clearly communicating reinforcers and punishers, providing staff with ongoing training, and periodic conducting self-evaluation. A lapse in any of these areas can greatly reduce the effectiveness of this model.

Subsequent chapters will explore the role of behavior therapy with cognitive therapy and social learning models. In reality, these three broad interventions are often blended together. **Stimulus control** and reinforcements are also used in **relapse prevention**, case management, and substance use treatment. These other models add key elements that were not inherent in the original classical and operant conditioning models; therefore, not typically included when outlining traditional behavior therapy. More recent advances will show humans learn and change their behavior in a variety of ways. That said, behavioral interventions are used in a variety of other learning models and are still relevant for correctional counseling today.

Box 8.1 **A Case Study: Jason**

This is a good time to introduce readers to Jason. Occasionally throughout the book, you will be asked to assume the role of Jason's case manager or counselor. In this capacity you will be asked to: (a) design a contingency contract for Jason (Box 8.2); (b) think about what certain counseling strategies would look like for Jason; and (c) devise a treatment plan.

But first, let's introduce you to him.

I. BACKGROUND AND SOCIAL HISTORY

Jason or "JT," as he likes to be called, is a 24-year-old male doing three to five years for burglary in his first stint at State Prison. JT first came into contact with the juvenile justice system when he was 14. Truancy, minor school vandalism, and several weeks of being

---

expelled for fighting, or as he referred to it, "standing up for his manhood," had twice placed him on probation. JT had a difficult family life. His mother was a quiet woman with little education. She worked hard on a factory assembly line and seemed to keep the family together, at least financially. Ten-hour days, however, left little energy or time for other parental functions. Jason's father had been married three times before he married JT's mother and had been known for his drinking, gambling, and occasional violence against his wife. He was often away from home for weeks at a time.

By the time JT was 18, his older brother Joe was doing a five-year stretch for assault and battery, his fourth offense. JT's younger sister, Mary, had taken a different path. Although frequently ridiculed by her father, Mary continued to make the honor roll in high school, dreaming of one day becoming a high school language teacher, a dream that had recently come true. JT and Mary were only two years apart in age and had always been close, although JT disdained her educational goals, claiming that "an education on the streets" is what it takes to get ahead in this world. JT, Joe, and Mary all were well above average in intelligence, although Mary was the only one who seemed to be trying to take advantage of her abilities.

Jason dropped out of school in the tenth grade. He regrets that decision now, but at the time, he felt that school was boring and he did not like his teachers.

II. OFFENDING HISTORY

Although this is Jason's first prison term, it is his fourth adult conviction. His juvenile record shows two adjudications, one for assault and another for vandalism and truancy. At age 19, Jason was convicted of assault and placed on probation. By age 22, Jason had two additional convictions, both for burglary. In all of his past offenses, Jason has acted in the company of other associates involved in the justice system.

III. CURRENT OFFENSE

Jason was convicted of robbery. With two friends, he robbed a pharmacy in a nearby neighborhood. The trio took $855 in cash from the pharmacist at gunpoint. This is Jason's first offense involving the use of a weapon.

You are JT's prison counselor. His disciplinary reports have consisted of relatively minor infractions such as "mouthing off" at his laundry supervisor and stealing fruit from the kitchen to make a kind of alcoholic beverage. His records indicate that he is in good physical health. The severity of Jason's antisocial behavior has escalated over time. This is his second violent offense as an adult, and his first involving a weapon. Jason displays some feelings of inferiority but demonstrated a good deal of false bravado during his initial interview.

Box 8.2 The Case of JT: A Contingency Contract

The contingency contract discussed in this box is based on the case study of Jason, which was presented in Box 8.1. As explained earlier, contingency contracts make a desired privilege contingent upon the demonstration of certain behaviors that correctional staff wish to reinforce.

For example:

TREATMENT PLAN—EXAMPLE

Goals of the Behavioral Approach (for Jason):

To make more frequent contact with family members.
To strengthen Jason's relationship with Mary.
To demonstrate respect for Mary's accomplishments.

Approach:

Jason will participate in several contingency contracts, upon which ultimately home furloughs are made contingent on: (a) increased contact with family members (phone and letters); (b) requesting visits from family members, particularly Mary; and (c) demonstrating key relationship skills (as taught in the social skills program). These contracts should be set forth in manageable increments of change and self/social responsibility. At first, we will not reinforce Jason with home furloughs, but rather with increased library privileges.

Complementary counseling sessions will address: (a) what responsibility to family members means; (b) rejection of irresponsible behaviors; (c) the skills associated with responsible relationships; and (d) reasons for respecting those who attain career accomplishments in prosocial ways.

APPROACH—EXAMPLE

Behavioral contracts, or contingency contracts, typically contain the following elements:

1. Statement of the role of both the client and the counselor.
2. Clear description of the behavior(s) expected from the client.
3. Clear description of the reward(s) associated with such behaviors.
4. Identification of the criteria to be used to determine success or failure in achieving each goal.
5. Criteria for altering the contract.

Figure 8.4 shows an example of a simple behavioral contract that can be used in a counseling session.

For this part of Jason's treatment plan, this contract might look like Figure 8.5.

CONTRACT

TASK

WHO: Jason

TASK: Call Mary;

WHEN: 15 min., once a week, 3 weeks

HOW WELL:

I will call Mary once a week to see if she will eat me. I have to try at least 3x before I give up for the week

REWARD

WHO: Counselor

TASK: 1 hr. extra library time per week

WHEN: 3 weeks

HOW MUCH:

After Jason calls Mary once a week for 3 weeks. He should try to talk for 10-15 minutes

SIGNATURE: Jason Smith   DATE: 4/20/15

SIGNATURE: Joseph Jones   DATE: 4/20/15

COMMENTS ON AGREED UPON TASK: _____

AGREED UPON REVISIONS TO TASK: Task will be revised if Mary is unavailable to answer her calls.

FIGURE 8.5 Completed contingency contract.

Discussion Questions

1. Give examples of overt and covert behaviors.
2. Define classical and operant conditioning and discuss how they differ.
3. Explain how you have experienced positive and negative reinforcement. Have you used it on someone else either knowingly or not? If so, how.
4. What's the difference between positive/negative reinforcers and positive/negative punishers? When should each be used?

5. What is the difference between a token economy and a level system? When would you use one or the other?

6. What are other types of institutional and community corrections reinforcers?

7. What other technology could be used during treatment with correctional populations?

ONLINE LEARNING ENHANCEMENTS

Online Video Lectures

Khan Academy: Positive and Negative Reinforcement and Punishment
www.khanacademy.org/test-prep/mcat/behavior/learning-slug/v/operant-conditioning-positive-and-negative-reinforcement-and-punishment

Study.com: Token Economies Definitions & Examples
https://study.com/academy/lesson/token-economy-in-the-classroom-definition-examples-quiz.html

Relevant TED Talks

Peggy Andover: The Difference between Classical Conditioning and Operant Conditioning
www.ted.com/talks/peggy_andover_the_difference_between_classical_and_operant_conditioning/transcript?language=en

Matt Vogl: How Virtual Reality Can Improve Your Mental Health
www.ted.com/talks/matt_vogl_how_virtual_reality_can_improve_your_mental_health?language=en

Relevant Websites

Example Behavior Contracts
www.pbisworld.com/tier-2/behavior-contract/

Reinforcement Strategies
https://intensiveintervention.org/sites/default/files/Reinforcement_Strategies_508.pdf

GLOSSARY OF KEY TERMS

aversion therapy   a behavioral intervention in which clients are voluntarily exposed to stimuli related to a problem behavior while simultaneously being subjected to some form of discomfort

behavioral approaches   therapeutic approaches, such as classical conditioning and operant conditioning, that target behavior change using various techniques to predict and control the relationship between actions and environmental stimuli

behaviorism an academic school of psychology that emphasizes the role of environmental stimuli on influencing behavior through conditioning and learning processes

classical conditioning a learning process in which a conditioned stimulus is repeatedly paired with an unconditioned stimulus to elicit a conditioned response (new behavior) from a client

conditioned response a learned response to a previously neutral stimulus

conditioned stimulus a previously neutral stimulus that eventually triggers a conditioned response after repeated pairings with an unconditioned stimulus

contingency contract a contract that specifies the behavioral responsibilities of the client and others who are responsible for administering reinforcements; such contracts make a desired privilege contingent upon the demonstration of certain behaviors that correctional staff wish to reinforce

covert sensitization a form of classical conditioning in which the behavior therapist creates a fantasy for the client in which aversive elements are woven into a story involving the desired object/behavior

exposure therapy a form of classical conditioning in which clients are repeatedly exposed to negative stimuli in an attempt to eliminate any fear or anxiety associated with such stimuli

extinction the gradual weakening of a conditioned response that results in the behavior decreasing or desisting

law of effect principle behaviors that are followed by positive results are most likely to become established while those that are followed by negative results will decrease

negative reinforcement one of two types of reinforcers associated with operant conditioning; the removal of an unpleasant stimulus in an attempt to increase the frequency of a desired behavior

operant conditioning a method of learning that involves modifying behavior by the judicious use of rewards

positive reinforcement one of two types of reinforcers associated with operant conditioning; the addition of a pleasing stimulus in an attempt to increase the frequency of a desired behavior

punishment the unconditioned stimulus in aversive conditioning; punishments should be used only if the therapist wishes to quickly eliminate some undesirable behavior in a client

relapse prevention the cognitive-behavioral interventions used with patients in addiction recovery to reduce the likelihood of a relapse, or addiction behavior

stimulus control the process of ensuring that antecedent events are in place to encourage clients to behave in a certain manner

token economy a frequently employed operant conditioning model in which targeted behaviors are reinforced with *tokens*, which can later be exchanged for more meaningful rewards; part of a contingency management model

unconditioned response a natural, unlearned response to an unconditioned stimulus

unconditioned stimulus a stimulus that elicits a response without any prior learning taking place

CHAPTER 9

Cognitive Interventions

Lori Brusman Lovins, Patricia Van Voorhis, and Emily J. Salisbury

KEY TERMS

acceptance

activating event

all-or-nothing thinking

antisocial cognitions

automatic thoughts

behavior chain

catastrophizing

cognitive behavioral therapy (CBT)

cognitive model

cognitive restructuring

cognitive skills

cognitive therapy

consequences

conventional reasoning

core beliefs

criminal thinking styles

gender-responsive programming

generalize

graduated practice

grounding

irrational belief

mindfulness interventions

modeling

moral dilemmas

moral education programs

overgeneralization

physiological cues

postconventional reasoning

preconventional reasoning

proactive

problem-solving

program fidelity

rational belief

rational emotive behavior therapy (REBT)

reducers

role-play

self-efficacy

self-statements

self-talk

shoulding

skill acquisition

skill application

social learning

stages of moral judgment

thinking reports

virtual reality (VR)

DOI: 10.4324/9780367808266-12

Cognitive interventions focus on the ways in which people think. The **cognitive model** proposes that it is dysfunctional thinking that influences feelings and behavior, and when individuals think in a more realistic and adaptive way, they experience fewer problem behaviors (Beck, 2021). Simply stated, thinking controls behavior. If we want to behave differently, we must change the way we think.

Thinking, of course, involves a broad array of *processes and skills*. Cognitive skills include things like social or coping skills, problem-solving skills, anger control, and conflict-resolution skills. The cognitive model is also concerned with what we think, or the *content* of our thoughts. This involves identifying the specific thoughts and corresponding beliefs that lead to maladaptive actions. As Donald Meichenbaum, a well-known cognitive psychologist, once explained to a group of college students: "Our thoughts often operate as cognitive templates that can be carried from situation to situation" (Meichenbaum, 1986). If we believe, for example, that stealing from our next-door neighbor is wrong, we probably will refrain from stealing at other times when the opportunity is presented.

Most of us do not need to be reminded of how our thoughts often exacerbate difficult situations. If I fear public speaking, for example, but the course I am taking requires a class presentation, what I tell myself about this presentation impacts my behavior. Telling myself *"I am terrible at public speaking, I am going to fail, everyone will laugh at me"* exacerbates my fear and impacts my ability to perform well. Hence, cognitions represent a constant stream of thoughts used to interpret our day-to-day situations. Given this, cognitions are also known to play a major role in psychological problems such as depression (Beck, Rush, Shaw, & Emory, 1979), anxiety disorders (Beck & Emory, 1985), and personality disorders (Linehan, 1993), just to name a few. Importantly, those who commit crimes on a repeated basis are known to have thoughts that support antisocial behavior (Barriga, Landau, Stinson, Liau, & Gibbs, 2000; Elliott & Verdeyen, 2002; Samenow, 1984; Walters, 1990, 2012; Walters & Cohen, 2016, Yochelson & Samenow, 1976), and internalized antisocial moral values (Jennings, Kilkenny, & Kohlberg, 1983; Kohlberg, 1976). In conjunction, people who repeatedly commit crimes often possess very limited problem-solving and other cognitive skills (Bonta & Andrews, 2017; Gendreau et al., 1996; Ross & Fabiano, 1985).

Cognitive therapy (CT) was developed by Aaron Beck in the 1960s. This was around the same time that Albert Ellis was constructing rational emotive behavior therapy (REBT). Beck and Ellis are identified as forefathers in developing the cognitive model. These therapies will be discussed in more detail below. Today, the term cognitive therapy is often used interchangeably with **cognitive behavioral therapy (CBT)**. CBT interventions use a structured, short-term, present-oriented approach that targets dysfunctional thinking to change behavior (Beck, 2021), and as noted, are used to treat an array of psychological and behavioral disorders. An interesting study out of the United Kingdom examined the impact of a single, 60–70 minute CBT session to treat prisoners experiencing acute insomnia. Following the 1-hour session, they found not only significant improvements in sleep but also a reduction in symptoms of depression and anxiety (Randall, Nowakowski, & Ellis, 2019). While certainly most CBT interventions are longer than an hour, this study demonstrates that short-term, targeted cognitive interventions can be highly effective.

Cognitive behavioral therapy (CBT) includes elements of both cognitive and behavioral theories (see Chapter 8). This chapter will focus on the cognitive end of this model, demonstrating the importance of identifying the thoughts and beliefs that drive behavior, and then restructuring or learning new cognitive skills for managing risky situations. With cognitive approaches, correctional practitioners work with individuals or groups to change antisocial thinking to develop more prosocial, functional behavior patterns. Note that this chapter will interchangeably use cognitive interventions and CBT.

COGNITIVE INTERVENTIONS IN CORRECTIONAL SETTINGS

During the past few decades, cognitive behavioral treatment modalities have become a preferred approach to counseling and therapy. This is especially true in our current climate of health care and the advent of "managed care," in which recipients of mental health services are encouraged by insurance providers to remedy problems in as few sessions as possible. Cognitive therapies are viewed as "here and now" approaches that are among the most efficient and expedient therapies available. It is also a preferred approach as there is ample evidence to support the effectiveness of cognitive models in changing a range of maladaptive behaviors, including more than 2,000 outcome studies on the effectiveness of CBT (Beck, 2021).

The growing interest in cognitive therapies for justice-involved juveniles and adults is equally understandable. First, like studies on the use of CBT to address mental and behavioral health concerns, numerous meta-analyses of cognitive interventions in correctional settings have shown the programs to be highly effective (Andrews et al., 1990; Antonowicz & Ross, 1994; Garrett, 1985; Izzo & Ross, 1990; Koehler, Losel, Akoensi, & Humphreys, 2012; Lipsey, 1992, 2009; MacKenzie, 2006), including seven meta-analyses devoted solely to cognitive behavioral programs (Landenberger & Lipsey, 2005; Lee et al., 2012; Lipsey, Chapman, & Landenberger, 2001; Pearson, Lipton, Cleland, & Yee, 2002; Tong & Farrington, 2006; Wilson, Allen, & MacKenzie, 2000; Wilson, Bouffard, & MacKenzie, 2005). It would be difficult to fault the efficiency, clarity, and effectiveness of these methods.

Second, like the behavioral strategies discussed in Chapter 8, cognitive interventions deal with client characteristics that are identifiable (thoughts and feelings) and observable (behavior). Thus, cognitive strategies are easier to use because these characteristics are clearer than the interpretation of unconscious motives, fears, and anxieties targeted by traditional therapies such as Freud's psychoanalysis. In relation to this, because most correctional agencies can afford to hire only a few psychologists, clinical social workers, or licensed counselors, many correctional counseling functions, including case management and group facilitation, are conducted by non-clinicians. Cognitive methods have proven to be quite valuable in this regard. Agencies have found that they can efficiently train nonclinical staff to use the cognitive methods. This is especially true in the case of the cognitive skills programs, in which the training of case managers, probation officers, and others is often conducted through in-service training sessions. Programs delivered by non-clinicians tend to follow structured, often scripted manuals, looking more like classrooms than therapy sessions. Corrections, however, is not the only field that has trained nonclinical practitioners in cognitive interventions. CBT interventions can be found in places such as medical offices, schools, vocational programs, and self-help groups, and are delivered by a range of trained professionals, paraprofessionals, and peer specialists (Beck, 2021). While not considered "therapy sessions" when delivered by non-clinicians, CBT interventions can be adapted for use in a range of situations to help individuals change maladaptive behaviors.

A third reason for the popularity of cognitive behavioral programs has to do with what we know about individuals that engage in criminal behavior. There has been decades of research on the predictors of criminal conduct. A consistent finding is that antisocial cognitions is a major risk factor for criminal behavior (Andrews, Zinger, Hoge, Bonta, Gendreau, & Cullen, 1990; Bonta & Andrews, 2017). Hence, individuals who engage in behaviors such as aggression, drug use, and theft often possess antisocial cognitions that justify these behaviors, as well as negative thinking about laws and law enforcement in general (Walters, 2016). Thus, if antisocial cognitions are major drivers to criminal conduct, and the goal is to reduce antisocial behaviors, an intervention that targets these cognitions makes sense.

COGNITIVE RESTRUCTURING APPROACHES

Cognitive and cognitive behavioral approaches generally fit into one of two models: cognitive restructuring, in which interventions endeavor to change the content of thoughts, attitudes, and beliefs (i.e., what we think); and cognitive skills, in which interventions seek to improve cognitive processes—the structure and form of reasoning (i.e., how we think) rather than its content. The division is not always clear. Some programs target both content and process. Cognitive skills programs, developed by Ross and Fabiano (1985), Goldstein, Glick, and Gibbs (1998), and Bush, Taymans, and Glick (1998), to name just a few, target both cognitive processes and antisocial thinking.

We will begin with the cognitive restructuring approach, reviewing the foundational work of Aaron Beck's (1962) cognitive therapy and Albert Ellis's (1962) rational emotive behavior therapy. We then move to individuals who applied the cognitive model to forensic populations. We will review the work of Yochelson and Samenow (1976) who focus on antisocial thinking errors, as well as the more recent work of Walters (2012) on criminal lifestyle theory.

Cognitive Therapy

Aaron Beck was trained as a psychoanalyst in the 1950s. Psychoanalytic therapy was originally developed by Sigmund Freud, and seeks to identify and minimize the effect of unconscious forces (e.g., the id, ego, super-ego) on behavior. Beck began his career by working to empirically validate the effectiveness of this model in an effort to add legitimacy to the field of psychology. When, to his surprise, he could not, he sought other explanations for depression (Beck, 2021). In his clinical practice, he found that his depressed patients often had negative and distorted cognitions, leading to his development of cognitive therapy (CT) as a treatment. He proposed that dysfunctional thinking was common to all psychological problems, and by teaching individuals to evaluate their thinking, and develop more realistic and adaptive thought patterns, their mood and behaviors would improve.

Beck argued that situations do not cause individuals to feel or respond in a particular way, rather it is how they construe (or interpret) the situation. Beck identified "automatic thoughts" or the spontaneous, almost reflexive words or images that go through a person's mind as a situation arises. These thoughts are not deliberative, rather they represent immediate interpretations of the situation one is experiencing. Automatic thoughts can be contrasted with core beliefs, which are the global or overgeneralized ways that individuals see the world. These beliefs are foundational to the way in which individuals interpret situations. For example, if my core belief is that I do not deserve to be loved, when a situation arises such as being rejected, my automatic thoughts of "*I'm not surprised. What was I thinking? No one will ever love me.*" are drawn from that core belief of not deserving love.

Cognitive theorists argue it is faulty thoughts and beliefs that leads to maladaptive behaviors. Let us look at another quick example:

SITUATION:	I'm getting yelled at by my boss for coming to work late.
AUTOMATIC THOUGHTS:	"*I know he's not yelling at me.*"
	"*What is his problem?*"
	"*Who does he think he is?*"
CORE BELIEF:	I won't be disrespected.
BEHAVIOR:	I swear at my boss.

These examples demonstrate how automatic thoughts are the initial thoughts that come to mind in a situation, and these thoughts are informed by a person's core beliefs. These distorted thoughts then lead to maladaptive behaviors. Thoughts and beliefs are therefore a primary target in cognitive therapy. CT teaches individuals to evaluate the validity of these thoughts. How accurate is the thought? Clients undergoing therapy may even be asked to investigate these thoughts. For example, if you indicate that your boss must hate you because he always complains about your work, you may be asked to explore the validity of that thought. You might be asked to observe your boss' interaction with coworkers to see if he corrects others' behavior as well. If yes, than the assertion that your boss "hates you" can be dispelled; if no, and you do seem to be the unfair target of your boss' complaints, then you explore ways to manage your thoughts, such as telling yourself, "*He's at it again, but I'm not going to let him get the better of me,*" or "*So what if he has a beef with me; I know I do a good job.*" Beck argues that correcting erroneous thoughts or adjusting maladaptive thoughts is part of the process of cognitive restructuring, and doing so can improve mood and behavior, leading to a more functional life.

Rational Emotive Behavior Therapy

Rational emotive behavior therapy (REBT) was initially devised by Ellis in the 1950s. Like cognitive therapy, REBT is concerned with emotions and thoughts that impair our existence. Part of the reason the REBT model has resonated, both in and outside of a correctional context, is the simplicity of the core model—the ABCs of REBT.

A	Activating Event	A situation, external event or triggering event.
B	Beliefs	A thought sequence that follows the event.
C	Consequences	Emotions and behaviors that result from the beliefs.

Let us say, for example, that the client experiences an unpleasant occurrence, a failure, or a rejection. REBT refers to this as an **activating event** and seeks to assess how the client makes sense of this experience.

In an unhealthy thought sequence, an **irrational belief** follows an activating event. Suppose a client asks someone out, and is rejected (activating event): "*Isn't it awful that she rejected me? I am worthless. No desirable woman will ever accept me. I don't deserve to be loved*" (beliefs). Several troubling emotional states may result from this irrational belief sequence. The client feels anxious, depressed, and hopeless (consequence). In a healthy thought sequence, however, the activating event is followed by a **rational belief**: "*It's a shame that she rejected me, but maybe she was not the one for me.*" The **consequences** of this rational belief may be the emotional states of disappointment or annoyance, but these states are far more manageable and transient than those that build from irrational beliefs.

According to Ellis, rational beliefs increase positive feelings and minimize pain. They are accurately related to real (not imagined) events. Irrational beliefs decrease happiness and maximize pain. In most cases, irrational beliefs are distorted perceptions of the activating event. They prevent the client from fulfilling his or her desires in the future. Ellis believed that irrational beliefs could be challenged and changed.

Like CT, REBT teaches the client that emotional states are not a result of the activating events, but rather the result of irrational beliefs. That is, these beliefs are often more damaging than the activating event itself. In other words, the harm is not in being rejected, it is what you tell yourself about being rejected. The client must be taught to dispute the irrational beliefs. Why is it awful? How am I worthless? Where is the evidence that no one will ever love me? Why am I less deserving of love than anyone else? Once the client can substitute rational beliefs for irrational beliefs, he or she will be happier and should make healthier decisions.

In a similar vein, Burns (1980) listed some common irrational ways of thinking. In **all-or-nothing thinking**, for example, things are viewed as black or white. A less-than-perfect performance is a failure. In **overgeneralization**, one negative event is seen as a never-ending pattern of defeat. In **catastrophizing**, individuals exaggerate the importance of something. For example, a person says, "*This is the worst thing that could have happened to me,*" when it is far from the worst thing. In **shoulding**, individuals either beat themselves up for what they "should" be doing, "*I should be a better mother.*" Ellis might respond to this statement with, "*Where is it written that you should be different from what you are?*" Shoulding oneself evokes feeling of guilt rather than motivating change by saying "*I would like to be a better mother.*" Shoulding can also be applied to others, "*You should be a better provider.*" This irrational thought evokes feelings of anger and blame, and does not serve to address the problem.

The REBT counselor is active, persuasive, educational, directive, and, at least in the Ellis model, hardheaded. Unlike Beck, who focuses on testing the accuracy of thoughts through observations and disputing those that are erroneous or unproductive, REBT involves disputing the client's irrational beliefs based on logic alone. The counselor may seem confrontational, but, in being confrontational, he or she confronts the beliefs, not the client. The client must be taught to continually observe and challenge his or her own belief system. REBT does not deal with the client's early history, unconscious thoughts and desires, non-verbal behavior, dreams, or any transference that occurs in the counseling situation, as would a psychoanalytic model. According to REBT, such early experiences affect clients in the present only because the clients themselves perpetuate them. Ellis states that the goals of REBT are to leave clients with a minimum of anxiety (self-blame) and hostility (blaming others), and to give them methods of self-observation and self-assessment that will ensure that they continue to be minimally anxious and hostile.

REBT Case Example

Most of Ellis's work was with people who were not justice-involved, but in his early writing, Ellis (1979) discussed the case of an exhibitionist he treated. The client was a 28-year-old social worker who exposed himself several times a year. He was arrested twice and was on the verge of ruining his professional career. He was married for eight years, had two children, and functioned well at his job. He came to counseling under duress because the court ordered him to seek counseling or be sentenced to jail.

Ellis helped the client to identify his irrational beliefs. First, the client believed that he must perform well in life (both professionally and sexually), that he had to win the approval of others, and that he must be perfect. The demands he made upon himself led him to feel inadequate when he failed to satisfy his wife sexually. Ellis pointed out that some demands that we make upon ourselves are irrational. It would be rewarding and pleasant if we always performed well in our lives, but this is neither necessary nor realistic, and failing to always perform well is not a catastrophe.

Second, the client believed that his wife should not be so critical of him and ought not to deprive him sexually—that she was horrible and mean for doing so. He also thought that other women ought to give in to his sexual advances. Again, Ellis suggested it would be quite convenient if others did what we wanted them to do, but there is no rational reason they should. And they are not horrible people for not doing what we want. Third, he believed that life ought not to be such a hassle and that he could not stand the difficulties that life presented to him. In point of fact, Ellis pointed out that he could stand the difficulties, as can most of us, all the while as we say to ourselves "I can't stand this!"

These irrational beliefs led the client to experience emotions such as self-pity, depression, and anger. Ellis would often diagram the impact of beliefs on emotions and behavior according to the A (activating event), B (beliefs), C (consequences) model of REBT. Using this model, the client's irrational thinking could be mapped as in Box 9.1.

Box 9.1 Map of Client's Irrational Thinking

[A]ctivating Event:	Client's sexual advances toward his wife are rejected.
[B]eliefs—Irrational:	"She should be meeting my needs as a man."
	"She doesn't care about me."
	"She thinks I'm a loser—I am worthless." "I deserve to have my needs met." "Women are worthless."
[C]onsequences:	Fury/depression/self-pity/client exposes himself.

After challenging the irrational belief, a healthier sequence occurs:

[A]ctivating Event:	Client's sexual advances toward his wife are rejected.
[B]eliefs—Rational:	"Where is it written that she has to do what I want?"
	"This does not mean she doesn't care about me."
	"This is not a measure of my worth." "I wish she'd satisfy my needs now, but it doesn't mean they'll never be met." "Women deserve respect."
[C]onsequences:	Frustration and disappointment/client goes to sleep

Thus, Ellis treated the client by pointing out his irrational thinking and helping him to challenge each of its components. The client realized that he wanted certain outcomes (such as getting more approval from his wife), but he also realized that he did not have to obtain them. As he surrendered his "shoulds" and "oughts," and substituted preferences and wishes, his behavior became less compulsive and he felt better able to control his sexual impulses. Ellis accepted the client, while rejecting the behavior. He helped him get in touch with his hostility and depression, thereby reducing their intensity.

The Cognitive Model in Corrections

The important work of Beck, Ellis, and others gave way to the examination of cognitive restructuring strategies specific to **antisocial cognitions**. Antisocial cognitions consist of pro-criminal beliefs that go against the norms and rules of society. Examples of antisocial thoughts include, "*He deserved to be hit for looking at me the way he did,*" or "*everybody uses marijuana, why shouldn't I?*" or "*Did you see how she was dressed? She was asking for it.*" Some assert that those with a pattern of criminal behavior simply think differently from others. Included in this group is Yochelson and Samenow (1976), and later Samenow (1984, 2001). They published a three-volume work titled, *The Criminal Personality*, where they identified 52 thinking errors from their work with forensic patients at St. Elizabeth's Hospital. Like other cognitive theorists, they posited that changing antisocial behavior requires a change in erroneous and irresponsible thinking patterns. Examples of these thinking errors include:

"power thrust"—I believe I must be in control.
"uniqueness"—I believe that rules do not apply to me as I am better than others.
"victim stance"—I blame others for my behavior and view myself as the true victim.

Others have identified somewhat similar cognitive patterns among correctional clients (e.g., see Barriga et al., 2000; Elliott & Verdeyen, 2002; Ross & Fabiano, 1985; Sykes & Matza, 1957; Walters, 1990). Building on the work of Yochelson and Samenow, Walters (1995) developed the *Psychological Inventory of Criminal Thinking Styles* (PICTS) used to assess criminal attitudes. This tool is currently used by the Administrative Office of the U.S. Courts (i.e., federal probation) as part of their *Post-Conviction Risk Assessment* (PCRA) tool (Lowenkamp, Johnson, Holsinger, Van Benschoten, & Robinson, 2013). Like other cognitive models, Walters considered the content of thoughts important in explaining behavior, arguing that *negative attitudes toward authority, positive attitudes toward deviance,* and *criminal identity* predict criminal behavior. Box 9.2 presents examples of thoughts that fall into each of these three categories.

Like the cognitive model, Walters also considered thought processes. He conceptualized that criminal thought processes were either **proactive** (planned and goal-directed) or **reactive** (impulsive). Within these subtypes, Walters (1990) identified eight specific **criminal thinking styles,** seven of which were empirically predictive of criminal conduct. Box 9.3 lists and defines the seven specific thinking styles, and provides an example of each.

As discussed, cognitive theories purport that thoughts determine behavior. In his criminal lifestyle theory, Walters (1990) contends that early delinquency shapes criminal thinking, and criminal thinking, in turn, shapes later criminal behavior. Studies conducted by Walters supports his argument that the relationship between criminal thinking and criminal behavior is reciprocal rather than unidirectional (Walters and Cohen, 2016). This suggests that young

Box 9.2 Walters's Antisocial Thought Content Categories

Thought Content	Example Thoughts
Negative attitudes toward authority	"Cops are all dirty." "There're just out to get me." "Laws don't apply to me." "The system is rigged." "I don't answer to the man."
Positive attitudes toward deviance	"Stealing is such a rush." "I get to make my own schedule." "Sometimes you have to show them who's boss." "She deserved what she got." "Getting high is worth the risk."
Criminal identity	"I am who I am." "I'm expected to do certain things." "Where I come from, this is what we do." "This is the life I chose." "No one disrespects me."

Box 9.3 Walters's Criminal Thinking Styles

Criminal Thought Process	Thinking Style	Definition	Example Thoughts
Proactive Criminal Thinking	Mollification	Making excuses or blaming others for my behavior.	"I'm the real victim here—the system has screwed me."
	Entitlement	Feeling above the law or special. I deserve to have what I want.	"I won't take the job if I have to start at the bottom."
	Power Orientation	Asserting control, power, or dominance; power-thrusting or intimidating others.	"I pay the bills in this house. She will do what I say."
	Superoptimism	Believing I can get away with anything; unrealistic about consequences of crime.	"They'll never catch me."
Reactive Criminal Thinking	Cutoff	Ignoring responsible behaviors; being impulsive; an "I don't care" or "screw it" attitude.	"I know I should skip this party, but whatever, I could use a fun night."
	Cognitive Indolence	Lazy thinking or taking short-cuts around problems; looks for the easy way out; lacks critical thinking; irresponsible.	"If they notice the money is missing, I can just say I was robbed."
	Discontinuity	Getting off track or getting sidetracked or distracted from your goals; unpredictable.	"They want me to get a job—maybe I'll start looking next week."

individuals with low self-control may engage in criminal conduct out of impulsivity or peer pressure, and the conduct itself can lead to the development of criminal thinking patterns. Walters argues that these thinking styles must be addressed to desist from criminal behavior.

In summary, addressing antisocial thinking begins with identifying the *irrational beliefs, thinking errors,* or *criminal thinking styles* and then working with the individual to restructure the maladaptive thoughts by challenging the thoughts or beliefs. The next section will break this process down.

The Three Steps to Cognitive Restructuring

The basic steps of cognitive restructuring for clients in a correctional setting include the three steps shown in Figure 9.1.

Whether addressing a mental or behavioral health issue, or more specifically an issue of antisocial attitudes and beliefs, the general methods for cognitive restructuring are the same. You begin by assessing the maladaptive thoughts. Formalized, validated tools like the PICTS can be used to identify patterns of criminal thinking. Other common tools used to assess antisocial attitudes in the criminal justice field are the *Criminal Sentiments Scale-Modified* (CSS-M; Shields & Simourd, 1991) or the *TCU Criminal Thinking Scales* (Knight, Garner, Simpson, Morey, & Flynn, 2006). These instruments can be used to determine whether a client has a high degree of antisocial thinking, and what areas appear most problematic. While many correctional programs use formalized assessments such as these, many do not. Antisocial thoughts are often informally assessed by asking questions, such as, "*What were your thoughts just before you grabbed the wallet?*" or "*What did you tell yourself before you became physically aggressive?*" A cognitive model, such as Ellis's ABC model, can also be used to help identify faulty thinking.

Once the thought content is identified, the practitioner must in some way challenge the antisocial thought or belief. As discussed earlier, they may question whether the belief is accurate or true. This may work in situations where a person claims that "*everybody gets high,*" or "*all cops are dirty.*" In other situations, the antisocial thought may be true, but it is still not productive. Take the client who says, "*I punched him when he disrespected me … nobody's going to disrespect me.*" Here, the practitioner may ask, "*How does the attitude—I won't be disrespected—get you closer to your goals of maintaining your job and completing probation?*" Rather than debate whether the client was disrespected, the focus becomes how that way of thinking benefits that client.

Once antisocial thinking is identified and challenged, the final step is to assist the individual to begin replacing antisocial thoughts with prosocial alternatives. Clients who tell themselves "*everybody gets high*" are justifying their behavior by making it normative. In this situation, the practitioner might ask, "*What is a more realistic or accurate statement than 'everybody gets high'?*" The client may respond, "*some people get high and some people don't.*"

FIGURE 9.1 Steps to cognitive restructuring.

This counter thought makes it just a little harder to justify the behavior of getting high. In the situation where the client punched someone for being "disrespectful," a practitioner could state, *"The belief that you must always be respected seems to get you into trouble quite a bit. If you are in a situation where you feel like you are being disrespected, how can you counter the belief, 'I won't be disrespected'?"* The client may respond, *"This is not worth losing my freedom."*

The technique of cognitive restructuring is particularly important for correctional clients whose criminal behavior appears to be driven by an excess of antisocial attitudes. Some individuals find themselves constantly in trouble because they cannot control their anger or addiction, or cannot successfully manage antisocial peers, or they struggle to handle problems in their lives and revert to criminal behavior. In these instances, *cognitive skills training* (discussed in the next section) becomes especially useful. However, for clients who engage in criminal behavior because they think it is justified, or enjoy the power, or see themselves as a criminal, cognitive restructuring is important. Like any learned behavior, cognitive restructuring takes practice and clients only learn to combat their risky thoughts with much repetition with using counter (i.e., restructured) thinking.

Notwithstanding the popularity of programs designed to address antisocial thinking, some precautions are warranted. What happens, for example, if clients who do not display much antisocial thinking are admitted to a cognitive behavioral program in a correctional setting? There are many such clients. Those who possess prosocial values and are less prone to antisocial thinking should not be participating in these cognitive restructuring groups. Doing so only serves to teach them antisocial thinking as it is modeled by peers. Again, the risk effect is likely to be at work here. Programs of this nature are effective among higher-risk clients, but often make matters worse for low-risk ones (see Bonta & Andrews, 2017; Lipsey, 2009; Smith et al., 2009; Van Voorhis et al., 2013).

COGNITIVE SKILLS APPROACHES

Where *cognitive restructuring* seeks to change the content of reasoning, *cognitive skills* programs seek primarily to change the structure or process of one's reasoning. To fully understand the cognitive skills programs, it is important to understand the distinction between process and content. Cognitive restructuring programs target the content of one's thinking—*what* the actual thoughts are. Cognitive skills programs target the process of thinking—*how* thoughts are formulated. Impulsivity, for example, has a characteristic cognitive process or structure regardless of whether the impulsivity is applied to stealing a car or reckless driving. The process is similar. Common cognitive skill deficits for those who engage in antisocial behavior, for instance stealing, include a failure to think through the consequences of the behavior or a limited awareness of alternatives to stealing. From this view, cognitive skills programs place a greater emphasis on what clients are *not* thinking than on what they *are* thinking. It is also important to note that deficits in cognitive skills is not the same as deficits in intelligence. A person can be very intelligent but have a limited ability to process through the impact of their decisions.

Cognitive Skills Programs in Corrections

Individuals who engage in a pattern of antisocial behavior are more likely than not to have a range of skill deficit areas. These include factors such as impulsivity, poor problem-solving, low self-control, and poor social, coping, or emotional-regulation skills. In Walters's (1995) characterization of criminal thinking, he differentiates the *proactive* from the *reactive* criminal thinking process. Proactive criminal thinkers engage in criminal behavior to meet a specified goal. Reactive criminal thinkers are more impulsive, spontaneous, and reactionary to high-risk situations. As an example, you may have two individuals who assault another person. One may be a drug dealer who assaulted a member of his gang for withholding drugs (proactive); the other might be a person who assaults someone at a bar after having a drink spilled on him (reactive). The proactive criminal thinking process suggests the person dealing drugs justifies his violent behavior as a necessary part of his "job"; he must demonstrate his power when he is being tested. His aggression is planned, controlled, and goal-directed, not impulsive. The person who assaults a stranger at a bar did so impulsively, without considering the consequences of his actions. Cognitive skills programs tackle the antisocial thought process of a drug dealer, including power orientation and justifying harmful behavior, and help someone with impulsive aggression by teaching self-control and emotion regulation strategies.

There are a number of cognitive skills programs designed for justice-involved individuals. Most come in the form of a structured curriculum. Nearly all of these curricula have a tool for identifying risky thoughts, so that those thoughts can be targeted for change (cognitive restructuring). Examples of such tools are **thinking reports** (Bush & Bilodeau, 1993; Bush et al., 1998; Ross, Fabiano, & Ross, 1989), or **behavior chains** (University of Cincinnati Corrections Institute, 2011). Both of these tools have similar components. Clients are taught to identify high-risk situations, which are similar to the "A-antecedent" in Ellis's ABC model. High-risk situations are the external events or triggers that are precursors to criminal conduct. Next, these tools typically have clients identify *thoughts* evoked from the high-risk situation. These can include both "automatic thoughts" or core beliefs. This would be the "B-beliefs" in Ellis's ABC model. Next, clients identify the *feelings* that result from the thoughts/beliefs sparked by the high-risk situation. Subsequently, the client lists the *action*, which is the behavioral response to the situation, or what the client does. In a behavior chain, this is typically the antisocial act that the client engaged in. Finally, *consequences* are identified. These include both positive consequences to the action selected in the situation, as well as the negative consequences.

In Ellis's ABC model, *feelings*, *action*, and *consequences* would be encompassed in "C-consequences" as each of these areas are considered consequences of the irrational thoughts an individual experiences. The example below shows the components of a behavior chain. The University of Cincinnati Corrections Institute (UCCI) has designed an array of curricula for justice involved populations, including programs targeting general criminality, substance abuse, employment, sexual abuse, and family relationships. They have also modified select curricula to use with juveniles and those with mental illness or cognitive delay. A behavior chain is a key cognitive tool used in all of these curricula, as the process of identifying antisocial thinking patterns is the same, irrespective of the target area. Below is how the case described earlier could be applied to a behavior chain:

Example Behavior Chain:

SITUATION: Someone spills a drink on me at a bar.
THOUGHTS: *"Are you kidding me!"*
"Who does this guy think he is?"
"Everyone is staring at me."

"That idiot did this on purpose."
"He's messed with the wrong person."
"I won't be disrespected like this."

FEELINGS: Shock
                Embarrassment
                Rage
                Vengeful

ACTION: I punch the guy in the face.

CONSEQUENCES: +

                Some release of my pent-up rage.
                I showed that I am not a pushover.

                -

                The police were called.
                The guy pressed charges.
                I was arrested.
                I spent three nights in jail.
                My probation officer found out.
                I was kicked out of a favorite bar for good.
                My wife was disappointed and angry.

In a cognitive skills program, clients must complete behavior chains or thinking reports repeatedly throughout the program. Clients are taught to explore a range of high-risk situations that lead to antisocial behavior, and then these tools can be used to break down the cognitive process in each situation. Tools such as a behavior chain or thinking report can be used in multiple ways. First, it helps the client to identify which high-risk situations are problematic for them. Secondly, it identifies the specific thoughts that lead to antisocial behaviors. Clients are taught to think about what self-talk occurred prior to an antisocial action. With repeated application, they become skilled at paying attention to their internal dialogue. These tools also help them to identify the feelings that often emerge in the chain of events that lead to an antisocial choice. Do they often experience anger, anxiety, shame, or excitement before engaging in an antisocial behavior? This helps the practitioner identify whether skills in emotion regulation need to be taught.

Finally, these tools help clients think through the consequences of their choices. They consider the positive benefits of antisocial choices (e.g., feeling high, having fun, feeling excitement, releasing anger) as well as the negative consequences (e.g., legal consequences, disappointing family, loss of employment). Clients can then be taught micro-skills, for instance simply thinking through the consequences of a choice before acting, or applying a social skill, like avoiding trouble with others, before things go too far.

This takes us to the next major component of a cognitive skills program—teaching skills. Arnold Goldstein wrote a series of skills training curricula including *The EQUIP Program* (Gibbs et al., 1995), *Skillstreaming the Adolescent* (Goldstein & McGinnis, 1997), and *The Prepare Curriculum* (Goldstein, 1999). While these specific curricula are not as widely used today in correctional settings, Goldstein did lay the groundwork for the steps to teaching individuals prosocial skills, a model adopted by many commonly used curricula, such as *Aggression Replacement Training* (Goldstein et al., 1998; Glick & Gibbs, 2011), *Thinking for a Change* developed by the National Institute of Corrections (Bush et al., 1998), and the UCCI curricula series discussed above.

Examples of social and emotion-regulation skills taught in correctional settings that can be used to help individuals manage high-risk situations include:

understanding the feelings of others
apologizing
asserting yourself
deciding to say "No"
dealing with peer pressure
responding to criticism
recognizing your feelings
dealing with anger
using self-control

These skills are often broken down into distinct steps, some of which are thinking steps (steps that would occur internally), while others are action steps (steps others can see the individual doing). Below is an example from a UCCI curriculum.

Skill: Deciding to Say "No"
Step 1: Decide if the situation is risky for you. (Thinking)
Step 2: Think about different ways to say "No." (Thinking)
Step 3: Choose the best way to say "No" in the situation and do it. (Thinking & Action)
Step 4: If appropriate, suggest other things to do that are not risky. (Action)

With consideration of the structure to which Goldstein and colleagues devised many social skills, the next section will explore step-by-step how these social skills are taught.

Teaching Cognitive Skills

In a cognitive skills group, the facilitator often focuses on a single skill for clients to practice during the session. Clients select a situation personal to them that applies to the skill being taught, and they practice the skill using the identified skill steps. Of note, while in corrections cognitive skills are often taught in a group setting, these skills can and are taught in individual settings as well. This might include an individual therapy session with a correctional or substance abuse counselor, a case management session with a social worker, or during a visit with a probation officer. Regarding the latter, several models have been developed to teach probation officers how to use cognitive interventions, as well as other evidence-based core correctional practices, when working with those on community supervision. You may recall from Chapter 3 the examples of Canada's Strategic Training Initiative in Community Supervision (STICS; Bonta et al., 2011), Staff Training Aimed at Reducing Re-arrest (STARR) used by federal probation (Robinson et al., 2011), and Effective Practices in Community Supervision (EPICS; University of Cincinnati Corrections Institute, 2010). Whether in a group or one-to-one setting, the following steps are generally used to teach clients cognitive skills:

1. Introduce—discuss why the skill is important and how it would be beneficial in staying out of trouble.

2. Teach—review the skill steps, differentiating thinking from action steps.

3. **Modeling**—the practitioner models the skill steps using a relatable scenario to demonstrate how the skills steps should be followed.

4. **Role-play**—clients practice the skill.

5. Feedback—clients are given feedback on execution of the skill.

6. **Graduated practice**—clients are assigned additional practice opportunities through homework or advanced practice sessions.

Instructors are trained to teach both **skill acquisition** and **skill application**. Skill acquisition involves learning the skill, which is done though practicing the skill steps, as outlined above. Skill application ensures that the client can **generalize** the cognitive skills to a variety of situations. For example, a client may role-play the skill *Deciding to say "no"* using the situation: *a friend offers me drugs*. Generalizing the skill helps ensure that the client also knows to apply the skill when a *cousin suggests they shoplift*, or a *co-worker encourages theft at work*. The cognitive skills taught in these programs can be applied to an array of high-risk situations, so clients must learn to generalize them to many scenarios.

To ensure skill application, instructors ask that participants practice the skills using scenarios specific to their own situations. This ensures that initial practice of a skill is applicable to the client's life. Facilitators also provide opportunities for **graduated practice**, where the skill practice is more advanced and realistic.

One advanced cognitive skill that many curricula include is the skill of **problem-solving**. This skill is important as it is widely applicable to problems that arise for clients. For example, a client may have been recently released from jail with no money and rent due. Rather than turn to criminal activity, the skill of problem-solving could be applied. Juliana Taymans has been instrumental in developing steps of problem-solving in criminal justice settings. This skill can be used alone (*Problem-Solving*; Taymans, 2006; Taymans & Parese, 1998) or as part of a larger curriculum (*Thinking for a Change*; Bush et al., 1998). Other curricula, such as the UCCI curriculum series, also include steps of problem-solving, as does *Reasoning and Rehabilitation* (Antonowicz & Ross, 2005; Ross et al., 1989), and *Moving On* (Van Dieten, 1998), a gender responsive CBT-based curriculum. Broader therapeutic models, such as dialectical behavior therapy (Linehan, 1993), also incorporate the skill of problem-solving. The following are steps of problem-solving. These may be adapted slightly from one curriculum to another, but generally the following basic steps are included:

Step 1: Define the problem and identify goals.
Step 2: Brainstorm options for addressing the problem.
Step 3: Choose the best solution by considering the pros and cons of the options.
Step 4: Implement the solution.
Step 5: Evaluate how well the solution worked.

A quasi-experimental evaluation of problem-solving, conducted for the Virginia Department of Correctional Education, found that the program reduced disciplinary infractions committed by both community and institutionalized participants (Spiropoulos, Spruance, Van Voorhis, & Schmitt, 2006). These reductions occurred in four out of five research sites, and in some settings, write-ups for prison disciplinaries were as much as 20% lower for the problem-solving group than the comparison group.

Thinking for a Change also achieved favorable evaluation results (Aos, Miller, & Drake, 2006; Golden, 2002; Golden, Gatcheland, & Cahill, 2006; Lowenkamp, Hubbard, Makarios, & Latessa, 2009).

In recent years, innovators have explored how technology can be used to help deliver CBT-based interventions in correctional settings. As outlined in Chapter 8, virtual environments are being used as a behavioral treatment alternative for exposure therapy (Maples-Keller et al., 2017; Rothbaum et al., 2010), as well as other anxiety disorders. Box 9.4 describes a pilot program that Bobbie Ticknor conducted in 2013 called Virtual Environment for the Treatment of Offenders (VETO; Ticknor, 2017).

Box 9.4 Virtual Environment for the Treatment of Offenders (VETO)

Ticknor (2019) conducted a pilot study at a juvenile facility in Ohio, testing the use of **virtual reality (VR)** in the delivery of a traditional cognitive behavioral intervention. VR can be defined as computer-generated environments that uses 2D or 3D visualization software and transmission devices to provide user input within a virtual world (Ticknor & Tillinghast, 2011). This pilot represented a feasibility study to evaluate whether VR could be used to enhance traditional CBT for confined juveniles. Surveys were collected from participants to ascertain qualitative information on the impact of the program.

In the study, participants and a facilitator met for 1-hour cognitive skills training sessions, 3 days a week for 10 weeks. Laptops, headsets, and game controllers were purchased to display the virtual simulation and participants created personalized avatars via the program. A proprietary software called *InWorld* was used.

Findings from the surveys of the 10 participants showed that all of the juveniles who participated in the pilot study had been in traditional group treatment previously. When asked to compare treatment modalities, pilot participants reported that the VR environment, which included use of role-play to learn new skills, was more engaging than traditional groups. They also felt more open to discuss their experiences and to ask questions via the avatar.

With respect to program functionality, while the facilitator received basic training on how to use the software, it became clear that additional training was needed. This was particularly true for security features and other tools intended to optimize the virtual experience. Access had to be restricted for features such as messaging as well as the movement and functions of the avatar.

The group was conducted using a traditional social skills curriculum. Although the facilitator was able to successfully use the virtual environment for teaching, role-playing, and providing feedback, other features in the software were not used that may have increased the effectiveness of the treatment.

One key benefit cited for use of VR was the ability to have members in the group who were physically in different locations. Although participants were in the same physical space for most of the pilot, there were occasions where the group facilitator had to be off-site, and could connect to the group via a standard Wi-Fi connection. Another unique feature was the ability to record a session so that role-plays could be replayed for participants, and more specific feedback could be discussed.

Finally, resources for expanding the VR program were explored. Considerations in implementing a VR program included cost, room availability, and ongoing training needs. Of note, the semi-immersive technology option being piloted in VETO was significantly less costly than other simulation options, making it a more feasible option for correctional sites. Advances in VR technology, as well as cost reductions that would broaden its availability, will hopefully lead to additional pilots of how technology can expand treatment options in correctional settings (Ticknor, 2019).

In some cases, cognitive skills curricula used in correctional programs are augmented by other types of programming. In these programs, clients often participate in a cognitive skills program to form a foundation, but get referred to additional programming to address alternative needs or life skills such as money management, vocational skills, parenting, or community reintegration. Skills like writing a resumé, interviewing for a job, or caring for children become much more solid, however, when they are built on the foundation of sound cognitive skills. For example, skills in money management and even vocational training (MacKenzie, 2006) become clearer once clients have addressed problems with impulsivity and antisocial thinking. Additionally, some employment or parenting curricula use a CBT framework to help participants learn pertinent skills. Some of these skills can be taught through role-playing and modeling ascribed by the social learning approach (see Chapter 10), and then used in combination with the cognitive models (Hollin, 1990). In fact, we will continue by discussing a cognitive development theory and specific programs that integrate this theory with social learning and cognitive skills approaches.

Mindfulness Interventions

Mindfulness interventions are used to treat a broad range of health and mental health conditions, such as chronic pain, depression, anxiety, and substance use disorders, just to name a few. Mindfulness has been described by some as the third-wave approach to cognitive behavioral treatment interventions (Hayes, Follette, & Linehan, 2004). Mindfulness can be defined as "a process of openly attending, with awareness, to one's present moment experience" (Creswell, 2017, p. 493). There are two important features of mindfulness. The first is grounding, or paying attention to present body sensations, emotions, mental images, thoughts, or other perceptual experiences (noises, lights, etc.). The second is an attitude of openness or acceptance of one's present state. This acceptance is important, so present experiences are looked at with openness and curiosity, even when they are difficult (Creswell, 2017). Hence, approaches like cognitive restructuring are not used, as the intent is not to identify and replace negative self-talk, rather it is to accept that it is present, and simply observe rather than respond to it. The mental image has been used of observing one's thoughts, emotions, and physical sensations going by on a conveyor belt—watching them come and then go away.

Box 9.5 Grounding Exercises

Try one of these quick grounding exercises:

Sit in a comfortable position, close your eyes, and focus on your breathing. Feel the air enter your nose and mouth, listening to the sound it makes and noticing the way it feels. Feel the air exit your mouth. Simply observe the sensation of breathing in and breathing out.

Another grounding exercise is to take hold of an object. It could be any object within reach, like a pencil, glass, or book. Close your eyes and run your hands over the object. How does it feel (cool or warm)? What is the texture like (smooth, rough, soft, hard)? What is the object's shape (long, rounded, sharp edges, etc.)?

The objective is the intentional focus on your breathing or on an object that both distracts your mind from stressors and helps bring you to a calm emotional state.

Mindfulness interventions have been shown to reduce depression and anxiety, by turning awareness toward one's thoughts, feelings, and body experiences, diminishing rumination and self-judgment. A study of mindfulness-based cognitive therapy (MBCT) with women in custody found an improvement in symptoms of depression and anxiety, especially when mindfulness techniques were discussed *and* practiced (Song, Zhao, Lou, Wang, & Zheng, 2020). In substance abuse programs, a mindfulness strategy known as urge surfing is used to observe the rise and fall of cravings for drugs or alcohol. Rather than react to these cravings, the physical sensations, thoughts and feelings associated with the cravings are observed and accepted, until the craving dissipates. In correctional treatment settings, mindfulness interventions are often incorporated as a component of a treatment program, usually within programs that use a cognitive behavioral framework as the primary model. Examples seen in correctional environments include acceptance and commitment therapy (ACT) and dialectical behavior therapy (DBT). A curriculum called *Achieving Change Through Value-Based Behavior* (Zarling, Lawrence, & Orengo-Aguayo, 2017) was designed based on the ACT model, and is used in Iowa as the primary treatment intervention for individuals convicted of intimate partner violence (IPV) offenses.

Moral Development Approaches

Some would argue that moral education does not belong in a section on cognitive skills. However, in placing it here, we focus on the developmental changes in reasoning structures that human beings experience over the life course. Humans, according to Piaget (1948), Kohlberg (1976), Warren (1983), and others, progress from the relatively concrete cognitive reasoning structures of children to the more flexible thinking of adults. If our learning environment affords the experience to make such developmental progressions, we are likely to become "more skilled" than one who continues to engage in absolute, concrete forms of reasoning. Immature forms of reasoning create situations in which answers are either "yes" or "no," problems are viewed from single rather than multiple perspectives, one's capacity to understand the perspectives of others is seriously constrained, and moral decisions depend solely on concerns about external rewards and punishments. Hence why this approach has been applied to corrections.

Lawrence Kohlberg's **stages of moral development** (Kohlberg, Colby, Gibbs, Speicher-Dubin, & Candee, 1979) form a cognitive developmental classification system that classifies individuals according to the ways in which they think about justice, fairness, and "right" courses of action. As with other cognitive approaches, the six stages of moral judgment pertain to the form or process of reasoning rather than to actual choices that the reasoning might support. The classification process and the treatment model that follows involve assigning an individual to one of the stages on this developmental continuum of cognitive complexity.

Moral judgment theory shares assumptions common to several other ego and cognitive developmental theories as set forth by Loevinger (1966); Piaget (1948); Sullivan, Grant, and Grant (1957); and others. These theories maintain that cognitive development:

1. Involves changes in the qualitative thought process that describes the way one thinks (not what one thinks).

2. Occurs through a developmental sequence of stages that is the same for all people.

3. Occurs in the direction of increasing complexity (i.e., one's thinking becomes more complex with development).

4. Represents an underlying logic at each developmental stage that appears to be consistent across situations.

5. Occurs through stages that are hierarchical integrations that enable individuals to comprehend all stages below and one stage above their diagnosed stage of moral reasoning.

Because development can cease at any point along the continuum, a cross-section of the population, theoretically, would show a distribution of persons at all stages.

There are three levels of reasoning in the moral development continuum: preconventional, conventional, and postconventional. Each level is comprised of two stages. A brief overview of the stage characteristics follows:

Preconventional Reasoning:

Stage 1: Moral decision-making involves blind obedience to authority to avoid punishment, defer to power or prestige, and avoid trouble. The interests of other individuals are not recognized.

Stage 2: A "right" course of action at this stage is predicated upon such instrumental considerations as the avoidance of punishment and the furtherance of one's own self-interests. The attainment of these objectives, however, engages one in exchanges and deals with other persons. Thus, others are important in an instrumental sense, as parties to such a deal.

Conventional Reasoning:

Stage 3: Moral reasoning is internally motivated by loyalty to other people and by a desire to live up to what is expected by significant others. Reasoning at this stage reflects an application of the "Golden Rule" philosophy.

Stage 4: Decisions reflect a desire to maintain such social institutions as the family, the community, and the country as social systems. The roles and rules of these systems are salient.

Postconventional Reasoning:

Stage 5: Moral reasoning adheres to the utilitarian notion of a social contract or the need to weigh certain rights, values, and legal principles against the greatest good for the greatest number of people.

Stage 6: Such ethical principles of justice as the right to life and respect for the dignity of other persons as ends rather than means are used to generate moral decisions. These principles are maintained to exist in a consistent and universal manner that is exclusive of laws or circumstances.

In juvenile and adult populations, we seldom observe individuals who are reasoning at either Stage 1 or Stage 6. These are extreme cases. Stage-specific reasoning is perhaps clearer with an example for each of the stages. Let our example be of Tim, a boy who is deciding whether to steal a bicycle that he finds unlocked on a school playground. It is important to remember that Tim's stage of moral judgment is not determined by his choice to steal the bike or to not steal it. Instead, it is his thought process, or reasons for his choice, that determines his stage of moral judgment. In fact, there are stage-specific reasons for or against stealing. For example:

If Tim were identified at Stage 2, we might hear him say that he stole the bike because he wanted one, and no one was around, so he knew he would not get caught. If he decided not to steal the bike, he might say that he was afraid of getting caught and being punished.

If Tim were classified as Stage 3, relationships with others would be an important consideration in resolving this moral dilemma. He might decide to steal the bike, for example, so that he could be with his other friends who had bicycles. He might decide not to steal the bike out of concern for the bike owner who would be hurt by losing it. A "Golden Rule" mentality may be heard as he relates his reasoning. That is, because Tim knows that he would not like to have his own property stolen, he chooses not to steal another's bicycle.

At Stage 4, an individual places priority on the importance of maintaining social systems. Laws, of course, help in this regard. It is hard to find a Stage 4 decision that would justify stealing the bike. But a Stage 4 decision not to steal the bike would place priority on obeying laws, not to avoid punishment or the disappointment of others, but rather because laws are important to maintaining social order. Tim might consider what would happen if everyone just stole whatever they wanted to steal.

Finally, a Stage 5 decision against stealing the bike would focus on universal rights that should exist exclusive of laws or circumstances. Property is one such right. Thus, Tim might reason that the owner of the bicycle has a right to keep it, regardless of the laws or opinions of others, or for that matter, what might happen to Tim if he gets caught.

As we observe Kohlberg's developmental sequence of cognitive reasoning, we can also observe some important developmental gates where some earlier cognitive difficulties would cease to exist. Stage 2 individuals, for example, demonstrate an external locus of control—a right course of action is determined by what is occurring in the external environment, where the individual scans the situation to determine whether he or she will be rewarded or punished. By Stage 3, however, the individual thinks about his or her relationships with others, an internalized notion. Similarly, the Stage 3 individual is capable of empathizing with others who are like him or her. And by Stage 5, empathy is afforded to those who are not like the self. Empathy and internal locus of control are among the cognitive skills addressed in other cognitive behavioral models.

In correctional treatment programs that emerge from Kohlberg's stages of moral judgment, the most important goal is to try to achieve growth from Stage 2, preconventional reasoning, to the conventional reasoning of at least Stage 3. This is because prosocial, empathic orientations begin at Stage 3, as does the notion of an internalized value system or conscience. Imagine, for example, the child whose decision to cheat or not to cheat on a test is predicated upon an externalized consideration of whether the teacher is in the room (a Stage 2 decision), versus the child who bases the decision not to cheat on an internalized belief that cheating is wrong. In fact, research on moral judgment and delinquency reports that moral judgment stages are significantly lower among system-impacted juveniles than among those who are not involved in the system (Jennings, Kilkenny, & Kohlberg, 1983). Typically, a significantly higher proportion of juveniles in the system are diagnosed at Stage 2 than are those who are not justice-involved. Thus, the goal of facilitating development to Stage 3 appears to be well founded.

The interventions designed to do that, moral education programs, assume that growth in moral judgment is most likely to occur when an individual interacts with prosocial environmental factors that encourage growth. Specifically, Kohlberg has maintained that exposure to fair and participatory environments promotes moral development. Therefore, the moral education groups expose participants to moral dilemmas that are then discussed in groups of individuals who are each thinking through the various issues at different stages of moral judgment. It is hoped that, over time, the moral conflict, its discussion, and its resolution will advance individuals to the higher levels of reasoning demonstrated by their peers in the group.

Cognitive Interventions in Corrections that Incorporate Moral Education

Current applications of moral education use the moral discussion groups and the Kohlberg developmental theory in multimodal approaches, combined with other cognitive behavioral or social learning components. Employing moral education in conjunction with other approaches recognizes that the moral education groups add an important values-based component to the cognitive skills and cognitive restructuring programs. Values, after all, are internalized and with us on a consistent basis. Learned behaviors and cognitions, on the other hand, are vulnerable to the competing rewards associated with antisocial behavior; because crime can be so rewarding, one might be more likely to use a new prosocial skill if it is supported by an internalized moral argument (or conscience) (Goldstein & Glick, 1995). Goldstein and his associates apply this concept in a cognitive behavioral program called Aggression Replacement Training® (ART) (Goldstein et al., 1998; Glick & Gibbs, 2011). Evaluation studies of ART find it to be an effective approach (Aos et al., 2006; Gunderson & Svartdal, 2006; Goldstein & Glick, 1995; Goldstein et al., 1998).

ART consists of three components:

1. *Skillstreaming.* This first module teaches a wide range of social skills, using the model for teaching skills discussed above, as originally developed by Goldstein and Glick.

2. *Anger control training (ACT).* This module teaches participants to recognize signs of anger in time to control it. Participants complete "hassle logs," which are similar to behavior chains, but with a focus on precursors to anger. Participants identify **physiological cues** (e.g., tense jaw, flushed face, clenched hands, upset stomach, etc.) that will alert them to early indicators of anger. Cognitive self-talk is also incorporated, as clients learn **self-statements** designed to lower anger arousal, such as *"chill out"* or *"calm down."* Cognitive skills, called **reducers** provide participants with emotion-regulation strategies, for instance, deep breathing and visualization. Finally, participants are taught to regularly self-evaluate how well they controlled their anger.

3. *Moral Reasoning.* The program's use of moral education is similar to Kohlberg's original model. Clients discuss and attempt to resolve moral dilemmas. Some of the dilemmas are standard to the Kohlberg model (e.g., the man who steals a drug to save his dying wife, or the "lifeboat dilemma"). Other dilemmas tap issues that may come up within the group or the correctional environment.

An additional example of a program that integrates the cognitive model with moral education is moral reconation therapy (MRT; Little & Robinson, 1986). MRT uses several group and workbook exercises designed to develop and improve moral reasoning through 16 graded moral and cognitive stages. MRT can be divided into shorter components but is somewhat less structured than other cognitive behavioral curricula. The flexibility of this curriculum allows facilitators to conduct open groups, where participants can enter at any time, as each member is working on their own stage. This is particularly desirable in correctional settings, such as residential or community-based programs, where having participants on a waiting list for treatment entry is problematic. This intervention is most likely to be used in general correctional settings or substance abuse treatment facilities. Evaluation results on MRT are mixed (Aos et al., 2006; Armstrong, 2003; Finn, 1998).

WIDESCALE APPLICATION OF THE COGNITIVE MODEL

The focus of the chapter up to this point has been on describing the cognitive model in general, and then on its application to a justice-involved population. It is important to note that within this "justice-involved population" there are many important subgroups. The question becomes, does this model still work for individuals who fall outside the typical corrections demographic of adult males. There is evidence to suggest that a cognitive behavioral model works with women (Duwe & Clark, 2015; Gehring, Van Voorhis, & Bell, 2010), juveniles (Lipsey, 1992; Lipsey & Wilson, 1998; Lipsey, 2009), and those with chronic mental illness (Morgan, Kroner, Mills, Bauer, & Serna, 2014; Van Horn et al., 2019). This section will focus on the application of a cognitive model to justice-involved females, as despite being effective, there are important program modifications needed for this population. The other area of focus for this section will be application of the cognitive model on a global scale. Use of CBT is not exclusive to the United States. In fact, the risk, need, responsivity (RNR) model, which serves as a foundation to effective correctional practices, was conceptualized by a group of Canadian scholars (see Bonta & Andrews, 2017). This section will also explore research on use of the cognitive model with justice-involved individuals outside of the United States.

Application to System-Impacted Women

It is important to stress that most of the programs discussed above were developed for justice-involved males and evaluated on male populations. Even in the largest **meta-analysis** conducted to date, Mark Lipsey (2009) cautions that the vast majority of studies available to his review were of programs attended by males. Thus, nearly 20 years after the early meta-analyses (e.g., Andrews et al., 1990), only 4% of the studies consisted of all-female samples (Lipsey, 2009). In response, a number of scholars maintain that traditional, correctional client-based, cognitive-restructuring groups should be re-evaluated for women (Bloom et al., 2003; Chesney-Lind, 1998). These concerns are especially pertinent to the antisocial thinking programs. Researchers have noted, for example, that women are less likely than men to possess the prototypical antisocial thinking (Barriga, Landau et al., 2000; Erez, 1988). Further, Carol Gilligan (1982) is well known for her critique of Kohlberg's stages of moral judgment, discussed earlier. Gilligan's research suggested that women's moral development was more likely to revolve around concerns for their relationships and their own decisions in the context of relationships. Additionally, antisocial thinking does not appear to be as strong a risk factor among women as among men. In our research on women's risk assessment, for example, the effects of antisocial thinking on recidivism are inconsistent across studies. We do, however, notice that other cognitions, such as self-efficacy, empowerment/responsibility, and anger, are more consistently related to women's recidivism (Van Voorhis et al., 2010).

Most of the concerns regarding cognitive behavioral programs do not involve whole-scale abandonment of the approach for women. There are, after all, clinical dimensions of both the social learning and the cognitive behavioral approach that are meaningful to the treatment of both male and female clients, such as positive reinforcement, modeling, generalization, and therapeutic relationships (Worell & Remer, 2003). However, **gender-responsive programming** initiatives in both the United States and Canada note that correctional programs for women should target the risk factors that more accurately describe women's pathways to crime. There is evidence to do so. Gobeil et al. (2016) conducted a meta-analysis with traditional cognitive behavioral programs versus those that also had gender-responsive components and found that those that were gender-responsive in nature were more effective in reducing women's recidivism than the more traditional CBT programs. Thus, instead of placing a priority on whether women are blaming their victims, a more productive focus of cognitive behavioral treatment might target **self-efficacy**/empowerment, healthy relationships and family issues, parental stress, trauma and abuse, and environmental safety (Blanchette & Brown, 2006; Bloom et al., 2003; Van Voorhis et al., 2010).

Program curricula are being redesigned to do just that. For example, *Moving On*, a cognitive curriculum developed by Marilyn Van Dieten (1998), integrates cognitive behavioral techniques with social learning, ecological, and relational approaches. The primary goal of the program is to provide women with crime-free alternatives and choices by assisting them to recognize and mobilize both personal and community resources. The program presents a series of topics that move from a broad understanding of what influences behavior (e.g., culture, society, family, relationships) to the more personal topics associated with self-change. Specific modules in the program include: (a) help women identify negative self-talk and substitute it with positive cognitions; (b) teach women valuable decision-making, problem-solving, social, self-management, and stress-relief skills; and (c) assist women's reintegration into the community. A review of the program module topics demonstrates that the cognitive model can be incorporated into gender-responsive programming. Two recent evaluations of the program found that it reduced women's recidivism (Duwe & Clark, 2015; Gehring et al., 2010).

Seeking Safety is another cognitive behavioral program for individuals who have experiences trauma, abuse, PTSD, and substance use (Najavits, Weiss, & Liese, 1996). While it has been used with both men and women, it is especially relevant to female clients because they suffer from these comorbid disorders at higher rates than men. This program has been well researched among male and female veterans (Cook, Walser, Kane, Ruzek, & Woody, 2006), low-income urban women (Hein, Cohen, Litt, Miele, Capstick, 2004), incarcerated women (Zlotnick, Najavits, Rohsennow, & Johnson, 2003), and in other settings.

Simply put, cognitive behavioral programming has moved beyond the "one size fits all" focus on antisocial thinking to additional treatment targets. Programs are being fit to specific populations and needs, and evaluation research is beginning to show favorable results. For more detail on interventions for justice-involved women, see Chapter 13.

Application Across the Globe

The cognitive model has been used widely in the United States, but also incorporated into correctional programs internationally. As noted, Canadian researchers were at the forefront of developing the model for effective correctional treatment in outlining the principles of effective intervention (Gendreau, 1996a), also known as the risk, need, responsivity (RNR) model (Andrews et al. 1990, Bonta & Andrews, 2017). The responsivity principle within this model calls for evidence-based models of intervention, namely, behavioral and cognitive strategies.

As such, many countries within Western culture integrate the cognitive model into treatment for their justice-involved populations. For Europe specifically, Koehler, Hamilton, and Losel (2013) conducted an international survey of European correctional treatment programs for young clients and found that, similar to North America, many different approaches were used, and adherence to effective practice principles varied widely. Yet, also like North America, the majority of programs surveyed reported adopting a cognitive behavioral approach to treatment. In terms of program fidelity, survey results suggested that process and outcome evaluations of program effectiveness were rare. In fact, they report that most of the studies came from Britain, and in many European countries, they found no evaluation studies of justice-involved youth. Beyond Western countries, program evaluations in correctional settings are even less common.

To examine the effectiveness of a cognitive model among a European population, Koehler and colleagues (2012) conducted a meta-analysis, or study of studies, on the effects of juvenile justice treatment in Europe. Consistent with findings from meta-analyses conduced in the United States and Canada, they found that (1) overall treatment worked, (2) cognitive behavioral models increased the treatment effect, and (3) models that adhered to RNR revealed the strongest effect. This research suggests that the Western world seems to subscribe to a similar philosophy about effective treatment models in corrections, although application of these models is likely to vary from one country to the next.

THE EFFECTIVENESS OF COGNITIVE BEHAVIORAL PROGRAMS—THE ROLE OF PROGRAM INTEGRITY

Throughout this chapter, we have presented much evidence of the effectiveness of cognitive behavioral programs for correctional clients. This optimism pertains to clients as a whole as well as to specific types of clients, such as those convicted of sex offenses (Hall, 1995), women (Gehring et al., 2010; Spiropoulos et al., 2006), substance users (Pearson & Lipton, 1999), and individuals with chronic mental illness (Morgan et al., 2014; Van Horn et al., 2019). In response, the implementation of cognitive behavioral programs and their curricula has been widespread. Two meta-analyses of cognitive behavioral programs note that the most effective treatment programs were small demonstration projects, studied, in some cases, by the very individuals who developed the curricula. When the programs were expanded to entire agencies and evaluated by outside researchers, however, the treatment effect diminished considerably (see Lipsey et al., 2001; Tong & Farrington, 2006; Wilson, Gallagher, & Mackenzie, 2000). Similar findings are shown in meta-analyses of the effects of program quality on client outcomes (see Lipsey, 2009; Lowenkamp et al., 2006; Nesovic, 2003).

The likely explanation for such findings faults the treatment integrity of the expanded programs. During the pilot phase of these programs, facilitators were probably carefully trained and monitored. Most importantly, the small demonstration sites were able to keep close tabs on program quality. Understandably, some of the initial focus on quality was lost when these programs were implemented agency-wide to larger groups of participants, and by individuals not directly involved with the development of the program.

How does this happen? If an agency wants to implement a given cognitive behavioral program, they invest in extensive staff training, purchase manuals, and start delivering the program. But does this assure that trained facilitators understand the training, keep to the basic program design, maintain good relationships with the participants, or are adept at using the core skills of the cognitive behavioral and social learning approaches (e.g., modeling, practice, feedback, and reinforcement)? Will staff be retrained if they have not retained these skills? Will some agencies, due to budgetary constraints, fail to train staff at all?

To illustrate, a recent evaluation of Reasoning and Rehabilitation found no significant difference between the program participants and members of the comparison group. As shown in Figure 9.2, the 12-month recidivism rates (rearrest) for those in Reasoning and Rehabilitation was 36% as compared to 38% for the comparison group (Van Voorhis et al., 2002). Further examination of Figure 9.2, however, finds that some of the Reasoning and Rehabilitation programs worked better than others. Groups in which leaders maintained good classroom control (structure) achieved recidivism rates of 19% instead of the 36% achieved by all of the participants. Additionally, use of appropriate cognitive behavioral techniques (practice and feedback) increased the effectiveness of the program. Groups in which participants had the opportunity to practice in all of the sessions evidenced a recidivism rate of 24% instead of 36%. It is not clear what was occurring in the less successful programs, but less participation suggests that perhaps the group leader was doing most of the talking rather than helping participants practice new ways of thinking and behaving. Understandably, those who completed the program also had much lower recidivism rates (25%). In sum, while policymakers and practitioners are optimistic about the cognitive behavioral approach, much needs to be done to guarantee that the programs are delivered according to their design.

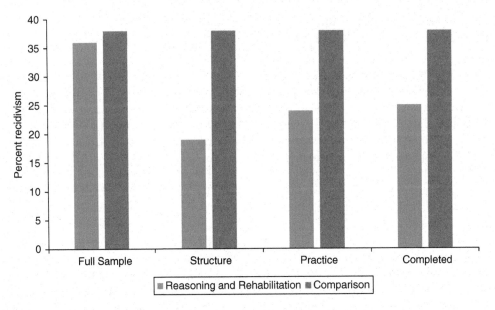

FIGURE 9.2 Effects of program quality on client outcomes.
Source: Van Voorhis et al. (2002)

Finally, Lowenkamp and colleagues (2006) conducted a study using over 3,000 justice-involved clients and 38 residential treatment programs. Using an instrument designed to measure program fidelity, they were interested in examining the relationship between program integrity and program effectiveness. They found a modest 4% reduction in recidivism across the 38 programs for those who successfully completed treatment. Using the Correctional Program Assessment Inventory (CPAI; see Chapter 4) as a measure of program integrity, they found a strong correlation between **program fidelity** and a reduction in recidivism. This research suggests that programs that use an effective model (such as CBT) and implement that model with fidelity/integrity are more likely to have clients who benefit from treatment engagement.

CONCLUSION

Cognitive and cognitive behavioral therapies have achieved much respect among mental and behavioral health providers and correctional practitioners. They are among the most successful treatment models presently available. Correctional agencies have discovered that they can train correctional practitioners, including some who may not have clinical degrees, to use the models effectively. In part, this may be attributable to the fact that cognitive interventions offer a demystified system of therapy, in comparison to an approach such as psychoanalysis. Indeed, many of the popular "self-help" books currently in print are based on cognitive therapy techniques. At the same time, many of the in-service training opportunities for correctional treatment practitioners emphasize cognitive therapy and cognitive counseling. Program materials (e.g., treatment manuals, lesson plans, assessments, and training modules) are readily available for CBT-based approaches. The counseling techniques and group treatments can be short-term, although more intensive treatment is needed for higher risk/higher need individuals.

These comments are not intended to oversimplify the cognitive approach. Cognitive therapies require active and directive counselors who challenge the irrational thoughts and irresponsible behaviors of their clients, while continuing to value their humanity and dignity. Given the reliance that criminal justice agencies have on nonclinical practitioners, it is also important that agencies train staff in basic cognitive theory and techniques, outside the application of this model to a particular curriculum. Foundational training will help ensure that practitioners understand what they are looking for and how to effectively address it using a cognitive model, outside a scripted curriculum.

Finally, agencies could also incur serious problems with treatment integrity if, in the course of relying too much on the simplicity of cognitive therapy, they omit adequate training and the development of treatment manuals to save resources. In such instances, programs known to be effective are observed to be "ineffective" when in fact they were not implemented according to the design (Lowenkamp et al., 2006; Van Voorhis et al., 1995; Van Voorhis et al., 2002). Just the same, the systems of counseling identified in this chapter have tremendous potential to change the antisocial thinking patterns and maladaptive behavior styles of correctional clients nationally and internationally. Because they target a set of factors known to be highly criminogenic (Andrews & Bonta, 2010), it is hardly surprising that research has found them to be effective.

Participation Exercises

Participation Exercise 1: Rational Emotive Behavior Therapy

Recall that rational emotive behavior therapy teaches clients to recognize how irrational thoughts or beliefs can lead to negative emotional states that impair our existence. This Participation Exercise is intended to help you become more aware of how your own thoughts influence your emotions.

Over the next few days, whenever you experience a strong emotion (positive or negative), reflect on what you were thinking at that moment. Record the *activating event*, your *thoughts and beliefs*, and the resulting *emotional state*.

Example:

Activating Event	Thoughts	Emotional State
You receive a low grade on an assignment	*"I am never going to be able to pass this course."* *"Maybe I should just drop out of school—I will never succeed."* *"I will never amount to anything."* *"I'm worthless."*	*Depression/ self-pity*

1. How did this exercise make you become more aware of your thoughts and beliefs?

2. What connection did you notice between your thoughts and your emotional state?

3. If the self-talk resulted in a negative emotional state, can you think of alternative thoughts that could be used to dispute or replace these irrational thoughts?

Participation Exercise 2: Antisocial Thinking

Now let us apply this exercise to people involved in the justice system. Read the list that follows describing some of the antisocial thoughts and beliefs often displayed by this population. Next, examine the list of Walters's criminal thinking styles below and identify which thinking style *best* fits the client statement. Some statements may apply to more than one style, but try to pick the best fit so that each thinking style is used once.

Criminal Thought Process	Thinking Style	Definition
Proactive Criminal Thinking	Mollification	Making excuses/blaming others for my actions.
	Entitlement	Feeling above the law or special. I deserve what I want.
	Power Orientation	Asserting control, power, or dominance; power-thrusting or intimidating others.
	Superoptimism	Believing I can get away with anything; unrealistic about consequences of crime.
Reactive Criminal Thinking	Cutoff	Ignoring responsible behaviors; being impulsive; an "I don't care" or "screw it" attitude.
	Cognitive Indolence	Lazy thinking or taking short-cuts around problems; looks for the easy way out; lacks critical thinking; irresponsible.
	Discontinuity	Getting off track or getting sidetracked or distracted from your goals; unpredictable.

Client Thought	Thinking Style?
1. "I don't care that I stole from him. His insurance will cover it."	
2. "Sometimes you just have to show them who's boss."	
3. "I knew skipping work and getting high with my coworker was a bad idea, but we were stressed out and needed a break."	
4. "I'm supposed to start treatment this week, but I'm not feeling like it."	
5. "I'm late for work again—I'll just say I forgot to clock in."	
6. "My friends would never give me up."	
7. "They owed me that money. I saved that company plenty more than I took."	

Participation Exercise 3: Cognitive Skills

In this Participation Exercise, you will practice the steps of problem-solving as it applies to two common high-risk situations for correctional clients. For each of the situations described below, imagine that you are the probation officer working with this client during a supervision session. Work through each of the steps of problem-solving as you would with the client.

Situation #1

John is on probation and has a court-ordered condition to abstain from alcohol and other drugs. A close family member has recently passed, and John knows there is going to be drugs and alcohol at the funeral.

Situation #2

Mary shows up on time for her scheduled office visit with her probation officer. She reported that she is having trouble at work. She keeps getting yelled at by her boss and believes he does not like or trust her because of her criminal history. She said work is stressing her out and making her want to go back to using. Maintaining employment is a condition of Mary's probation.

Problem-Solving Steps	Instructions
Step 1: Define the problem and identify goals.	Clearly state the client's problem and identify goals the client has related to this problem—what does the client want or need?
Step 2: Brainstorm options for addressing the problem.	Think of several options, realistic or not, prosocial or antisocial, anything goes.
Step 4: Choose the best solution by considering the pros and cons of the options.	Next to each option, list the pros and cons of that option for the client; circle the best option.
Step 5: Implement the solution.	Write down what steps the client would need to take to implement the solution you choose.
Step 6: Evaluate how well the solution worked.	Pretend the client executed the solution, and it went well (or not); write how you would praise use of the skill.

Discussion Questions

1. How would you describe the theory behind the cognitive therapies?

2. What makes these therapies so popular today?

3. Think of your favorite crime show or movie. Identify a criminal act in the movie. Complete the ABC model on that criminal act. If the "beliefs" are not stated, take a guess at what irrational thoughts led to the criminal action. Be sure you list the feelings, action, and external consequences under "C."

4. Think of an occasion when you made a choice you were not proud of (e.g., yelled at someone, lied about something, did not meet a commitment). Try to complete a behavior chain. Begin by writing down the action you are not proud of on the *action* line. Then work backwards, identifying the *situation* that triggered your action, your *thoughts* and your *feelings* before you acted, and then write down the positive and negative *consequences* after your action took place.

5. Think about the last time you experienced a strong negative emotion (e.g., sadness, anger, anxiety). Can you recall what thoughts went through your mind before or during the experience? Write them down. Can you dispute them—that is, point out the irrational elements in them? Finally try to restructure or change your thoughts into more rational thoughts.

6. Describe the techniques and goal of moral education interventions.

7. Explain the difference between a cognitive restructuring program and a cognitive skills program.

8. What role do antisocial thinking styles play in crime causation?

9. How effective are cognitive behavioral programs with female correctional clients?

10. How do correctional programs lose their integrity?

Key to Participation Exercise 2

1. M; 2. PO; 3. C; 4. D; 5. CI; 6. S; 7. E.

GLOSSARY OF KEY TERMS

acceptance   accepting one's present state with openness and curiosity

activating event   a situation or trigger, often unpleasant or risky, which evokes both an internal response (thoughts/feelings) and an external response (behavior); the "A" in rational emotive behavior therapy's ABC model

all-or-nothing thinking   a common irrational way of thinking in which an individual views things as either black or white

antisocial cognitions   thoughts or beliefs that go against the laws or rules in society, or that cause harm to others; also called criminal thinking

automatic thoughts   spontaneous, almost reflexive words or images that go through a person's mind as a situation (or activating event) arises

behavior chain   a tool for identifying risky thoughts, so that those thoughts can be targeted for change; consists of *situation, thoughts, feelings, action,* and *consequences;* a pictorial form of a thinking report

catastrophizing   a common irrational way of thinking in which individuals exaggerate the importance of an event or situation by assuming that it is far worse than it actually is

cognitive behavioral therapy (CBT)   a compilation of cognitive and behavior therapy which recognizes that cognitions, as well as behaviors, are learned and that behavior is prompted, supported, mediated, and reinforced by cognitions; the major goal of CBT approaches is to change patterns of thinking or behavior that are detrimental to clients

cognitive model   a model that proposes that it is dysfunctional thinking that influences feelings and behavior, and when individuals think in a more realistic and adaptive way, they experience fewer problem behaviors

cognitive restructuring   a model of cognitive or cognitive behavioral approaches in which interventions endeavor to change the content of beliefs, values, and attitudes (i.e., what we think)

cognitive skills   a model of cognitive or cognitive behavioral approaches in which interventions seek to improve cognitive processes—the structure and form of reasoning (i.e., how we think) rather than its content

cognitive therapy (CT)   developed by Aaron Beck in the 1960s; he proposed that dysfunctional thinking was common to all psychological problems, and by teaching individuals to evaluate their thinking, and develop more realistic and adaptive thought patterns, their mood and behaviors would improve.

consequences   results of our thoughts/beliefs; in REBT's ABC model, consequences include emotions and behaviors that result from beliefs (B); in the behavior chain, consequences are defined as the positive and negative outcomes of one's action

conventional reasoning   one of three levels of reasoning in the moral development continuum in which prosocial, empathic orientations and the notion of an internalized value system or conscience begin (Stage 3); and an individual begins to place priority on the importance of maintaining social systems (Stage 4)

core beliefs   the global or overgeneralized ways that individuals see the world; they are foundational to the way in which individuals interpret situations.

criminal thinking styles   a model developed by Glenn Walters that describes seven specific criminal thinking styles that are empirically predictive of criminal conduct; these thinking styles are identified via a validated assessment called the Psychological Inventory of Criminal Thinking Styles (PICTS)

gender-responsive programming   interventions that target risk factors that more accurately reflect women's pathways to crime

generalize   the ability to apply a cognitive skill to a variety of risky situations

graduated practice   role-play that is more realistic or advanced, so that it better simulates real-world experiences

grounding   paying attention to present body sensations, emotions, mental images, thoughts, or other perceptual experiences

irrational belief   a distorted perception of an activating event that occurs in an unhealthy thought sequence; irrational beliefs decrease happiness and maximize pain

mindfulness interventions   interventions that incorporate the process of openly attending, with awareness, to one's present moment experience

modeling demonstration of a skill by someone proficient in use of the skill; in cognitive skills interventions, the group facilitator/practitioner models the skill steps using a relatable scenario to demonstrate how the steps should be followed

moral dilemmas situations in which an individual must make a difficult choice between two or more courses of action that conflict with one's moral principles

moral education programs interventions designed under the assumption that growth in moral judgment is most likely to occur when an individual interacts with prosocial environmental factors that encourage growth

overgeneralization a common irrational way of thinking in which one negative event is seen as a never-ending pattern of defeat

physiological cues bodily cues that serve to alert individuals to their feelings of anger (e.g., tense jaw, flushed face, clenched hands, stomach feelings, etc.) while they still have time to control such anger; these are taught in the ART (and other) CBT-based curricula

postconventional reasoning one of three levels of reasoning in the moral development continuum in which moral reasoning adheres to a notion of universal rights that should exist exclusive of laws or circumstances (Stage 5); and such ethical principles of justice as the right to life and respect for the dignity of other persons as ends rather than means are used to generate moral decisions (Stage 6)

preconventional reasoning one of three levels of reasoning in the moral development continuum in which blind obedience to authority is employed only to avoid trouble or punishment without any consideration of the interests of others (Stage 1); and the right course of action is predicated on avoidance of punishment or to further one's own self-interests (Stage 2)

proactive a planned or goal-directed criminal thought process; one of two criminal thought process subtypes (proactive and reactive) conceptualized in Walters's criminal thinking styles

problem-solving an advanced cognitive skill that is widely applicable to a range of risky situations and whose steps are taught in a number of cognitive behavioral curricula

program fidelity the degree to which a program adheres to the design of the original model; also called program integrity; can impact the effectiveness of a program

rational beliefs perceptions that occur in healthy thought processes; rational beliefs increase positive feelings, minimize pain, and are accurately related to real (not imagined) events

rational emotive behavior therapy (REBT)   a foundational, popular cognitive restructuring approach that teaches clients to recognize how irrational thoughts or beliefs can lead to negative emotional states that impair our existence

reducers   strategies that are taught in anger control training as a means of helping individuals reduce levels of anger; such strategies may include visualization of peaceful scenes, deep breathing, thinking about the consequences of acting out anger, and counting backward

role-play   a mechanism used for practicing cognitive skills; in cognitive skills interventions, the client role-plays skills by following skill steps, after the skill has been demonstrated by the group facilitator/practitioner

self-efficacy   one's self-confidence that they are able to change a behavior; a human trait associated with success

self-statements   internal statements that can serve to "trigger" anger or, with the incorporation of anger control training methods, lower anger arousal with the use of calming phrases

self-talk   talk or thoughts that are directed toward oneself; can be taught as a cognitive skill that helps clients identify negative self-talk and substitute it with positive cognitions

shoulding   a common irrational way of thinking in which individuals try to motivate themselves by saying "I must…" or "I ought…," and so feel guilty when they do not

skill acquisition   a goal of cognitive skills training that involves learning the skill, which is done though practicing the skill steps

skill application   a goal of cognitive skills training which ensures that the client can generalize the cognitive skills to a variety of situations

social learning   an approach to counseling and therapy which maintains that observational learning is the most common form of human learning; social learning approaches provide clients with (a) role models with good relationship skills; (b) opportunities to practice newly learned skills and behaviors; (c) specific performance feedback; and (d) client reinforcement for learning the new behaviors

stages of moral judgment   the six stages of Lawrence Kohlberg's cognitive developmental classification system that classifies individuals according to the ways in which they think about justice, fairness, and "right" courses of action

thinking reports   a tool for identifying risky thoughts, so that those thoughts can be targeted for change; often consists of *situation, thoughts, feelings, behavior,* and *consequences*, and sometimes includes new or restructured thoughts; similar purpose as a behavior chain

virtual reality computer-generated environment that uses 2D or 3D visualization software and transmission devices to provide user input within a virtual world; used to treat psychological conditions such as anxiety disorders and piloted in a correctional setting as another mode to offering CBT-based interventions

CHAPTER 10

Social Learning Interventions

Patricia Van Voorhis and Emily J. Salisbury

Classical conditioning and operant conditioning, presented in Chapter 8, are not the only models of human learning. In fact, direct learning (operant conditioning) is not even the predominant mode of human learning. According to Albert Bandura (1977), most of the learning achieved by humans occurs through a process of **observational learning**. That is, notwithstanding the importance of reinforcement, punishment, and stimuli to learning, most of what we have learned over the course of our lifetimes has been learned vicariously, through observing and imitating others. From this perspective, **role models** and the process of **modeling** are crucial (Bandura, 1977). Social learning approaches integrate a number of the learning concepts discussed in Chapter 8, but the emphasis is on modeling. Modeling provides a means for clients to observe and imitate the behaviors, or **goal behaviors**, that the therapy is designed to teach.

Social learning programs dominate correctional rehabilitation endeavors. Their popularity is largely due to their efficiency and their cost-effectiveness, but their effectiveness cannot be

DOI: 10.4324/9780367808266-13

overlooked. Meta-analyses reveal that social learning models, especially when combined with cognitive behavioral models, are among the most effective treatment approaches (Andrews et al., 1990; Antonowicz & Ross, 1994; Bonta & Andrews, 2017; Dowden & Andrews, 2000; Lipsey, 1992, 2009; Losel, 1995). Indeed, high-quality social learning/cognitive behavioral treatment approaches have achieved reductions in recidivism as high as 20% to 30% (Bonta & Andrews, 2017).

To understand the importance of modeling to learning, we need only think for a minute about our own learning experiences. To have learned directly or solely through rewards and punishments, through a gradual process of shaping, would have been extremely inefficient. We did not pick up our skills, be they athletic, verbal, social, or occupational, solely through such a process of trial and error. We observed other athletes or writing styles that we especially appreciated, or we remembered the social skills of those whom we perceived as popular. Then we imitated the skills of these role models and, through practice and reinforcement, we became increasingly proficient in using them.

The modeling provided by others facilitates our own learning in several ways, by:

1. demonstrating how to perform a new behavior—an invaluable assistance to the acquisition of totally new techniques and skills;

2. prompting or showing us how to use the behavior at the appropriate times;

3. motivating us, or increasing our desire to use a new skill or behavior—especially when the model is reinforced for his or her skill; and

4. disinhibiting us—modeled behavior reduces our anxiety and fear about using totally new skills, thereby reducing tendencies to avoid rather than practice the new skill (Spiegler & Guevremont, 2002).

Alternatively, models who are punished for certain behaviors usually dissuade us from imitating their behaviors. The notion of general deterrence, for example, is based on the assumption that, as we view others being punished, we will avoid committing the same behaviors that led to their fate.

We might recognize that we did not imitate everyone we met, or even many of the people we met. Instead, we imitated the behavior of people who appeared competent, attractive, and those who were rewarded. This was a highly idiosyncratic process. You may have sought to imitate the attractive athlete, for example, while the student across from you was impressed with the knowledge demonstrated by her math teacher, and the student in front of her thought that the person in the front row of the class had a special flair for dress and style. Simply put, not everyone is a good role model, and those who are important role models for others may not be so for us, and vice versa. We will devote considerable attention in this chapter to the qualities needed to be an effective role model to juvenile and adult correctional clients.

Unfortunately, modeling also promotes the learning of antisocial behavior. Indeed, having antisocial associates (or role models) is a strong risk factor for offending behavior in juveniles and adults (Akers, 2001; Bonta & Andrews, 2017; Elliot, Huizinga, & Ageton, 1985). Poor parental modeling is strongly associated with antisocial behavior (Patterson, 1982; Patterson, Reid, & Dishion, 1992), and modeling of aggressive behavior leads to aggression and hostility in those who view aggression (Bandura, 1973; Kirby, Milich, & Hundley, 2003; Patterson, 1982).

FIGURE 10.1 Clinical Supervisor Otto Williams Jr. explains the goals of a therapeutic community at a class at the fresh start drug rehabilitation program at Northern State Prison in Newark, New Jersey.
Source: AP Photo/Daniel Hulshizer.

Environments are also important to the social learning paradigm. Therapeutic communities, a popular treatment strategy in both correctional and mental health settings, emphasize the importance of all aspects of the environment in the treatment of clients (see Figure 10.1). In traditional therapeutic communities, for example, both staff and incarcerated clients are trained to act as appropriate role models. All staff members, not just the treatment staff, are considered potential models. To model fair and respectful relationship styles, an effort is made to substitute authoritarian roles and policies with fairer modes of communication and decision-making. Administrators also endeavor to remove the oppressive trappings of institutional living and to replicate, as much as possible, life outside the institution (Burdon, Farabee, Prendergast, Messina, & Cartier, 2002). A therapeutic community may even remove some of the architectural and design features of the traditional prison, reasoning that the program cannot teach people how to function democratically and fairly in an environment that is excessively authoritarian.

In contrast to some of the earlier forms of milieu therapy, contemporary therapeutic communities based upon a social learning model show clear signs of success. One such program, the Amity prison-based drug treatment therapeutic community in California, found that participants in the treatment group were significantly less likely than those in the control group to be returned to prison following release (Wexler, DeLeon, Kressel, & Peters, 1999; Wexler, Melnick, Lowe, & Peters, 1999). Moreover, those in the treatment group who completed the therapeutic community treatment *and* aftercare group were significantly less likely to return to prison compared to those who: (1) dropped out of treatment; or (2) completed treatment but not aftercare (Prendergast, Hall, Wexler, Melnick, & Cao, 2004).

Social learning interventions also take cognitive processes (i.e., one's thoughts, beliefs, values, and perceptions) into account. Indeed, much of our learning involves the thoughts that prompt and support our behavior or those that appraise the stimuli that are presented to us (Bandura, 1977). Cognitive behavioral approaches recognize that the effectiveness of rewards, punishments, role models, and almost all other environmental factors are highly dependent upon how the client perceives these factors. They also more deliberately target thoughts and thought processes. A more detailed account of cognitive behavioral approaches for correctional clients is presented in Chapter 9.

WHO MAKES A GOOD ROLE MODEL?

As noted earlier, only certain individuals function as effective role models. A growing body of research shows us the qualities of good role modeling. For example, the early research by Albert Bandura and his associates (Bandura, 1965, 1977; Bandura, Ross, & Ross, 1963; Bandura & Walters, 1963) found that the following factors affect whether a person will be imitated:

1. attractiveness;
2. competence; and
3. extent to which the person is rewarded.

Early research by Donald Andrews (1980) focused on how system-involved people learn prosocial attitudes and behavior. Note that Andrews's term for prosocial attitudes is "anticriminal sentiments." In a series of studies, Andrews manipulated learning environments, examining each in turn, to identify optimal modeling styles for teaching people prosocial sentiments and behaviors. Andrews found that it was not enough to simply be exposed to anticriminal individuals; one also needed to participate in a process that involved discussion of the prosocial values to experience attitudinal change. Thus, opportunities to view modeled interactions and to practice or respond to others, facilitated learning.

Additional findings spoke to the relationship qualities of the role models. Andrews found that individuals who were skilled in interpersonal relationships, those who were more open, warm, and understanding of the viewpoints of others, effected more learning than those who were less skilled in these relationship qualities. In one study he reported that the type of probation officer whose clients had the least recidivism after the program was one who modeled anticriminal behaviors and sentiments, but also possessed good relationship skills (Andrews, 1980).

As shown in Table 10.1, officers who scored low on relationship skills and who even tacitly modeled criminal sentiments tended to have clients whose behavior did not change over time. Interestingly, the clients of officers who had good relationship skills but modeled antisocial attitudes were found to have higher recidivism rates. The clients of officers with good relationship styles who also modeled anticriminal behaviors showed lower recidivism rates. The importance of the relationship skills of the role model is also seen in the final group. Officers who were low in relationship skills but strong in anticriminal modeling did not produce the desired recidivism reductions. Simply put, models with warm interpersonal styles were much more effective than those with more detached modes of relating to clients. The relationship skills and interpersonal sensitivity of role models is crucial. Without it, the modeled behaviors often are not learned. However, we must remember that role models with advanced relationship skills will facilitate the learned transfer of whatever behaviors

TABLE 10.1 Relationship style versus the message: what do correctional clients learn?			
		Firm, Fair, Warm	Distant
Content of Probation Officer's Message	**Prosocial**	Prosocial values, beliefs, and behaviors	No behavioral change
	Antisocial	Antisocial values, beliefs, attitudes, and behaviors	No behavioral change

Source: Andrews, D. (1980). Some experimental investigations of the principles of differential association through deliberate manipulations of the structures of service systems. *American Sociological Review, 45,* 448–462.

they are modeling. If an interpersonally warm counselor or peer models antisocial behavior, it is his or her behavior that will be learned.

In later writings, Bonta and Andrews (2017) further defined the qualities of effective modeling. Good role models are noted to be enthusiastic, open, and flexible, and they afford their clients the freedom to express their opinions and feelings. This does not mean that the counselor or correctional worker never expresses disapproval and always says what clients want to hear. At times, good relationship skills will require that correctional counselors express disapproval toward clients. This must be done without threatening the clients' psychological sense of well-being, and is only effective when a trusting and fair relationship has been established. If a client has missed an appointment or returned late from a weekend furlough, for example, we cannot afford the luxury of ignoring the behavior. We can and should be honest about our concern and should do so by limiting our comments to the behavior and its consequences—consequences to the client and to us as his or her supervisor. In this way, we critique the behavior, but not the person. We retain a belief in the client's ability to succeed and in his or her inherent worth as an individual.

The relationship qualities of good role modeling also involve maintaining an environment of mutual liking, respect, and caring, in which openness, warmth, and understanding are offered within the limits of appropriate interpersonal boundaries. You will recall the importance of these relational skills from Chapter 3. In fact, if these relationship qualities are in place, clients' compliance to conditions of supervision increases, resulting in fewer violations and revocations. For example, Skeem and colleagues (2007) found that probation officers who had caring, fair, trusting, and authoritative (but not authoritarian) relationship styles significantly reduced the number of technical violations and revocations of their clients. An authoritarian style is strict, demanding, and directive, while being unresponsive to clients' needs. Moreover, increases in officer "toughness" (reflecting an indifference to views and feelings, expectations of compliance, and punitiveness when expectations are not met) actually increased clients' likelihoods of violations and revocations. On the other hand, officers who were too permissive and lenient were also more likely to increase non-compliance (Andrews & Kiessling, 1980; Trotter, 1999). Thus, the quality of the dual role relationships (firm, fair, and caring through law enforcement and case management roles) correctional staff have with clients is critical.

In addition to relationship qualities, correctional counselors must give considerable attention to the manner in which prosocial behavior is modeled and antisocial behavior is discouraged. In demonstrations of behaviors, for example, role models must be clear. If possible, the model should indicate, even if this has to be done verbally, that he or she is rewarded for using the behavior being modeled. In turn, the counselor must attend to rewarding or praising the client for demonstrating new behaviors. As discussed in the next section, reinforcement, a primary component of the operant conditioning paradigm, is also a key to social learning interventions. Clients must work in a reinforcing and encouraging environment. Moreover, if new behaviors or skills are difficult or fear-inducing, counselors should empathize with the client's fear, yet highlight the benefits of the new skill in achieving long-term goals. Where appropriate, counselors may also relate a time when they had, but overcame, a similar fear.

We might also give some attention to techniques of reinforcement and disapproval. Reinforcement often takes the form of praise. Bonta and Andrews (2017) recommend that such praise be strong, emphatic, and immediate statements of approval, support, and agreement with the client's statements or behavior. Non-verbal expressions such as eye contact, smiles, or a sharing of experiences are also sound techniques of approval. Additionally, some time should be given to a cogent statement of why approval of the client's actions is being offered—what is good about the behavior? Reactions of this nature, of course, should be strong enough to distinguish the counselor's responses as a reinforcement rather than a pleasant manner of behavior.

Bonta and Andrews (2017) recognize the occasional need to disapprove of a client's behavior in effective ways. Indeed, the probation officers studied in Andrews's earlier research—those who had good relationship skills—nevertheless did not make reinforcing comments indiscriminately; they did so in a contingent manner (Andrews, 1980). Correctional counselors are advised to make clear, emphatic, and immediate statements of disapproval or disagreement. These reactions should follow the behavior or the counselor's knowledge of the behavior in a close time proximity— not several days later. Clients must receive a clear explanation of the counselor's reasons for disapproval. This might also include a suggestion of a prosocial alternative to the attitude or behavior to which the counselor objects. Disapproval should stand in stark contrast to a counselor's more satisfying relationship with the client (or else it will not be recognized as disapproval). Finally, the relationship should return to a more positive regard once the client again demonstrates prosocial behavior.

In summary, Bonta and Andrews (2017) suggest that "anticriminal modeling" include the following:

1. Learn to recognize antisocial thinking patterns and be able to differentiate them from prosocial modes of thinking (see Chapter 9 for antisocial thinking errors). Recognize also that specific offenses, for example, sex offenses, violent sex offenses, spouse abuse, hate crimes, and more general forms of violence, have their own cognitions and supporting language (e.g., "She was coming on to me"). Do not show tacit approval of these orientations.

2. Correct any negative attitudes toward police, courts, and correctional agencies.

3. Do not tolerate or become lax toward rule-breaking behaviors or "ends justify the means" orientations.

4. The antisocial expressions of case managers may promote the recidivism of their clients. Be attentive to your own antisocial expressions (e.g., cynicism regarding the criminal justice system).

5. Do not attempt "con talk" in an effort to become closer to clients.

6. Model "anticriminal expressions:"
   (i)   emphasize negative consequences of offending behavior;
   (ii) reject antisocial cognitions (see Chapter 9); and
   (iii) identify the "risks" of associating with antisocial others or of accepting the belief systems of antisocial others.
7. Encourage association with "prosocial others."
8. Encourage clients to avoid "high-risk" situations.
9. Model good self-management skills: examining one's own conduct, thinking before acting, thinking about the consequences of one's own behavior, setting realistic standards for oneself, and working on avoidance and denial patterns.
10. Insist on attendance and the completion of assignments listed in the treatment plan.
11. Focus on criminogenic expressions and behavior and the behaviors that may lead to recidivism rather than the behaviors that are simply irritating (e.g., loud mannerisms).
12. Reinforce prosocial expressions, for example, responsible work habits.

This section has portrayed modeling as an essential therapeutic skill. Without too much thought, one could imagine a number of behaviors that counselors or other staff could engage in that would serve just the opposite function—subtly reinforcing clients for their antisocial acts. Imagine, for example, the halfway house case manager who wants too much to be liked by the residents of the institution, who smiles at a resident's use of aggressive language, who espouses the "boys will be boys" orientation, and who fails to react to language and behaviors that are exploitive of women. Picture the counselor who supports a weekend furlough for a resident who has "had a bad week," all the while ignoring the fact that the resident has failed to accomplish any of his or her goals for the week. Imagine the probation officer who jokes about "beating the system," or tells the client, "just keep the judge happy," instead of supporting the prosocial value of the conditions of probation. How about the group home adviser who gives little thought to the antisocial peers with whom the client is allowed to congregate or allies with the client against other staff members? Unfortunately, these behaviors are not uncommon in correctional settings, and neither is the reinforcement of such acts. Some criminogenic orientations may even be well supported in our culture.

For some, the approaches recommended in this section may seem too structured, perhaps too rigid. The costs of modeling antisocial behavior, however, are high, even when our behavior seems inadvertent. Further, the need for consistency is greater for justice-involved people than it might be for more responsible individuals. Perhaps we can afford occasional lapses with children who typically demonstrate prosocial thinking and behavior, but with conduct-disordered children or children with other behavioral difficulties we cannot afford to be inconsistent (Patterson, 2003; Samenow, 1989). With juveniles or adults involved in the system, the outcome is equally certain—antisocial modeling on our part, no matter how subtle, is likely to perpetuate or encourage antisocial attitudes or behavior.

THE PROCESS OF OBSERVATIONAL LEARNING

Notwithstanding its importance, the skill of the role model is only one of the factors influencing observational learning. Learning is a process, and social learning is a more complex process than we observed with the classical and operant models. To illustrate this process, Albert Bandura (1977) set forth the sequence of factors affecting the success of observational learning.

Figure 10.2 assumes that a goal behavior has already been modeled. It goes without saying, perhaps, that the behavior will not be learned if the observer pays no attention to the modeled event. Thus, the first box in Figure 10.2 shows that such attention depends on the qualities of the modeling and the characteristics of the observer. Modeling stimuli must be distinctive. That is, the model has to be noticed. At the same time, the model cannot be so different from the observer as to be a novelty. We are more likely to imitate people we want to be like; clowns, or many other types of entertainment, are likely to be viewed for their entertainment value rather than imitated. **Affective valence** refers to the emotional reaction to the behavior being demonstrated. If the modeled behaviors invoke fear or anxiety, they are less likely to be imitated than behaviors that appear to be enjoyable. We might, for example, be more interested in modeling our behavior after a tennis instructor than the model who is preparing us to cope with an upcoming dental procedure.

Similarly, complex goal behaviors will be approached with less enthusiasm than a task for which we have a high degree of **self-efficacy** or confidence in our ability to perform. Conversely, if we undermine self-efficacy, as when we tell girls they are not good at math, we should not be surprised when our modeling of a solution to a math problem produces anxiety or avoidance.

The word "prevalence" in Figure 10.2 refers to the prevalence of role models. Ideally, we would hope that our clients will see goal behaviors modeled outside of our treatment groups as well as within them. Environments are extremely important in this regard. Indeed, treatment efforts are often discouraged by:

1. parents and family members who model behaviors that oppose those that we are trying to teach (e.g., aggressive behaviors);

2. institutional staff who are not trained to reinforce or serve as models for the goal behaviors or (worse yet) those who model the very antisocial behaviors and attitudes that we are trying to prevent; and

3. peers who encourage youth to revisit antisocial behavior.

Finally, the higher the **functional value** or usefulness of the modeled goal behavior, the more likely it is to be adopted. How valuable, for example, will better behavior and new skills be?

Whether an observer pays attention to a modeled goal behavior also has a lot to do with the characteristics of the observer. At a minimum, observers need to have the **sensory capacities** to see and hear the model. Just the same, observational learning has been used in mental health settings in which patients evidence intellectual, neurological, and other physical and mental impediments to attentiveness. Such difficulties must be planned for, however, because **arousal levels** also affect learning; both hyperaroused and inattentive, lethargic clients will have difficulty attending to the modeled behaviors. Moreover, the client's attitude or **perceptual set** toward the model, the behavior being modeled, the other clients in the program, and the whole idea of participating in this particular treatment program need to be considered. Have similar experiences been reinforced in the past, or were they onerous ordeals that affected the client's desire to participate in the present experience? Bad

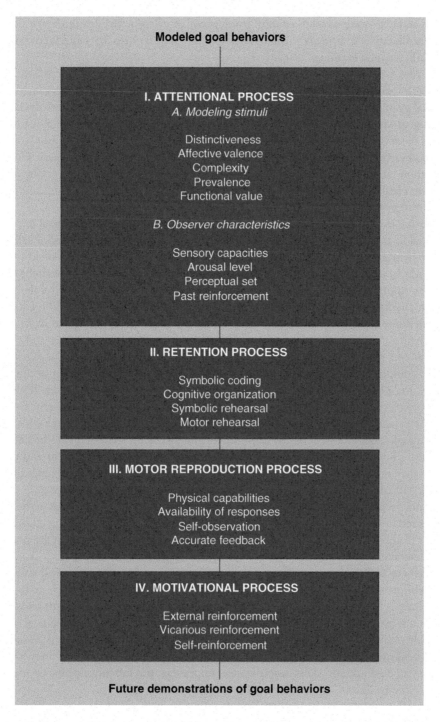

FIGURE 10.2 The process of observational learning.
Source: Bandura, A. (1977). Self-efficacy: Toward a unifying theory of behavioral change. *Psychological Review, 94,* 191–215.

attitudes and expectations on the part of learners will interfere with even the best of learning situations. Clients who bring with them negative stereotypes of teachers and fellow students have a difficult time learning.

If all goes well, and the client has paid attention to the modeling, he or she still must remember or mentally retain the experience. The event must be mentally organized in an individual's mind to be retained sufficiently in memory. Can the individual verbally describe the skill/goal behavior? **Symbolic coding** refers to any of a number of strategies for translating an observed behavior into memory. Certainly, translating the behavior into words and remembering the words is one way. We are also likely to retain visual imagery. **Cognitive organization** will also occur as we relate the event to others or we evaluate certain qualities of the event (e.g., the tone of the role model's voice, style of dress, etc.) and assess our interest in the entire matter.

Practicing the modeled goal behavior is an important task; behavior rehearsal or practice is essential to the process of observational learning. Rehearsal can occur symbolically, such as when clients review modeled events in their imagination (**symbolic rehearsal**). Clients should also have the opportunity to actually demonstrate and practice the behaviors in treatment (**motor rehearsal**). The most common form of motor rehearsal is **role-playing**, in which clients are given the opportunity to repeat the goal behaviors, while counselors and sometimes other clients assume complementary roles for the purpose of practicing the behaviors.

The success of this practice phase of learning is highly dependent on the factors listed in the third component of Bandura's model (Figure 10.2). It goes without saying, perhaps, that the client must be physically (and mentally) capable of performing the behavior. If he or she does not possess the physical capabilities to replicate the entire behavior exactly, he or she should be capable of **component responses** so that approximations to the behavior can be demonstrated. One seldom perfectly duplicates a golf instructor's swing on the first attempt, for example, but there ought to be some attempt at a swing that the instructor and the student can then react to with accurate feedback and accurate self-observation. Hopefully, such feedback and additional practice will improve the golf swing over time.

Bandura's scheme also deals with a client's motivation for using the behavior in the future. As discussed in Chapter 8, operant conditioning theory maintains that reinforced behaviors are more likely to be repeated than those that are not reinforced or those that are punished. Reinforcement in this case can come in many forms. The counselor's praise, or **external reinforcement**, should occur in most situations. Observers of the role model will receive **vicarious reinforcement** as they note the role model's reinforcement and will come to expect similar rewards for their own demonstrations of the behavior. **Self-reinforcement** is extremely important. Especially when the goal behavior is valued behavior or has a good deal of functional utility, clients are likely to feel a strong sense of pride and satisfaction in accomplishing the new behavior. Some learned behaviors are likely to serve as reinforcements in themselves, for example, new athletic skills, assertiveness, improvements in study habits, or improved parental effectiveness.

Figure 10.2 omits some key issues. First, it says very little about the nature of the modeling process, which can be quite varied. Modeled behavior can involve a **live model**, or a **symbolic model**, such as one we might observe in a film, a book, or in our imagination. Some social learning processes also make use of **covert modeling**, a process that encourages clients to visualize their performance of the behaviors they want to perform. Role models can also engage in **participant modeling**, in which they perform the target behavior with the client.

An important consideration not yet addressed is the process of repeating the behaviors outside of the learning environment. As with other learning models, clients need to generalize the newly acquired behaviors outside of their therapy, in day-to-day living. Often general imitation as well as specific imitation of behaviors is desired. If, for example, a client is taught to avoid a specific high-risk situation, such as his friends at a local bar (specific imitation), the counselor will hope that he will learn to identify other high-risk situations and avoid those as well (general imitation). Generalization of learned skills is often a function of environmental considerations (Goldstein, Glick, Irwin, Pask-McCartney, & Rubama, 1989) or what is happening in the homes and neighborhoods of our clients. Will parents model and reinforce the goal behaviors, for example, or will they model dysfunctional alternatives?

Our overview of the structure of an observational learning process, or the social learning paradigm, should make a compelling case for treatment and program planning. Many of the correctional treatment settings we work in will be using this paradigm, but when is modeling being used effectively, and when is it not? In this regard, program planners and practitioners must ask a number of questions:

1. Are they employing and training skilled role models?
2. Are they identifying goal behaviors that their clients are able to perform, and if not, are they breaking complicated goal behaviors down into manageable components?
3. Are there sufficient opportunities for role-playing and practice?
4. Are staff reinforcing client behaviors and teaching clients to feel pride in their new-found skills?
5. Are staff in other areas of the correctional environment modeling the goal behaviors and reinforcing clients in using the new goal behaviors?
6. Have we made provisions for facilitating the generalization of newly learned behaviors to settings outside of the correctional environment?

SOCIAL LEARNING INTERVENTIONS IN CORRECTIONS AND PREVENTION

As a program in itself and as a component of other programs, social learning and modeling forms the mainstay of many mental health and correctional treatment endeavors. We could offer numerous examples but, for purposes of illustration, we focus on two: parent management training (Kazdin, 2000; Reid, Patterson, & Snyder, 2003) and structured learning training, also called skillstreaming (Goldstein et al., 1989).

Parent Management Training

Parent management training (PMT) is a treatment strategy for dealing with children and adolescents who exhibit conduct problems. The strategy was developed at the Oregon Social Learning Center (see Patterson, 1974, 1982), but has since been widely adopted and researched throughout the United States and internationally. PMT employs a social learning approach to train parents to alter their children's behavior at home. Most of this work has focused on children with oppositional defiant disorder, conduct disorder, and system-impacted juveniles, but the approach has also been used with children diagnosed with autism, attention-deficit/hyperactivity disorder (ADHD), intellectual disability, and other diagnoses.

Research on PMT has shown how poor parental discipline contributes to child behavioral problems (e.g., Patterson, 2003; Patterson et al., 1992) and how good parenting skills can prevent such problems (Kazdin, 2000; Reid et al., 2003). Keeping with the social learning paradigm that behavior is learned through observation, modeling, shaping, reinforcement, and punishment, child behavioral problems surely can be fostered by poor parental discipline. Specifically, parents: (1) allow children to escape punishment; (2) ignore (do not reinforce) good behavior; (3) do not monitor their children well enough to observe the behaviors that should be reinforced or punished; (4) do not set limits; and (5) punish inconsistently and coercively. When the child's aversive behavior escalates, parents demonstrate inappropriate levels of anger and aggression, which are then modeled to the child. This package of events then causes child behavioral problems to become more intense over time and begins to cause other problems in the child's life, including problems with academics, peer relationships, delinquency, and substance use.

Treatment for these behaviors begins with the parents; often one parent or a single parent attends either individual sessions or sessions with other parents. They are taught to identify antecedents or stimuli for prosocial behaviors they hope to teach their children. These may include verbal prompts and instructions and modeling. PMT seeks to develop positive behaviors to reduce the need for antisocial negative behaviors (Kazdin, 2000). It is necessary to show parents the importance of reinforcing good behaviors through the use of social reinforcement (e.g., praise), token reinforcements, or the process of making privileges contingent upon desired behavior. Reinforcement schedules are developed and maintained. Parents must also work to reduce undesired behavior, using brief time-outs, or loss of privileges, but the preference is for rewards and the fostering of positive behavior. Other strategies of operant conditioning are also taught to parents, including shaping, extinction, and how not to inadvertently reinforce inappropriate behavior.

The parents themselves may engage in role-play with the therapist or other group members as they work to learn new ways to set limits, praise, and interact with their children. They must learn to identify and observe their children's behavior over time, and to adhere to specific reinforcement schedules, especially early in the treatment process. This typically involves some degree of record-keeping that tracks behavior against the baselines. Later these schedules may become more intermittent and ultimately may be phased out. The therapy will also target the child's behavior in school, including classroom deportment, relationships with peers, and homework. School officials and teachers may become partners in the behavioral program.

The duration of treatment depends largely upon the severity of the child's behavioral problems. For milder cases, therapy can range from six to eight weeks; programs for more disturbed children last from 12 to 25 weeks (Kazdin, 1997). This treatment has also been found to be most effective during the preschool years (Bor, Najman, & O'Callaghan, 2001). PMT has been evaluated in many controlled studies and found to be effective in reducing behavioral problems in schools and homes (see Patterson, Dishion, & Chamberlain, 1993; Serketich & Dumas, 1996) and in foster care settings (Chamberlain, Fisher, & Moore, 2003; Chamberlain & Reid, 1994). Reductions in delinquency have also been observed (Bank, Marlowe, Reid, Patterson, & Weinrott, 1991; Dishion & Andrews, 1995). A meta-analysis found reductions in recidivism of approximately 22% for PMT and similar behavioral parent training programs (Piquero, Farrington, Welsh, Tremblay, & Jennings, 2008). Evaluations have also documented improvements in parenting skills. The strategy, however, is somewhat time-consuming and demanding. Understandably, families dealing with poverty, limited social support, parental histories of antisocial behavior, single parenting, and high levels of stress from other problems are at high risk of dropping out of the program (Kazdin, Mazurick, & Siegel, 1994).

Structured Learning Training/Skillstreaming

An example of a structured approach to social skills training is seen in Arnold Goldstein's **structured learning training** (Goldstein et al., 1989), later called **skillstreaming**. Skillstreaming is also one of three components of a treatment package called Aggression Replacement Training® (Goldstein et al., 1998) and part of a peer-helping approach referred to as EQUIP (Gibbs et al., 1995; see Chapter 9). Working on the assumption that justice-involved juveniles, especially aggressive ones, possess fewer social skills than juveniles who are not involved in the system, Goldstein and his associates set out a list of 50 essential social skills. These are shown in Box 10.1. Structured learning training/skillstreaming endeavors to teach these skills.

Box 10.1 Example of Structured Learning Skills for Adolescents

GROUP 1. BEGINNING SOCIAL SKILLS

a   Listening

b   Starting a conversation

c   Having a conversation

d   Asking a question

e   Saying thank you

f   Introducing yourself

g   Introducing other people

h   Giving a compliment

GROUP 2. ADVANCED SOCIAL SKILLS

a   Asking for help

b   Joining in

c   Giving instructions

d   Following instructions

e   Apologizing

f   Convincing others

GROUP 3. SKILLS FOR DEALING WITH FEELINGS

a   Knowing your feelings

b   Expressing your feelings

c   Understanding the feelings of others

d   Dealing with someone else's anger

e   Expressing affection

f   Dealing with fear

g   Rewarding yourself

GROUP 4. SKILL ALTERNATIVES TO AGGRESSION

a   Asking permission

b   Sharing something

c   Helping others

d   Negotiation

e   Using self-control

f   Standing up for your rights

g   Responding to testing

h   Avoiding trouble with others

i   Keeping out of fights

GROUP 5. SKILLS FOR DEALING WITH STRESS

a   Making a complaint

b   Answering a complaint

c   Sportsmanship after the game

d   Dealing with embarrassment

e   Dealing with being left out

f   Standing up for a friend

g   Responding to persuasion

h   Responding to failure

i   Dealing with contradictory messages

j   Dealing with an accusation

k   Getting ready for a difficult conversation

l   Dealing with group pressure

GROUP 6. PLANNING SKILLS

a   Deciding on something to do

b   Deciding on what caused a problem

c   Setting a goal

d   Deciding on your abilities

e   Gathering information

f   Ranking problems by importance

g   Making a decision

h   Concentrating on a task

Source: Goldstein, A., Glick, B., Irwin, M., Pask-McCartney, C., & Rubama, I. (1989). *Reducing Delinquency: Intervention in the Community.* New York: Pergamon Press.

Consistent with the social learning model, the staff use the teaching strategies of (1) modeling, (2) role-playing, (3) performance feedback, and (4) generalization training. The latter, generalization training, encourages the youths to practice newly learned skills in a variety of settings. In addition, each skill is broken down into several steps. Youths being taught negotiating skills (Skill 4,d), for example, proceed through the following six steps:

1.   Decide if you and the other person are having a difference of opinion.
2.   Tell the other person what you think of the problem.
3.   Ask the other person about what he or she thinks about the problem.
4.   Listen openly to his or her answer.
5.   Think about why the other person might feel this way.
6.   Suggest a compromise.

Similarly, youths learning to deal with group pressure (Skill 5,l) engage in the following four steps:

1.   Think about what the group wants to do and why.
2.   Decide what you want to do.
3.   Decide how to tell the group what you want to do.
4.   Tell the group what you have decided.

Most of the writings of Arnold Goldstein and his frequent co-author Barry Glick stress the importance of the stages of social learning. Modeling, for example, should employ either live role models or videos of models demonstrating each of the skill steps. Moreover, the modeling should occur in a variety of settings to assure the transfer or generalization of the skill to real-life experiences outside of the correctional environment.

Role-playing provides an opportunity to practice or rehearse the skill immediately after it has been modeled. In role-playing, youth participants choose co-actors to play the role of a significant other who might be relevant to the youth's use of the skill in real life. Before engaging in the role-play, the main actor must describe how the skill would actually be used in his or her life, and that becomes the scenario for role-playing. Trainers must, of course, assure that the main actor and co-actor do not, for some reason, discontinue the role-playing prematurely, prior to covering all of the steps to the skill. Each group member must engage in role-playing each skill taught and must identify a situation relevant to his or her home environment.

Performance feedback is an essential follow-up to each of the role-playing exercises. Whenever possible, trainers must offer praise and encouragement. The feedback, however, is highly structured, and much attention is devoted to commenting on whether specific steps were actually demonstrated to an effective degree. Trainers, in other words, cannot limit their comments to general evaluative remarks; for example, "That was nice, Joe" is not sufficient.

The written accounts of Aggression Replacement Training® and structured learning training devote considerable attention to techniques for assuring that the newly learned skills are generalized outside the training settings. The program designers warn of the many flawed program efforts in which youths demonstrated new behaviors in correctional settings, but failed to use them upon returning home. Thus, transfer training identifies a number of techniques for encouraging the endurance of new prosocial skills. One strategy involves over-learning, or the use of more learning trials than those needed to obtain an initial indication of the skill. Participants find themselves learning a single skill in a variety of ways, including role-playing in different situations, observing the practice of others, writing the skill steps, and engaging in multiple homework assignments. In addition, the training attempts to replicate life situations similar to those experienced in the home environments of the group participants.

New behaviors are difficult to sustain when program participants return to environments that either fail to reinforce prosocial behaviors or reinforce the antisocial behaviors that the program sought to discontinue. Therefore, Goldstein and his associates attempted to show parents and family members the various skills taught to youths and to impress upon them the need to support their teachings in home settings. In one evaluation of a program that used skillstreaming, the family program did not increase the effectiveness of the overall programs over what the program had achieved for the youths alone (Goldstein et al., 1989). In part, this may have been due to the difficulty in securing the full participation of the families. Written accounts of the program suggested that families were overburdened with adversity; securing their participation may have required more effort than conducting the family program itself. More recent evaluations show more favorable results, especially when combined with other components of Aggression Replacement Training® (Goldstein et al., 1998) (see Drake, Aos, & Miller, 2009). See Box 10.2 for a case study.

Box 10.2 The Case of Jason: A Social Learning Approach

The social learning approaches discussed in this box are based on the case study of Jason, presented in Box 6.2. The essence of a social learning intervention is the strategy of prosocial modeling coupled with opportunities for practice and appropriate use of reinforcement and punishment (Bonta & Andrews, 2017). These techniques should take place in structured group sessions as well as in day-to-day interactions with correctional staff.

TREATMENT PLAN—EXAMPLE
The Goals of a Social Learning Approach (for Jason):

To develop appropriate conflict management skills.
To understand and identify high-risk situations.
To associate with prosocial individuals and avoid antisocial individuals.

Approach:
Jason will take part in a social skills course, in which he will focus on skills of conflict management and avoiding antisocial individuals.

Goals will also be approached through staff's ongoing adherence to the techniques of prosocial modeling.

APPROACH—EXAMPLE
As noted before, Jason will participate in a social skills course (see Goldstein et al., 1989). He will receive instruction in a variety of social skills, but will focus on those pertaining to conflict management and association with positive, prosocial people. The following exemplifies a class session in which Jason and other group members are taught the skill of compromising.

1. *Modeling*: Co-leaders model a discussion between two persons in conflict.

COUNSELOR A (JASON): When you change the channel in the TV room, without asking me, I get very angry. sometimes you interrupt shows that I am really interested in, and then I don't get to see what happened.

COUNSELOR B (HORACE): I guess it is hard to miss a favorite show. I know, I don't like it when someone does that to me. However, you are often watching TV, Jason. Whenever, a big show comes on, like a big game, or great movie, you are already in the room watching something else. I've missed some great shows this year.

COUNSELOR A (JASON): *Listens to Horace's concerns and indicates that he hears them.* Well, I like to watch TV a lot, and you do seem to like sports more than I do. Maybe we can work this out in a dorm meeting. Maybe, at the beginning of the week, we could talk about what really good shows are coming up. And then let the group vote on what shows they want to schedule the TV for. If a show is not on the schedule, and I am watching something else, I get to continue to watch my show. But you could talk to me about changing, like tell me what is on and ask if you can change it. But if I'm there first, I don't have to say yes.

COUNSELOR B (HORACE): That sounds ok. Let's talk to the others about it tonight.

2. *Role-play (Practice)*: Jason practices role-playing a similar conflict with another group member. They attempt to demonstrate the skills of:

(a) expressing anger;

(b) listening to the perspective of the other person;

(c) relating their understanding of the other's position; and

(d) suggesting mutually beneficial alternatives.

3. *Receiving Feedback*: Group leaders and other group members comment on the role-playing. They offer praise when possible and suggestions when warranted (e.g., try not to use blaming language, speak to your own feelings, and do not make assumptions about the motives of other people, etc.).

4. *Generalization Training*: Group leaders give members homework. In this case, for example, they might ask Jason and other group members to practice similar conflict resolution strategies outside of the group. Over time, the members should practice these lessons in increasing levels of difficulty.

5. *Feedback on Homework Assignments*: At the next meeting, group members discuss their practice outside of the group. Leaders and group members provide feedback.

In addition to the social skills classes, staff use the techniques of good role modeling and appropriate use of reinforcements and punishments (see Bonta & Andrews, 2017). In Jason's case, these might involve:

Staff refusing to reinforce any antisocial comments that Jason might offer (e.g., "That lady was insured for that TV"). Staff should also indicate to Jason that such communications are inappropriate and likely to be contributing to his troubles.

Insisting on Jason's compliance with prison rules as well as his conformity to the rules of group participation. Staff should not allow the enforcement of rules to drift and become inconsistent.

The staff should model prosocial behaviors in their interactions with inmates. They also should not imitate or smile at Jason's criminogenic expressions, or indicate that they too sometimes "go over the line."

Encourage Jason's association with prosocial individuals—his sister, perhaps. Point out that his association with antisocial individuals is high-risk behavior and usually leads him to trouble.

Offer Jason praise and encouragement when he accomplishes important tasks (e.g., responsible work habits or a new social skill).

CONCLUSION

We began our presentation of learning therapies in Chapter 8, with accounts of the radical behavioral interventions of classical conditioning and operant conditioning. In this chapter, learning is shown as a process that can occur vicariously as we observe the experiences of others. We learn, in other words, from role models in our environment. In recent years, correctional programs have made wide use of this learning paradigm. And when the social learning models have been delivered according to design, they are among the most successful programming options currently available. This chapter has stressed that programs based on social learning theory evidence a high degree of treatment integrity when they employ effective role models who possess good relationship skills, provide ample opportunities for role-playing, offer feedback toward refining initial attempts, reinforce accomplishments, and generalize learned behaviors to real-life situations.

In the next chapter we consider the importance of integrating families and larger systems into treatment interventions. Seldom do justice-involved individuals come from healthy, prosocial familial environments. Thus, it becomes important to understand how a more holistic approach may be appropriate for some clients.

Discussion Questions

1. What relationship skills must a person possess to be an effective role model?
2. Think for a minute about the most effective teachers you have had over the years. In what ways did their classes demonstrate the principles of effective modeling? How did they utilize the various steps of the social learning process?
3. What is the rationale behind teaching the skills listed in Box 10.1 to correctional clients?
4. Identify the important components or steps of the social learning process.
5. What is meant by "anticriminal modeling"? In what ways do case managers or counselors sometimes inadvertently demonstrate criminal modeling?
6. According to PMT, what are the skills of good parenting?

GLOSSARY OF KEY TERMS

affective valence   a factor in the process of observational learning that refers to the emotional reaction to a behavior being demonstrated

arousal levels   individual degrees of alertness or responsiveness to stimuli; affect clients' abilities to learn and attend to modeled behaviors

cognitive organization   a factor in the process of observational learning that refers to how one relates an observed event to others or evaluates certain qualities of the event (e.g., the tone of the role model's voice, style of dress, etc.)

component responses   a factor in the process of observational learning that refers to a client's ability to perform approximations of a modeled behavior when they are physically unable to replicate the entire behavior exactly

covert modeling   a form of modeling that encourages clients to visualize their performance of the behaviors they want to perform

external reinforcement   the act of praising a client during the observational learning process

functional value   the usefulness of a modeled goal behavior in the process of observational learning

general imitation   the process of practicing learned skills and behaviors across multiple scenarios outside of the learning environment

generalize   the process of repeating learned behaviors outside of the learning environment

goal behaviors   ideal behaviors that are taught and modeled through the process of observational learning

live model   an actual individual who demonstrates or acts out modeled behavior

modeling   a behaviorally-based procedure that involves the use of models to demonstrate a particular behavior or attitude that an individual would like to acquire

motor rehearsal   the act of demonstrating and practicing learned behaviors in a treatment setting

observational learning   a process of learning attitudes or behaviors vicariously, through observing and imitating others

participant modeling   an observational learning technique in which role models perform target behaviors with clients

perceptual set   a client's predisposed attitude toward models, the behaviors being modeled, the other clients in a given program, and the whole idea of participating in that particular treatment program

role models   individuals or groups who inspire others to imitate their attitudes and behaviors; can be live or symbolic

role-playing   a therapeutic exercise in which clients are given the opportunity to repeat goal behaviors, while counselors and sometimes other clients assume complementary roles for the purpose of practicing the behaviors

self-efficacy   an individual's confidence in their ability to perform tasks or behaviors

self-reinforcement   a process in which individuals reward and reinforce their own behavior when a certain standard of performance has been attained

sensory capacities   an observer's ability to see and hear the model in the process of observational learning

specific imitation   the process of practicing specific learned skills and behaviors outside of the learning environment

structured learning training/skillstreaming   a social skills training method for juveniles that endeavors to teach 50 essential social skills through modeling, role-playing, performance feedback, and generalization training

symbolic coding strategies employed in translating an observed behavior into memory

symbolic model figurative role models, such as those observed in films, books, or in one's imagination, who serve to demonstrate or act out modeled behavior

symbolic rehearsal the process of practicing or reviewing modeled events in one's imagination

therapeutic communities an in-patient residential program for targeting substance use using a social learning treatment strategy in correctional and mental health settings in which staff and clients are trained to act as appropriate role models and life outside the institution is replicated as much as possible

vicarious reinforcement an observational learning process in which observers of the role model note the model's reinforcement and will come to expect similar rewards for their own demonstrations of the goal behavior

CHAPTER 11

Family Interventions

Patricia Van Voorhis, Emily J. Salisbury, and Michael Braswell

KEY TERMS

boundaries	multisystemic treatment (MST)
communications therapy	mystification
disengaged boundaries	object relations
double bind	psychodynamic family therapy
dyads	reframing
enmeshed system	rigid boundaries
family structure	scapegoats
family system	strategic family therapy
family therapy	structural family therapy
homeostasis	subsystems
individuate	therapeutic paradox
metacommunication	"working through" process

Family environments and the quality of family life are often cited in the development of antisocial behavior in a variety of ways, including the failure to form adequate parent-child attachments (Baumrind, 1985; Bowlby, 1988), exposing children to violence in the home (Banyard, Williams, Saunders, & Fitzgerald, 2008; Thornberry, Lizotte, Krohn, Farnsworth, & Jang, 1994), excessive conflict (Katz & Gottman, 1993), inadequate child socialization and parenting skills (Larzelere & Patterson, 1990; Loeber & Dishion, 1983; Patterson & Dishion, 1985), and dysfunctional styles of interaction. From a systemic perspective, a justice-involved youth or adult may be a symptom of a very troubled family system. In such cases, problem behavior serves functional purposes for the family, such as when delinquency takes the family's attention away from a faltering marriage (Henggeler, 1982; Minuchin, 1985). The relevance of the family to criminal behavior is perhaps most poignantly evident when members commit acts of violence against each other as demonstrated in child and spouse abuse.

Concerns for family issues also must extend beyond the etiology of criminal behavior to concern for what happens after a conviction or adjudication of a family member. Often by necessity, the day-to-day business of criminal justice agencies does much to threaten the stability of families. Criminal and family courts separate hundreds of families each day. Juvenile

DOI: 10.4324/9780367808266-14

justice agencies have been criticized both for prematurely separating children from their biological families and for prematurely returning institutionalized youths to families that cannot offer a better alternative to the institution. Institutions further aggravate the problem when they limit visitations, forbid contact visits, fail to place detained people in close geographical proximity to their families, and neglect family issues in the course of treatment.

In one survey of incarcerated parents, 60% reported being incarcerated more than 100 miles from their home. Moreover, 57% of fathers and 54% of mothers reported having no visits from their children (Mumola, 2000). For mothers especially, retaining custody after a period of incarceration has become far more difficult. The Adoption and Safe Families Act of 1997 terminated parental custody after a child has been in foster care for at least 15 of the past 22 months. The law affects incarcerated parents as well as those in treatment for some forms of mental illness or substance use (Bloom et al., 2003).

Ironically, when the period of incarceration and separation is over, the individual's chances of returning to a normal life often depend on how well the family is functioning by the end of the ordeal (Hairston, 2002) and how much support the family is able to offer (Nelson, Deess, & Allen, 1999). Given the observation that many marriages dissolve after two years of incarceration (Brodsky, 1975), and that contact with family members diminishes over the length of a prison sentence (Lynch & Sabol, 2001), we can expect that many people who are incarcerated long-term will not be returning to supportive family settings. Even in cases that do not result in separation, the stressors of police and court proceedings usually prove to be a severe jolt to most families. In all of the examples cited above, it is clear that much is expected of the families involved with system-impacted juveniles and adults. It is hoped that effective family therapy programs, along with emerging prisoner reentry policies and some of the family-strengthening programs mentioned toward the end of this chapter, can assist families in need.

The prospect of a justice-involved person's return to a law-abiding life is even more complicated than the issue of whether the family adjusts to his or her arrest and disposition. Success may also depend upon the individual's participation in some form of treatment, the quality of family life prior to treatment, and the nature of the family's involvement in the treatment process. In many cases, the policy of treating the family member while ignoring the family's problems wastes time and money. Correctional counselors and case managers frequently express the frustrating claim that their clients improve during treatment only to get worse upon returning to families lacking affection, adequate supervision of children, support, and open communication (Janeksela, 1979; Klein, Alexander, & Parsons, 1977). Early writings on family therapy note similar results among other challenging clients, including people diagnosed with schizophrenia (Bateson, Jackson, Haley, & Weakland, 1956), drug addiction (Hirsch & Imhof, 1975; Stanton, 1994), anorexia (Minuchin, Rosman, & Baker, 1978), and alcoholism (Meeks & Kelly, 1970; Steinglass, 2004).

The treatment of a troubled family member can have an unfavorable impact on the family as well. These members of a family often play an important role in maintaining familiar but unhealthy patterns of interaction between family members (Hoffman, 1981). As a result, if the troubled member becomes well, the family system may be threatened unless other members have participated in the change process. Family members may want to return to a less painful status quo arrangement of living together in discord rather than risking a move beyond familiar traditions to greater personal and interpersonal growth. The family therapy literature presents numerous examples of instances in which the improved behavior of the problematic member shocked families into unhealthy compensating behaviors, such as identifying new family "scapegoats" or withdrawing from therapy (Napier & Whitaker, 1980; Sameroff, 1989). The family system has a reality that is more than the sum total of member characteristics. If the family system is at fault, it is futile to treat only one symptom of its problems.

The following case study demonstrates the power of the family system.

Carter, a 14-year-old male, and his parents were referred for counseling as a result of his increasing acting-out behavior, particularly at school. Until recently, the teen-ager apparently had been a reasonably well-behaved and productive student. During the last several weeks, however, both his parents and school officials became alarmed. Verbal disrespect to teachers, plummeting grades, and finally joyriding with several of his friends in a stolen car brought Carter and his family to the attention of the juve-nile court.

Carter's family consisted of a mother, father, older sister, and younger brother. Carter's father was an assistant manager at a department store. Severe economic dep-rivation as a child had resulted in his becoming a "workaholic," always being prepared for the possible return of "hard times." He was caught between his genuine concern for his son and his compulsive need for greater economic security. Carter's mother was at home, spending the majority of her time caring for Carter's younger brother, who was severely intellectually challenged. Carter's older sister, who was a senior in high school, seemed less affected by the current family dilemma. She and Carter apparently had very little to do with each other.

Carter indicated he both loved and hated his younger brother. He felt guilty—that perhaps it should have been him rather than his brother who was severely intellectu-ally disabled. Just the same, he resented the disproportionate amount of attention his brother received, yet knew it was necessary. Being in the middle, he felt extra pressure to help with his brother's care, but being in the middle also meant that there was little time and attention left for him from his parents. Carter particularly felt neglected by his father.

As counseling began to include Carter and his parents, communication between them improved. Carter and his father grew closer and began to schedule "special" time together. When this initially occurred, Carter's mother began to experience anxiety. Focusing on her need for special time appeared to resolve her feelings of being more isolated from Carter and his father. Subsequent follow-up counseling sessions seemed to indicate that the family was functioning effectively. Carter's grades and behavior had improved. Three months later, an urgent telephone call from his mother revealed that Carter had struck one of his teachers and that he had been suspended from school. During the last several weeks, Carter's behavior had deteriorated rapidly, coinciding with his father's move to another state to take a more economically secure position. The family was to join him at Christmas in their new home.

Carter's prospects seemed bleak. His father was absent from the family in an attempt to improve their economic position with a new job. His absence left a void in Carter's life due to his need for a relationship with his father, and at the same time placed additional pressure on an already overtaxed mother. In the father's absence, the family system had to adjust and realign itself, a situation that did not lend itself to Carter's continued improvement.

The field of **family therapy** considers individual modes of therapy to be too narrow and inattentive to the impact of relationships, families, and their respective systems on family members. Family therapy approaches are consistent with the major tenets of social psychology, community psychology, environmental psychology, and social ecology, which assert that individuals cannot be understood apart from their interactions with group, social, and cultural forces in their environments (Bronfenbrenner, 1979). From this view, behavioral problems are seen as having multiple causes that involve families, schools, neighborhoods, workplaces, and peer groups (Zigler, Taussig, & Black, 1992). This is also a hallmark tenet of the social work perspective—the importance of persons in their environments.

Traditional therapies are also faulted for their failure to recognize the potency of group change, especially at the level of the family system. The family is often the key to long-term change because in most instances it exercises its influence over the entire life span (Larzelere & Patterson, 1990; Loeber & Dishion, 1983; Sampson & Laub, 1993). While the growing awareness of the family's role in the etiology and treatment of antisocial behavior is reflected in treatment developments that involve families in the correctional process, the criminal justice system's use of this approach is perhaps not what it should be. This is unfortunate in view of the growing number of favorable evaluation results. In fact, the effectiveness of family therapy is underscored in several reviews of the treatment evaluation literature (Andrews, Gordon, Hill, Kurkowski, & Hoge, 1993; Hazelrigg, Cooper, & Borduin, 1987; Kazdin, 1987; Loeber & Hay, 1994; Patterson et al., 1993; Shadish et al., 1993).

HISTORY AND OVERVIEW OF FAMILY THERAPY

The history of family therapy, as a field, spans less than 50 years (Nichols & Schwartz, 2006). Until relatively recently, in fact, family involvement in individual therapy was discouraged by such major figures as Freud, Rogers, and others as likely to contaminate the client-therapist relationship. Presumably, neurotic conflicts with other family members or perhaps a conscious or unconscious desire to win their approval would cause clients unwittingly to deny and distort their true feelings and impulses.

The earliest approaches to family therapy were problem-centered efforts to cure illnesses, particularly schizophrenia, by treating the family through group counseling techniques (Nichols & Schwartz, 2006). Initially, researchers attempted to identify prototypical patterns of family interaction to characterize each problem. But efforts to describe the "schizophrenogenic family" or the "alcoholic marriage" proved to be oversimplified. It soon became clear that family issues were not necessarily specific to the presenting problem. The common elements among such problem-centered families were more generally: (a) their presenting problem; and (b) the fact that the family functioned in a dysfunctional manner that served to perpetuate the presenting problem (Russell, Olson, Sprenkle, & Atilano, 1983). The exact nature of the dysfunction, however, varied from family to family.

Later years witnessed the development of several distinct treatment models. Notwithstanding their different approaches, each model held several fundamental assumptions regarding the importance of the systems within which we love, play, and work.

Some authors have faulted family therapy itself for being too narrow. These critics assert that family systems should not be the sole target of therapeutic intervention because families are comprised of individuals who possess varied individual strengths and problems, and some of these may affect family functioning more than others. They also observe that families exist in reciprocal relationships with extra-family systems such as schools, work settings, and neighborhoods. Any one of these outside systems may significantly influence the quality of family life or impede the progress of family therapy (Henggeler & Borduin, 1990). Such concerns launched Multisystemic Therapy® (Henggeler & Borduin, 1990), an eclectic approach that combines several of the family therapy models, discussed below, with: (a) individual approaches for a troubled family member (if needed) and (b) other community services (e.g., childcare and school advocacy).

Family therapy is viewed today as a significant field of mental health. Services that address a diverse array of problems are available through many private and public mental health programs. The term "family therapy" would be misleading, however, if it suggested that these services are obtained solely by intact nuclear families. Family therapy is more accurately viewed as a treatment modality designed to address the problems that result from the manner in which individuals perceive and manage their relationships. Such services may be retained by a variety of living units, including single-parent homes, gay and cohabitating couples, single people, and reconstituted families.

Good approaches to family therapy must also modify their approach to reflect ethnic diversity. This is not just because the criminal justice system deals with much diversity but also because the context of the family differs so dramatically across ethnic groups. Ethnicity affects role expectations, family values, concepts of morality, religiosity, needs, and perceptions of life events. Although most of the writing on family therapy addresses the needs of the white, middle-class family living in the general, not justice-involved, population, the move to ethnically responsive approaches is apparent (Ho, 2003; Kumpfer, 1999; Parra-Cardona, Sharp, & Wampler, 2008).

Schools of family therapy differ primarily in their treatment focus, or the type of family problem that is addressed in therapy. In organizing the complex array of methods, Guerin (1976) divides strategies into two basic schools: psychodynamic and systems-based technologies. The psychodynamic approaches include the individual, group, and experiential therapies of Ackerman (1966), Zuk (1975), Whitaker (1976), and others. Systems-based approaches encompass the communications (or strategic) methods of Haley (1976) and Satir (1972), as well as the structural strategies developed by Minuchin (1974) and Bowen (1978). Absent from Guerin's early classification scheme are social learning models, for example, the work of such behaviorists as Alexander and Parsons (1982); Sexton and Alexander (2000); Patterson (1974, 1982); Gordon and Arbuthnot (1987); Gordon, Arbuthnot, Gustafson, and McGreen (1988); and Kumpfer, DeMarsh, and Child (1989); and the multisystemic treatments of Henggeler and Borduin (1990). These will also be discussed in this chapter.

Despite the uniqueness of each of the family therapy models identified above, many share in varying degrees the belief that the family should be viewed as a system. A number of concepts that have emerged from early studies of the family as a system continue to be viewed as fundamental to family therapy today. Families are seen as having a unity that is greater than the sum of the individual personalities comprising the system. As a result, when a family approaches therapy with a troubled member, the family system *as well as* the individual is assumed to be in need of help.

The treatment of a system follows from a different causal paradigm than that used in the individual, non-systemic therapies summarized earlier. Non-systemic models employ a linear approach to therapy. In other words, they assume that problem behaviors follow a simple cause-and-effect relationship. The assumption is that if we intervene with the cause of a problem, we will alleviate the resulting problem. Systems therapies, in contrast, view problem behaviors as circular, reciprocal, and interrelated. Symptoms are part of a multi-causal relationship system (Nichols & Schwartz, 2006). It is not simply that a child's behavior problem adversely affects other family members; other family members also affect the child.

In understanding systems therapies, it is important to understand the qualities of systems. Patricia Minuchin (1985) summarizes these as follows:

1. *Any system is an organized whole, and elements within the system are necessarily inter-dependent.* Because of their interdependence, the system cannot be fully understood by assessing only an individual member of the system. The system is more than the sum of its parts; the behaviors of members of the system exist in a context.

2. *Patterns in a system are circular rather than linear.* The behaviors of members, in other words, exist in larger chains of circular, reciprocal, and spiraling interactions. This picture argues against blaming individual family members for the family's problems.

3. *Systems have homeostatic features that maintain the stability of their patterns.* Over time, behaviors of system members can become consistent and predictable. Systems appear to prefer this steady state, and may experience stress when change is needed. In a variety of ways, systems may also seek to resist change.

4. *Evolution and change are inherent in open systems.* Systems need to change over time. The family system that raises small children, for example, needs to be different from the system that sends these same children to high school. Open systems are more likely to grow and change than closed, isolated systems. Open systems exchange information with the environment outside the system. In doing so, they become more adaptive. Closed systems appear to experience more psychosocial difficulties such as abuse or incest (Alexander, 1973). Because there is no opportunity to question abusive or other dysfunctional behaviors (the family is not interacting sufficiently with the outside environment), these behaviors may also come to be viewed by family members as normal or justifiable.

5. *Complex systems are composed of subsystems.* These subsystems carry out distinct roles within the system. The roles of the parental subsystem, for example, are different from those of the sibling subsystem.

6. *The subsystems within a larger system are separated by boundaries, and interactions across these boundaries are governed by implicit rules and patterns.* Some of these rules are socially prescribed. Most societies require that parents supervise children. Other rules may be developed within the system, for example, "we don't talk to anyone about family matters." Boundaries are discussed further in the section on structural family therapy, but for now they refer to the borders that differentiate one system from other systems. Likewise, they are the borders that differentiate the system's various subsystems (e.g., parents, children, and various dyads). We refer to these boundaries as open, closed, or semi-permeable. As will be seen shortly, the appropriateness of a given boundary, rule, or pattern depends on the nature of the subsystem.

What can a system do to bring about difficulties for one or more of its members? Any number of things. In striving for homeostasis, or a balanced, steady state of equilibrium, family systems "elect" (although not necessarily consciously) members to help stabilize the system in its ongoing patterns (Sameroff, 1989). One case history of a family's experience in therapy, for example, describes David and Carolyn Brice's desperate attempts to cope with their oldest daughter's acting-out behaviors (Napier & Whitaker, 1980). Daughter Claudia's extreme unhappiness with her parents was shown in her constant battles with her mother, late and long disappearances from home, sexually acting-out, and a frightening preoccupation with death. Fairly early in therapy, co-therapists helped the parents to see that Claudia's behavior functioned to keep the Brice family together. The Brices' marriage had cooled down several years prior to the onset of Claudia's problems and had ceased to meet the needs of either partner. Claudia's dramatic behavior served to unite her parents emotionally in their concern for her, while conveniently allowing them to escape the problems of their marriage. Claudia's behavior, in this case, maintained a certain degree of homeostasis in a dysfunctional system. Oddly, as Claudia's behavior improved after this revelation, the Brices' son, Don, began acting out. Dysfunctional systems often unconsciously defend against the cure of one of their members by electing another scapegoat, or by taking the family or individual members out of therapy to maintain homeostasis. As might be expected, Don's behavior also improved rather quickly, but resolution of the marital difficulties consumed the remainder of the therapy process.

Much of our knowledge of family systems was advanced by Murray Bowen (1978). Bowen maintained that troubled families create dysfunctional system boundaries and communication processes. Members may become "fused" into an undifferentiated mass. In this sense of "stuck-togetherness," individuals lose their sense of uniqueness. Such fused or enmeshed individuals function in emotionally reactive, as opposed to rational, ways. Poor boundaries between individuals, in this case, make it difficult for individuals to understand themselves. It becomes difficult for members to be aware of where they leave off and other family members begin. In other words, I may have a strong sense of "who we are" as a family, but little or no idea of "who I am" as an individual. Such a system may become closed, blocking outside sources of information and maintaining a distorted sense of reality. Members also may communicate through a process of "triangulation," in which emotions cease to be a two-way exchange. Instead, a three-person system is formed. The wife, for example, may tell her daughter, rather than her husband, about the frustrations of her marriage. While this process may succeed in ventilating emotions, it fails to resolve conflicts and is not healthy for the daughter.

The perspective of the family as a system represents a new paradigm in psychotherapy, a dramatic shift from linear to circular causality in which the individual can no longer be viewed as an individual personality formed by discrete events from his or her past. According to the systems paradigm, individual behavior is largely the result of the social context that is often dominated by the family. The causes are ongoing and circular, the turbulent products of all of the interlocking relationships, roles, rules, communication patterns, boundaries, and habits that families develop.

The following sections provide brief overviews of five major family therapy models:

1. psychodynamic
2. communications
3. structural
4. social learning approaches
5. multisystemic family therapy

While this discussion of pure approaches may serve to clarify the various models, they may also offer a distorted view of the typical therapeutic process. Most applications are eclectic. In day-to-day practice, therapists often borrow techniques and perspectives from several models. Moreover, the models themselves are not mutually exclusive.

PSYCHODYNAMIC FAMILY THERAPY

The earliest forms of family therapy were conducted from a psychodynamic perspective. These models had their origins in the work of Freud and Adler, but credit for theoretical and treatment developments pertinent to family therapy is directed to the later work of Ackerman (1966), Boszormenyi-Nagy and Ulrich (1981), Stierlin (1977), Sullivan (1953), and Dicks (1963). Although psychodynamic therapists do not dismiss systems theory entirely, they adhere primarily to traditional perspectives on unconscious forces.

The most important focus in **psychodynamic family therapy** is on object relations. "Object" in this case refers to the person and his or her relationships with others, particularly intimate others. "Object relations" is defined by Westen (1991) as "a set of cognitive and affective processes that mediate interpersonal functioning in close relationships." Object relations theory maintains that components of family life, especially those relevant to the child's relationship with his or her mother, are internalized. Throughout the course of a lifetime, internalized parent-child interactions are then held to influence the functioning of later interpersonal relationships as well as one's perception of self. The form of these representations changes over time, moving from infantile dependence or merger with the mother, to independence, to interdependency with others, to an ideal of mutual exchange (Liebert & Spiegler, 1994). Healthy development requires that people move away from the dependence of childhood to the interdependence of adulthood—to **individuate**, in other words. In addition, intimate relationships of adults often reflect repetitions of issues affecting past relationships as well as the adequacy with which children separate, or individuate, from parents. Problems with object relations may be manifested in a variety of dysfunctional patterns, including difficulties with:

1. failure to individuate or separate from parents (e.g., intense dependency);
2. conflict management;
3. formation of trusting relationships;
4. ability to delay gratification;
5. tolerance of closeness or separation;
6. confidence; and
7. self-esteem.

People may also carry over an inaccurate sense of themselves and others into new relationships. The repetition of dysfunctional scripts from the "home of origin" (Barnhill & Longo, 1978), projective identification, or transference of parental characteristics onto others (Boszormenyi-Nagy and Ulrich, 1981) can mar adult relationships.

As with individual psychodynamic approaches, psychodynamic family therapists strive to uncover, clarify, and interpret unconscious material from the past. Once this material is brought into consciousness, therapists can help clients to "work through" or translate their newfound understanding into productive, more functional behaviors. The identification of unconscious material may occur more efficiently in family therapy than in individual therapy. In individual therapy, clues from the unconscious areas of the personality emerge from observations of a client's free associations, defense mechanisms, dream therapy, and from transference. Transference occurs when aspects of past relationships and transactions are transferred to the therapist during therapy. The transference can then be observed and interpreted for the client. In family therapy, however, transference may occur among family members as well as to the therapist. Family members may also direct projective identifications onto other members. Some of these projections may encourage antisocial behavior. A father, for example, may gratify his own aggressive instincts and fantasies through the aggressive behaviors of his son. Such projections and other defenses are likely to be more frequent in family therapy than in individual therapy (Nichols & Schwartz, 2006).

Psychodynamic therapists may have to attend to the history of each family member to discover the sources of family difficulties. The "working through" process may also be more complex, but somewhat faster, because there are more opportunities for it to occur in the family therapy setting than in individual therapy.

Although psychodynamic family therapy boasts a rich theoretical literature and numerous case studies, evaluations have not found the psychodynamic approach to be as effective as other models (Andrews et al., 1993; Shadish et al., 1993). We also recognize that the object relations perspective of the psychodynamic approach is criticized by many, particularly scholars who study feminist theory and gender, as placing too much blame on mothers. Whether we focus on the "mother blaming" problem or not, psychodynamic interventions stand apart from more modern approaches to family therapy, which recognize a wider range of factors at work in contributing to delinquent and criminal behaviors (Pardeck, 1989).

COMMUNICATIONS FAMILY THERAPY

Interest in the communications of families began as research (rather than as therapy) with the work of Gregory Bateson (Bateson et al., 1956), Donald Jackson (1967), Jay Haley (1976), and Virginia Satir (1967). As the term suggests, communications therapists help families by studying and improving upon the manner in which members communicate with each other. This has involved not only a study of the actual words transmitted in family communication but "metacommunication" as well. Metacommunication refers to a second level of communication that can convey as much information as the verbal content of a conversation. Words say one thing, and other factors, such as voice tone and body language, say another. Family therapists have learned that metacommunication can complicate family interactions in ways that can create problems for a family system.

Early examples of these transactions can be viewed in Bateson's classic therapies with individuals diagnosed with schizophrenia, which noted numerous instances in which family members would convey one thought verbally (e.g., "I love you") and just the opposite nonverbally (e.g., non-emotive tone, lack of physical contact, etc.). This phenomenon is known as the "double bind." For example, Bateson and associates (1956) relate the story of a mother's visit with her son who was recovering from a schizophrenic episode. The mother stiffened when the young boy put his arm around her, but when he withdrew, she asked, "Don't you love me anymore?" When he blushed, she quipped, "Why are you so easily embarrassed and afraid of your feelings?" The visit resulted in the patient's becoming upset and assaultive later in the day. Similar confusion is caused by a process called "mystification," in which family members distort the experiences of other members by denial or relabeling. For example, a parent may say to a child, "You must be tired" rather than "You're feeling angry." In such environments, children are not trained to communicate or to recognize feelings.

Communications therapy, and the strategic therapies that evolved from the communications model, typically work from a systems perspective. Therapists believe that they cannot understand family interactions until they understand the family's role patterns, stability, levels of communication, and governing processes from a systems perspective. Such processes are generally believed to maintain homeostasis in the family. As a result, therapists are very sensitive to both the processes and form of information exchange rather than to the specific content of the interaction.

The most direct approach to alerting family members to dysfunctional communication styles is seen in the treatment techniques of Virginia Satir (1967). Her strategy typically involved identifying and clarifying the numerous complicated and tangled messages of her clients. After identifying the sources of confusion, she corrected patterns by modeling clearer messages, and encouraging communication of personal statements ("I" rather than "you" or "we"), differentiation of opinion from fact or principle, and direct communication to other members rather than about other members. The communication material most frequently identified by Satir concerns emotions and affect. She maintained that being in touch with feelings and communicating them in a clear manner (and allowing others to do the same) is a key to healthy family life as well as to the self-esteem of family members.

To understand how our discussion of thoughts and emotions may affect our sense of self, listen to the following two ways in which a father might communicate anger toward his son:

Without "I statements":

"You know, you can really get angry with a kid who is too lazy to study or go out and get a job."

With "I statements":

"My son's lack of motivation makes me angry. He is too lazy to study or go out and get a job. This is frustrating to me, because I'd like to think he is better than that."

What do we hear from the remark that uses the "I statement"? We hear more ownership of the feelings of frustration and anger. The "you statement" pushes the anger aside; perhaps it reflects some belief that the father is not entitled to feel angry. In using the "I statement," however, the father is more likely to own and acknowledge his anger, and to give himself permission to feel angry. Perhaps he will also face the fact that his son is having difficulty taking responsibility for his schooling and work. Denying the frustration, however, is not going to be helpful.

Haley (1976) later criticized the directness of Satir and others as ineffective and naive. Families and individuals, he maintains, are often resistant to change, and they are not able to change on the basis of information alone. They get "stuck" in dysfunctional patterns. What does it mean to be stuck? Well, imagine the same situation in which a college-aged child does little else besides sit at the computer, watch television, or party with friends. There may have been several family fights over the situation, and many counseling sessions, but still the youth continues to sit, with no intention of obtaining postsecondary training or education. He continues to let his parents support him.

Haley's approach in such a situation involved changing the rules, games, and power basis at work in the family system. He is known for his use of the **"therapeutic paradox."** For example, if instead of allowing a client to offer an excuse repeatedly, a counselor simply agrees with the excuse (e.g., Client: "I am not smart enough to get through college"; Counselor: "Gee, maybe you aren't."), the client is placed in a bind between agreeing that he or she is incompetent or admitting that with some changes (like going to class and reading the required texts), he or she really could assume adult responsibilities. Because many clients in this situation would refuse to actually believe that they are incompetent, they are left with the realization that "I can't handle this job or this course" was an excuse that allowed them to stay stuck, and to avoid working harder. This strategy gains some power for the therapist, which Haley found was needed to encourage clients' use of problem-solving rather than destructive, blaming, or rationalizing behaviors.

Haley also attempted to portray specific family members in more acceptable terms by relabeling, or **reframing**, the motivations of family members (e.g., a parent checking on a child's progress is a reflection of love and concern rather than nagging). In recent years, Haley's work has been termed **strategic family therapy** and currently is viewed as an offshoot of communications therapy.

STRUCTURAL FAMILY THERAPY

Salvador Minuchin's **structural family therapy** (Minuchin, 1974) began with the families of system-involved boys at Wiltwyck School, Esopus, New York. Later, as Director of the Philadelphia Child Guidance Clinic, the model expanded to address a more diverse array of families (Minuchin et al., 1978). This work has since devoted a good deal of time to Hispanic families (Kurtines & Szapocznik, 1996) and to families living in poverty (Minuchin, Colapinto, & Minuchin, 2006).

Borrowing heavily from systems theory, the goal of structural family therapy is to alter the patterns of family **subsystems** and their boundaries. **Family structure** is a term pertaining to the stable and enduring interactions that occur in family settings. Over time, according to Minuchin, families develop habitually utilized rules and patterns of interaction. The husband who encourages his wife to "tell the story about whatever" and then proceeds to interrupt her with corrections of petty, peripheral details is a fitting example. Such an interaction has happened before, and bored listeners may be subjected to several repeat performances in a single evening unless they wisely extricate themselves from the situation. Some structures are universal (e.g., parents protect children) and others are uniquely characteristic of specific families (e.g., Mom controls).

Structural family therapy also targets **boundaries** within the family system. The nature of family subsystems and their boundaries is a treatment target that has not been discussed elsewhere in this book. Just the same, it is an extremely important problem to address. There are numerous subsystems within a family, including individuals, parents, children, spouses, specific **dyads**, and alliances or conspiracies. Figure 11.1 shows just a few of these. Family boundaries dictate the roles of members and the terms of their participation. The permeability of subsystem boundaries is one concern of the structural therapist.

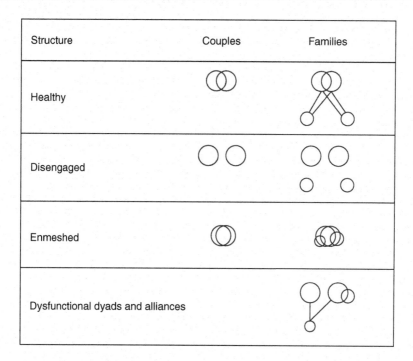

Structure	Couples	Families
Healthy		
Disengaged		
Enmeshed		
Dysfunctional dyads and alliances		

FIGURE 11.1 Couple and family subsystems.

What those boundaries should look like depends on the nature of the system. Intimate relationships, for example, share a good deal of space, but not all aspects of one's personhood. As shown in Figure 11.1 the "healthy couple" has shared space and separate space. In the healthy family, children do not share the same intimate space that the adult couple does.

Rigid boundaries between subsystems indicate that the subsystems are extremely independent of each other (see Figure 11.1). Such subsystems are also considered disengaged. **Disengaged boundaries** are highly appropriate to some situations—when strangers sit together on a bus, perhaps. In fact, how do you feel when an individual shares the most personal aspects of his or her life with you during a first meeting? It is usually somewhat uncomfortable. An element of disengagement, at least at first, is more comfortable. But in the context of intimate relationships, disengagement often seems hurtful to at least one of the partners because it seems to indicate a lack of interest on the part of the other partner. Of course, it may also indicate that both of them are uninterested. The husband who regularly shows no concern for his wife's grief exemplifies "disengagement." In disengaged families or subsystems, then, members may also appear oblivious to the effects of their behaviors on other members. Add children to the mix, as shown in the third column in Figure 11.1, and the system is probably evidencing elements of neglect. All members are very independent, but that is not the appropriate relationship between parents and young children.

The **enmeshed system**, on the other hand, displays a high degree of support, interdependence, warmth, affection (or quasi-affection), and control—too much. Boundaries between subsystems are diffuse—not very clear. Often, this discourages the independence of members of the subsystem and adversely affects their abilities to cope with difficulties outside of the subsystem. Enmeshed systems also may interfere with the individuation of children. Members sound, feel, and act alike. Over time, individuals may not have a separate sense of their own feelings and responsibilities. For example, it may be the case that "we are angry" rather than "I am angry." As a result, individuals may have a poor sense of how to cope with their own feelings, needs, desires, and stresses. Neither type of boundary configuration (disengaged or enmeshed) solves family problems well, as neither is flexible enough to sustain change, explore alternatives, or support the growth of individual members.

Finally, there is the issue of who is allied with whom and the appropriateness of those alliances. The last diagram in Figure 11.1 shows a child sharing intimate space with an adult, while the age-appropriate adult partners are disengaged. This figure depicts a situation of physical or emotional incest. In contrast, the family diagram at the top, showing a more healthy system, shows adult partners sharing intimate space, but giving children some degree of space in a relationship that is affectionate, protective, and parental.

Structural family therapy endeavors to reorder dysfunctional family structures in a manner that:

1. establishes a clear generational distinction between parents and children (e.g., the children and parents are not peers);

2. realigns dysfunctional subsystems (e.g., a parent-child dyad working against the other parent); and

3. develops semipermeable, flexible boundaries that are neither enmeshed nor disengaged.

The therapist proceeds through the following stages:

1. "Joining" the family system to form a new therapeutic system with the family. The therapist is a member of this system, but respects the authority of the parents, accommodates individual reactions to others and the therapeutic situation, and demonstrates acceptance and understanding.

2. Encouraging enactments of family interactions and observing spontaneous episodes of interactions.

3. Diagnosing structure, subsystems, and boundary configurations (e.g., who says what to whom and in what way?).

4. Realigning the structures as a participant (e.g., shaping the competence of a family member, enabling subsystems to assume appropriate roles).

5. Realigning subsystems and boundaries (e.g., strengthening boundaries between parents and children, loosening boundaries between spouses, encouraging open discussion of difficulties, etc.).

Structural family therapy also has been integrated into social learning approaches in Alexander and Parsons' (1982) functional family therapy approach, and into Henggeler and Borduin's (1990) multisystemic family therapy. Both are discussed below.

BEHAVIORAL AND SOCIAL LEARNING MODELS

Authorities recognize numerous behavioral differences between antisocial and prosocial families. Alexander and his colleagues, for example, note that antisocial families in comparison to prosocial ones are less talkative, utilize fewer positive interruptions, are more defensive and less supportive, and are less active (Alexander & Parsons, 1982). In addition, antisocial homes appear to set too many rules that are enforced inconsistently. Conflict management in such families is often unsatisfactory and characterized by an inability to negotiate resolutions, or to differentiate rules from requests. Patterson and his colleagues note such additional behaviors as a parental tendency to reinforce deviant ("coercive") behaviors, punish in an inconsistent manner, or neglect to monitor children's behavior (Patterson, 1982; Patterson & Fleischman, 1979).

Applications of family therapy with families that are justice-involved widely recognize social learning and behavioral programs as promising strategies in the prevention and treatment of antisocial behavior (e.g., see Andrews et al., 1990; Andrews et al., 1993; Gendreau & Ross, 1987; Kumpfer, 1999; Olson, Russell, & Sprenkle, 1980). These programs are grounded in theories of operant conditioning and social learning (Chapters 8 and 10). Their interventions, for the most part, target observable behavioral problems that occur in the family setting and appear to be related to the delinquent or antisocial behavior of the children in the family. These include: (a) communication problems; (b) poor parenting skills (e.g., monitoring and appropriate use of rewards and punishments); (c) problems with conflict management; and (d) day-to-day home management skills.

For example, a treatment goal for specialists at the Oregon Social Learning Center (OSLC), founded by pioneering child psychologist Gerald Patterson, is to improve the parenting skills of parents of children with conduct problems. Most important in this regard is strengthening the parents' ability to use appropriate methods of operant conditioning or contingency management. Parents of such children are often observed to: (a) insufficiently monitor/track children's behavior; (b) spend little time with children; (c) not back up threats and admonitions; (d) punish in an inconsistent manner (e.g., only when they are in a bad mood); (e) have poor control over their own anger; (f) be inconsistent with each other; (g) nag; (h) be overly permissive; and (i) fail to make rewards contingent upon good behavior.

Programs at the OSLC teach parents to define, record, and monitor coercive behaviors. Parents are encouraged to discontinue negative reinforcement of coercive behaviors (e.g., giving in to the child's whining), to administer rewards contingent upon prosocial behaviors, and to administer appropriate and effective punishments in response to coercive behaviors. Therapists endeavor to reduce the overall number of punitive responses while improving their effectiveness. Punishment is considered necessary, but family members are trained to reduce their tendency to punish with anger, and learn to make greater use of techniques such as time-outs, withdrawal of privileges, allowance reductions, and increased work assignments. Parents are also instructed in more general principles of child management to identify normative child behaviors and to utilize effective tactics of negotiation and compromise (Patterson, Chamberlain, & Reid, 1982). The results of these interventions have been favorable, even among high-risk youths (Bank et al., 1991; Dishion & Andrews, 1995; Fisher & Gilliam, 2012). The OSLC model has also been developed for foster care parents (Chamberlain, 2003) called Multidimensional Treatment Foster Care (MTFC), which has demonstrated effectiveness across the United States, Europe, and Scandinavia (Fisher & Gilliam, 2012).

In another evidence-based behavioral approach, Karol Kumpfer (Pawnee) and associates developed the **Strengthening Families Program** (SFP; Kumpfer, 1999), an approach that strengthens the skills of parents, children, and the family as a whole. SFP is conducted in a

14-week program that was initially designed for drug use prevention with children ages six through 12 of substance using parents. It is now considered to be appropriate for troubled families regardless of whether substance use is an issue. The model has since been tailored to rural, Indigenous, and urban African-American families (Kumpfer, 1999) and to Hispanic and Asian families. Modifications have also resulted in a shorter program, a school-based program, and a program for low-income parents.

The program builds skills related to family relationships, parenting skills, and social and life skills. Skills taught to parents in a separate module include strategies of child reinforcement and attention, communication, substance use education, problem-solving, and limit-setting. Children are taught skills of communication, understanding feelings, social skills, problem-solving, resisting peer pressure, compliance with parents, and developmentally appropriate substance use education. The family sessions address problems, plan recreation, and reinforce positive behavior. SPF has been found to be effective with substance-using parents as well as ethnically diverse parents.

A third example, **functional family therapy** (FFT), is more broadly targeted to the operations of the family as a system (Alexander & Parsons, 1973, 1982; Alexander, Waldron, Newberry, & Liddle, 1988). FFT is one of the first family therapy approaches for antisocial children and is still widely used with families of justice-involved and high-risk children (Sexton & Alexander, 2000). We place it within a behavioral category of family therapy because most meta-analyses do, and because the program works with family skills and targets specific family behaviors. Even so, there are some decidedly unique qualities to this program. For example, concerns for the family as a system are clear. Generally speaking, the goal of this short-term behavioral family intervention program is to improve the functioning of the system by fostering reciprocity among family members, by developing effective communication skills and reducing negativity, and by teaching family members how to deal effectively with circumstances that bring about family conflict and delinquent behaviors. Family therapists model, prompt, and reinforce such behaviors as clear communication of feelings, differentiation of rules from requests, use of negotiation strategies, especially as they pertain to parenting adolescents (e.g., curfew, choice of friends, etc.), and the development of solution-oriented communication styles (e.g., interrupting for clarification, additional information, or feedback).

Functional family therapy is primarily grounded in social learning theory but borrows from the structural family therapy and a multisystemic approach. Consistent with structural family therapy, time in therapy is also devoted to understanding what function problem behaviors have in the family system. Many of the behaviors that are treated are those that fit into a larger family systemic context; once their function is understood, therapy seeks to find an appropriate alternative. In addition, an operant model is employed, especially with families that have young children and adolescents. Short- and long-term effects on family interaction styles and on recidivism have been favorable (e.g., see Alexander & Parsons, 1982; Barton, Alexander, Waldron, Turner, & Warburton, 1985; Gordon et al., 1988; Sexton & Turner, 2010). Treatment gains for the group studied by Gordon and his associates, however, were diminished over a longer follow-up period (Gordon et al., 1995).

This approach has also been modified to be responsive to lower income, multicultural families, and to address a variety of behavioral problems, including delinquency, aggression, and substance abuse.

MULTISYSTEMIC TREATMENT

Multisystemic treatment (MST; Henggeler & Borduin, 1990) emphasizes the importance of assessing and treating child and adolescent conduct disorders by addressing a broad spectrum of family problems. Treatment of family systems from this approach must consider all factors that contribute to the child's behavioral problems, including the problems of specific individuals as well as the influence of extrafamilial systems. Proponents of the multisystemic approach believe that traditional forms of family therapy are too simplistic. That is, the approaches described above: (a) fail to consider the importance of the problems of individual family members and extrafamilial systems (e.g., schools, peers, neighbors, and workplaces); (b) fail to consider individual developmental issues (e.g., the cognitive maturity of children); and (c) are too reluctant to borrow, when appropriate, from the individual treatment models. In contrast to the family systems paradigm, MST maintains that the family system may not always be the sole cause of the dysfunctional behaviors of individuals within the system. Moreover, there may be a need to use multiple family therapy approaches, including structural family therapy (Minuchin, 1974) and behavioral parent training (Patterson, 1982), while at the same time treating some family members for their individual problems (e.g., antisocial peers, inadequate social skills, substance use, and poor mental health). In this way, MST continues to value the notion of a family system, but sees the family as part of a wider array of systems that also affect the family system. Moreover, a family member with severe behavioral, health, or other difficulties can affect the family system so seriously that it makes sense to devote most of the therapeutic attention to that individual member of the system.

In sum, MST offers multiple modalities of treatment. Nine principles guide the MST approach (Henggeler et al., 1998):

1. Understand the family's identified problems within a broader systemic context (e.g., schools, neighborhood, extended families).
2. Understand the family's positive and systemic strengths and use them as levers for change.
3. Encourage responsible behavior and discourage irresponsible behavior among family members.
4. Keep interventions present- and action-oriented, targeting specific and well-defined problems.
5. Target sequences of behaviors that contribute to the identified problems. Consider behavioral sequences that occur within the family system and with the multiple systems that interact with the family (e.g., school, extended family, neighborhood).
6. Keep interventions appropriate to the developmental level and needs of young family members.
7. Require daily or weekly intervention-based efforts from family members.
8. Continuously evaluate the effectiveness of the interventions from multiple perspectives. Assure that service providers assume accountability for overcoming barriers to successful outcomes.
9. Promote treatment generalization beyond the period of treatment to long-term maintenance of therapeutic change. Empower caregivers to address family members' needs across multiple systemic contexts.

The multisystemic approach occurs over the following sequence of strategies:

1. *An Initial Assessment* is conducted with the child's parents or parent. This interview results in a description of the child's behavior in the context of the strengths and weaknesses of the child as well as the child's environment. This includes a description of the strengths and weaknesses of the: (a) school; (b) child's abilities; (c) parents' marriage; (d) peer and social network; (e) siblings; (f) parenting skills; and (g) quality of the interrelationship between these entities.

2. *A Treatment Plan* is produced that sets a system of interventions in place that builds on the existing strengths of the child and the other systems.

3. *Goals of Treatment:* Whereas other family therapies may recommend additional treatments such as assessments for attention deficit disorder, or substance use treatment for one family member, multisystemic treatment is likely to involve the family therapist in these aspects of the treatment plan as opposed to referring the clients to other providers.

MST seeks to be flexible and recognizes that different combinations of risk factors are at work with different families. Interventions are individualized. In some cases, treatment may appear to be little more than problem-solving, such as when a plan is developed to see that children are supervised after school. In other instances, the treatment may include therapeutic meetings with the entire family, marital therapy with the parents, or a parenting skills class (see Figure 11.2). Finally, treatment plans may involve a number of outside community services that are not therapeutic in nature, such as childcare, transportation, recreation centers, school interventions, or job development.

In most cases, the intervention is intensive, lasting four to six months, where service is available to the family 24 hours a day, seven days a week. The family is assisted by a professional master's- or doctoral-level therapist and a caseworker. Both are supervised by a psychologist or psychiatrist. The intervention is not tied to any standard modality of family therapy; strategic family therapy, structural family therapy, and cognitive behavioral therapy have all been used, depending upon the family's needs.

Clearly, MST is held in high regard. Licensed MST programs exist throughout the United States and internationally. Evaluations of MST also show that this approach is effective for treating serious and chronic system-impacted juveniles (Borduin et al., 1995; Henggeler, Clingempeel, Brondino, & Pickrel, 2002; Henggeler, Melton, & Smith, 1992; Mann, Borduin, Henggeler, & Blaske, 1990), even in inner-city, lower-class, high-crime neighborhoods (Henggeler et al., 1986). Its use with delinquency and antisocial behavior has been well tested. In a 20-year follow-up study of serious and violent antisocial youth, adolescents participating in MST, versus those receiving individual treatment, had favorable outcomes that extended well into their adult years. The youth who received MST had significantly lower rates of felony recidivism, misdemeanor recidivism, and family-related civil suits (Sawyer & Borduin, 2011).

MST was initially used with the families of children with behavioral problems. Later applications found MST to be a useful treatment for other clinical problems (Henggeler & Lee, 2003; Sundell et al., 2008), including substance abuse (Henggeler, Pickrel, Brondino, & Crouch, 1996; Randall, Henggeler, Cunningham, Rowland, & Swenson, 2001), juvenile sex offending (Borduin, Henggeler, Blaske, & Stein, 1990), and abusive parenting (Brunk, Henggeler, & Whelan, 1987).

In contrast to the other family therapy models discussed in this section, MST offers a distinct focus on case coordination as well as therapy. "Intervention with other systems" is really an academic way of saying that MST gets needed help to the family, helping it to resolve crises with schools, financial well-being, mental health, substance use, and so on. There is no pretense that family therapy alone will resolve the other hardships faced by these families or that families can even participate in family therapy if more competing threats are present.

FIGURE 11.2 An incarcerated person at the Davidson County Correctional Development Center, who is serving time for auto theft, holds a computerized baby for the first time during a parenting class at the prison in Nashville, Tennessee. The class teaches participants responsibility and patience with realistic dolls that cry, burp, and urinate.
Source: AP Photo/*The Tennessean*, Shelley Mays.

In this regard, MST is consistent with the well-known family preservation approaches (Nelson, 1991) that seek to keep problem children out of the juvenile justice and foster care systems. Homebuilders is perhaps the most well-known model of this type (Haapala & Kinney, 1988). The service time is limited (four to six weeks) with caseworkers coordinating concrete services such as food, transportation, and childcare. Counseling from a variety of modalities is also available (e.g., cognitive behavioral, communications). Most of the counseling and caseworker services are provided in the home, or scheduled in a nearby office or neighborhood during a time that is convenient to the family (Kinney, Haapala, Booth, & Leavitt, 1991).

Particularly for families flooded by adversity, the "wraparound" services model makes good sense. In these models, families participating in family counseling or substance use treatment are less likely to be overwhelmed by having to find their own way to meet other essential needs. In some cases, the need for wraparound services may be chronic, needed off and on for the duration of a lifetime, as with some forms of mental illness, intellectual disability, and advanced forms of alcohol and other drug addiction.

This is a note of caution. The writings on the multiservice programs often read as if service and therapy are linear—they have a beginning (when the client or clients are in crisis), a middle (when counseling or services are delivered), and an end (when everyone gets better). Many families in such situations, however, do not get better and cannot be dropped at the end of the prescribed "short-term" intervention. They may become stabilized for periods of time, but require services again at a later time. In such cases, the partners must plan for ongoing services.

FAMILY THERAPY AND CRIMINAL JUSTICE APPLICATIONS

Involving family members in the rehabilitation or reintegration of someone who is involved in the justice system appears to be especially appropriate:

1. Whenever we observe the family to be intertwined in the etiology of offending behavior (which occurs frequently).
2. In many instances of family violence.
3. When a family member is abusing alcohol or other drugs.
4. When we want to facilitate an institutionalized family member's return to family life.

A view of the family therapies as they address these specific problems offers an improved understanding of criminal justice-related applications of family therapy. One danger in discussing family therapy as an approach to family violence, substance abuse, and criminal behavior, however, is in assuming that there are prototypical family styles and treatment approaches for each problem. In fact, sources discourage thinking in terms of the "alcoholic family," the "violent family," or the "delinquent family." They maintain that it is reasonable to expect dysfunctional interactions in such families, but important to encourage careful observation and diagnosis of each family (Aldarondo & Strauss, 1994; Russell et al., 1983). Because there are many paths to the problems listed above, it is not very helpful to match treatments to problems as if all families with a given symptom encompass the same treatment issues.

For families seeking assistance in the resettlement and reconnection of a family member who was recently incarcerated, they may find the interactive game *Recharge: Beyond the Bars* helpful. It is a card deck with thoughtful, pre-designed questions and interactions that facilitate greater connection, empathy, reflection, and growth between players. The game was designed by psychotherapist, Leslie R. Robinson, as a social communication game to heal and transform relationships.

DOMESTIC VIOLENCE

Child Abuse

In response to increasing concern about child abuse and adverse childhood events, family therapists and researchers have targeted the following focal concerns: (a) dynamics that promote abuse; (b) interactional contributions of the child victim to abusive situations; (c) marital discord; (d) aggressive sibling interactions; (e) factors related to alcohol and other drugs; (f) child sexual abuse, including incest; (g) poor self-image of the parents; and (h) parents' psychological vulnerability to stress. Situational stressors also contribute to the problem (see Baird, Wagner, & Neuenfeldt, 1992; Saunders & Azar, 1989). These include: (a) excessive number of children; (b) employment and economic problems; (c) poor home and financial management skills; (d) young age of the mother; (e) emotional loss resulting from death or separation; (f) chronic illness of a parent; (g) rapid life changes; and (h) social isolation.

Given the wide array of interacting factors at work in child abuse, it is not surprising that experts suggest that treatment take place on multiple levels (e.g., individual, familial, and community; Becker et al., 1995). As noted earlier, multisystemic approaches in particular have been tested and found to be an effective means of family preservation (Schoenwald & Henggeler, 1997) and treating abusive parents (Brunk et al., 1987; Swenson, Schaeffer, Henggeler, Faldowski, & Mayhhew, 2010). Even so, almost all of the other approaches to family therapy have been found to be appropriate in the treatment of abusive and neglectful families. A portion of the work at the Oregon Social Learning Center, for example, deals with abuse precipitated by explosive behaviors in children and parents' inability to control them. Here, parents are taught more effective parenting practices (Patterson, 1982). Structural and communications therapies also have a history of being effective methods for dealing with child abuse (Minuchin, 1974; Pardeck, 1989).

These results do not necessarily pertain to children who have been sexually abused in incestuous relationships. Here, sources disagree about whether the child should be treated in a family system that includes the abuser. Any use of family therapy in such situations must secure the protection and empowerment of the victim relative to the power held by the abuser or perhaps even the parental system (Barrett, Trepper, & Fish, 1990). In fact, it is not uncommon to offer family therapy separately to the victim, the perpetrator, and the non-abusing parent (Collins & Collins, 1990), or to treat the perpetrator alone in individual or group therapy.

Sagatun (2007) examined the effects of a self-help program that included people convicted of incest and focused on their sense of responsibility for the incest, change in family relationships, and subsequent rates of recidivism. Results included clients feeling more responsible for their crimes and decreasing recidivism. As might be expected, the program was less successful in keeping families intact.

Finally, skills training approaches emanating from both the social learning and the cognitive behavioral models form a strong foundation for improving the parenting practices of abusive parents. One program, Project 12-Ways, teaches basic home-related skills (e.g., shopping, menu planning, cleaning) to the parents who have been accused of child neglect (Lutzker, 1990). The behavioral skills approaches can also be used in this regard to improve parent-child interactions (McLaren, 1988), problem-solving (Howing, Wodarski, Gaudin, & Kurtz, 1989), and interactional skills of a general nature (Kinney et al., 1991).

Intimate Partner Violence

Violence among intimate partners continues to be a significant global problem and has not declined in the last five decades despite numerous clinical, social, and institutional efforts to reduce it (Wagers & Radatz, 2020). The National Intimate Partner and Sexual Violence Survey from the U.S. Centers for Disease Control and Prevention estimates that roughly 30% of women and 25% of men experience intimate partner violence (IPV) at some point in their lifetimes (Smith et al., 2017). Although IPV is a highly nuanced and complex behavioral problem that is difficult to disentangle, some research indicates that perpetration of IPV occurs at equal rates by men and women (Desmarais, Reeves, Nicholls, Telford, & Fiebert, 2012). Yet, women are far more likely to experience severe violence and harm compared to men based on myriad studies across multiple disciplines (Wagers & Radatz, 2020). For instance, IPV was a precipitating factor in 48% of all homicides of females compared to 9% of males based on the National Violence Death Reporting System (Fowler, Jack, Lyons, Betz, & Petrosky, 2018). Moreover, women are six times more likely to be murdered by an intimate partner than men (Cooper & Smith, 2011).

Treatment programs to address IPV began emerging in the late 1970s during the clarion call of the feminist movement. Because of the rapid growth of offending treatment programs, many different approaches were developed. The Duluth Model, a frequently utilized feminist psychoeducational approach (Pence & Paymar, 1993), was developed in the early 1980s. Other approaches to treat IPV included psychodynamic, attachment-focused, dialectical behavior therapy, and cognitive behavioral therapy (CBT; Wagers & Radatz, 2020). Most treatment interventions today use an eclectic, hybridized approach using multiple modalities, but the most common combinations include the Duluth Model and CBT (Cannon, Hamel, Buttell, & Ferreira, 2016).

The primary aim of IPV treatment programs is to reduce recidivism through perpetrator behavior changes, in an effort to increase victim safety. Most programs are generally structured around a weekly group setting for 3–12 months in which facilitators assist clients through manualized curricula to teach new skills and alternatives to violence (Wagers & Radatz, 2020). These programs were originally designed for treating male perpetrators of IPV against female partner victims, with very little direction on how to adapt programs to female perpetrators and LGBTQI+ victim-perpetrator relationships, and persons with disabilities. The reality is that typically most IPV perpetrators are sentenced to a "one-size-fits-all" approach that does not appropriately reflect the diverse needs within this population (Hamel, 2020). Unique needs are most typically addressed on an as-needed basis, and oftentimes result in staff working individually with such clients rather than through standardized programming (Cannon et al., 2016). For more details on how best to modify such programs for the LGBTQI+ community, readers are encouraged to read Brenda

TABLE 11.1 Holtzworth-Munroe and Stuart's batterer typologies

Batterer Typology	Characteristics
Family-Only	Limit violence to the family Lowest risk of injury Low frequency and severity of violence Little childhood trauma
Generally Violent/Antisocial	Psychopathic characteristics Uses moderate to severe violence Extensive offending history Likely to have substance abuse problems Likely to have experienced severe childhood abuse
Dysphoric/Borderline	Moderate offending—falls between the previous two Uses moderate to severe violence Experienced severe parental rejection Moderate interparental violence during childhood

Source: Holtzworth-Munroe, A., & Stuart, G.L. (1994). Typologies of male batterers: Three subtypes and the differences among them. *Psychological Bulletin, 116,* 476–497.

Russell's text (2020) *Intimate Partner Violence and the LGBT+ Community: Understanding Power Dynamics.*

Holtzworth-Munroe and Stuart (1994) are known for a classic study that identified three types of perpetrators of IPV, which they called "batterers": family-only batterers, generally violent/antisocial batterers, and dysphoric/borderline batterers (see Table 11.1; Holtzworth-Munroe & Meehan, 2002). By establishing which group a perpetrator falls into, we can better create a treatment program for the client (Dixon & Browne, 2003).

Therapy with partners who engage in IPV must address the following types of problems (Saunders & Azar, 1989; Stith & Rosen, 1990): (a) inability to express feelings and emotions; (b) emotional dependence; (c) alcohol and other drug abuse; (d) heightened adherence to masculine sex-role stereotypes; (e) lack of assertiveness; (f) social isolation; (g) poor coping skills; and (h) habitual communication and behavioral patterns that escalate into violent interactions. Often, techniques of crisis management are practiced prior to beginning more long-term therapy. The first goal must always be to stop the violence. In addition, therapists are quick to encourage their clients to use local community support services and programs, such as self-help groups (e.g., Batterers Anonymous, Parents Anonymous), parenting skills workshops, hotlines, marriage-enrichment programs, and services that offer relief time for parents (Gaudin, Wodarski, Arkinson, & Avery, 1991).

Without blaming victims for an abuser's decision to use violence, most family therapists recognize that there are reciprocal dynamics to many of the target problems listed above. Thus, even though limits have to be set with perpetrators of violence, couples who wish to stay married are encouraged to address the problems of family violence together (Rosen, Matheson, Stith, McCollum, & Locke, 2007), thus taking a systems view to its solution (Chamow, 1990; Simpson, Doss, Wheeler, & Christensen, 2007). Indeed, many of the published accounts of family therapy recommend a systemic or an ecosystemic approach (e.g., see Flemons, 1989; Nichols & Schwartz, 2006). This perspective is not necessarily inconsistent with feminist concerns for protecting victims, taking a strong stand against violent behavior, and avoiding victim-blaming (Stith & Rosen, 1990). Interventions target most of the problem areas enumerated above. In addition to addressing many of the sources of family stress (e.g., finances, parental issues), conjoint (structural and strategic family therapy) marital therapy appears to be the predominant approach, assuming, of course, that the couple wish to stay together. Unfortunately, the effectiveness of family therapy as a response to intimate partner violence has not been widely researched.

We remind readers that an alternative approach of treating only the perpetrator may also be effective. For example, clients may benefit from skills training, including anger management (Edleson & Grusznski, 1988; Hamberger & Hastings, 1988), other cognitive behavioral approaches (Saunders, 1996), and support groups for both victims and batterers (Petrik, Gildersleeve-High, McEllistrem, & Subotnik, 1994). In recognizing the relevance of family therapy as a vehicle for treating family violence, however, one cannot ignore the fact that the safety of family members, as well as their future well-being, must be given priority over efforts to improve the quality of their relationships. Often the removal of abusive members from the home, out-of-home placements, legal aid, career planning for a life without one's spouse, therapy for the victim, and self-help and support groups provide more appropriate alternatives (Saunders & Azar, 1989).

SUBSTANCE ABUSE

Numerous authorities implicate the family in the etiology and maintenance of addictive behaviors (Kaufman & Kaufman, 1992; Stanton, Todd, & Associates, 1982). Steinglass, Bennett, Wolin, and Reiss (1987) observed that alcohol was often central to many of the interactions in families of alcoholics. The family, for example, that saved discussions, arguments, displays of warmth, and complaints for times when drinking was occurring often allowed their interactions to be marred by the effects of drinking. Studies have found that families with an alcoholic parent who are able to maintain family rituals (i.e., dinner time, holiday celebrations, vacations) undisrupted by the alcoholism, are significantly less likely to have children who become alcoholics (Steinglass et al., 1987). By contrast, families in which such rituals were disrupted by the alcoholism were far more likely to pass on alcoholic behavior to the next generation.

In addition, addictions are considered among the behaviors that maintain dysfunctional homeostasis within family systems (Steinglass et al., 1987). Scapegoating, resistance to therapy, poor communication, family modeling of substance abusing behavior, problems with late individuation and separation, and poor parenting practices are not uncommon among such families. Moreover, when family dynamics are at least helping to support an addiction, counselors and case managers need to pay attention. Case managers, social workers, probation officers, and institutional treatment staff may unintentionally become entangled in the family's efforts to maintain homeostasis, thereby perpetuating the problem. They may also thwart treatment efforts by failing to maintain the distance needed to keep from becoming a member of a family triangle, one involving the therapist, the client, and the probation officer (Mowatt, Van Deusen, & Wilson, 1985).

Accounts of family therapy approaches to alcohol and other drug abuse report some encouraging results (Connell, Dishion, Yasui, & Kavanagh, 2007; Hogue, Dauber, Samuolis,

& Liddle, 2006), but there have not been many methodologically sound studies of the effectiveness of family therapy with this population. While family treatments seem to span all five strategies discussed previously, applications of structural and conjoint approaches (a combination of structural and strategic therapies) seem most common (Kaufman & Kaufman, 1992).

Until the early 1970s, family therapy with alcoholics consisted primarily of marital therapy. Then several studies noted that the involvement of the alcoholic's family greatly improved the alcoholic's chances of success (Janzen, 1977). Published accounts describe the use of the conflict management and communication strategies of Satir and Ackerman (Meeks & Kelly, 1970), social learning and behavioral approaches (Cheek, Franks, Laucious, & Burtle, 1971), and systems therapy (Berenson, 1986).

Family therapy for families with adolescent substance users appears to be more developed than similar services for adult clients (Liddle & Dakof, 1995). Stanton et al. (1982; Stanton, 1994), however, are credited with conducting one of the most comprehensive studies of the effectiveness of family therapy with adult substance use. Testing the effects of a family therapy model that combined structural family therapy with strategic family therapy, the authors found this model to be far more effective in reducing drug use than non-family treatment and family education (a movie). Other research with adolescents also found structural family therapy highly effective in reducing drug use and associated behavioral problems (Szapocznik, Kurtines, Foote, Perez-Vidal, & Harvis, 1983). This program also improved family functioning. As noted earlier, most of Szapocznik's research is with Hispanic families. Similar findings were noted among non-Hispanic participants as well (Joanning, Thomas, Quinn, & Mullen, 1992).

Successes of family therapy are not limited to structural and communication models. Friedman (1989) reports excellent outcomes (reductions in drug use) for functional family therapy with families of adolescent drug users (Alexander & Parsons, 1982). Behavioral family therapies have been found effective in several small studies (e.g., Azrin, Donohue, Betsalel, Kogan, & Acierno, 1994). In addition, we have already noted the success of MST with substance users (e.g., Henggeler et al., 1991; Henggeler et al., 1996; Henggeler et al., 2002; Henggeler et al., 2006).

The problem of clients dropping out of treatment appears to plague many correctional treatment programs, and those focused on substance use is no exception. However, a number of studies have found that, for a variety of reasons, family therapy approaches appear to have greater client retention rates than individual therapies (Joanning et al., 1992; Liddle & Dakof, 1995). Family treatment drug courts (FTDCs) represent an emerging approach in treating families involved in child welfare who have substance abuse problems. Results indicate that FTDC parents enter treatment more quickly, remain in treatment longer, and complete more substance use treatment sessions. Perhaps most promising, children of FTDC parents were more likely to be reunited with their parents compared to children of non-FTDC parents (Green, Furrer, Worcel, Burrus, & Finigan, 2007). Additional information on family therapy for substance use can be found in Chapter 12.

WHEN A FAMILY MEMBER IS INCARCERATED

Although sources have long maintained that incarcerated people who remain involved with families during incarceration make better parole adjustment than those who are emotionally separated from their families, programs offering family therapy or family services are fairly recent developments. Undoubtedly, incarceration causes a myriad of problems for incarcerated people and families. In addition to the problem of separation itself, families may be unable to obtain adequate information regarding such matters as the status of legal proceedings, visitation policies, transportation to the institution, results of parole reviews, and other necessary information (Christian, 2005). Economic problems abound. Emotional stress, guilt, sexual frustration, anger, and depression threaten what may already be unstable relationships. There is a need to redefine the marital relationship in the absence of the incarcerated spouse, and to decide, unencumbered by self-doubt and denial, whether to continue the marriage. In response to the very thought of a wife's infidelity, incarcerated people may engage in acting-out behavior or depressive withdrawal. Their fear of rejection may prompt them to prematurely reject their spouse or family first. Denial and an intense desire to keep a relationship intact may also result in an unrealistic view of their marriages and families, and avoidance of the difficulties that do exist (Kaslow, 1987). Such views create additional stress on families when loved ones are released from prison.

And what about children of incarcerated people? As noted previously, incarceration periods of greater than 15 months seriously affect a parent's chance of regaining custody upon release unless the children have been with a relative of the parent. Community service providers note, however, that this is no guarantee of a smooth transition back into parenthood upon prison release. For example, tired relatives may be quick to return children to parental custody at a time when the newly released individual must find safe housing, work, childcare, and abide by a myriad of parole requirements, including participation in treatment programs. A great resource for families responsible for children of incarcerated parents is the

FIGURE 11.3 Nursery inside Prison Světlá nad Sázavou in the Czech Republic.
Photo credit: Emily Salisbury

Incarceration Toolkit available online from Sesame Street (www.sesamestreet.org/toolkits/incarceration?language=en).

A survey of correctional agencies in the United States (LIS, Inc., 2002), reports that only about 27 states have a policy of considering proximity to family in the assignment of people to prison settings, and only 16 states offer to assist family visitation efforts by furnishing transportation and lodging. Agencies were much less likely to furnish space for overnight visits with children and spouses. Even fewer agencies provide nurseries where newborns may be with their mothers for a period of time following birth.

Classes designed to strengthen parenting skills are growing in number. The same survey indicated that they were available to women in 95% of the agencies surveyed and to men in 85% of the agencies surveyed. Most of these are conducted without the children present. However, children's participation is available to women in 61% of the agencies and to men in 26% of the agencies. One innovative treatment effort consisted of individual and group therapy for incarcerated fathers that addressed the impact of their absence from the family system and ways of communicating with their children while in prison. Benefits included improved parenting skills involving both justice-involved juveniles and incarcerated fathers (Magaletta & Herbst, 2001).

Family unification and support efforts for visitation and prison nurseries appear to be stronger in countries throughout Europe and Asia compared to the United States, though some prison systems in the U.S. have model programs, such as the Oregon Department of Corrections program called Through a Child's Eyes (TACE), which include carnival-like family event days for incarcerated women and men. In addition, the longest running prison nursery in the United States was founded in 1901 at Bedford Hills Correctional Facility in New York. Similar prison nurseries can be found in several other U.S. states and throughout the world. Figure 11.3 shows a nursery inside Prison Světlá nad Sázavou, a women's facility in the Czech Republic.

Community services to families received a big boost under the Federal Coming Home Initiative developed by the U.S. Department of Justice. This initiative forms partnerships among several key federal agencies, such as Housing and Urban Development and Health and Human Services. Federal grants to all states now fund state models that in many cases also promote partnerships with state-level agencies, including corrections, substance use, housing, employment, and mental health. The National Institute of Corrections has contributed to this effort through its Transition from Prison to Community Initiative (Parent & Barnett, 2003), which provides a model (mostly a case management model) for reintegrating people into the community following incarceration. Attention to family issues is not the only service provided under the new initiatives, but it is not difficult to see the relevance of programs such as MST, Family Preservation, and other multiservice models.

CONCLUSION

In conclusion, the vast literature of family therapy suggests that it is one of the interventions that has had some success in reducing recidivism and improving family functioning. In the current funding climate, however, family therapy continues to make only modest inroads toward addressing the needs of people involved in the justice system. While it is clear that it is relevant to those needs, and that evaluations of its effectiveness generally have been favorable, family therapy does not seem to be readily available nor to be routinely considered by court and correctional officials as a viable component of a treatment plan. Current government and private reimbursement policies offer no encouragement. State policies that result in greater reimbursement for state institutional placements than for community-based options, and insurance policies that favor medical treatment over mental health treatment or individual treatment over family treatment, both serve to discourage the use of family-level interventions.

This chapter does not mean to extol family therapy as the panacea that will work with all individuals who approach family and criminal courts. Certainly not all clients are amenable to family therapy. Some families of system-impacted youth may be hostile and defensive to the idea of participating in therapy. In numerous cases, parental concern for their children is either nonexistent or too limited to initiate any work at the family level. In addition, some people may have exhausted their families by the time they come to the attention of the criminal justice system. Finally, a significant number of families face stressors that are more intense than the criminality of a family member. Understandably, families attempting to survive the exhausting demands of poverty and unemployment will evidence little motivation for family therapy. However, this still leaves a significant portion of adult and juvenile cases in need of family-level interventions. While family therapy is a more complex and expensive endeavor than individual therapy, it is often the more sensible choice and cost effective in the long run. The alternative is to treat one member of a pathological family for symptoms of a much larger problem.

Discussion Questions

1. Why is the family "system" such a powerful unit? How could such a system contribute to an adolescent becoming involved in the justice system? How could such a system help rehabilitate an antisocial family member?

2. Compare the communications model of family therapy with the structural model. What are the advantages and disadvantages of each? Which do you prefer?

3. What are the advantages of multisystemic family therapies over some of the other models discussed in this chapter?

4. Discuss the use of family therapy interventions with child abuse. What kind of interventions seem to work best with this problem area?

5. How could a family therapy program be useful with incarcerated people and their families? What would be some unique aspects and limitations of such a program?

ONLINE LEARNING ENHANCEMENTS

Google the words "Coffee Creek Through a Child's Eyes" and view the images from the family unification event hosted by the Oregon Department of Corrections. Consider how the images contrast with the stereotypical image and idea of "inmate" mothers. How do the images make you feel differently?

GLOSSARY OF KEY TERMS

boundaries   borders within the family system that differentiate its various subsystems

communications therapy   a form of family therapy that typically works from a systems perspective; communications therapists seek to study and improve upon the manner in which family members communicate with each other

disengaged boundaries   boundaries within the family system that denote emotional detachment, independence, and obliviousness among members; such disengagement may be indicative of child neglect

double bind   a phenomenon in which family members convey to each other one thought verbally and just the opposite non-verbally

dyad   a family subsystem that consists of a pair of individuals (e.g., married couple, parent-child)

enmeshed system   a family system in which unclear boundaries and excessive degrees of support, interdependence, warmth, affection (or quasi-affection), and control are exhibited; the enmeshed system discourages the independence of members of the subsystem and adversely affects their abilities to cope with difficulties outside of the subsystem

family structure   a term pertaining to the stable and enduring interactions that occur in family settings

family system   a familial unit in which members exhibit varying degrees of interdependence and whose realities are more than the sum total of member characteristics

family therapy   a therapeutic field in which family systems, rather than individuals, are targeted for treatment; family therapy operates under the assumption that individual modes of therapy are too narrow and inattentive to the impact of relationships, families, and their respective systems on family members

homeostasis   a balanced, steady state of equilibrium within family systems

individuate   a component of healthy development in which people move away from the dependence of childhood to the interdependence of adulthood

metacommunication   a second level of communication involving voice tone, body language, and other factors that can convey as much information as the verbal content of a conversation

multisystemic treatment (MST)   a treatment program that emphasizes the importance of assessing and treating child and adolescent conduct disorders by addressing a broad spectrum of family problems; treatment of family systems from the MST approach must consider all factors that contribute to the child's behavioral problems, including the problems of specific individuals as well as the influence of extrafamilial systems

mystification   a process in which family members distort the experiences of other members by denial or relabeling

object relations   a set of cognitive and affective processes that mediate interpersonal functioning in close relationships

psychodynamic family therapy   a form of family therapy that incorporates a psychodynamic perspective pioneered by Freud and Adler; psychodynamic family therapy is characterized by an interest in unconscious aspects of individual personality development as well as the social/family context in which individual and relational dysfunction develops

reframing   a process of relabeling the motivations of family members to portray them in more acceptable terms

rigid boundaries   boundaries in which family subsystems are extremely independent of each other

scapegoats   people who are blamed for the wrongdoings or faults of others

strategic family therapy   an offshoot of communications therapy in which clients are encouraged to employ problem-solving strategies to address problematic symptoms within the family rather than destructive, blaming, or rationalizing behaviors

structural family therapy   a form of family therapy that addresses problems within families by altering the patterns of subsystems and their boundaries

subsystems   self-contained systems within the larger family system (e.g., parents, children, and various dyads)

therapeutic paradox   a therapeutic technique in which clients are directed by the therapist to continue undesired symptomatic behavior, and even increase it, to indicate that they have voluntary control over such behavior

"working through" process   a psychodynamic process in which the therapist assists the client in identifying, exploring, and coping with problems

PART IV

Effective Correctional Interventions for Special Populations

Up to this point in the book, we have presented a variety of theories and strategies of correctional intervention. In these next four chapters we devote considerable attention to the treatment of specific justice-involved populations—substance-dependent clients, justice-involved women, people convicted of sex offenses, and those who display severely antisocial and psychopathic behavior. Because many innovative practices have been developed for these groups in recent years, these chapters have been revised considerably over recent editions of this book.

Chapter 12 reviews approaches to the treatment of substance dependence. Chapter 13 provides an overview of emerging approaches for women involved in the system. Chapter 14 provides an explanation of the pathways to sex offending and approaches for treatment and community management. Finally, Chapter 15 describes the complexities of intervening with severely antisocial and psychopathic clients, while also providing a discussion of the most promising methods of treatment and practical advice for practitioners. These chapters are intended to be responsive to practitioners and policymakers who face increasing pressures to address the risk/need factors of these populations. As we review these strategies, however, it is striking to note that social learning and cognitive behavioral models continue to form the core of these programs. Just the same, a good deal of attention has been devoted to tailoring the social learning and cognitive behavioral models to the unique features of these populations. Additionally, all four groups require sound assessment strategies, and an emerging array of assessments allow practitioners to better understand their risk factors. Finally, increasing attention is given to the growing realization that abuse and trauma play a role in the etiology of these problems. One now sees program components designed to help calm clients, including mindfulness and meditation and various approaches to accommodate neurological problems. It is in the treatment of people convicted of sex offenses, substance use, and women, especially, that we see most of the innovations in the field of correctional treatment.

DOI: 10.4324/9780367808266-15

CHAPTER 12

Treating Clients with Substance Abuse

Patricia Van Voorhis, Myrinda Schweitzer, and Gail Hurst

KEY TERMS

abstinence violation effect (AVE)

aftercare

aversion therapies

behavioral family therapies

communications therapy

community reinforcement approach
  (CRA)

contingency contracts

covert sensitization

culturally competent

disease model

drug courts

educational model

family systems models

harm-reduction approaches

high-risk situations

identified patient

methadone maintenance

multisystemic family therapy

peer encounters

psychodynamic family therapies

relapse prevention

relational model of self

self-help groups

sponsors

stages of change

substance abuse

substance dependence

temperance model

theory of addiction

theory of trauma

theory of women's
  psychosocial development

therapeutic communities

According to estimates, illicit drug and alcohol addiction affect most people in the criminal justice system (Mumola & Karberg, 2006). In fact, during the 1990s, with help from the "war on drugs" and mandatory sentencing policies, substance users accounted for 20% of the growth in state prison populations (Office of National Drug Control Policy, 2003) and 72% of the growth in federal prison populations (Bureau of Justice Statistics, 2001). At the same time, substance use is known to place justice-involved people at clear risk for future offending (Bureau of Justice Statistics, 1992; Gendreau et al., 1996). From this perspective, substance-using individuals place a heavy demand on all correctional agencies.

Fortunately, advances in the technology of substance use treatment offer much support to correctional efforts to provide viable treatment. These include developments in assessments,

DOI: 10.4324/9780367808266-16

treatment models, relapse prevention strategies, medication-assisted treatment, drug courts, and methods for accommodating client responsivity. In addition, research shows a clearer picture of "what works" in the treatment of this very important social problem (Anglin & Hser, 1990; Miller et al., 2003; Pearson & Lipton, 1999).

None of this is to suggest that treatment of addiction is a straightforward endeavor. There are many "paths" to substance use and many different types of substance users (Wanberg & Milkman, 1998). For example, we now recognize that effective treatment should accommodate the client's readiness to change. That is, interventions designed for people who are in denial about the existence of an addiction should differ from those delivered to clients who are actively seeking to change or those who hope to maintain sobriety (Stinson & Clark, 2017). Likewise, a debate continues about what should be the underlying philosophy of treatment, particularly whether we should consider substance use a disease or a learned behavior (Miller & Hester, 2003). Substance use interventions and supervision strategies should also vary by client risk and whether the client is substance-dependent or a substance abuser (Marlowe, 2009). Finally, while most treatment models adhere to a requirement of abstinence from addictive substances, others advocate **harm-reduction approaches**, such as controlled drinking, methadone maintenance, and needle-exchange programs (MacCoun, 1998; Marlatt, Blume, & Parks, 2001; Marlatt & Witkiewitz, 2002).

This chapter offers an overview of the main approaches and philosophies to treating the substance-using correctional client. As in the treatment of other mental health problems, most interventions rest on the theoretically based systems of therapy discussed in earlier chapters (e.g., psychodynamic, radical behavioral, family, social learning, and cognitive behavioral approaches). In this chapter, we also discuss assessment, responsivity, support groups, continuity of care, and harm-reduction models. With few exceptions, treatments for drug addictions are not viewed as distinct from those for alcohol addictions, because the addiction is the treatment target—more so than the addictive substance (Wanberg & Milkman, 1998).

MODELS OF SUBSTANCE ABUSE

The wide array of interventions for substance abuse differ rather dramatically in terms of their definitions of who the substance user is and how he or she came to become addicted to alcohol or other drugs. Treatment implications, of course, follow from each model's core philosophy. In discussing the history and patterns of treatments for alcoholism, for example, Miller and Hester (2003) set forth the 11 models shown in Box 12.1. Many of the models also apply to other types of drug abuse.

Box 12.1 Models of Alcohol Intervention

MORAL MODEL

Probably the longest-standing conceptualization of alcoholism views it as a sin, incurred as the result of personal choice. To this day, some religious faiths continue to hold this view. Even Alcoholics Anonymous defines alcoholism as a "spiritual deficit." This perspective suggests that alcoholism and other addictions be addressed through various means of spiritual direction and social control, including criminal sanctions.

TEMPERANCE MODEL

Through the late 1800s to the repeal of Prohibition in 1933, alcoholism was viewed as caused by a harmful drug—alcohol. Although the temperance movements of those days had support from many religious circles, they did not necessarily fault the drinker. Instead, they blamed alcohol and its destructive qualities. "Treatment" from this perspective did not require treatment of the alcoholic but rather legislation that prohibited use and distribution of alcohol, a policy not unlike current approaches to illegal drugs.

DISEASE MODEL

Conceptualizing alcoholism as a disease began with the end of Prohibition and the formation of Alcoholics Anonymous. The **disease model** views alcoholics as physiologically distinct from non-alcoholics in that their biological makeup renders them incapable of drinking in moderation. With this condition, drinking progresses to a point where the drinker acquires an irreversible compulsion to drink, which can only be arrested through abstinence. "Recovery" from the disease requires recognition of the condition and its effects, abstinence, and support from other recovered alcoholics. In the United States, the disease model receives strong support from medical arenas as a disease requiring medical treatment. The disease model is less widely supported outside of the United States.

EDUCATIONAL MODEL

This approach views alcoholism as caused by ignorance of the harms and effects of alcohol. Indeed, in the United States, education has long been one of the common preventive approaches to addiction. Its applicability appears most relevant to primary prevention efforts, strategies that are administered to the general population.

CHARACTEROLOGICAL MODEL

Most relevant to psychodynamic interventions, this model asserts that alcoholism results from fundamental personality problems. One can fault developmental difficulties such as fixation of normal psychological development, early trauma, excessive use of certain defense mechanisms, and other factors. For some clinicians and scholars, this model has initiated a search for the "alcoholic personality" or the "addictive personality." Treatment from this perspective would involve resolution or interpretation of underlying conflicts and sources of anxiety.

CONDITIONING MODEL

Alcoholism and other addictions are learned through the same behavioral mechanisms through which other behaviors are learned. Causation, then, is rooted in classical and operant conditioning models of learning. Drinking and other types of drug use are reinforced through peer approval, tension reduction, improved social confidence, and festivity (operant conditioning). At the same time, addicts come to appreciate the various stimuli of addictive behaviors, for example, certain friends, settings, and paraphernalia (classical conditioning). Treatment involves reconditioning, contingency management, and stimulus control.

SOCIAL LEARNING/COGNITIVE BEHAVIORAL MODEL

As noted in Chapters 9 and 10, behaviors can be learned vicariously in the presence of peers and others who model a behavior that is then imitated. Both the behaviors and the cognitions associated with substance abuse may be learned in this manner. Treatment models operating from this approach teach new skills, particularly coping skills, and seek to alter individuals' relationships with their environments and the individuals with whom they associate. In addition, these interventions endeavor to change thought patterns that are viewed as associated with addictive behavior. The social learning/cognitive behavioral model is becoming the preferred approach to treating the substance-using correctional client.

BIOLOGICAL MODELS

Not to be confused with the disease models, these approaches attempt to identify and target specific genetic or physiological causes of alcoholism. Since the 1970s, biological research has: (a) identified inherited risk factors of alcoholism; (b) identified abnormal forms of metabolizing alcohol; (c) studied brain sensitivity to alcoholism; and (d) studied the manner in which drinking escalates to alcoholism. Treatment from this approach may involve genetic counseling, counseling abstinence, or controlled drinking.

GENERAL FAMILY SYSTEMS MODEL

This model views substance abuse as occurring within dysfunctional family systems. That is, addiction is just one symptom of family dysfunction. Treatment addresses the needs of all family members as members of a system. Treatment targets may include enabling behaviors, poor boundaries among family members, communication problems, and trust issues.

SOCIOCULTURAL MODELS

These models recognize that some social environments and cultures support alcohol and other drug abuse more than others. What follows from the sociocultural model are attempts to regulate drinking establishments and alcohol/drug distribution patterns to prevent undue encouragement of substance use. Thus, illegal drugs, liquor taxation, licensure requirements for bars and restaurants, advertising restrictions, regulation of hours for drinking establishments, and age restrictions are examples of sociocultural efforts to control alcohol and other drug use.

PUBLIC HEALTH MODEL

This approach seeks to integrate important aspects of the models listed above. The public health model encourages a multifaceted approach to addictions, focusing on: (a) the agent (alcohol/illegal drugs), (b) the host (the substance user), and (c) the micro- and macro-environments (family, peers, and society). The public health model advocates simultaneous attention to the hazardous nature of alcohol, individual susceptibilities to alcohol, and social policies that regulate its distribution.

Source: Miller, W., & Hester, R. (2003). Treatment for alcohol problems: Toward an informed eclecticism. In R. Hester & W. Miller (Eds.), *Handbook of Alcoholism Treatment Approaches* (3rd ed.). Boston: Allyn & Bacon.

In practice, interventions for substance-abusing clients are more likely to be eclectic than to conform to a single policy or model of service delivery. Even so, some of the models differ dramatically on such issues as: (a) who is responsible for the addiction (the addict or a disease that the addict cannot help having); (b) whether the addict is a moral individual; (c) whether abstinence is required; or (d) what should be targeted in treating the addiction (knowledge, physiological factors, spirituality, social support, social skills, or cognitions).

Importantly, the choice of what model to implement often manifests itself at policy levels, such as when agencies debate whether they should support the disease model or cognitive behavioral approaches. Cost is another factor. Over the years, the federal government has instituted major funding initiatives, including the Treatment Accountability for Safer Communities (TASC) programs during the 1970s and the Residential Substance Abuse Treatment (RSAT) programs of the 1990s. New federal and state agencies have been created to address the massive problems associated with alcohol and other drug use in the United States. One of the most recent funding initiatives is from the National Institutes of Health, called the Helping to End Addiction Long-term (HEAL) Initiative, which is specific to ending opioid addiction in the United States. Opioid addiction has been surging for decades and was made tragically worse during the coronavirus epidemic. According to the Centers for Disease Control and Prevention, 87,000 Americans died from drug overdoses between September 2019 and September 2020, which eclipsed the number from any year since the opioid epidemic began in the 1990s (Ahmad, Rossen, & Sutton, 2021). Of course, many treatment programs were forced to close their doors during the pandemic, or become significantly more limited in service provision with limited bed space and availability. To be true, the United States and other countries will be dealing with the aftermath of addiction during the COVID-19 pandemic for years to come.

Even so, the National Criminal Justice Treatment Practices Survey (Taxman, Perdoni, & Harrison, 2007) detected two disturbing trends. First, the overwhelming majority of justice-involved clients receive low-intensity substance use educational programs, regardless of whether services are administered in the community or in correctional facilities. Such programs have not been widely studied and clearly are not among the most effective programs at reducing recidivism and addictive behaviors. Second, for various reasons, surprisingly small proportions of substance-using clients who need treatment actually receive the programs, even when such programs are available.

THERAPEUTIC MODALITIES

In keeping with the main approach to this text, we focus on the treatment models themselves that are most frequently used with forensic offending populations, offering an overview of substance abuse treatment from each of the treatment systems discussed in earlier chapters. While psychodynamic therapy for addiction is a common modality for treating substance use, it is infrequently used among offending populations. Therefore, we begin with the behavioral approach.

Behavioral Approach

Strategies appearing under the rubric of classical or operant conditioning include aversion therapies, contingency contracting, token economies, covert sensitization, stimulus control, and community reinforcement. Some of these approaches stand alone as substance use interventions in themselves; others are components of such other programs as therapeutic communities or relapse prevention programs.

Use of these strategies makes sense for a variety of reasons. One has only to think about how alcohol and other drug use actually conforms to classical and operant conditioning to see the applicability of both learning models to the treatment of alcohol and drug use. Addiction can be viewed as being encouraged and maintained by the addictive substances and their effects. Drinking, for example, is often encouraged by such antecedents (stimuli) as days of the week, times of the day, activities associated with drinking, familiar drinking establishments, drinking buddies, certain meals, and emotional states. Similarly, drinking is reinforced by such effects as reduction in stressful feelings, a "buzz," increased social comfort, and peer approval. Radical behavioral therapies seek to reverse these processes by controlling the stimuli that encourage substance use and by reinforcing controlled drinking, abstinence, and other prosocial substitute behaviors.

Classical conditioning therapies for substance use treatment consist primarily of aversion therapy and stimulus control. Aversion therapies work directly with a client's desire for an addictive drug; they attempt to reverse these desires. These early approaches paired aversive stimuli with consumption of alcohol or other drugs. The aversive stimuli included drug-induced nausea, drug-induced breathing difficulties (apnea), foul odors, and electric shock (Wilson, 1987). The goal of treatment was to cause clients to associate the addictive substance with the aversive stimulus, thereby developing an avoidance reaction to the alcohol or other drug. Given the pain and stress associated with these approaches, however, more recent applications of aversion therapy use a more benign form of classical conditioning: covert sensitization.

As described in Chapter 8, covert sensitization employs aversive imagery rather than aversive experiences. Clients imagine the aversive events or feelings rather than directly experiencing them. Sometimes, however, a nauseating odor may be used to accompany the images. Rimmele, Miller, and Dougher's (2003) approach to covert sensitization with people who abuse alcohol includes the following steps: (a) preliminary assessment; (b) constructions of various scenes specific to each client; (c) administration of stimulus scenes; (d) administration of sensitization or aversive scenes; and (e) administration of escape or avoidance scenes. The preliminary assessment obtains information concerning a client's drinking preferences, patterns, and motivations. A variety of drinking scenes incorporate the situations and details that would typically accompany a client's drinking habits. The aversive scenes construct situations that find the client experiencing either nausea or strong emotional reactions (e.g., embarrassment, disgust, guilt, or horror). Rimmele and colleagues (2003) offer the following poignant example of one such scene:

> [After leaving the bar] you have just entered your car, and are preparing to back out of the driveway, on your way to the store. With one hand on the hot steering wheel, you reach forward to insert the key in the ignition. As you feel it slide in, you swallow and notice the taste of beer in your mouth. You can smell it, as if you just swallowed a large sip. You turn the key, and the engine surges to life. As you pull the shift lever into reverse, you glance over your shoulder to make sure it is clear behind the car. The car gives a sickening lurch as if you ran over a small bump. The taste of beer is strong in your mouth as you open the door and look toward the back of the car. You are horrified to see a small foot sticking out from behind your rear tire. You jump from the car, and find a small crumpled body pinned under the rear of the car. You're down on your hands and knees, and as you peer under the car, you can clearly see the blood puddling under the small child's body. There is no movement, and you cannot tell if the child is alive. The smell of beer is strong on your breath, and the smell mixes with the warm odor of blood on the ground. You are horrified, you cannot think straight, as you stare at the broken body. You notice that the child's arms are bent unnaturally, and you see the stark white color of bone protruding through the clothing. The sour taste of beer surges into your mouth, and burning fear and horror fills you, as you see the child's limbs give a series of twitches.

The aversive scene is constructed to elicit a strong response from the client. When this occurs, the client informs the therapist or demonstrates that he or she is uncomfortable. The therapist then shows an aversion relief scene (getting help for the child) or an escape scene (never going to the bar in the first place). The goal to be achieved after exposure to several stimulus and aversive scenes, however, is to have this escape scene become a conditioned response. Ultimately, the client will come to express the desire to escape before the conclusion of the aversive scene or perhaps even before the aversive scene begins. In successful therapy, the conditioned response will occur for the client in similar situations outside of therapy.

Applications of classical conditioning are also seen in relapse prevention programs. One of the goals of relapse prevention is to alert clients to situations (or stimuli) that place clients at a higher risk of relapse than if they were not in the presence of such stimuli. Initially, we may encourage clients to avoid such stimuli, but in the case of family holidays and other situations, this is not always possible. In the terminology of the relapse prevention approach, such times are referred to as **high-risk situations**. Treatment involves helping clients to identify their own "high-risk" situations and to develop coping skills and plans for dealing with them (Marlatt & Barrett, 2004; Parks, Marlatt, & Anderson, 2001). Anecdotally, these are referred to as the "people, places, and things" that are likely to lead to high-risk situations.

Unfortunately, excessive alcohol or other drug use is reinforced by the effects of such use. Drinking, for example, may lead to immediate reward/reinforcement (a "buzz," tension reduction, or peer approval). Although use may also be followed by negative consequences, these usually are delayed (e.g., physical discomfort, disease, social disapproval, financial loss, decreased self-esteem). Operant conditioning models attempt to change the ways in which substance use is reinforced. These approaches are seen primarily as components of other approaches. For example, therapeutic communities (described further below) may make use of token economies or other systems of behavioral rewards and punishments (see Chapters 8 and 10) as a means of increasing accountability and responsibility. In these cases, residents progress through levels of treatment and earn privileges as rewards for using prosocial substitute behaviors. Residents are rewarded with things such as restaurant coupons for positive achievements, while also being held accountable for negative behaviors (Inciardi & Lockwood, 1994).

Additional examples of operant conditioning include community reinforcement and contingency contracting. Many therapies integrate behavioral contracts (contingency contracts) in which access to jobs, family, friends, recreation, and other community reinforcers are contingent upon the client's ongoing sobriety (Smith & Meyers, 2003). A contingency contract is often used with adolescents or following an intervention (see Smith & Meyers, 2003).

The community reinforcement approach (CRA) (Hunt & Azrin, 1973; Miller, Meyers, & Hiller-Sturmhofel, 1999) seeks to provide people addicted to alcohol with the incentives (reinforcements) to stop drinking. This involves disrupting positive reinforcements for drinking and developing positive reinforcements for sobriety. In the early phases of CRA, therapists work to increase clients' motivation to stop drinking. An "inconvenience review" inventories all of the problems associated with the client's drinking, including work, marital, and health problems. Identification of the client's "high-risk situations" and drinking-related reinforcements is also done early in therapy. A number of additional approaches are selected that are planned to increase the client's sources of positive reinforcement for not drinking. For example, these could include reducing the client's alcohol-induced isolation and increasing his or her hobbies, recreational outlets, and social interactions with friends who do not drink. Help in removing barriers to positive pursuits may also be given, such as when the client is assisted with employment efforts or with coping and social skills. Sometimes relationship counseling is offered through CRA along with teaching family members to use reinforcers (e.g., spending time with the client during times of sobriety and not while under the influence). CRA has also been used with other kinds of drug-using clients.

Finally, recognizing that sobriety removes a major source of enjoyment (reinforcement) from a client's life, relapse prevention programs recommend the introduction of new sources of enjoyment. Clients should have, in other words, a healthy balance between "shoulds" and "wants" (Marlatt & Gordon, 1985). This finds therapists encouraging clients to make lifestyle changes that develop new interests and sources of enjoyment, as well as new groups of friends. Otherwise, focusing on the deprivations of sobriety, and creating a life overburdened by "shoulds" could increase the likelihood of relapse.

Where do the radical behavioral approaches stand in terms of their effectiveness? The earlier classical conditioning and aversion models have not fared well. In addition, the idea that people addicted to substances can be punished into not using alcohol or other drugs has been shown to be ineffective. Studies are somewhat more supportive of the incentive-based models (Miller, Andrews, Wilbourne, & Bennett, 1998). In a meta-analysis of behavioral and cognitive behavioral programs, researchers found programs to be effective in reducing recidivism and drug use, but the cognitive behavioral/social learning programs were more effective than programs that relied primarily on the behavioral model (Pearson et al., 2002). We now turn to these approaches.

Social Learning and Cognitive Behavioral Approaches

Many recent advances in substance use treatment utilize social learning approaches and cognitive behavioral approaches. As discussed in Chapters 9 and 10, these treatment models overlap; cognitive therapies use role models and reinforcement to model new cognitive skills, and social learning approaches often target cognitive patterns.

As noted earlier, however, the fundamental vehicle for change within a social learning paradigm is the role model who can be imitated by others and offer feedback to those who are trying to change. Role models have a long history in substance use treatment. Members of AA and NA, for example, are encouraged to work with "sponsors." These are AA or NA members who have been in recovery for a significant period of time. Through their own example, sponsors also offer other members the opportunity to see that sobriety can have its rewards. Sponsors model skills of relationship-building, responsibility, and support, although not as formally as role models might in the social learning approaches discussed below. As will be seen, a good deal of attention must also be given to the thought processes of people addicted to substances, particularly how their thinking supports or does not support their recovery.

Therapeutic Communities

Therapeutic communities (TCs) have become a common form of treatment for system-impacted clients diagnosed with substance use disorder (DeLeon, 2000; Inciardi & Lockwood, 1994). TCs are inpatient forms of treatment in which clients spend three months to one year in a residential setting (either community-based inpatient or a unit within a prison). The philosophy of most TCs is that substance use is learned from environmental influences and experiences such as underemployment, poverty, job stress, and marital discord (Milhorn, 1990). In fact, residents in therapeutic communities are viewed as being in need of habilitation as a population of individuals whose skill deficits, vocational strengths, and level of psychological disturbance is more pronounced than correctional clients in other treatment settings (Shore, 2004). Addiction is viewed as a disorder of the whole person. That is, the problem is the person, not the drug (Pan, Scarpitti, Inciardi, & Lockwood, 1993).

TC staff members may be former substance users who have themselves been resocialized in therapeutic communities (Pan et al., 1993; Schuckit, 2006). While staff are expected to act as peer role models and encourage mutual self-help, the traditional therapeutic community model also seeks to use all aspects of the environment (e.g., leadership, staff's use of authority, rules) as "models" to residents (Jones, 1968). The objectives of TCs involve changing negative patterns of behavior, thinking, and feelings that act as predispositions to drug abuse (Pan et al., 1993). There is a strong emphasis on the clients' help in maintaining the community (Milhorn, 1990). TCs also seek to use positive forms of peer influence. Often TCs employ a staged model approach in which clients progress to higher levels as they demonstrate improved individual and social responsibility. Other types of treatment found within the TC include tutorial learning sessions, remedial and formal education classes, and vocational training (Anglin & Hser, 1990).

Over time, the term "therapeutic community" has come to mean many different things. In fact, one comprehensive evaluation of drug treatment programs reported that the TCs represented in the large sample of studies did not offer uniform approaches to treating substance abuse (Pearson & Lipton, 1999). This sometimes creates confusion about just what intervention is represented by therapeutic communities (Taxman & Bouffard, 2002). We see in some TCs a design that focuses on cognitive behavioral intervention, social learning, and positive peer culture. The TCs run by the Federal Bureau of Prisons in the United States, for example, are cognitive behavioral. Moreover, it is not unusual for TCs to use the same cognitive behavioral curricula that are used for general justice-involved populations.

While peer role-modeling and mutual self-help are components of many TCs, some TCs achieved notoriety through role-modeling practices that strayed far from the criteria set forth in Chapter 10. Most criticized in this regard is a highly confrontational procedure known as **peer encounters**, where much of the "therapy" consisted of staff and peers challenging the behavior of an addicted person. Such groups also required members' adherence to the ideology of the group. For example, Synanon, a program established in the 1960s for heroin addicts, used confrontational strategies closely patterned after those used in Guided Group Interaction. Founders of Synanon claimed that the peer group was an important vehicle for breaking through the manipulation, denial, and lying common to addictive behaviors. Peer encounters were seen as a way of "heightening a resident's awareness of the images, attitudes, and conduct that need to be modified" (Pan et al., 1993). Others viewed the Synanon brand of peer encounter as dangerous. Instead, clients with substance use disorders are believed to require consistency, empathy, and firm but non-punitive confrontation. Most TCs have moved away from inappropriate levels of confrontation to approaches that stress mutual helping.

With the exception of overly confrontive programs, TCs have shown favorable results in a meta-analysis (Drake et al., 2009; Pearson & Lipton, 1999), as well as in separate evaluations (Knight, Simpson, & Hiller, 1999; Martin, Butzin, Saum, & Inciardi, 1999; Pelissier et al., 1998; Prendergast et al., 2004; Warren, Evans, Dolan, & Norton, 2004; Welsh, 2007; Wexler et al., 1999). The most effective programs are those that provide community-based aftercare following release (Griffith, Hiller, Knight, & Simpson, 1999).

TCs within women's prisons are increasingly encouraged to transform into empowerment communities using gender-responsive principles (see Chapter 13) due to the relational aggression that can often occur among confined female populations. An innovative example of this was the Program of HOPE (Healing Opportunities Promoting Empowerment) administered by the Pathfinder Network in Coffee Creek Correctional Facility in Oregon. The program was so well received by clients that other incarcerated women in the facility verbally indicated they would stay in prison longer to try and gain access to the program because they knew it would address what they really needed for battling their substance use (e.g., prior and current trauma, self-efficacy, unhealthy intimate relationships, etc.).

Coping and Social Skills Training

Used in a variety of situations, including approaches to non-abusing correctional clients, cognitive behavioral programs that teach coping and social skills have clear applicability to substance-using clients. These programs target a number of the common social and coping skill deficiencies among this population. These include problem-solving (Beck, Wright, Newman, & Liese, 1993), self-efficacy (Marlatt, 1985; Wanberg & Milkman, 1998), and a variety of skills pertinent to social competency and emotional control (Monti, Rohsenow, Colby, & Abrams, 2005). Relapse prevention programs focus on skills pertinent to recognizing and dealing with high-risk situations (Annis & Davis, 2003; Marlatt & Barrett, 2004; Parks et al., 2001).

The basic steps to skills training in the substance use programs are similar to those mentioned in Chapter 10. For example, Monti and associates (2005) set forth the following steps to teaching the skill of refusing a drink:

1. The group leader gives a *rationale* for acquiring the skill by explaining that being pressured for a drink is a "high-risk" situation. Clients are reminded that alcohol is so readily available that they are likely to encounter situations in which drinks will be offered. Turning down the drink is not easy, but requires specific skills.

2. The group leader gives *guidelines* for using the skill, including: saying "no" in a clear manner; suggesting an alternative; avoiding excuses or acting indecisively; and making eye contact with the person offering the drink.

3. The group leader *models* an ineffective and then an effective response to a sample situation.

4. The group members *role-play* responses to similar situations.

5. The group members are *reinforced* for effective demonstrations of the skill or components of the skill.

6. The group members receive constructive *feedback* on how the skill might be improved.

7. The group members are encouraged to *comment on their own use of the skill.*

8. The group members *rehearse the skill in increasingly difficult situations.*

Additional skills taught in these types of programs include giving positive feedback, giving criticism, receiving criticism, listening, conversational skills, developing sober supports, conflict resolution skills, non-verbal communication, expressing feelings, assertiveness, refusing requests, coping with cravings, managing negative thinking, relaxation, and managing stress.

Relapse Prevention Training

A subset of the skills training programs deals exclusively with relapse prevention. This extremely important innovation in substance use intervention has come to be recognized as a major stage of therapy, which does not occur until clients have initiated change toward abstinence. The goal of relapse prevention is to maintain that change (Annis & Davis, 2003). Underlying most relapse prevention programs is Albert Bandura's theory of self-efficacy (1978), which holds that self-efficacy greatly facilitates clients' efforts to cope. In the case of substance use, it is assumed that self-efficacy is crucial to coping with high-risk situations and maintaining sobriety. That is, clients who are confident in their skills for coping with a high-risk situation are less likely to relapse than those who are not (Annis & Davis, 2003; Parks et al., 2001).

The importance of self-efficacy is illustrated in Figure 12.1. A high-risk situation either elicits an effective coping response or results in a lapse into drinking or other drug use. The two situations, however, have different effects on self-efficacy. Successful coping— avoiding the lapse—increases self-efficacy and the expectancy of positive outcomes in future situations. Ineffective coping decreases self-efficacy, increasing the positive expectancies for the effects of the alcohol or other drug, and ultimately increasing the likelihood of full relapse. Additional goals of relapse prevention include teaching clients to recognize and cope with high-risk situations and preventing a lapse from deteriorating into a relapse.

These approaches recognize that the road to recovery often occurs in fits and starts, and that a lapse is not as important as a relapse. Lapses do, however, result in guilt, feelings of

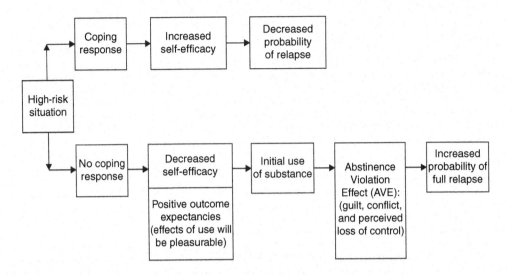

FIGURE 12.1 Cognitive behavioral model of the relapse process.
Source: Marlatt, G., & Barrett, K. (2004). Relapse prevention. In M. Galanter & H. Kleber (Eds.), *Textbook of Substance Abuse Treatment* (3rd ed.). Washington, DC: American Psychiatric Press.

failure, and perceived loss of control—feelings that Marlatt and Gordon (1985) classically referred to as the **abstinence violation effect (AVE)**. Unless addressed, AVEs lead to demoralization, reduced self-efficacy, and the loss of one's motivation to remain abstinent. Thus, relapse prevention devotes considerable attention to helping clients prevent lapses and full-blown relapses from reduced self-efficacy.

Following recognition of the nature of the situations that are likely to lead to relapse, clients work to develop and rehearse plans for coping with each type of situation. In doing so, they develop an inventory of their existing strengths, such as their support network (e.g., friends, family, therapists, support groups), their knowledge of times in which they had been able to cope, or their cognitive strengths (e.g., a belief in self-discipline). Discussions, role-playing, and homework assignments are used to encourage clients to draw on these coping skills and to develop new skills. For each problem situation, clients and therapists work on a tentative plan of action for how they will deal with the event. Clients plan ahead and rehearse alternative responses, become mentally prepared, and practice in increasingly difficult situations. Over time, the client is exposed to more difficult and more varied situations, with the goal of achieving mastery of these situations and building confidence or self-efficacy. The goal is to increase self-efficacy over time. The process usually includes assessments of clients' self-efficacy at different times throughout the relapse prevention therapy (Annis & Graham, 1988).

The types of coping skills and alternative approaches to high-risk situations include: assertiveness, stress management, relaxation training, anger management, communication skills, marital therapy, and social and dating skills. Clients are encouraged to focus on their successes. With growing self-efficacy, relapse, if it occurs, may be less likely to lead to a full return to one's full substance use pattern. Marlatt and Barrett (2004) also teach clients to modify cognitive reactions to lapses and AVEs to prevent a single lapse from becoming a relapse. In particular, clients are taught to restructure or reframe self-defeating attitudes or reactions to lapses, recognizing, for example, that recovery is a learning process that takes time. In addition to the methods for dealing with specific situations, they also encourage lifestyle-balancing strategies. For example, meditation, mindfulness, and exercise are viewed as strengthening a client's overall coping capabilities and reducing the intensity of urges.

Relapse prevention can be a stand-alone program as a general self-control approach, but it is typically used as a post-treatment strategy. Empirical studies indicate that the model, in most cases, reduces recidivism (Parks et al., 2001).

Family Therapy Approaches

Few would question whether families are seriously affected by the substance abuse of a family member. In addition to coping with the stress of living with a person who is abusing alcohol or other drugs, family members are viewed as having key roles in supporting the client's efforts to recover. In many instances, family members have developed behaviors that initially helped them to cope with their addicted family member but later proved to be dysfunctional. For example, some members may have inadvertently enabled a family member to drink or use other drugs by making up excuses as to why the member cannot go to work, taking over his or her family responsibilities, purchasing alcohol, or refusing to allow other family members to discuss the issue. Finally, having inherited a physiological predisposition to addiction, and having lived in an addicted family system, some family members must also examine their own susceptibility to addiction.

Family therapy for alcoholism and other drug addiction spans the family therapy models presented in Chapter 11; these include psychodynamic, behavioral, communications, and family systems approaches. Key to family therapy for substance use is the assumption that the substance-using client, technically referred to as the "identified patient" (IP) is not the only person in the family who is in need of therapy. Because the system is an entity that is considered to be as troubled as members within the system, it may not work to treat one member apart from the system.

Each of the family therapy models discussed below views alcoholism or other drug addiction in a different manner. **Psychodynamic family therapies** assess the IP and other family members in terms of histories and "family of origin" issues. In this way, therapy attempts to help family members understand how past relationships and problems may be replayed in the present. In addition, therapists may attempt to identify and interpret members' resistance to change. Interestingly, members other than the IP will often demonstrate behaviors, habits, or communication patterns (e.g., denial, inability to deal with conflict, or reluctance to discuss angry reactions) that prevent change in the IP or the family system (Anderson & Stewart, 1983). Transference, projective identification, and countertransference must also be interpreted and incorporated into tasks that help to set new behaviors in place.

Some consider the psychodynamic model of family therapy to be inadequate for the treatment of addiction because it is not a "here and now" approach (Kaufman, 1985). In addition, substance use requires more of an active emphasis on limit-setting and coping with present-day crises than is focused on in the psychodynamic approach.

Behavioral family therapies rely mostly on a social learning theoretical framework. From this perspective, the family is alerted to behaviors that may be reinforcing excessive drinking or other drug use, such as enabling or providing too much attention to the IP. Similarly, family members may be shielding the IP from the consequences of his or her drug use; in experiencing no costs to his or her excessive use, the addict continues to use. The family learns of sequences of behaviors that may be setting up stimulus-response patterns for substance use, for example, poor communication and conflict resolution strategies that then precipitate excessive drinking.

Behavioral family approaches encourage members to set specific behavioral goals, such as to stop "taking care" of the alcoholic, to maintain "family detoxification," or to rehearse alternative behavioral sequences (e.g., better communication patterns). Thus, the IP and family members: (a) become alert to the behaviors that stimulate drinking or other drug use; (b) rearrange contingencies (e.g., reinforce sobriety); (c) monitor sobriety rather than ignore alcohol and other drug abuse; and (d) learn new skills for interacting with one another (e.g., assertiveness, problem-solving, refraining from blaming) (McCrady, 1990). Behavioral family therapy approaches are widely used, especially for treating adolescent substance use (Kaufman, 1985).

Family systems models seek to identify family routines, regulatory behaviors, rituals, or problem-solving strategies that have developed to deal with substance abuse within the family (Steinglass et al., 1987). Unfortunately, when family matters become directed primarily toward coping with the alcoholism or other drug addiction of a family member, other important family functions, such as child-rearing, support, and the family's financial well-being, may suffer. Such processes also encourage the intergenerational transmission of substance abuse. One of the goals of family systems therapy is to change "alcoholic family systems" to "families with an alcoholic member." An "alcoholic family system," according to Steinglass (2004), organizes itself around its core issue of dealing with an alcoholic member or members. In contrast, a "family with an alcoholic member" is not organizing most of its activities and behaviors to accommodate the alcoholic.

Another goal of family systems therapy is to alter the family "structures" that sustain addiction. From this model, family therapy targets problem-solving strategies and dysfunctional family roles (e.g., a child who has assumed adult responsibilities). At the same time, it seeks to restore an appropriate family hierarchy (parents supervise children) and appropriate boundaries to family relationships (e.g., extending some separation to overly enmeshed systems and shifting alliances) (Kaufman, 1985).

Communications therapy can also apply to the task of treating family systems. Here, altering dysfunctional family communication patterns helps to create more healthy family structures. Such changes may include: (a) discontinuing the practice of triangulation (e.g., talking *to* someone rather than *about* someone); (b) communicating directly to individuals rather than expecting them to read minds; (c) accurately describing problems rather than renaming them or "mystifying" them; and (d) clarifying the intentions of another person rather than making assumptions.

Finally, **multisystemic family therapy** addresses the family systems issues discussed above, but also provides intensive "wraparound" services to families in which substance use or other problems have diminished the family's ability to meet the basic needs of its members or work with extrafamilial systems in a healthy manner (Henggeler et al., 1996; Randall et al., 2001).

In addition to these five family therapy models, families coping with substance abuse may benefit from the following:

1. *Support Groups for Family Members.* As discussed later in this chapter, self-help groups exist for family members. These are specific to the family member's role within the family;

there are groups for spouses, young children, teenagers, and adult children. These groups paralleled the development of Alcoholics Anonymous and while they are specific to the developmental needs of family members, they use many of the same principles as AA, including 12 steps and sponsorship.

2. *Interventions and Confrontations.* This client population often resists treatment until long after their behavior has become destructive and costly to those around them. Interventions offer one method for motivating uncooperative addicts to change. Family interventions are typically facilitated by a substance use counselor who provides opportunities for family members, employers, and friends to confront the addict about his or her behavior. These individuals explain how the behaviors have hurt them and their relationships with the addict. Some give an ultimatum that ongoing commitment to their relationship with the addict will require the addict to participate in treatment and maintain abstinence. Such sessions are not announced ahead of time to the addict/alcoholic, and they often conclude with the person in need of help leaving for residential treatment either immediately or shortly after the intervention. Substance use therapists hold three or four preparatory sessions with participants prior to conducting the intervention (O'Farrell, 2003).

DRUG COURTS

Drug courts emerged in the late 1980s to deal with the influx of cases generated by the "war on drugs." The courts, which have proliferated dramatically during the past 20 years, differ tremendously across jurisdictions. Some divert defendants contingent upon their completion of therapy and/or refraining from future offending; others suspend a sentence based on similar contingencies.

Both juvenile and adult drug courts exist. In contrast to other criminal courts, the bench has a greater role in case monitoring and supervision. That is, people return to court for routine status checks, relapse, failure to attend treatment, or other problematic behavior. In some cases, the judge may issue a continuance and the formulation of a modified plan of treatment. In more serious cases, a deferred sentence may be imposed or a defendant may proceed to conviction. In all cases, judicial authority and therapeutic jurisprudence is used as a tool for encouraging compliance with drug court conditions (U.S. General Accounting Office, 1997). Drug courts are intended to offer a more reasonable and less costly response to substance use than incarceration.

It is important to realize that drug courts themselves are administrative rather than therapeutic entities. They are part of a larger group of problem-solving courts such as mental health courts, but cannot be associated with any specific type of treatment modality (e.g., behavioral, cognitive behavioral). Specific modalities vary considerably across courts; some offer multiple therapeutic options and others offer no therapy (Bouffard & Taxman, 2004; Goldkamp, White, & Robinson, 2001).

Generally, the courts have shown some effectiveness in reducing drug-related offenses (Listwan, Sundt, Holsinger, & Latessa, 2003). A meta-analysis summarizing outcomes across 22 studies, for example, reported an average reduction in recidivism of 7.5% (Lowenkamp, Holsinger, & Latessa, 2002). Another meta-analysis of 38 studies noted that the overall reduction in recidivism was 26% (Wilson, Mitchell, & MacKenzie, 2003). In all of these studies, there were too few programs to test the effectiveness of specific program modalities.

FIGURE 12.2 Singer-songwriter James Taylor hugs drug court graduate Valerie Carter during a ceremony honoring 100 graduates of the Pinellas County (Florida) Adult Drug Court.
Source: AP Photo/John Pendygraft, Pool.

However, Wilson and associates (2003) note that the most effective courts: (a) provided a clear incentive for completing the program, such as rewarding clients with either dismissed charges, deferred sentencing, or completion of a condition of probation and (b) relied on a single service provider. Other reports have shown that courts using single service providers are often adhering to cognitive behavioral interventions (Peyton & Gossweiler, 2001). Researchers also note that sufficient "dosage," or length of time in the drug court program, matters (Peters, Haas, & Hunt, 2001). A few examples of the causes of relapse after graduation from drug courts have been found to be family problems, lack of social support, and employment difficulties (McCarthy & Waters, 2003). See Figure 12.2.

THE IMPORTANCE OF SUPPORT GROUPS

Self-help groups and support groups have become important adjuncts to therapy for a vast array of personal, medical, and social problems. The prototype for self-help groups is Alcoholics Anonymous (AA), formed in Ohio in 1935. The approach of AA fits within the "disease model." Alcoholism is viewed as a physical, mental, and spiritual disease. AA also assumes that alcoholism has a common set of symptoms, genetic basis, and a disease progression. Total cure of the disease is not possible; one can only arrest its development through lifetime abstinence.

AA operates on a 12-step model, encouraging alcoholics to grow from an initial acknowledgment of the fact that alcohol is making their lives unmanageable to: (a) a reliance on spiritual support to assist in the recovery process; (b) acknowledgment of "defects of character" and how these have harmed others; (c) making amends to people whom they have harmed; (d) ongoing spiritual involvement; and (e) a commitment to helping other people addicted to alcohol.

AA does not view itself as engaging in a psychological model of therapy. In fact, one of the Twelve Traditions of AA states: "AA should remain forever non-professional." Still, one sees in the 12 steps a number of the therapeutic goals of well-established clinical approaches, including: (a) dealing with denial; (b) reliance on role models; and (c) development of coping strategies and healthier relationships with others (McCrady & Irving, 2003). Some maintain that AA shares similarities with behavioral and cognitive behavioral therapies. Both AA and behavioral skills approaches, for example, emphasize avoidance of settings in which drinking takes place (i.e., "high-risk situations"), coping skills for high-risk situations, social support, improvement of relationships through communication training, and the development of new social networks. Both AA and cognitive behavioral programs endeavor to change self-defeating thoughts and thought processes, such as "either-or thinking" (also called "stinkin' thinkin'") and self-centered definitions of situations.

In contrast to AA, however, the cognitive behavioral models see substance abuse as more complex than a disease with a common set of symptoms and causes. From the cognitive behavioral model, there are many types of substance users. Moreover, some of the messages given by AA and Narcotics Anonymous (NA) (such as substance abuse is a disease that one has no control over or one that a higher power will control) run contrary to the messages of most cognitive behavioral approaches, which offer a more direct approach to client responsibility.

Since the beginning of AA, other groups have formed to offer support and self-help for other types of substance use, for example, NA, Cocaine Anonymous (CA); and for specific types of individuals, for example, LGBTQI+ and gender-specific groups, such as Women for Sobriety. Groups for family members offer important support services, especially to those who may not be able to afford the family approaches discussed previously. Such groups are usually specific to the family role and age of the family member, for example, Alanon (for spouses), Alateen, Alatot, and Adult Children of Alcoholics.

Does this mean that AA or NA can be the only "therapy" offered within a correctional agency? Unfortunately, this happens in corrections, either on an ongoing basis in some cases or during periods of fiscal constraint when agencies cut more intensive forms of therapy to save money. For a number of reasons, AA/NA cannot be advocated as the only form of substance abuse treatment that an agency needs to provide. First, it has not and cannot be subjected to an appropriate degree of evaluation research. In fact, its organizing principles discourage tests of its effectiveness. Second, there is no supervision of groups and how they are conducted. There are guidelines for such groups, and the national organizations hope to encourage adherence to them, but, without oversight, groups, particularly justice-involved groups, can "drift" into more antisocial directions. Just the same, effective support groups can be important supplements to more intensive substance use treatment.

PHARMACOLOGICAL APPROACHES

Pharmacological agents offer a well-known approach to the treatment of alcohol and opiate addictions and are subsumed under the umbrella term of medication-assisted treatment (MAT). There are several drugs used for these purposes. Chief among these is extended-release naltrexone (i.e., Vivitrol), a narcotic antagonist that blocks the euphoric effects of opiates and is also used in the treatment of alcohol addiction. However, naltrexone is not recommended for people with other health conditions, which is why it must be carefully administered among offending populations. Methadone and Suboxone are two other drugs used in MAT but are less frequently endorsed by correctional organizations because they both have addiction potential in and of themselves. These medications are used to reduce the painful symptoms of opioid withdrawal and help clients wean off opioids gradually over time.

Vivitrol (with substance use counseling) is becoming the preferred MAT intervention among prison administrators and correctional staff because there is no potential for misuse and addiction. It is a monthly medication and can be injected prior to release from prison and maintained in the community, and has demonstrated empirical effects in reducing relapse among criminal justice populations (Lee et al., 2016).

Methadone maintenance is a form of outpatient treatment that involves giving patients daily doses of methadone, under supervision, as a substitute for such opiates as heroin, morphine, and Percodan (Caulum, 1994). Dosages of methadone are closely monitored; ideally, doses are gradually reduced until the patient is drug free (Marion & Coleman, 1991). The duration of methadone maintenance is generally longer than the duration of other treatment modalities; clients may stay in methadone treatment for three years or more (Nurco, Kinlock, & Hanlon, 1993). Many programs will provide additional services, such as vocational training and drug counseling. Such programs are aimed at reducing antisocial behavior, reducing needle-borne diseases (e.g., AIDS and hepatitis), and enhancing vocational and social stability (Landry, Smith, & Morrison, 1994). Similar programs have resulted in significant reductions in recidivism (Kinlock, Gordon, Schwartz, & O'Grady, 2008).

Of all drug treatment options, methadone maintenance appears to be the most controversial. Many argue that methadone clients have simply shifted their dependence to a legal narcotic. Other critics warn that some methadone clients may "continue to use heroin and other drugs intermittently, and continue to commit crimes, including the sale of their take-home methadone" (Institute of Medicine, 1990). From an alternative standpoint, methadone maintenance may be viewed as a long-term therapy similar to the treatment of any other chronic health disorder. That is, just as the diabetic needs insulin, the addict needs methadone for treatment (Milhorn, 1990). Still, methadone maintenance has been found to be an effective strategy in reducing withdrawal symptoms and drug cravings.

Outpatient methadone treatment ranges from one-time assessment and referrals to drop-in and "rap" centers to outpatient therapeutic communities. Clients in outpatient TCs usually report three days per week for two to three hours (Milhorn, 1990). Services found in outpatient methadone programs are similar to those in the TC; group and individual counseling are available. Because outpatients continue to live in the community and have more ready access to drugs, they usually receive more frequent urine tests (Milhorn, 1990).

The goals of methadone maintenance are somewhat different from the goals of the other forms of substance use treatment. Most interventions seek to reduce consumption to zero, but the overriding goal of methadone maintenance is to reduce drug use by an appreciable amount (Institute of Medicine, 1990). The goal of totally reducing the use of drugs is lower on the list of priorities in most methadone maintenance programs. Secondary goals include improving productivity, social behavior, and psychological well-being (Anglin & Hser, 1990).

In this sense, methadone maintenance programs appear to be focusing on harm reduction rather than abstinence. As a harm-reduction method, methadone maintenance has more in common with needle-exchange programs, controlled drinking, and "safe use" educational programs, than with the interventions covered throughout this chapter. The harm-reduction strategies are well-received outside of the United States, but in the United States they are seen as "sending the wrong message" (MacCoun, 1998). Perhaps they also run counter to public preferences for retributive and deterrent approaches.

RESPONSIVITY CONSIDERATIONS

As noted in Chapters 6 and 13, good treatment programs usually address the responsivity principle (Bonta & Andrews, 2017). Recall that a program attends to the general responsivity of its clients when it chooses program approaches that are suitable to system-impacted populations. Specific responsivity addresses client characteristics that are likely to affect the client's ability to participate in a program. The program staff should then consider these factors when "matching" clients to appropriate programs or program components. In doing so, case managers and counselors will seek to remove any known barriers to treatment, such as transportation, and provide programs that accommodate responsivity issues such as anxiety, readiness to change, co-occurring disorders and others.

What client differences should we focus on? In answering this question, we must consider the nature of the criminogenic need that we are treating. Specific responsivity characteristics important to substance use treatments, for example, may not be the same characteristics that should be considered when addressing client literacy. In addition, we cannot accommodate every client characteristic because there would not be enough program resources to differentiate among numerous client characteristics. We have to set priorities.

We have selected five types of client responsivity characteristics as important to substance use programming: (a) motivation for change; (b) comorbidity; (c) ethnicity; (d) gender; and (e) intensity of the addiction (abuse versus dependence).

Motivation for Change and Motivational Interviewing

Programs should recognize that clients differ in their readiness to change substance using behaviors, and should therefore consider the client's stage of change (Miller & Rollnick, 2002; Prochaska & DiClemente, 1986; Wanberg & Milkman, 1998). Prochaska and DiClemente (1986), for example, set out five stages of change, and each stage suggests different treatment goals. The definition of each stage along with the treatment recommendations for each stage are shown in Table 12.1.

It would be preferable to have an assessment tool for classifying clients into one of the five stages, but early attempts to do so have either been unsuccessful or have not yet been completed. These include the Stages of Change Readiness and Treatment Eagerness Scale (SOCRATES) (Miller & Tonigan, 1996); the Adult Self-Assessment Questionnaire (AdSAQ) (Wanberg & Milkman, 1993); and additional work in Canada by Serin and Kennedy (1997). For this reason, a client's stage of change must still be determined through clinical judgment after a careful discussion with the correctional client.

Once staff have identified which stage of change the client is in, a strategy called Motivational Interviewing (Miller & Rollnick, 2013; see Chapter 3) can aid in reaching the treatment goals outlined in Table 12.1. Motivational Interviewing is a client-centered,

TABLE 12.1 Stages of change		
Stage	*Definition*	*Treatment Goal*
Precontemplation	People do not intend to change, because: (a) they do not think they have a problem; (b) they are defensive; and (c) are discouraged about their ability to change.	Consciousness raising, e.g., interventions, observations, interpretations of substance use-related life events. Awareness of defenses.
Contemplation	People intend to change in the foreseeable future (within the next six months). They seem more confident in their ability to change. Still, they are ambivalent about the values of change, e.g., benefits do not clearly outweigh the costs.	Education and evaluation of the costs of their addiction. Self-appraisal of values toward themselves and addiction.
Preparation	People intend to change within the next month, and are more confident that they can control their addiction. They have a plan to change and are willing to take small steps toward change.	Same as precontemplation, plus some counterconditioning and stimulus control to begin to reduce the use of addictive substances.
Action	People engage in behaviors that demonstrate change, such as abstaining from alcohol or other drugs.	Emphasis on self-liberation, self-efficacy, increased use of counterconditioning and stimulus control, contingency management, formation of support systems.
Maintenance	People work to consolidate gains achieved during the action phase to prevent relapse. They have attained self-efficacy toward dealing with high-risk situations.	Relapse prevention: Identification of high-risk situations, continued building of self-efficacy, strategies for coping with high-risk situations and relapse.

Source: Prochaska, J., & DiClemente, C. (1986). Toward a comprehensive model of change. In W. Miller & N. Heather (Eds.), *Treating Addictive Behaviors: Processes of Change.* New York: Plenum.

directive method for enhancing intrinsic motivation to change. Specifically, Motivational Interviewing offers staff a set of skills to help move an individual through the stages of change. It has been widely adopted in the field of corrections (Stinson & Clark, 2017).

Two important skill sets in Motivational Interviewing are that of OARS and FRAMES (Miller & Rollnick, 2013). These are explained in Tables 12.2 and 12.3.

Many individuals come to treatment programs in the precontemplation stage; that is, they do not believe they have a problem or need treatment. Using Motivational Interviewing techniques, we can meet these individuals at their stage of change and use OARS to help them recognize the benefits of participating in treatment.

Let us consider Mary, who has just been referred to a substance use treatment program. Mary arrives for her first appointment and it is clear that she is angry. Staff quickly identify that she is in the precontemplation stage as she complains that she does not have a problem using cocaine, and that her probation officer only sent her to the program because he does not like her. Consider the exchange below.

TABLE 12.2 OARS

Open-ended questions	Questions that require more than a simple yes/no or one-word answer.
Affirmations	Compliments or statements of appreciation and understanding.
Reflective listening	A statement of understanding that involves reflecting back to the individual what they said.
Summarizing	Review of the previously discussed information that can be tied with current information or used to shift the focus to a new topic.

Source: Miller, W., & Rollnick, S. (2013). *Motivational Interviewing: Helping People Change* (3rd ed.). New York: Guilford.

TABLE 12.3 FRAMES

Skill	Definition	Example
Feedback	is given to the individual regarding his or her personal risk or impairment following an assessment of substance use and related problems.	"Results of the assessment we completed last week show that your use occurs more than other adults your age."
Responsibility	for change is placed entirely on the individual. The client has the choice to either continue using or change.	"Thanks for coming in today. I was wondering if we could talk more about your use of cocaine during the session today?"
Advice	should be given to the individual in a nonjudgmental manner only if the individual has given the staff permission to give advice. Advice should be suggested, not told to the individual.	"Can I tell you what I have seen in past situations? Most have found that change does not occur over night and it is helpful to work together on your change process."
Menu	of options for change and treatment alternatives is identified by the staff and client together.	"You certainly have some options here. The first decision is to continue to attend treatment or to stop altogether."
Empathetic	counseling using reflective listening is shown to the client through warmth and understanding.	"I can see that you are angry about having to attend treatment. Let's talk about that."
Self-efficacy	is created within the individual to encourage change.	"How did you remain clean and sober for two years before?"

Source: Miller, W. (1999). Enhancing motivation for change in substance abuse treatment. *Treatment Improvement Protocol (TIP) Series 35* (DHHS Publication No. (SMA) 99–3354, pp. 1–213), Rockville, MD: U.S. Department of Health and Human Services.

MARY: I don't have a problem and don't want to be here! I don't need this.

STAFF: So what you are saying is that you believe you are OK.

MARY: That's right, I don't need you!

STAFF: Yet, you are mandated by the court to be here.

MARY: Who cares about the court, I don't want to be here.

STAFF: What happens if you don't come?

MARY: I don't have a choice, I have to come.

STAFF: Plenty of people don't show up to their treatment programs. What happens to them?

MARY: They get sent to prison.

STAFF: OK, so if you don't show up, you can go to prison.

MARY: I can't go to prison.

STAFF: Let's look at the other side. What happens if you show up?

MARY: I'll go to prison anyway. I know I am going to mess up.

STAFF: So if you don't show up, you go to prison, and if you show up, you are going to go to prison?

MARY: Yeah! I am doomed!

STAFF: Which one is more likely to lead to going to prison?

MARY: Not showing up.

STAFF: This is a pretty tough situation: either don't show up and you will definitely go to prison, or show up and you might go to prison. What do you think you will do?

MARY: I think I will show up and see what happens.

STAFF: Sounds like you are willing to give this a try.

The counselor in this situation used open-ended questions to help Mary identify potential consequences of not attending treatment. She also used reflective listening to show Mary that she understood her and that she heard her concerns. During the summary, toward the end of the interview, the counselor used empathy when she acknowledged the difficult situation Mary was in. Ultimately, using OARS helped Mary decide to give treatment another chance.

While OARS are specific techniques that can be used to facilitate the change process, FRAMES are a set of skills staff use throughout the individual's movement through the stages of change. First, it is important that feedback be provided in a constructive nonconfrontational way. Counselors are taught to *roll with resistance* rather than arguing with the client. Arguing only serves to build client resistance, and overpowers the client's responsibility to change. Second, the client plays an active role in the decision to change. As such, staff should present the client with choices throughout the change process rather than tell the client what he or she needs to do. This also reflects the importance of presenting the client with a menu of options to choose from, both regarding change and treatment alternatives. Similarly, advice should be provided in a simple, clear manner that reflects the stage the individual is in. At times, counselors may *create discrepancies* by suggesting that some client behaviors are getting in the way of client goals. It is important to stress that the discrepancy is one that underscores the client's ambivalence concerning the discrepancies between his or her behaviors and his or her goals. "Creating discrepancy" refers to the client's ambivalence, not the counselor's.

Non-judgmental statements show the client that staff see where they are, but also encourage the client to continue moving through the stages of change. The counselor must show genuine understanding or empathy for the client's situation. Lastly, efforts to build the individual's confidence in their ability to change and to develop new skills should take the form of reinforcing any positive changes. Counselors should be reinforcing *change talk* as well as changes in behavior. They should be building self-efficacy whenever possible.

Responding to Co-occurring Disorders

A second set of client considerations attempts to target the problems and individual conditions that co-occur with substance use. As noted, particularly by the proponents of cognitive interventions, the paths to and problems resulting from substance abuse are many. Some clients who are involved in the justice system drink for greater enjoyment of social situations; others seek to medicate depression and stress. Some have experienced employment and/or marital problems; others have not. Some have incurred tissue and organ damage as a result of their substance use, and others have not (Wanberg & Milkman, 1998). Each of these problems identifies important treatment targets and excludes others. Accommodating these differences requires correctional agencies to use client-specific assessment strategies, such as: (a) the Adult Substance Use Survey (Wanberg, 1993); (b) the Symptom Checklist 90 (Derogatis, 1977); (c) the Life Situation Questionnaire (Wanberg, 1995); (d) the Offender Profile Index (Inciardi, McBride, & Weinman, 1993); and (e) the Addiction Severity Index (McLellan et al., 1992).

The choice of treatment, at this point, depends upon what is actually co-occurring with the substance use. Many types of mental health and physical health problems will need to be stabilized prior to beginning substance use treatment. Treatment providers may also wish to consider curricula that integrate concerns for co-occurring mental health (Covington, 2002) or trauma issues (Najavits et al., 1996). Few such curricula exist, however.

Multicultural Treatment

Substance use intervention services would do well to consider the needs and strengths specific to diverse populations by accommodating factors pertinent to race, gender, and social class, and LGBTQI+ needs. Within these broad categories of diversity, substance use can have different meanings, contexts, associated norms, traditions, and antecedents (see Wanberg & Milkman, 1998). Tools for accommodating such differences, however, are fairly new to correctional programming. In fact, many of the needs assessments specific to special populations are only now being conducted.

The questions posed by these groups, however, are numerous. For example, what considerations should be taken in building the self-efficacy of groups that have experienced racial, sexual, or class discrimination? The fact that such images are internalized by minority clients and reinforced by society poses additional challenges to programs attempting to build self-efficacy. Counselors and correctional staff, for example, should be sensitive to social stereotypes that may portray such individuals as "low achievers" (Wallace, 1991). On the other hand, how shall we capitalize on the cultural competence of groups who, by virtue of their cultural identity, may enjoy strong levels of family and community support and spiritual strength?

Furthermore, some ethnic groups may have values that discourage participation in therapy. While mental health services in Western societies appear to value work ethics, individualism, action orientations, self-disclosure, scientific method, and competition, these may not be as highly valued among certain ethnic groups. Differences in language, communication style, use of body language, and verbal skills may also contribute to misunderstandings (Sue & Sue, 2002).

It is unfortunate that treatment needs of specific groups are under-researched, but the following offers a few concerns (Wanberg & Milkman, 1998):

- While African-American males do not appear to differ from other ethnic groups in terms of the consequences and symptoms of their drug use, they experienced the largest increase in incarceration rates during the 1980s.
- Latino women are more likely than Latino men to be shamed within their own culture for substance use.
- Studies have not confirmed differences in alcohol metabolism between Native American groups and other ethnic groups in the United States.
- Women tend to become heavy drinkers at a later age than men.
- Women are more likely than men to: (a) drink alone; (b) use alcohol with other drugs; and (c) use alcohol and other drugs for purposes of medication.
- Childhood abuse of girls is more likely to result in a progression from child abuse to depression to substance abuse to crime, than it is for boys (Covington, 2002; McClellan, Farabee, & Crouch, 1997; Salisbury & Van Voorhis, 2009).

While more research is needed to move away from a "one size fits all" approach to substance use treatment, and much needs to be done to design culturally-specific and gender-specific treatment programs, a number of suggestions can be offered:

- Diversity awareness training with the goal of developing "culturally competent" staff, who appreciate diversity, adapt to differences, and seek culturally specific understanding of others.
- Adherence to a model of non-judgmental interactions.
- Ongoing sensitivity to one's own areas of ethnocentrism and bias, and appreciation for the need to self-evaluate one's attention to diversity issues.
- Openness to culturally sensitive treatment models. Attention to culturally relevant curricula and program materials.
- Use of culturally fair assessments, especially the avoidance of assessments that have not been normed for use with certain populations.
- Attention to diversity in hiring.
- Sensitivity in dress and office environments, for example, avoiding expression of expensive tastes when dealing with economically disadvantaged clients.
- Attention to needs such as childcare, transportation, disabilities, homelessness.
- Sensitivity to the influences of discrimination and prejudice on clients.

Gender Responsivity

A number of state and federal policy initiatives have focused on the treatment needs of justice-involved women—substance-using women, especially. The 1980s "war on drugs" has been especially hard on women in poverty (Austin, Bruce, Carroll, McCall, & Richards, 2000). Women's prison populations have grown at a faster pace than men's, and most of this is attributable to increases in the number of females using substances (Beck, 2000). Incarcerated women are also more likely than males to have coexisting psychiatric disorders (Peters, Strozier, Murrin, & Kearns, 1997; Messina, Burdon, Hagopian, & Prendergast, 2006; Pelissier, 2004; Sacks, 2004; Staton-Tindall et al., 2007). They also evidence less antisocial thinking than men (Staton-Tindall et al., 2007). In prison, women are more likely than men to test HIV-positive, and to have substance use patterns that are closely linked to their relationships with men (Langan & Pelissier, 2001; Peters et al., 1997).

Readers familiar with the gender-responsive risk factors (Chapters 6 and 13) will recognize that although we are now discussing women's issues under the broad heading of responsivity, a number of scholars assert that these issues speak more to gender-responsive risk than to responsivity. In fact, the field is currently endeavoring to sort out whether these needs are truly responsivity issues (Bonta & Andrews, 2017) or whether they are risk factors specific to women (Salisbury et al., 2016; Van Voorhis, 2012).

For women, substance use often co-occurs with depression and abuse (Covington, 2002; McClellan et al., 1997; Salisbury & Van Voorhis, 2009; Staton-Tindall et al., 2007). That alone should put a decidedly different face on the types of substance use programs they receive (Bloom et al., 2003). Covington (2002), for example, proposed an approach that operates from three theoretical perspectives:

1. The **theory of addiction.** For women, addiction must be seen holistically (as a function of factors such as genetic predisposition, poor health, shame, isolation, and abuse). Addiction is a disease rather than the result of a disorder (including cognitive disorders).

2. The **theory of women's psychosocial development.** Women develop through relationships and mutuality. Relationships factor into their substance use and must be considered in their treatment and recovery.

3. The **theory of trauma.** A history of abuse predisposes women to substance use.

From this perspective on the causation of women's substance use, Covington (2002) developed the following guiding principles of women's treatment:

1. Develop and use women-only groups.
2. Recognize the multiple issues involved, and establish a comprehensive, integrated, and collaborative system of care.
3. Create an environment that fosters safety, respect, and dignity.
4. Develop and use a variety of therapeutic approaches.
5. Focus on women's competences and strengths.
6. Individualize treatment plans, and match treatment to women's strengths and issues.

Programs based on this model include *Helping Women Recover* (Covington, 2008a) and *Beyond Trauma* (Covington, 2003) and have achieved favorable evaluation results (Messina, Grella, Cartier, & Torres, 2010). Additional programs are starting to recognize the importance of addressing comorbid disorders of post-traumatic stress disorder (PTSD) and substance use disorder (SUD), for example, Seeking Safety (Najavits et al., 1996) (see Chapter 13).

Another approach targeted specifically to women is a modified therapeutic community, Forever Free, which utilizes a disease model approach augmented by modules on self-esteem, anger management, assertiveness training, healthy relationships, abuse, PTSD, codependency, parenting, and healthy sex (Hall, Prendergast, Wellish, Patten, & Cao, 2004). Both Seeking Safety and Forever Free have been favorably evaluated.

Key to the new directions for women's programming and therapy is the relational model of self. This theory was developed through research conducted at the Stone Center for Developmental Studies at Wellesley College, Wellesley, Massachusetts (Miller, 1976; Gilligan, 1982). The relational model recognizes that men and women form self-identity differently. Women do so through attachments and connections with others, and men are more comfortable with separation and individuation. With substance-using justice-involved women, sharing the additional burdens of poverty, unemployment, single parenting, and child custody, it is not difficult to see the importance of the "wraparound services" discussed in Chapter 11 (Bloom et al., 2003) or community centers that house both women and their children (Van Wormer, 2002).

Substance Dependence versus Substance Abuse

Correctional agencies and drug courts are beginning to consider the important distinction between substance dependence and substance abuse. Substance dependence or addiction involves a compulsive urge to use alcohol or other drugs that is often accompanied by neurological damage to the brain. The symptoms of substance dependence include intense cravings, withdrawal symptoms when levels of the substance decline in the blood, and uncontrolled binges with any use of the substance. Serious psychiatric disorders often co-occur with substance dependence. In contrast, individuals considered to be engaged with substance abuse have none of the above symptoms, and the decision to use or not use is under their control; the clinical need to have the substance of choice is much lower than for the substance-dependent individual. The treatment needs of substance abuse are very different from those of the substance-dependent individual. Marlowe (2009) sets forward a number of guidelines for each group.

It is the substance-dependent individual who is in most need of intensive substance abuse treatment. These individuals require detoxification, and can benefit from the skills-based approaches discussed in this chapter. Those addicted to opiates should participate in medication-assisted treatment. Practitioners must recognize that goals such as abstinence and employment are less attainable than they are for the person who abuses substances but is not dependent; these should be considered long-term goals. Attendance at programs and compliance with other conditions, which are attainable, should be the focus of program reinforcement and punishment. Of course, supervision levels should depend upon the client's overall risk score. Many will require residential placements.

People without dependence do not require the intensive clinical services that are needed for substance-dependent individuals. They do not have a physical need for the drug and likely their use is not co-occurring with mental illness. If they are at high risk of additional offending, they are better served by the cognitive behavioral programs targeted to general criminogenic needs (e.g., antisocial thinking, employment, antisocial associates). Abstinence is an attainable correctional requirement because they do not have physical cravings. Low-risk substance users may receive preventive services or early intervention in the form of a substance use education program that teaches the dangers and progression of substance abuse. Exposing substance-abusing individuals to costly clinical approaches is unnecessary.

CONTINUITY OF CARE

If used to their full potential, there are many resources to address substance abuse. We hope that has become apparent throughout this chapter. So many improvements to programs, assessments, and services have occurred over the past several decades that it is hard to imagine criminal justice agencies assuming the full burden of providing substance use services. It is equally apparent that no agency should be providing a single "one size fits all" approach to substance use, given the myriad pathways to abuse and the different stages in the therapeutic process. Moreover, in recent years, the field of criminal justice has done a better job of recognizing that substance abuse is a chronic problem. Substance use therapy does not have a beginning, a middle, and an end. Abstinence often occurs in stops and starts, and most "recovering" substance users recognize that they have a lifelong potential for relapsing.

The notion of "continuity of care" fits this situation quite well. Continuity of care refers to a push to go further and provide a seamless continuum of care based on evidence-based practices for clients addicted to alcohol and other drugs (VanderWaal, Taxman, & Gurka-Ndanyi, 2008). A seamless continuum of care is described as a systems approach that consists of services offered at each phase of the client's movement throughout the criminal justice system. The emphasis is on the coordination of services at each phase, such as screening and assessment, treatment planning, long-term case management, ongoing compliance management, judicial involvement, evidence-based drug treatment programs, and aftercare. With the focus on the specific services rather than on the organization providing the services, collaboration among the individual agencies providing services is essential (Eisenberg & Fabelo, 1996). The individual agencies then come together with a common goal: to reduce antisocial behavior through attention to the client's alcohol and/or other drug use.

Partnerships between criminal justice agencies and community treatment providers are essential. Transition services from prison to community are also often guided by this notion. As noted in the earlier discussions of therapeutic communities and other interventions, the provision of continuity of care should also involve prison transition services referring clients to community treatment providers for ongoing post-prison services. Figure 12.3 illustrates this model.

Looking at Figure 12.3 it is clear that both the criminal justice agencies and the treatment providers should work closely together to deliver services. Taking a closer look at those services, an individual is identified as having a substance use problem usually through an initial screening and then a more thorough assessment. A comprehensive assessment is used to identify the severity and nature of the drug abuse, any related problems, and any identified skills that can aid in the treatment process. Once the assessment is completed, a treatment plan is developed that follows the principles of risk, need, and responsivity and considers the client's needs, problems, strengths, and resources identified during the assessment process.

VanderWaal et al. (2008) suggest that a case manager be assigned to the client to ensure that all parties involved are working to accomplish the treatment goals. Specifically, the case manager works with criminal justice and treatment teams to monitor, manage, and increase compliance with treatment and criminal justice requirements. Judicial supervision, graduated sanctions, and random drug testing can all help ensure ongoing treatment compliance. Clients should be involved in a treatment program that helps them move through any resistance, build motivation, develop prosocial coping skills, and receive reinforcement for any progress made.

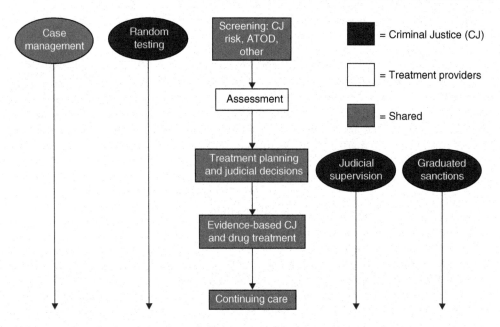

FIGURE 12.3 Seamless inter-agency collaboration model.
Source: VanderWaal, C.J., Taxman, F.S., & Gurka-Ndanyi, M.A. (2008). Reforming drug treatment services to offenders: Cross-system collaboration, integrated policies, and a seamless continuum of care model. *Journal of Social Work Practice in the Addiction, 8* (1), 127–153.

The last phase of this continuum of care is aftercare. Aftercare, while often the most neglected phase, is considered to provide continuing care to the clients to prevent relapse and maintain changes made during the treatment phase (VanderWaal et al., 2008). Throughout this chapter, we have noted that aftercare greatly increases the effectiveness of substance use treatment.

EFFECTIVENESS OF SUBSTANCE USE INTERVENTIONS

The earliest evaluations of programs for substance-using correctional clients showed overly high relapse rates, but research now supports a number of specific program models and programmatic conditions. Literature reviews supporting behavioral, social learning, and cognitive behavioral approaches (Anglin & Hser, 1990; Institute of Medicine, 1990; Monti et al., 2005; Prendergast, Anglin, & Wellisch, 1995; Wexler & Lipton, 1993) have since been supported by meta-analyses (Miller et al., 2003; Pearson & Lipton, 1999). Specifically, Miller and his associates (2003) report that the most successful programs are behavioral and cognitive behavioral approaches, such as social skills training, community reinforcement, behavior contracting, relapse prevention, and motivational enhancement. Marital therapy is more likely to "work" when behavioral and communication treatment models are also used. The least successful approaches consist of educational, unspecified general counseling models, psychotherapy, and confrontational approaches.

Despite these favorable results, experts warn that there is no "magic bullet" or single treatment that is effective with everyone (Palmer, 1992). A growing body of literature suggests rather generically that some treatment is better than no treatment (Harris & Miller, 1990; Prendergast et al., 1995). For example, in a comparative evaluation of three well-known treatment models—cognitive behavioral therapy, motivational enhancement, and Facilitated 12-Step programming—authors of Project MATCH reported that all three achieved client improvements (Project MATCH Research Group, 1997). Similar findings were noted in an earlier study when Brandsma, Maultsby, and Welsh (1980) compared AA, insight therapy, and behavioral therapy among court-referred subjects. All treatment groups achieved more favorable results on drinking and legal problems than members of a comparison group. With justice-involved populations, therapeutic communities, once considered ineffective, have recently shown more favorable outcomes. The new TC models, however, are very different from their predecessors and tend to provide cognitive behavioral approaches.

CONCLUSION

Correctional agencies appear to be assuming increasing responsibility for treating substance-abusing clients. At the same time, it may seem that these same clients consume very large proportions of correctional treatment budgets. In response, new organizational structures have been developed, such as drug courts, drug testing, and day-reporting centers. Improved therapies and treatments show encouraging outcomes.

Even with these advances, however, few substance-abusing clients actually receive treatment relative to the number who have substance abuse histories (Beck, 2000; Taxman et al., 2007). It makes little sense to ignore the tremendous advances in the technology of assessing and treating this population. Yet there are many ways in which this happens. First, the demand for such services is high and overwhelming to many agencies. In such settings, the treatment needs of some clients may never be met. Second, some agencies have misinterpreted options such as drug courts, day treatment, and drug testing as treatments in themselves when they really are not. Without effective treatment programs, they simply contain and surveil substance-using behaviors without changing them. Third, in an effort to move all substance-using clients into some form of treatment, agencies often contract with outside providers (e.g., mental health agencies, hospitals, or private therapists) without knowing what is actually occurring in the contract programs. Important questions must be asked of such service providers, such as: Are they using an established model of treatment known to be effective with substance-using correctional clients? Are their assessments normed and validated to system-impacted populations? Do they operate from other principles of effective intervention? (see Chapters 4, 6, and 13). Finally, correctional officials need to take a "helicopter" view of these services, asking whether they cover the needs of different types of substance users, such as those who deny the need for services, those who suffer from related brain injury and other co-occurring problems (e.g., mental health, PTSD), those who need relapse prevention services, those who need social support, and others.

Discussion Questions

1. Compare and contrast the various models of substance use treatment.
2. Discuss pharmacological and cognitive behavioral treatment approaches to the problem of substance use. What are the advantages and disadvantages of each?

3. What are medication-assisted treatment programs? How are they used?

4. What treatment targets should be considered in treating the family members of substance users?

5. Why is self-efficacy important in the maintenance of abstinence?

6. What factors should be taken into account when counselors consider the responsivity principle for substance-using clients?

7. Should substance use programs be modified for ethnic groups and women? How should this be done?

8. Explain the difference between substance abuse and substance dependence. How should treatments for these two conditions be different?

ONLINE LEARNING ENHANCEMENTS

Johann Hari, "Everything You Think You Know About Addiction is Wrong"
With over 17 million views, this TED talk by journalist Johann Hari outlines what he believes really causes addiction—to everything from cocaine to smartphones—and how can we overcome it. Johann Hari has seen our current methods fail firsthand, as he has watched loved ones struggle to manage their addictions. He started to wonder why we treat addicts the way we do—and if there might be a better way. As he shares in this deeply personal talk, his questions took him around the world, and unearthed some surprising and hopeful ways of thinking about an age-old problem. www.ted.com/talks/johann_hari_everything_you_think_you_know_about_addiction_is_wrong?language=en

SAMHSA GAINS Webinar: Preventing Opioid Overdose at Reentry Through Jail- and Community-Based Programs
Formerly incarcerated individuals with opioid use disorder are at high risk for death by overdose during the first two weeks after reentering the community. This webinar covers five critical activities that jail- and community-based programs can engage in to ensure continuity of care and the necessary supports to lower the risk of overdose during this transition. Specific program examples around jail-based treatments and healthcare, community-based in-reach activities, and specialized case management are shared. www.youtube.com/watch?v=KgU4kHQbph0&list=PLBXgZMI_zqfTZLFkwVAUAypnpsWWc_G9b&index=16

GLOSSARY OF KEY TERMS

abstinence violation effect (AVE) feelings of guilt, failure, and perceived loss of control that occur as a result of lapses during the substance use recovery process

aftercare the last phase of the continuum of care; during this phase, clients are provided continuing care to prevent relapse and maintain changes made during the treatment phase

aversion therapies classical conditioning therapies for substance use that work directly with a client's desire for an addictive drug, attempting to reverse such desires; aversion therapies pair aversive stimuli (e.g., drug-induced nausea, electric shock) with consumption of alcohol or other drugs, the goal of which is to cause clients to associate the addictive substance with the aversive stimulus

behavioral family therapies a family therapy approach to substance use treatment that relies mostly on a social learning theoretical framework; behavioral family therapies alert the family to behaviors that may be reinforcing the substance-using client's excessive drinking or other drug use, encouraging members to work toward ceasing such behavior

communications therapy a family therapy approach to substance use treatment that involves altering dysfunctional family communication patterns to help create more healthy family structures

community reinforcement approach (CRA) a form of substance use treatment that utilizes a radical behavioral approach to provide alcohol users with incentives (reinforcements) to stop drinking; CRA targets alcohol addiction through the disruption of positive reinforcements for drinking and the development of positive reinforcements for sobriety

contingency contracts behavioral contracts, given to substance-using clients by therapists, in which access to jobs, family, friends, recreation, and other community reinforcers are contingent upon the client's ongoing sobriety

covert sensitization a form of classical conditioning in which the behavior therapist creates a fantasy for the client in which aversive elements are woven into a story involving the desired object/behavior

culturally competent a characteristic of therapists and staff who appreciate diversity, adapt to differences, and seek culturally specific understanding of others when treating substance-using clients

disease model a model of alcohol intervention that conceptualizes alcoholism as a disease; the disease model views alcoholics as physiologically distinct from non-alcoholics in that their biological makeup renders them incapable of drinking in moderation

drug courts judicially supervised court dockets that provide a sentencing alternative of treatment combined with supervision for people living with serious substance use disorders; drug courts vary considerably across jurisdictions, with some diverting clients contingent upon their completion of therapy and/or refraining from future offending and others suspending sentences based on similar contingencies

educational model a model of alcohol intervention that views alcoholism as caused by ignorance of the harms and effects of alcohol; the educational model utilizes education as a preventive approach to addiction

family systems models family therapy approaches to substance use that seek to identify family routines, regulatory behaviors, rituals, or problem-solving strategies which have developed to deal with substance use within the family

harm-reduction approaches a substance use treatment approach that advocates for methods such as controlled drinking, methadone maintenance, and needle-exchange programs rather than complete abstinence from addictive substances

high-risk situations situations (or stimuli) that place clients at a higher risk of relapse than if they were not in the presence of such stimuli

identified patient the identified substance-using client in family therapy approaches to substance use treatment

methadone maintenance a form of outpatient treatment that involves giving patients daily doses of methadone, under supervision, as a substitute for opiates such as heroin, morphine, and Percodan

multisystemic family therapy a form of family therapy that addresses substance use by targeting family systems and structures that sustain addiction as well as providing intensive "wraparound" services to such families

peer encounters a highly confrontational procedure where much of the therapy consists of staff and peers challenging the behavior of an addict

psychodynamic family therapies family therapy approaches to substance use in which the identified patient and other family members are assessed in terms of histories and "family of origin" issues to help family members understand how past relationships and problems may be replayed in the present

relapse prevention the act of helping clients initiate and maintain change toward abstinence from substance use

relational model of self a form of women's programming and therapy that recognizes that men and women form self-identity differently, with women doing so through attachments and connections with others, and men through separation and individuation

self-help groups mutual support groups in which members share a common personal, medical, or social problem; self-help groups serve as an important adjunct to therapy, particularly in the case of clients with drug or alcohol addictions

sponsors AA or NA members who have been in "recovery" for a significant period of time; through their own example, sponsors offer other members the opportunity to see that sobriety can have its rewards by modeling skills of relationship-building, responsibility, and support

stages of change   the five stages of client readiness to change substance-using behaviors, including precontemplation, contemplation, preparation, action, and maintenance; each stage suggests different treatment programs, recommendations, and goals for substance-using clients

substance abuse   a condition, as opposed to substance dependence, in which the decision to use or not use is under one's control; the clinical need to have the substance of choice is much lower than for the substance-dependent individual

substance dependence   a condition that involves a compulsive urge to use alcohol or other drugs that is often accompanied by neurological damage to the brain; symptoms of substance dependence include intense cravings, withdrawal symptoms when levels of the substance decline in the blood, and uncontrolled binges with any use of the substance

temperance model   a perspective, prominent through the late 1800s to the repeal of Prohibition in 1933, which views alcoholism as being caused by a harmful drug—alcohol—rather than the drinker; this perspective prioritizes legislation that prohibits the use and distribution of alcohol rather than treatment of the user

theory of addiction   a theoretical perspective which asserts that for women, addiction must be seen holistically (as a function of factors such as genetic predisposition, poor health, shame, isolation, and abuse); this perspective views addiction as a disease rather than the result of a disorder

theory of trauma   a theoretical perspective which asserts that a history of abuse predisposes women to substance use

theory of women's psychosocial development   a theoretical perspective which asserts that women develop through relationships and mutuality; relationships factor into women's substance use and must be considered in their treatment and recovery

therapeutic communities   an in-patient residential program for targeting substance use using a social learning treatment strategy in correctional and mental health settings in which staff and clients are trained to act as appropriate role models and life outside the institution is replicated as much as possible

CHAPTER 13

Treating System-Involved Women

Emily J. Salisbury

A growing recognition exists across criminal justice agencies to provide interventions tailored to the unique life circumstances of system-involved women. Much of this recognition is a direct result of the staggering increase in the number of women who entered the U.S. criminal justice system in the last 30 years. Indeed, between 1977 and 2004, the female incarceration rate surged by 757%, a figure that almost doubled the male incarceration growth rate of 388% for the same time period (Frost, Greene, & Pranis, 2006). Additionally, the rate of women under probation supervision rose 30% between 1995 and 2010, while for men the comparative rate of increase was only 8.4% (Bonczar, 1997; Glaze & Bonczar, 2011). Women now comprise one-quarter of all people on probation in the United States (Glaze & Bonczar, 2011).

Despite these dramatic influxes, women are not committing more crimes and have not become more violent than in years past. In fact, a variety of public policies during the 1980s and 1990s contributed to the likelihood of women, particularly poor women of color, being under some form of correctional supervision. For example, the enduring "war on drugs," the significant overhaul of welfare "reform" policies under the Clinton administration, mandatory arrest strategies for domestic violence, adoption of mandatory minimum sentencing guidelines for drug and property offenses, and zero-tolerance policies in schools all served to widen the criminal and juvenile justice funnel for girls and women (Chesney-Lind & Irwin, 2008).

Women involved in the justice system, when broadly compared with their male counterparts, reflect a relatively "low-risk" but "high-need" population. This is not to suggest

DOI: 10.4324/9780367808266-17

that women are not capable of violence or that men do not have an assortment of treatment needs. Rather, the likelihood of dangerous and violent behavior committed by women is far less than what we see with men, and criminogenic needs (e.g., antisocial attitudes, antisocial associates, substance use) often develop and manifest differently across gender. Moreover, because women and men are socialized to behave in congruence with established gender roles and norms, gendered trajectories to crime and ongoing recidivism exist (Daly, 1992; Salisbury & Van Voorhis, 2009). As a result, supervision and treatment interventions for women must reflect these distinctions. In fact, Gobeil et al. (2016) determined through a meta-analysis that gender-responsive programming interventions were significantly more likely to reduce women's recidivism in comparison to gender-neutral interventions.

WOMEN'S UNIQUE CRIMINOGENIC PATHWAYS AND NEEDS

To be successful in supervising and treating women, staff must have a complete understanding of the numerous challenges women faced prior to their entry into the justice system and how surviving them manifests behaviorally in custody and treatment settings. Qualitative, life-history interviews with system-impacted women consistently reveal lives of extreme poverty, multiple forms of child abuse and ongoing adult victimization, low educational achievement, mental illness (e.g., depression, anxiety, post-traumatic stress disorder, borderline personality disorder), self-medicating behavior with alcohol or other drugs, unhealthy intimate relationships, parental stress, and low levels of self-esteem and self-efficacy (Arnold, 1990; Browne, Miller, & Maguin, 1999; Chesney-Lind & Rodriguez, 1983; Daly, 1992; Gilfus, 1992; Owen, 1998; Richie, 1996). Moreover, research statistically supports the self-reported stories heard from women—many of these needs intersect in ways that significantly increase the likelihood of recidivism for women in the justice system (McClellan et al., 1997; Reisig et al., 2006; Salisbury & Van Voorhis, 2009).

For example, with a sample of women on probation in Missouri, Salisbury and Van Voorhis (2009) analyzed three commonly narrated pathways toward their probation revocation and subsequent incarceration for a two-year period:

1. A **child abuse pathway** revealed that self-reported abuse during childhood by the women facilitated their subsequent revocation and incarceration. Although child abuse was not directly related to future incarceration, it was related to their histories of mental illness and substance use, which then led to their current depression/anxiety and substance use, and, in turn, facilitated their probation failures.

2. A **relational pathway** demonstrated that some women's paths to revocation began with problems surrounding a dysfunctional intimate relationship. Unhealthy relationships, characterized by losses in personal power, were related to reductions in self-efficacy and women becoming victims of intimate partner abuse, resulting in ensuing depression/anxiety and substance use.

3. A **social and human capital pathway** highlighted that women's paths to incarceration also began with a lack of social support from families, dysfunctional intimate relationships, and low educational attainment. These three problems intersected to create reductions in women's self-efficacy, as well as difficulties in maintaining employment and financial independence, leading to supervision failure and incarceration.

Importantly, the people on probation in the Salisbury and Van Voorhis (2009) study were relatively low-risk women. Of the 304 women in the sample who were tracked for recidivism after two years, only 52 (17.1%) women were incarcerated. Moreover, the majority of incarcerations were for probation violations (73.1%), not new crimes or convictions. Thus, the women were likely not incarcerated because they posed significant danger to public safety, but because their needs, as revealed in the three pathways, were not adequately addressed.

In response to the growing evidence revealing that girls and women are less dangerous and have distinct needs, there has been a significant paradigm shift toward supervision and treatment programs that are **gender-responsive**. Although the term *gender-responsive* may initially seem misleading because the perspective focuses on the issues of women and not men, the term was intentionally chosen to place a "gendered" lens on correctional and criminal justice systems. The term also suggests that one gender is not more important than the other—even if most criminal justice policy begins with men in mind. Moreover, many of the scholars who developed the gender-responsive paradigm anticipate the research on women to eventually improve criminal justice policies for men as well.

THEORETICAL FOUNDATIONS TO THE GENDER-RESPONSIVE PERSPECTIVE

Individuals who wish to fully understand the gender-responsive perspective and gendered pathways of justice-involved women must first grasp the theoretical foundations upon which this paradigm has been established. First, a discussion of the **relational theory** of women's psychological development is presented, as it has become a core theory in explaining female criminality. Within this relational framework, two additional theoretical concepts are presented: **holistic addiction theory** and the **theory of trauma**. These theories create a basis for understanding system-impacted females' widespread experiences with trauma, substance use, and mental health.

Relational Theory

Beginning with Jean Baker Miller's classic 1976 work, *Toward a New Psychology of Women*, the psychological development of women became understood through a unique perspective separate from traditional explanations of men's psychological development. Miller (1976), along with Carol Gilligan (1982) and others at the Stone Center at Wellesley College, developed a new theory of women's psychology, which challenged the idea that healthy psychological development is defined solely by separation and autonomy from others. These scholars argued that women have an alternative route to achieving healthy psychological growth. According to Miller (1976), women's identities are primarily formed through connections with others. A woman's growth is manifested through the types of relationships she has, and her sense of self-worth is defined by interconnections with others. Thus, connection, rather than disconnection, is central to women's development.

Women's need for fostering relationships and caring for others was long criticized by traditional moral reasoning theorists as being a sign of weakness and deficiency, essentially impeding women's psychological growth (Kaplan, 1984). Because women had difficulty separating themselves from others when presented with moral dilemmas, they were characterized as being unable to achieve higher-order cognitive maturity (Kohlberg, 1984; see Chapter 9). This foregone conclusion led Carol Gilligan (1982) to propose that women were not morally deficient, but the theoretical explanations were flawed. "[T]he failure of women to fit existing models of human growth may point to a problem in the representation, a limitation in the conception of the human condition, an omission of certain truths about life" (Gilligan, 1982, pp. 1–2).

According to Miller (1986), healthy relationships are mutual, empathic, and empowering for all individuals involved. The two key features of true connections include mutuality and empathy. Mutuality refers to the ability of each person in the relationship to represent his or her own feelings and thoughts creating mutual influence and mutual responsiveness. Empathy denotes a complex ability to engage in another's thoughts and feelings, without losing sight of his or her own cognitive and affective experiences (Covington, 2008b).

Miller (1986) proposed that mutual, empathic, and empowering relationships produce five psychological effects for all participants: (1) increased zest and vitality; (2) empowerment to act (i.e., personal agency); (3) knowledge of self and others; (4) self-worth; and (5) a desire for more connection. Thus, healthy relationships generate self-esteem, self-efficacy, and continuous connections with others.

Although generally girls are socialized to be more empathic toward others than boys (Gilligan, Lyons, & Hanmer, 1990), females who are involved in the system, particularly those who are incarcerated, have suffered repeatedly from non-empathic relationships. These relationships either promote a lack of empathy for both the self and others, or an exaggerated empathy for others and no empathy for the self (Covington, 2008b). The lack of self-empathy that is produced as a result of unsatisfying relationships as it relates to self-esteem and self-efficacy may be one route through which mental illness and substance use are fostered. For example, Miller (1988) portrayed women's experiences of condemned isolation in which a woman feels isolated in her primary relationships because significant others in her life fail to validate and adequately respond to her attempts at connecting. This woman believes she is the sole cause of problems within the relationship, and, as a result, feels there is no possibility of improving the relational situation. This leads to intense feelings of shame, self-blame, and guilt, which may result in drug use, since drugs essentially become a method of coping with extreme hope- and helplessness (Miller, 1988). Kaplan (1984), also from the Stone Center, reported that women who were disconnected from others or who had difficulty forming healthy relationships experienced major depressive characteristics such as low self-esteem. These features often led to substance-using behaviors, which served to fill women's relational void.

Relational theory was renamed and reframed in the mid-1990s to relational-cultural theory in an attempt to highlight the nuances, and cultural identities, of African-American women (Quinn & Grumbach, 2015). The field is (finally) beginning to understand that this does not go far enough to truly address the specific needs of women of color. For example, Quinn and Grumbach (2015) argue that incorporating solution-focused therapy and critical race theory with relational-cultural theory will more appropriately encompass the most effective ways to engage with women of color, particularly African-American women. Solution-focused therapy (Macdonald, 2011) has similar tenets as Motivational Interviewing (Chapter 3), as both are rooted in positive psychology. For instance, both approaches embrace the values that the client is the expert in their own lives, and that they already possess the strengths to reach their therapeutic goals, with guidance from mental health professionals.

The theoretical assumptions of critical race theory (CRT; Bell, 1995) are outlined in Box 13.1 and can surely contribute toward improving outcomes for African-American women (and men) in treatment. Because there has been a tremendous amount of political rhetoric about what CRT is, and is not, due in large part to a moral panic and fear of conservatives in the United States losing sociopolitical power, it is important to understand the theory's basic foundations. In short, CRT challenges the notions that (a) color blindness will eliminate racism, (b) racism is a matter of individuals, not systems, and (c) one can fight racism without paying attention to sexism, homophobia, economic exploitation, and other forms of oppression and injustice (Valdes, Culp, & Harris, 2002 as cited in Quinn & Grumbach, 2015).

Box 13.1 Central Assumptions of Critical Race Theory

Reproduced from Quinn and Grumbach (2015)

1. **Endemic racism.**

   Rather than accepting racism as abnormal or individualistic, racism is an ordinary occurrence for people of color, permeates all aspects of social life, and race-based ideology is threaded throughout society.

2. **Race is a social construction.**

   Race is a contrived system of categorizing people according to physical attributes with no correspondence to genetic or biologic reality and acknowledges the force of its meaning and implications. Race is a social construction without a fixed objective definition and exists primarily for purposes of social stratification, as race is first determined based on set criteria believed to be external to the concept.

3. **Differential racialization.**

   This tenet is based on the idea that dominant social discourses and people in power can racialize groups of people in different ways at different times, depending on historic, social, or economic need.

4. **Interest convergence/materialist determinism.**

   Racism brings material advantage to the majority race, and progressive change regarding race occurs only when the interests of the powerful happen to converge with those of the racially oppressed.

5. **Voices of color.**

   The dominant group's accounting of history routinely excludes minority perspectives to justify and legitimize its power. This silencing of alternative experiences serves to minimize the interplay of power and oppression across time and place. CRT advocates are writing of history to include the lived reality of oppressed groups from their perspectives and in their own words to challenge liberalist claims of neutrality, color blindness, and universal truths.

6. **Antiessentialism/intersectionality.**

   This is the acknowledgment of the intersectionality of various oppressions and suggests that a primary focus on race can eclipse other forms of exclusion. CRT theorists contend that analysis without a multidimensional framework can replicate the very patterns of social exclusion it seeks to combat and lead to the essentializing of oppressions.

Holistic Addiction Theory

A growing body of knowledge continues to suggest that the etiology of substance use varies significantly across gender. Women's drug use, abstinence, and relapse seem to be more closely tied with intimate relationships compared to men's substance-related behaviors (Hser, Anglin, & Booth, 1987; Hser, Anglin, & McGlothlin, 1987; Rosenbaum, 1981). Research studies have shown that women are oftentimes introduced to drugs by dominant male figures in their lives, including family members, friends, or lovers (Henderson & Boyd, 1995; Henderson, Boyd, & Mieczkowski, 1994; Sun, 2007; Van Wormer, 2001). Further, a woman's drug of choice may actually transform psychologically into an object of love or affection to the relationally isolated woman. Addiction can be understood as a type of relationship, where the woman is in an intense obsession with the drug (Covington, 2008b). According to Covington and Surrey (1997), "It is a kind of love relationship in which the object of addiction becomes the focus of a woman's life" (p. 338). Because turning to substances is such a common choice for women who experience non-empathic, dysfunctional relationships, a theory of addiction that embraces this reality is supported by the extant gender-responsive literature.

Patterns of drug abuse, onset of use, psychosocial characteristics, and physiological effects have all shown to be unique across gender (Blume, 1990; Nelson-Zlupko, Kauffman, & Dore, 1995). Compared to males, females describe the onset of substance use as being more sudden and intense rather than gradual, as is seen more often with men (Center for Substance Abuse Treatment [CSAT], 1999). Furthermore, males tend to initiate drug use for pleasure-seeking purposes, whereas females generally begin use as a way to numb physical or psychological pain often due to physical or sexual abuse (CSAT, 1999; Reed, 1985). Women are also apt to be addicted to multiple substances with greater regularity (Celentano & McQueen, 1984), and are more likely to use drugs in isolated, private settings (Marsh & Miller, 1985; Reed, 1985). Even during recovery, gender differences have been reported. Ryan (1981) noted that while recovering men frequently emphasize the problems caused by the consequences of drug use, recovering women more often struggle with the stressors that led to their drug use.

Drug using, system-involved women are much more likely than similarly situated men to have histories of sexual abuse, co-occurring mental disorders, lower self-esteem, and more acute drug abuse histories (Henderson, 1998; Langan & Pelissier, 2001; Messina, Burdon, & Prendergast, 2003; Owen & Bloom, 1995; Peters et al., 1997). Moreover, the severity of substance abuse and addiction has been shown to be a stronger predictor of antisocial behavior for women than for men (Dowden & Brown, 2002; McClellan et al., 1997).

Because the etiology of substance use and misuse varies across gender, many researchers suggest that treatment issues for addiction are similarly quite different for women than they

FIGURE 13.1 Graduates from the Women in Recovery program are greeted at the Oklahoma City State Capitol. Women in Recovery is an alternative to incarceration for non-violent, system-involved women with alcohol and other drug addictions.
Source: AP Photo/*The Oklahoman*, Paul B. Southerland.

are for men (Bloom et al., 2003; Covington & Surrey, 1997; Hagan, Finnegan, & Nelson-Zlupko, 1994; Henderson, 1998; Messina et al., 2003; Peters et al., 1997; Reed, 1987; Wellisch, Prendergast, & Anglin, 1996). Essentially, a **holistic theory of addiction** recognizes that (1) addicted women differ from their male counterparts in several significant ways, and (2) women's substance abusing behavior is a complex problem for which a multifaceted treatment model should be implemented. Such a holistic model focuses on simultaneously treating women's co-occurring addiction and mental illness needs, while incorporating a relational therapeutic perspective that recognizes the primary causal role of victimization and trauma. See Figure 13.1.

Theory of Trauma

A report published by the Centers for Disease Control and Prevention (Black et al., 2011) reported that close to one in five women in the United States (18.3%) have experienced rape or attempted rape in their lifetimes. This startlingly high figure applies to non-offending women in the general population; the estimates for justice-involved women are consistently much higher. When assessing multiple forms of trauma, most research studies conclude that 77% to 90% of incarcerated women report extensive histories of emotional, physical, and sexual abuse (Messina & Grella, 2006). As a result, **trauma theory** has become a critical perspective in the understanding and treatment of system-involved women. This perspective originated from the general psychiatric and psychological literatures and is useful in directing treatment providers toward appropriate and effective treatment modalities for coping with trauma. Trauma theory is also relevant to the treatment of substance use disorders since alcohol and other drug use is such a common coping strategy for trauma survivors.

Trauma can result from many different events, not necessarily involving violence. It can result from witnessing violence or from being stigmatized due to gender, race, poverty, or many other social positions (Covington, 2008b). Trauma is defined not only by an overwhelming event but also by an individual's reactions to that event. Reactions to traumatic events can vary significantly across individuals, and even though anxiety- and fear-based reactions are assumed by many correctional professionals to be the common symptoms, they are not always present. In fact, according to the DSM-5 (American Psychiatric Association, 2013), the most prominent clinical characteristics of psychological distress after a traumatic event include: (1) a lack of pleasure or the ability to experience it (i.e., anhedonia); (2) a state of unease or general dissatisfaction with life (i.e., dysphoria); (3) externalizing angry and aggressive symptoms; or (4) dissociative symptoms such as feelings of being detached from oneself. For women, trauma can alter a female's relational experiences and significantly hinder her psychological development (Covington, 2008b; Herman, 1992).

The cumulative impact of trauma has also been emphasized in the literature. Root (1994) suggested that the effects of trauma often occur over the course of a lifetime, particularly for women of color. For example, African-American women may be subjected to various forms of insidious trauma such as racial and class discrimination throughout their lives. Continuous trauma can trigger survival behaviors that are easily misunderstood to be pathological if their etiology is not apparent (Root, 1994).

From a psychiatric perspective, trauma survivors have a significant disconnection from themselves and from others (Herman, 1992). According to Herman (1992), victims of trauma frequently feel unsafe in relation to others, as well as within their own bodies. Further, victims' cognitions and emotions are self-perceived to be chaotic and out of control. This holds true for survivors of many different types of traumatic events including combat veterans, Holocaust victims, battered women, and rape survivors. Therefore, the model of treatment is similar across varying types of traumatic experiences.

TRANSLATING THE GENDER-RESPONSIVE PERSPECTIVE INTO PRACTICE

Legal concerns about ensuring equity across gender should be focused not on having the same policies and programming, but ensuring that policies and programming work *equally well* for women as they do men (Buell & Abbate, 2020). Because the vast majority of policies in the correctional system were originally designed for men and applied to women under the false assumption that both groups behave similarly, there are significant disadvantages for women in many correctional policy areas (i.e., supervision strategies, custody classification, risk/needs assessment, treatment interventions, reentry services). In response, since the mid-1990s the National Institute of Corrections (NIC) has committed to an ongoing gender-responsive initiative developing a body of knowledge on how to effectively manage and intervene with justice-involved women. By compiling existing knowledge from research and practice with women, a set of guiding gender-responsive principles were developed to inform correctional policy and practice (see Box 14.2; Bloom et al., 2003). These principles have also been incorporated into the United Nations Rules for the Treatment of Women Prisoners and Noncustodial Measures for Women Offenders (the Bangkok Rules) adopted by the United Nations in 2010 (United Nations, 2010).

Box 14.1 Gender-Responsive Principles for Women

GENDER MAKES A DIFFERENCE
Recognizing gender means accepting a broad spectrum of social and environmental disparities between men and women who are involved in the justice system.

ENVIRONMENTS MUST BE BASED ON SAFETY, RESPECT, AND DIGNITY
Women have suffered extreme amounts of physical and emotional abuse throughout their lives. Correctional settings should be trauma-informed and trauma-responsive to create safe, trusting environments and facilitate behavioral change.

RELATIONSHIPS ARE CENTRAL TO WOMEN'S LIVES
Policies and practices should be relationally focused and promote healthy connections.

SERVICES MUST BE COMPREHENSIVE, INTEGRATED, AND CULTURALLY RELEVANT
Holistic and culturally sensitive services should address the intersection of needs commonly observed among women, rather than addressing each need in isolation of others.

PROVIDE OPPORTUNITIES TO IMPROVE WOMEN'S SOCIOECONOMIC STATUS
Financial independence for women and their children should be a primary goal.

COLLABORATE WITH COMMUNITY RESOURCES
Mobilize community resources for comprehensive, wraparound services.

Source: Bloom, B., Owen, B., & Covington, S. (2003). *Gender Responsive Strategies: Research, Practice, and Guiding Principles for Women Offenders*. Washington, DC: U.S. Department of Justice, National Institute of Corrections.

Programs and interventions that are gender-responsive go beyond simply having female caseloads. Rather, they recognize and embrace the realities of girls' and women's lives. Because established norms and gender-roles socialize women and men to generally behave in distinct ways (e.g., women's pathways into and out of crime are often fundamentally different than men's pathways, women serve time in incarcerated settings in distinct ways than men), they should not be assessed, supervised, and treated in exactly the same fashion. Differences suggest that women need distinct types of custody environments, unique levels of supervision, and various services and programs focusing on multiple aspects of women's lives.

For instance, avoiding re-traumatization is essential during women's behavioral change and recovery process. This becomes particularly difficult to accomplish in criminal justice settings where the day-to-day operations involve demanding and vociferous speech, intense bodily searches, isolation, and restraint. These and other stimuli can trigger traumatic reactions and cause further harm to trauma survivors. As a result, research and policy initiatives have begun to investigate the potential benefits of implementing trauma-informed services, particularly with women (e.g., see Harris & Fallot, 2001; WCDVS [Women's Cooccurring Disorders and Violence Survey] funded by SAMHSA).

Trauma-Informed Policies, Supervision, and Treatment

The extreme amount of trauma in system-impacted women's lives has led scholars and practitioners to advocate for all treatment *and supervision* strategies with women to be trauma-informed (Covington & Bloom, 2007). Trauma-informed policies and services are those that are influenced by an understanding of the impact of interpersonal violence and victimization on women's development and lives (Elliott, Bjelajac, Fallot, Markoff, & Reed, 2005). A trauma-informed organization will ensure that all staff, including receptionists, line staff, and administrators, are trained to understand the prevalence of abuse and victimization in correctional clients' lives, as well their various detrimental effects on human behavior. Agency-wide education and training are used to safeguard that every interaction between staff and clients aids in the recovery process and avoids re-traumatization (Harris & Fallot, 2001). Because of the high prevalence of abuse and victimization in women's lives and the inability to distinguish who has or has not experienced trauma, it has been suggested that a policy of universal precautions be implemented among service agencies. That is, best practices are those that treat all women as if they are trauma survivors (Elliott et al., 2005). The importance of implementing trauma-informed services has been deemed so critical to service delivery that some suggest that programs that fail to become trauma-informed are by default "trauma-denied," or denying the existence and significance of trauma in women's lives (Elliott et al., 2005).

Gender-Responsive Risk/Needs Assessment

Although some of the traditional, gender-neutral risk/needs assessments originally designed for men have been validated on women populations (e.g., the Level of Service/Case Management Inventory [Andrews et al., 2004], COMPAS [Brennan, Dieterich, & Ehret, 2009]), given the mounting evidence surrounding the gendered pathways research, these assessments have not been enough to provide an accurate portrayal of the scope of women's criminogenic needs. Evidence supporting the additional needs and strengths that agencies should be assessing with female populations comes from research developed at the University of Cincinnati and the NIC, which resulted in the construction and validation of a gender-responsive risk/needs assessment instrument intentionally designed for system-involved women (see Chapter 6; Van Voorhis et al., 2008; Van Voorhis et al., 2010; Wright et al., 2007).

Among these studies, issues surrounding child and adult abuse/victimization, depression/ anxiety, dysfunctional relationships, parental stress, and self-esteem/self-efficacy were investigated to determine their importance in facilitating women's recidivism. The suite of Women's Risk Need Assessment (WRNA) instruments have been successfully validated in several states across the United States and with various female correctional populations, including those on probation, incarcerated women, pre-release incarcerated women, and those on parole and post-release community supervision. It has also been adopted internationally in Singapore, England, the Czech Republic, and Namibia. The WRNAs can either be used as stand-alone assessments for agencies that have not adopted a dynamic, gender-neutral risk/need tool, or as a supplement for agencies that have invested in another validated instrument, but that seek to provide gender-responsive supervision and treatment. Additionally, research results from the WRNA instruments informed an automated gender-responsive supplement to the COMPAS, called the COMPAS Women (Northpointe Institute for Public Management, Inc., n.d.).

The Service Planning Instrument for Women (SPIn-W) is another gender-responsive risk/ needs assessment instrument and case planning tool. Developed by Orbis Partners (n.d.), the instrument is designed to complement the Collaborative Case Work for Women (CCW-W; formerly called the Women Offender Case Management Model; Orbis Partners, 2006; see Table 13.1) developed by the same company. Comprised of 11 domains, the SPIn-W measures women's criminogenic needs and strengths as a first step toward applying the overall CCW-W.

Gender-Responsive Treatment Curricula

Curricula that are (1) gender-responsive, (2) cognitive behavioral in nature, and (3) based on the principles of effective treatment intervention are most desirable with female correctional populations. Table 13.1 presents curricula that are currently the most promising for women in the criminal justice system. Although some gender-responsive interventions listed were initially created with nonoffending populations in mind (e.g., Beyond Trauma, Helping Women Recover), they have subsequently been integrated among female correctional populations with success.

Turning back to the Collaborative Case Work for Women curriculum (Van Dieten, 2008), this intervention is designed to apply the six guiding gender-responsive principles outlined in Box 14.1. Developed for the NIC by Orbis Partners, the goals of CCW-W are to reduce the recidivism of incarcerated or community-supervised women and to improve the health and well-being of women and their families. An outcome evaluation of CCW-W (formerly WOCMM) with women on probation from the state of Connecticut demonstrated that women who received the model had significantly lowered recidivism rates after a year (31.6% rearrested) in comparison to women who did not receive the model (42.5% rearrested; Millson, Robinson, & Van Dieten, 2010).

Another program that continues to gain evaluation support is Lisa Najavits's Seeking Safety (Najavits, 2002a, 2002b) curriculum, a cognitive behavioral psychotherapy program for women suffering from dual diagnoses of substance abuse and post-traumatic stress disorder (PTSD). The curriculum emphasizes that the primary clinical need from both disorders is safety. Safety is broadly defined in the program and includes abstinence from substances, reductions in self-harmful behaviors, and ending dangerous relationships. Several research studies have revealed the program's effectiveness in reducing psychopathology and recidivism with female correctional populations (Lynch, Heath, Mathews, & Cepeda, 2012; Zlotnick, Johnson, & Najavits, 2009; Zlotnick et al., 2003).

Gender-Responsive Program Assessment

As more programs move toward gender-responsive orientations for female populations, it becomes important to guide agencies on how best to provide supervision and services in a

TABLE 13.1 Gender-responsive interventions for women correctional populations

Program	Developer	Theoretical Foundations	Treatment Targets
Beyond Trauma	Stephanie Covington	Relational Trauma	Coping with trauma Cognitive skills Healthy relationships Parenting
Female Offender Treatment and Employment Program (FOTEP)	Mental Health Systems, Inc.	Relational Trauma	Case management and reentry Education Employment/financial Independence Substance abuse Mental health Parenting
Forever Free	Mental Health Systems, Inc.	Cognitive behavioral	Substance abuse Healthy relationships Post-traumatic stress disorder (PTSD) Anger management Parenting Self-esteem
Helping Women Recover	Stephanie Covington	Relational Trauma Holistic addiction	Substance abuse Coping with trauma Healthy relationships
La Bodega de la Familia; Vera Family Justice Program*	Vera Institute of Justice (Carol Shapiro)	Family systems Relational Positive psychology (strength-based)	Case management and reentry Family and social support
Moving On	Orbis Partners, Inc. (Marilyn Van Dieten)	Relational Cognitive behavioral	Motivation for change Healthy relationships Antisocial attitudes Cognitive skills Stress management
Seeking Safety	Lisa Najavits	Relational Trauma Holistic addiction Cognitive behavioral	Substance abuse Coping with trauma PTSD
Collaborate Case Work for Women	Orbis Partners, Inc. (Marilyn Van Dieten)	Relational Trauma Cognitive behavioral Positive psychology (strength-based)	Case management and reentry Family and social support Health and well-being

Note: *Although this program was not developed with an underlying gender-responsive perspective, it includes many of its elements. It is also effective with male offending populations.

gender-responsive milieu. Recently, two instruments were developed to assess a program's therapeutic integrity, or fidelity, to gender-responsive perspectives. First, the Gender-Informed Practices Assessment (GIPA) was developed through a cooperative agreement between NIC and the Center for Effective Public Policy. As noted in Box 13.2, the GIPA is comprised of 12 domains and is intended to guide correctional administrators in the development of both evidence-based (i.e., gender-neutral principles of effective correctional intervention) and gender-responsive practices.

Second, a tool specifically designed for assessing gender-responsive adherence of programs with juvenile girls was created by the Oregon Coalition of Advocates for Equal Access for Girls (2011). The Gender-Responsive Standards and Assessment Tool for Girls' Programs and Services (G-SAT) assesses four areas: (1) facility, (2) staffing, (3) programs and services for girls, and (4) administration/leadership. The tool is not only useful for assessing juvenile justice programs but also child welfare, mental health, and residential alcohol and other drug programs.

Box 13.2 Gender-Informed Practices Assessment (GIPA) Domains

DOMAIN 1: LEADERSHIP AND PHILOSOPHY
Addresses the extent to which executive leadership and facility management demonstrate commitment to both evidence-based and gender-informed practice for women in critical ways.

DOMAIN 2: EXTERNAL SUPPORT
Examines the external support from system stakeholders, funders, and community partners for the agency's mission regarding gender-informed and evidence-based practices for women.

DOMAIN 3: FACILITY
Examines multiple aspects of a facility's location, physical design, and conditions with regard to their gender-appropriateness for women.

DOMAIN 4: MANAGEMENT AND OPERATIONS
A frequent challenge to administrators responsible for women is the integration of gender-informed practices in every aspect of operations with the facility's security requirements.

DOMAIN 5: STAFFING AND TRAINING
A well-run facility is grounded in a workforce that is committed to the facility's mission, and hired and trained to carry out the daily requirements of gender-informed practice. In difficult budget times, agency and facility leadership are challenged to value and maintain a commitment to gender-responsive training and staff development.

DOMAIN 6: FACILITY CULTURE
Examines the facility environment and assesses the extent to which incarcerated people and staff feel physically and emotionally safe and respected. It also explores the "reporting culture" of formal and informal methods to report sexual, physical, and emotional abuse.

DOMAIN 7: OFFENDER MANAGEMENT

This domain examines the gender-appropriateness and clarity of rules and expectations, the methods for motivating positive behaviors, and the disciplinary practices of the facility.

DOMAIN 8: ASSESSMENT AND CLASSIFICATION

Examines gender-informed procedures for determining custody level, assessing dynamic risks and needs, and identifying vulnerable and predatory incarcerated clients (PREA draft standard).

DOMAIN 9: CASE AND TRANSITIONAL PLANNING

Appropriate case and transition planning involves a process of addressing incarcerated clients' individual and unique needs, particularly those that impair humane prison adjustment and those that are related to future offending (i.e., risk factors, criminogenic needs). The role of case management in this process is to match women to programs and services according to their assessed need for such services.

DOMAIN 10: RESEARCH-BASED PROGRAM AREAS

Examines each of the core programs of the facility along six dimensions: gender-responsive intent, evidence-based foundation, availability of manuals and treatment guides, use of clear criteria for program eligibility, efforts to monitor outcomes, and quality assurance.

DOMAIN 11: SERVICES

Reviews six critical service areas with regard to important attributes of gender-informed practice. The six areas are medical, mental health, transportation, food, legal services, and victim services.

DOMAIN 12: QUALITY ASSURANCE AND EVALUATION

Explores the extent to which the agency and facility use quality assurance methods to review and improve all functional units.

CONCLUSION

Although the knowledge base regarding the most effective ways to supervise and treat justice-involved women is not as advanced as the body of work established with men, there is nevertheless enough research wisdom to know that traditional, gender-neutral strategies are insufficient in addressing the realities of women's lives. Indeed, our correctional system would look quite different if we began with women in mind, knowing that most are far less dangerous, yet still in need of significant services. If we accept the premise that "gender makes a difference," our correctional policies and interventions would similarly reflect this philosophy.

At the same time, we cannot afford to ignore the wealth of evidence that emerged over the last 30 years from the Canadian correctional psychologists who developed the principles of effective intervention and the risk-need-responsivity model (Bonta & Andrews, 2017; Gendreau, 1996b). While it is true that most of the evidence from this research agenda focused on males, much of it is also relevant to females. Improving supervision and treatment of women means embracing both gender-responsive principles as well as the knowledge from traditional, gender-neutral principles of effective intervention.

Discussion Questions

1. What intervention needs do women have that differ from men?
2. Even though both system-impacted women and men suffer from addiction, why should it be treated differently with women?
3. If our correctional system started with women in mind instead of men, how do you think it would look different?
4. What is critical race theory and how can it be integrated with gender-responsive interventions?

ONLINE LEARNING ENHANCEMENTS

Emily Salisbury, "Judging Societies by Women's Prisons," TEDx
This TEDx was delivered during a gender-responsive event at the Washington Corrections Center for Women in Gig Harbor, Washington. In this talk, Emily Salisbury asks people to consider the positive social impacts that can occur by adopting policies and procedures in prisons that start with women in mind. Given that incarcerated women are oftentimes dismissed or ignored among prison systems, Salisbury illustrates the social and legal consequences of placing policies on women that were originally designed for men. Fortunately, gender-responsive solutions exist to help agencies adopt more effective policies, creating a safer society for all of us. www.youtube.com/watch?v=IJwlyf7rCtU

To see the entire event series, which included TEDx talks by currently incarcerated women (at the time of filming), see www.youtube.com/playlist?list=PLz7pK3zKqJ26JKcg xZcaV0JOLwI10li5o

Healing Neen: **A Film About Trauma, Healing, and Resilience**
After surviving a childhood of abuse and neglect, Tonier "Neen" Cain lived on the streets for two nightmarish decades, where she endured unrelenting violence, hunger, and despair while racking up 66 criminal convictions related to her addiction. Incarcerated and pregnant in 2004, treatment for her lifetime of trauma offered her a way out … and up. Her story illustrates the consequences that untreated trauma has on individuals and society at-large, including mental health problems, addiction, homelessness, and incarceration. Today, she is a nationally renowned speaker and educator on the devastation of trauma and the hope of recovery. It is recommended that educators watch the film independently to determine its appropriateness for their classroom, and provide a content warning and debriefing after the film. https://vimeo.com/15851924

GLOSSARY OF KEY TERMS

anhedonia   a lack of pleasure or the ability to experience it

child abuse pathway   one of three common pathways toward women's probation revocation in which women reported that abuse during childhood facilitated their subsequent revocation and incarceration

condemned isolation   an experience in which a woman feels isolated in her primary relationships because significant others in her life fail to validate and adequately respond to her attempts at connecting; women experiencing condemned isolation believe that they are at fault for problems within the relationship and, as a result, feel there is no possibility of improving the relational situation

gender-responsive   a perspective in which a "gendered" lens is placed on correctional and criminal justice systems; gender-responsive correctional supervision and treatment plans consider the unique criminogenic pathways and needs of female and male populations

holistic addiction theory   a theoretical concept in which it is suggested that women's drug use, abstinence, and relapse seem to be more closely tied with intimate relationships compared to men's substance-related behaviors; this theory recognizes that: (1) addicted women differ from their male counterparts in several significant ways, and (2) women's substance-using behavior is a complex problem for which a multifaceted treatment model should be implemented, including a focus on simultaneously treating women's co-occurring addiction and mental illness needs, while incorporating a relational therapeutic perspective that recognizes the primary causal role of victimization and trauma

relational pathway   one of three common pathways toward women's probation revocation in which women's paths to revocation begin with problems surrounding a dysfunctional intimate relationship

relational theory   a theoretical concept in which it is suggested that the psychological development of women, unlike that of men, is manifested through the types of relationships they have, and their sense of self-worth is defined by interconnections with others; connection, rather than disconnection, is central to women's development

social and human capital pathway   one of three common pathways toward women's probation revocation in which it is suggested that women's paths to incarceration began with a lack of social support from families, dysfunctional intimate relationships, and low educational attainment; these three issues create reductions in self-efficacy, as well as difficulties in maintaining employment and financial independence, leading to supervision failure and incarceration

theory of trauma   a theoretical concept that emphasizes the prevalence of trauma in the histories of justice-involved women; this theory is a critical perspective in the understanding and treatment of women involved in the justice system, as it is useful in directing treatment providers toward appropriate and effective treatment modalities for coping with trauma as well as the treatment of substance use disorders

trauma-informed   a framework that emphasizes an understanding of the impact of interpersonal violence and victimization on women's development and lives; it is recommended by scholars and practitioners that treatment and supervision strategies with justice-involved women, as well as correctional policies and services, be trauma-informed

universal precautions   a policy recommendation in which service agencies treat all women as if they are trauma survivors due to the high prevalence of abuse and victimization in women's lives and the inability to distinguish who has or has not experienced trauma

CHAPTER 14

Treating Clients Who Commit Sex Offenses

Patricia Van Voorhis and Whitney Howey

KEY TERMS

attachment disorder	eye movement desensitization and
behavioral strategies	reprocessing (EMDR)
civil commitment	neurological deficits
client confidentiality	polygraph
clinical interview	relapse prevention
cognitive behavioral therapy	risk assessments
cognitive distortions	role-playing
containment	self-regulation and self-management
dialectical behavior therapy (DBT)	social learning theory
dynamic risk/needs	social skills training
empathy training	The Good Lives Model
	therapeutic alliance

In 2019, 459,310 rapes and sexual assaults occurred in the United States. Over the five-year period spanning from 2015 to 2019, this figure has ranged from a low of 298,410 in 2016, to a high of 734,630 in 2018 (Bureau of Justice Statistics, 2019). In addition, the Adverse Childhood Experiences Study (ACE) estimated that one in four girls and one in six boys will be sexually assaulted by the age of 18 (Anda, Dube, Giles, & Felitti, 2003). Juveniles who commit sexual offenses account for more than 35% of sexual offenses against minors, with the overwhelming majority (93%) being male (Finkelhor, Ormrod, & Chaffin, 2009). Women represent between 1% and 5% of arrests/convictions for sexual offense perpetration, though this number underrepresents the reality of females who commit sexual offenses (Sandler & Freeman, 2011). Nearly one in five college women are raped over what is now projected to be a five-year stay in college (Fisher, Cullen, & Turner, 2000). In the majority of cases, offenses were committed by someone known to the victim. Moreover, many offenses are not represented in these figures because they were never reported (see English, 2004). On average, only about 25% of rapes and sexual assaults were reported to police in 2018 and only about 34% in 2019 (Bureau of Justice Statistics, 2019).

DOI: 10.4324/9780367808266-18

Although people who commit sex offenses share some of the characteristics of the general justice-involved population, they also represent a unique group of individuals. They are assumed by many to be untreatable and predatory (Quin, Forsyth, & Mullen-Quinn, 2004), and many are subjected to some of the strictest containment and commitment policies our society administers. Yet, knowledge of the complex causes of their behavior continues to grow, and that knowledge, in turn, has generated new treatment strategies and more optimism about whether they can be successfully treated.

A COMPLEX ARRAY OF CAUSES AND THEORIES

Approaches to the treatment of this very serious problem must recognize that the causes of sex offending are varied and complex. The earliest explanations emerged from psychoanalytic theories. Indeed, Freud had a good deal to say about sex. These historical theories spanned the typical array of psychoanalytical culprits from castration anxiety (an Oedipal conflict causing a boy to fear his father will cut off his penis to punish the boy's attachment to his mother), to seductive mothers, faulty ego and superego development, excessive id drives involving aggression and libidinal urges, unresolved trauma, and neurotic conflicts. As will be seen, today's paradigms are more complex, and most account for the influence of learning, neurological impairments, the formation of cognitive distortions, attachment disorders, problems with intimacy, anxiety, and anger. Many of these causes are interrelated.

Behavioral Theories

Behavioral theories of sex offending recognize that learning plays an important role in the development of sexual behaviors. A classically conditioned stimulus for inappropriate sexual behavior can form following the repeated pairing of sexuality with a traumatic or disturbing event. The intense emotional response formed through such processes may then impact later attempts at sexual gratification. A child who is repeatedly molested may have been brought to climax and had such sexual experiences reinforced, thereby setting an operant conditioning paradigm into motion. Sexual fantasies may be reinforced through masturbation and may then develop into more harmful behaviors (Maletzky, 1991). Sexually inappropriate attitudes and behaviors may also be modeled by peers, relatives, and gang members.

Attachment Disorders

Many people who commit sex offenses show some form of **attachment disorder** (Stirpe, Abracen, Stermac, & Wilson, 2006). John Bowlby's (1969, 1988) pioneering work in attachment theory teaches that childhood attachments to parents are fundamental to normal childhood development. Secure attachments are more likely to result in **self-regulation and self-management** skills. Insecure attachments promote behavioral, emotional, and cognitive dysregulation (see Anechiarico, 2015). Feelings of anxiety, emotional dependency, and anger may result from attachment and separation issues in childhood. Traumatic attachments and separations that involve child abuse may also result in character and neurological disorders. Sometimes outcomes manifest themselves in poorly regulated behaviors, emotional problems, and cognitive distortions that support sex offending behaviors.

Treatment professionals must be concerned with emotional issues that prevent people who commit sex offenses from forming age-appropriate intimate relationships. Intimate relationships may be marred by the low self-esteem that results from poor attachments and social anxiety. Individuals with such emotional problems may develop exploitive relationship styles, where others are used thoughtlessly to meet one's own needs (Marshall & Marshall, 2010). While many, especially those who molest children, are able to acquire sexual and marital partners, their relationships may be conflictual and fearful, with limited sexual satisfaction and poor conflict management skills. Specifically, among people who molest children, many have limited social competency skills with respect to close relationships, limited self-confidence, and empathy failure may also lead to continued offending (Hudson & Ward, 2000). Sex offending can be viewed as a defensive attempt to respond to intimacy and attachment disorders and emotional loneliness (Ward, Hudson, & Marshall, 1995).

Cognitive Distortions

As discussed in Chapter 9, **cognitive distortions** and limitations in cognitive skills are important preludes to dysfunctional behavior. Antisocial attitudes and distorted views of others and one's personal responsibilities are learned. They then stimulate behaviors. These attitudes also allow inappropriate behaviors to continue because the thoughts minimize guilt, anxiety, shame, and other inhibitors. Individuals who commit sex offenses appear to evidence characteristic attitudes, distortions, and beliefs that play a potent role in their behavior. For example, many minimize or distort the damage of their behavior on others (Hudson & Ward, 2000). People who molest children may feel they have actually done some good for their victims. They may view children in sexualized terms or may feel that children are more emotionally safe than adults. Women may be seen as sex objects and a woman saying no to a sexual encounter may be distorted by a person prone to engaging in sexual assault, by "seeing" that a woman's body language is consenting rather than listening to their contradictory verbal refusal (Polaschek & Ward, 2002). People who commit serial rape may also have difficulties reading the social cues of women. Remorse may be minimal.

Neurological Deficits

Neurological deficits, especially those associated with abuse and neglect, are increasingly coming to the attention of treatment providers (see Longo, 2015). Child maltreatment can adversely affect brain development and functioning. For example, victims of physical and sexual abuse are more likely than others to sustain temporal lobe damage. High exposure to cortisol stress hormones may also alter neurons in the hippocampus and limbic areas of the brain (Teicher, 2002). Such assaults to healthy brain development are now known to have permanent effects on such functions as stress management, learning new skills, adapting to adversity, and a host of other self-management skills (Shonkoff et al., 2011; Teicher, 2002).

Mental Health Problems and Developmental Disorders

Although people convicted of sex offenses demonstrate a number of cognitive and emotional problems and many have been diagnosed with post-traumatic stress disorder (PTSD) and personality disorders, most do not suffer from serious forms of mental illness or developmental disorders (Schwartz, 2011). Across a number of studies, approximately 50% of those studied had been diagnosed with mood disorders and approximately one-third suffered from PTSD related to their own victimizations. Serious mental illness (SMI) and developmental disorders, however, are only noted in subgroups of this population.

Typologies of People Convicted of Sex Offenses

As can be seen above, people who commit sex offenses comprise a very heterogeneous group of system-impacted people and should not be treated as if they are all alike. Sorting this long list of traits into knowledge that is of clinical value can pose a challenge to therapists and counselors. It would be rare for all of the attributes listed above to be observable in a single individual. It is perhaps more useful to think of the sex offending population in terms of types or subgroups where individuals are more similar to others in the subgroup than they are to the entire group. Beginning in the 1970s, a number of scholars began to classify individuals who commit sex offenses into typologies that identified meaningful subgroups of this population. Some felt that, for treatment purposes, the types helped to organize a vast array of information into group similarities that more readily lent themselves to treatment approaches.

One important distinction is between people who molest children and people who commit rape. There are distinct typologies for these populations that portray clear emotional and personality differences. Individuals who molest children are more likely to display feelings of inadequacy, limited social skills, isolation and loneliness, and passivity in adult relationships (Marshall, 1993). Individuals who commit rape, on the other hand, offend as an act of anger and hostility (Hudson & Ward, 2000). As might be expected, the cognitive attributions used to rationalize their offenses are different. Those who molest children are more likely to display cognitive distortions that deny the impact of their behavior on childhood victims; people who rape are more likely to blame women and demonstrate distorted impressions of them.

Groth's typology of pedophiles (1979) distinguished between fixated and regressed pedophiles. Fixated pedophiles have been attracted to children rather than to age-appropriate sexual partners for their entire lives. Generally, fixated pedophiles have not reached psychosexual maturity, do not appear to be socially competent, and their attraction to children is compulsive. Fixated individuals typically involve male victims whom they are not related to, and their actions are premeditated.

In contrast, regressed pedophiles have had sexual relationships with age-appropriate partners, but have experienced a number of stressors that have threatened their self-esteem and confidence. Such stressors may include unemployment, marital problems, loneliness, isolation, or illness. Their sexual involvement with children begins in adulthood and is more likely to involve incest with a female victim. Their recidivism rate is not as high as that observed for fixated pedophiles, and they are more likely to feel remorse for their actions.

Although the distinction between fixated and regressed was designed by Groth to represent a continuum, fixated pedophiles are viewed to be more dangerous, more likely to abuse young boys, and to have the most victims and the highest rate of recidivism (Abel & Rouleau, 1990; Marques, Day, Nelson, & West, 1994).

An extensive review done by Lim, Wahab, Kumar, Ibrahim, and Kamaluddin (2021) focused on factors more commonly associated with criminality among people who have sexually abused children. Two terms were used in this review to classify people who have sexually abused children according to the nature of the abuse: those who made physical contact to sexually abuse children and those who used online platforms to sexually abuse children (Lim et al. 2021). Additional differences among contact offenders and child pornography offenders goes beyond opportunity (e.g., greater access to either children or the internet), including higher indicators of antisociality among those who have committed contact child sexual abuse (Babchishin, Hanson, & VanZuylen, 2015). Finally, people who commit child pornography offenses are more likely to have greater victim empathy than contact offenders (Babchishin et al., 2015).

In attempting to characterize another group of people who commit sex offenses, Groth's typology of rapists (1979) stressed that anger, rather than sexual desire, is the primary motivation for rape. People who commit rape were further classified according to the motivation for the anger: (a) discharge of rage and frustration; (b) a display of power, dominance, and authority; (c) a display of anger that is a panic reaction to humiliation; and (d) erotic anger. Psychological profiles of different offenders who have abused children are important to understand and are lacking in most typologies (Lim et al., 2021). Personality traits, cognitive distortion, empathy, and impulsivity are the more established psychological profiles that are often linked to criminality of child sexual abuse (Lim et al., 2021). It has also proven helpful to distinguish between acquaintance and stranger rapes. Most people know their victims, and acquaintance rapes, while still coercive, are typically less violent than stranger rapes (Polaschek, Ward, & Hudson, 1997).

These typologies, while descriptive, must be viewed with caution. First, the types themselves, such as "regressed," invite stereotypes (Schwartz, 2011) that stop short of providing the full etiology of an individual's behavior. Readers will recognize, for example, that they appear to be more descriptive of the offense than the personal attributes that should be addressed in therapeutic settings. For example, there is little reference to childhood abuse and trauma, neurological impairments, attachment disorders, cognitive distortions, emotional and self-regulatory issues because many of these dynamics were put forward by later research conducted after the development of the typologies. Second, traditional typologies have difficulties fitting in complex behaviors of people who have sexually abused children when they are classified into a specific/discrete group (Lim et al., 2021). Finally, the typologies have proven difficult to validate (Schwartz, 2011) and are derived from limited samples of offenders (Lim et al., 2021).

Considerations for Typologies of Females Convicted of Sex Offenses

For the development of crime prevention strategies and rehabilitative services, it is important to understand typologies of people who have offended (Sandler & Freeman, 2007). Matthews, Matthews, and Speltz (1989) devised the first well-known typology specifically for females convicted of sex offenses. This typology included three categories for females convicted of sex offenses: (a) teacher/lover, (b) predisposed, and (c) male-coerced. The most comprehensive typology for females convicted of sex offenses was developed by Vandiver and Kercher (2004), though had similarities with Matthews and colleagues' typology. Vandiver and Kercher (2004) identified six categories of females who committed sex offenses: (1) teacher/lover; (2) non-criminal homosexual offender; (3) sexual predators;

(4) young adult child exploiters; (5) motivated by economic gain offender; and (6) aggressive homosexual offender.

1. Teacher/lover: experiences lack of intimacy and seeks emotional compensation from adolescent victims.

2. Non-criminal homosexual offender: not likely to have a criminal record; victimizes adolescent females.

3. Sexual predator: preference for prepubescent male victims (average 11 years old), most likely to be arrested for subsequent sexual offenses.

4. Young adult child exploiter: most likely to be arrested for sexual offense of young victims (average seven years old); no preference for male or female victims and more likely to be related to victims.

5. Motivated by economic gain offender: typically older female; targets older victims; arrested numerous times; antisocial personality traits present.

6. Aggressive homosexual offender: older female sexually assaulting adult female victims; more likely to have a pre-established relationship with their victim.

Females convicted of sexual offenses are a highly heterogeneous group and research with limited data continues to evolve (Sandler & Freeman, 2007). As a result, these must be viewed with caution.

MODALITIES OF SEX OFFENDING THERAPY

As with other approaches to correctional therapy, there is no one treatment modality that works with everyone who commits sex offenses. Unfortunately, this is a fairly recent observation with respect to the treatment of the sex offending population. During the 1960s and 1970s, therapies over simplistically used single psychotherapeutic techniques such as psychosurgery, psychoanalysis, hypnosis, or behavioral approaches (Lester, 1982). It was generally assumed that decreasing deviant sexual arousal was all that was needed to decrease deviant sexual offending. This task was typically accomplished through physiological strategies and behavioral strategies. By the 1980s and 1990s, the number of needs treated by sex offending programs began to expand to fit the array of needs discussed above. Programs became multimodal and comprehensive. Most now contain an identifiable cognitive behavioral component and most recently have incorporated attention to trauma and neurological issues.

Physiological Approaches

The goal of decreasing deviant sexual arousal was at its worst when treatment involved little more than surgical castration or stereotactic brain surgery, which altered the area of the brain that controlled sex drives (Schorsch, Galedary, Haag, Hauch, & Lohse, 1990). Physical castration procedures began in the late 1800s. More recently they have been opposed by Article 3 of the European Convention of Human Rights, Amnesty International, and the American Civil Liberties Union.

However, chemical castration using antiandrogens such as Depo-Provera or gonadotrophin-releasing hormones such as Leuprorelin, both of which cause a decrease in male sex drive, are taken electively in a number of U.S. states and foreign countries, often in exchange for reduced sentences. In fact, in 2012, more than 100 individuals diagnosed with pedophilia elected to take Leuprorelin in the United Kingdom. In doing so, one claimed that "Without the drugs, I wouldn't stand a chance. With the drugs, it's helped me to have a clear mind. I don't want to see every woman as a sexual object; I want to see her for who she is. I've never been able to do that before. It's always been me, me, me" (Aetkenhead, 2013). Although chemical castration is still used on a voluntary basis in some states, a number of court cases have limited the extent to which people can elect the procedure. Incarcerated people are considered to be a protected class and under enough duress to question whether their consent can be made freely. Although still available as a treatment, few experts would argue that chemical castration or other physiological approaches to reduce arousal is sufficient in itself to treat people convicted of sex offenses. When used, these procedures typically supplement newer psychotherapeutic treatments.

Behavioral Approaches

A number of behavioral strategies have been employed to address deviant sexual arousal. These approaches are described in greater detail in Chapter 8. The behavioral methods use aversive therapies, covert sensitization, aversive imagery, or operant conditioning. Through various approaches, they essentially involve unlearning existing deviant sexual behaviors, which themselves are viewed to be learned behaviors. As with the physiological approaches, however, the behavioral modalities have given way to more modern therapies. When used, they tend to be an adjunctive approach used in conjunction with other therapies, primarily cognitive behavioral modalities. Even the proponents of behavioral modalities are quick to assert that they should be part of a multimodal, holistic treatment process (Maletzky, 1991).

Aversive sex offending therapies seek to help clients associate deviant sexual stimuli and unacceptable sexual behaviors with aversive, unpleasant stimuli. The aversive stimuli may include electrical shocks, vomit-inducing drugs, drugs that cause temporary paralysis, and foul odors (Maletzky, 1991). The treatment process involves presenting the client with a verbal, video, or pictorial image of an unacceptable potential victim that is paired with the unpleasant stimulus. Over time and several repetitions, the child or the behavior comes to be associated with the aversive smell, taste, or other unpleasant stimuli. It is hoped that the association will cause children to lose their attractiveness to potential perpetrators. When used, aversive procedures are used primarily with compulsive behaviors such as pornography, pedophilia, and exhibitionism. They may be used prior to other modalities to stabilize the client until more prosocial behaviors are internalized. Some report their use in combination with other medications (Ball & Seghorn, 2011).

As with other forms of aversion therapy, the use of direct aversive stimuli may be viewed as harmful, painful, and inhumane. Covert sensitization or aversive imagery replaced the need to require clients convicted of sex offenses to directly experience aversive stimuli. Developed by Cautela in the 1960s (Maletzky, 1991), imagery is used to view rather than experience the pairing of unconditioned and conditioned stimuli. Clients may view pictures or hear graphic stories of some imagined sexual act followed by a negative consequence involving perhaps terror, anxiety, or nausea. The clients may also imagine adverse consequences such as being discovered by one's wife or employer or being reported to the police. The scenarios may also include escape scenes where individuals may imagine avoiding or turning away from the sexual behaviors, thereby averting all adverse outcomes.

Aversive conditioning, covert sensitization, and aversive imagery are intense therapies that require a thorough understanding of the client. Scenarios and rehearsals must match the form of deviant arousal, the types of behaviors committed, and the stimuli leading up to them. An intensive period of therapy must be followed by less frequent follow-up treatments, and even then the extinction of the effect is a distinct possibility. If the aversive stimuli are omitted and the client returns to earlier behaviors, the impact of the unconditioned stimulus (e.g., a nauseous odor) will become weaker and weaker until it disappears. Moreover, it may not be that difficult for the client to engage in the old behaviors.

Sources debate the effectiveness of behavioral therapies for clients who commit sex offenses. These approaches have limited databases and "current" treatment programs tend to use more cognitive behavioral approaches (Lösel & Schmucker, 2005).

Cognitive Behavioral Approaches

Since the 1980s, cognitive behavioral therapy and social learning theory approaches have been vital in the treatment of clients convicted of sex offenses. As noted previously, many clients hold beliefs, values, and attitudes that instigate and maintain their behavior; many harbor the dysfunctional attitudes needed to minimize or excuse their harms. It is also necessary to recognize that clients may also adhere to some of the cognitive distortions held by the justice-involved (non-sex offending) population with respect to crime in general. Or they may amplify the inappropriate sexual attitudes heard in society and not be able to keep such cognitions from affecting their behavior (McCrady et al., 2008). One of the intents of cognitive behavioral sex offending groups is to uncover these thinking errors, explain how they affect one's behavior, and correct them. Cognitive behavioral approaches seek to confront cognitive distortions that underlie the problematic behavior (Beech, Bartels, & Dixon, 2013).

Cognitive behavioral sex offending programs also move beyond this cognitive restructuring model to help clients build new thought processes, such as empathy for others, and the social skills needed to engage in prosocial, adult companionship. Murphy (1990) identified three types of cognitive training that were essential to the treatment of clients who commit sex offenses:

1. **Empathy training**: It is important for sex offending groups to introduce group members to the harms of their actions. This may involve therapeutic discussions with representatives from victims services groups. Clients may also be asked to read and discuss written accounts from survivors or view news accounts or other media in therapy sessions.

2. **Role-playing**: The approach will ask the group member to play a role other than himself or herself in a skit. Perhaps he or she will play the role of a police officer, a family member, or a victim, while the therapist or another group member plays the offender. Assuming the role of another human being who was hurt by the client's behavior may greatly assist the client's efforts to understand the feelings of others and to develop empathy for them. Role-playing may also help to identify the cognitive distortions that are expressed in the skit.

3. **Social skills training**: Many sex offending clients have poor social skills. They may experience difficulties talking to peers, especially to women. Additionally, it may be difficult to initiate social opportunities, resolve differences, be assertive, and get needs met in prosocial ways. Without these skills, it is very difficult for them to develop healthy adult relationships. The process of social skills training is outlined in the social learning chapter (Chapter 10). Clients generally practice behaviors that are demonstrated by therapists, other group members, or in videos. Their rehearsals and practice should continue outside of the treatment setting as they practice initiating and maintaining conversations with other adults in real-world settings.

Group members should have the opportunity to discuss their experiences in groups or in individual therapy. These approaches must focus on the formation of relationships and the process of building intimacy with others (Shursen, Brock, & Jennings, 2008), while at the same time being reminded of the rights of others (Ward, 2007).

It should be noted that very few programs only utilize a cognitive behavioral approach to the exclusion of all other possible modalities (Schwartz, 2011). One that came closest to doing so was the Sex Offender Treatment and Evaluation Project (SOTEP), which began in California in 1981. SOTEP was mandated by the California legislature and designed by the California Department of Mental Health. Clients were under the supervision of the state's Department of Corrections and had been convicted of child molestation or rape. In the course of each week in treatment, they participated in one hour of individual therapy, two hours with members of the nursing staff, and four and a half hours of relapse prevention. Additional training included stress management, relaxation techniques, sex education, anger management, and social skills training. Treatment was followed by an additional year in the Sex Offender Aftercare Program.

SOTEP was the subject of a large-scale experimental evaluation. The initial results found favorable results for the treatment groups. However, after more long-term follow-up, the final report indicated that the relapse prevention component was ineffective and that the overall treatment effect was not meaningful (Marques, Wiederanders, Day, Nelson, & Van Ommeren, 2005). Nevertheless, similar programs have actually found reductions in recidivism for the treatment groups (Hanson et al., 2002; Lösel & Schmucker, 2005).

Relapse prevention programs were initially developed for use in substance use therapy as a form of aftercare (Marlatt & Gordon, 1985). These programs were designed to help clients continue to use the skills that they learned in treatment. The model used with sex offending clients is similar in theory to that used with people addicted to illicit substances (see Chapter 12). Toward the end of (and sometimes during) the treatment program, clients are helped to develop a list of the psychological and situational factors that could "trigger" reoffending. The list should be unique to each individual. It should be carried with the client at all times and given to supervising authorities. A very important part of the relapse prevention component involves teaching the clients ways to avoid high-risk situations or cope with high-risk situations that cannot be avoided (Pithers, Marques, Gibat, & Marlatt, 1983). Relapse prevention programs have been a vital part of cognitive behavioral sex offending programs for over 20 years (Laws, Hudson, & Ward, 2000).

A number of concerns have been raised about the efficacy of relapse prevention for people who commit sex offenses. First, there is some concern that, notwithstanding their popularity, relapse prevention programs may not be very effective in reducing recidivism (Laws, 2003). Second, relapse prevention may overestimate the motivation of some clients to change and may not be a good fit for the types of clients who are highly motivated to engage in harmful sexual behaviors and those who conduct a good deal of planning prior to their offenses.

The self-regulation model of sex offending treatment was proposed by Ward and Hudson (2000) as an alternative to relapse prevention, which takes a more complex view of sex offending. According to Ward and Hudson, sex offending clients are much more diverse than the early relapse prevention models assumed. Most importantly, Ward and Hudson faulted traditional relapse prevention models for assuming that all clients are motivated to stop when, in fact, many want to continue to engage in sexually exploitive behavior. A key factor in their behavior involves their self-regulation skills and their goals. Self-regulation enables individuals to engage in goal-directed behaviors. Goals may involve attaining desired situations or feelings (acquisitional goals) or avoiding undesirable ones (inhibitory goals). Regardless of which goal is desired, the goal-directed behaviors involve cognitive scripts that guide the behavior, and a client who is engaged in choosing, monitoring, modifying, and evaluating his or her behavior. All of these actions fit well within the cognitive behavioral model of offending: goals, cognitive scripts, feelings, reactions, and evaluations of how well one's behavior and thoughts worked to achieve desired goals.

According to Ward and Hudson (2000), there are three types of symptoms of dysfunctional self-regulation:

1. Individuals may lose control over their emotions or their behavior and begin to act in a disinhibited manner.

2. Individuals may attempt to control their behavior but do so in a way that is not effective.

3. Individuals may possess effective strategies of self-control but direct these skills toward antisocial goals.

When these dysfunctional modes of self-regulation are combined with the clients' goals (acquisitional or inhibitory) and goal-directed strategies, four separate strategies to sex offending are revealed. The strategies also depict distinctions among clients in terms of their cognitive distortions, degree of offense planning, evaluations of their actions (favorable or unfavorable), and the types of situations that lead to unlawful sexual encounters. The four pathways are as follows:

Avoidant-Passive Pathway: Individuals offending within this pathway do not wish to commit a sexual offense; their goal actually is to avoid it. However, they cannot exercise effective coping strategies, and are likely to engage in negative thought processes that then disinhibit behavior and cause them to lose control and act impulsively. They do not have a good deal of confidence in their ability to control their behavior. Their offenses are planned covertly, and they fail to anticipate times when they are getting too close to high-risk situations. Their desires make them anxious, and they may try to distract themselves from them. They experience guilt and anxiety after the offense. Because sexual desire, excitement, and anxiety are not managed, their recidivism potential is high. Individuals operating in the avoidant-passive pathway are more appropriate for the traditional relapse prevention model because they seek to avoid inappropriate sexual behavior.

Avoidant-Active Pathway: This person may also be appropriate to the traditional relapse prevention model because he or she also wants to avoid the commission of a sex offense. This individual makes an active attempt to control reactions that threaten loss of control (e.g., arousal or fantasy). In this case, the individual expects that his or her control strategies will work, but they do not, and, in some cases, they increase the likelihood of an offense. Often negative emotions may instigate an offense. For example, the individual could be angry about an insult or a rejection. Anger might have been amplified by alcohol. He may have used pornography to redirect his urge away from an actual victim, but he is only encouraging the urge.

Approach-Automatic Pathway: This individual has an acquisitional goal to commit a sex offense and does not desire to avoid it. However, the behavior is impulsive and well based on a learned cognitive schema that supports the behavior. These may involve negative attitudes toward women or a sense of entitlement. The offense is activated by situational stimuli that the individual may not fully understand. The offense may also have been planned in a crude manner. The individual looks forward to the event and derives pleasure following it.

Approach-Explicit Pathway: The sexual assault represents an acquisitional goal for this person as well. This individual is capable of self-regulation. However, his self-regulatory skills are directed toward antisocial acquisition goals. Sexual aggression is well entrenched in this individual's belief and value system. Offenses are planned deliberately and sometimes meticulously. The individual may groom the victim over time, offer gifts, and lure them into close proximity. These individuals also react positively to the incident.

These types portray divergent pathways to sex offending, and not all of them are amenable to the traditional relapse prevention approach. For example, motivations inherent in the two approach types identify a client who is not motivated to avoid a relapse. A good deal of treatment targeted to beliefs, values, and empathy training appear warranted for these individuals. Additionally, at least one of the types, the Approach Explicit Pathway, already possesses the self-management skills that relapse prevention is designed to teach. Treatments also must recognize that the nature of the cognitive distortions addressed in treatment must differ according to whether the client is classified into an avoidant or an approach pathway. The attitudes evidenced by the approach model are supportive of sexually exploitive behavior. They depict a well-entrenched lifestyle that the client is not ashamed of. Treatment would entail changing these attitudes along with other dynamics of the offense pathway such as deviant sexual arousal.

Increased coping skills may be an appropriate approach for avoidant types. Avoidant types likely will need to develop greater self-esteem, intimacy skills, and self-efficacy (confidence that their behavior is under their control). Individuals demonstrating an avoidant-passive approach will need to have attention called to the fact that their denial is not working; they will need to develop new strategies for preventing relapses. These clients may not need to be motivated to change their behaviors, since they already have the desire to stop.

Incorporating Treatments for Brain Injuries and Trauma

In recognizing and treating diverse types of sex offenses, the self-regulation approach brings us back to statements made earlier in this chapter: People convicted of sex offenses are a truly diverse and heterogeneous group of individuals. In fact, while we have discussed the treatment of behavior, cognitions, and social skills, we have said little about such causal factors as attachment disorder, brain injuries, and neurological disorders resulting from abuse and attachment disorders. Such disorders in themselves may set off the self-regulation issues seen in the sex offending population.

With these far more complex causal connections coming to our attention in more recent years, is it essential that we stay entrenched in the cognitive behavioral perspective that targets only thinking and skill sets, or is it important to branch out to other treatment modalities?

In one sense, cognitive behavioral approaches are appropriate for many clients with neurological disorders. In fact, concrete repetition, behavior rehearsal, and generalization to increasingly more difficult cognitive and behavioral processes may be very appropriate for clients with neurological issues. This approach clearly involves a long and laborious learning process compared with the efficiency with which a young child learns, but it is key to the development of new neural pathways (Arden & Linford, 2009).

Another approach for some types of neurological issues resulting from abuse and trauma is seen in **eye movement desensitization and reprocessing (EMDR;** Shapiro, 1995). EMDR is noted to be a valuable tool for improving brain functioning following trauma. Although not a therapy in itself, EMDR often helps clients to be more emotionally available to ongoing therapy and future emotional attachments.

It may also make sense to consider modalities that more finely target attachment and dysregulation, such as **dialectical behavioral therapy (DBT;** Dimeff & Linehan, 2001). The focus of DBT remains on skills relevant to emotional, behavioral, and cognitive regulation. DBT focuses on stress management, distress acceptance, and emotional control. Clients are taught skills of interpersonal effectiveness. The program also uses mindfulness and meditation to train the mind to be calm and focused and to tolerate stress without making matters worse. This approach represents a departure from general correctional programs focused on criminogenic needs, but one can see the appropriateness of such strategies to Ward and Hudson's avoidant types. One sees similar directions in emerging programs for system-involved women (see Chapter 13), especially those dealing with depression and trauma (Covington, 2003). In an overview of sex offending programs, Schwartz (2011) reminds us that most programs that describe themselves as cognitive behavioral programs are really a blend of modalities.

Additional Considerations for Treatment of Females

Risk-need-responsivity principles are used for treating the female population similarly to the male population, but with greater emphasis on general recidivism due to females typically having a lower risk of sexually reoffending. Interventions also place an emphasis on preventing child abuse given the high possibility of caregiver roles among females (Cortoni, 2015). Another focal point of treatment should be historical risk factors, which more strongly affect females who commit sexual offenses compared to males who commit sex offenses. These include prior victimization (trauma interventions), substance abuse, and mental health problems (Andrews & Bonta, 2010a; Cortoni, 2015). Women who commit sexual offenses require stronger and more meaningful social connections for treatment to be effective. Treatment must target factors that contributed to their initial offending, such as low self-esteem, unhealthy relationships, unhealthy sexual expression, anger management problems, and unhealthy communication styles (Andrews & Bonta, 2010a; Cortoni, 2015). Other considerations identified for the treatment of females fall into four broad domains: (1) cognitive: address cognitive distortions, beliefs about sexual offending, address gender stereotypes; (2) emotional: regulate effective emotional responses to situations; (3) sexual: healthy sexual regulation and sexual interest; and (4) relational: increase healthy relationships and build coping mechanisms (Cortoni, 2015).

Additional Considerations for Treatment of Juveniles

Juveniles who commit sexual offenses encompass a multitude of unique personality traits, psychopathologies, demographic features, and childhood histories (Fox & DeLisi, 2018). Treatment of juveniles should be individualized and based on the etiology of the sexual behavior problem. Cognitive behavioral strategies are commonly used with juveniles and some areas of treatment include: social skills training, impulse control, role-playing, teaching healthy sexuality, improving anger management skills, challenging and changing thinking errors (cognitive distortions), increasing empathy for victims, and relapse prevention (Ryan, Hunter, & Murrie, 2012). Trauma considerations are of importance when discussing the treatment of juveniles who commit sexual offenses. The treatment of juveniles who commit sexual offenses is not the same as treatment of adults, and therefore, should not be reflected/implemented as such.

KEY COMPONENTS OF SEX OFFENDING THERAPY

The Therapeutic Alliance

The importance of the therapeutic alliance between a client and a therapist has been discussed at many points throughout this book. The quality of that relationship is key to whether therapeutic change occurs. In the case of many sex offending clients, however, the importance of the therapeutic alliance gains added significance (Marshall et al., 2003; Yates, 2004). As discussed earlier, many are diagnosed with attachment disorders, experience difficult peer and adult relationships, and have poor relationship skills. Attachment and intimacy deficits then may affect self-regulation and create narcissistic defenses, where one's needs are not met in mutually reciprocal relationships but rather through the exploitation of others (Anechiarico, 2015).

Because the therapeutic alliance may represent a client's first introduction to a healthy relationship, it is an extremely important vehicle for change. The therapeutic relationship is an opportunity for clients to experience themselves being understood by another person and self-affirmed. Defenses may soften and begin to yield to mutual understanding and new cognitive orientations. As a healthy relationship is built, needs are met in reciprocal styles and a more stable self-esteem may form. The same may be said for relational and emotional processing in group settings. Good therapeutic groups provide secure connections to others, a feeling of being understood, and opportunities to voice and receive empathic responses. These provide attachment-building processes and the development of new relational styles that may then provide a more secure foundation for later intimate relationships. They also help to build the confidence needed to initiate future relationships.

Notwithstanding the importance of the therapeutic relationship to sex offending therapy, a number of professional requirements make this a more difficult relationship to develop than standard therapeutic relationships. In contrast to other counseling situations, sex offense counselors and therapists cannot offer much in the way of client confidentiality to their clients. Sex offending clients are expected to waive the right to the confidentiality of most if not all of the content that would typically be held to be confidential in a counseling setting. An increasing number of jurisdictions courts, correctional agencies, social services, law enforcement, child welfare, social services, mental health, and healthcare agencies use the information in a collaborative manner to promote public safety. Another challenge is that the sex offending client treatment often is not voluntary. Clients are often pressured into treatment by legal mandates or the pressure to avoid a stricter sentence. Once in treatment, treatment goals may be reached by agents of the court or criminal justice agencies rather than through collaboration between client and therapist.

Ethics do not exist in a vacuum, however. The profession maintains that clients be informed of the nature of the programs, procedures, and interventions as well as their risks and benefits. Treatment decisions should be informed by formal interviews and assessments leading to the formation of an individualized treatment plan. The client should be informed of all treatment goals and afforded opportunities to have questions answered. Finally, a number of states formally recognize the specialized nature of sex offending interventions and require that counselors and therapists undergo specialized training and certification (Center for Sex Offender Management [CSOM], 2008).

Assessments

Sex offending clients require a thorough assessment of their background and needs prior to the beginning of therapy. They present treatment programs with a complex array of needs and characteristics. At the same time, there are many program modalities that can be matched to these needs but matching the wrong needs to the wrong modalities is likely to be harmful. For example, therapists working with the self-regulation model (described before) must conduct assessments needed to classify clients into one of the four pathways prior to beginning treatment (Yates & Kingston, 2011). In another example, the State of Maine's RULE program provides treatments in eight domains: physical (e.g., mental illness, neurological); behavioral (e.g., deviant sexual arousal); emotional (e.g., anger, fear, grief); cognitive (distortions and faulty coping skills); family dynamics; interpersonal (social skills); societal messages; and spiritual. A thorough assessment is needed to determine which clients will receive which treatment options (Schwartz, 2015).

When assessing people convicted of sex offenses, the information gained can be grouped into four areas (Lester, 2014):

1. *social history* (i.e., employment history; hobbies and interests; family relationships, composition, attachments, and structure; significant life events; and ethnicity);

2. *psychological and social problems* (i.e., history of trauma and abuse; psychiatric diagnoses; substance use, emotional difficulties, history of non-sexual offending and antisocial behavior);

3. *sexual development* (i.e., sexual history and experience; attitudes toward sex; sexual knowledge and preference; sexual dysfunction; age of onset of puberty and adjustment to puberty; sexual and intimate relationships; and history of sexual victimization); and

4. *sexual patterns of offending* (i.e., history of sexual offending; attitudes toward the victim and the offense; masturbatory and sexual fantasies; use of force and physical aggression; willingness to engage in treatment; and ability to specify treatment goals) (Maletzky, 1991).

For example, research suggests that the type of masturbatory fantasy (age-appropriate vs. deviant) relates to the factors such as presence of hostility, likelihood of recidivism, type of offense, and treatment prospects (DiGiorgia-Miller, 2007; Looman, Serran, & Marshall, 2011).

A clinical interview is the most widely used technique to obtain information about the client, and it should be the first step of treatment. Interviewers should be aware that sex offending clients may use post-offense rationalizations and distort reports of their offenses (Beech et al., 2013). For example, they may blame others, including victims, for their acts. They may minimize their actions by taking responsibility for only parts of an incident (Maletzky, 1991). Interviewers should also expect denial, rationalizations, and claims of seduction. Treatment should address these types of defenses and seek to encourage the client to deal with them and other problems openly and honestly. Interviewers may learn of more offenses than what appears on official records. Schwartz (2015) observes that it is not unusual for previously undisclosed victims to come to the attention of treatment providers during the interview and over the course of treatment.

The assessment should not rely solely on the clinical interview. Assessors should also obtain additional information from significant others, including wives, girlfriends, and family members (Maletzky, 1991). Additional records should prove useful. These may include prior psychological and medical records as well as police and victim reports. When examining these records, evaluators should search for patterns of disruptive behavior, antisocial acts, inappropriate sexual incidents, use of violence or force during the acts, and the duration and frequency of the acts (Maletzky, 1991).

A thorough psychiatric examination should also take place. Clients with psychiatric disorders must receive treatment for mental health disorders in addition to treatment for the psychological and behavioral problems associated more specifically with the sexual behavior. As noted later in this section, the clinical interview should also be accompanied by risk and needs assessments designed specifically for people who commit sex offenses.

Once a more common feature of sex offending assessments and treatment programs, the penile plethysmography (PPG) has come into some disfavor and has undergone a number of recent legal and ethical challenges. Penile plethysmography (also known as phallometry) has been used to determine arousal patterns in male clients who are exposed to sexual content in the form of pictures, movies, or audio accounts (Maletzky, 1991), by measuring penile erection responses (Marshall & Fernandez, 2000). PPG has several problems associated with it. First, it is by no means clear that sexual offending clients differ from non-offending clients in penile responses to deviant sexual stimuli. For example, Marshall and Fernandez (2000) share studies resulting in inconsistent differences between clients convicted of rape and non-offending clients. In fact, when considering differences between these two populations, there is better evidence for differences in social skills, intimacy, loneliness, self-esteem, and cognitive distortions than in PPG responses (Marshall, 1996). Sex offending clients are more likely to differ from each other than from non-offending populations (Sperber, 2004).

Second, there are ethical problems associated with its use. There is concern that showing deviant sexual stimuli may actually encourage deviant sexual tendencies rather than treat them. Moreover, the stimuli or images shown to the client while participating in PPG are degrading to women and depict children as sexual objects. Adolescent male clients are particularly worthy of concern in this regard (Marshall, 1996). Third, in a ruling that questioned the appropriateness of the PPG unless narrowly tailored to a compelling government interest, the U.S. Court of Appeals for the Second Circuit recently vacated a lower court ruling requiring a person convicted of a sex offense to submit to PPG testing. The three-judge appellate court wrote that the PPG crossed the line of humane treatment and civil liberties (*United States v. McLaurin*, 731 F.3d 258 [2d Cir. 2013]).

Polygraph techniques, on the other hand, are used more frequently with people convicted of sex offenses. Post-adjudication polygraph examinations are fairly commonly used for purposes of managing adult and juvenile sex offending populations. The polygraph serves a surveillance function that allows criminal justice agencies to determine whether the individual is engaging in any ongoing sexual offenses. For purposes of post-conviction supervision, the polygraph is used to varying degrees in the federal system and in all states. People may have to submit to one to six tests per year. The polygraph's use as a preconviction tool for evidentiary purposes is less common.

Perhaps carelessly termed "the lie detector" by a San Francisco newspaper in the 1920s, the polygraph nevertheless records physiological responses caused by the autonomic nervous systems (ANS). The ANS automatically creates physiological responses when one becomes anxious as a result of misrepresenting one's actions or becomes even modestly concerned about telling a lie. The polygraph provides a way to record these electrodermal, cardiovascular, respiratory activities over the course of a series of questions posed by the examiner. Questions are skillfully formulated and scored by trained and certified examiners. They are individualized to the circumstance of each individual and begin with a pretest that sets a baseline for further questioning.

Notwithstanding its frequent use, the polygraph also has been the subject of a number of legal challenges (see Blackstone, 2015). Some famous individuals have actually passed the polygraph, including Gary Ridgeway, the Green River Killer, and the double agent who spied for the Soviet Union, Aldrich Aimes. Its accuracy is the subject of much scientific debate (see National Academy of Sciences [NAS], 2003).

Over time, a number of classification schemes have also been devised to assist the process of matching clients to appropriate treatments. Several have been presented before as typologies. These also appear to be coming into disfavor. Although it is abundantly clear that not all sex offending clients are alike, a number of sources suggest that many clients could be classified into more than one type or could change types over time (Robertiello & Terry, 2007; Schwartz, 2011). For example, Heil, Ahlmeyer, and Simons (2003) found that 78% of people who molested children also admitted to sexually victimizing adults. In their review of classification schemes that have been proposed for people convicted of rape, people who molest children, sex offending females, sex offending juveniles, and people convicted of cyber offenses, Robertiello and Terry also noted that the schemes have not changed much over the years. Alternatively, actuarial assessments with ratings on numerous characteristics may prove much more useful for treatment purposes than single types because the assessments better fix the complex array of sex offending client characteristics.

Although emerging sex offending therapies appear to be more specialized than most correctional treatment approaches, many authorities continue to recommend they follow the risk-needs-responsivity (RNR) approach (Anechiarico, 2015; Schwartz, 2015). That is: (1) intensive services should be reserved for those at highest risk to reoffend (the risk principle); (2) the needs that should be addressed are those in which treatment has been found to reduce recidivism (the needs principle); and (3) interventions should match client learning styles and their capabilities to successfully participate in programming (the responsivity principle).

Adherence to the risk principle requires the use of valid risk assessment instruments. Risk assessment has become an important tool for correctional practitioners (see Chapter 6). It was recognized early on, however, that some sex offending clients score low on general correctional risk assessments such as the LSI-R even though they may be at high risk of committing additional sex offenses (Hanson & Bussiere, 1998). Although many sex offending clients look like a typical justice-involved client, many more do not. It is not unusual for program participants to include the clergy, medical doctors, wealthy businesspeople, college professors, and bankers (Schwartz, 2015). In response, several risk assessment tools have been developed specifically for people convicted of sex offenses.

Some of the risk factors for sex offending clients are similar to those for non-sex offending clients. However, researchers have noted the value of the following risk factors, which are unique to people who commit sex offenses: (1) prior sex offenses; (2) involvement of stranger victims; and (3) the existence of any male victims (Hanson & Bussiere, 1998). Positive responses to these items place sex offending clients at higher risk of committing more offenses. To date, several static sex offending risk assessments have been developed, including: (1) the Static-99 (Hanson & Thornton, 1999); (2) the Static-99R (Helmus, Thornton, Hanson, & Babchishin, 2012); (3) the Rapid Risk Assessment for Sexual Offense Recidivism (RRASOR; Hanson, 1997); and (4) the Sex Offender Risk Appraisal Guide (SORAG; Quinsey, Harris, Rice, & Cormier, 1998).

While these static risk assessments are useful in helping to determine supervision levels and whether a client needs to be in intensive treatment, they do nothing to recommend specific sex offending treatments. In other words, they do not identify dynamic risk/needs factors that can be addressed by treatment programs. This realization led to the development

TABLE 14.1 General Correctional Client Dynamic Risk/Needs Assessment compared to a Sex Offending Client Dynamic Risk/Needs Assessment

General Correctional Client Dynamic Risk Factors (LSI-R)	Sex Offending Client Dynamic Risk Need Factors (Stable 2007)
Education/Employment	Significant social relationships
Financial	Capacity for stable relationships
Family/Marital	Emotional identification with children
Accommodations	Hostility toward women
Leisure/Recreation	General social rejection
Companions	Lack of concern for others
Alcohol/Drug	Impulsivity
Emotional/Personal	Poor problem-solving skills
Antisocial attitudes	Negative emotionality Sex drive/sex preoccupation Sex as coping Deviant sexual preferences Cooperation with supervision

of the Sex Offender Need Assessment Rating (SONAR; Hanson & Harris, 2000) and its most recent version the Stable 2007 (Hanson, Harris, Scott, & Helmus, 2007). Such dynamic risk/needs instruments continue to include the static predictors of recidivism but add consideration for needs that predispose clients to future offenses. Table 14.1 compares the dynamic risk/needs factors pertinent to general correctional populations (as noted on the LSI-R) with those contained on the Stable 2007. In fact, few of the attributes listed on the Stable 2007 also appear on the LSI-R. Therefore, although the needs principle still pertains to sex offending clients, a unique group of dynamic risk factors must be addressed.

Assessment of Females Who Commit Sexual Offenses

The use of assessment tools that are specific to females is important and should be utilized whenever possible. However, there are currently not many validated gender-specific risk assessment tools for this population (Cortoni, Hanson, & Coache, 2010), and there is considerable need for one. Notably, sexual risk assessments are typically normed on males who commit sexual offenses and then applied to females who commit sexual offenses (Cortoni & Gannon, 2016). The Level of Service Inventory Revised (LSI-R) is used among the offending female population to measure protective factors and general recidivism (Vess, 2011). The use of dynamic and static risk assessment measures with the female population that are normed for males (listed in above section) should be on a case-by-case basis and recognized as not validated with the female population (Cortoni & Gannon, 2016).

Assessment of Juveniles Who Commit Sexual Offenses

The risk-need-responsivity model is also used with juveniles who commit sexual offenses as guidance for treatment/intervention needs. General recidivism is assessed and considered when recommending treatment needs in juveniles who commit sexual offenses. It is important to note that the same risk assessment tools that are used in adults are not best practice if used with juveniles. The three most commonly used sexual risk assessments used with juveniles are the Juvenile Sex Offender Assessment Protocol-II (JSOAP-II), the Estimate of Risk of Adolescent Sexual Offense Recidivism (ERASOR), and the Juvenile Sexual Offense Recidivism Risk Assessment Tool-II (JSORRAT-II; Rich, 2017).

Containment Approaches

Whether they are programs for sex offending clients or the general correctional population, successful treatment programs should take place in correctional settings that provide an appropriate degree of structure and supervision over clients. In other words, high-risk clients are not only recommended to receive intensive psychological and psychoeducational services, but these must take place within a level of supervision and containment appropriate to their risk level.

Not surprisingly, this reasoning is amplified for sex offending clients. Some maintain that treatment is not enough. For example, some treatment providers observe that "without the leverage of the criminal justice system's consequences for noncompliance, they could not work with sex offenders" (English, 2004). In response, a number of states have adopted containment and civil commitment laws to assure the adequate risk management of people who commit sex offenses. These laws seek to incapacitate the individual through a repertoire of criminal justice sanctions, services, and policies, including sex offender registration and proximity restrictions, mandatory identification techniques including mandatory DNA testing, specialized probation and parole caseloads, mandatory post-conviction polygraph examination, electronic monitoring, longer periods of confinement, and multiagency community partnerships. The clearest example of these approaches exists in a supervision model called the Containment Approach, which was designed by researchers at the Colorado Division of Criminal Justice (English, Jones, & Patrick, 2003). The Containment Approach is a five-pronged approach to managing sex offending clients that includes:

1. an underlying philosophy that places a priority on victim protection, reparation, and public safety;
2. reliance upon multiagency coordination and cooperation;
3. a supervision model that emphasizes risk management individualized to the needs of each client;
4. a consistent set of multiagency policies and protocols; and
5. quality control mechanisms addressed to program monitoring and evaluation.

Interagency cooperation, from the standpoint of the containment model, involves sex offending treatment programs, law enforcement, probation and parole agencies, schools, hospital and emergency room personnel, attorneys, social services, rape crisis centers and other victim advocates, polygraph examiners, researchers, and departments of corrections (see Figure 14.1). Case management is tailored to each client. However, the privilege of

FIGURE 14.1 A sign directing visitors to the Farmington Correctional Center and Missouri Sexual Offender Treatment Center. Missouri's controversial sex offending rehabilitation and treatment program is a civil involuntary commitment program for the treatment of sexually violent predators.
Source: AP Photo/James A. Finley.

community supervision typically involves the client's waiving his or her right to confidentiality so that information about risk and treatment issues can be shared across various community stakeholders. Typically, three functions share important information in a synergistic and collaborative manner: (1) criminal justice supervision; (2) treatment providers; and (3) polygraph examiners. The shared information includes such matters as preferred victims, offense patterns and history, and the frequencies of deviant sexual arousal. The teams design requirements and restrictions, policies regarding home visits, monitoring requirements, and consequences for non-compliance. Treatment providers are expected to provide information on the client's offense sequence and high-risk situations. As noted earlier, this is information that in many therapeutic situations would be considered to be confidential. Containment models are expected to provide quick responses to changes in an individual's risk status as well as ongoing verification of the individual's behavior and reports of any minimization and denials of behavior. Post-conviction polygraph monitoring is used in most states and is admissible by judicial discretion in state courts in at least 21 states.

Of far more concern than the community containment models are the sex offending **civil commitment** laws that currently are operational in more than 20 states. These began in Washington state in 1990 following a series of sex crimes that resulted in the murder of several children. In most of these programs, people convicted of sex offenses can be civilly committed, or subjected to selective incapacitation, if three criteria are present: (1) the individual has committed a qualifying sex crime; (2) is suffering from a mental abnormality or personality disorders that likely will cause him or her to commit future sex crimes; and (3) is high risk for recidivism. In a number of the states with civil commitment statutes, few if any people have been released since committed. For example, in Minnesota's program, only two of 700 clients had been conditionally released as of 2012 (Brant, Wilson, & Prescott, 2015). In a study that sought to estimate the recidivism potential of the Minnesota clients, Duwe (2014) estimated that only 18% would actually commit a new offense. The inaccuracy of the prediction is largely due to the discretionary nature of two of the three commitment criteria: (1) identifying who has a mental abnormality that likely will cause him or her to commit future sex crimes; and (2) determining who is at high risk for recidivism with a high enough degree of certainty to warrant such long-term commitments. The civil commitment laws are under legal review in a number of jurisdictions.

The Good Lives Model

The Good Lives Model (GLM; Ward & Gannon, 2006) is a holistic framework of offender rehabilitation. The GLM is a strengths-based approach to offender rehabilitation and focuses on building capabilities and strengths in people to reduce their risk of reoffending. The framework is responsive to individuals' particular abilities, interests, and goals and has been adopted as a framework by several treatment programs for people who commit sexual offenses.

According to the GLM, people offend because they are attempting to secure some kind of valued outcome in their life. Therefore, a primary treatment goal is to conceptually identify and understand what a good life is for the client, formulate socially acceptable ways to obtain goals of having a good life, and translate it into a good lives rehabilitation plan. Treatment is individually tailored to assist in implementation of a client's specific good lives intervention plan, while addressing criminogenic needs that might be blocking "goods fulfilment." Good lives rehabilitation plans are collaboratively created with practitioners, and interventions might include building internal capacity and skills, building external resources, and social supports.

The model assumes that all individuals have similar aspirations and needs, and the overall goal is to help each person acquire the skills required to succeed and thrive in the world. A core theoretical assumption is that criminal behavior represents a maladaptive attempt to meet life values (Ward & Stewart, 2003). A strong emphasis is placed on the agency of the person, with a requirement for clients to actively pursue satisfying their good lives plan and values in a manner that does not harm others. Therefore, rehabilitation is focused on increasing skills, knowledge, and opportunities for them to meet their needs.

THE EFFECTIVENESS OF SEX OFFENDING TREATMENT PROGRAMS

The common view of sex offending clients is that they cannot be treated. Early scientific studies supported that view (see Furby, Weinrott, & Blackshaw, 1989; Quinsey, Harris, Rice, & LaLumiere, 1993). With the advent of new cognitive behavioral approaches, however, this opinion is changing. One of the first studies to show that some programs were effective was a meta-analysis conducted by Hall (1995). In recent years, meta-analyses have been viewed by many as the "gold standard" for determining whether a program is effective in reducing recidivism. This is because reductions in recidivism or lack thereof are summarized across studies. A summary statistic called the effect size then is used to represent the "consensus of opinion." A strong effect size shows not only that a certain type of program was effective, but that it was consistently effective or effective in more than one setting. Hall found that 19% of the clients who completed treatment recidivated, compared to 29% of the comparison group subjects. Cognitive behavioral programs and those using hormonal treatments were found to be more effective than behavioral programs. It should be noted, however, that Hall's review included only 12 published studies. Other published studies had to be eliminated because either there were no comparison groups or because the groups had too few participants.

In later years, more experimental studies were conducted and produced more synthesized research findings. These converged on the observation that the recidivism rates of treated sex offending clients are lower than those for clients who are untreated (Aos et al., 2006; Gallagher, Wilson, Hirschfield, Coggeshall, & MacKenzie, 1999; Hanson et al., 2002; Hanson, Bourgon, Helmus, & Hodgson, 2009; Lösel & Schmucker, 2005).

The studies conducted by Hanson and his associates are especially instructive. The first, conducted in 2002, was a meta-analysis of 43 studies. In total, the researchers compared 5,078 treated clients to 4,376 untreated ones and found that the treated ones had a recidivism rate of 12%, versus 17% for the untreated clients. Although results were favorable, treatment effects for sex offending clients are not as strong as those for programs for the general correctional population. A later study conducted by Hanson and his associates involved only 22 studies. These studies afforded an opportunity to examine whether the principles of effective intervention (risk, needs, and responsivity; Bonta & Andrews, 2017) differentiated successful programs from unsuccessful ones. Generally, results were more favorable for programs following the needs and responsivity principles than those that did not. Adherence to the risk principle did not appear to matter. Hanson observed that the more successful programs took place after 1980, with the advent of cognitive behavioral and relapse prevention programs.

A few precautions should be noted. First, many of the evaluations omitted clients who did not complete the programs from the samples. Second, there do not appear to be any studies in which large, statewide interventions were found to be successful. Large-scale programs may be losing control of program quality as they go to scale in statewide interventions. This was surely the case in the California SOTEP program discussed earlier (Marques et al., 2005). Finally, it must be understood that the effect sizes are more pertinent to the treatment programs than to the containment and civil commitment programs. For example, a recent study of the restrictive laws in New York state found that they had no appreciable impact on the incidence of sex offending by first-time or previously convicted sex offending clients (Sandler, Freeman, & Socia, 2008). This would not be altogether surprising if the programs represented an exclusive reliance on punishment and surveillance. Punishment and surveillance programs are widely known to have a limited effect on recidivism, unless they include strong rehabilitative components (Aos et al., 2006; Cullen & Gendreau, 2000).

Effectiveness of Treating Juveniles

Some form of treatment is generally provided to juveniles who commit sexual offenses (Lab, Shields, & Schondel, 1993), though it may range from services provided in the community to residential intervention, or even being placed in lockdown facilities where treatment is available. The best method of measuring the effectiveness of a treatment is to statistically compare sexual recidivism rates for those who completed a treatment program and those who received no treatment. However, very few studies have been conducted to evaluate the effectiveness of treatment with juveniles who have commit a sexual offense (Worling & Curwen, 2000). A meta-analysis based on nine studies completed by Reitzel and Carbonell (2006) on the effectiveness of treatment for juveniles who have committed a sexual offense yielded an effect size of 0.43, which is considered a moderate effect size. This result indicates that juveniles who received treatment compared to those who did not were statistically less likely to recidivate. Meta-analyses are not without criticisms and limitations. However, research supports lower recidivism among juveniles who commit sexual offenses compared to adults (Lobanov-Rostovsky, 2015).

CONCLUSION

Options for treating people convicted of sex offenses have improved considerably over the past 30 years, and sex offending treatment continues to be a rapidly changing field. Just the same, sex offending clients continue to be considered a challenging population to treat. They, themselves, bring many of the challenges, but sex offending client management programs bring additional roadblocks that treatment practitioners must work around. These include waivers of confidentiality and mandatory treatment requirements, societal mythologies and stereotypes, and political obstacles. While it is no longer entirely accurate to assert that people who commit sex offenses are untreatable, treatment programs have become expensive and highly specialized. Additionally, treatment practitioners often must be highly credentialed and prepared to work as team members with other community specialists and stakeholders.

Discussion Questions

1. Identify and discuss some of the ways that sex offending therapies have improved since the 1980s.

2. How might behavioral and physiological treatments be used today?

3. In what way do attachment disorders affect people who commit sex offenses?

4. Is it enough to require sex offending clients to participate in cognitive behavioral programs and nothing else?

5. Some believe that sex offending clients can be cured through punishment and "get tough" strategies alone. Do you agree?

6. What problems with relapse prevention does the self-regulation model attempt to resolve?

7. What are some differences between general typologies and typologies of females specifically?

8. What types of criticisms have been voiced about the PPG and polygraph examination?

9. Typology, assessment, and treatment of juveniles who commit sexual offenses has long been mirrored after adults. What are the key differences between juveniles and adults who commit sex offenses?

10. How effective is sex offending treatment in comparison to general correctional treatment programs?

11. Why might treatment practitioners choose not to give sex offending clients the same risk assessment as they give to non-sex offending clients?

GLOSSARY OF KEY TERMS

attachment disorder   a disorder that arises from the unavailability of normal socializing care and attention from primary caregivers in early childhood; individuals with insecure attachments often exhibit poorly regulated behaviors, emotional problems, and cognitive distortions that support sex offending behaviors

behavioral strategies   various approaches to address deviant sexual arousal (e.g., aversive therapies, covert sensitization, aversive imagery, or operant conditioning) that involve unlearning existing deviant sexual behaviors, which themselves are viewed to be learned behaviors

civil commitment   a legal process through which people convicted of sex offenses are incapacitated through a repertoire of criminal justice sanctions, services, and policies, including sex offender registration and proximity restrictions, mandatory identification techniques including mandatory DNA testing, specialized probation and parole caseloads, mandatory post-conviction polygraph examination, electronic monitoring, longer periods of confinement, and multiagency community partnerships

client confidentiality a standard principle in the therapeutic relationship in which counselors and therapists are not permitted to reveal information about their clients to a third party without the consent of the client or a clear legal reason

clinical interview an important first step in the treatment process that involves the counselor or therapist asking the client questions to obtain pertinent information about them

cognitive behavioral therapy (CBT) focuses on confronting and changing cognitive distortions and behavior

cognitive distortions exaggerated or irrational thought patterns involved in the onset and perpetuation of psychopathological states, especially those more influenced by psychosocial factors

containment the action of keeping something harmful under control or within limits

dialectical behavior therapy (DBT) type of cognitive behavioral therapy that focuses on teaching regulation skills such as stress management, distress acceptance, and emotional control

dynamic risk/needs risk factors and needs that are changeable throughout the life course and can be addressed by treatment programs

empathy training teaching perspectives and experiences of others, including possible impacts of harmful behavior

eye movement desensitization and reprocessing (EMDR) a tool that is used to target trauma memories while also focusing on external stimuli

neurological deficits abnormality of a body area, such as the brain, spinal cord, muscles, or nerves

polygraph a tool used to detect physiological responses in the body, used as a lie detector

relapse prevention a model originally developed for substance abuse to aid in identifying high-risk situations and coping mechanisms to prevent relapse

risk assessments a tool to evaluate risk for re-offense

role-playing   changing one's character or persona as a perspective-taking technique in psychotherapy

self-regulation and self-management   the ability to control emotions, thoughts, and behaviors

social learning theory   learning occurs through observing and imitating others, as well as through observing rewards and punishments

social skills training   teaching the implementation of appropriate and healthy interpersonal effectiveness skills

The Good Lives Model (GLM)   a strengths-based approach to offender rehabilitation that focuses on the client's abilities and goals for their lives

therapeutic alliance   the ongoing relationship built between the therapist and client

CHAPTER 15

Treating Clients with Severe Antisocial Behavior and Psychopathy

Emily J. Salisbury

KEY TERMS

amygdala
antisocial personality disorder (APD)
Comprehensive Assessment of Psychopathic Personality (CAPP)
Factor 1, Facet 1: Interpersonal
Factor 1, Facet 2: Affective
Factor 2, Facet 3: Lifestyle

Factor 2, Facet 4: Antisocial
four-factor model
neuropsychological deficits
psychopathy
Psychopathy Checklist–Revised, Second Edition (PCL-R, 2nd ed.)
six-dimensional model
therapeutic alliance

Although much of the general public might characterize all justice-involved people as "severely antisocial," in fact, most are not designated as such. Correctional and mental health staff must be able to identify, supervise, and treat clients who are more likely to engage in harm and violence against others in institutions and in the community. Thus, the term "severely antisocial" in this chapter refers to those who are diagnosed with antisocial **personality disorder (APD)** according to the DSM-5 (American Psychiatric Association, 2013) or who are identified as having psychopathic traits according to a reliable and valid assessment instrument, such as the *Psychopathy Checklist–Revised, Second Edition* (PCL-R, 2nd ed.) (Hare, 2003). While the PCL-R, 2nd edition, is not the only assessment instrument used to assess for psychopathy, it is the most widely used in clinical and research settings. This chapter refers to the clinical conceptualization of psychopathy rather than the legal conceptualization.

The primary aim of this chapter is to provide an overview of the most effective methods for treating severely antisocial correctional clients. Many clinicians and correctional staff falsely conclude that intervening with severely antisocial clients is hopeless and harmful, especially with psychopathic ones (Rice, Harris, & Cormier, 1992). However, the latest

DOI: 10.4324/9780367808266-19

research literature on treating seriously violent individuals often diagnosed with psychopathy has been among the fastest growing areas of publication interest in correctional and forensic psychology in the last decade. Without a doubt, careful assessment, diagnosis, supervision, and treatment are absolutely necessary with this population due to their greater propensity to physically harm and emotionally manipulate others. Yet, it is *because* of this greater propensity to harm others that mandates we determine the most effective ways to intervene. Indeed, "Continuing to ignore the development of evidence-based programmes for psychopaths is equivalent to neglecting patients with most lethal forms of cancer" (Ogloff & Wood, 2010, p. 170).

DISTINGUISHING ANTISOCIAL PERSONALITY DISORDER AND PSYCHOPATHY

Although the *Diagnostic and Statistical Manual of Mental Disorders: Fifth Edition* (DSM-5; American Psychiatric Association, 2013) suggests that APD and psychopathy are interchangeable terms reflecting the same diagnosis, the forensic psychological research literature makes a distinction between the two diagnoses and theoretical constructs. For instance, Ogloff (2006) states that the diagnostic criteria for each disorder are different enough to warrant viewing each as a unique construct, but there is certainly some conceptual overlap. The DSM-5 characterizes psychopathy as a "specifier" of APD—therefore, psychopathy is not technically a "diagnosis" per se, but is rather subsumed under a diagnosis of APD. Diagnostic criteria for APD can be found in Box 15.1.

However, there is still widespread debate on whether psychopathy is a type of APD or a distinct construct and diagnosis—most forensic psychologists consider psychopathy to be distinct. Even though APD is considered a personality disorder in the DSM-5, Ogloff (2006) argues that the diagnostic criteria for APD primarily center around antisocial and offending behavior, whereas criteria for diagnosing psychopathy typically focus more on personality deficits.

Individuals diagnosed with APD and/or psychopathy display a lifelong behavioral pattern that demonstrates a disregard for and violation of the rights of others. Diagnosed individuals often seek to gain power, money, or sex through the manipulation, dominance, and exploitation of others, but they often mimic a normal, functioning person. They are characterized as callous and calculating people who frequently engage in emotional manipulation and physical aggression for their own personal gain, with little remorse. In fact, two of the hallmark books published on psychopathy were titled, *The Mask of Sanity* (Cleckley, 1941) and *Without Conscience* (Hare, 1993). As such, psychopathic correctional clients' supervision and treatment needs require special consideration and extreme caution.

Prevalence and Cultural Differences

Measuring the prevalence of APD is challenging given the various assessments available to diagnose the disorder and the debate surrounding whether APD and psychopathy essentially reflect the same construct, or if psychopathy should be considered a more violent extreme of APD (Warren & South, 2006). The forensic psychological scholarship generally supports the latter conclusion (Sellbom & Drislane, 2020). For instance, Ogloff and Wood (2010) argue that careful clinical practice dictates that an individual who is diagnosed as having APD should subsequently be assessed for psychopathy. Thus, psychopathy is considered a more extreme personality disorder than antisocial personality disorder.

Box 15.1 Diagnostic Criteria for Antisocial Personality Disorder (APD)

A. A pervasive pattern of disregard for and violation of the rights of others, occurring since age 15 years, as indicated by three (or more) of the following:

1. Failure to conform to social norms with respect to lawful behaviors as indicated by repeatedly performing acts that are grounds for arrest.

2. Deceitfulness, as indicated by repeated lying, use of aliases, or conning others for personal profit or pleasure.

3. Impulsivity or failure to plan ahead.

4. Irritability and aggressiveness, as indicated by repeated physical fights or assaults.

5. Reckless disregard for safety of self or others.

6. Consistent irresponsibility, as indicated by repeated failure to sustain consistent work behavior or honor financial obligations.

7. Lack of remorse, as indicated by being indifferent to or rationalizing having hurt, mistreated, or stolen from another.

B. The individual is at least age 18 years.

C. There is evidence of conduct disorder with onset before age 15 years.

D. The occurrence of antisocial behavior is not exclusively during the course of schizophrenia or bipolar disorder.

Source: American Psychiatric Association (2013). *Diagnostic and Statistical Manual of Mental Disorders* (5th ed.). [DSM-5] Washington, DC: American Psychiatric Publishing, American Psychiatric Association, p. 659.

The DSM-5 indicates that prevalence rates of APD are between 0.2% and 3.3% of the general population. This is largely consistent with estimates from the National Epidemiologic Survey on Alcohol and Related Conditions, which estimates that approximately 7.6 million people in the United States have APD (Grant et al., 2004). However, studies investigating high-risk populations (e.g., males with alcohol use disorder, patients from substance abuse clinics, incarcerated people, and forensic patients) demonstrate far higher prevalence estimates of APD—greater than 70% (American Psychiatric Association, 2013).

Prevalence estimates of psychopathy in the general population are similar to those of APD. Using a screening version of the PCL-R, Coid, Yang, Ullrich, Roberts, and Hare (2009) estimate that the prevalence of psychopathy in the British general population is between

0.6% and 2.3% (3.7% in men, 0.9% in women). These estimates are largely consistent with other studies of prevalence in the general population in the United States (Blair, Mitchell, & Blair, 2005; Hare, 2003). While the prevalence of APD and psychopathy increases dramatically when examining prison populations, far more incarcerated people appear to have APD than psychopathy. Hare (1998) found that up to 70% to 80% of people in prison met the criteria for APD, while only 20% met the cut-off score for classification as a psychopath on the PCL-R.

It is well established in the research literature that males exhibit the behavioral traits of APD and psychopathy much more frequently in comparison to females (Coid et al., 2009; Grant et al., 2004; Washburn et al., 2007). Indeed, men are twice as likely to be diagnosed with APD, yet the likelihood of being diagnosed decreases with age for both genders (Flynn, Craddock, Luckey, Hubbard, & Dunteman, 1996). Results from a study of 137 incarcerated women in a maximum-security prison found that 23 (17%) of the women met criteria for an APD diagnosis only, 21 (15%) met criteria for psychopathy only (measured as a cut-off score of 25 or greater on the PCL-R), 44 (32%) met diagnostic criteria for both APD and psychopathy, and 49 (36%) women met no criteria for either diagnosis (Warren & South, 2006). These results support the argument that APD and psychopathy should be treated distinctly, even with incarcerated women.

The vast majority of research on psychopathy has been conducted with Caucasian justice-involved populations. Therefore, drawing firm conclusions about possible distinctions in the prevalence of severely antisocial behavior across race and ethnicity is difficult. However, perhaps more important is the question of whether psychopathy manifests itself similarly across racial groups. Well-designed research studies investigating this hypothesis are starting to emerge, suggesting little difference in how psychopathy operates across race.

For example, using a sophisticated, longitudinal sample from the Pittsburgh Youth Study (PYS), Vachon, Lynam, Loeber, and Stouthamer-Loeber (2011) found that juvenile and adult correlates of psychopathy (e.g., demographics, personality traits, substance abuse, APD symptoms) did not differ for Black men compared to white men, nor for men who were convicted or not convicted of crimes. These results provide preliminary support that the assessment and treatment of psychopathy may be similar for whites and Blacks, regardless of their offending history. Nevertheless, more research studies are needed in this area to reach firm conclusions.

CONCEPTUALIZATIONS OF PSYCHOPATHY FOR ASSESSMENT

There continues to be debate among scholars regarding the precise aspects that comprise the theoretical construct of psychopathy, but most experts agree that it is made up of more than one single dimension (Sellbom & Drislane, 2020). Rather, psychopathy is frequently viewed as either a four-factor model consistent with the work of Robert D. Hare and colleagues (Wong & Hare, 2005), or a six-dimensional model developed by Cooke, Hart, Logan, and Michie (2012). But see also the work of Lilienfeld and Andrews (1996), which provided a preliminary validation of a self-report assessment of psychopathy titled the Psychopathy Personality Inventory. The PPI-Revised (Lilienfeld & Widows, 2005) has been well validated for use with various forensic and justice-involved samples (e.g., see Hughes, Stout, & Dolan, 2013).

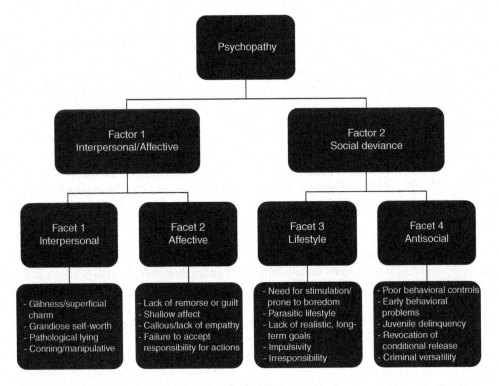

FIGURE 15.1 Scale structure of the PCL-R, 2nd ed. (Hare, 2003).

Clinicians that follow the four-factor (or facet) model of psychopathy (see Figure 15.1) will likely adopt the most widely used assessment instrument for identifying psychopathy, the *Psychopathy Checklist–Revised*, 2nd edition (PCL-R, 2nd ed.; Hare, 2003). The instrument has been validated across the globe in varying countries beyond North America, including Latin America (Folino & Hare, 2005; León-Mayer, Folino, Neumann, & Hare, 2015), Western Europe (Moltó, Poy, & Torrubia, 2000), and Scandinavia (Douglas, Strand, Belfrage, Fransson, & Levander, 2005; Sturup et al., 2013). Moreover, versions of the Psychopathy Checklist have been incorporated into a number of general risk assessment instruments predicting violence, general sexual offending, and sexual violence. These instruments include the Violence Risk Appraisal Guide (VRAG; Quinsey et al., 2006), the Sex Offender Risk Appraisal Guide (SORAG; Quinsey, Rice, & Harris, 1995), the Domestic Violence Risk Appraisal Guide (DVRAG; Hilton, Harris, Rice, Houghton, & Eke, 2008), the Historical-Clinical-Risk-20 (HCR-20; Webster, Douglas, Eaves, & Hart, 1997), and the Sexual Violence Risk-20 (SVR-20; Boer, Hart, Kropp, & Webster, 1997).

The PCL-R, 2nd edition, includes 20 items (see Box 15.2) that are scored through collateral file review of the client's historical behavior, discussions with persons who know the client well, and a semi-structured interview with the actual client. For each item in Box 15.2, the score can range between 0 and 2. Therefore, the total maximum score is 40 points. In North America, when an individual receives a score that is higher than 30 points, he or she is considered psychopathic. European clinicians often adopt a cut-off score of 25 or higher (Malatesti & McMillan, 2010).

Box 15.2 Items from *Psychopathy Checklist–Revised*: Second Edition (Hare, 2003)

1. glibness/superficial charm
2. grandiose sense of self-worth
3. need for stimulation/proneness to boredom
4. pathological lying
5. conning/manipulative
6. lack of remorse or guilt
7. shallow affect
8. callous/lack of empathy
9. parasitic lifestyle
10. poor behavioral controls
11. promiscuous sexual behavior
12. early behavior problems
13. lack of realistic, long-term goals
14. impulsivity
15. irresponsibility
16. failure to accept responsibility for own actions
17. many short-term marital relationships
18. juvenile delinquency
19. revocation and conditional release
20. offending versatility

While the PCL-R initially was formulated as a two-factor model (Hare, 1991), including only the Interpersonal/Affective (Factor 1) and Social Deviance (Factor 2) factors, ongoing research has demonstrated that a four-factor (or four-facet) model provides a more superior statistical fit for the instrument (Hill, Neumann, & Rogers, 2004; Neumann, Hare, & Neuman, 2007). Therefore, the two original factors were disaggregated further into the facets shown in Figure 15.1, including (1) Factor 1, Facet 1: Interpersonal; (2) Factor 1, Facet 2: Affective; (3) Factor 2, Facet 3: Lifestyle; and (4) Factor 2, Facet 4: Antisocial.[1]

There are debates on whether psychopathy should be conceptualized as a person either having psychopathy or not having psychopathy—many scholars argue it should be measured as the degree to which a person has psychopathy (Sellbom & Drislane, 2020). This has implications for using the cutoff scores of an instrument like a PCL-R. While it would be easier for a clinician to say a person has psychopathy if they score higher than 30 points, because of the multidimensionality of the construct, many argue it is not that easy to clearly state. These are debates that are still being worked through among the psychopathy scholarship today.

Alternatively, the conceptual map of psychopathy proposed by Cooke and colleagues (2012) is a model that includes six domains that reflect the basic areas of personality and personality functioning. Figure 15.2 shows Cooke et al.'s (2012) **Comprehensive Assessment of Psychopathic Personality (CAPP)**, which includes 33 symptoms of psychopathy, defined by three adjectives (or adjectival phrases) within six functional domains (i.e., Attachment, Behavioral, Cognitive, Dominance, Emotional, and Self).

INTEGRATING RISK, NEEDS, AND RESPONSIVITY

Justice-involved clients with psychopathy, and those with APD, are viewed by the correctional rehabilitation field as individuals who are "the highest of the high risk" clients, and with the strongest need for intervention. But they are also viewed as the most difficult to treat from a responsivity perspective. In fact, some scholars argue that psychopathy is both a risk factor and a responsivity factor (Ogloff & Wood, 2010). Unfortunately, limited research has been conducted on the application of the risk, needs, and responsivity principles to manage and treat clients with psychopathy safely, despite scholars pointing attention to this need (Ogloff & Wood, 2010; Wong & Burt, 2007).

What has been established is that psychopathic clients have similar criminogenic needs as other serious, high-risk, violent clients, albeit at a higher depth and level (Skeem, Monahan, & Mulvey, 2002; Wong & Hare, 2005). Most interventions have been successful with this population when targeting the risk factors for violence, rather than the antisocial personality characteristics of this population (e.g., superficial charm, grandiose sense of self-worth, pathological lying, conning/manipulative, etc.). In other words, interventions that focus on the Social Deviance (Factor 2) dimensions of psychopathy, rather than the Interpersonal/Affective dimension (Factor 1) have demonstrated greater treatment effectiveness (Wong, Gordon, Gu, Lewis, & Olver, 2012; Wong & Olver, 2015). Indeed, there is no empirical evidence demonstrating that the personality characteristics of psychopathy can be eliminated. Instead, the treatment of psychopathy is focused on reducing the risk of future violence and offending (Ogloff & Wood, 2010; Skeem et al., 2002), much like it would be with individuals deemed severely antisocial, but without a diagnosis of psychopathy. As a result, it is necessary to implement a dynamic risk/need assessment instrument such as those discussed in Chapter 6 to know precisely which criminogenic needs should be integrated into a treatment plan.

Nevertheless, antisocial personality characteristics and how they manifest behaviorally cannot be ignored in the delivery of services, and they are largely viewed through a lens of general and specific responsivity principles. For instance, delivering cognitive behavioral treatment in a group setting will prove challenging, though not impossible, with even one psychopathic client in the room because of the greater likelihood that he or she will attempt to manipulate the learning environment and other clients' attitudes toward the intervention or facilitator.

Moreover, system-involved people with psychopathic traits have **neuropsychological deficits** (Beaver, Vaughn, Barnes, DeLisi, & Boutwell, 2012; Kiehl, 2006; Raine & Yang, 2006) that preclude their ability to cognitively and emotionally process information and develop emotionally meaningful connection with others, presenting significant challenges in

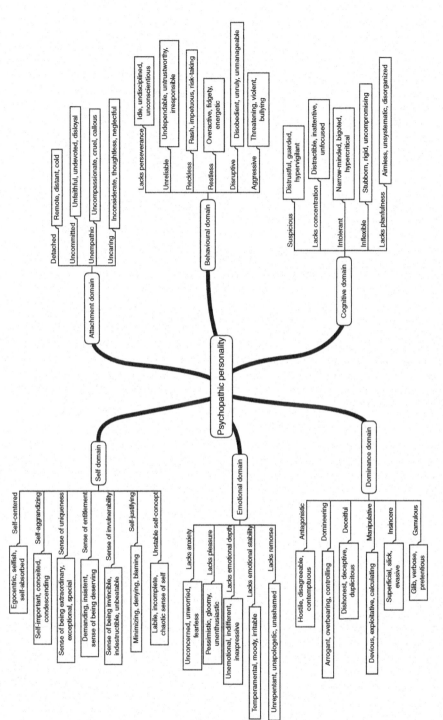

FIGURE 15.2 Comprehensive Assessment of Psychopathic Personality (CAPP).

Source: Cooke, D. J., Hart, S. D., Logan, C., & Michie, C. (2012). Explicating the construct of psychopathy: Development and validation of a conceptual model, the Comprehensive Assessment of Psychopathic Personality (CAPP). *International Journal of Forensic Mental Health, 11*, 242–252, DOI: 10.1080/14999013.2012.746759

the therapeutic process of self-reflection, empathy, and motivation (Polascheck, 2006; Seto & Quinsey, 2006). For instance, research has pointed to structural and functional impairment in the frontal lobes and prefrontal cortex of the brain as key correlates of psychopathy (Gorenstein, 1982; Raine, Lencz, Bihrle, LaCasse, & Colletti, 2000). These areas of the brain are responsible for emotional processing and flexible control of cognitive and motor abilities in goal-directed behavior (Rogers, 2006). Further, Blair et al. (2005) indicate that dysfunction in the **amygdala** portion of the brain is a key neurological cause of psychopathy. Abnormalities in the amygdala may explain psychopathic individuals' reported difficulty in certain forms of learning and in their inability to behaviorally display emotions.

These neurological deficits manifest into personality characteristics and behaviors that present challenges forming a **therapeutic alliance** (Wong & Hare, 2005). Building trust and rapport with a psychopathic correctional client should be approached in a fundamentally different manner, and will manifest very distinctly compared with less seriously antisocial clients, and staff should always be aware of the early signs of manipulation with this population.

PRACTICAL ADVICE FOR TREATING SEVERELY ANTISOCIAL AND PSYCHOPATHIC CORRECTIONAL CLIENTS

While there is preliminary evidence in support of treating the criminogenic needs of psychopathic individuals as they relate to violence and offending (Ogloff & Wood, 2010; Olver, Lewis, & Wong, 2013; Wong & Olver, 2015), correctional counselors and practitioners must approach working with this population with extreme caution. The potential for physical and emotional harm is far too great working with psychopathic clients to not take measured steps in their behavioral management. Harris and Rice (2006) provided critical words of advice for practitioners building safe rapport with psychopaths, which generally also apply to any client known to be severely antisocial in behavior.

Box 15.3 Advice for Building Safe Rapport with Clients with Psychopathy (adapted from Harris & Rice, 2006)

1. Read Hare (1998) to understand the nature of psychopaths.

2. Reputation matters—leopards rarely change their spots.

3. Never take a psychopathic client's word at face value—always confirm his or her assertions against official records and key informants.

4. Do not just attend to how he or she behaves around you—carefully observe how he or she treats everyone.

5. Beware of flattery.

6. Be very suspicious if a psychopathic individual asks you to break a rule, no matter how minor, or to keep an illicit confidence.

7. Talk to a colleague about your relationship with him or her. If your trusted colleague says things do not sound right, beware. Get supervision immediately.

Of course, before engaging in any treatment intervention with psychopathic clients, a comprehensive evaluation should be administered using a standardized and validated assessment for identifying psychopathy (e.g., PCL-R, 2nd ed.). Moreover, additional clinical assessments may be warranted to assess other mental health conditions, such as co-occurring mental illness, substance use disorders, paraphilic disorders (e.g., sexual masochism disorder, pedophilic disorder), or malingering (e.g., feigning illness).

Any intervention that might take place with justice-involved clients should be cognitive behavioral in nature and target violent behavior (Factor 2) rather than antisocial personality components (Factor 1; Ogloff & Wood, 2010; Wong & Olver, 2015). The criminogenic needs of psychopathic and severely antisocial people become the central focus of treatment, with staff closely observing antisocial characteristics that might interfere with treatment engagement and fidelity. With psychopathic sex offending clients, cognitive behavioral approaches and relapse prevention strategies are likely to show more effectiveness than strategies targeting clients' empathy and affective needs (Ogloff & Wood, 2010).

In addition, Wong and Hare (2005) argue that the treatment of psychopathy can be conducted in a group setting, but with careful caveats. They suggest that having a proportion of the participants be non-psychopathic, high-risk, violent clients would help ease the group dynamic. Wong and Hare (2005) also encourage rolling, or open, group entry to allow for individuals who are further along in the stages of change to serve as learning models for those in earlier stages.

Finally, staff must be well trained and supervised to work effectively with this population. Treating psychopathic and severely antisocial individuals is extremely complex and requires a skill level and expertise that is often hard to find in clinicians and psychologists. Additionally, adequate funding and resources are required to be successful. Seto and Quinsey (2006) suggest high staff ratios so that thoughtful supervision can take place and to reduce the likelihood of staff being deceived and manipulated.

CONCLUSION

Despite the "therapeutic nihilism" (Wong & Olver, 2015) that has existed in the field regarding the treatment of severely antisocial correctional clients, and those with psychopathy in particular, there is preliminary evidence supporting the efficacy of treatment interventions when they focus on reducing future violence and offending. Additionally, it would not be wise to dismiss the five decades of research on the principles of effective intervention (e.g., risk, needs, and responsivity principles) with antisocial individuals. How these principles can be effectively applied with psychopathic clients is still admittedly in a relative state of infancy.

Nevertheless, even though there is still discussion in the literature regarding how "treatable" psychopathic clients are, this should not dissuade the field from trying to determine effective interventions focused on reducing future violence and offending. Improvement in understanding the etiological causes of psychopathy will help in determining favorable treatment interventions for the future. As more studies are conducted on the neurological, neuropsychological, biosocial, and genetic causes of psychopathy, a greater acceptance of those who suffer from it will emerge. But the bottom line for correctional counselors, social workers, and staff working with these populations is that careful clinical training and supervision are required to create safe and effective interventions.

Discussion Questions

1. How do the criteria for diagnosing antisocial personality disorder differ from the criteria for diagnosing psychopathy using the PCL-R, 2nd Edition?

2. Explain why the prevalence rate of justice-involved people suffering from APD and psychopathy is far higher than with the general public.

3. What are dimensions of psychopathy according to the four-factor model and the six-dimensional model?

4. Specifically address why it is more challenging to intervene with psychopathic and severely antisocial clients than with less serious offending clients.

5. Should the principles of risk, needs, and responsivity be applied to psychopathic individuals?

6. Why might it be more effective to intervene in Factor 2 characteristics of psychopaths than in Factor 1 characteristics?

7. What special skills must correctional staff have in working with severely antisocial clients to be successful?

ONLINE LEARNING ENHANCEMENTS

Dr. Shadd Maruna's lecture "What are Psychopaths For?" argues that there are a number of debates among this literature base. These debates are important for clinicians to understand and to determine their values and views around this controversial label and topic. www. youtube.com/watch?app=desktop&v=oHuyldmcMJs

GLOSSARY OF KEY TERMS

amygdala   an almond-shaped mass of gray matter inside each cerebral hemisphere of the brain, involved with the experiencing of emotions (including fear, anxiety, and aggression), the processing of memory, and decision-making

antisocial personality disorder (APD)   a mental health disorder characterized by a pervasive pattern of disregard for and violation of the rights of others; unlike psychopathy, criteria for diagnosing APD typically focus more on antisocial and offending behavior

Comprehensive Assessment of Psychopathic Personality (CAPP)   a conceptual map of psychopathy that includes 33 symptoms of the disorder, defined by three adjectives (or adjectival phrases) within six functional domains (i.e., Attachment, Behavioral, Cognitive, Dominance, Emotional, and Self)

four-factor model   a model of psychopathy in which four dimensions (Interpersonal, Affective, Lifestyle, Antisocial) are used to identify the disorder, typically with the use of the PCL-R 2nd ed. assessment instrument

neuropsychological deficits deficiencies in the brain and nervous system that interfere with one's cognition, emotional processing, and behaviors

psychopathy a personality disorder characterized by persistent antisocial behavior, impaired empathy and remorse, and bold, disinhibited, and egotistical traits; unlike APD, criteria for diagnosing psychopathy typically focus more on personality deficits

Psychopathy Checklist–Revised, **Second Edition (PCL-R 2nd ed.)** a popular, valid, and reliable assessment instrument that is used in the diagnosis of psychopathy

six-dimensional model a model of psychopathy in which six dimensions (i.e., Attachment, Behavioral, Cognitive, Dominance, Emotional, and Self), outlined in the CAPP instrument, are used to identify the disorder

therapeutic alliance the cooperative working relationship between therapists and clients; this relationship is often difficult to form when treating psychopathic clients, as many of them possess neurological deficits that manifest into challenging and manipulative personality characteristics and behaviors

NOTE

1   Factor 1, Facet 1: Interpersonal – one of four facets of psychopathy found in the *Psychopathy Checklist–Revised*, 2nd edition (PCL-R, 2nd ed.); this facet is concerned with the identification of interpersonal deficits associated with psychopathy, including glibness/superficial charm, grandiose self-worth, pathological lying, and conning/manipulative

Factor 1, Facet 2: Affective – one of four facets of psychopathy found in the PCL-R, 2nd ed.; this facet is concerned with the identification of affective deficits associated with psychopathy, including lack of remorse or guilt, shallow affect, callous/lack of empathy, and failure to accept responsibility for actions

Factor 2, Facet 3: Lifestyle – one of four facets of psychopathy found in the PCL-R, 2nd ed.; this facet is concerned with the identification of deviant lifestyle traits associated with psychopathy, including, need for stimulation/prone to boredom, parasitic lifestyle, lack of realistic, long-term goals, impulsivity, and irresponsibility

Factor 2, Facet 4: Antisocial – one of four facets of psychopathy found in the PCL-R, 2nd ed.: this facet is concerned with the identification of antisocial traits associated with psychopathy, including poor behavioral controls, early behavioral problems, juvenile delinquency, revocation of conditional release, and criminal versatility

References

Abel, G., & Rouleau, J. (1990). The nature and extent of sexual assault. In W. Marshall, D. Laws, & H. Barbaree (Eds.), *Handbook of Sexual Assault: Issues, Theories and Treatment of the Offender* (pp. 9–12). New York: Plenum Press.

Abram, K. M., Teplin, L. A., McClelland, G. M., & Dulcan, M. K. (2003). Comorbid psychiatric disorders in youth in juvenile detention. *Archives of General Psychiatry, 60,* 1097–1108.

Abreu, D., Parker, T., Noether, C., Steadman, H., & Case, B. (2017). Revising the paradigm for jail diversion for people with mental and substance use disorders: Intercept 0. *Behavioral Sciences & the Law, 35,* 380–395.

Ackerman, N. (1966). Family psychotherapy—Theory and practice. *American Journal of Psychotherapy, 20,* 405–414.

Aetkenhead, D. (2013). Chemical castration: The soft option? *The Guardian,* January 18.

Agee, V. (1987). *The Treatment Program at Paint Creek Youth Center.* Bainbridge, OH: Unpublished manuscript, Paint Creek Youth Center.

Ahmad, F. B., Rossen, L. M., & Sutton P. (2021). *Provisional Drug Overdose Death Counts.* National Center for Health Statistics. Retrieved from www.cdc.gov/nchs/nvss/vsrr/drug-overdose-data.htm

Akers, R. (2001). Social learning theory. In R. Paternoster & R. Bachman (Eds.), *Explaining Criminals and Crime* (pp. 192–210). Los Angeles: Roxbury.

Aldarondo, E., & Strauss, M. (1994). Screening for physical violence in couples therapy: Methodological, practical, and ethical considerations. *Family Process, 33,* 425–439.

Alessi, S. M. (2013). Contingency management. In P. M. Miller (Ed.), *Interventions for addiction: Comprehensive addictive behaviors and disorders* (pp. 37–46). Elsevier.

Alexander, J. (1973). Defensive and supportive communications in normal and deviant families. *Journal of Consulting and Clinical Psychology, 40,* 223–231.

Alexander, J., & Parsons, B. (1973). Short-term behavioral intervention with delinquent families: Impact on family process and recidivism. *Journal of Abnormal Psychology, 81,* 219–225.

Alexander, J., & Parsons, B. (1982). *Functional Family Therapy.* Belmont, CA: Brooks/Cole.

Alexander, J., Pugh, C., & Parsons, B. (1998). *Functional Family Therapy: Book Three in the Blueprints and Violence Prevention Series.* Boulder: University of Colorado, Center for the Study and Prevention of Violence.

Alexander, J., Waldron, J., Newberry, A., & Liddle, N. (1988). Family approaches to treating delinquents. Mental illness, delinquency, addictions, and neglect. In E. Nunnally & C. Chilman (Eds.), *Families in Trouble Series* (pp. 128–145). Newbury Park, CA: Sage.

Alonzo-Vaughn, N., Bradley, R., & Cassavaugh, M. (2015). PBIS in Arizona Department of Juvenile Corrections: How tier II practices build upon tier 1. *Residential Treatment of Children and Youth, 32,* 321–333.

American Bar Association (ABA). (1989). *ABA Criminal Justice and Mental Health Standards.* Washington, DC: American Bar Association.

American Bar Association (ABA). (2011). *ABA Standards for Criminal Justice: Treatment of Prisoners* (3rd ed.). Washington, DC: American Bar Association.

American Correctional Association. (2021). *Performance-Based Expected Practices for Adult Correctional Institutions* (5th ed.). Alexandria, VA: American Correctional Association.

American Counseling Association. (2014). *2014 ACA Code of Ethics*. Alexandria, VA: American Counseling Association.

American Psychiatric Association. (2000). *Diagnostic and Statistical Manual of Mental Disorders* Text Revision (4th ed.). [DSM-IV-TR] Washington, DC: American Psychiatric Association.

American Psychiatric Association. (2013). *Diagnostic and Statistical Manual of Mental Disorders* (5th ed.). [DSM-5] Washington, DC: American Psychiatric Publishing, American Psychiatric Association.

Anda, D., Dube, S., Giles, W., & Felitti, V. (2003). The relationship of exposure to childhood sexual abuse to other forms of abuse, neglect and household dysfunction during childhood. *Child Abuse and Neglect, 26*, 625–639.

Anderson, C., & Stewart, S. (1983). *Mastering Resistance: A Practical Guide to Family Therapy*. New York: Guilford.

Andrews, D. (1980). Some experimental investigations of the principles of differential association through deliberate manipulations of the structures of service systems. *American Sociological Review, 45*, 448–462.

Andrews, D. (1995). The psychology of criminal conduct and effective treatment. In J. McGuire (Ed.), *What Works: Reducing Re-offending*. New York: John Wiley.

Andrews, D., & Bonta, J. (1995). *The Level of Supervision Inventory—Revised (LSI-R)*. North Tonawanda, NY: Multi-Health Systems.

Andrews, D. A., & Bonta, J. (2010). Rehabilitating criminal justice policy and practice. *Psychology, Public Policy, and Law, 16*, 39–55.

Andrews, D., & Kiessling, J. (1980). Program structure and effective correctional practice: A summary of CaVic research. In R. Ross & P. Gendreau (Eds.), *Effective Correctional Treatment* (pp. 439–463). Toronto: Butterworths.

Andrews, D., & Wormith, S. (1989). Personality and crime: Knowledge destruction and construction in criminology. *Justice Quarterly, 6*, 289–309.

Andrews, D., Bonta, J., & Hoge, R. (1990). Classification for effective rehabilitation: Rediscovering psychology. *Criminal Justice and Behavior, 17*, 19–52.

Andrews, D., Bonta, J., & Wormith, S. (2004). *The Level of Service/Case Management. Inventory (LS/CMI): User's Manual*. Toronto: Multi-Health Systems.

Andrews, D., Dowden, C., & Gendreau, P. (1999). *Clinically Relevant and Psychologically Informed Approaches to Reduced Re-Offending: A Meta-Analytic Study of Human Service, Risk, Need, Responsivity, and Other Concerns in Justice Contexts*. Unpublished manuscript. Ottawa: Carleton University.

Andrews, D., Gordon, D., Hill, J., Kurkowski, K., & Hoge, R. (1993). *Program Integrity, Methodology, and Treatment Characteristics: A Meta-Analysis of Effects of Family Intervention with Young Offenders*. Unpublished manuscript. Ottawa: Carleton University.

Andrews, D., Zinger, I., Hoge, R., Bonta, J., Gendreau, P., & Cullen, F. (1990). Does correctional treatment work? A psychologically informed meta-analysis. *Criminology, 28*, 369–404.

Anechiarico, B. (2015). The primary aim of sex offender treatment: Translating criminogenic needs into a treatment strategy. In B. Schwartz (Ed.), *The Sex Offender: Insights on Treatment and Policy Developments*, Vol. VIII (pp. 2–1–2–20). Kingston, NJ: Civic Research Institute.

Anglin, D., & Hser, Y. (1990). Treatment of drug abuse. In M. Tonry & J. Wilson (Eds.), *Drugs and Crime* (pp. 393–460). Chicago: University of Chicago Press.

Annis, H., & Davis, C. (2003). Relapse prevention. In R. Hester & W. Miller (Eds.), *Handbook of Alcoholism Treatment Approaches: Effective Alternatives* (3rd ed.) (pp. 176–194). Boston: Allyn & Bacon.

Annis, H., & Graham, J. (1988). *Situation Confidence Questionnaire (SCQ): User's Guide.* Toronto: Addiction Research Foundation of Ontario.

Antonowicz, D., & Ross, R. (1994). Essential components of successful rehabilitation programs for offenders. *International Journal of Offender Therapy and Comparative Criminology, 38,* 97–104.

Antonowicz, D., & Ross, R. (2005). Social problem-solving deficits in offenders. In M. McMurran & J. McGuire (Eds.), *Social Problem Solving and Offending: Evidence, Evaluation and Evolution* (pp. 91–120). New York: John Wiley.

Aos, S., Miller, M., & Drake, E. (2006). *Evidence-based Adult Corrections Programs: What Works and What Does Not.* Olympia: Washington State Institute for Public Policy.

Arboleda-Florez, J., & Holley, H. (1989). Predicting suicide behaviours in incarcerated settings. *Canadian Journal of Psychiatry, 34,* 668–674.

Arden, J., & Linford, L. (2009). *Brain-based Therapy with Adults.* Hoboken, NJ: John Wiley.

Ardino, V. (2012). Offending behaviour: The role of trauma and PTSD. *European Journal of Psychotraumatology, 3,* 1–4.

Armstrong, T. (2003). The effects of moral reconation therapy on the recidivism of youthful offenders: A randomized experiment. *Criminal Justice and Behavior, 30*(6), 668–687.

Arnold, R. (1990). Processes of victimization and criminalization of Black women. *Social Justice, 17,* 153–166.

Austin, J. (1986). Evaluating how well your classification system is operating: A practical approach. *Crime & Delinquency, 32,* 302–333.

Austin, J., & McGinnis, K. (2004). *Classification of High-Risk and Special Management Prisoners: A National Assessment of Current Practices.* Washington, DC: National Institute of Corrections.

Austin, J., Bruce, M., Carroll, L., McCall, P., & Richards, S. (2000). *The Use of Incarceration in the United States: A Policy Paper Presented by the National Policy Committee to the American Society of Criminology.* Columbus, OH: American Society of Criminology.

Ax, R., & Morgan, R. (2002). Internship training opportunities in correctional psychology: A comparison of settings. *Criminal Justice and Behavior, 29,* 332–347.

Ayllon, T., & Azrin, N. (1968). *The Token Economy: A Motivational System for Therapy and Rehabilitation.* New York: Appleton-Century-Crofts.

Azrin, N., Donohue, B., Betsalel, V., Kogan, E., & Acierno, R. (1994). Youth drug abuse treatment: A controlled outcome study. *Journal of Child and Adolescent Substance Abuse, 3,* 1–16.

Babchishin, K. M., Hanson, R. K., & VanZuylen, H. (2015). Online child pornography offenders are different: A meta-analysis of the characteristics of online and offline sex offenders against children. *Archives of Sexual Behavior, 44,* 45–66.

Backer, T., Davis, S., & Soucy, G. (Eds.), (1995). *Reviewing the Behavioral Science Knowledge Base on Technology Transfer.* (NIDA Research Monograph 155). Rockville, MD: U.S. Department of Health and Human Services, Public Health Service, National Institutes of Health.

Baird, C., Wagner, D., & Neuenfeldt, D. (1992). *Using Risk Assessment to Structure Decisions about Services. Protecting Children: The Michigan Model.* NCCD Focus, March. San Francisco: National Council on Crime and Delinquency.

Ball, C., & Seghorn, T. (2011). Diagnosis and treatment of exhibitionism and other sexual compulsive disorders. In B. Schwartz (Ed.), *Handbook of Sex Offender Treatment* (pp. 35-1–35-17). Kingston, NJ: Civic Research Institute.

Bandura, A. (1965). Influence of models' reinforcement contingencies on the acquisition of imitative responses. *Journal of Personality and Social Psychology, 1,* 589–595.

Bandura, A. (1973). *Aggression: A Social Learning Analysis.* Englewood Cliffs, NJ: Prentice Hall.

Bandura, A. (1977). Self-efficacy: Toward a unifying theory of behavioral change. *Psychological Review, 94,* 191–215.

Bandura, A. (1978). Reflections on self-efficacy. *Advances in Behavioral Research and Therapy, 1,* 237–269.

Bandura, A., & Walters, R. (1963). *Social Learning and Personality Development.* New York: Holt, Rinehart & Winston.

Bandura, A., Ross, D., & Ross, S. (1963). Vicarious reinforcement and imitative learning. *Journal of Abnormal and Social Psychology, 67,* 601–607.

Bank, L., Marlowe, J., Reid, J., Patterson, G., & Weinrott, M. (1991). A comparative evaluation of parent training interventions for families of chronic delinquents. *Journal of Abnormal Child Psychology, 19,* 15–33.

Banyard, V. L., Williams, L. M., Saunders, B. E., & Fitzgerald, M. M. (2008). The complexity of trauma types in the lives of women in families referred for family violence: Multiple mediators of mental health. *American Journal of Orthopsychiatry, 78,* 394–404.

Baranyi, G., Cassidy, M., Fazel, S., Priebe, S., & Mundt, A. P. (2018). Prevalence of Posttraumatic Stress Disorder in Prisoners. *Epidemiological Review, 40,* 134–145.

Barnhill, L., & Longo, D. (1978). Fixation and regression in the family life cycle. *Family Process, 17,* 469–478.

Barrett, M., Trepper, T., & Fish, L. (1990). Feminist-informed family therapy for the treatment of intrafamily child sexual abuse. *Journal of Family Psychology, 4,* 151–166.

Barriga, A., Landau, J., Stinson, B., Liau, A., & Gibbs, J. (2000). Cognitive distortions and problem behaviors in adolescents. *Criminal Justice and Behavior, 27*(1), 36–56.

Barton, C., Alexander, J., Waldron, H., Turner, D., & Warburton, J. (1985). Generalizing treatment effects of functional family therapy: Three replications. *American Journal of Family Therapy, 13,* 16–26.

Bateson, G., Jackson, D., Haley, J., & Weakland, J. (1956). Toward a theory of schizophrenia. *Behavioral Science, 1,* 251–264.

Baumrind, D. (1985). Familial antecedents of adolescent drug use: A developmental perspective. In C. Jones & R. Battjes (Eds.), *Etiology of Drug Abuse: Implications for Prevention* (pp. 13–44). (NIDA Research Monograph 56). Washington, DC: U.S. Government Printing Office.

Beaver, K. M., Vaughn, M. G., Barnes, J. C., DeLisi, M., & Boutwell, B. B. (2012). The neuropsychological underpinnings to psychopathic personality traits in a nationally representative and longitudinal sample. *Psychiatric Quarterly, 83,* 145–159.

Beck, A. (2000). *Prisoners in 1999.* Washington, DC: U.S. Department of Justice, Bureau of Justice Statistics.

Beck, A. T. (1962). Reliability of psychiatric diagnoses: A critique of systematic studies. *American Journal of Psychiatry, 119,* 210–216.

Beck, A. T., & Emory, G. (1985). *Anxiety Disorders and Phobias: A Cognitive Perspective.* New York: Basic Books.

Beck, A., Rush, A., Shaw, B., & Emory, G. (1979). *Cognitive Therapy of Depression.* New York: Guilford.

Beck, A., Wright, F., Newman, C., & Liese, B. (1993). *Cognitive Therapy of Substance Abuse.* New York: Guilford.

Beck, J. S. (2021). *Cognitive Behavior Therapy: Basics and Beyond* (3rd ed.). New York: Guilford Press.

Becker, J. V., Alpert, J. L., BigFoot, D. S., Bonner, B. L., Geddie, L. F., Henggeler, S. W., Kaufman, K. L., & Walker, C. E. (1995). Empirical research on child abuse treatment: Report by the Child Abuse and Neglect Treatment Working Group, APA. *Journal of Clinical Child Psychology, 24,* 23–46.

Bedell, P. S., So, M., Morse, D. S., Kinner, S. A., Ferguson, W. J., & Spaulding, A. C. (2019). Corrections for academic medicine: The importance of using person-first language for individuals who have experienced incarceration. *Academic Medicine, 94,* 172–175.

Beech, A. R., Bartels, R. M., & Dixon, L. (2013). Assessment and treatment of distorted schemas in sexual offenders. *Trauma, Violence & Abuse, 14,* 54–66.

Belisle, L., (2021). Exploring the Role of Adverse Childhood Experiences (ACEs) Among Gendered Racial/Ethnic Groups of Justice-Involved Youth. (Publication No. 4121) [Doctoral Dissertation, University of Nevada]. UNLV Theses, Dissertations, Professional Papers, and Capstones. Retrieved from https://digitalscholarship.unlv.edu/thesesdissertations/4121

Belknap, J. (2007). *The Invisible Woman: Gender, Crime, and Justice.* Wadsworth Cengage Learning.

Belknap, J., & Holsinger, K. (2006). The gendered nature of risk factors for delinquency. *Feminist Criminology, 1*, 48–71. https://doi.org/10.1177/1557085105282897

Bell, D. A. (1995). Who's afraid of critical race theory? *University of Illinois Law Review, 4*, 893–910.

Benedict, A. (2014). *Using Trauma-Informed Practices to Enhance Safety and Security in Women's Correctional Facilities.* Center for Effective Public Policy, National Resource Center on Justice-Involved Women. Retrieved from https://bja.ojp.gov/sites/g/files/xyckuh186/files/Publications/NRCJIW-UsingTraumaInformedPractices.pdf

Ben-Porath, Y. S., & Tellegen, A. (2020). *Minnesota Multiphasic Personality Inventory-3.* Minneapolis, MN: Pearson Assessments.

Berenson, D. (1986). The family treatment of alcoholism. *Family Therapy Today, 1*, 1–2, 6–7.

Berg, R. J., & Quinney, R. (Eds.), (2005). *Storytelling Sociology: Narrative as Social Inquiry.* Boulder, CO: Lynne Rienner.

Black, M. C., Basile, K. C., Breiding, M. J., Smith, S. G., Walters, M. L., Merrick, M. T., Chen, J., & Stevens, M. R. (2011). *The National Intimate Partner and Sexual Violence Survey (NISVS), 2010 Summary Report.* Atlanta, GA: National Center for Injury Prevention and Control, Centers for Disease Control and Prevention.

Blackstone, K. (2015). Polygraph with adjudicated sex offenders. In B. Schwartz (Ed.), *The Sex Offender: Insights on Treatment and Policy Developments,* Vol. VIII (pp. 6–1–6–38). Kingston, NJ: Civic Research Institute.

Blair, J., Mitchell, D., & Blair, K. (2005). *The Psychopath, Emotion, and the Brain.* Malden, MA: Blackwell Publishing.

Blanchette, K., & Brown, S. L. (2006). *The Assessment and Treatment of Women Offenders: An Integrative Perspective.* Chichester, UK: Wiley.

Blasko, B. L., Friedmann, P. D., Giuranna Rhodes, A., & Taxman, F. S. (2015). The parolee-parole officer relationship as a mediator of criminal justice outcomes. *Criminal Justice and Behavior, 42*, 722–740.

Bloom, B., Owen, B., & Covington, S. (2003). *Gender Responsive Strategies: Research, Practice, and Guiding Principles for Women Offenders.* Washington, DC: U.S. Department of Justice, National Institute of Corrections.

Blume, S. B. (1990). Chemical dependency in women: Important issues. *American Journal of Drug and Alcohol Abuse, 16*, 297–307.

Boer, D. P., Hart, S. D., Kropp, P. R., & Webster, C. D. (1997). *Manual for the Sexual Violence Risk-20: Professional Guidelines for Assessing Risk of Sexual Violence.* Vancouver: British Columbia Institute on Family Violence.

Bogue, B., Nandi, A., & Jongsma, A. (2003). *The Probation and Parole Treatment Planner.* Hoboken, NJ: John Wiley.

Bohn, M. (1979). Classification of offenders in an institution for young adults. *FCI Research Reports,* 1–31.

Bonczar, T. P. (1997). *Bureau of Justice Statistics Special Report: Characteristics of Adults on Probation, 1995.* Washington, DC: Bureau of Justice Statistics.

Bonta, J. (1996). Risk-needs assessment and treatment. In A. T. Harland (Ed.), *Choosing Correctional Options that Work: Defining the Demand and Evaluating the Supply* (pp. 18–32). Thousand Oaks, CA: Sage.

Bonta, J. (2002). Offender risk assessment: Guidelines for selection and use. *Criminal Justice and Behavior, 29*, 355–379.

Bonta, J., & Andrews, D. A. (2017). *The Psychology of Criminal Conduct* (6th ed.). New York: Routledge.

Bonta, J., Bourgon, G., Rugge, T., Scott, T. L., Yessine, A. K., Gutierrez, L., & Li, J. (2010). *The Strategic Training Initiative in Community Supervision: Risk-need-responsivity in the real world.* Ottawa, ON, Canada: Public Safety Canada.

Bonta, J., Bourgon, G., Rugge, T., Scott, T. L., Yessine, A. K., Gutierrez, L., & Li, J. (2011). An experimental demonstration of training probation officers in evidence-based community supervision. *Criminal Justice and Behavior, 38*, 1127–1148. https://doi.org/10.1177/0093854811420678

Bonta, J., Law, M., & Hanson, R. (1998). The prediction of criminal and violent recidivism among mentally disordered offenders: A meta-analysis. *Psychological Bulletin, 123*–142.

Bonta, J. S., Wallace-Capretta, S., & Rooney, J. (2000). A quasi-experimental evaluation of an intensive rehabilitation supervision program. *Criminal Justice and Behavior, 27,* 312–329.

Boppre, B. (2019). Improving corrections strategies for women at the margins: Recommendations for an intersectionally-responsive approach. *Corrections: Policy Practice, and Research, 4,* 195–221.

Bor, W., Najman, J. M., & O'Callaghan, M. (2001). *Aggression and the Development of Delinquent Behavior in Children.* Canberra: Australian Institute of Criminology.

Bordnick, P. S., Copp, H. L., Traylor, A., Graap, K. M., Carter, B. L., Walton, A., & Ferrer, M. (2009). Reactivity to cannabis cues in virtual reality environments. *Journal of Psychoactive Drugs, 41,* 105–112.

Bordnick, P. S., Elkins, R. L., Orr, T. E., Walters, P. & Thyer, B. A. (2004). Evaluating the relative effectiveness of three aversion therapies designed to reduce craving among cocaine abusers. *Behavioral Interventions, 19,* 1–24.

Borduin, C., Henggeler, S., Blaske, D., & Stein, R. (1990). Multisystemic treatment of adolescent sexual offenders. *International Journal of Offender Therapy and Comparative Criminology, 34,* 105–113.

Borduin, C., Mann, B., Cone, L., Henggeler, S., Fucci, B., Blaske, D., & Williams, R. (1995). Multisystemic treatment of serious juvenile offenders: Long-term prevention of criminality and violence. *Journal of Consulting and Clinical Psychology, 63,* 569–578.

Boszormenyi-Nagy, I., & Ulrich, D. (1981). Contextual family therapy. In A. Gurman & D. Kniskern (Eds.), *Handbook of Family Therapy* (pp. 187–211). New York: Brunner/Mazel.

Botella, C., Fernandez-Alvarez, J., Guillen, V., Garcia-Palacios, A. & Banos, R. (2017). Recent progress in virtual reality exposure therapy for phobias: A systematic review. *Current Psychiatry Reports, 19,* 1–13.

Botella, C., García-Palacios, A., Villa, H., Baños, R. M., Quero, S., Alcañiz, M., & Riva, G. (2007). Virtual reality exposure in the treatment of panic disorder and agoraphobia: Controlled study. *Clinical Psychology & Psychotherapy, 14,* 164–175.

Bouffard, J., & Taxman, F. (2004). Looking inside the "black box" of drug court treatment services using direct observations. *Journal of Drug Issues, 34*(1), 195–218.

Bourgon, G., & Armstrong, B. (2005). Transferring the principles of effective intervention to a "real world" setting. *Criminal Justice and Behavior, 32,* 3–25.

Bourgon, G., Chadwick, N., & Rugge, T. (2020). Beyond core correctional practice: Facilitation prosocial change through the Strategic Training Initiative in Community Supervision. In S. Wormith, L. A. Craig, & T. E. Hogue (Eds.), *The Wiley Handbook of What Works in Violence Risk Management: Theory, Research and Practice* (pp. 505–523). Hoboken, NJ: Wiley-Blackwell.

Bowen, M. (1978). *Family Therapy in Clinical Practice.* New York: Aronson.

Bowker, A. (1994). Handle with care: Dealing with offenders who are mentally retarded. *FBI Law Enforcement Bulletin,* July, 12–16.

Bowlby, J. (1969). *Attachment and Loss.* New York: Basic Books.

Bowlby, J. (1988). *A Secure Base: Clinical Implications of Attachment Theory.* London: Routledge & Kegan Paul.

Bralley, J., & Prevost, J. (2001). Reinventing community supervision: Georgia parole's results-driven supervision. *Corrections Today, 63*(2), 120–125.

Brandsma, J., Maultsby, M., & Welsh, R. (1980). *Outpatient Treatment of Alcoholism: A Review and Comparative Study.* Baltimore: University Park Press.

Brant, J., Wilson, R., & Prescott, D. (2015). Doubt about SVP programs: A critical review of sexual offender civil commitment in the United States. In B. Schwartz (Ed.), *The Sex Offender: Insights on Treatment and Policy Developments,* Vol. VI11 (pp. 5–1–5–29). Kingston, NJ: Civic Research Institute.

Braswell, M., Miller, L., & Cabana, D. (2006). *Human Relations and Corrections* (5th ed.). Prospect Heights, IL: Waveland.

Braswell, M., & Whitehead, J. (2002). In the beginning was the student: Teaching peacemaking and justice issues. *Crime & Delinquency, 48*(2), 333–349.

Brennan, T., Breitenbach, M., & Dieterich, W. (2008). Explanatory taxonomy of adolescent delinquents: Identifying several social psychological profiles. *Journal of Quantitative Criminology, 24,* 179–203.

Brennan, T., Breitenbach, M., Dieterich, W., Salisbury, E., & Van Voorhis, P. (2012). Women's pathways to serious and habitual crime: A Person-Centered analysis incorporating gender responsive factors. *Criminal Justice and Behavior, 39,* 1481–1508.

Brennan, T., Dieterich, W., & Ehret, B. (2009). Evaluating the predictive validity of the COMPAS risk and needs assessment system. *Criminal Justice and Behavior, 36,* 21–40.

Brennan, T., Dieterich, W., & Oliver, W. (2006). *COMPAS: Technical Manual and Psychometric Report Version 5.0.* Traverse City, MI: Northpointe Institute.

Brodsky, S. (1975). *Families and Friends of Men in Prison: The Uncertain Relationship.* Lexington, MA: D. C. Heath.

Bronfenbrenner, U. (1979). *The Ecology of Human Development: Experiments by Nature and Design.* Cambridge, MA: Harvard University Press.

Brown, S. L., Robinson, D., Wanamaker, K. A., & Wagstaff, M. (2020). Strengths matter: Evidence from five separate cohorts of justice-involved youth and adults across North America. *Criminal Justice and Behavior, 47,* 1428–1447.

Browne, A., Miller, B., & Maguin, E. (1999). Prevalence and severity of lifetime physical and sexual victimization among incarcerated women. *International Journal of Law and Psychiatry, 22,* 301–322.

Brunk, M., Henggeler, S., & Whelan, J. (1987). Comparison of multisystemic therapy and parent training in the brief treatment of child abuse and neglect. *Journal of Consulting and Clinical Psychology, 55,* 311–318.

Buchanan, R., Whitlow, K., & Austin, J. (1986). National evaluation of objective prison classification systems: The current state of the art. *Crime & Delinquency, 32,* 272–290.

Bucklen, K. B., Duwe, G., & Taxman, F. (2021). *Guidelines for Post-Sentencing Risk Assessment.* Washington, DC: National Institute of Justice, U.S. Department of Justice. Retrieved from: www.ojp.gov/pdffiles1/nij/300654.pdf

Buell, M., & Abbate, J. (2020, January/February). Same is not equal: Policy and practice for justice-involved women. *American Jails,* 8–14.

Burdon, W., Farabee, D., Prendergast, M., Messina, N., & Cartier, J. (2002). Prison-based therapeutic community substance abuse programs: Implementation and operational issues. *Federal Probation, 66*(3), 3–8.

Bureau of Justice Statistics. (1992). *Compendium of Federal Justice Statistics, 1989.* Washington, DC: U.S. Department of Justice.

Bureau of Justice Statistics. (2001). *Federal Drug Offenders, 1999, with Trends, 1984–1999 (NCRJ-154043).* Washington, DC: Bureau of Justice Statistics.

Bureau of Justice Statistics. (2006). *Drug Use and Dependence, State and Federal Prisoners, 2004 (NCJ-213530).* Washington, DC: U.S. Government Printing Office.

Bureau of Justice Statistics. (2019). Criminal victimization. Generated using the NCVS Victimization Analysis Tool and www.bjs.gov. Sept., 2020.

Burns, D. (1980). *Feeling Good.* New York: Morrow.

Buser, M. (2020, November 2). The ethical conflict of social work within a carceral system. *Filter.* Retrieved from https://filtermag.org/social-work-carceral-system/

Bush, J., & Bilodeau, B. (1993). *OPTIONS: A Cognitive Change Program.* Washington, DC: National Institute of Corrections.

Bush, J., Taymans, J., & Glick, B. (1998). *Thinking for a Change.* Washington, DC: National Institute of Corrections.

Bush, N. E., Armstrong, C. M., & Hoyt, T. V. (2019). Smartphone apps for psychological health: A brief state of the science review. *Psychological Services, 16*(2), 188–195.

Butcher, J., Dahlstrom, W., Graham, W., Tellegen, A., & Kaemmer, B. (1989). *Manual for the Restandardized Minnesota Multiphasic Personality Inventory: MMPI-2. An Interpretative and Administrative Guide.* Minneapolis: University of Minnesota Press.

Cannon, C., Hamel, J., Buttell, F. P., & Ferreira, R. (2016). A survey of domestic violence perpetrator programs in the United States and Canada: Findings and implications for policy and intervention. *Partner Abuse, 7*, 226–276.

Caputo, G. A. (2004). Treating sticky fingers: An evaluation of treatment and education for offenders. *Journal of Offender Rehabilitation, 38*, 49–68.

Carr, K., Hinkle, B., & Ingram, B. (1991). Establishing mental health and substance abuse services in jails. *Journal of Prison and Jail Health, 10*, 77–89.

Carson, E. A. (2020). *Prisoners in 2019.* Washington, DC: Bureau of Justice Statistics.

Carson, E. A., & Cowhig, M. P. (2020a). *Mortality in Local Jails, 2000–2016 — Statistical Tables.* Washington, DC: Bureau of Justice Statistics.

Carson, E. A., & Cowhig, M. P. (2020b). *Mortality in State and Prisons, 2001–2016 — Statistical Tables.* Washington, DC: Bureau of Justice Statistics.

Cattell, R., & Cattell, A. (1973). *Culture Fair Intelligence Tests.* San Diego, CA: EdiTS.

Caulum, S. (1994). *Drug and Alcohol Treatment Options.* Washington, DC: Paper presented to the National Association of Sentencing Advocates.

Celentano, D. D., & McQueen, D. V. (1984). Multiple substance use among women with alcohol-related problems. In S. C. Wilsnack & L. J. Beckman (Eds.), *Alcohol Problems in Women* (pp. 97–116). New York: Guilford.

Center for Addiction and Mental Health. (1999). *1999 Resources.* Toronto: Center for Addiction and Mental Health.

Center for Criminal Justice Research. (2009). *Ohio Risk Assessment System (ORAS).* Cincinnati: Center for Criminal Justice Research.

Center for Sex Offender Management (CSOM). (2008). *The Comprehensive Approach to Sex Offender Management.* Silver Spring, MD: Center for Effective Public Policy.

Center for Substance Abuse Treatment (CSAT). (1999). *Substance Abuse Treatment for Women Offenders: Guide to Promising Practices.* Rockville, MD: U.S. Department of Health and Human Services.

Chadwick, N., Dewolf, A., & Serin, R. (2015). Effectively training community supervision officers: A meta-analytic review of the impact on offender outcome. *Criminal Justice and Behavior, 42*, 977–989. http://doi.org/10.1177/0093854815595661

Chamberlain, P. (2003). The Oregon Multidimensional Treatment Foster Care model: Features, outcomes, and progress in dissemination. (Moving evidence-based treatments from the laboratory into clinical practice). *Cognitive and Behavioral Practice, 10*, 303–312.

Chamberlain, P., Fisher, P., & Moore, K. (2003). Multidimensional treatment foster care: Applications of the OSLC intervention model to high-risk youth and their families. In J. Reid, G. Patterson, & J. Snyder (Eds.), *Antisocial Behavior in Children and Adolescents: A Developmental Analysis and Model for Intervention* (pp. 203–218). Washington, DC: American Psychological Association.

Chamberlain, P., & Reid, J. B. (1994). Differences in risk factors and adjustment for male and female delinquents in treatment foster care. *Journal of Child and Family Studies, 3*, 23–39.

Chamow, L. (1990). The clinician's role in treating spouse abuse. *Family Therapy, 17*, 123–128.

Chaple, M., Sacks, S., McKendrick, K., Marsch, L. A., Belenko, S., Leukefeld, C., Prendergast, M., & French, M. (2014). Feasibility of a computerized intervention for offenders with substance use disorders: A research note. *Journal of Experimental Criminology, 10*(1), 105–127.

Cheek, F., Franks, C., Laucious, J., & Burtle, V. (1971). Behavior-modification training for wives of alcoholics. *Quarterly Studies of Alcoholism, 32*, 456–461.

Chesney-Lind, M. (1998). Women in prison: From partial justice to vengeful equity. *Corrections Today, 60*(7), 66–73.

Chesney-Lind, M. (2000). What to do about girls? Thinking about programs for young women. In M. McMahon (Ed.), *Assessment to Assistance: Programs for Women in Community Corrections* (pp. 139–170). Lanham, MD: American Correctional Association.

Chesney-Lind, M., & Irwin, K. (2008). *Beyond Bad Girls: Gender, Violence, and Hype*. New York: Routledge.

Chesney-Lind, M., & Rodriguez, N. (1983). Women under lock and key. *Prison Journal, 63*, 47–65.

Cho, S., Ku, J., Park, J., Han, K., Lee, H., Choi, Y. K., Jung, Y.-C., Namkoong, K., Kim, J.-J., Kim, I. Y., Kim, S. I., & Shen, D. F. (2008). Development and verification of an alcohol craving- induction tool using virtual reality: Craving characteristics in social pressure situation. *CyberPsychology & Behavior, 11*, 302–309.

Christian, J. (2005). Riding the bus: Barriers to prison visitation and family management strategies. *Journal of Contemporary Criminal Justice, 21*, 31–48.

Clark, R. E. (2004). The classical origins of Pavlov's conditioning. *Integrative Physiological & Behavioral Science, 39*(4), 279–294.

Clear, T. (1988). Statistical prediction in corrections. *Research in Corrections, 1*, 1–39.

Cleckley, H. (1941). *The Mask of Sanity*. St. Louis, MO: C. V. Mosby.

Clem, J. M., Prost, S. G., & Thyer, B. A. (2015). Does wilderness therapy reduce recidivism in delinquent adolescents? A narrative review. *Journal of Adolescent and Family Health, 7*, 1–20.

Clements, C., McKee, J., & Jones, S. (1984). *Offender Needs Assessments: Models and Approaches*. Washington, DC: National Institute of Corrections.

Clodfelter, T. A., Holcomb, J. E., Alexander, M. A., Marcum, C. D., & Richards, T. N. (2016). A case study of Staff Training Aimed at Reducing Rearrest (STARR). *Federal Probation, 80*(1), 30–38.

Coid, J. W., Yang, M., Ullrich, S., Roberts, A., & Hare, R. D. (2009). Prevalence and correlates of psychopathic traits in the household population of Great Britain. *International Journal of Law and Psychiatry, 32*, 65–73.

Collins, H., & Collins, D. (1990). Family therapy in the treatment of child sexual abuse. In M. Rothery & G. Cameron (Eds.), *Child Maltreatment: Expanding Our Concept of Helping* (pp. 231–245). Hillsdale, NJ: Lawrence Erlbaum.

Comartin, E. B., Nelson, V., Smith, S., & Kubiak, S. (2021). The criminal/legal experiences of individuals with mental illness along the Sequential Intercept Model: An eight-site study. *Criminal Justice and Behavior, 48*, 76–95.

Conley, R., Luckasson, R., & Bouthilet, G. (1992). *The Criminal Justice System and Mental Retardation: Defendants and Victims*. Baltimore: P. H. Brookes.

Connell, A. M., Dishion, T. J., Yasui, M., & Kavanagh, K. (2007). An adaptive approach to family intervention: Linking engagement in family-centered intervention to reductions in adolescent problem behavior. *Journal of Consulting and Clinical Psychology, 75*, 568–579.

Cook, J., Walser, R., Kane, V., Ruzek, J., & Woody, G. (2006). Dissemination and feasibility of a cognitive behavioral treatment for substance use disorders and post-traumatic stress disorder in the veterans administration. *Journal of Psychoactive Drugs, 38*, 89–92.

Cooke, D. J., Hart, S. D., Logan, C., & Michie, C. (2012). Explicating the construct of psychopathy: Development and validation of a conceptual model, the Comprehensive Assessment of Psychopathic Personality (CAPP). *International Journal of Forensic Mental Health, 11*(4), 242–252.

Cooper, A., & Smith, E. L. (2011). *Homicide Trends in the United States, 1980–2008*. Washington, DC: U.S. Department of Justice, Bureau of Justice Programs.

Corley, M. (1996). Correctional education programs for adults with learning disabilities. *Linkages, 3*(2), 1–25, National Adult Literacy & Learning Disabilities Center. Retrieved January 24, 2003, from the National Institute for Literacy.

Cortoni, F. (2015). What is so special about female sexual offenders? Introduction to the special issue on female sexual offenders. *Sexual Abuse, 27*, 232–234.

Cortoni, F., & Gannon, T. (2016). Female sexual offenders: An overview. In A. Phenix & H. Hoberman (Eds.), *Sexual Offending: Predisposing Antecedents, Assessments and Management* (pp. 213–224). New York: Springer.

Cortoni, F., Hanson, R. K., & Coache, M. E. (2010). The recidivism rates of female sexual offenders are low: A meta-analysis. *Sexual Abuse, 22,* 387–401.

Council of State Governments. (2002). *Criminal Justice/Mental Health Consensus Project.* Lexington, KY: CSG. Retrieved from www.ojp.gov/pdffiles1/nij/grants/197103.pdf

Covington, S. (2002). Helping women recover: Creating gender-responsive treatment. In S. Straussner & S. Brown (Eds.), *The Handbook of Addiction Treatment for Women* (pp. 52–72). San Francisco: Jossey-Bass.

Covington, S. (2003). *Beyond Trauma: A Healing Journey for Women.* Center City, MN: Change Companies.

Covington, S. (2008a). *Helping Women Recover: A Program for Treating Substance Abuse. Facilitator's Guide—Revised Edition for Use in the Criminal Justice System.* San Francisco: Jossey-Bass.

Covington, S. (2008b). The relational theory of women's psychological development: Implications for the criminal justice system. In R. T. Zaplin (Ed.), *Female Offenders: Critical Perspectives and Effective Interventions* (2nd ed., pp. 135–164). Sudbury, MA: Jones and Bartlett.

Covington, S., & Bloom, B. E. (2007). Gender-responsive treatment and services in correctional settings. In E. Leeder (Ed.), *Inside and Out: Women, Prison, and Therapy* (pp. 9–34). New York: Haworth Press.

Covington, S., & Surrey, J. (1997). The relational model of women's psychological development: Implications for substance abuse. In S. Wilsnack & R. Wilsnack (Eds.), *Gender and Alcohol: Individual and Social Perspectives* (pp. 335–351). New Brunswick, NJ: Rutgers University Press.

Creswell, D. J. (2017). Mindfulness Interventions. *Annual Reviews of Psychology,* (68) 491–516.

Cullen, F., & Gendreau, P. (2001). From nothing works to what works: Changing professional ideology in the 21st century. *The Prison Journal, 81,* 313–338.

Cullen, F., Wright, J., & Applegate, B. (1996). Control in the community: The limits of reform? In A. Harland (Ed.), *Choosing Correctional Interventions that Work: Defining the Demand and Evaluating the Supply* (pp. 69–116). Newbury Park, CA: Sage.

Cullen, F. T., & Gendreau, P. (2000). Assessing correctional rehabilitation: Policy, practice, and prospects. In J. Horney (Ed.), *Criminal Justice 2000: Changes in Decision Making and Discretion in the Criminal Justice System* (pp. 109–175). Washington, DC: U.S. Department of Justice, National Institute of Justice.

Cullen, F. T., Jonson, C. L., & Mears, D. (2017). Reinventing community corrections. In M. Tonry & D. Nagin (Eds.), *Reinventing American Criminal Justice* (pp. 27–93). Chicago: University of Chicago Press.

Cullen, F. T., Pratt, T. C., Turanovic, J. J., & Butler, L. (2018). When bad news arrives: Project HOPE in a post-factual world. *Journal of Contemporary Criminal Justice, 34,* 13–34. https://doi.org/10.1177/1043986217750424

Daly, K. (1992). Women's pathways to felony court: Feminist theories of lawbreaking and problems of representation. *Southern California Review of Law and Women's Studies, 2,* 11–52.

Dass, R., & Gorman, P. (1985). *How Can I Help? Stories and Reflections on Service.* New York: Alfred A. Knopf.

Davis, L. M., Bozick, R., Steele, J. L., Saunders, J., Miles, J. N. V. (2013). *Evaluating the Effectiveness of Correctional Education: A Meta-analysis of Programs that Provide Education to Incarcerated Adults.* RAND Corporation.

DeHart, D., Lynch, S., Belknap, J., Dass-Brailsford, P., & Green, B. (2013). Life history models of female offending: The roles of serious mental illness and trauma in women's pathways to jail. *Psychology of Women Quarterly, 38,* 138–151.

DeLeon, G. (2000). *The Therapeutic Community: Theory, Model, and Method.* New York: Springer.

DeMatteo, D., Filone, S., & Davis, J. (2015). Substance use and crime. In B. L. Cutler & P. A. Zapf (Eds.), *APA Handbook of Forensic Psychology* (pp. 325–349). Washington, DC: American Psychological Association.

Denkowski, G., & Denkowski, K. (1985). The mentally retarded offender in the state prison system: Identification, prevalence, adjustment, and rehabilitation. *Criminal Justice and Behavior, 12,* 55–76.

Derogatis, L. (1977). *SCL-90 Administration: Scoring and Procedures Manual.* Baltimore: Johns Hopkins University Press.

Derogatis, L. (1994). *Brief Symptom Inventory: Administration, Scoring, and Procedures Manual.* Minneapolis: National Computer Systems.

Desmarais, S., Reeves, K. A., Nicholls, T. I., Telford, R. P., & Fiebert, M. S. (2012). Prevalence of physical violence in intimate relationships, Part 1: Rates of male and female victimization. *Partner Abuse, 3,* 140–169. https://doi.org/10.1891/1946-6560.3.2.140

Dicks, H. (1963). Object relations theory and marital studies. *British Journal of Medical Psychology, 36,* 125–129.

Dierkhising, C. V., Ko, S. J., Woods-Jaeger, B., Briggs, E. C., Lee, R., & Pynoos, R. S. (2013). Trauma histories among justice-involved youth: Findings from the National Child Traumatic Stress Network. *European Journal of Psychotraumatology, 4(1),* 1–12. http://dx.doi.org/10.3402/ejpt.v4i0.20274

DiGiorgio-Miller, J. (2007). Emotional variables and deviant sexual fantasies in adolescent sex offenders. *Journal of Psychiatry and Law, 35*(Summer), 109–124.

Dignam, J. T. (2003). Correctional mental health ethics revisited. In T. J. Fagan & R. K. Ax (Eds.), *Correctional Mental Health Handbook* (pp. 39–56). Thousand Oaks, CA: Sage.

Dilulio, J. (1991). *No Escape: The Future of American Corrections.* New York: Basic Books.

Dimeff, L., & Linehan, M. (2001). Dialectical behavior therapy in a nutshell. *California Psychologist, 34,* 10–13.

Dishion, T., & Andrews, D. (1995). Preventing escalation in problem behavior with high-risk young adolescents: Immediate and one-year outcomes. *Journal of Consulting and Clinical Psychology, 63,* 538–548.

Dixon, L., & Browne, K. (2003). The heterogeneity of spouse abuse: A review. *Aggression and Violent Behavior, 8,* 107–130.

Douglas, K. S., Strand, S., Belfrage, H., Fransson, G., & Levander, S. (2005). Reliability and validity evaluation of the Psychopathy Checklist: Screening Version (PCL:SV) in Swedish correctional and forensic psychiatric samples. *Assessment, 12,* 145–161.

Dowden, C., & Andrews, D. (2000). Effective correctional treatment and violent reoffending: A meta-analysis. *Canadian Journal of Criminology, 42,* 449–467.

Dowden, C., & Andrews, D. A. (2004). The importance of staff practice in delivering effective correctional treatment: A meta-analytic review of core correctional practice. *International Journal of Offender Therapy and Comparative Criminology, 48,* 203–214. https://doi.org/10.1177/0306624X03257765

Dowden, C., Antonowicz, D., & Andrews, D. (2003). The effectiveness of relapse prevention with offenders: A meta-analysis. *International Journal of Offender Therapy and Comparative Criminology, 47,* 516–528.

Dowden, C., & Brown, S. L. (2002). The role of substance abuse factors in predicting recidivism: A meta-analysis. *International Journal of Crime, Psychology, and Law, 8,* 243–264.

Drake, E. K., & Aos, S. (2012). *Confinement for technical violations of community supervision: Is there an effect on felony recidivism?* Olympia: Washington State Institute for Public Policy. Retrieved from www.wsipp.wa.gov/ReportFile/1106/Wsipp_Confinement-for-Technical-Violations-of-Community-Supervision-Is-There-an-Effect-on-Felony-Recidivism_Full-Report.pdf

Drake, E., Aos, S., & Miller, M. (2009). Evidence-based public policy options to reduce crime and criminal justice costs: Implications in Washington State. *Victims and Offenders, 4,* 170–196.

Drapeau, M., Korner, A. C., & Brunet, L. (2004). When the goals of therapists and patients clash: A study of pedophiles in treatment. *Journal of Offender Rehabilitation, 38,* 69–80.

Duwe, G. (2014). To what extent does civil commitment reduce sexual recidivism? Estimating the selective incapacitation effects in Minnesota. *Journal of Criminal Justice, 42,* 193–202.

Duwe, G., & Clark, V. (2015). Importance of program integrity: Outcome evaluation of a gender responsive, cognitive behavioral program for female offenders. *Criminology and Public Policy, 14,* 301–328.

Eckhouse, L., Lum, K., Conti-Cook, C., Ciccolini, J. (2019). Layers of bias: A unified approach to understanding problems with risk assessment. *Criminal Justice and Behavior, 46,* 185–209.

Edleson, J., & Grusznski, R. (1988). Treating the men who batter: Four years of outcome data from the Domestic Abuse Project. *Journal of Social Service Research, 12,* 3–22.

Eisenberg, M., & Fabelo, T. (1996). Evaluation of the Texas Correctional Substance Abuse Treatment Initiative: The impact of policy research. *Crime & Delinquency, 42*(2), 296–308.

Elliott, D. E., Bjelajac, P., Fallot, R. D., Markoff, L. S., & Reed, B. G. (2005). Trauma-informed or trauma denied: Principles and implementation of trauma-informed services for women. *Journal of Community Psychology, 33,* 461–477.

Elliott, D., Huizinga, D., & Ageton, S. (1985). Reconciling race and class differences in self-reported and official estimates of delinquency. *American Sociological Review, 45,* 95–110.

Elliott, W. (2002). Managing offender resistance to counseling. *Federal Probation, 66,* 172–178.

Elliott, W., & Verdeyen, V. (2002). Game *Over! Strategies for Managing Inmate Deception.* Lanham, MD: American Correctional Association.

Elliott, W., & Walters, G. (1991). Coping with offenders' resistance to psychoeducational presentations on the criminal lifestyle. *Journal of Correctional Education, 42,* 172–177.

Elliott, W., & Walters, G. (1997). Conducting psychoeducational interventions with drug abusing offenders: The Lifestyle Model. *Journal of Drug Education, 27,* 307–319.

Ellis, A. (1962). *Reason and Emotion in Psychotherapy.* Secaucus, NJ: Lyle Stuart.

Ellis, A. (1979). The sex offender. In H. Toch (Ed.), *Legal and Criminal Psychology.* New York: Holt, Rinehart & Winston.

English, K. (2004). The containment approach to managing sex offenders, *Seton Hall Law Review, 34,* 1255–1272.

English, K., Jones, L., & Patrick, I. (2003). Community containment of sex offender risk: A promising approach. In B. J. Winick & J. W. LaFond (Eds.), *Protecting Society from Dangerous Offenders: Law, Justice, and Therapy* (pp. 265–277). Washington, DC: American Psychological Association.

Erez, E. (1988). Myth of the new female offender: Some evidence from attitudes toward law and justice. *Journal of Criminal Justice, 16*(6), 499–509.

Exner, J. (2002). *The Rorschach: A Comprehensive System* (Vol. 1) (4th ed.). New York: John Wiley.

Eysenck, H., & Eysenck, M. (1983). *Mindwatching: Why People Behave the Way They Do.* New York: Anchor.

Farabee, D. (2005). *Rethinking Rehabilitation: Why Can't We Reform Our Criminals?* Washington, DC: AEI Press.

Feeley, M., & Simon, J. (1992). The new penology: Notes on the emerging strategy of corrections and its implications. *Criminology, 30,* 449–474.

Fernandez, M., McClain, D., Brown Williams, B., & Ellison, P. (2015). PBIS in Georgia Department of Juvenile Justice: Data dashboard and radar reports utilized for team data based decision-making with facility team leader perspectives. *Residential Treatment for Children & Youth, 21,* 334–343.

Finigan, M. (1998). *An Outcome Evaluation of the Multnomah County S.T.O.P. Drug Diversion Program.* Portland, OR: NPC Research.

Finkelhor, D., Ormrod, R., & Chaffin, M. (2009). *Juveniles Who Commit Sex Offenses Against Minors.* Washington, DC: U.S. Office of Juvenile Justice Delinquency Prevention.

Finn, P. (1998). *The Delaware Department of Corrections Life Skills Program.* Washington, DC: U.S. Department of Justice, Office of Justice Programs.

First, M. B., Williams, J. B. W., Benjamin, L. S., & Spitzer, R. L. (2015). *User's Guide for the SCID-5-PD (Structured Clinical Interview for DSM-5 Personality Disorder).* Arlington, VA: American Psychiatric Association.

First, M. B., Williams, J. B. W., Karg, R. S., & Spitzer, R. L. (2015a). *Structured Clinical Interview for DSM-5 Disorders, Research Version (SCID-5-RV).* Arlington, VA: American Psychiatric Association.

First, M. B., Williams, J. B. W., Karg, R. S., & Spitzer, R. L. (2015b). *Structured Clinical Interview for DSM-5 Disorders, Clinician Version* (SCID-5-CV). Arlington, VA: American Psychiatric Association.

Fisher, B., Cullen, F., & Turner, M. (2000). *The Sexual Victimization of College Women*. Washington, DC: Office of Justice Programs, National Institute of Justice.

Fisher, P. A., & Gilliam, K. S. (2012). Multidimensional Treatment Foster Care: An alternative to residential treatment for high risk children and adolescents. *Psychosocial Intervention, 21*, 195–203.

Flemons, D. (1989). An ecosystemic view of family violence. *Family Therapy, 16*, 1–10.

Flynn, P. M., Craddock, S. G., Luckey, J. W., Hubbard, R. L., & Dunteman, G. H. (1996). Comorbidity of antisocial personality and mood disorders among psychoactive substance-dependent treatment clients. *Journal of Personality Disorders, 10*, 56–67.

Folino, J. O., & Hare, R. D. (2005). Listado revisado para verificación de la psicopatía: su estandarización y validación en la Argentina. *Acta Psiquiátrica y Psicológica de América Latina, 51*, 94–104.

Fowler, K. A., Jack, S. P. D., Lyons, B. H., Betz, C. J., & Petrosky, E. (2018). Surveillance for violent deaths: National violent death reporting system, 18 states 2014. *Morbidity and Mortality Weekly Report, 67*, 1–36. https://doi.org/10.15585/mmwr.ss6702a1

Fox, B., & DeLisi, M. (2018). From criminological heterogeneity to coherent classes. *Youth Violence and Juvenile Justice, 16*, 299–318.

Frawley, P. J., Howard, M. O., and Elkins, R. L. (2017). Aversion Therapies, Chapter 61. *Principles of Addiction Medicine* (6th ed.). Chevy Chase, MD: The American Society of Addiction Medicine, Inc.

French, S., & Gendreau, P. (2006). Reducing prison misconducts. *Criminal Justice and Behavior, 33*, 185–218.

Friedman, A. (1989). Family therapy vs. parent groups: Effect on adolescent drug abusers. *American Journal of Family Therapy, 17*, 335–347.

Frost, N. A., Greene, J., & Pranis, K. (2006). *Hard Hit: The Growth in the Imprisonment of Women, 1977–2004*. New York: Institute on Women & Criminal Justice, Women's Prison Association.

Furby, L., Weinrott, M., & Blackshaw, L. (1989). Sex offender recidivism: A review. *Psychological Bulletin, 105*, 3–30.

Gallagher, C., Wilson, D., Hirschfield, P., Coggeshall, M., & MacKenzie, D. (1999). A quantitative review of the effects of sex offender treatment on sexual reoffending. *Corrections Management Quarterly, 3*, 19–29.

Garrett, C. (1985). Effects of residential treatment on adjudicated delinquents: A meta-analysis. *Journal of Research in Crime & Delinquency, 22*, 287–308.

Gaudin, J., Wodarski, J., Arkinson, M., & Avery, L. (1991). Remedying child neglect: Effectiveness of social network interventions. *Journal of Applied Social Sciences, 15*, 97–123.

Gehring, K., & Van Voorhis, P. (2014). Needs and pretrial failure: Additional risk factors for female and male pretrial defendants. *Criminal Justice and Behavior, 41*, 943–970.

Gehring, K., Van Voorhis, P., & Bell, V. (2010). "What works" for female probationers? An evaluation of the moving on program. *Women, Girls and Criminal Justice, 11*(1), 6–10.

Gendreau, P. (1995). Technology transfer in the criminal justice field. In T. Backer, S. Davis, & G. Soucy (Eds.), *Reviewing the Behavioral Science Knowledge Base on Technology Transfer* (pp. 198–208). (NIDA Research Monograph 155). Rockville, MD: U.S. Department of Health and Human Services, Public Health Service, National Institutes of Health.

Gendreau, P. (1996a). Offender rehabilitation: What we know and what needs to be done. *Criminal Justice and Behavior, 23*, 144–161.

Gendreau, P. (1996b). The principles of effective intervention with offenders. In A. Harland (Ed.), *Choosing Correctional Options that Work: Defining the Demand and Evaluating the Supply* (pp. 117–130). Thousand Oaks, CA: Sage.

Gendreau, P., & Andrews, D. (1990). Tertiary prevention: What the meta-analysis of the offender treatment literature tells us about what works. *Canadian Journal of Criminology, 32*, 173–184.

Gendreau, P., & Andrews, D. (2001). *Correctional Program Assessment Inventory (CPAI-2000)*. Saint John: University of New Brunswick.

Gendreau, P., French, S., & Gionet, A. (2004). What works (what doesn't work): The principles of effective correctional treatment. *Journal of Community Corrections, 13,*27–30.

Gendreau, P., & Goggin, C. (1991). *Evaluation of Correctional Service of Canada Substance Abuse Programs.* (Research Report No. 16). Ottawa: Research and Statistics Branch, Correctional Service of Canada.

Gendreau, P., & Goggin, C. (1996). Principles of effective correctional programming with offenders. *Forum on Corrections Research, 8*(3), 38–40.

Gendreau, P., Goggin, C., French, S., & Smith, P. (2006). Practicing psychology in correctional settings. In A. Hess & I. Weiner (Eds.), *The Handbook of Forensic Psychology* (3rd ed.) (pp. 722–750). Hoboken, NJ: Wiley.

Gendreau, P., Goggin, C., & Fulton, B. (2000). Intensive supervision in probation and parole. In C. R. Hollin (Ed.), *Handbook of Offender Assessment and Treatment* (pp. 195–204). Chichester, UK: John Wiley.

Gendreau, P., Goggin, C., & Smith, P. (2001). Implementation guidelines for correctional programs in the real world. In G. A. Bernfeld, D. Farrington, & A. Leschied (Eds.), *Offender Rehabilitation in Practice* (pp. 247–268). Chichester, UK: John Wiley.

Gendreau, P., Goggin, C., & Smith, P. (2002). Is the PCL-R really the "unparalleled" measure of offender risk? *Criminal Justice and Behavior, 29,* 397–126.

Gendreau, P. & Listwan, S. J. (2018). Contingency management programs in corrections: Another panacea? *Journal of Contemporary Criminal Justice, 34*(1), 35–46.

Gendreau, P., Listwan, S. J., Kuhns, J. B., & Exum, M. L. (2014). Making prisoners accountable: Are contingency management programs the answer? *Criminal Justice and Behavior, 41,* 1079–1102.

Gendreau, P., Little, T., & Goggin, C. (1996). A meta-analysis of the predictors of adult offender recidivism: What works? *Criminology, 34,* 575–607.

Gendreau, P., Paparazzi, M., Little, T., & Goddard, M. (1993). Does "punishing smarter" work? An assessment of the new generation of alternative sanctions in probation. *Forum on Corrections Research, 5,* 31–34.

Gendreau, P., & Ross, R. (1979). Effective correctional treatment: Bibliotherapy for cynics. *Crime & Delinquency, 25,* 463–489.

Gendreau, P., & Ross, R. (1987). Revivification of rehabilitation: Evidence from the 1980s. *Justice Quarterly, 4,* 349–409.

Gendreau, P., & Smith, P. (2007). Influencing the "people who count": Some perspectives on the reporting of meta-analytic results for prediction and treatment outcomes with offenders. *Criminal Justice and Behavior, 34,* 1536–1559.

Gendreau, P., & Smith, P. (2012). Assessment and treatment strategies for correctional institutions. In J. Dvoskin, J. Skeem, R. Novaco, & K. Douglas (Eds.), *Using social science to reduce violent offending* (pp. 157–178). Oxford: Oxford University Press.

Gibbs, J., Potter, G., & Goldstein, A. (1995). *The EQUIP Program: Teaching Youth to Think and Act Responsibly through a Peer-Helping Approach.* Champaign, IL: Research Press.

Gilfus, M. E. (1992). From victims to survivors to offenders: Women's routes of entry and immersion into street crime. *Women & Criminal Justice, 4,* 63–90.

Gillam, D. G., & Yusuf, H. (2019). Brief motivational interviewing in dental practice. *Dental Journal, 7,* 51–60. https://doi.org/10.3390/dj7020051

Gilligan, C. (1982). *In a Different Voice: Psychological Theory and Women's Development.* Cambridge, MA: Harvard University Press.

Gilligan, C., Lyons, N., & Hanmer, T. (1990). *Making Connections: The Relational Worlds of Adolescent Girls at Emma Willard School.* Cambridge, MA: Harvard University Press.

Glaze, L. E., & Bonczar, T. P. (2011). *Probation and Parole in the United States, 2010.* Washington, DC: Bureau of Justice Statistics.

Glick, B., & Gibbs, J. (2011). *ART: A Comprehensive Intervention for Aggressive Youth* (3rd ed.). Champaign, IL: Research Press.

Gobeil, R., Blanchette, K., & Stewart, L. (2016). A meta-analytic review of correctional interventions for women offenders: Gender-neutral versus gender-informed approaches. *Criminal Justice and Behavior, 43*(3), 301–322.

Golden, L. (2002). *Evaluation of the Efficacy of a Cognitive Behavioral Program for Offenders on Probation: Thinking for a Change.* Dallas: University of Texas Southwestern Medical Center at Dallas.

Golden, L., Gatcheland, R., & Cahill, M. (2006). Evaluating the effectiveness of the National Institute of Corrections' "Thinking for a Change" program among probationers. *Journal of Offender Rehabilitation, 43*, 55–73.

Goldkamp, J., White, M., & Robinson, J. (2001). Do drug courts work? Getting inside the drug court black box. *Journal of Drug Issues, 31*(1), 27–72.

Goldstein, A. P. (1999). *The Prepare Curriculum: Teaching Prosocial Competencies* (Revised ed.). Champaign, IL: Research Press.

Goldstein, A. P., & Glick, B. (1995). *The Prosocial Gang: Implementing Aggression Replacement Training.* Thousand Oaks, CA: Sage.

Goldstein, A. P., Glick, B., & Gibbs, J. (1998). *Aggression Replacement Training: A Comprehensive Intervention for Aggressive Youth* (Revised ed.). Champaign, IL: Research Press.

Goldstein, A. P., Glick, B., Irwin, M., Pask-McCartney, C., & Rubama, I. (1989). *Reducing Delinquency: Intervention in the Community.* New York: Pergamon.

Goldstein, A. P., & McGinnis, E. (1997). *Skillstreaming the Adolescent: New Strategies and Perspectives for Teaching Prosocial Skills.* Champaign, IL. Research Press.

Gordon, D., & Arbuthnot, J. (1987). Individual, group, and family interventions. In H. Quay (Ed.), *Handbook of Juvenile Delinquency* (pp. 290–324). New York: Wiley.

Gordon, D., Arbuthnot, J., Gustafson, K., & McGreen, P. (1988). Home-based behavioral-systems family therapy with disadvantaged juvenile delinquents. *American Journal of Family Therapy, 16*, 243–255.

Gordon, D., Graves, K., & Arbuthnot, J. (1995). The effects of functional family therapy for delinquents on adult criminal behavior. *Criminal Justice and Behavior, 22*, 60–73.

Gorenstein, E. E. (1982). Frontal lobe functions in psychopaths. *Journal of Abnormal Psychology, 91*, 368–379.

Grant, B. F., Hasin, D. S., Stinson, F. S., Dawson, D. A., Chou, S. P., & Ruan, W. J. (2004). Prevalence, correlates, and disability of personality disorders in the United States: Results from the National Epidemiologic Survey on Alcohol and Related Conditions. *Journal of Clinical Psychiatry, 65*, 948–958.

Gray, S. R. (1995). A comparison of verbal satiation and minimal arousal conditioning to reduce deviant arousal in the laboratory. *Sexual Abuse: A Journal of Research and Treatment, 7*, 143–153.

Green, B. L., Furrer, C., Worcel, S., Burrus, S., & Finigan, M. W. (2007). How effective are family treatment drug courts? Outcomes from a four-site national study. *Child Maltreatment, 12*, 43–59.

Green, B. L., Miranda, J., Daroowalla, A., & Siddique, J. (2005). Trauma exposure, mental health functioning and program needs of women in jail. *Crime and Delinquency, 51*, 133–151.

Greenfeld, L. A., & Snell, T. L. (1999). *Women Offenders.* Washington, DC: Bureau of Justice Statistics.

Greenspan, R. L., & Loftus, E. F. (2020). Eyewitness confidence malleability: Misinformation as post-identification feedback. *Law and Human Behavior, 44*, 194–208 https://doi.org/10.1037/lhb0000369

Griffith, J., Hiller, M., Knight, K., & Simpson, D. (1999). A cost-effectiveness analysis of in-prison therapeutic community treatment and risk classification. *The Prison Journal, 79*(3), 352–368.

Groth, N. (1979). *Men Who Rape: The Psychology of the Offender.* New York: Basic Books.

Groth-Marnat, G. (2003). *Handbook of Psychological Assessment* (4th ed.). New York: John Wiley.

Grove, W., & Meehl, P. (1996). Comparative efficiency of informal (subjective, impressionistic) and formal (mechanical, algorithmic) prediction procedures: The clinical statistical controversy. *Psychology, Public Policy, and Law, 2*(2), 293–323.

Guerin, P. (1976). *Family Therapy: Theory and Practice.* New York: Gardner.

Gunderson, K., & Svartdal, F. (2006). ART in Norway: Outcome evaluation of 11 Norwegian student projects. *Scandinavian Journal of Educational Research, 50,* 63–81.

Haapala, D., & Kinney, J. (1988). Avoiding out-of-home placement of high-risk status offenders through the use of intensive home-based family preservation services. *Criminal Justice and Behavior, 15,* 334–348.

Hagan, T., Finnegan, L., & Nelson-Zlupko, L. (1994). Impediments to comprehensive treatment models for substance-dependent women: Treatment and research questions. *Journal of Psychoactive Drugs, 26,* 163–171.

Hairston, C. (2002). *Prisoners and Families: Parenting Issues during Incarceration.* Washington, DC: Paper presented at the Urban Institute's From Prison to Home Conference, January 30–31.

Haley, J. (1976). *Problem-Solving Therapy.* San Francisco: Jossey-Bass.

Hall, E., Prendergast, M., Wellish, J., Patten, M., & Cao, Y. (2004). Treating drug-abusing prisoners: An outcomes evaluation of the Forever Free program. *The Prison Journal, 84,* 81–105.

Hall, G. (1995). Sexual offender recidivism revisited: A meta-analysis of recent treatment studies. *Journal of Consultant and Clinical Psychology, 63,* 802–809.

Hamberger, L., & Hastings, J. (1988). Skills training for treatment of spouse abusers: An outcome study. *Journal of Family Violence, 3,* 121–130.

Hamel, J. (2020). Beyond gender: Finding common ground in evidence-based batterer intervention. In B. Russell (Ed.), *Intimate Partner Violence and the LGBT+ Community: Understanding Power Dynamics* (pp. 195–223). New York: Springer Publishing.

Haney, C. (2003). Mental health issues in long-term solitary and supermax confinement. *Crime & Delinquency, 49,* 124–156.

Hanson, K., Harris, A., Scott, T., & Helmus, L. (2007). *Assessing the risk of sexual offenders on community supervision: The Dynamic Supervision Project.* (User Report No. 2007–05). Ottawa: Public Safety Canada.

Hanson, R. K. (1997). *The Development of a Brief Actuarial Risk Scale for Sexual Offense Recidivism.* (User Report No. 1997–2004). Ottawa: Department of the Solicitor General of Canada.

Hanson, R. K., Bourgon, G., Helmus, L., & Hodgson, S. (2009). *A Meta-analysis of the Effectiveness of Treatment for Sexual Offenders: Risk, Need, and Responsivity.* Ottawa: Public Safety Canada.

Hanson, R. K., & Bussiere, M. T. (1998). Predicting relapse: A meta-analysis of sexual offender recidivism studies. *Journal of Consulting and Clinical Psychology, 66,* 348–362.

Hanson, R. K., Gordon, A., Harris, A. J. R., Marques, J. K., Murphy, W., Quinsey, V. L., & Seto, M. C. (2002). First report of the Collaborative Outcome Data Project on the effectiveness of psychological treatment for sex offenders. *Sexual Abuse, 14,* 169–194.

Hanson, R., & Harris, A. (2000). *The Sex Offender-Need Assessment Rating (SONAR): A Method for Measuring Change in Risk Levels.* (User Report No. 2000–2001). Ottawa: Solicitor General Canada.

Hanson, R. K., & Morton-Bourgon, K. E. (2004). *Predictors of Sexual Recidivism: An Updated Meta-analysis.* Ottawa, Ontario: Public Safety and Emergency Preparedness Canada.

Hanson, R., & Thornton, D. (1999). *Static 99: Improving Actuarial Risk Assessments for Sex Offenders.* (User Report No. 1999–2002). Ottawa: Solicitor General Canada.

Hardyman, P., Austin, J., & Peyton, J. (2004). *Prisoner Intake Systems: Assessing Needs and Classifying Prisoners.* Washington, DC: National Institute of Corrections.

Hardyman, P., Austin, J., & Tulloch, O. (2002). *Revalidating External Prison Classification Systems: The Experience of Ten States and Model for Classification Reform.* Washington, DC: National Institute of Corrections.

Hardyman, P., & Van Voorhis, P. (2004). *Developing Gender-Specific Classification Systems for Women Offenders.* Washington, DC: National Institute of Corrections.

Hare R. (1991). *The Hare Psychopathy Checklist–Revised.* Toronto: Multi-Health Systems.

Hare, R. (1993). *Without Conscience: The Disturbing World of the Psychopaths among Us.* New York: Pocket Books.

Hare, R. (1998). Psychopaths and their nature. In T. Millon, E. Simonsen, M. Birket-Smith, & R. Davis (Eds.), *Psychopathy: Antisocial, Criminal, and Violent Behavior* (pp. 188–212). New York: Guilford.

Hare, R. (2003). *Hare Psychopathy Checklist—Revised* (2nd ed.). North Tonawanda, NY: Multi-Health Systems.

Harlow, C. (2003). *Education and Correctional Populations: Bureau of Justice Statistics Special Report.* Washington, DC: U.S. Government Printing Office.

Harrell, A., & Cavanagh, S. (1998). *Drug Courts and the Role of Sanctions: Findings from the Evaluation of the D.C. Superior Court Drug Intervention Program.* Washington, DC: Paper presented at the NIJ Research in Progress Seminar Series.

Harris, G. T. (1995). *Overcoming Resistance: Success in Counseling Men.* Lanham, MD: American Correctional Association.

Harris, G. T., & Rice, M. E. (2006). Treatment of psychopathy: A review of empirical findings. In C. Patrick (Ed.), *Handbook of Psychopathy* (pp. 555–572). New York: Guilford.

Harris, K., & Miller, W. (1990). Behavioral self-control training for problem drinkers: Components of efficacy. *Psychology of Addictive Behaviors, 4,* 82–90.

Harris, M., & Fallot, R. D. (2001). Envisioning a trauma-informed service system: A vital paradigm shift. In M. Harris & R. D. Fallot (Eds.), *Using Trauma Theory to Design Service Systems* (pp. 3–22). San Francisco: Jossey-Bass.

Harris, P. (1988). The Interpersonal Maturity Level Classification System: I-Level. *Criminal Justice and Behavior, 15,* 58–77.

Hawken, A. & Kleiman, M. A. R. (2009). *Managing Drug Involved Probationers with Swift and Certain Sanctions: Evaluating Hawaii's HOPE.* (No. 229023). Washington, DC: National Institute of Justice.

Hawken, A., Kulick, J., Smith, K., Mei, J., Zhang, Y., Jarman, S., Yu, T., Carson, C., & Vial, T. (2016). *HOPE II: A follow-up to Hawaii's HOPE evaluation.* (No. 249912). Washington, DC: National Institute of Justice.

Hawton, K., Linsell, L., Adeniji, T., Sariaslan, A., & Fazel, S. (2014). Self-harm in prison in England and Wales: An epidemiological study of prevalence, risk factors, clustering, and subsequent suicide. *The Lancet, 383,* 1147–1154.

Hayes, S. C., Follette V. M., Linehan, M. (2004). *Mindfulness and Acceptance: Expanding the Cognitive-Behavioral Tradition.* New York: Guilford Press.

Hays, P. A., & Iwamasa, G. Y. (2006). *Culturally Responsive Cognitive-Behavioral Therapy: Assessment, Practice, and Supervision.* Washington, DC: American Psychological Association.

Hazelrigg, M., Cooper, H., & Borduin, C. (1987). Evaluating the effectiveness of family therapies: An integrative review and analysis. *Psychological Bulletin, 101,* 428–442.

Heil, P., Ahlmeyer, S., & Simons, D. (2003). Crossover sexual offenses. *Sexual Abuse, 15,* 221–236.

Hein, D., Cohen, L., Litt, L., Miele, G., & Capstick, C. (2004). Promising empirically supported treatments for women with comorbid PTSD and substance use disorders. *American Journal of Psychiatry, 161,* 1426–1432.

Helmus, L., Thornton, D., Hanson, R., & Babchishin, K. (2012). Improving the predictive accuracy of the Static-99 and Static 2002 with older sex offenders: Revised age weights. *Sexual Abuse: A Journal of Research and Treatment, 24,* 64–101.

Henderson, D. J. (1998). Drug abuse and incarcerated women: A research review. *Journal of Substance Abuse Treatment, 15,* 579–587.

Henderson, D. J., & Boyd, C. (1995). Women and illicit drugs: Sexuality and crack cocaine. *Health Care for Women International, 16,* 113–124.

Henderson, D. J., Boyd, C., & Mieczkowski, T. (1994). Gender, relationships and crack cocaine. *Research in Nursing and Health, 17,* 265–272.

Henggeler, S. (Ed.), (1982). *Delinquency and Adolescent Psychopathology: A Family-Ecological Systems Approach.* Littleton, MA: Wright.

Henggeler, S., & Borduin, C. (1990). *Family Therapy and Beyond: A Multisystemic Approach to Treating the Behavior Problems of Children and Adolescents.* Pacific Grove, CA: Brooks/Cole.

Henggeler, S., & Lee, T. (2003). Multisystemic treatment of serious clinical problems. In A. Kazdin (Ed.), *Evidence-based Psychotherapies for Children and Adolescents* (pp. 301–324). New York: Guilford.

Henggeler, S., Borduin, C., Melton, G., Mann, B., Smith, L., Hall, J., Cone, L., & Fucci, B. R. (1991). Effects of multisystemic therapy on drug use and abuse in serious juvenile offenders: A progress report from two outcome studies. *Family Dynamics of Addiction Quarterly, 1,* 40–51.

Henggeler, S., Clingempeel, G., Brondino, M., & Pickrel, S. G. (2002). Four-year follow-up of multisystemic therapy with substance-abusing and substance-dependent juvenile offenders. *Journal of American Academy of Child and Adolescent Psychiatry, 41,* 868–874.

Henggeler, S., Halliday-Boykins, C., Cunningham, P., Randall, J., Shapiro, S., & Chapman, J. (2006). Juvenile drug court: Enhancing outcomes by integrating evidence-based treatments. *Journal of Consulting and Clinical Psychology, 74,* 42–54.

Henggeler, S., Melton, G., & Smith, L. (1992). Family preservations using multisystemic therapy: An effective alternative to incarcerating serious juvenile offenders. *Journal of Consulting and Clinical Psychology, 60,* 953–961.

Henggeler, S., Pickrel, S., Brondino, M., & Crouch, J. (1996). Eliminating (almost) treatment dropout of substance abusing or dependent delinquents through home-based multisystemic therapy. *American Journal of Psychiatry, 153,* 427–428.

Henggeler, S., Rodick, J., Borduin, C., Hanson, C., Watson, S., & Urey, J. (1986). Multisystemic treatment of juvenile offenders: Effects on adolescent behavior and family interaction. *Developmental Psychology, 22,* 132–141.

Henggeler, S., Schoenwald, S., Borduin, C., Rowland, M., & Cunningham, P. (1998). *Multisystemic Treatment of Antisocial Behavior in Children and Adolescents.* New York: Guilford.

Henggeler, S., Schoenwald, S., & Pickrel, S. (1995). Multisystemic therapy: Bridging the gap between university- and community-based treatment. *Journal of Consulting and Clinical Psychology, 63,* 709–717.

Hepburn, J. (1989). Prison guards as agents of social control. In L. Goodstein & D. MacKenzie (Eds.), *The American Prison: Issues in Research and Policy* (pp. 191–208). New York: Plenum.

Herman, J. (1992). *Trauma and Recovery.* New York: Harper Collins.

Hester, R., & Miller, W. (Eds.) (2003). *Handbook of Alcoholism Treatment Approaches: Effective Alternatives* (3rd ed.). Boston: Allyn & Bacon.

Hill, C. D., Neumann, S. C., & Rogers R. (2004). Confirmatory factor analysis of the Psychopathy Checklist: Screening Version in offenders with axis I disorders. *Psychological Assessment, 16,* 90–95.

Hilton, N. Z., Harris, G. T., Rice, M. E., Houghton, R. E., & Eke, A. W. (2008). An in depth actuarial assessment for wife assault recidivism. *Law and Human Behavior, 32,* 150–163.

Hineline, P. N., & Rosales-Ruiz, J. (2013). Behavior in relation to aversive events: Punishment and negative reinforcement. In G. J. Madden (Ed.), *APA Handbook of Behavior Analysis: Methods and Principles* (pp. 483–512). Washington, DC: American Psychological Association.

Hirsch, R., & Imhof, J. (1975). A family therapy approach to the treatment of drug abuse and addiction. *Journal of Psychedelic Drugs, 7,* 181–185.

Hislop, J. (2001). *Female Sex Offenders: What Therapists, Law Enforcement, and Child Protection Services Need to Know.* Ravensdale, NJ: Issues Press.

Ho, M. K. (2003). *Family Therapy with Ethnic Minorities* (2nd ed.). Newbury Park, CA: Sage.

Hodges, J., Guiliotti, N., & Porpotage, F. M., II (1994). *Juvenile justice bulletin: Improving literacy skills of juvenile detainees.* Washington, DC: Office of Justice Programs. Office of Juvenile Justice and Delinquency Prevention.

Hoffman, L. (1981). *Foundations of Family Therapy.* New York: Basic Books.

Hoffman, P. (1983). Screening for risk: A revised Salient Factor Score (SFS-81). *Journal of Criminal Justice, 11*, 539–547.

Hoge, R., Leschied, A., & Andrews, D. (1993). *An Investigation of Young Offender Services in the Province of Ontario: A Report of the Repeat Offender Project.* Toronto: Ministry of Community and Social Services.

Hogue, A., Dauber, S., Samuolis, J., & Liddle, J. H. A. (2006). Treatment techniques and outcomes in multidimensional family therapy for adolescent behavior. *Journal of Family Psychology, 20*, 535–543.

Hollin, C. (1990). *Cognitive-Behavioral Interactions with Young Offenders.* New York: Pergamon.

Holtfreter, K., Reisig, M. D., & Morash, M. (2004). Poverty, state capital, and recidivism among women offenders. *Criminology and Public Policy, 3*, 185–208.

Holtzworth-Munroe, A., & Meehan, J. C. (2002). *Typologies of Maritally Violent Men: A Summary of Current Knowledge and Suggestions for Future Research.* Paper presented at National Research Council Workshop, Washington, DC: Committee on Law and Justice, National Institute of Justice, Office of Justice Programs, U.S. Department of Justice.

Holtzworth-Munroe, A., & Stuart, G. L. (1994). Typologies of male batterers: Three subtypes and the differences among them. *Psychological Bulletin, 116*, 476–497.

Houston, J. (1998). *Making Sense with Offenders' Personal Constructs, Therapy, and Change.* New York: Wiley.

Howard, M. O. (2001). Pharmacological aversion treatment of alcohol dependence. Production and prediction of conditioned alcohol aversion. *American Journal of Drug and Alcohol Abuse 27*, 561–585.

Howing, P., Wodarski, J., Gaudin, J., & Kurtz, P. (1989). Effective interventions to ameliorate the incidence of child maltreatment. *Journal of Consulting and Clinical Psychology, 51*, 424–431.

Hser, Y., Anglin, M., & Booth, M. (1987). Sex differences in addict careers: 3. Addiction. *American Journal of Drug and Alcohol Abuse, 13*, 231–251.

Hser, Y., Anglin, M., & McGlothlin, W. (1987). Sex differences in addict careers: 1. Initiation of use. *American Journal of Drug and Alcohol Abuse, 13*, 33–57.

Hubbard, D. J. (2007). Getting the most out of correctional treatment: Testing the responsivity principle on male and female offenders. *Federal Probation, 71*, 2.

Hudson, S. M, & Ward, T. (2000). Interpersonal competency in sex offenders. *Behavior Modification, 24*, 494–527.

Hughes, M. A., Stout, J. C., & Dolan, M. C. (2013). Concurrent validity of the Psychopathic Personality Inventory-Revised and the Psychopathy Checklist: Screening version in an Australian offender sample. *Criminal Justice and Behavior, 40*, 802–813.

Humphries, K. & Kilmer, B. (2020). Still HOPEful - Reconsidering a failed replication of a swift, certain, and fair approach to reducing substance use among individuals under criminal justice supervision. *Addiction, 115*, 1973–1977.

Hunt, G., & Azrin, N. (1973). A community-reinforcement approach to alcoholism. *Behavior Research and Therapy, 11*, 91–104.

Inciardi, J., & Lockwood, D. (1994). When worlds collide: Establishing CREST Outreach Center. In B. Fletcher, J. Inciardi, & A. Horton (Eds.), *Drug Abuse Treatment: The Implementation of Innovative Approaches* (pp. 63–78). Westport, CT: Greenwood.

Inciardi, J., McBride, D., & Weinman, B. (1993). The assessment and referral of criminal justice clients: Examining the focused offender disposition program. In J. Inciardi (Ed.), *Drug Treatment and Criminal Justice* (pp. 149–193). Newbury Park, CA: Sage.

Institute of Medicine. (1990). Treating drug problems. In D. Gerstein & H. Harwood (Eds.), *Treating Drug Problems.* Washington, DC: National Academy Press.

Izzo, R., & Ross, R. (1990). Meta-analysis of rehabilitation programs for juvenile delinquents: A brief report. *Criminal Justice and Behavior, 17*, 134–142.

Jackson, D. (1967). The myth of normality. *Medical Opinion and Review, 3*, 28–33.

James, N. (2015). Risk and Needs Assessment in the Criminal Justice System. *Risk and Needs Assessment in the Criminal Justice System*, i–29.

Janeksela, G. (1979). Mandatory parental involvement in the treatment of "delinquent" youth. *Juvenile and Family Court Journal, 30*, 47–54.

Janzen, C. (1977). Families in treatment of alcoholism. *Journal of Studies on Alcoholism, 38*, 114–130.

Jenness, V., Sexton, L., & Sumner, J. (2019). Sexual victimization against transgender women in prison: Consent and coercion in context. *Criminology, 57*, 603–631.

Jennings, W., Kilkenny, R., & Kohlberg, L. (1983). Moral development theory and practice for youthful and adult offenders. In W. Laufer & J. Day (Eds.), *Personality Theory, Moral Development and Criminal Behavior* (pp. 281–355). Lexington, MA: Lexington Books.

Jesness, C. (1996). *The Jesness Inventory Manual*. North Tonawanda, NY: MultiHealth Systems.

Jesness, C. (2003). *The Jesness Inventory-Revised: Technical Manual*. North Tonawanda, NY: Multi-Health Systems.

Jesness, C., & Wedge, R. (1983). *Classifying Offenders: The Jesness Inventory Classification System*. Sacramento: Youth Authority.

Joanning, H., Thomas, F., Quinn, W., & Mullen, R. (1992). Treating adolescent drug abuse: A comparison of family systems therapy, group therapy, and family drug education. *Journal of Marital & Family Therapy, 18*, 345–356.

Jolivette, K., & Nelson, C. M. (2010). Adapting positive behavioral interventions and supports for secure juvenile justice settings: Improving facility-wide behavior. *Behavioral Disorders, 36*, 28–42.

Jolivette, K., Swoszowski, N. C., McDaniel, S. C., & Duchaine, E. L. (2016). Using positive behavioral interventions and supports to assist in the transition of youth from juvenile justice facilities back to their neighborhood school: An illustrative example. *Journal of Correctional Education, 67*(2), 9–24.

Jones, A. (2018). Correctional control 2018: Incarceration and supervision by state. [Press release]. Northampton, MA: Prison Policy Initiative. Retrieved from: www.prisonpolicy.org/reports/correctionalcontrol2018.html#:~:text=An%20estimated%204.5%20million%20adults,as%20much%20attention%20as%20incarceration

Jones, M. (1968). *Beyond the Therapeutic Community*. New Haven, CT: Yale University Press.

Jones, P. (1996). Risk prediction in criminal justice. In A. Harland (Ed.), *Choosing Correctional Options that Work: Defining the Demand and Evaluating the Supply* (pp. 33–68). Thousand Oaks, CA: Sage.

Kahle, L. L., & Rosenbaum, J. (2021). What staff need to know: Using elements of gender responsive programming to create safer environments for system-involved LGBTQ girls and women. *Criminal Justice Studies, 34*, 1–15.

Kaplan, A. G. (1984). *The "Self in Relation": Implications for Depression in Women*. (Publication No. 14). Wellesley, MA: Stone Center.

Kaplan, H., & Sadock, B. (2000). *Modern Synopsis of Comprehensive Textbook of Psychiatry* (7th ed.). Baltimore: Lippincott, Williams & Wilkins.

Kaslow, F. (1987). Couples or family counseling for prisoners and their significant others. *American Journal of Family Therapy, 15*, 352–360.

Katz, L., & Gottman, J. (1993). Patterns of marital conflict predict children's internalizing and externalizing behaviors. *Developmental Psychology, 29*, 940–950.

Kauffman, K. (1988). *Prison Officers and their World*. Cambridge, MA: Harvard University Press.

Kaufman, E. (1985). *Substance Abuse and Family Therapy*. Orlando, FL: Grune & Stratton.

Kaufman, E., & Kaufman, P. (1992). *Family Therapy of Drug and Alcohol Abuse* (2nd ed.). Needham Heights, MA: Allyn & Bacon.

Kazdin, A. (1987). *Conduct Disorders in Childhood and Adolescence*. Homewood, IL: Dorsey.

Kazdin, A. (1997). Parent management training: Evidence, outcomes, and issues. *Journal of the American Academy of Child and Adolescent Psychiatry, 36*(10), 1349–1357.

Kazdin, A. (2000). *Parent Management Training*. Washington, DC: American Psychological Association.

Kazdin, A., Mazurick, J., & Siegel, T. (1994). Treatment outcomes among children with externalizing disorder who terminate prematurely versus those who complete psychotherapy. *Journal of the American Academy of Child and Adolescent Psychiatry, 33*, 549–557.

Kellogg, C. E., & Morton, N. W. (1978). *Revised Beta Examination* (2nd ed.). Cleveland, OH: Psychological Corporation.

Kellogg, C. E., & Morton, N. W. (2009). *Beta III: A Non-Verbal Measure of Cognitive Abilities in Adults*. San Antonio, TX: Pearson.

Kennealy, P. J., Skeem, J. L., Manchack, S. M., & Louden, J. E. (2012). Firm, fair, and caring officer-offender relationships protect against supervision failure. *Law and Human Behavior, 36*, 496–505. https://doi.org/10.1037/h0093935

Kennedy, D. (1984). Suicide while in police custody. *Journal of Police Science and Administration, 12*, 191–200.

Khoury, L., Tang, Y. L., Bradley, B., Cubells, J. F., & Ressler, K. J. (2010). Substance use, childhood traumatic experience, and Posttraumatic Stress Disorder in an urban civilian population. *Depression and Anxiety, 27*, 1077–1086.

Kiehl, K. A. (2006). Cognitive neuroscience perspective on psychopathy: Evidence for paralimbic system dysfunction. *Psychiatry Research, 142*, 107–128.

Kimball, K. A., Jolivette, K., & Sprague, J. R. (2017). Agency-stakeholder reflections: Perspectives of statewide adoption of the PBIS framework in juvenile facilities. *Journal of Correctional Education, 68*, 17–36.

Kinlock, T., Gordon, M., Schwartz, R., & O'Grady, K. (2008). A study of methadone maintenance for male prisoners: 3-month post-release outcomes. *Criminal Justice and Behavior, 35*, 34–47.

Kinney, J., Haapala, D., Booth, C., & Leavitt, S. (1991). The homebuilders model. In E. Tracy, D. Haapala, J. Kinney, & P. Pecora (Eds.), *Intensive Family Preservation Services: An Instructional Sourcebook* (pp. 15–49). Cleveland, OH: Mandel School of Applied Social Sciences.

Kirby, E., Milich, R., & Hundley, M. (2003). Attributional biases in aggressive children and their mothers. *Journal of Abnormal Psychology, 112*, 698–708.

Kirsch, I., Jungeblut, A., Jenkins, L., & Kolstad, A. (1993). *Adult Literacy in America: A First Look at the Results of the National Adult Literacy Survey*. Washington, DC: U.S. Government Printing Office.

Klein, N., Alexander, J., & Parsons, B. (1977). Impact of family systems intervention on recidivism and sibling delinquency: A model of primary prevention and program evaluation. *Journal of Consulting and Clinical Psychology, 45*, 469–474.

Knight, D., Simpson, D., & Hiller, M. (1999). Three-year incarceration outcomes for in-prison therapeutic community treatment in Texas. *The Prison Journal, 79*(3), 337–351.

Knight, K., Garner, B. R., Simpson, D. D., Morey, J. T., & Flynn, P. M. (2006). An assessment of criminal thinking. *Crime & Delinquency, 52*, 159–177.

Koehler, J. A., Hamilton, L. & Losel, F. A. (2013). Correctional treatment programmes for young offenders in Europe: A survey of routine practice. *European Journal on Criminal Policy and Research, 19*, 387–400.

Koehler, J. A., Losel, F., Akoensi, T. D., & Humphreys, D. K. (2012). A systematic review and meta-analysis on the effects of young offender treatment programs in Europe. *Journal of Experimental Criminology, 9*, 19–43.

Kohlberg, L. (1976). Moral stages and moralization. In T. Lickona (Ed.), *Moral Development and Behavior* (pp. 31–53). New York: Holt, Rinehart & Winston.

Kohlberg, L. (1984). *The Psychology of Moral Development* (Vol. 2). San Francisco: Harper & Row.

Kohlberg, L., Colby, A., Gibbs, J., Speicher-Dubin, B., & Candee, D. (1979). *Standard Form Scoring Manual*. Cambridge, MA: Harvard University Press.

Kopp, S. (1977). *Back to One: A Practical Guide for Psychotherapists*. Palo Alto, CA: Science and Behavior Books.

Kreshel, P. J. (1990). John B. Watson at J. Walter Thompson: The legitimation of "Science" in advertising. *Journal of Advertising, 19*(2), 49–59.

Kropp, P., Hart, S., Webster, C., & Derek Eaves, M. (1997). *Spousal Assault Risk Assessment Guide (SARA).* North Tonowanda, NY: Multi-Health Systems.

Kumpfer, K. (1999). *Strengthening America's Families: Exemplary Parenting and Family Strategies for Delinquency Prevention.* Washington, DC: U.S. Department of Justice, Office of Justice Programs, Office of Juvenile Justice and Delinquency Prevention.

Kumpfer, K., DeMarsh, J., & Child, W. (1989). *Strengthening Families Program: Children's Skills Training Curriculum Manual, Parent Training Manual, Children's Skill Training Manual, and Family Skills Training Manual.* [Unpublished manuscript]. Salt Lake City, UT: Social Research Institute, University of Utah.

Kurtines, W., & Szapocznik, J. (1996). Family interaction patterns: Structural family therapy within contexts of cultural diversity. In E. Hibbs & P. Jensen (Eds.), *Psychosocial Treatments for Child and Adolescent Disorders: Empirically Based Strategies for Clinical Practice* (pp. 671–696). Washington, DC: American Psychological Association.

Kurtz, E., & Ketcham, K. (2002). *The Spirituality of Imperfection: Storytelling and the Search for Meaning.* New York: Bantam Books.

Lab, S. P, Shields, G., & Schondel, C. (1993). Research note: An evaluation of juvenile sexual offender treatment. *Crime and Delinquency, 39,* 543–553.

Lab, S., & Whitehead, J. (1990). From "nothing works" to the "appropriate works": The latest step in the search for the secular grail. *Criminology, 28,* 405–417.

Labrecque, R. M., & Smith, P. (2017). Does training and coaching matter? An 18-month evaluation of a community supervision model. *Victims & Offenders, 12,* 233–252. https://doi.org/10.1080/15564886.2015.1013234

Landenberger, N. A., & Lipsey, M. W. (2005). The positive effects of cognitive-behavioral programs for offenders: A meta-analysis of factors associated with effective treatment. *Journal of Experimental Criminology, 1,* 451–476.

Landry, M., Smith, D., & Morrison, M. (1994). *Understanding Drugs of Abuse: The Process of Addiction Treatment and Recovery.* Washington, DC: American Psychiatric Press.

Langan, N. P., & Pelissier, B. (2001). Gender differences among prisoners in drug treatment. *Journal of Substance Abuse, 13,* 291–301.

Larzelere, R., & Patterson, G. (1990). Parental management: Mediator of the effects of SES on early delinquency. *Criminology, 28,* 301–323.

Latessa, E. J., Smith, R., Lempke, R., Makarious, M., & Lowenkamp, C. (2010). The creation and validation of the Ohio Risk Assessment System (ORAS). *Federal Probations, 74,* 16–22.

Latessa, E. J., Smith, P., Schweitzer, M., & Labrecque, R. M. (2013). *Evaluation of the Effective Practices In Community Supervision model (EPICS) in Ohio.* Cincinnati, OH: Center for Criminal Justice Research, University of Cincinnati. www.uc.edu/content/dam/uc/ccjr/docs/reports/Final%20OCJS%20Report%202.22.13.pdf

Lattimore, P. K., MacKenzie, D. L., Zajac, G., Dawes, D., Arsenault, E., & Tueller, S. (2016). Outcome findings from the HOPE demonstration experiment: Is swift, certain, and fair an effective supervision strategy? *Criminology & Public Policy, 15,* 1103–1141.

Lauritsen, J. L., Sampson, R. J., & Laub, J. H. (1991). The link between offending and victimization among adolescents. *Criminology, 29,* 265–292. https://doi.org/10.1111/j.1745-9125.1991.tb01067.x

Laws, D. (2001). Olfactory aversion: Notes on procedure, with speculations on its mechanism of effect. *Sexual Abuse: A Journal of Research and Treatment, 13,* 275–287.

Laws, D. (2003). The rise and fall of relapse prevention. *Australian Psychologist, 38,* 22–30.

Laws, D., Hudson, S., & Ward, T. (2000). *Remaking Relapse Prevention with Sex Offenders: A Sourcebook.* Thousand Oaks, CA: Sage.

Lee, J. D., Friedmann, P. D., Kinlock, T. W., Nunes, E. V., Boney, T. Y., Hoskinson, R. A., Wilson, D., McDonald, R., Rotrosen, J., Gourevitch, M. N., Gordon, M., & Fishman, M. (2016). Extended-release naltrexone to prevent opioid relapse in criminal justice offenders. *New England Journal of Medicine, 374*, 1232–1242.

Lee, S., Aos, S., Drake, E., Pennucci, A., Miller, M., & Anderson, L. (2012). *Return on Investment: Evidence-based Options to Improve Statewide Outcomes, April 2012.* (Document No. 12–04–1201). Olympia: Washington State Institute for Public Policy.

León-Mayer, E., Folino, J. O., Neumann, C., & Hare, R. D. (2015). The construct of psychopathy in a Chilean prison population. *Revista Brasileira de Psiquiatria, 37*, 191–196.

Lester, D. (1982). The treatment of exhibitionists. *Corrective and Social Psychiatry, 28*(3), 94–98.

Lester, D. (2014). Treating sexual offenders. In P. Van Voorhis & Emily Salisbury (Eds.), *Correctional Counseling and Rehabilitation* (8ᵗʰ ed.) (pp. 245–264). Waltham, MA: Elsevier.

Levenson, J. S., & Macgowan, M. J. (2004). Engagement, denial, and treatment progress among sex offenders in group therapy. *Sexual Abuse: Journal of Research and Treatment, 16*, 49–63.

Levenson, R. (1988). Development in the classification process. *Criminal Justice and Behavior, 15*, 24–38.

Liddle, H., & Dakof, G. (1995). Efficacy of family therapy for drug abuse: Promising but not definitive. *Journal of Marital & Family Therapy, 21*, 511–543.

Liebert, R., & Spiegler, M. (1994). *Personality: Strategies and Issues.* Pacific Grove, CA: Brooks/Cole.

Lilienfeld, S. O., & Andrews, B. P. (1996). Development and preliminary validation of a self-report measure of psychopathic personality traits in noncriminal populations. *Journal of Personality Assessment, 66*, 488–524.

Lilienfeld, S. O., & Widows, M. R. (2005). *PPI-R: Psychopathic Personality Inventory Revised: Professional Manual.* Lutz, FL: Psychological Assessment Resources, Inc.

Lim, Y. Y., Wahab, S., Kumar, J., Ibrahim, F., & Kamaluddin, M.R. (2021). Typologies and psychological profiles of child sexual abusers: An extensive review. *Children (Basel), 8*, 333.

Linehan, M. M. (1993). *Cognitive-behavioral Treatment of Borderline Personality Disorder.* New York: Guilford Press.

Linhorst, D. M., McCutchen, T. A., & Bennett, L. (2003). Recidivism among offenders with developmental disabilities participating in a case management program. *Research in Developmental Disabilities, 24*, 210–230.

Lipsey, M. (1992). Juvenile delinquency treatment: A meta-analytic inquiry into the variability of effects. In T. Cook, H. Cooper, D. Cordray, H. Hartmann, L. Hedges, R. J. Light, T. A. Louis, & F. Mosteller (Eds.), *Meta-Analysis for Explanation* (pp. 83–127). New York: Russell Sage Foundation.

Lipsey, M. (2009). The primary factors that characterize effective interventions with juvenile offenders: A meta-analytic overview. *Victims and Offenders, 4*, 124–147.

Lipsey, M., Chapman, G., & Landenberger, N. (2001). Cognitive-behavioral programs for offenders. *Annals (of the American Academy of Political and Social Science), 578* (November), 144–157.

Lipsey, M. W., & Cullen, F. T. (2007). The effectiveness of correctional rehabilitation: A review of systematic reviews. *Annual Review of Law and Social Science, 3*, 297–320.

Lipsey, M., & Wilson, D. (1993). The efficacy of psychological educational and behavioral treatment: Confirmation from meta-analysis. *American Psychologist, 48*, 1181–1209.

Lipsey, M., & Wilson, D. (2001). *Practical Meta-Analysis.* Thousand Oaks, CA: Sage.

Lipsey, M. W., & Wilson, D. (1998). Effective Intervention for Serious Juvenile Offenders: A Synthesis of Research, in R. Loeber and D. P. Farrington (Eds.), *Serious and Violent Juvenile Offenders: Risk Factors and Successful Interventions* (pp. 313–345). Newbury Park, CA: Sage.

LIS, Inc. (2002). *Services for Families of Prison Inmates.* Longmont, CA: National Institute of Corrections.

Listwan, S., Sperber, K., Spruance, L., & Van Voorhis, P. (2004). Anxiety in correctional settings: It's time for another look. *Federal Probation, 68*(1), 43–50.

Listwan, S., Sundt, J., Holsinger, A., & Latessa, E. (2003). The effect of drug court programming on recidivism: The Cincinnati experience. *Crime & Delinquency, 49*(3), 389–411.

Listwan, S., Van Voorhis, P., & Ritchey, P. (2007). Personality, criminal behavior, and risk assessment: Implications for theory and practice. *Criminal Justice and Behavior, 34*(1), 60–75.

Listwan-Johnson, S., Gentry Sperber, K., Murphy Spruance, L., & Van Voorhis, P. (2004). High anxiety offenders in correctional settings: It's time for another look. *Federal Probation, 68*, 43–50.

Little, G., & Robinson, K. (1986). *Juvenile MRT: How to Escape Your Prison.* Memphis, TN: Eagle Wing Books.

Little, K., & Schneidman, E. (1959). Congruencies among interpretations of psychological test and anamnestic data. *Psychological Monographs: General and Applied, 73*, 1–42.

Lobanov-Rostovsky, C. (2015). Recidivism of juveniles who commit sexual offenses. *SOMAPI Research Brief.* Washington, DC: Office of Justice Programs.

Loeber, R., & Dishion, T. (1983). Early predictors of male delinquency. *Psychological Bulletin, 94*, 68–99.

Loeber, R., & Hay, D. (1994). Developmental approaches to aggression and conduct problems. In M. Rutter & D. Hay (Eds.), *Development through Life: A Handbook for Clinicians* (pp. 488–516). Oxford, UK: Blackwell Scientific Publications.

Loevinger, J. (1966). The meaning and measurement of ego development. *American Psychologist, 21*, 195–217.

Longo, R. (2015). Trauma and its impact on the brain: An overview. In B. Schwartz (Ed.), *The Sex Offender: Insights on Treatment and Policy Developments* (Vol. VIII) (pp. 1–1–1–22). Kingston, NJ: Civic Research Institute.

Looman, J., Serran, G., & Marshall, W. (2011). Mood conflict and deviant sexual fantasies. In B. Schwartz (Ed.), *Handbook of Sex Offender Treatment* (pp. 7–1–7–16). Kingston, NJ: Civic Research Institute.

Lösel, F. (1995). Increasing consensus in the evaluation of offender rehabilitation? Lessons from recent research synthesis. *Psychology, Crime & Law, 2*, 19–39.

Lösel, F., & Schmucker, M. (2005). The effectiveness of treatment for sexual offenders: A comprehensive meta-analysis. *Journal of Experimental Criminology, 1*, 117–146.

Lovins, B. K., Cullen, F. T., Latessa, E. J., & Jonson, C. L. (2018). Probation officer as a coach: Building a new professional identity. *Federal Probation, 82*, 13–19.

Brusman Lovins, L. B., Lowenkamp, C. T., Latessa, E. J., & Smith, P. (2007). Application of the risk principle to female offenders. *Journal of Contemporary Criminal Justice, 23*(4), 383–398.

Lowenkamp, C. T. (2004). *A Program-Level Analysis of the Relationship between Correctional Program Integrity and Treatment Effectiveness.* [Unpublished doctoral dissertation]. University of Cincinnati.

Lowenkamp, C. T., Holsinger, A., & Latessa, E. (2002). *Are Drug Courts Effective? A MetaAnalytic Review.* Cincinnati, OH: University of Cincinnati.

Lowenkamp, C. T., Holsinger, A., Robinson, C. R., & Alexander, M. (2014) Diminishing or durable treatment effects of STARR? A research note on 24-month re-arrest rates. *Journal of Crime and Justice, 37*, 275–283. https://doi.org/10.1080/0735648X.2012.753849

Lowenkamp, C. T., Hubbard, D., Makarios, M., & Latessa, E. (2009). A quasiexperimental evaluation of "Thinking for a Change": A "real-world" application. *Criminal Justice and Behavior, 36*, 137–146.

Lowenkamp, C. T., Johnson, J. L., Holsinger, A. M., Van Benschoten, S. W., & Robinson, C. R. (2013). The federal post-conviction risk assessment (PCRA): A construction and validation study. *Psychological Services, 10*(1), 87–102.

Lowenkamp, C. T., & Latessa, E. (2002). *Evaluation of Ohio's Community-based Correctional Facilities and Halfway House Programs.* Cincinnati, OH: University of Cincinnati.

Lowenkamp, C. T., Latessa, E., & Smith, P. (2006). Does correctional program quality really matter? The importance of adhering to the principles of effective intervention. *Criminology and Public Policy, 5*, 201–220.

Lozoff, B. (1999). *Deep and Simple.* Durham, NC: Human Kindness Foundation.

Lutzker, J. (1990). Behavioral treatment of child neglect. *Behavior Modification, 14*, 301–315.

Lynch, J., & Sabol, W. (2001). *Prisoner Reentry in Perspective*. Washington, DC: Urban Institute.

Lynch, S. M., Heath, N. M., Mathews, K. C., & Cepeda, G. J. (2012). Seeking safety: An intervention for trauma-exposed incarcerated women? *Journal of Trauma and Dissociation, 13*, 88–101.

MacCoun, R. (1998). Toward a psychology of harm reduction. *American Psychologist, 53*, 1199–1208.

Macdonald, A. L. (2011). *Solution-Focused Therapy: Theory, Research, and Practice*. Thousand Oaks, CA: Sage.

MacKenzie, D. (1989). Prison classification: The management and psychological perspectives. In L. Goodstein & D. MacKenzie (Eds.), *The American Prison: Issues in Research and Policy* (pp. 163–189). New York: Plenum.

MacKenzie, D. (2006). *What Works in Corrections: Reducing the Criminal Activities of Offenders and Victims*. New York: Cambridge University Press.

Magaletta, P. R., & Herbst, D. P. (2001). Fathering from prison: Common struggles and successful solutions. *Psychotherapy: Theory, Research, Practice, Training, 38*, 88–96.

Magaletta, P. R., Patry, M. W., Dietz, E. F., & Ax, R. K. (2007). What is correctional about clinical practice in corrections? *Criminal Justice and Behavior, 34*, 7–21.

Malatesti, L., & McMillan, J. (2010). Defending PCL-R. In L. Malatesti & J. McMillan (Eds.), *Responsibility and Psychopathy: Interfacing Law, Psychiatry, and Philosophy* (pp. 79–91). New York: Oxford University Press.

Maletzky, B. (1991). *Treating the Sexual Offender*. Newbury Park, CA: Sage.

Manchak, S. M., Skeem, J. L., & Rook, K. S. (2014). Care, control, or both? Characterizing major dimensions of the mandated treatment relationship. *Law and Human Behavior, 38*, 47–57.

Mann, B., Borduin, C., Henggeler, S., & Blaske, D. (1990). An investigation of systemic conceptualizations of parent-child coalitions and symptom change. *Journal of Consulting and Clinical Psychology, 58*, 336–344.

Mann, R. E., Hanson, R. K. & Thornton, D. (2010). Assessing risk for sexual recidivism: some proposals on the nature of psychologically meaningful risk factors. *Sex Abuse, 22*, 191–217.

Maples-Keller, J. L., Bunnell, B. E., Kim, S. J., & Rothbaum, B. O. (2017). The use of virtual reality technology in the treatment of anxiety and other psychiatric disorders. *Harvard Review of Psychiatry, 25*, 103–113.

Marion, T., & Coleman, K. (1991). Recovery issues and treatment resources. In D. Daly & M. Raskin (Eds.), *Treating the Chemically Dependent and their Families*. Newbury Park, CA: Sage.

Marlatt, G. (1985). Cognitive factors in the relapse process. In G. Marlatt & J. Gordon (Eds.), *Relapse Prevention: Maintenance Strategies in the Treatment of Addictive Behaviors* (pp. 128–200). New York: Guilford.

Marlatt, G., & Barrett, K. (2004). Relapse prevention. In M. Galanter & H. Kleber (Eds.), *Textbook of Substance Abuse Treatment* (3rd ed.) (pp. 285–299). Washington, DC: American Psychiatric Press.

Marlatt, G., Blume, A., & Parks, G. (2001). Integrating harm reduction therapy and traditional substance abuse treatment. *Journal of Psychoactive Drugs, 33*(10), 13–21.

Marlatt, G., & Gordon, J. (Eds.). (1985). *Relapse Prevention: Maintenance Strategies in the Treatment of Addictive Behaviors*. New York: Guilford.

Marlatt, G., & Witkiewitz, K. (2002). Harm reduction approaches to alcohol use: Health promotion, prevention, and treatment. *Addictive Behaviors, 27*(6), 867–886.

Marlowe, D. (2009). Evidence-based sentencing for drug offenders: An analysis of prognostic risks and criminogenic needs. *Chapman Journal of Criminal Justice, 1*(1), 167–201.

Marlowe, D. B., & Kirby, K. C. (1999). Effective use of sanctions in drug courts: Lessons from behavioral research. *National Drug Court Institute Review, 2*, 1–32.

Marlowe, D. B., Shannon, L. M, Ray, B., Turpin, D. B., Wheeler, G. A., Newell, J., & Lawson, S. G. (2018). Developing a culturally proficient intervention for young African American men in drug court: Examining feasibility and estimating an effect size for Habilitation Empowerment Accountability Therapy (HEAT). *Journal for Advancing Justice, 1*, 109–130.

Marques, J. K., Day, D., Nelson, C., & West, M. (1994). Effects of cognitive-behavioral treatment of sex offender recidivism: Preliminary results of a longitudinal study. *Criminal Justice and Behavior, 21,* 28–54.

Marques, J. K., Wiederanders, M., Day, D. M., Nelson, C., & van Ommeren, A. (2005). Effects of relapse prevention program on sexual recidivism: Final results from California's Sex Offender Treatment and Evaluation Project (SOTEP). *Sexual Abuse: Journal of Research and Treatment, 17,* 79–107.

Marsh, K., & Miller, N. A. (1985). Female clients in substance abuse treatment. *International Journal of the Addictions, 20,* 995–1019.

Marshall, W. L. (1993). The treatment of sex offenders: What does the outcome data tell us? A reply to Quinsey, Harris, Rice, and LaLumiere. *Journal of Interpersonal Violence, 8,* 524–530.

Marshall, W. L. (1996). Assessment, treatment, and theorizing about sex offenders. *Criminal Justice and Behavior, 23,* 162–199.

Marshall, W. L., & Fernandez, Y. M. (2000). Phallometric testing with sexual offenders. *Clinical Psychology Review, 20,* 807–822.

Marshall, W. L., & Marshall, L. E. (2010). Attachment and intimacy in sexual offenders: an update. *Sexual and Relationship Therapy, 25,* 86–90.

Marshall, W. L., Marshall, L. E., Serran, G., & Fernandez, Y. (2006). *Treating Sexual Offenders: An Integrated Approach.* New York: Routledge.

Marshall, W. L., Serran, G., Fernandez, Y., Mulloy, R., Mann, R., & Thornton, D. (2003). Therapist characteristics in the treatment of sex offenders: Tentative data on their relationship with indices of behavior change. *Journal of Sexual Aggression, 9,* 25–30.

Martin, S., Butzin, C., Saum, C., & Inciardi, J. (1999). Three-year outcomes of therapeutic community treatment for drug-involved offenders in Delaware. *The Prison Journal, 79*(3), 294–320.

Martinson, R. (1974). What works? Questions and answers about prison reform. *The Public Interest, 35,* 22–54.

Masters, J., Burish, T., Hollon, S., & Rimm, D. (1987). *Behavior Therapy: Techniques and Empirical Findings* (3rd ed.). New York: Harcourt Brace Jovanovich.

Masterson, M. (2020, February 19). Lawsuit: Female Prisoner Says She Was Raped by Transgender Inmate. *WTTW News.* Retrieved from https://news.wttw.com/2020/02/19/lawsuit-female-prisoner-says-she-was-raped-transgender-inmate

Mathews, R., Matthews, J., & Speltz, K. (1989). *Female Sexual Offenders: An Exploratory Study.* Brandon, VT: Vermont Safer Society Press.

Matson, J., & DiLorenzo, T. (1984). *Punishment and its Alternatives: A New Perspective for Behavior Modification.* New York: Springer.

McCarthy, S., & Waters, T. F. (2003). Treating substance abuse offenders in the Southwestern United States: A report evaluating the long-term effectiveness of the Yuma County Adult Drug Court. *Journal of Offender Rehabilitation, 37,* 163–177.

McClellan, D. S., Farabee, D., & Crouch, B. M. (1997). Early victimization, drug use, and criminality: A comparison of male and female prisoners. *Criminal Justice and Behavior, 24,* 455–476.

McCollum, A. (1994). Prison college programs. *The Prison Journal, 74,* 15–51.

McCrady, B. (1990). The marital relationship and alcoholism. In R. Collins, K. Leonard & J. Searles (Eds.), *Alcohol and the Family: Research and Clinical Practice.* New York: Guilford.

McCrady, S., & Irving, S. (2003). Self-Help Groups. In R. Hester & W. Miller (Eds.), *Handbook of Alcoholism Treatment Approaches* (3rd ed.). Boston: Allyn & Bacon.

McCrady, F., Kaufman, K., Vasey, M. W., Barriga, A. Q., Devlin, R. S., & Gibbs, J. C. (2008). It's all about me: A brief report of incarcerated adolescent sex offender's generic and sex-specific cognitive distortions. *Sexual Abuse, 20,* 261–271.

McGuire, R. J. (2002). *Evidence-based Programming Today.* Boston, MA: Draft Paper for the International Community Corrections Association (ICCA) Annual Conference 2002.

McInnis, W., Dennis, W., Myers, M., O'Connell Sullivan, K., & Jongsma, A. (2002). *The Juvenile Justice and Residential Care Treatment Planner*. Hoboken, NJ: John Wiley.

McLaren, L. (1988). Fostering mother-child relationships. *Child Welfare, 67*, 343–365.

McLellan, A., Kushner, H., Metzger, D., & Peters, F. (1992). Fifth Edition of the Addiction Severity Index. *Journal of Substance Abuse Treatment, 9*, 199–213.

McMackin, R. A., Tansi, R., & LaFratta, J. (2004). Recidivism among juvenile offenders over periods ranging from one to twenty years following residential treatment. *Journal of Offender Rehabilitation, 38*, 1–15.

Meehl, P. (1954). *Clinical versus Statistical Prediction*. Minneapolis: University of Minnesota Press.

Meeks, D., & Kelly, C. (1970). Family therapy with the families of recovering alcoholics. *Quarterly Journal of Studies on Alcohol, 31*, 399–413.

Megargee, E., & Bohn, M. (1979). *Classifying Criminal Offenders: A New System Based on the MMPI*. Beverly Hills, CA: Sage.

Megargee, E., Carbonell, J., Bohn, M., & Sliger, G. (2001). *Classifying Criminal Offenders with the MMPI-2: The Megargee System*. Minneapolis: University of Minnesota Press.

Meichenbaum, D. (1986). Cognitive behavior modification. In F. H. Kanfer, & A. P. Goldstein (Eds.), *Helping People Change: A Textbook of Methods* (pp. 346–380). New York: Pergamon.

Merkt, H., Wangmo, T., Pageau, F., Liebrenz, M., Devaud Cornaz, C., & Elger, B. (2021). Court-mandated patients' perspectives on the psychotherapist's dual loyalty conflict—Between ally and enemy. *Frontiers in Psychology, 11*, 1–15.

Messina, N., Burdon, W., Hagopian, G., & Prendergast, M. (2006). Predictors of prison-based treatment outcomes: A comparison of men and women participants. *American Journal of Drug and Alcohol Abuse, 32*, 7–28.

Messina, N., Burdon, W., & Prendergast, M. (2003). Assessing the needs of women in institutional therapeutic communities. *Journal of Offender Rehabilitation, 37*, 89–106.

Messina, N., & Grella, C. (2006). Childhood trauma and women's health outcomes in a California prison population. *American Journal of Public Health, 96*, 1842–1848.

Messina, N., Grella, C., Cartier, J., & Torres, S. (2010). A randomized experimental study of gender-responsive substance abuse treatment for women in prison. *Journal of Substance Abuse Treatment, 38*, 97–107.

Milhorn, T. H. (1990). *Chemical Dependence*. New York: Springer-Verlag.

Miller, F. G., & Lazowski, L. E. (1999). *The Substance Abuse Subtle Screening Inventory-3 (SASSI-3) Manual*. Springfield, IN: The SASSI Institute.

Miller, J. (1976). *Toward a New Psychology of Women*. Boston: Beacon.

Miller, J. (1986). *What Do We Mean by Relationships? Work in Progress No. 22*. Wellesley, MA: Stone Center, Working Paper Series.

Miller, J. (1988). *Connections, Disconnections, and Violations. Work in Progress No. 33*. Wellesley, MA: Stone Center, Working Paper Series.

Miller, J., & Maloney, C. (2013). Practitioner compliance with risk/needs assessment tools: A theoretical and empirical assessment. *Criminal Justice and Behavior, 40*, 60–71.

Miller, W. R. (1999). Enhancing motivation for change in substance abuse treatment. *Treatment Improvement Protocol (TIP) Series 35* (DHHS Publication No. (SMA) 99-3354, pp. 1–213). Rockville, MD: U.S. Department of Health and Human Services.

Miller, W. R., Andrews, N. R., Wilbourne, P., & Bennett, M. E. (1998). A wealth of alternatives: Effective treatments for alcohol problems. In W. R. Miller & N. Heather (Eds.), *Treating Addictive Behaviors: Processes of Change* (2nd ed., pp. 203–216). New York: Plenum Press.

Miller, W. R., Brown, J., Simpson, T., Handmaker, N., Bien, T., Luckie, L., Montgomery, H. A., Hester, R. K., & Tonigan, J. S. (2003). What works? A methodological analysis of the alcohol treatment outcome literature. In R. K. Hester & W. Miller (Eds.), *Handbook of Alcoholism Treatment Approaches* (3rd ed.) (pp. 12–44). Boston: Allyn & Bacon.

Miller, W. R., & Hester, R. (2003). Treatment for alcohol problems: Toward an informed eclecticism. In R. K. Hester & W. Miller (Eds.), *Handbook of Alcoholism Treatment Approaches* (3rd ed.) (pp. 1–12). Boston: Allyn & Bacon.

Miller, W. R., Meyers, R., & Hiller-Sturmhofel, S. (1999). The community reinforcement approach. *Alcohol Research and Health, 23*(2), 116–120.

Miller, W. R., & Rollnick, S. (2002). *Motivational Interviewing: Preparing People for Change* (2nd ed.). New York: Guilford.

Miller, W. R., & Rollnick, S. (2013). *Motivational Interviewing: Helping People Change* (3rd ed.). New York: Guilford.

Miller, W. R., & Tonigan, J. (1996). Assessing drinker's motivation for change: The Stages of Change Readiness and Treatment Eagerness Scale (SOCRATES). *Psychology of Addictive Behaviors, 10,* 81–89.

Millon, T., Grossman, S., & Millon, C. (2015). *Millon Clinical Multiaxial Inventory-IV.* Bloomington, MN: Pearson Assessments.

Millson, B., Robinson, D., & Van Dieten, M. (2010). *Women Offender Case Management Model: The Connecticut Project.* Ottawa: Orbis Partners.

Minuchin, P. (1985). Families and individual development: Provocations from the field of family therapy. *Child Development, 56,* 289–305.

Minuchin, P., Colapinto, J., & Minuchin, S. (2006). *Working with Families of the Poor* (2nd ed.). New York: Guilford.

Minuchin, S. (1974). *Families and Family Therapy.* Cambridge, MA: Harvard University Press.

Minuchin, S., Rosman, B., & Baker, L. (1978). *Psychosomatic Families: Anorexia Nervosa in Context.* Cambridge, MA: Harvard University Press.

Mitchell, C., & Egan, J. (1995). *Quality of Instruction Inventory.* Boston: Department of Corrections, Program Services Division.

Moffat, C. T. (2011). Helping those in need: Human service workers. *Occupational Outlook Quarterly,* 23–32.

Mohr, W. K., Martin, A., Olson, J. N., Pumariega, A. J., & Branca, N. (2009). Beyond point and level systems: Moving toward child-centered programming. *American Journal of Orthopsychiatry, 79*(1), 8–18.

Moltó, J., Poy, R., & Torrubia, R. (2000). Standardization of the Hare Psychopathy Checklist-Revised in a Spanish prison sample. *Journal of Personality Disorders, 14,* 84–96.

Monti, P., Rohsenow, D., Colby, S., & Abrams, D. (2005). Coping and social skills training. In R. K. Hester & W. Miller (Eds.), *Handbook of Alcoholism Treatment Approaches* (3rd ed.) (pp. 176–194). Boston: Allyn & Bacon.

Morash, M. (2010). *Women on Probation and Parole.* Boston, MA: Northeastern University Press.

Morash, M., Bynum, T., & Koons, B. (1998). *Women Offenders: Programming Needs and Promising Approaches.* Washington, DC: National Institute of Justice.

Morgan, R. D. (2003). Basic mental health services: Services and issues. In T. J. Fagan & R. K. Ax (Eds.), *Correctional Mental Health Handbook* (pp. 59–72). Thousand Oaks, CA: Sage.

Morgan, R. D., Fisher, W. H., Duan, N., Mandracchia, J. T., & Murray, D. (2010). Prevalence of criminal thinking among state prison inmates with serious mental illness. *Law and Human Behavior, 34,* 324–336.

Morgan, R. D., Kroner, D. G., Mills, J. F., Bauer, R. L. & Serna, C. (2014). Treating Justice Involved Persons with Mental Illness: Preliminary evaluation of a comprehensive treatment program. *Criminal Justice and Behavior, 41,* 902–916.

Moriarty, M. (2008). Book Review of "Heart of the Matter: The Role of Attitude in Teaching," by Arthur D. Willis, Marcia M. Greenberg & Jo Ann Larsen (Albany, Publishers Solutions, 2007). *Contemporary Justice Review, 11*(4), 463–465.

Mowatt, D., Van Deusen, J., & Wilson, D. (1985). Family therapy and the drug using offender. *Federal Probation, 49,* 28–34.

Mumola, C. (2000). *Incarcerated Parents and Their Children.* Washington, DC: Bureau of Justice Statistics.

Mumola, C., & Karberg, J. (2006). *Drug Use and Dependence, State and Federal Prisoners, 2004.* Washington, DC: Bureau of Justice Statistics.

Munetz, M., & Griffin, P. (2006). Use of the Sequential Intercept Model as an approach to decriminalization of people with serious mental illness. *Psychiatric Services, 57,* 544–549

Murphy, W. (1990). Assessment and modification of cognitive distortions in sex offenders. In W. Marshall, D. Laws, & H. Barbaree (Eds.), *Handbook of Sexual Assault Issues, Theories and Treatment of the Offender.* New York: Plenum.

Myers, L., & Jackson, D. (2002). *Reality Therapy and Choice Theory: Managing Behavior for Today, Developing Skills for Tomorrow.* Lanham, MD: American Correctional Association.

Najavits, L. M. (2002a). *Seeking Safety: A Treatment Manual for PTSD and Substance Abuse.* New York: Guilford.

Najavits, L. M. (2002b). Seeking safety: Therapy for trauma and substance abuse. *Corrections Today, 64,* 136–141.

Najavits, L. M., Weiss, R., & Liese, B. (1996). Group cognitive behavioral therapy for women with PTSD and substance use disorder. *Journal of Substance Abuse Treatment, 13,* 13–22.

Napier, A., & Whitaker, C. (1980). *The Family Crucible.* New York: Bantam Books.

National Academy of Sciences (NAS). (2003). *The Polygraph and Lie Detection.* Washington, DC: National Academies Press.

National Association of Social Workers (NASW). (2021). *Code of Ethics of the National Association of Social Workers.* Washington, DC: NASW.

National Commission on Correctional Health Care. (2002). *The Health Status of Soon-to-be Released Inmates, Volume 1.* Washington, DC: U.S. Department of Justice, National Institute of Justice. Retrieved from: www.ncjrs.gov/pdffiles1/nij/grants/189735.pdf

National Commission on Correctional Health Care. (2015). *Standards for Mental Health Services in Correctional Facilities.* Chicago: National Commission on Correctional Health Care.

National Institute of Correctional Education. (2004). *The United Nations Economic and Social Council Resolution 20.* Retrieved from the National Institute of Correctional Education.

National Institute of Corrections. (1979). *Classification Instruments for Criminal Justice Decisions, Volume 3: Institutional Custody.* Washington, DC: National Institute of Corrections.

Nelson, K. (1991). Populations and outcomes in five family preservation programs. In K. Wells & D. Biegel (Eds.), *Family Preservation Services: Research and Evaluation* (pp. 72–91). Newbury Park, CA: Sage.

Nelson, M., Deess, P., & Allen, C. (1999). *The First Month Out: Post-Incarceration Experiences in New York City.* New York: Vera Institute of Justice.

Nelson-Zlupko, L., Kauffman, E., & Dore, M. M. (1995). Gender differences in drug addiction and treatment: Implications for social work intervention with substance-abusing women. *Social Work, 40,* 45–54.

Nesovic, A. (2003). *Psychometric Evaluation of the Correctional Program Assessment Inventory (CPAI).* [Unpublished doctoral dissertation]. Ottawa: Carleton University.

Neumann, C. S., Hare, R. D., & Newman, J. P. (2007). The super-ordinate nature of the Psychopathy Checklist-Revised. *Journal of Personality Disorders, 21,* 102–117.

Nichols, M., & Schwartz, R. (2006). *Family Therapy: Concepts and Methods* (7th ed.). Needham Heights, MA: Allyn & Bacon.

Noonan, M. E., & Ginder, S. (2014). *Mortality in Local Jails and State Prisons, 2000–2012: Statistical Tables.* Washington, DC: Bureau of Justice Statistics, U.S. Department of Justice.

Northpointe Institute for Public Management, Inc. (n.d.). COMPAS Women: Comprehensive offender assessment, classification, and case management. Retrieved from www.northpointeinc.com/pdf/Womens%20COMPAS%20Flyer%20Front.pdf

Nurco, D., Kinlock, T., & Hanlon, T. (1993). *Drug Abuse Treatment in the United States: Nature, Status, and New Directions.* Paper presented at the Medical and Surgical Faculty of Maryland 4th Annual Conference on Addiction, December.

O'Farrell, T. (2003). Marital and family therapy. In R. K. Hester & W. Miller (Eds.), *Handbook of Alcoholism Treatment Approaches* (3rd ed.). Boston: Allyn & Bacon.

Office of National Drug Control Policy (2003). *National Drug Control Strategy.* Washington, DC: ONDCP, The White House.

Ogloff, J. R. P. (2006). The psychopathy/Antisocial Personality Disorder conundrum. *Australian and New Zealand Journal of Psychiatry, 40,* 519–528.

Ogloff, J. R. P., & Wood, M. (2010). The treatment of psychopathy: Clinical nihilism or steps in the right direction? In L. Malatesti & J. McMillan (Eds.), *Responsibility and Psychopathy: Interfacing Law, Psychiatry, and Philosophy* (pp. 155–181). New York: Oxford University Press.

Olson, D., Russell, C., & Sprenkle, D. (1980). Marital and family therapy: A decade review. *Journal of Marriage and the Family, 42,* 973–993.

Olver, M., Lewis, K., & Wong, S. C. P. (2013). Risk reduction treatment of high-risk psychopathic offenders: The relationship of psychopathy and treatment change to violent recidivism. *Personality Disorder: Theory, Research and Treatment, 4,* 160–167.

Opris, D., Pintea, S., García-Palacios, A., Botella, C., Szamosközi, Ş., & David, D. (2012). Virtual reality exposure therapy in anxiety disorders: A quantitative metaanalysis. *Depression and Anxiety, 29*(2), 85–93.

Orbis Partners. (n.d.). *Gender-responsive Assessment (SPIn-W).* Retrieved from www.orbispartners.com/assessment/gender-responsive-spin-w

Orbis Partners. (2000). *Youth Assessment Screening Inventory (YASI).* Ottawa: Orbis Partners.

Orbis Partners. (2003). *Service Planning Instrument (SPIn).* Ottawa: Orbis Partners.

Orbis Partners. (2005). *Service Planning Instrument for Women (SPIn-W).* Ottawa: Orbis Partners.

Orbis Partners. (2006). *Women Offender Case Management Model (Prepared for the National Institute of Corrections).* Ottawa: Orbis Partners.

Oregon Coalition of Advocates for Equal Access for Girls. (2011). *Gender-Responsive Standards and Assessment Tool for Girls' Programs and Services.* Portland, OR: National Crittendon Foundation.

O'Reilly, S., O'Reilly, J., & O'Reilly, T. (Eds.) (2002). *The Road Within: True Stories of Transformation and the Soul.* San Francisco: Travelers' Tales.

Owen, B. (1998). *In the Mix: Struggle and Survival in a Women's Prison.* Albany, NY: SUNY Press.

Owen, B., & Bloom, B. (1995). Profiling women prisoners: Findings from national surveys and a California sample. *The Prison Journal, 75,* 165–185.

Pacini, M., Maremmani, A. G. I., & Maremmani, I. (2020). The conceptual framework of dual disorders and its flaws. *Journal of Clinical Medicine, 9,* 1–11.

Palmer, T. (1974). The Youth Authority's Community Treatment Project. *Federal Probation, 38,* 3–14.

Palmer, T. (1978). *Correctional Intervention and Research.* Lexington, MA: D. C. Heath.

Palmer, T. (1992). *The Re-emergence of Correctional Intervention.* Newbury Park, CA: Sage.

Palmer, T. (2002). *Individualized Intervention with Young Multiple Offenders: The California Community Treatment Project.* Hampton, CT: Garland.

Pan, H., Scarpitti, F., Inciardi, J., & Lockwood, D. (1993). Some considerations on therapeutic communities in corrections. In J. Inciardi (Ed.), *Drug Treatment and Criminal Justice* (pp. 30–43). Newbury Park, CA: Sage.

Paparozzi, M. A., & Gendreau, P. (2005). An intensive supervision program that worked: Service delivery, professional orientation, and organizational supportiveness. *The Prison Journal, 85,* 445–466. https://doi.org/10.1177/0032885505281529

Pardeck, J. (1989). Family therapy as a treatment approach to child abuse. *Family Therapy, 16,* 113–120.

Parent, D., & Barnett, L. (2003). *Transition from Prison to Community Initiative.* Washington, DC: National Institute of Corrections.

Parkinson, A., Dulfano, I., & Nink, C. (2003). *Removing Barriers: Research-based Strategies for Teaching Those Who Learn Differently.* Centerville, UT: Management and Training Corporation Institute.

Parks, G., Marlatt, G., & Anderson, B. (2001). Cognitive-behavioral alcohol treatment. In H. Nick & T. Peters (Eds.), *International Handbook of Alcohol Dependence and Problems* (pp. 69–86). New York: John Wiley.

Parra-Cardona, J. R., Sharp, E. A., & Wampler, R. S. (2008). Changing for my kid: Fatherhood experiences of Mexican-origin teen fathers involved in the Justice System. *Journal of Marital & Family Therapy, 34,* 369–387.

Patterson, D. A, Hughes, M., Maher, N., Shen, Y., Shore-Fitzgerald, C., & Wang, Y. (2017). Computerized behavioral interventions: Current products and recommendations for substance use disorder treatment. *Journal of Social Work Practice in the Addictions, 17,* 339–351.

Patterson, G. (1974). Intervention for boys with conduct problems: Multiple settings, treatments, and criteria. *Journal of Consulting and Clinical Psychology, 42,* 471–481.

Patterson, G. (1982). *A Social Learning Approach: Coercive Family Process.* Eugene, OR: Castalia.

Patterson, G. (2003). Early development of coercive family process. In J. Reid, G. Patterson & J. Snyder (Eds.), *Antisocial Behavior in Children and Adolescents: A Developmental Analysis and Model for Intervention.* Washington, DC: American Psychological Association.

Patterson, G., Chamberlain, P., & Reid, J. (1982). A comparative evaluation of a parent-training program. *Behavior Therapy, 13,* 638–650.

Patterson, G., & Dishion, T. (1985). Contributions of families and peers to delinquency. *Criminology, 23,* 63–79.

Patterson, G., Dishion, T., & Chamberlain, P. (1993). Outcomes and methodological issues relating to treatment of antisocial children. In T. Giles (Ed.), *Handbook of Effective Psychotherapy* (pp. 43–88). New York: Plenum.

Patterson, G., & Fleischman, M. (1979). Maintenance of treatment effects: Some considerations concerning family systems and follow-up data. *Behavior Therapy, 10,* 168–185.

Patterson, G., Reid, J., & Dishion, T. (1992). *Antisocial Boys.* Eugene, OR: Castalia.

Pavlov, I. P. (1927). *Conditioned Reflexes: An Investigation of the Physiological Activity of the Cerebral Cortex* (G. Anrep, Trans.). London: Oxford University Press.

Pearson, F., & Lipton, D. (1999). A meta-analytic review of the effectiveness of corrections-based treatments for drug abuse. *The Prison Journal, 79*(4), 384–410.

Pearson, F., Lipton, D., Cleland, C., & Yee, D. (2002). The effects of behavioral/cognitive-behavioral programs on recidivism. *Crime & Delinquency, 48*(3), 476–496.

Pelissier, B. (2004). Gender differences in substance use treatment entry and retention among prisoners with substance use histories. *American Journal of Public Health, 94,* 1418–1424.

Pelissier, B., Gaes, G., Camp, S., Wallace, S., O'Neil, J., & Saylor, W. (1998). *TRIAD Drug Treatment Evaluation Project Six-Month Interim Report.* Washington, DC: Federal Bureau of Prisons, Office of Research and Evaluation.

Pence, E., & Paymar, M. (1993). *Education Groups for Men Who Batter.* New York: Springer Publishing.

Perkinson, R., & Jongsma, A. (2006). *The Addiction Treatment Planner.* Hoboken, NJ: John Wiley.

Peters, R., Haas, A., & Hunt, W. (2001). Treatment "dosage" effects in drug court programs. In J. Hennessy & N. Pallone (Eds.), *Drug Courts in Operation* (pp. 63–72). New York: Haworth.

Peters, R., & Matthews, C. (2003). Substance abuse treatment programs in prisons and jails. In T. J. Fagan & R. K. Ax (Eds.), *Correctional Mental Health Handbook.* Thousand Oaks, CA: Sage.

Peters, R., Strozier, A., Murrin, M., & Kearns, W. (1997). Treatment of substance-abusing jail inmates: Examination of gender differences. *Journal of Substance Abuse Treatment, 14,* 339–349.

Petersilia, J. (2003). *When Prisoners Come Home: Parole and Prisoner Reentry.* Oxford: Oxford University Press.

Petersilia, J. (2007). Employ behavioral contracting for "earned discharge" parole. *Criminology & Public Policy, 6*, 807–814.

Petrik, N., Gildersleeve-High, L., McEllistrem, J., & Subotnik, L. (1994). The reduction of male abusiveness as a result of treatment: Reality or myth? *Journal of Family Violence, 9*, 307–316.

Pettus, C., Veeh, C., Renn, T., & Kennedy, S. C. (2021). The well-being development model: A theoretical model to improve outcomes among criminal justice system-involved individuals releasing from incarceration. *Social Service Review, 95*, 413–468.

Pettus-Davis, C. (2021). Support4Families: A proposed intervention model to support families of individuals returning home after incarceration. *Families in Society: The Journal of Contemporary Social Services, 102*, 316–332. https://doi.org/10.1177/1044389420970008

Pettus-Davis, C., Dunnigan, A., Veeh, C., Howard, M. O., Scheyett, A. M., & Roberts-Lewis, A. (2017). Enhancing social support post-incarceration: Results from a pilot randomized controlled trial. *Journal of Clinical Psychology, 73*, 1226–1246.

Peyton, E., & Gossweiler, R. (2001). *Treatment Services in Adult Drug Courts: Report on the 1999 National Drug Court Treatment Survey.* Washington, DC: National Institute of Justice.

Phelps, M. S. (2017). Mass probation: Toward a more robust theory of state variation in punishment. *Punishment & Society, 19*, 53–73. https://doi.org/10.1177/1462474516649174

Piaget, J. (1948). *The Moral Judgment of the Child.* Glencoe, IL: The Free Press.

Pimlott Kubiak, S., Beeble, M. L., & Bybee, D. (2009). Using the K6 to assess the mental health of jailed women. *Journal of Offender Rehabilitation, 48*, 296–312.

Piquero, A., Farrington, D., Welsh, B., Tremblay, R., & Jennings, W. (2008). *Effects of Early Family Parent Training Programs on Antisocial Behavior and Delinquency: A Systematic Review.* Stockholm: Swedish Council for Crime Prevention.

Pithers, W., Marques, J., Gibat, C., & Marlatt, D. (1983). Relapse prevention with sexual aggressives: A self-control model of treatment and maintenance of change. In J. Greer & I. Stuart (Eds.), *The Sexual Aggressor: Current Perspectives on Treatment* (pp. 214–239). New York: Van Nostrand Reinhold.

Polascheck, D. (2006). Violent offender programmes: Concept, theory, and practice. In C. R. Hollin & E. J. Palmer (Eds.), *Offending Behavior Programmes: Development, Application, and Controversies* (pp. 113–154). New York: Wiley.

Polaschek, D. L. L., & Ward, T. (2002). The implicit theories of potential rapists: What our questionnaires tell us. *Aggression and Violent Behavior, 7*, 385–406.

Polaschek, D. L., Ward, T., & Hudson, S. (1997). Rape and rapists: Theory and treatment. *Clinical Psychology Review, 17*, 117–144.

Pollock, J. M. (1998). *Counseling Women in Prison.* Thousand Oaks, CA: Sage.

Pope, L., & Delany-Brumsey, A. (2016). *Creating a Culture of Safety: Sentinel Event Reviews for Suicide and Self-Harm in Correctional Facilities.* Brooklyn, NY: Vera Institute of Justice. www.vera.org/publications/culture-of-safety-sentinel-event-suicide-self-harm-correctional-facilities

Porter, D. (2021, June 29). After suit, New Jersey to house inmates based on gender ID. Retrieved from https://apnews.com/article/nj-state-wire-new-jersey-89816d8a82cca2b7ffe74ca122088da9

Prendergast, M., Anglin, D., & Wellisch, J. (1995). Treatment of drug-abusing offenders under community supervision. *Federal Probation, 59*, 66–75.

Prendergast, M., Hall, E., Wexler, H., Melnick, G., & Cao, Y. (2004). Amity Prison-Based Therapeutic Community: 5-Year Outcomes. *The Prison Journal, 84*, 36–60.

Prendergast, M., Podus, D., Finney, J., Greenwell, L., & Roll, J. (2006). Contingency management for treatment of substance use disorder: A meta-analysis. *Addictions, 101*, 1546–1560.

Prins, S. (2014). The prevalence of mental illness in U.S. state prisons: A systematic review. *Psychiatric Services, 65*, 862–872.

Prochaska, J., & DiClemente, C. (1986). Toward a comprehensive model of change. In W. Miller & N. Heather (Eds.), *Treating Addictive Behaviors: Processes of Change* (pp. 3–27). New York: Plenum.

Project MATCH Research Group. (1997). Matching alcoholism treatment to client heterogeneity: Project MATCH post-treatment drinking outcomes. *Journal of Studies on Alcohol, 58,* 7–29.

Purkiss, M., Kifer, M., Hemmens, C., & Burton, V. (2003). Probation officer functions—a statutory analysis. *Federal Probation, 67*(1), 12–24.

Quay, H. (1984). *Managing Adult Inmates: Classification for Housing and Program Assignments.* College Park, MD: American Correctional Association.

Quay, H., & Parsons, R. (1972). *The Differential Behavioral Classification of the Juvenile Offender.* Washington, DC: U.S. Department of Justice.

Quinn, C. R., & Grumbach, G. (2015). Critical race theory and the limits of relational theory in social work with women. *Journal of Ethnic and Cultural Diversity in Social Work, 24,* 202–218.

Quinn, J. F, Forsyth, C. J, & Mullen-Quinn, C. (2004). Societal reaction to sex offenders: A review of the origins and results of the myths surrounding their crimes and treatment amenability. *Deviant Behavior, 25,* 215–232.

Quinsey, V. L., Harris, G. T., Rice, M. E., & Cormier, C. (1998). *Violent Offenders: Appraising and Managing Risk.* Washington, DC: American Psychological Association.

Quinsey, V. L., Harris, G., Rice, M. E., & Cormier, C. (2006). *Violent Offenders: Appraising and Managing Risk* (2nd ed.). Washington, DC: American Psychological Association.

Quinsey, V. L., Harris, G. T., Rice, M. E., & LaLumiere, M. (1993). Assessing treatment efficacy on outcome studies of sex offenders. *Journal of Interpersonal Violence, 10,* 85–105.

Quinsey, V. L., Rice, M. E., & Harris, G. T. (1995). Actuarial prediction of sexual recidivism. *Journal of Interpersonal Violence, 21,* 85–105.

Raine, A., Lencz, T., Bihrle, S., LaCasse, L., & Colletti, P. (2000). Reduced prefrontal gray matter volume and reduced autonomic activity in Antisocial Personality Disorder. *Archives of General Psychiatry, 57,* 119–127.

Raine, A., & Yang, Y. (2006). The neuroanatomical bases of psychopathy: A review of brain imaging findings. In C. J. Patrick (Ed.), *Handbook of Psychopathy* (pp. 278–295). New York: Guilford.

Randall, J., Henggeler, S., Cunningham, P., Rowland, M., & Swenson, C. (2001). Adapting multi-systemic therapy to treat adolescent substance abuse more effectively. *Cognitive and Behavioral Practice, 8,* 359–366.

Randall, C., Nowakowski, S. & Ellis, J.G. (2019). Managing acute insomnia in prison: Evaluation of a "one-Shot" cognitive behavioral therapy for insomnia (CBT-I) Intervention. *Behavioral Sleep Medicine, 17,* 827–836.

Raskin White, H. (2016). Substance use and crime. In K. J. Sher (Ed.), *The Oxford Handbook of Substance Use and Substance Use Disorders: Volume 2* (pp. 347–378). Oxford, UK: Oxford University Press.

Raskin White, H., Loeber, R., Stouthamer-Loeber, M., & Farrington, D. P. (1999). Developmental Associations between Substance Use and Violence. *Development and Psychopathology, 11,* 785–803.

Reed, B. G. (1985). Drug misuse and dependency in women: The meaning and implications of being considered a special population or minority group. *International Journal of the Addictions, 20,* 13–62.

Reed, B. G. (1987). Developing women-sensitive drug dependence treatment services: Why so difficult? *Journal of Psychoactive Drugs, 19,* 151–164.

Reid, J., Patterson, G., & Snyder, J. (Eds.), (2003). *Antisocial Behavior in Children and Adolescents: A Developmental Analysis and Model for Intervention.* Washington, DC: American Psychological Association.

Reisig, M. D., Holtfreter, K., & Morash, M. (2006). Assessing recidivism risk across female pathways to crime. *Justice Quarterly, 23,* 384–405.

Reitzel, L. R., & Carbonell, J. L. (2006). The effectiveness of sexual offender treatment for juveniles as measured by recidivism: A meta-analysis. *Sexual Abuse, 18,* 401–421.

Rice, M. E., Harris, G. T., & Cormier, C. A. (1992). An evaluation of a maximum security therapeutic community for psychopaths and other mentally disordered offenders. *Law and Human Behavior, 16,* 399–412.

Rich, P. (2017). *Working with Sex Offenders: A Guide for Practitioners.* London: Routledge.

Richie, B. E. (1996). *Compelled to Crime: The Gender Entrapment of Black Battered Women.* New York: Routledge.

Rimmele, D., Miller, W., & Dougher, M. (2003). Aversion therapies. In R. Hester & W. Miller (Eds.), *Handbook of Alcoholism Treatment Alternatives: Effective Alternatives* (3rd ed.). Boston: Allyn & Bacon.

Riva, G., Wiederhold, B. K., & Mantovani, F. (2018). Neuroscience of virtual reality: From virtual exposure to embodied medicine. *Cyberpsychology, Behavior, and Social Networking, 22*(1), 82–96.

Robertiello, G., & Terry, K. J. (2007). Can we profile sex offenders? *Aggression and Violent Behavior, 12,* 508–518.

Robinson, C. R., Lowenkamp, C. T., Holsinger, A. M., VanBenschoten, S., Alexander, M., & Oleson, J. C. (2012). A random study of Staff Training Aimed at Reducing Re-arrest (STARR): Using core correctional practices in probation interactions. *Journal of Crime and Justice, 35,* 167–188. https://doi.org/10.1080/0735648X.2012.674823

Robinson, C. R., VanBenschoten, S., Alexander, M., & Lowenkamp, C. T. (2011). A random (almost) study of Staff Training Aimed at Reducing Re-arrest (STARR): Reducing recidivism through intentional design. *Federal Probation, 75*(2), 95–107.

Rogers, R. (2006). The functional architecture of the frontal lobes: Implications for research with psychopathic offenders. In C. Patrick (Ed.), *Handbook of Psychopathy* (pp. 313–333). New York: Guilford.

Root, M. P. (1994). Reconstructing the impact of trauma on personality. In L. Brown & M. Ballou (Eds.), *Personality and Psychopathology: Feminist Reappraisals* (pp. 229–265). New York: Guilford.

Rosen, K. H., Matheson, J. L., Stith, S. M., McCollum, E. E., & Locke, L. D. (2007). Negotiated time-out: A de-escalation tool for couples. *Journal of Marital Therapy, 29,* 291–298.

Rosenbaum, M. (1981). When drugs come into the picture, love flies out the window: Women addicts' love relationships. *International Journal of the Addictions, 16,* 1197–1206.

Rosenthal, R., & DiMatteo, M. (2001). Meta-analysis recent developments in quantitative methods for literature reviews. *Annual Review of Psychology, 52,* 59–82.

Rosenthal, R., & Rubin, D. B. (1979). A note on percent variance explained as a measure of the importance of effects. *Journal of Applied Social Psychology, 9,* 395–396.

Ross, R., & Fabiano, E. (1985). *Time to Think: A Cognitive Model of Delinquency Prevention and Offender Rehabilitation.* Johnson City, TN: Institute of Social Science and Arts.

Ross, R., Fabiano, E., & Ross, R. (1989). *Reasoning and Rehabilitation: A Handbook for Teaching Cognitive Skills.* Ottawa: Flix Desktop Services.

Rothbaum, B. O., Rizzo, A. S., & Difede, J. (2010). Virtual reality exposure therapy for combat-related post-traumatic stress disorder. *Annals of the New York Academy of Sciences, 1208,* 126–132.

Russell, B. (2020). *Intimate Partner Violence and the LGBT+ Community: Understanding Power Dynamics.* New York: Springer Publishing.

Russell, C., Olson, D., Sprenkle, D., & Atilano, R. (1983). From family symptom to family system: Review of family therapy research. *American Journal of Family Therapy, 11,* 3–14.

Ryan, E. P., Hunter, J. A, & Murrie, D. C. (2012). *Juvenile Sex Offenders: A Guide to Evaluation and Treatment for Mental Health Professionals.* Oxford: Oxford University Press.

Ryan, V. S. (1981). Differences between males and females in drug treatment programs. In A. J. Schecter (Ed.), *Drug Dependence and Alcoholism: Social and Behavioral Issues* (pp. 789–801). New York: Plenum Press.

Saar, M. S., Epstein, R., Rosenthal, L., & Vafa, Y. (2015). *The Sexual Abuse to Prison Pipeline: The Girls' Story.* Center on Poverty and Inequality: Georgetown Law. Retrieved from www.law.georgetown.edu/poverty-inequality-center/wp-content/uploads/sites/14/2019/02/The-Sexual-Abuse-To-Prison-Pipeline-The-Girls%E2%80%99-Story.pdf

Sacks, J. (2004). Women with co-occurring substance use and mental disorders (COD) in the criminal justice system: A research review. *Behavioral Sciences and the Law, 22,* 449–466.

Sadeh, N., & McNiel, D. E. (2015). Posttraumatic Stress Disorder increases risk of criminal recidivism among justice-involved persons with mental disorders. *Criminal Justice and Behavior, 42*, 573–586.

Sagatun, I. J. (2007). Attributional effects of therapy with incestuous families. *Journal of Marital & Family Therapy, 8*, 99–104.

Salisbury, E. J., Boppre, B., & Kelly, B. (2016). Gender-responsive risk and need assessment: Implications for justice-involved women. In F. S. Taxman (Ed.), *Handbook on Risk and Need Assessment: Theory and Practice* (Volume 1: Handbook Series sponsored by the Division on Corrections and Sentencing, American Society of Criminology) (pp. 220–243). New York: Routledge.

Salisbury, E. J., Sundt., J., & Boppre, B. (2019). Mapping the Implementation Landscape: Assessing the Systemic Capacity of Statewide Community Corrections Agencies to Deliver Evidence-Based Practices. *Corrections: Policy, Practice and Research, 4*, 19–38.

Salisbury, E. J., & Van Voorhis, P. (2009). Gendered pathways: A quantitative investigation of women probationers' paths to incarceration. *Criminal Justice and Behavior, 36*, 541–566.

Samenow, S. (1984). *Inside the Criminal Mind.* New York: Times Books.

Samenow, S. (1989). *Before It's Too Late.* New York: Times Books.

Samenow, S. (2001). Understanding the criminal mind: A phenomenological approach. *Journal of Psychiatry & Law, 29*(3), 275–293.

Sameroff, A. (1989). Commentary: General systems and the regulation of development. In M. Gunnar & E. Thelen (Eds.), *Systems and Development: The Minnesota Symposia on Child Psychology* (pp. 219–235). Hillsdale, NJ: Lawrence Erlbaum.

Sampson, R., & Laub, J. (1993). *Crime in the Making: Pathways and Turning Points through Life.* Cambridge, MA: Harvard University Press.

Sandhu, D., & Rose, J. (2012). How do therapists contribute to therapeutic change in sex offender treatment: An integration of the literature. *Journal of Sexual Aggression, 18*(3), 269–283.

Sandler, J. C., & Freeman, N. J. (2007). Topology of female sex offenders: A test of Vandiver and Kercher. *Sexual Abuse, 19*, 73–89.

Sandler, J. C., & Freeman, N. J. (2011). Female sex offenders and the criminal justice system: A comparison of arrests and outcomes. *The Journal of Sexual Aggression, 17*, 61–76.

Sandler, J. C., Freeman, N. J., & Socia, K. M. (2008). Does a watched pot boil? A time-series analysis of New York State's Sex Offender and Registration Law. *Psychology, Public Policy and Law, 14*, 284–302.

Satir, V. (1967). *Conjoint Family Therapy.* Palo Alto, CA: Science and Behavior Books.

Satir, V. (1972). *Peoplemaking.* Palo Alto, CA: Science and Behavior Books.

Saunders, D. (1996). Feminist-cognitive-behavioral and process-psychodynamic treatments for men who batter: Interaction of abuser traits and treatment models. *Violence and Victims, 11*, 393–414.

Saunders, D., & Azar, S. (1989). Treatment programs for family violence. In L. Ohlin & M. Tonry (Eds.), *Family Violence* (pp. 481–546). Chicago: University of Chicago Press.

Sawyer, A., & Borduin, C. (2011). Effects of multisystemic therapy through midlife: A 21.9-year follow-up of a randomized clinical trial with serious and violent juvenile offenders. *Journal of Consulting and Clinical Psychology, 79*(5), 643–652.

Schoenwald, S., & Henggeler, S. (1997). Combining effective treatment strategies with family-preservation models of service delivery. In R. Illback & C. Cobb (Eds.), *Integrated Services for Children and Families: Opportunities for Psychological Practice* (pp. 121–136). Washington, DC: American Psychological Association.

Schorsch, E., Galedary, G., Haag, A., Hauch, M., & Lohse, H. (1990). *Sex Offenders: Dynamics and Psychotherapeutic Strategies.* New York: Springer-Verlag.

Schuckit, M. (2006). *Drug and Alcohol Abuse: Clinical Guide to Diagnosis and Treatment.* New York: Plenum Medical Book Co.

Schwartz, B. (2011). Characteristics and typologies of sex offenders. In B. Schwartz (Ed.), *Handbook of Sex Offender Treatment* (pp. 2-1–2-33). Kingston, NJ: Civic Research Institute.

Schwartz, B. (2015). The R.U.L.E. Program: An integrative approach to treating adult, male sex offenders. In B. Schwartz (Ed.), *The Sex Offender: Insights on Treatment and Policy Developments* (Vol. VIII) (pp. 13-1–13-24). Kingston, NJ: Civic Research Institute.

Seligman, M. (2002). *Authentic Happiness: Using the New Positive Psychology to Realize your Potential for Lasting Fulfillment.* New York Times: The Free Press.

Sellbom, M., & Drislane, L. E. (2021). The classification of psychopathy. *Aggression and Violent Behavior, 59,* 1–10. https://doi.org/10.1016/j.avb.2020.101473

Selzer, M. (1971). The Michigan Alcoholism Screening Test: The quest for a new diagnostic instrument. *American Journal of Psychiatry, 127*(12), 1653–1658.

Semel, R. A. (2016). Incorporating the Jesness Inventory-Revised (JI-R) in a best-practice model of juvenile delinquency assessments. *Journal of Forensic Psychology Practice, 16*(1), 1–23.

Serin, R., & Kennedy, S. (1997). *Treatment Readiness and Responsivity: Contributing to Effective Correctional Programming.* Ottawa: Correctional Services of Canada.

Serketich, W., & Dumas, J. (1996). The effectiveness of behavioral parent training to modify antisocial behavior in children: A meta-analysis. *Behavioral Therapy, 27,* 171–186.

Seto, M. C., & Quinsey, V. L. (2006). Toward the future: Translating basic research into prevention and treatment strategies. In C. Patrick (Ed.), *Handbook of Psychopathy* (pp. 589–601). New York: Guilford.

Sexton, T., & Alexander, J. (2000). *Functional Family Therapy. Juvenile Justice Bulletin.* Washington, DC: Office of Justice and Delinquency Prevention.

Sexton, T., & Turner, C. (2010). The effectiveness of functional family therapy for youth with behavioral problems in a community practice setting. *Journal of Family Psychology, 24*(3), 339–348.

Shadish, W., Montgomery, L., Wilson, P., Wilson, M., Bright, I., & Okwumabua, T. (1993). Effects of family and marital psychotherapies: A meta-analysis. *Journal of Consulting and Clinical Psychology, 61,* 992–1002.

Shapiro, F. (1995). *Eye Movement Desensitization and Reprocessing. Basic Principles, Protocols, and Procedures.* New York: Guilford.

Sherman, L., Gottfredson, D., MacKenzie, D., Eck, J., Reuter, P., & Bushway, S. (1997). *Preventing Crime: What Works, What Doesn't, What's Promising.* Washington, DC: National Institute of Justice, U.S. Department of Justice.

Shields, I. W., & Simourd, D. J. (1991). Predicting predatory behavior in a population of young offenders. *Criminal Justice and Behavior, 18,* 180–194.

Shipley, W., Gruber, C., Martin, T., & Klein, A. (2009). *Shipley-2.* Los Angeles: Western Psychological Services.

Shonkoff, J., Garner, A., & the Committee on Psychosocial Aspects of Child and Family Health, Committee on Early Childhood, Adoption, and Dependent Care, and Section on Developmental and Behavioral Pediatrics. (2011). The lifelong effects of early childhood adversity and toxic stress. *Pediatrics,* Online Issn: 1098-4275.

Shore, J. (2004). Community-based treatment. In M. Galanter & H. Kleber (Eds.), *Textbook of Substance Abuse Treatment* (3rd ed.). Washington, DC: American Psychiatric Press.

Shursen, A., Brock, L. J., & Jennings, G. (2008). Differentiation and intimacy in sex offender relationships. *Sexual Addiction & Compulsivity, 15,* 14–22.

Simourd, D. (1997). Criminal sentiments scale-modified and pride in delinquency: Psychometric properties and construct validity of two measures of criminal attitudes. *Criminal Justice and Behavior, 24,* 52–70.

Simourd, D. (2004). Use of dynamic risk/need assessment instruments among long-term incarcerated offenders. *Criminal Justice and Behavior, 31*(3), 306–323.

Simpson, L. E., Doss, B. D., Wheeler, J., & Christensen, A. (2007). Relationship violence among couples seeking therapy: Common couple violence or battering? *Journal of Marital & Family Therapy, 33,* 270–283.

Skeem, J. L., Eno Louden, J., Polaschek, D., & Camp, J. (2007). Assessing relationship quality in mandated community treatment: Blending care with control. *Psychological Assessment, 19,* 397–410.

Skeem, J. L., Louden, J. E., Polaschek, D., & Camp, J. (2007). Assessing relationship quality in mandated community treatment: Blending care with control. *Psychological Assessment, 19,* 397–410. https://doi.org/10.1037/1040-3590.19.4.397

Skeem, J. L., & Manchak, S. (2008). Back to the future: From Klockars' model of effective supervision to evidence-based practice in probation. *Journal of Offender Rehabilitation, 47,* 220–247. https://doi.org/10.1080/10509670802134069

Skeem, J. L., Monahan, J., & Mulvey, E. (2002). Psychopathy, treatment involvement, and subsequent violence among civil psychiatric patients. *Law and Human Behavior, 26,* 577–603.

Smith, C., Algozzine, B., Schmid, R., & Hennly, T. (1990). Prison adjustment of youthful inmates with mental retardation. *Mental Retardation, 28,* 177–181.

Smith, J., & Meyers, R. (2003). The community reinforcement approach. In R. Hester & W. Miller (Eds.), *Handbook of Alcoholism Treatment Approaches* (3rd ed.). Boston: Allyn & Bacon.

Smith, P., Gendreau, P., & Swartz, K. (2009). Validating the principles of effective intervention: A systematic review of the contributions of meta-analysis in the field of corrections. *Victims & Offenders, 4,* 148–169.

Smith, P., Goggin, C., & Gendreau, P. (2002). *The Effects of Prison Sentences and Intermediate Sanctions on Recidivism: General Effects and Individual Differences.* Ottawa: Solicitor General of Canada: A Report to the Corrections Research Branch.

Smith, P., Schweitzer, M., Labrecque, R. M., & Latessa, E. J. (2012). Improving probation officers' supervision skills: An evaluation of the EPICS model. *Journal of Crime and Justice, 35,* 189–199. https://doi.org/10.1080/0735648X.2012.674826

Smith, S. G., Chen, J., Basile, K. C., Gilbert, L. K., Merrick, M. T., Patel, N., Walling, M., & Jain, A. (2017). *The National Intimate Partner and Sexual Violence Survey (NISVS): 2010–2012 State Report.* National Center for Injury Prevention and Control, Center for Disease Control. www.cdc.gov/violenceprevention/pdf/NISVS-StateReport Book.pdf

Snape, L., & Atkinson, C. (2016). The evidence for student-focused motivational interviewing in educational settings: A review of the literature. *Advances in School Mental Health Promotion, 9,* 119–139. https://doi.org/10.1080/1754730X.2016.1157027

Song, X, Zhao, H., Lou, T., Wang, Y. & Zheng, M. (2020). Comparison of mindfulness with and without practice among women in custody. *Criminal Justice and Behavior, 48,* 1111–1126.

Sorbello, L., Eccleston, L., Ward, T., & Jones, R. (2002). Treatment needs of female offenders: A review. *Australian Psychologist, 37*(37), 198–205.

Sperber, K. (2004). *Potential Applications of an Existing Offender Typology to Child Molesting Behaviors.* [Unpublished doctoral dissertation]. University of Cincinnati.

Spiegler, M., & Guevremont, D. (2002). *Contemporary Behavior Therapy* (4th ed.). Pacific Grove, CA: Brooks/Cole.

Spiegler, M., & Guevremont, D. (2010). *Contemporary Behavior Therapy* (5th ed.). Belmont, CA: Wadsworth.

Spiropoulos, G., Spruance, L., Van Voorhis, P., & Schmitt, M. (2006). Pathfinders vs. problem solving: Comparative effects of cognitive-behavioral programs for men and women offenders. *Journal of Offender Rehabilitation, 42*(3), 69–94.

Spohr, S. A., Taxman, F. S. & Walters, S. T. (2015). The relationship between electronic goal reminders and subsequent drug use and treatment initiation in a criminal justice setting. *Addictive Behaviors, 51,* 51–56.

Stanchfield, P. (2001). Clarifying the therapist's role in the treatment of the resistant sex offender. In B. K. Welo (Ed.), *Tough Customers: Counseling Unwilling Clients.* Lanham, MD: American Correctional Association.

Stanton, M. (1994). *Family Therapy for Drug Abuse.* Philadelphia, PA: Paper presented at the National Conference on Marital and Family Therapy Outcome and Process Research: State of the Science.

Stanton, M., Todd, T., & Associates. (1982). *The Family Therapy of Drug Abuse and Addiction.* New York: Guilford.

Staton-Tindall, M., Garner, B., Morey, J., Leukefeld, C., Krietemeyer, J., Saum, C., & Oser, C. (2007). Gender differences in treatment engagement among a sample of incarcerated substance abusers. *Criminal Justice and Behavior, 34,* 1143–1156.

Steadman, H. J., Osher, F. C., Clark Robbins, P., Case, B., & Samuels, S. (2009). Prevalence of serious mental illness among jail inmates. *Psychiatric Services, 60,* 761–765.

Steadman, H. J., Silver, E., Monahan, J., Appelbaum, P. S., Clark Robbins, P., Mulvey, E. P., Grisso, T., Roth, L. H., & Banks, S. (2000). A classification tree approach to the development of actuarial violence risk assessment tools. *Law and Human Behavior, 24,* 83–100.

Steinglass, P. (2004). Family therapy. In M. Galanter & H. Kleber (Eds.), *Textbook of Substance Abuse Treatment* (3rd ed.). Washington, DC: American Psychiatric Press.

Steinglass, P., Bennett, L., Wolin, S., & Reiss, D. (1987). *The Alcoholic Family.* New York: Basic Books.

Stierlin, H. (1977). *Psychoanalysis and Family Therapy.* New York: Jason Aronson.

Stinson, J. D., & Clark, M. D. (2017). *Motivational Interviewing with Offenders: Engagement, Rehabilitation and Reentry.* New York: Guilford Press.

Stirpe, T., Abracen, J. Stermac, L., & Wilson, R. (2006). Sexual offenders' state-of-mind regarding childhood attachments: A controlled investigation. *Sexual Abuse: A Journal of Research and Treatment, 18,* 289–302.

Stith, S., & Rosen, K. (1990). Family therapy for spouse abuse. In S. Stith, M. Williams, & K. Rosen (Eds.), *Violence Hits Home: Comprehensive Treatment Approaches to Domestic Violence.* New York: Springer.

Sturup, J., Edens, J. F., Sorman, K., Karlberg, D., Fredriksson, B., & Kristiansson, M. (2013). Field reliability of the Psychopathy Checklist-Revised among life sentenced prisoners in Sweden. *Law and Human Behavior, 38,* 315–324.

Sue, D. W., & Sue, D. (2002). *Counseling the Culturally Diverse: Theory and Practice* (4th ed.). New York: Wiley.

Sullivan, C., Grant, M., & Grant, D. (1957). The development of interpersonal maturity: An application to delinquency. *Psychiatry, 20,* 373–385.

Sullivan, H. (1953). *The Interpersonal Theory of Psychiatry.* New York: Norton.

Sun, A-P. (2007). Relapse among substance-abusing women: Components and processes. *Substance Use and Misuse, 42,* 1–21.

Sundell, K., Hansson, K., Lofholm, C. A., Olsson, T., Gustle, L. H., & Kadesjo, C. (2008). The transportability of multisystemic therapy to Sweden: Short-term results from a randomized trial of conduct-disordered youths. *Journal of Family Psychology, 22,* 550–560.

Swenson, C., Schaeffer, C., Henggeler, S., Faldowski, R., & Mayhhew, A. (2010). Multisystemic therapy for child abuse and neglect: A randomized effectiveness trial. *Journal of Family Psychology, 24*(4), 497–507.

Sykes, G., & Matza, D. (1957). Techniques of neutralization: A theory of delinquency. *American Sociological Review, 22,* 664–670.

Szapocznik, J., Kurtines, J. W., Foote, F., Perez-Vidal, A., & Hervis, O. (1983). Conjoint versus one-person family therapy: Some evidence for the effectiveness of conducting family therapy through one person. *Journal of Consulting and Clinical Psychology, 51,* 889–899.

Taxman, F. S. (2014). Second generation of RNR: The importance of systemic responsivity in expanding core principles of responsivity. *Federal Probation, 78*(2), 32–40. Retrieved from https://search.ebscohost.com/login.aspx?direct=true&AuthType=shib&db=edshol&AN=edshol.hein.journals.fedpro78.21&site=eds-live&scope=site&custid=s6281220

Taxman, F. S., & Belenko, S. (2012). *Implementing Evidence-Based Practices in Community Corrections and Addiction Treatment.* New York: Springer.

Taxman, F. S., & Bouffard, J. (2002). Assessing therapeutic integrity in modified therapeutic communities for drug-involved offenders. *The Prison Journal, 82*(2), 189–212.

Taxman, F. S., & Coudy, M. (2015). Risk tells us who, but not what or how: Empirical assessment of the complexity of criminogenic needs to inform correctional programming. *Criminology and Public Policy, 14,* 71–102.

Taxman, F. S., Perdoni, M., & Harrison, L. (2007). Drug treatment services for adult offenders: The state of the state. *Journal of Substance Abuse Treatment, 32,* 239–254.

Taxman, F. S., Shepardson, E. S., & Bryne, J. M. (2004). *Tools of the trade: A guide to incorporating science into practice.* Washington, DC: U.S. Department of Justice, National Institute of Corrections.

Taxman, F. S., Soule, D., & Gelb, A. (1999). Graduated sanctions: Stepping into accountable systems and offenders. *The Prison Journal, 79*(2), 182–204.

Taymans, J. (2006). Interpersonal problem-solving skills—A step-by-step process to enhance pro-social information processing. In B. Glick (Ed.), *Cognitive Behavioral Interventions for At Risk Youth* (pp. 9–1–9–17). Kingston, NJ: Civic Research Institute.

Taymans, J., & Parese, S. (1998). *Problem Solving Skills for Offenders: A Social Cognitive Intervention.* Washington, DC: George Washington University.

Teicher, M. (2002, March). The neurobiology of child abuse. *Scientific American,* 68–75.

Teplin, L. A., Abram, K. M., McClelland, G. M., Mericle, A. A., Duncan, M. K., & Washburn, J. J. (2006). *Psychiatric Disorders of Youth in Detention.* Washington, DC: U.S. Department of Justice, Office of Juvenile Justice and Delinquency Prevention.

Thornberry, T., Lizotte, A., Krohn, M., Farnsworth, M., & Jang, S. (1994). Delinquent peers, beliefs, and delinquent behavior: A longitudinal test of interactional theory. *Criminology, 94,* 47–83.

Thorndike, E. L. (1898). Animal intelligence: An experimental study of the associative processes in animals. *Psychological Monographs: General and Applied, 2*(4), i–109.

Ticknor, B. (2018). *Virtual Reality and the Criminal Justice System: Exploring the Possibilities for Correctional Rehabilitation.* Lanham, MD: Lexington Books.

Ticknor, B. (2019). Virtual reality and correctional rehabilitation: A game changer. *Criminal Justice and Behavior, 46*(9), 1319–1336.

Ticknor, B., & Tillinghast, S. (2011). Virtual reality and the criminal justice system: New possibilities for research, training, and rehabilitation. *Journal of Virtual Worlds Research, 4,* 4–44.

Tong, L., & Farrington, D. (2006). How effective is the "Reasoning and Rehabilitation" program in reducing reoffending? A meta-analysis of evaluations in four countries. *Psychology, Crime, and Law, 12,* 3–24.

Travis, J., & Lawrence, S. (2002). *Beyond the Prison Gates: The State of Parole in America.* Washington, DC: The Urban Institute.

Trotter, C. (1999). *Working with Involuntary Clients: A Guide to Practice.* Thousand Oaks, CA: Sage.

United Nations Rules for the Treatment of Women Prisoners and Non-custodial Measures for Women Offenders (the Bangkok Rules), G.A. Res. 65/229, annex, adopted Dec. 21, 2010, U.N. Doc. A/Res/65/229 (March 16, 2011).

University of Cincinnati Corrections Institute (UCCI). (2010). *Effective Practices in Community Supervision (EPICS).* Cincinnati, OH: Criminal Justice Research Center, University of Cincinnati.

University of Cincinnati Corrections Institute. (2005). *Correctional Program Checklist.* Cincinnati, OH: UCCI.

University of Cincinnati Corrections Institute. (2011). *Cognitive-Behavioral Intervention-Core Adult Curriculum Description.* Cincinnati, OH: UCCI. https://cech.uc.edu/about/centers/ucci/products/interventions/group-interventions.html

University of Cincinnati Corrections Institute. (2015). *Correctional Program Checklist 2.0.* Cincinnati, OH: UCCI.

University of Cincinnati Corrections Institute. (n.d.). *Effective practices in community supervision.* University of Cincinnati Corrections Institute. Retrieved from www.uc.edu/content/dam/uc/corrections/docs/Training%20Overviews/EPICS.pdf

U.S. General Accounting Office. (1997). *Drug Courts: Overview of Growth, Characteristics and Results.* Washington, DC: U.S. General Accounting Office.

Vachon, D. D., Lynam, D. R., Loeber, R., & Stouthamer-Loeber, M. (2011). Generalizing the nomological network of psychopathy across populations differing on race and conviction status. *Journal of Abnormal Psychology, 121,* 263–269.

Valdes, F., Culp, J. M., & Harris, A. P. (2002). Battles waged, won, and lost: Critical race theory at the turn of the millennium. In F. Valdes, J. M. Culp, & A. P. Harris (Eds.), *Crossroads, Directions, and a New Critical Race Theory* (pp. 1–6). Philadelphia, PA: Temple University Press.

Van der Kolk, B. A., Roth, S., Pelcovitz, D., Sunday, S., & Spinazzola, J. (2005). Disorders of extreme stress: The empirical foundation of a complex adaptation to trauma. *Journal of Traumatic Stress, 18,* 389–399.

VanderWaal, C. J., Taxman, F. S., & Gurka-Ndanyi, M. A. (2008). Reforming drug treatment services to offenders: Cross-system collaboration, integrated policies, and a seamless continuum of care model. *Journal of Social Work Practice in the Addiction, 8*(1), 127–153.

Van Dieten, M. (1998). *Applying the Principles of Effective Correctional Interventions.* Presentation to NIC Workshop on Effective Interventions with High Risk Offenders. July.

Van Dieten, M. (2008). *Women Offender Case Management Model.* Washington, DC: National Institute of Corrections.

Vandiver, D. M, & Kercher, G. (2004). Offender and victim characteristics of registered female sexual offenders in Texas: A proposed typology of female sexual offenders. *Sexual Abuse, 16,* 121–137.

Van Horn, S.A, Morgan, R.D., Brusman Lovins, L. Littlefield, A.D., Hunger, J.T., Gigax, G. and Ridley, K. (2019). Changing Lives and Changing Outcomes: "What Works" in an intervention for justice-involved persons with mental illness. *Psychological Services 16,* 693–700.

Van Ness, D., & Strong, K. H. (2015). *Restoring Justice: An Introduction to Restorative Justice* (5th ed.). New York: Routledge (Anderson).

Van Voorhis, P. (1987). Correctional effectiveness: The high cost of ignoring success. *Federal Probation, 51,* 56–62.

Van Voorhis, P. (1994). *Psychological Classification of the Adult Male Prison Inmate.* Albany, NY: SUNY Press.

Van Voorhis, P. (2006). Comprehensive evaluation of cognitive behavioral programs in corrections. In B. Glick (Ed.), *Cognitive Behavioral Interventions for At Risk Youth.* Kingston, NJ: Civic Research Institute.

Van Voorhis, P. (2012). On behalf of women offenders: Women's place in the science of evidence-based practice. *Criminology and Public Policy, 11*(2), 111–145.

Van Voorhis, P., Cullen, F., & Applegate, B. (1995). Evaluating interventions with violent offenders: A guide for practitioners and policymakers. *Federal Probation, 59,* 17–28.

Van Voorhis, P., & Groot, B. (2010). *Predictive Validity of Women's COMPAS Scales among Incarcerated Women in California.* Cincinnati, OH: Center for Criminal Justice Research.

Van Voorhis, P., & Presser, L. (2001). *Classification of Women Offenders: A National Assessment of Current Practices.* Washington, DC: National Institute of Corrections.

Van Voorhis, P., Salisbury, E., Wright, E., & Bauman, A. (2008). *Achieving Accurate Pictures of Risk and Identifying Gender-Responsive Needs: Two New Assessments for Women Offenders.* Washington, DC: National Institute of Corrections.

Van Voorhis, P., & Spiropoulos, G. (2003). *Evaluation of Adult Work-Release Services.* Cincinnati, OH: University of Cincinnati, Center for Criminal Justice Research.

Van Voorhis, P., Spiropoulos, G., Ritchie, P. N., Seabrook, R., & Spruance, L. (2013). Identifying areas of specific responsivity in cognitive behavioral programs. *Criminal Justice and Behavior, 40,* 1250–1279.

Van Voorhis, P., Spruance, L., Ritchie, N., Listwan, S., Seabrook, R., & Pealer, J. (2002). *The Georgia Cognitive Skills Experiment: Outcome Evaluation, Phase II.* Cincinnati, OH: University of Cincinnati, Center for Criminal Justice Research.

Van Voorhis, P., Wright, E., Salisbury, E., & Bauman, A. (2010). Women's risk factors and their contributions to existing risk/needs assessment: The current status of gender responsive assessment. *Criminal Justice and Behavior, 37*(3), 261–288.

Van Wormer, K. (1999). The strengths perspective: A paradigm for correctional counseling. *Federal Probation, 63*(1), 51–59.

Van Wormer, K. (2001). *Counseling Female Offenders and Victims: A Strengths-Restorative Approach.* New York: Springer.

Van Wormer, K. (2002). Addictions and women in the criminal justice system. In S. Straussner & S. Brown (Eds.), *The Handbook of Addiction Treatment for Women* (pp. 470–486). San Francisco: Jossey-Bass.

Vess, J. (2011). Ethical practice in sex offender assessment. *Sexual Abuse, 23*, 381–396.

Viglione, J., Rudes, D., & Taxman, F. (2015). Misalignment in supervision: Implementing risk/needs assessment instruments in probation. *Criminal Justice and Behavior, 42*, 263–285.

Wagers, S., & Radatz, D. L. (2020). Emerging treatment models and programs in intimate partner violence treatment: An introduction. *Partner Abuse, 11*, 202–227.

Walker, S. (2001). *Sense and Nonsense about Crime and Drugs* (5th ed.). Belmont, CA: Wadsworth.

Wallace, B. (1991). *Crack Cocaine: A Practical Treatment Approach for the Chemically Dependent.* New York: Brunner/Mazel.

Walsh, E. (2003). Legal and ethical issues related to the mental health treatment of incarcerated persons. In R. K. Schwartz (Ed.), *Correctional Psychology: Practice, Programming, and Administration.* New York: John Wiley.

Walters, G. D. (1990). *The Criminal Lifestyle: Patterns of Serious Criminal Conduct.* Newbury Park, CA: Sage.

Walters, G. D. (1995), The Psychological Inventory of Criminal Thinking Styles (PICTS). Part I: Reliability and preliminary validity. *Criminal Justice and Behavior, 22*, 307– 325.

Walters, G. D. (2001). Overcoming offender resistance to abandoning a criminal lifestyle. In B. K. Welo (Ed.), *Tough Customers: Counseling Unwilling Clients.* Lanham, MD: American Correctional Association.

Walters, G. D. (2012). Criminal thinking and recidivism: Meta-analytic evidence on the predictive and incremental validity of the Psychological Inventory of Criminal Thinking Styles (PICTS). *Aggression and Violent Behavior, 17*, 272–278.

Walters, G. D. (2016). Proactive and reactive criminal thinking, psychological inertia, and the crime continuity conundrum. *Journal of Criminal Justice, 46*, 45–51.

Walters, G. D., & Cohen, T. H. (2016). Criminal thought process as a dynamic risk factor: Variable-and person-oriented approaches to recidivism prediction. *Law and Human Behavior, 40*, 411–419.

Wanberg, K. (1993). *The Adult Substance Use Survey (ASUS).* Arvada, CO: Center for Addictions Research and Evaluation.

Wanberg, K. (1995). *The Life Situation Questionnaire.* Arvada, CO: Center for Addictions Research and Evaluation.

Wanberg, K., & Milkman, H. (1993). *The Adult Self Assessment Questionnaire (AdSAQ).* Arvada, CO: Center for Addictions Research and Evaluation.

Wanberg, K., & Milkman, H. (1998). *Criminal Conduct and Substance Abuse Treatment: Strategies for Self-Improvement and Change.* Thousand Oaks, CA: Sage.

Ward, T. (2007). On a clear day you can see forever: Integrating values and skills in sex offender treatment. *Journal of Sexual Aggression, 13*, 187–201.

Ward, T., & Gannon, T.A. (2006). Rehabilitation, etiology, and self-regulation: The comprehensive good lives model of treatment for sexual offenders. *Aggression and Violent Behavior, 11*, 77–94.

Ward, T., & Hudson, S. (2000). A self-regulations model of relapse prevention. In D. Laws, S. Hudson, & T. Ward. (Eds.), *Remaking Relapse Prevention with Sex Offenders: A Sourcebook* (pp. 79–101). Thousand Oaks, CA: Sage.

Ward, T., Hudson, S., & Marshall, W. (1995). Attachment style and intimacy deficits in sexual offenders: A theoretical framework. *Sex Abuse: A Journal of Research and Treatment, 7*, 317–335.

Ward, T., & Maruna, S. (2007). *Rehabilitation.* London: Routledge.

Ward, T., & Stewart, C.A. (2003). The treatment of sex offenders. *Professional Psychology, Research and Practice, 34*, 353–360.

Warren, F., Evans, C., Dolan, B., & Norton, K. (2004). Impulsivity and self-damaging behaviour in severe personality disorder: The impact of democratic therapeutic community treatment. *Therapeutic Communities: International Journal for Therapeutic and Supportive Organizations, 25*, 55–71.

Warren, J. I., & South, S. C. (2006). Comparing the constructs of Antisocial Personality Disorder and psychopathy in a sample of incarcerated women. *Behavioral Sciences and the Law, 24*, 1–20.

Warren, M. (1971). Classification of offenders as an aid to efficient management and effective treatment. *Journal of Criminal Law, Criminology and Police Science, 62*, 239–268.

Warren, M. (1983). Application of Interpersonal Maturity Theory to offender populations. In W. Laufer & J. Day (Eds.), *Personality Theory, Moral Development, and Criminal Behavior* (pp. 23–50). Lexington, MA: Lexington Books.

Warren, M., & the Staff of the Community Treatment Project. (1966). *Interpersonal Maturity Level Classification: Diagnosis and Treatment of Low, Middle, and High Maturity Delinquents.* Sacramento: CA: Youth Authority.

Washburn, J. J., Romero, E. G., Welty, L. J., Abram, K. M., Teplin, L. A., McClelland, G. M., & Paskar, L. D. (2007). Development of antisocial personality disorder in detained youths: The predictive value of mental disorders. *Journal of Consulting and Clinical Psychology, 75*, 221–231.

Watson, J. B. (1913). Psychology as a behaviorist views it. *Psychological Review, 20*, 158–177.

Way, B. B., Miraglia, R., & Sawyer, D. A. (2005). Factors related to suicide in New York State prisons. *International Journal of Law and Psychiatry, 28*, 207–221.

Webster, C. D., Douglas, K. S., Eaves, D., & Hart, S. D. (1997). *HCR-20: Assessing Risk for Violence* (version 2). Burnaby, BC: Mental Health Law and Policy Institute, Simon Fraser University.

Wechsler, D. (2008). *Wechsler Adult Intelligence Scale* (4th ed.). San Antonio, TX: Pearson.

Wellisch, J., Prendergast, M., & Anglin, M. D. (1996). Needs assessment and services for drug-abusing women offenders: Results from a national survey of community-based treatment programs. *Women in Criminal Justice, 8*, 27–60.

Welo, B. K. (2001). Taking care of yourself in the process: Counselor self-care in brutal environments. In B. K. Welo (Ed.), *Tough Customers: Counseling Unwilling Clients.* Lanham, MD: American Correctional Association.

Welsh, W. (2007). A multisite evaluation of prison-based therapeutic community drug treatment. *Criminal Justice and Behavior, 34*, 1481–1498.

Westen, D. (1991). Social cognition and object relations. *Psychological Bulletin, 109*, 429–455.

Wexler, H., DeLeon, G., Kressel, D., & Peters, J. (1999). The Amity Prison T C Evaluation: Reincarceration outcomes. *Criminal Justice and Behavior, 26*, 147–167.

Wexler, H., & Lipton, D. (1993). From reform to recovery advances in prison drug treatment. In J. Inciardi (Ed.), *Drug Treatment and Criminal Justice* (pp. 209–227). Newbury Park, CA: Sage.

Wexler, H., Melnick, G., Lowe, L., & Peters, J. (1999). Three-year reincarceration outcomes for Amity in-prison therapeutic community and aftercare in California. *The Prison Journal, 79*, 321–336.

Whetzel, J., & Lowenkamp, C. T. (2011). Who cares what offenders think? New insight from offender surveys. *Federal Probation, 75*(2), 13–15.

Whitaker, C. (1976). The family is a four-dimensional relationship. In P. Guerin (Ed.), *Family Therapy: Theory and Practice.* New York: Gardner.

Whitehead, J., Jones, M., & Braswell, M. (2008). *Exploring Corrections in America* (2nd ed.). Newark, NJ: LexisNexis Matthew Bender (Anderson).

Whitehead, J., & Lab, S. (1989). *A Response to Does Correctional Treatment Work?* [Unpublished paper].

Wilkinson, G., & Robertson, G. (2006). *The Wide-Range Achievement 4 (WRAT-4) Professional Manual.* Lutz, FL: Psychological Assessment Resources.

Wilson, D. B., Allen, L., & MacKenzie, D. (2000). *A Qualitative Review of Structures, Group-Oriented, Cognitive-Behavioral Programs for Offenders.* [Unpublished manuscript]. College Park: University of Maryland.

Wilson, D.B, Bouffard, L.A., & MacKenzie, D.L. (2005). A quantitative review of structure, group-oriented, cognitive-behavioral programs for offenders. *Criminal Justice and Behavior, 32,* 172–204.

Wilson, D. B., Gallagher, C., & MacKenzie, D. (2000). A meta-analysis of corrections-based education, vocation, and work programs for adult offenders. *Journal of Research in Crime and Delinquency, 37*(4), 347–368.

Wilson, D. B., Mitchell, O., & MacKenzie, D. L. (2003). *A Systematic Review of Drug Court Effects on Recidivism.* [Unpublished manuscript].

Wilson, D. B., Mitchell, O. & MacKenzie, D. L., (2007). A systematic review of drugs court effects on recidivism. *Journal of Experimental Criminology, 2*(4), 459–487.

Wilson, J. (1987). Strategic opportunities for delinquency prevention. In J. Wilson & G. Loury (Eds.), *From Children to Citizens* (pp. 291–311). New York: Springer-Verlag.

Wilson, M. (2019, November 4). Oregon Transgender Prisoner Must be Housed Along with Other Transgender or NonCisgender Prisoners. *Prison Legal News.* Retrieved from www.prisonlegalnews.org/news/2019/nov/4/oregon-transgender-prisoner-must-be-housed-alone-or-other-transgender-or-noncisgender-prisoners/

Wilson, S. J., & Lipsey, M. (2000). Wilderness challenge programs for delinquent youth: A meta-analysis of outcome evaluations. *Evaluation and Program Planning, 23,* 1–12.

Winkler, G. (1992). Assessing and responding to suicidal jail inmates. *Community Mental Health Journal, 28,* 317–326.

Wodahl, E., Ogle, R., & Heck, C. (2011). Revocation trends: A threat to the legitimacy of community-based corrections. *The Prison Journal, 91*(2), 207–226.

Wolff, N., & Shi, J. (2012). Childhood and adult trauma experiences of incarcerated persons and their relationship to adult behavioral health problems and treatment. *International Journal of Environmental Research and Public Health, 9,* 1908–1926.

Wong, S. C. P., & Burt, G. (2007). The heterogeneity of incarcerated psychopaths: Differences in risk, need, recidivism, and management approaches. In H. Hervé and J. C. Yuille (Eds.), *The Psychopath: Theory, Research, and Practice* (pp. 461–484). Princeton, NJ: Lawrence Erlbaum.

Wong, S. C. P., & Hare, R. D. (2005). *Guidelines for a Psychopathy Treatment Program.* Toronto: Multi-Health Systems.

Wong, S. C. P., Gordon, A., Gu, D., Lewis, K., & Olver, M. E. (2012). The effectiveness of violence reduction treatment for psychopathic offenders: Empirical evidence and a treatment model. *International Journal of Forensic Mental Health, 11,* 336–349.

Wong, S. C. P., & Olver, M. E. (2015). Risk reduction treatment of psychopathy and applications to mentally disordered offenders. *CNS Spectrums, 20,* 303–310.

Worell, J., & Remer, P. (2003). *Feminist Perspectives in Therapy: Empowering Diverse Women* (2nd ed.). Hoboken, NJ: John Wiley.

Worling, J. R, & Curwen, T. (2000). Adolescent sexual offender recidivism: Success of specialized treatment and implications for risk prediction. *Child Abuse & Neglect, 24,* 965–982.

Wormith, J. S., & Zidenberg, A. M. (2018). The historical roots, current status, and future applications of the risk-need-responsivity model (RNR). In *New Frontiers in Offender Treatment* (Anonymous, Trans.) (pp. 11–41). New York: Springer.

Wozniak, J. F., Braswell, M. C., Vogel, R. E., & Blevins, K. R. (2008). *Transformative Justice: Critical and Peacemaking Themes Influenced by Richard Quinney.* Washington, DC: Lexington Books.

Wright, E. M., Salisbury, E. J., & Van Voorhis, P. (2007). Predicting the prison misconducts of women offenders: The importance of gender-responsive needs. *Journal of Contemporary Criminal Justice, 23,* 310–340.

Wright, E. M., Van Voorhis, P., Salisbury, E. J., & Bauman, A. (2012). Gender-responsive lessons learned and policy implications for women in prison: A review. *Criminal Justice and Behavior, 39,* 1612–1632.

Wright, K., Clear, T., & Dickson, P. (1984). Universal application of probation risk-assessment instruments: A critique. *Criminology, 33,* 113–134.

Yates, P. (2004). Treatment of adult sexual offenders: A therapeutic cognitive-behavioral model of intervention. In R. Geffner, K. Franey, T. Arnold, & R. Falconer (Eds.), *Identifying and Treating Sex Offenders: Current Approaches, Research, and Techniques* (pp. 195–232). Binghamton, NY: Haworth.

Yates, P., & Kingston, D. (2011). Pathways to sexual offending. In B. Schwartz (Ed.), *Handbook of Sex Offender Treatment* (pp. 17-1–17-15). Kingston, NJ: Civic Research Institute.

Yochelson, S., & Samenow, S. (1976). *The Criminal Personality, Vol. I: A Profile for Change.* New York: Jason Aronson.

Yonas, D., & Garland, T. (1994). Recognizing and utilizing ethnic and cultural diversity in counseling approaches. In P. Kratcoski (Ed.), *Correctional Counseling and Treatment* (3rd ed.). Prospect Heights, IL: Waveland.

Zapf, P., Golding, S., & Roesch, R. (2006). Criminal responsibility and the insanity defense. In I. Weiner & A. K. Hess (Eds.), *Handbook of Forensic Psychology* (pp. 332–363). Hoboken, NJ: John Wiley.

Zarling, A., Lawrence, E. & Orengo-Aguayo, R. E. (2017). Achieving Change Through Value Based Behavior [Unpublished Curriculum]. University of Iowa Research Foundation.

Zhong, S., Senior, M., Yu, R., Perry, A., Hawton, K., Shaw, J., & Fazel, S. (2021). Risk factors for suicide in prisons: A systematic review and meta-analysis. *The Lancet Public Health, 6,* e164–e174.

Zigler, E., Taussig, C., & Black, K. (1992). Early childhood intervention: A promising preventative for juvenile delinquency. *American Psychologist, 47,* 997–1006.

Zlotnick, C., Johnson, J., & Najavits, L. M. (2009). Randomized controlled pilot study of cognitive-behavioral therapy in a sample of incarcerated women with substance use disorder and PTSD. *Behavior Therapy, 40,* 325–336.

Zlotnick, C., Najavits, L. M., Rohsennow, D. J., & Johnson, D. M. (2003). A cognitive-behavioral treatment for incarcerated women with substance abuse disorder and post-traumatic stress disorder: Findings from a pilot study. *Journal of Substance Abuse Treatment, 25,* 99–105.

Zuk, G. (1975). *Process and Practice in Family Therapy.* Haverford, CT: Psychology and Behavioral Science Books.

Author Index

Note: Page numbers in *italic* denote figures and in **bold** denote tables.

Subject Index

Note: Page numbers in *italic* denote figures and in **bold** denote tables.

inappropriate interventions 59–60; meta-analyses 18, 44, *57*, *58*, 123, 167, 187, 188, 189, 200, 210–211, 258, 265–266, 321–322; principles of effective intervention 57–59, 122–126, *123*; program deficiencies 60–64; relapse prevention 309–310; sex offender treatments 309–310, 321–322; social learning interventions 199–200, 201, 210–211; staff issues 62–64; substance abuse interventions 60–61, 258, 265–266, 278–279; therapeutic integrity/program fidelity 60–64, 66, 190, 196, 295–297
empathy 11, 131, 139, 287; accurate 50, 53
empathy training 308, 311, 324
enmeshed systems 231–232, *231*, 247
EQUIP Program *177*, 211
ethics 29–32; client definition 30; codes of 29–30; competence boundaries 31; confidentiality 13, 31–32, 313–314, 324; dual/multiple relationships 31, 39; sex offender treatments 313–314, 315–316; treatment versus security dichotomy 13, 16, 30, 40; validity 110–112, *111*, 118
ethnicity *see* racially and ethnically responsive approaches
ethnocentrism 34, 39
evidence-based corrections 42, 54
Evocation, in Motivational Interviewing 52, 54
exposure therapy 163
external reinforcement *207*, 208, 217
extinction 147, 163, 308
eye movement desensitization and reprocessing (EMDR) 312, 324

family structure 230–232, *231*, 247
family systems 221–222, 247; subsystems and boundaries 230–232, *231*, 246, 248
family systems therapies 224–226, 254, 264, 282
family therapy 220–246, 247; behavioral and social learning models 209–211, 224, 232–234, 239, 240, 242, 243–246, 263–264, 281; case study 222; child abuse 239; communications therapy 224, 228–230, 239, 246, 264, 281; drug courts 243–244; functional family therapy (FFT) 232, 234, 243; history and overview 223–227; during incarceration 243–245; intimate partner violence (IPV) 240–241, **241**; multisystemic

treatment (MST) 224, 232, 234, 235–238, *237*, 239, 247–248, 264, 282; parent management training (PMT) 209–211; psychodynamic therapy 224, 227–228, 240, 248, 263, 282; skills training 240; strategic therapy 224, 229, 230, 242, 243, 248; Strengthening Families Program (SFP) 233–234; structural therapy 224, 230–232, *231*, 234, 239, 242–243, 248; substance abuse 242–243, 263–265; support groups 264–265, 267; systems therapies 224–226, 254, 264, 282
family treatment drug courts (FTDCs) 243
Federal Coming Home Initiative 245
Female Offender Treatment and Employment Program (FOTEP) **295**
fixated pedophiles 304
Fluency-Based Computer-Delivered Program for Behavioral Intervention and Assessment 156–157
Forever Free program 275–276, **295**
four-factor model 329, 330–332, *330*, 336
FRAMES skills 270, **271**, 272
functional family therapy (FFT) 232, 234, 243
functional value 206, *207*, 217

gender identification 98
Gender Informed Needs Assessment (GINA) 104
gender responsivity 7–8, 34, 35, 117, 195, 284–298, 299; assessments 95–96, 100, 104–105, 110, 112, 118, 124–125, 293–294, 318; case planning/management 129; cognitive behavioral interventions 187–188; critical race theory (CRT) 287, 288–289; effectiveness of gender-responsive initiatives 294–297; gender-responsive principles 291–292; holistic addiction theory 289–290, *290*, 299; relational model of self and 276, 282; relational theory 286–287, 299; sex offender treatments 312–313; substance abuse interventions 129, 260, 274–276, 289–290, *290*, 294, **295**; substance use support groups 267; supervision and sanctions 129; trauma theory 275, 283, 290–291, 300; trauma-informed services 292–293, 300; treatment curricula 294, **295**; women's criminogenic pathways and needs 96, 104, 285–286, 299